Adobe Illustrator 6.0 Masterworks

Sharyn Venit

MIS: PRESS

A Subsidiary of
Henry Holt and Co., Inc.

First Edition—1996

Printed in the United States of America.

Library of Congress Cataloging-in-Publication Data

Venit, Sharyn.
    Adobe Illustrator 6.0 masterworks / by Sharyn Venit.
        p.   cm.
    ISBN 1-55828-446-X
    1. Computer graphics. 2. Adobe Illustrator (Computer file)
    3. Macintosh (Computer)—Programming.
    T385.V455   1996
    006.6'869—dc20   96-6188
                                                              CIP

10 9 8 7 6 5 4 3 2 1

Associate Publisher: *Paul Farrell*

Managing Editor: *Cary Sullivan*	**Production Editor:** *Stephanie Doyle*
Development Editor: *Andrew Neusner*	**Technical Editor:** *Diane Burns*
Copy Edit Manager: *Shari Chappell*	**Copy Editor:** *Thomas Crofts*

Dedication

To the artist in each of us who struggles to translate
beautiful visions into printable images.

Acknowledgements

First and foremost, I am deeply grateful to all the artists who contributed their work to this edition: Robin Bort, Sandee Cohen, Scott Crouse and Scotty's Inc., Stephen Czapiewski at OOMM Studios, Eve Elberg at Eve Design, Susan Equitz, Steven Gordon, GordonMaps, Ben Gorman (Navajo silversmith), Doug Heinlein and Imagination Pilots Entertainment, Paul McBride Mahan, Rob Marquardt and Benyas AD Group, Curt Mobley, Linda Oates, Alvin O'Sullivan, Arthur J. Saarinen and AVID, Karen Rosenstein, Larry Rosenstein, Sue Sellars at Two Blue Heron Studios, Ian Shou, Karin Sletten (photographs), Gary Allen Smith, Gary Symington, Marina Thompson, Ray Villarosa and OHS, Scott Winkowski, Sandra Wooten (photograph), Lester Yocum, and dr. Zox.

My greatest thanks also to Diane Burns for her meticulous technical edits on the manuscript, and to Maureen Cooney, Rebecca Scott, Gail Evans, and Gary Marzolf for their help with the manuscript. Special appreciation to Linda Oates for her support, Carole McClendon for her guidance, and to Andy Neusner and Stephanie Doyle at MIS:Press for being so easy to work with.

Sharyn

Contents

Chapter 1

What Is Adobe Illustrator?

Adobe Illustrator is a powerful illustration tool with strong built-in typographic and color capabilities. Illustrator lets you build artwork by layering lines, curves, and shapes called *paths* one on top of the other. The closest analogy to traditional, non-computer-assisted graphic arts is paper collage, where you cut out and layer different shapes made of colored or patterned paper. But Illustrator offers much more flexibility than traditional collage; it lets you produce results that would be either impossible or enormously time-consuming to produce traditionally.

Working with paths is much easier and more flexible than working with paper cut-outs. Unlike a paper cut-out, you can go back and change the shape of the path at any time, change the line and fill specifications, and make exact copies of the path to use elsewhere in your artwork. You can use Illustrator's transformation tools to scale, rotate, skew, and reflect paths to precise percentages and angles. You can even have Illustrator generate a series of intermediate shapes and colors by blending one path to another.

Illustrator is a production tool as well as a design tool. Once your paper collage was completed, if you wanted to reproduce it in print you'd need to have it photographed, then have color separations made from the photograph. With Illustrator, you can print composite proofs in shades of gray on monochrome printers or in color on color printers, and you can print final color separations directly to film on a PostScript imagesetter. All the color pages in this book were produced using Illustrator and a PostScript imagesetter.

System Requirements

Minimum system requirements for Adobe Illustrator 6.0 include:

➤ a 68K-based Macintosh computer with 4 megabytes of application RAM or a Power Macintosh with 6.6 megabytes of application RAM

➤ System 7.0 or later

➤ a 640 × 480 or larger display

➤ a hard disk

➤ either a floppy disk drive or a CD-ROM drive

Requirements for using the Adobe Illustrator 6.0 Deluxe CD-ROM include

➤ a CD-ROM drive

➤ QuickTime 2.1 extension, which is included

➤ 4 megabytes of application RAM

➤ a 640 × 480 or larger color display

NOTE Adobe Illustrator also runs under Windows on PC systems, and Illustrator files can be transferred between the two systems. If you are using Illustrator under Windows, most of the commands and functions described here work the same way on both systems, except the **Command** key (**~CD**) on the Macintosh is equivalent to the **Control** key on the PC, and the **Control** key on the Macintosh is the equivalent of the **Alt** key on the PC.

Memory

For optimal performance, Adobe recommends 6 megabytes of application RAM for 68K-based systems and 9 megabytes of application RAM for Power Macintosh systems. You can increase the amount of memory available to Illustrator by disabling any Startup documents (INIT files) you are currently using by dragging them out of the Extensions folder (in the System folder) and by reducing the size of the RAM cache in the Memory control panel.

Hard Disk Space

The complete Illustrator package, including tutorial files and examples, uses more than 18 Mb of hard disk space. If you install only the minimum number of files needed to run the program, you can reduce the space required to about 6 Mb.

Color Monitor

For accurate display of on-screen color, a 24-bit video card is desirable or on-board VRAM for 16- and 24-bit color, but Illustrator will attempt to display color as accurately as possible using an 8-bit video card.

PostScript Printer

A PostScript printer is highly recommended. Illustrator will print the screen representation of your artwork to non-PostScript printers, but these printers cannot reproduce hairlines or many of Illustrator's special PostScript effects. Illustrator can also print to PostScript imagesetters for high-quality final output and can print slides on PostScript-compatible film recorders, such as LaserGraphics LFR, Agfa Matrix with Chromascript RIP, and the Solitaire series from Management Graphics.

Scanner

A scanner is a useful tool, but not an essential one. Flatbed scanners allow you to create image files of line art and gray scale or color continuous-tone images, like photographs. You can import these image files into Illustrator and incorporate them in your artwork as is, use them as templates, or use Illustrator's Autotrace tool to trace them. If you want to scan photographic images, you should use a scanner that captures 8 bits per pixel for black-and-white photographs or 24 bits per pixel for color photographs.

Examples of Graphics Designed in Illustrator

The wine label shown in Figure 1.1 illustrates some of Illustrator's features. Additional examples of Illustrator artwork are shown in Figure 1.2. See also the color plates and the Case Studies in the last chapter of the book.

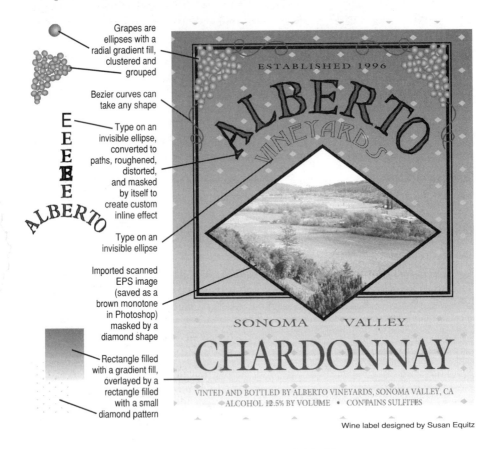

Grapes are ellipses with a radial gradient fill, clustered and grouped

Bezier curves can take any shape

Type on an invisible ellipse, converted to paths, roughened, distorted, and masked by itself to create custom inline effect

Type on an invisible ellipse

Imported scanned EPS image (saved as a brown monotone in Photoshop) masked by a diamond shape

Rectangle filled with a gradient fill, overlayed by a rectangle filled with a small diamond pattern

Wine label designed by Susan Equitz

Figure 1.1 A wine label created in Adobe Illustrator.

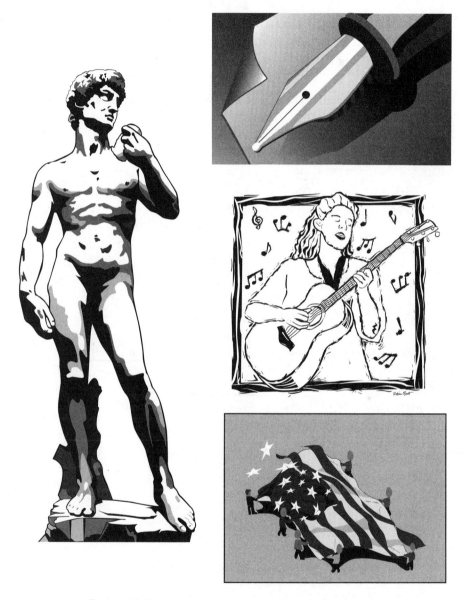

Figure 1.2 Examples of artwork created in Adobe Illustrator.

Illustrator's Key Features

Paths and Bezier Curves

Illustrator is built around the PostScript page description language, which has become an industry standard in computer-assisted publishing and prepress. Lines, curves, and shapes created in Illustrator are called paths, and they are based on a system called *Bezier curves*. You will learn more about paths in the tutorial in Chapter 4, but here are some basic concepts.

A path can be a single point, a series of points that define a curved or straight line, or a complex closed shape. To define a straight line you simply click the mouse button to place the end-points, called *anchor points*. Curved lines have anchor points too, but they also have additional points called *direction handles*. To draw a curve, you click to place an anchor point, then drag a direction handle away from the anchor point in the direction that is tangent to the curve you are drawing.

Each curve segment is defined by two anchor points and two direction handles, one associated with each anchor point. (See Figure 1.3) The resulting curves, called *Bézier curves* after the mathematician Pierre Bézier, are very accurate, and easy to control. You create paths by clicking anchor points and dragging direction handles. You can mix straight lines and curve segments and make paths open or closed. An *open path* has two end-points. A *closed path* forms one continuous line with any number of anchor points but no end-points.

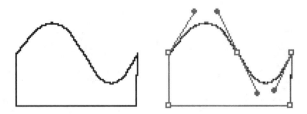

Figure 1.3 A curved path with anchor points and direction handles.

You can give different line weights to paths, from the finest line your printer can print up to a 1000-point line, and make the line any color you want. You can specify a fill as a solid color, a pattern, or a smooth gradation from one color to another. You can also specify no line and no fill. A path with no line and no fill will be invisible in the final artwork.

Illustrator 6.0 introduces a **Path Pattern** command that lets you place patterns along a path to create borders, frames, and other graphic elements.

6.0 NEW FEATURE

You can make two or more paths into a compound path to create see-through "windows." In the wine label, the diamond shape in the center of the label was joined with the outer rectangle of the label to form a compound path, thus opening a diamond-shaped window through to the scanned image. You can also mask artwork (including scanned images) with a path, so that only the part of the artwork framed by the path shows in the artwork. This cookie-cutter effect is called a *mask* or, in PostScript language, a *clipping path*.

You can display artwork on the screen in either Preview mode—to see how it looks when printed—or in Artwork mode—to see a "wireframe" view of the paths.

Fill Patterns

In addition to filling paths with solid color, Illustrator lets you specify *gradient fills*, which blend smoothly from one color to another. You can choose the starting color, the ending color, and the direction in which the colors blend. You can also create blends of multiple colors. The wine label contains a graduated fill blending from a dark shade at the top of the label to a light shade at the bottom.

When you want to blend shapes as well as colors, you can create blends, which are a series of intermediate shapes with intermediate colors between the two paths being blended.

You can create pattern fills composed of repeating, or *tiled* designs. You create the pattern elements as you would any other Illustrator artwork. Once you have defined a tile design, you can apply it as a pattern fill to any closed path. The small diamonds in the wine label are an example of a tiled pattern.

 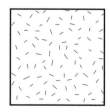 

Figure 1.4 Examples of solid, patterned, and gradient fills.

Compound paths are paths that have been joined into a single object. One use of these is to create transparent holes in a path, such as the diamond-shaped hole in the wine label, showing a scanned image that is actually positioned behind the rectangle of the label. Another is to apply a single graduated or patterned fill to several paths.

Typographic Controls

Illustrator also offers amazing typographic controls. You can adjust the font size and leading in increments of 1/100 of a point, and control word spacing, letter spacing, baseline shifting, and kerning. You can apply color to type and use the transformation tools to rotate, reflect, scale, and *shear* (skew) type just as you would any other path.

You can type text along a path. The baseline of the type follows the shape of the path. You can use this feature for effects like the circular text commonly found on buttons or for names of roads or rivers on maps, or any other place where you want to run text along a curve or arbitrary line.

You can convert type into *outlines*—editable paths whose anchor points and direction handles you can move to change the actual letter shapes. You can modify the shapes of the letterforms and use the converted type as a mask. The letters in the name *Alberto* on the wine label were converted to paths.

Imported Images

You can import scanned images such as line art, black-and-white photographs, and color photographs and make them part of your artwork, as was done with the Sonoma Valley scene on the wine label. You can even mask a photo-realistic image with a path. This is like cutting a shape out of a photograph and pasting it into your collage. Imported color images print in color on color printers and separate correctly when you print color separations from Illustrator and other color separation programs such as Adobe Separator, PrePrint, QX, and SpectreSeps.

Illustrator 6.0 significantly expands the number of file types that can be imported into an Illustrator document, from a limited range of EPS formats only to include thoselisted at the top of the next page.

6.0 NEW FEATURE

- ➤ Any PostScript file, regardless of originating application
- ➤ TIFF formats
- ➤ Any file saved in Adobe Photoshop format (version 2.5 or later)
- ➤ Adobe Portable Document Format (PDF)
- ➤ Any format supported by an Adobe Photoshop plug-in module
- ➤ PICT 1 & 2

Spot and Process Color

Illustrator allows you to work with spot color, process color, or a mixture of both. *Spot color* is color that will be reproduced in the final printed artwork by printing with a specially mixed ink that exactly matches the desired color. *Process color* is color that will be reproduced in the final printed artwork by overprinting percentages of four separate inks: cyan, magenta, yellow, and black.

The four-color process provides an economical means of reproducing a wide spectrum of color using only four inks, it is necessary for printing color continuous-tone images such as photographs. Each spot color uses a separate ink, so illustrations that contain more than three colors usually use process color instead of spot color, because each additional ink color used increases the cost of the print job. Sometimes designers plan to use a spot color in addition to process color. For example, many corporate logos use a custom color that cannot be exactly reproduced using process color, and the corporation or its advertising agency will often insist that the color be exact. Illustrator lets you mix spot and process color and will generate as many color separations as are necessary.

Illustrator 6.0 introduces the ability to print color separations directly, rather than going through Adobe Separator.

6.0 NEW FEATURE

You can define custom colors using four-color process percentages (cyan, magenta, yellow, and black), or you can choose from a built-in library of more than 700 colors from the Pantone Color Matching System, an industry standard for spot color. You can also access other color libraries, including FOCOLTONE, TOYO, and TRUMATCH.

High-Resolution Output

Illustrator benefits from a property of the PostScript page-description language, namely, device-independence. This means that a PostScript printer will always reproduce the artwork as accurately as it can, limited only by the resolution of the printer. You can use PostScript laser printers to proof your artwork and PostScript color printers to print color composites before printing final artwork on a high-resolution imagesetter, and you can be sure that the results from the imagesetter will be the same as they were from the laser printer, only better.

Illustrator Interface

Many of Illustrator's features cannot be seen in the final artwork, but they help in its creation. Figure 1.5 shows the wine label in Figure 1.1, as it appears in the Illustrator window.

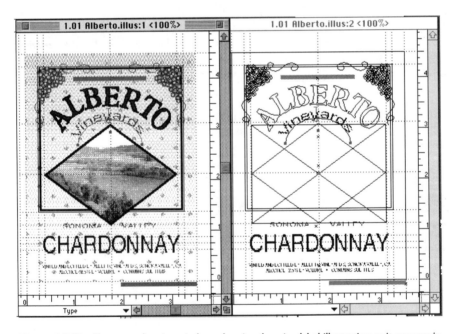

Figure 1.5 The Illustrator drawing window, showing the wine label illustration as it appears in Illustrator in Preview mode (left) and as wireframe artwork.

Tools

Illustrator displays a Toolbox on the screen with icons that represent tools very similar in function to the traditional tools you might find on an artist's drafting table, such as a pen, scissors, a paintbrush, a paint bucket, a magnifying glass, and a ruler. The Toolbox also includes many tools that offer functions that are impossible with traditional tools, such as transformation tools to rotate, scale, reflect, or shear objects, and a Blend tool that creates new shapes or colors based on a combination of two starting shapes or colors. These and other tools are used throughout this book.

Illustrator 6.0 adds new plug-in tools including the Knife, Star, Polygon, Spiral, and Twirl tools. Third-party plug-in developers can now easily add tools to this palette or create palettes of their own.

NOTE

Alignment Aids

Illustrator has features that help you position your artwork accurately. You can display rulers along the top and left sides of the drawing window and choose the unit of measurement they use. Dotted lines in the ruler track the horizontal and vertical position of the mouse cursor as you move it.

You can drag nonprinting guides from the ruler and make them a distinctive color, so that you don't mistake them for part of the artwork. If you turn on the **Snap to Guides** feature, the guides exert a magnetic-like pull on elements in the drawing: if you drag an object within a specified distance of a guide, it snaps precisely into alignment with the guide.

Illustrator 6.0's new Align palette combines key features of the Align and Distribute filers into an intuitive and simple palette.

NOTE

Palettes

Illustrator's *palettes* are windows that float above the drawing window. As with other windows, you can move a palette around the screen by dragging its title bar, resize it by dragging the resize box, or close it by clicking its close box. You open palettes by choosing them from the Windows menu. The Information, Layers, Paint Style, Gradient, Paragraph, and Character palettes all contain scrolling lists of available items that you can choose with a single mouse click, and each has a pop-up menu that lets you create, edit, copy, and remove items from the palette:

➤ The Paint Style palette provides an easy way to define colors and apply them to lines and fills in your artwork with one or two mouse clicks. You'll find this is the palette you use most often.

➤ An Information palette displays the vertical and horizontal coordinates of the mouse cursor or the position of the currently selected element. When you drag an element, the Information palette displays the original position, the current position, and the angle and distance between the original and current positions.

➤ The Layers palette lets you put different elements of your artwork on different layers. You can give each layer a name, change the stacking order of layers, move elements from one layer to another, make layers temporarily invisible, and choose which layers to print. You can choose to make only the current drawing layer active, in which case you effectively lock all the other layers against accidental changes, or you can make all the visible layers active. When you work with complex illustrations, Illustrator's layers save time and confusion by letting you turn off all layers except those on which you are currently working. This makes the screen redraw faster and prevents you from selecting other elements of the artwork by accident.

➤ The Character and Paragraph palettes let you change type specifications by clicking on entries in these windows which can remain open while you are working with type.

➤ A Tab Ruler palette offers a convenient alternative to menu commands for setting tabs in text.

➤ The new Align palette introduced in Illustrator 6.0 combines key features of the Align and Distribute filters from version 5.5, and offers a simple and intuitive tool for aligning objects.

➤ The Control palette in Illustrator 6.0 displays numerical information about the location, size, rotation angle, and scaling percentage of a selected object, and lets you change the object by editing these fields—a welcome improvement over the Info palette of earlier versions that simply displayed information without letting you change it.

Palettes snap to each other, to the edges of the screen, and to the document window in Illustrator 6.0.

NOTE

New Features in Illustrator 6.0

Illustrator 6.0 builds upon the strengths of earlier versions and adds improvements in performance, a more streamlined user interface, and new functionality. The following sections describe some of the important new features Illustrator 5.5 users will encounter in Illustrator 6.0. These features are described in detail throughout this book. They include the long-awaited ability to print color separations directly from Illustrator, the new palettes described in the previous section, and integration with other applications, including Adobe Photoshop.

New API

Version 6.0 incorporates a new Adobe API that includes core technology designed to extend product functionality by leveraging the use of plug-ins across Adobe products and multiple platforms. In addition, the new API supports:

➤ Existing Adobe Illustrator 5.x plug-ins and new plug-ins designed for version 6.0

➤ All Adobe Photoshop filters and file formats

➤ It integrates third-party plug-in filters as interactive palettes and tools within the filter menu

Enhanced Image Support

Adobe Illustrator 6.0 provides a host of new import capabilities, including:

➤ TIFF and Adobe Photoshop 2.5 or later and runs Adobe Photoshop and compatible filters

➤ Adobe Illustrator versions 1, 88, 3, 5, 6

➤ The Adobe Portable Document Format (PDF)

➤ EPS

➤ Any format supported by an Adobe Photoshop plug-in module

➤ PICT 1&2, plus many more

➤ Rasterize converts Adobe Illustrator artwork to pixel-based images

➤ Colorize 1-bit TIFF images

Adobe Solution with Cross-Product Integration

Version 6.0 provides improved integration capabilities with other leading Adobe products, including:

➤ Drag and Drop between Adobe Photoshop 3.0.4 and Adobe Illustrator 6.0

➤ Support for Adobe Fetch™, the leading visual database for cataloging digital media

➤ Support for Adobe Acrobat 2.0, including editing PDF files

➤ Launching Adobe Illustrator EPS files within Adobe PageMaker 6.0

➤ Support for PostScript ™ on the Clipboard

Built-in Production Capabilities

Version 6.0 features integrated production capabilities such as:

➤ Built-in color separation

➤ The ability to interpret PostScript files regardless of native application

New Tools and Palettes

➤ The expanded Tools palette contains plug-in tools with special functions, including the Knife, Star, Polygon, Spiral, and Twirl tools. Third-party plug-in developers can easily add tools to this palette or create palettes of their own.

➤ The Eyedropper tool can now sample colors from within any open document—not just the current document.

➤ The new Control palette identifies the location (x,y), the width and height, and the rotation and scaling of the selected object(s). Editing each of those fields will affect the selected objects.

➤ The new Align palette combines key features of the Align and Distribute filters into an intuitive and simple palette.

➤ Palettes now snap to each other, to the edges of the screen, and to the document window for exact placement.

New Filters and Commands

Adobe Illustrator 6.0 adds several new features and capabilities, from new plug-ins to performance improvements, in several key areas:

➤ The **Path Patterns** command let users place patterns along paths, a unique method of creating borders, frames, unique shapes and graphic design elements. The patterns generated are fully editable vector artwork. For example, a pattern applied to a path can be colored, resized, and transformed just like other Adobe Illustrator artwork.

➤ The Clean Up Artwork filter gives users options for making artwork less "messy," including the selection and removal of stray points, removal of unpainted objects, and removal of empty text paths.

➤ A Zig Zag filter distorts paths by moving them in a perpendicular pattern from selected path(s).

➤ The new **Transform Each** command combines Move Each, Rotate Each, and Scale Each into one filter, now accessed from the Arrange menu.

➤ **Saturate** combines the Saturate, Saturate More, Desaturate, and Desaturate More filters.

➤ **Arithmetic in Numeric Fields** lets users perform addition and subtraction within any text fields in which numbers are used.

➤ **Expand** turns patterns and gradients into objects.

Illustrator–One Tool in the Studio

Illustrator is only one component of a full publishing system that includes a computer and a printer, and might also include:

➤ Scanner
➤ Added printer fonts

➤ Other graphics software

➤ Page layout software

Illustrator can interact with all these elements by importing and exporting graphics and type.

Illustrator and Fonts

Try to use PostScript fonts if possible when you work with type in Illustrator. PostScript fonts are available from many vendors, including Adobe Systems, Bitstream, and Monotype. To use a PostScript font, you must have both the screen (bitmap) font and the printer (outline) font on your computer.

NOTE

You can also use TrueType fonts, which function the same as PostScript fonts, but it is recommended that you don't install both PostScript and TrueType versions of the same fonts.

You can also use bitmap fonts (screen fonts for which you have no printer fonts), but you cannot convert them to outlines (one of Illustrator's useful features), and they will appear jagged or will be printed in Courier font on the final output.

Utility programs like 5th Generation Software's Suitcase II and Alsoft's Master Juggler let you keep your fonts anywhere on your hard disk and load and unload them at any time.

For more information on fonts, see Chapter 8.

Illustrator and Scanned Images

Earlier versions of Illustrator allowed you to import scanned images saved in EPS (Encapsulated PostScript) format, and open PICT file formats, and to print them as part of the artwork. You could also open bitmap and PICT-format images as templates that could be traced, but not printed as part of the artwork.

You cannot alter the contrast and brightness of imported color images, but you can scale, rotate, reflect, or shear them; choose halftone screens; and print process-color separations so that the color image is reproduced properly in the final printed piece. You can crop a scanned image by masking it with a shape drawn in Illustrator.

NOTE

When you incorporate scanned images into your artwork, be sure to scan them at a resolution suitable for your final output. For grayscale images, a resolution of approximately 125 % of the line screen frequency setting you will use in the printed piece is recommended. For example, if you will be printing with a screen having 133 lines per inch (lpi), an image scanned at 150 dots per inch will yield good results. Scanning at a higher resolution will increase the size and complexity of the file without providing any significant improvement in image quality.

Opening PostScript Artwork from Other Sources

6.0 NEW FEATURE

You can open PostScript artwork created in any other program that produces PostScript file formats, including files saved in earlier versions of Adobe Illustrator. Alternatively, you can import Encapsulated PostScript (EPS) art using the **Place Art** command. Illustrator 6 lets you open or place (import) any PostScript file, regardless of originating application, and edit the components of the artwork.

Illustrator and Page-Layout Applications

You can use Illustrator artwork in Macintosh page-layout applications such as Adobe PageMaker and QuarkXPress. You can save Illustrator artwork as an EPS file, a format accepted by most Macintosh page-layout applications, with the option of previewing the artwork on a Macintosh in black and white or color or on an IBM system.

NOTE

If you include a preview image in the EPS file, the image will be displayed in the page-layout program and will print correctly. If you do not include a preview image, the page-layout application will display a gray box having the same dimensions as the image, and the image may not print correctly.

Transferring Illustrator Artwork to IBM PC Documents

You can save Illustrator documents in an EPS format that can be read by most page-layout programs that run under DOS or Windows on PC compatibles. You can also include a preview image of the artwork in the EPS file.

Summary

The best way to learn Illustrator's features and capabilities is to try using them. If you have never used Illustrator before, try going through the tutorials in the next chapters, trying the features and steps as you read. If you have used earlier versions of Illustrator, you might want to skim the next chapters and read only the version 6.0 icon sections.

Chapter 2

Basic Concepts

This is a reference chapter describing the document window, menus, and basic mouse operations. It includes optional exercise steps that will take you through some basic Macintosh and Illustrator operations without attempting to comprehensively explain every tool and command.

6.0 NEW FEATURE

If you are already familiar with Illustrator 5.5 or earlier versions, you can simply skim this and other chapters for new commands and features, identified with a 6.0 icon in the margin. If you are familiar with the Macintosh computer and with other drawing applications on the Macintosh (such as MacDraw or MacroMedia FreeHand), we suggest you read quickly through this chapter to get an idea of how Illustrator compares to the other applications you know. If you have never used a drawing application, you should go through the steps in this chapter using Illustrator on the computer. (If you have never used a Macintosh, you may need to refer to Apple Computer's manuals for the Macintosh operating environment to find information not presented in this book.)

Installing Illustrator

Because Adobe Illustrator offers a vast array of features and capabilities, it is a large program that is shipped on several diskettes. During the installation process, the pieces on these disks are assembled into one large program file on your hard disk (along with other files that support Adobe Illustrator).

The installation process is simple—you insert the installation disk in the floppy disk drive and double-click the **Install** icon, and then follow the prompts to insert the other disks that come with the package. The installation program also lets you choose where to install the program (on which hard disk, in which folder), and whether to install the full package (Easy Install) or to save space on your hard disk by not installing all of the printer drivers, sample files, and tutorial files that come with Adobe Illustrator (Custom Install).

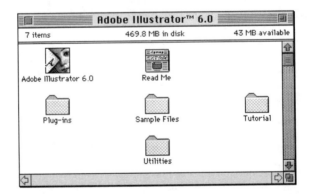

Figure 2.1 The Adobe Illustrator 6.0 folder is automatically created on your hard disk.

If you accept the installation defaults, a folder named Adobe Illustrator 6.0 is created on your hard disk that contains all the elements you have chosen to install.

Adobe Illustrator 6.0 deluxe comes on a CD-ROM, but you still must go through the process of installing the program on your hard drive—you cannot run it from the CD-ROM directly.

6.0 NEW FEATURE

Starting Illustrator

There are several ways you can start Illustrator:

➤ The most common method of starting a program is to double-click the program icon. This is the usual shortcut to the alternative of clicking the application icon once to select it and then choosing **Open** from the File menu (**File > Open**).

➤ Under System 7, you can start any application from the Apple menu (see next section), so you don't have to bother finding and opening folders on the desktop.

➤ You can also start Adobe Illustrator by double-clicking an Illustrator document icon. This method simultaneously opens the document and starts the program—but if you are following the steps of this tutorial, it is better to start with a blank page.

The next section begins a series of steps that you can simply read to get an overview of Illustrator's features, but if you are learning Illustrator for the first time it would be better to follow the steps on your own computer.

NOTE

EXERCISE: START ILLUSTRATOR FROM THE DESKTOP

This first procedure for starting Illustrator is always available, as compared to the other methods we'll describe which require some preparatory steps. Here we use the term *Desktop* to refer to the basic Macintosh screen that is displayed when no other applications are running. Under System 7, you can switch from any running application to this display by choosing **Finder** from the Applications menu at the top right corner of the screen.

1. Display the desktop. Quit all active applications, or choose **Finder** from the list of active applications on the Applications menu. If the current applications have open windows that obscure the desktop icons referred to in the next steps, you may need to move or resize those windows or quit those applications in order to see the icons. Of course, if you're running other applications already, then you probably don't need the explanation in the next steps!

2. Open the **Hard Disk** icon from the desktop. Double-click the icon that represents the hard disk on which you installed Illustrator to open that window, if it is not already open (see Figure 2.2).

Adobe Illustrator™ 6.0   Adobe Illustrator 6.0

Figure 2.2 Adobe Illustrator 6.0 folder (left) and application icon (right) when viewed by icon on the desktop.

3. Double-click the **Illustrator** folder icon to open it. If you accepted the normal defaults in installing Illustrator, you will find a folder named "Adobe Illustrator 6.0" on the hard disk. Open the Illustrator folder by double-clicking the icon or the name (see Figure 2.2). If the hard disk window displays its contents as a list—View menu commands **By Name**, **By Size**, **By Kind**, or **By Date**—you can also open the folder by clicking on the right-pointing arrow icon left of the name.

4. Double-click the **Illustrator** program icon. Double-click the **Illustrator** program icon to start Illustrator. Illustrator displays the opening screen shown in Figure 2.5 (later in this chapter).

Figure 2.3 The Adobe Illustrator 6 alias icon in the Apple Menu Items folder.

Starting Illustrator from the Apple Menu

The Apple menu is always displayed at the upper-left corner of your screen, no matter what application you are currently running. There are three ways to start Illustrator from the Apple menu—whether or not the Desktop or Finder window is currently displayed.

➤ You can set up Illustrator to appear as a command on the menu.

➤ You might find Illustrator listed under the Recent Applications submenu of the Apple menu.

➤ You might find a Illustrator document under the Recent Documents submenu of the Apple menu.

The first method requires some preparatory steps, which are described here. The other two alternatives apply only if you are running under System 7.5 or higher and if Illustrator was recently running on your system, and you're invited to try them for yourself.

In these next steps, you create an alias of the Illustrator program icon and move it into the Apple Menu Items folder. You could, instead, move the actual program icon into that folder, but it's a good idea to keep the original program icons in the folders created when they are installed if the installation includes a lot of other related files that the program might use when running—such as Illustrator's plug-ins.

The first three steps are the same as in the previous section.

1. Display the desktop.
2. Open the Hard Disk icon from the desktop.
3. Double-click the **Illustrator** folder icon to open it.
4. Click once on the **Illustrator** program icon to select it.
5. Choose **File > Make Alias**, or use the keyboard shortcut **Command+M**.
6. Drag the alias icon from the Illustrator folder into the Apple Menu Items folder, which is in the System folder (Figure 2.3).

7. Now—or whenever you want in the future—you can start Illustrator by choosing **Adobe Illustrator 6 Alias** from the Apple menu (Figure 2.4).

Figure 2.4 The Adobe Illustrator 6 Alias command on the Apple menu.

Starting Illustrator Automatically

You can have Illustrator start up automatically whenever you start your Macintosh by adding the Illustrator application icon or its alias to the Startup Items folder in the System folder.

The first five steps are the same as in the previous sidebar. Then do the following:

6. Drag the alias icon from the Illustrator folder into the Startup Items folder, which is in the System folder.

7. Now Illustrator will start automatically whenever you start your system.

Whatever method you use, when you start the Illustrator program, the opening screen displays the Adobe logo and information about your version of Illustrator. Once the program has started, the information window closes and a row of menu titles is displayed along the top of the screen (see Figure 2.6).

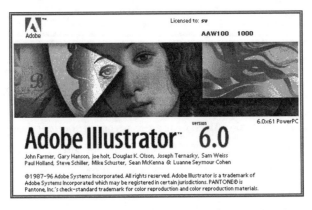

Figure 2.5 The opening screen shows Illustrator's version and your registration name and number.

Examining the Document Window

When you first start Illustrator, the screen displays information about the version you are using. The screen then shows a blank page of a new document on the screen with the name "Untitled art 1" on the title bar (if you started Illustrator from the program icon) or the name of the open document (if you started Illustrator by double-clicking a document icon on the desktop). This is the *document window* (a term common to many Macintosh applications), and it shows the work area or *Artboard* (a common graphic design term that has been adopted in the Adobe documentation).

A quick look at the document window and the palettes on the screen will give you an idea of the versatility of Adobe Illustrator.

NOTE

The **pointer** shows the current position of the mouse and is used for selecting commands and objects on the Artboard or pasteboard.

The Title Bar

The document window has a *title bar* showing the name of the document, and the percent of actual size displayed on the screen is shown in brackets next to the file name—usually <50%> for a new letter-size file displayed on a 13-inch screen in Fit in Window view (**Command+M**).

You can move the whole document window by dragging the title bar. The title bar also includes a *close box* and a *zoom box*—standard Macintosh interface features.

Menu Titles

Pull-down menu titles appear on the menu bar listing Adobe Illustrator's command categories. If you position the mouse pointer over a menu name and hold down the mouse button to open a menu, you'll see that some of the command names are gray and cannot be selected because no object is selected, or because some other condition required by the command is not met.

EXERCISE: TO MAKE SURE YOU'RE IN SYNC...

If you are examining the document window for the first time, choose the following commands from the menus to make your screen look like the ones shown in this chapter:

➤ Choose **View > Fit in Window** (if it is not already in Fit in Window view), or use the keyboard shortcut **Command+M**.

➤ Choose **View > Preview**, or use the keyboard shortcut **Command+Y**.

➤ Choose **Window > Show Toolbox** if the Toolbox is not displayed, or use the keyboard shortcut **Command+Control+T**.

We use the > symbol to indicate a *menu > command > submenu* sequence throughout this book. You choose a command by first positioning the mouse on the menu name at the top of the screen, then holding the mouse button and dragging down the menu to highlight the command you want and then releasing the mouse button.

NOTE

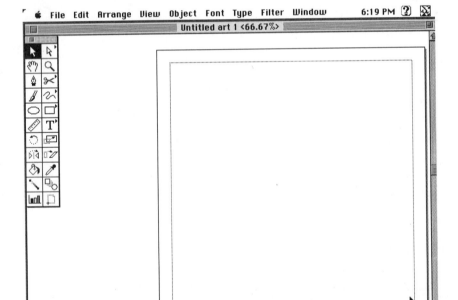

Figure 2.6 Adobe Illustrator displays a blank page when you first start the program.

The Artboard

The page image, or Artboard, shows the edges of the paper, with a dotted line showing the limits of the print area that apply to the printer that is currently selected through **Apple > Chooser**. The normal default size for the page is US Letter size—8.5 × 11 inches—but you can specify any size from 2 inches (144 points) up to 120 inches (8640 points, or 720 picas) by choosing **File > Document Setup (Command+Shift+D)**.

The area surrounding the page image serves as a *pasteboard* for storage of text and graphics while you work. You can use this area as an active storage area while you are building the artwork, or you can use it as a more permanent storage area for the document—an alternative to using the Scrapbook and other sources for commonly used elements.

Specifying the Artboard Size

Normally, the Artboard size is the same as the page size (or paper size) specified in the Page Setup dialog box (**File > Page Setup**), unless otherwise specified through the startup file or the Document Setup dialog box (see Chapter 10). Illustrator lets you specify sizes up to 120 inches square. You'll learn more about the dimensions of the work area later in this chapter, under "Displaying Rulers."

You can change the Artboard size independently of the page size by choosing **File > Document Setup** and selecting from predefined page sizes in the pop-out list (for letter, legal, or tabloid size), or you can enter your own custom measurements. If the Document Setup dimensions differ from the Page Setup dimensions, you can set the tiling options in the Document Setup dialog box to view and print parts of pages. If you click **Use Page Setup**, then the Artboard will automatically match the specifications in the Page Setup dialog box and will change whenever Page Setup is changed. You can change the units shown in the Dimensions area by choosing from the Ruler Units pop-out list in the dialog box.

The Artboard is initially centered in the page size (print) area, but you can reposition the artwork within the printable area using the Page tool (described in Chapter 11).

The Status Line

The *Status Line* at the bottom-left corner of the document window displays the name of the current tool, the date and time, the amount of free memory, or the number of undos—depending on the selection you make from the status bar's pop-up menu.

EXERCISE: MAKE A SELECTION FROM THE STATUS BAR MENU

If you want to view the names of the tools as you choose them during this tutorial, and a tool name is not already displayed in the Status Line, then position the mouse over the arrow on the Status Line and hold down the mouse button to display the pop-up menu. Then keep holding the mouse button as you drag to highlight **Current Tool** on the menu, and release the mouse button.

The Toolbox and Other Palettes

The screen might also display a Toolbox, a Layers palette, an Information palette, a Paint Style palette, a Gradient palette, a Character or Paragraph palette, a Tab ruler, an Align palette, Plug-in tools, and/or a Control palette—depending on how your defaults are set up or how your screen looked when you last quit the program. (You'll learn later in this book how to change the defaults for displaying these windows.)

The Macintosh Interface

Windows and palettes can be moved and sized on the screen. You can have more than one document *window* open at a time, but the active document window will usually display *on top of* any other document windows (unless you have arranged them side-by-side). If you close a document window, you are closing the document. *Palettes*, on the other hand, are always displayed on top of the active window, and each palette is related to the active document only. You can close any palette without closing the active document.

Examining the Tools in the Toolbox

Adobe Illustrator's Toolbox is much like a conventional artist's assortment of drawing tools, but pens, rulers, protractors, and knives are replaced by icons, which you select to perform the artist's work.

EXERCISE: TO MAKE SURE YOU'RE IN SYNC...

If the Toolbox is not already displayed on your screen, you can display a hidden Toolbox by choosing **Window > Show Toolbox** when the Toolbox is not displayed, or by using the keyboard shortcut **Command+Control+T**.

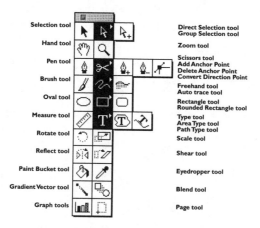

Figure 2.7 The Toolbox.

The Toolbox is a separate window on the screen. You can drag the Toolbox by its title bar to any position on the screen. You can also close the tool palette by clicking its **Close** box or by choosing **Window > Hide Toolbox**. To redisplay the Toolbox after you close it, choose **Window > Show Toolbox**. If you use these commands often, you will quickly prefer to use the keyboard shortcut **Command+Shift+T** to show or hide the Toolbox.

EXERCISE: DRAW SOMETHING

Follow these steps to draw a rectangle on the Artboard:

1. Click on the **Rectangle** tool in the Toolbox to select it.

2. Position the pointer anywhere on the Artboard.

3. Hold down the mouse button and drag diagonally.

4. Release the mouse button when the rectangle is the size you want.

Quitting and Resuming This Tutorial: At any time during this tutorial, you can choose *Quit* to exit Illustrator. You do not need to save your work.

6.0 NEW

Basic Mouse Operations

In order to use commands and tools, you must become familiar with two mouse operations. First, position the mouse pointer on the screen and then (1) click the mouse button once or twice or (2) drag the mouse while holding down the mouse button. You will use each of these operations in working with Adobe Illustrator, sometimes combining these operations with holding the **Shift** key, **Option** key, **Command** key, or **Spacebar**. The terms used to define these actions are summarized here:

➤ *Click*—First move the mouse without holding any keys or the mouse button in order to position the pointer over an object, then press the mouse button once and release it immediately.

➤ *Double-click*—First move the mouse without holding any keys or the mouse button in order to position the pointer over an object, then press the mouse button twice, quickly.

➤ *Drag*—First move the mouse without holding any keys or the mouse button in order to position the pointer over an object, then hold down the mouse button and move the mouse to a new position, then release the mouse button.

➤ *Shift+click*—Click the mouse button while holding the **Shift** key down.

➤ *Command+click*—Click the mouse button while holding the **Command** key down.

➤ *Option+click*—Click the mouse button while holding the **Option** key down.

➤ *Control+click*—Click the mouse button while holding the **Control** key down.

➤ *Shift+Option+click (and other combinations)*—Click the mouse button while holding two or more keys down.

➤ *Shift+drag*—Drag the mouse while holding the mouse button and the **Shift** key down.

➤ *Option+drag*—Drag the mouse while holding the mouse button and the **Option** key down.

➤ *Shift+Option+drag (and other combinations)*—Drag the mouse while holding the mouse button and two or more keys down.

Introduction to Commands

Using commands from the menus is one of three ways of creating or modifying artwork in Adobe Illustrator—the other two, using tools or using palettes, are explained in later chapters. We put these first in the sequence because they are the most obvious to new users—you can see them on the screen and the command names are usually descriptive of what they do.

There are certain features that are common to all menus and commands on the Macintosh, and these are described in the next section. Subsequent sections describe individual commands in the order they appear on the menus, and the menus are listed in the order they appear at the top of the screen in Illustrator.

6.0 NEW FEATURE

Commands are described briefly in this chapter. More detailed descriptions of most commands appear in later chapters.

Choosing a Command

Adobe Illustrator, like all applications that run on a Macintosh, displays a menu bar at the top of the screen, listing the names of the menus of available commands. Commands are displayed below each menu title when a menu is open.

➤ To select a command, position the mouse pointer over the menu title, hold down the mouse button, drag down the menu until the desired item is highlighted, then release the mouse button.

➤ You choose a command from a *submenu* —indicated by a right-pointing arrow after the command name—by first positioning the mouse on the menu bar at the top of the screen to open the first menu, then dragging down the menu to highlight a command with an arrow next to it. This opens the submenu. Still holding the mouse button, drag down the submenu to highlight the command you want and then release the mouse button.

Some of the command names displayed on the menus are followed by ellipses (...). A dialog box will be displayed whenever you use one of these commands. Commands that are not followed by ellipses have an immediate result that cannot be canceled unless the **Undo** command is available.

NOTE

As you gain proficiency with Illustrator, you will find it is generally faster to use keyboard shortcuts or to use a tool or a palette (if it is already displayed on the screen) to accomplish tasks that can also be done through the menus. However, for commands that have no equivalent tool or shortcut or palette entry, you must use menus.

Keyboard Shortcuts

Some commands can be selected using keyboard shortcuts instead of the mouse. Shortcuts are listed on the menus next to the commands that have shortcuts. A clov er or "freeway" symbol (xxx) represents the **Command** key, an up arrow symbol indicates the **Shift** key, and a caret symbol (^) represents the **Option** key. For example, the keyboard equivalent of **Type > Alignment > Center is Command+Shift+C**.

		Type	
		Size	▶
		Leading	▶
✓Left	⌘⇧L	**Alignment**	▶
Center	⌘⇧C	Tracking...	⌘⇧K
Right	⌘⇧R	Spacing...	⌘⇧0
Justify	⌘⇧J		
Justify Last Line	⌘⇧B	Character...	⌘T

Figure 2.8 Type menu, with Alignment command submenu displayed, shows keyboard shortcuts for eight commands.

Dialog Box Entries

Commands followed by an ellipsis (...) on the menu list result in the display of a dialog box on the screen, offering the opportunity to select from various options, enter information required by the command, or cancel the command. Some dialog boxes can be moved around on the screen by dragging the title bar, just as any other window can be moved. A dialog box may contain any or all of the following:

➤ Boxes for typing text or numbers.

➤ Pop-out menus that let you choose from a list of alternatives.

➤ Check boxes that let you choose one or more options from a list.

➤ Radio buttons (small circular buttons that are used to select one option from a list of several mutually exclusive choices).

➤ Larger rectangular option buttons that close the dialog box, offering options such as **OK** and **Cancel**, or that open additional dialog boxes.

➤ Scrolling lists of fonts or file names.

➤ Warnings or messages.

Some of the general procedures that apply to all dialog boxes are described here. Specific dialog box entries are described in detail throughout this book.

Text Boxes

If there are any text boxes for typing text or numbers in the dialog box, the cursor will normally be positioned in the first such box when the dialog box opens. You can move the cursor from one text box to another by clicking on the text label that describes the entry, using the mouse to position the pointer inside the text box and clicking to position the cursor, or by pressing the **Tab** key. You can select text inside a text box by clicking on the text label that describes the entry to select all the text, using the mouse to drag the cursor over the text, double-clicking to select a word, or tabbing into the text box to select all of the text.

EXERCISE: MAKE ENTRIES IN A TEXT BOX

1. Choose **File > Document Setup** to display a dialog box with text entry fields.

2. **Tab** through the fields to see which ones get highlighted.

3. Change the Output resolution to match your printer, if you like.

NOTE

Pressing the **Tab** key in any dialog box jumps you from one text box to the next. Entries in any other areas usually require the mouse.

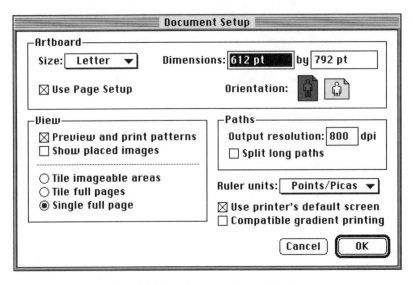

Figure 2.9 The Document Setup dialog box.

Pop-Out Menus

Some text boxes are framed by a drop-shadow and include a down-pointing arrow, indicating that you can choose from a list of alternatives by holding the mouse button as you click on the text box to display the pop-out list, then drag the mouse to make your selection.

EXERCISE: CHOOSE FROM A POP-OUT MENU

1. In the Document Setup dialog box, position the mouse pointer over the Size pop-out menu and hold down the mouse button to view the list of page sizes.

2. Make sure **Letter** size is selected when you release the mouse button.

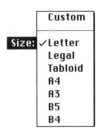

Figure 2.10 Pop-out list of page sizes in Document Setup dialog box.

Check Boxes

You can choose one or more options from a list that displays check boxes. Options that are selected show an **x** inside the box. An empty check box indicates that the option is not selected. Check boxes are toggles: clicking on an empty box selects the option, clicking on a box with an **x** deselects the option. You can also select or deselect these options by clicking on the text label that describes the entry.

EXERCISE: CLICK ON CHECK BOXES

Click on the **Show Placed Images** check box in the Document Setup dialog box to select it.

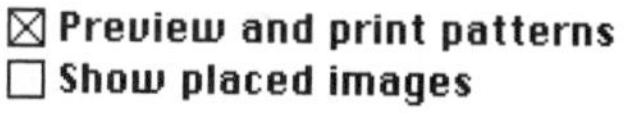

☒ Preview and print patterns
☐ Show placed images

Figure 2.11 Check boxes from the Document Setup dialog box.

Radio Buttons

Small circular buttons are used to select one option from a list of several mutually exclusive choices. The current selection is indicated by a dark circle inside the button. You can change the selection by clicking on another button in the list or by clicking anywhere on the text label that describes that option.

EXERCISE: CLICK ON RADIO BUTTONS

1. Click on the **Tile Imageable Area** radio button in the Document Setup dialog box. You see that selecting one radio button automatically deselects the others.

2. Click on **Single** full page to reselect it (the normal default).

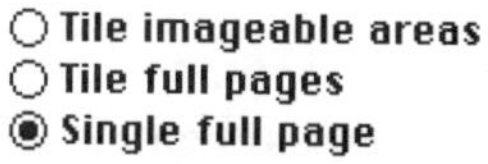

○ Tile imageable areas
○ Tile full pages
◉ Single full page

Figure 2.12 Radio buttons from the Document Setup dialog box.

Rectangular Option Buttons

Larger rectangular option buttons are used to close the dialog box, offering options such as **OK** and **Cancel**, or to open additional dialog boxes. Often, one rectangular button is framed in a double-rule border, indicating that pressing the **Return** key will have the same effect as clicking on that button.

EXERCISE: PRESS RETURN TO SELECT THE OK OPTION

Press **Return** to select the **OK** option button—the button framed in a double-rule border. In the Document Setup dialog box, press **Return** to close the dialog box.

Figure 2.13 Control buttons from the Document Setup dialog box.

Scrolling Lists

Lists of fonts or file names are often displayed in a small window within the dialog box, with scroll bars on the right for moving up or down the list. You select from a scrolling list by using the scroll bar (if necessary) to find the name you wish to select, then clicking on the name to highlight it. In some cases, you can jump ahead in a long alphabetical list by typing the first letter of the name you wish to choose.

EXERCISE: VIEW A SCROLLING LIST

1. Choose **File > Save** (**Command+S**). The first time you use this command, the Save Document as dialog box is displayed.

2. If the current folder includes many other folders and documents, you can use the scroll bar on the right of the list to view more names.

If there are fewer than five folders and/or documents, the scroll bars are not functional, but the next steps might yield longer lists.

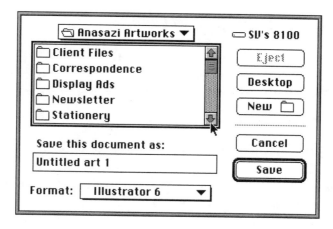

Figure 2.14 The Save document as dialog box shows a scrolling list of folders.

EXERCISE: SAVE YOUR WORK (OPTIONAL)

We have been working on artwork that has not yet been saved—indicated by the fact that the title bar shows it as "Untitled." This means that the artwork is stored in the computer's memory but not yet on a disk. If the power should fail suddenly, you would lose all the work you have done so far. It's a good idea to save your documents often while you work.

Follow the two steps in the previous section. Then do the following:

3. Type **Practice Artwork** (or whatever name you choose) in the text box of the Save Document as dialog box.

4. You can choose the drive and folder in which to store the document using the techniques described in Chapter 10 in the description of the **Save as** command. Format options are also described in Chapter 10.

5. Click **Save** or press **Return** to close the dialog box.

NOTE

Quitting and Resuming This Tutorial: At any time during this tutorial, you can choose **Quit** to exit Illustrator. You do not need to save your work.

If you start this tutorial, then save your work and quit Illustrator, you could later choose **Open** from the File menu (**File > Open**) to open the document you saved and continue where you left off.

Warnings (Alerts) or Messages

If the dialog box displays only the text of a warning or message, you have the option of clicking **OK** (to indicate that you have read the message) or **Cancel** (to indicate that you have read the warning and you wish to cancel the current command).

EXERCISE: DISPLAY A WARNING

Choose **Basic Concepts** from the Help menu to display a message. Unless you have already installed the Help files from the Adobe Illustrator 6.0 Deluxe CD-ROM, Illustrator will display a message prompting you to load the deluxe disk. Click **Cancel** to close the dialog box. (If you have already installed the help files, Illustrator will display a help screen. Click the **Close** box in the upper left corner to close the window.)

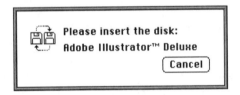

Figure 2.15 Dialog box with a message or warning.

Examining the Menus

You have already used some of Illustrator's commands in the previous steps. Illustrator's menus and commands are described in detail throughout this book, but we summarize them here to give you a quick overview of Illustrator's features.

As you read the next descriptions, open the menus on your screen by positioning the mouse pointer over a menu name on the menu bar and holding down the mouse button. Feel free also to choose commands that are followed by an arrow to view a submenu, or commands followed by ellipsis (...) to examine their dialog boxes. Click **Cancel** to close any dialog box.

The Macintosh Interface

Commands shown in gray are not currently available—in most cases this is because nothing is selected in the document window, or some other condition required for the command is not met.

The Apple Menu

As in other Macintosh applications, the Apple menu contains all of the Macintosh desk accessories that you have installed in your system folder, along with a commands specific to Illustrator called **About Adobe Illustrator...** and **About Plug-ins.** The figure shows the pull-down Apple menu.

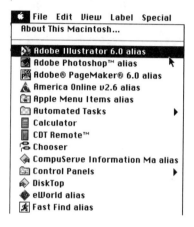

Figure 2.16 The Apple menu.

The next steps describe using the **About Illustrator** command to view the version and serial number—important information if you ever need help from Adobe Tech Support. Other sections in this book describe some of the Apple menu commands that are especially useful with Illustrator, including the Control Panel (for setting up color display in Chapter 6), and Chooser (that allows you access the network or to switch between several different printers as described in Chapter 11).

See earlier section on adding program names to the Apple Menu Items folder in the System folder under System 7. You can also add desk accessories to the Apple menu. Refer to your Macintosh user manual for more information on how to do this.

NOTE

EXERCISE: USE THE ABOUT ILLUSTRATOR COMMAND

1. Choose **About Illustrator** from the Apple menu to view information about the version and serial number.

2. Hold the **Option** key to start scrolling list of credits in the dialog box.

3. Click anywhere to close the dialog box.

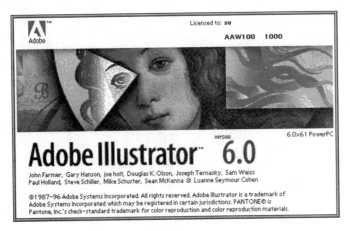

Figure 2.17 The About Illustrator dialog box.

The File Menu

NOTE

The File menu has commands that affect whole documents. It includes commands that are common to most Macintosh applications, such as **New, Open, Close, Save, Save as, Document Setup** (for the Artboard), **Page Setup** (for the paper and printer), **Print**, and **Quit**. Illustrator adds the following commands, not common to other applications:

➤ The **Revert to Saved** command cancels all changes made since the last time you saved the document.

➤ The **Place** command imports graphics from other applications.

➤ The **Import Styles** command lets you import paint styles from other Illustrator documents. The **Import Text** command imports text files.

➤ The Preferences submenu displays four preferences categories—General, Color Matching, Hyphenation Options, and Plug-ins—that let you change how Illustrator displays elements on the screen.

The **File** menu includes two new commands added in Illustrator 6.0:

➤ The **Separation Setup** command, introduced in Illustrator 6.0, lets you print color separations directly from Illustrator, instead of going through Adobe Separator or some other application as required by earlier versions.

➤ The **Document Info** command lists information about the document (file size, date modified, etc.) or about the contents of the document, such as objects, custom colors, patterns, gradients, and placed EPS files.

NOTE

You have already played with the *Document Setup* and *Save* commands. These and the other File menu commands are described in more detail in later chapters.

File   Edit   Arrange   View
New   ⌘N
Open...   ⌘O
Close   ⌘W
Save   ⌘S
Save As...
Revert to Saved
Place...
Import Styles...
Import Text...
Document Setup...   ⌘⇧D
Separation Setup...
Document Info...
Page Setup...
Print...   ⌘P
Preferences   ▶
Quit   ⌘Q

—6.0 ↑

Figure 2.18 The File menu.

The Edit Menu

The Edit menu includes commands that are common to most Macintosh applications, such as **Undo, Cut, Copy, Paste, Clear,** and **Select all**. Some of these commands affect the Macintosh Clipboard (a "storage area" in the computer's memory from which the contents can be retrieved using the **Paste** command) by cutting, copying to it, and pasting from it.

Illustrator adds **Redo, Select None, Paste in Front, Paste in Back, Show Clipboard,** and a selection of Publishing commands that hook into System 7's publishing feature (described in Chapter 7).

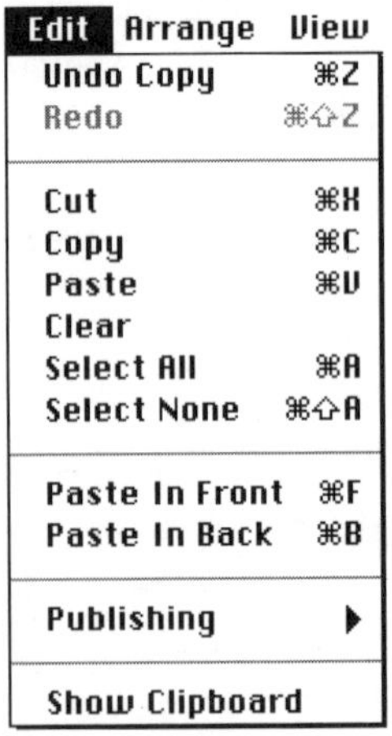

```
┌─────────────────────────────────┐
│ Edit  Arrange   View            │
├─────────────────────────────────┤
│ Undo Copy           ⌘Z          │
│ Redo               ⌘⇧Z          │
├─────────────────────────────────┤
│ Cut                 ⌘H          │
│ Copy                ⌘C          │
│ Paste               ⌘U          │
│ Clear                           │
│ Select All          ⌘A          │
│ Select None        ⌘⇧A          │
├─────────────────────────────────┤
│ Paste In Front      ⌘F          │
│ Paste In Back       ⌘B          │
├─────────────────────────────────┤
│ Publishing            ▶         │
├─────────────────────────────────┤
│ Show Clipboard                  │
└─────────────────────────────────┘
```

Figure 2.19 The Edit menu.

The Macintosh Interface

Although different applications have different menu commands, and hence different keyboard shortcuts, the **Command + key** equivalents for **Undo**, **Cut**, **Copy**, and **Paste** are constant throughout all Macintosh applications. Knowledge and use of these keyboard shortcuts is basic to Macintosh literacy—if you learn only four **Command+key** menu equivalents, they should be **Undo**, **Cut**, **Copy**, and **Paste**. These **Command+key** menu equivalents use the four keys located closest to the left-hand **Command** key: **Command+Z** is **Undo**, **Command+X** is **Cut**, **Command+C** is **Copy**, and **Command+V** is **Paste**.

The Macintosh Clipboard

The Clipboard is a "storage area" in the computer's memory from which the contents can be retrieved using the **Paste** command. The **Copy** command (**Command+C**) copies the selected objects to the Clipboard, leaving the objects in place as artwork and replacing whatever was previously in the Clipboard.

clear command   option move = copy

The **Cut** command (**Command+X**) deletes the selected object or objects from the Illustrator artwork and stores it in the Clipboard, replacing whatever was previously in the Clipboard. The cut object can be pasted back into the current file or another Illustrator file using the **Paste** command.

The **Paste** command (**Command+V**) pastes the contents of the Clipboard to the center of the active window, on top of all the other objects on the active layer. The pasted objects appear in the center of the screen and become the currently selected objects. All other objects are deselected.

To view the contents of the Clipboard, select **Edit > Show** Clipboard.

To Skip the Clipboard

The **Clear** command (and **Delete** or **Backspace** key) deletes all selected objects from the artwork. Cleared objects are not stored in the Clipboard. You must use the **Undo** command if you wish to reverse the command and retrieve the objects.

In Illustrator you can copy objects by holding the **Option** key as you move an object with a selection tool or when you use any of the transformation tools.

When to Cut

Use the **Cut** command whenever you wish to remove selected objects from the artwork and temporarily store them in the Clipboard. If you want to remove objects from the artwork but do not want to lose the contents of the Clipboard, select one of these alternatives to the **Cut** command:

➤ Press the **Delete** (or **Backspace**) key, or choose **Edit > Clear**. This action removes the selected objects from the artwork but it does not store them in the Clipboard.

➤ Before using the **Cut** command, move the contents of the Clipboard back to the artwork by choosing **Edit > Paste**.

➤ Drag the selected objects off to the side of the illustration for storage; they will remain part of the artwork until you delete them.

Undo and Redo in Illustrator

The **Undo** command (**Command+Z**) reverses the last operation you performed. The **Redo** command (**Command+Shift+Z**) reverses the last **Undo** operation you performed.

The text of the command that is displayed in the menu varies depending on the last operation. If the operation can be undone, the command becomes **Undo**, followed by the name of the action—for example, **Undo Clear**. If the action cannot be undone, **Undo** appears dimmed, indicating that the **Undo** command is disabled.

You can set up to 200 undo and redo levels, through the General Preferences dialog box (*File > Preferences > General*). This means that you can undo (and redo) up to 200 of the last operations you performed, in reverse order, by repeatedly choosing the **Undo** (or **Redo**) command. The default **Undo** level is set to **5**.

NOTE

EXERCISE: INCREASE THE NUMBER OF UNDOS

You can have more fun with this tutorial—take more chances and recover from your own mistakes—if you increase the number of **Undo** levels now. To do this:

1. Choose **File > Preferences > General**.

2. In the General Preferences dialog box, press the **Tab** key until the **Undo** levels value is highlighted (or drag over the value with the mouse to highlight it).

3. Type **20** as the number of undo levels.

4. Click **OK** or press **Return** to close the dialog box.

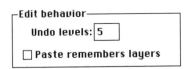

Figure 2.20 Undo levels in the General Preferences dialog box.

Copying Tricks in Illustrator

The **Copy** command is most useful when you want to store selected objects in the Clipboard for repeated use (over a short period), when you need to paste the copies between layers (not onto the top layer), and when you need to copy selected elements from one document to another.

Otherwise, you can copy objects by holding the **Option** key as you move an object with a selection tool or when you use any of the transformation tools (the Scale, Rotate, Reflect, and Shear tools). This is a more efficient method of copying objects when you want to align the copies or when you want to combine the copy procedure with a movement or a transformation before choosing **Arrange > Repeat Transform** to repeat the procedures. (See *The Selection Tools, The Scale Tool, The Rotate Tool, The Reflect Tool,* and *The Shear Tool* in Chapter 5 for methods of copying selections without storing them in the Clipboard.)

EXERCISE: COPY BY OPTION+DRAGGING

1. Click on the **Selection** tool (the solid black arrow pointer) in the Toolbox to select it.

2. Position the pointer on the rectangle you created earlier in these exercises.

3. Hold down the mouse button and the **Option** key as you drag the object to create a duplicate.

4. You can create additional copies, spaced the same distance apart, by choosing Arrange > Repeat Transform (**Command+D**).

Correcting Mistakes: Don't worry about making mistakes in these exercises. If you get into trouble, simply choose *Edit > Undo* (*Command+Z*) to back up as far as you want, or click the *Selection* tool and choose *Edit > Select None*, then go back and repeat whatever steps you need in order to catch up.

NOTE

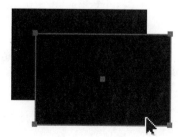

Figure 2.21 Option+drag to create a duplicate copy of an object.

Art work to pict

for use in word etc

Figure 2.22 Repeat Transform to create more duplicate, evenly spaced apart.

Converting Artwork to PICT Format

You can copy an Illustrator file into a PICT format which can then be pasted into Microsoft Word, PowerPoint, and some other (but not all) Macintosh applications that cannot handle PostScript formats. To do this, hold down the **Option** key and choose **Edit > Copy**, or press **Option+Command+C**. This action copies not only the PostScript information in the Illustrator file, but the screen bitmap as well, making it possible to paste the artwork into the other applications that support bitmap or PICT formats. This will work only if adequate memory is available.

Pasting in Illustrator

It's a good idea to select the layer onto which you wish to paste the object, either before or after using the Paste command. See the description of the Layers palette in Chapter 10. All pasted objects are selected when they appear on the screen. It's a good idea to use the **Undo, Cut, Send to Back, Bring to Front,** or **Group** command immediately, or move the pasted selections into position immediately, before clicking elsewhere and deselecting an ungrouped selection of pasted objects.

You cannot paste graphics from other applications into Illustrator. You can, however, paste text, provided that you first create an insertion point with one of the text tools.

WARNING

Using Select All and Select None

The **Select All** command (**Command+A**) selects all objects that are not locked or hidden, on all visible layers. Hidden or locked, will not be selected. You may then perform any action on them that will affect the objects as a group.

When you wish to select most but not all of the objects in a file, it often saves time to use **Select All**, then deselect those objects you do not wish to be selected by holding down the **Shift** key and clicking on them.

SHORTCUT

Edit > Select None (**Command+Shift+A**) lets you quickly deselect all objects in the document. This is a handy alternative to simply clicking on an empty part of the artwork, especially when objects fill the current screen display.

It is a good idea to deselect all objects whenever you want to create a new color, pattern, gradient, or paint style or change default settings without affecting anything in the current artwork.

NOTE

EXERCISE: EXAMINE THE CLIPBOARD

1. Choose **Edit > Select All** (**Command+A**).

2. Choose **Edit > Copy** (**Command+C**).

3. Choose **Edit > Show Clipboard** to examine the contents.

Figure 2.23 Use the **Copy** or **Cut** command to get Illustrator artwork into the Clipboard.

Displaying the Clipboard

The **Edit > Show/Hide Clipboard** command opens (or closes) the Clipboard window and displays its contents. You can also close the Clipboard window, or any active window, by clicking in the close box in the upper left corner of the window.

You can resize the Clipboard window and move it around the screen just like any other Mac window. This can be helpful if you want the Clipboard window always open but out of the way of your artwork.

The phrase *<n > artwork objects* appears in the Clipboard window when you choose the **Show Clipboard** command, where *<n >* is the number of objects in the Clipboard. If you cut or copy any text into the Clipboard while editing text, the text itself appears in the Clipboard window. If you hold the **Option** key down while you use the **Copy** command, the Clipboard window displays a bitmap version of the objects (see **Edit > Copy** for more details). You cannot edit the contents of the Clipboard window.

EXERCISE: CLOSE THE CLIPBOARD WINDOW

Choose **Edit > Hide Clipboard** to close it if it is still displayed.

The Arrange Menu

The Arrange menu lists commands that affect the position or appearance of objects on the Artboard.

➤ The **Repeat Transform** command repeats the last steps using the transformation tools.

➤ The **Move** command moves a selected object by a distance you specify numerically—as a more precise method of moving than simply dragging the object with the mouse.

➤ The **Transform Each** command lets you move, scale, or rotate individual objects withing a selection.

➤ The **Bring to Front** and **Send to Back** commands rearrange objects stacked within a layer.

➤ The **Group** command lets you associate several selected objects as one object—though you can still select and change individual items within a group, and **Ungroup** reverses the grouping.

➤ The **Lock** prevents a selected object from being selected or moved, and is reversed by **Unlock**.

➤ The **Hide** command makes selected objects invisible on the screen, and is reversed by **Show All**.

Arrange	View	Object	
Repeat Transform			⌘D
Move...			⌘⇧M
Bring To Front			⌘=
Send To Back			⌘-
Transform Each...			
Group			⌘G
Ungroup			⌘U
Lock			⌘1
Unlock All			⌘2
Hide			⌘3
Show All			⌘4

Com D
Com Sh M

Figure 2.24 The Arrange menu.

NOTE

You have already played with the *Repeat Transform* command. This and the other Arrange menu commands are described in more detail in later chapters.

The View Menu

New View

The View menu affects the way your artwork is displayed on the screen. These commands change the size of the page view in the document window, switch between viewing the artwork as it will print (Preview) and viewing the artwork as a system of lines and curves (Artwork), and hide or display other elements (template, rulers, and non-printing guides) on the screen. You can also Zoom In or Out, or jump to Actual Size (100%) or Fit in Window view of the whole page.

The **New View** command lets you name a window viewing the same document, and list that view name on the View menu. If you set up a 200% view of a particular spot in the artwork, for example, and then use **View > New View** to name that view, then when you change to other magnifications you can jump back to this same view by choosing the view name from the View menu. The **Edit**

View command lets you change the name of these views. None of these commands affects how the document looks when it is printed.

View	Object Font Type
✓Preview	⌘Y
Artwork	⌘E
Preview Selection	⌘⌥Y
Hide Template	⌘⇧W
Show Rulers	⌘R
Hide Page Tiling	
Hide Edges	⌘⇧H
Hide Guides	
Zoom In	⌘]
Zoom Out	⌘[
Actual Size	⌘H
Fit In Window	⌘M
New View...	⌘⌃V
Edit Views...	

Figure 2.25 The View menu.

NOTE

Some of the View menu commands are described here. The ***Show/Hide Template*** command is described in Chapter 7. The ***Show/Hide Page Tiling*** command is described in Chapter 11. And the ***New Views*** and ***Edit Views*** commands are described in Chapter 10. See also The ***Zoom Tool*** (described in Chapter 3) for other methods of changing magnifications of artwork.

Preview vs. Artwork Views

The **Preview Illustration** command (**Command+Y**) displays a preview image of the artwork in the active window—an approximation on the screen of how the artwork will look when it is printed. The **Artwork** command (**Command+W**) displays the Illustrator artwork as paths and anchor points only—without paint attributes—in the active window. The **Preview Selection** command (**Command+Option+Y**) displays a preview image of only the currently selected object or objects in the active window when the rest of the objects are shown in Artwork view. Previewing only the current selection is faster than previewing the whole illustration.

SHORTCUT

Working with a Preview window open may slow down processing as you work. If you wish to stop the page from previewing after you have invoked the ***Preview Illustration*** command, but before the screen has finished redrawing in Preview, press ***Command+(period)***.

EXERCISE: EXAMINE THE DIFFERENCE BETWEEN PREVIEW AND ARTWORK VIEWS

1. Choose **View > Fit in Window** (**Command+M**) to view the whole Artboard.

2. Choose **View > Artwork** (**Command+W**) to display a wire-frame view of the rectangles you created in earlier steps.

Figure 2.26 An illustration shown in two different views: Artwork and Preview

3. Choose **edit > Select None** to deselect all objects.

4. Choose View > Preview Selection (**Command+Option+Y**).

5. Click on one of the rectangles with the Selection tool to view its preview.

n Artwork view, you must click on a path to select an object—not on the area inside the shape.

NOTE

Viewing the Template

A template is a bitmap or PICT file that you use as a nonprinting background for aligning or tracing artwork. The **Show Template** command (**Command+E**) displays both the Illustrator artwork and your template in the active window. The template appears on screen when you use this command, but it will not print. This command is grayed if no template is associated with the active Illustrator document. If the template is already displayed, the menu command displays as Hide Template.

See Chapter 10 for methods of loading or changing templates.

NOTE

Displaying Rulers

We earlier described the Artboard—the outline of the page size—that appears in the document window surrounded by a pasteboard, and how the dimensions of the Artboard can be changed. You can also see the dimensions easily by displaying rulers on the screen.

The **Show/Hide Rulers** command (**Command+R**) displays (or hides) rulers along the inside of the scroll bars in the active window. The **View > Show Rulers** command displays a horizontal ruler (identified as the **X-axis** in the Information and Control palettes) and a vertical ruler (the **Y-axis**). The rulers—and the Information and Control palettes—measure position from a zero point, normally the bottom left corner of the page.

The unit of measure shown on the rulers is the same as that selected in the Document Setup dialog box, displayed when you choose **File > Document Setup**. Points is the normal default when you start Illustrator. You can also set the measurement system (Inches, Centimeters, or Picas/Points) using **File > Preferences > General**. When the unit of measure is points (the default), the rulers display either picas or picas and points, depending on the zoom scale.

As you move the pointer, dotted lines in the rulers track your movements to indicate the current position. When the rulers are displayed, you can drag horizontal and vertical guides from them into the artwork window. These appear as dashed lines and exhibit the same properties as guide objects created with the **Make Guide** command (see Chapter 10).

NOTE

Hiding the rulers has no effect on existing ruler guides, but you must show the rulers again to create new guides.

EXERCISE: EXAMINE THE RULERS

1. Choose **View > Show Rulers** (**Command+R**) if you do not see a ruler at the right and bottom of your screen display.

2. Move the mouse around to see how markers on the rulers reflect the current mouse position.

NOTE

You can also use the Information palette to view the cursor position, as in the next steps.

EXERCISE: CREATE RULER GUIDES

To create a horizontal or vertical guide:

1. Choose **Window > Show Info** (**Command+Option+I**) to display the Information palette if it is not already displayed on the screen.

2. Move the mouse around to see how markers on the palette numbers reflect the current mouse position.

3. Position the mouse pointer over the appropriate ruler.

4. Hold down the mouse button and drag into the artwork area. A ruler guide appears as a dashed line—check the position against the rulers and in the Information palette.

5. Release the mouse button when the guide is in the desired position.

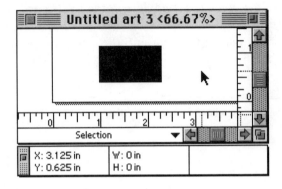

Figure 2.27 The Information palette and markers on the rulers reflect the current mouse position—or the position of objects as you move them.

NOTE

You can change the zero point by positioning the mouse pointer over the intersection of the rulers at the bottom right corner of the page and dragging new axes onto the pasteboard or the page—as described in Chapter 10—but please leave the zero point at the bottom left corner of the page for now in order to more easily follow the steps later in this tutorial.

Hiding Paths and Anchor Points

When an object is selected, Illustrator normally displays the object's anchor points and, in Preview mode, the path as a selection edge. You can hide these elements, so they are not displayed when an object is selected, by using the **Hide Edges** command (**Command+Shift+H**).

EXERCISE: HIDE AND THEN SHOW THE EDGES

1. Choose **View > Preview** (**Command+Y**).

2. Click on the **Selection** tool and click on one of the rectangles you created earlier to select it. Notice the anchor points and path are displayed in blue (on a color monitor).

3. To hide edges and anchor points on selected objects, choose **View > Hide Edges** (**Command+Shift+H**). This is a more accurate representation of how the object looks when printed.

4. To make the edges and anchor points visible again, choose **View > Show Edges** (**Command+Shift+H**).

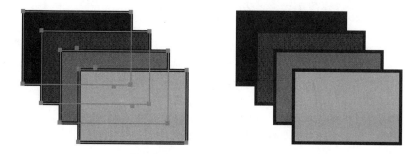

Figure 2.28 Selected object with edges and anchor points showing (left) and hidden (right).

Showing and Hiding Guides

You can create nonprinting lines on the screen by dragging ruler guides from the rulers (as done earlier) or by applying the **Make Guides** command to drawn objects. You can hide these guides, to simplify the screen display, by using the **Hide Guides** command.

EXERCISE: HIDE AND DISPLAY THE GUIDES

1. To hide all the guides in the Artboard, choose **View > Hide Guides**.

2. To make the guides visible again, choose **View > Show Guides**.

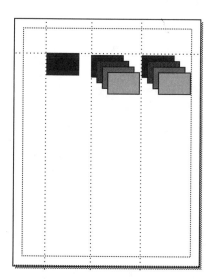 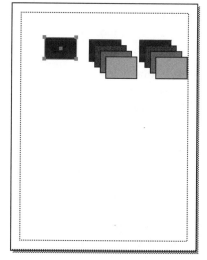

Figure 2.29 Artboard with guides showing (left) and hidden (right).

Cmn] [

Changing the View Magnification

There are several ways to enlarge or reduce your view of the Artboard on the screen:

➤ The **View > Zoom In** (**Command+]**) and **Zoom Out** (**Command+[**) commands offer alternatives to using the Zoom tools. These commands zoom in or out in the same increments as the Zoom tools, which is determined by the Zoom tool preferences settings (see Chapter 10).

➤ The **Actual Size** command (**Command+H**) displays the file in its actual size in the active window. The file is centered in the active window and scaled so that one screen pixel represents one point (approximately 1/72nd of an inch).

➤ The **Fit in Window** command (**Command+M**) displays the entire Artboard—up to 120 inches on each side—centered, in the active window.

NOTE

The **Zoom** commands maintain the same objects at the center of the screen. To zoom into an area that is not centered on the screen, use the Zoom tool, described in Chapter 3. If you are repeatedly switching between several views, set up multiple open windows (**Window > New Window**), or custom views (**View > New View**).

EXERCISE: CHANGE THE DISPLAY MAGNIFICATION

Cmn
+

1. To enlarge your view of the artwork relative to the center of the screen, simply type **Command+]**—the keyboard shortcut to choosing **View > Zoom In**.

2. To reduce your view of the artwork relative to the center of the screen, simply type **Command+[**—the keyboard shortcut to choosing **View > Zoom Out**. Press these keys as many times as necessary to see how far you can zoom out.

3. To view the illustration in actual size, choose **View > Actual Size**, press **Command+H,** or **Double-click** on the Zoom tool icon (if visible) in the toolbox. Actual size is shown in the first view in the accompanying figure.

4. Choose **View > Fit in Window**, or press Command+M, or double-click on the **Hand tool** icon in the toolbox, to fit the entire illustration into the active window. (Note that this does not select the Hand tool, but leaves the currently selected tool in effect.)

Figure 2.30 Artwork in Actual Size and Fit in Window views.

The Object Menu

The Object menu commands change the appearance of selected objects.

➤ The **Paint Style** command displays the Paint Styles palette, through which you can change the fill and line style of elements created using Illustrator's drawing tools,

➤ The **Custom Colors**, **Pattern**, and **Gradient** commands let you create and apply new colors, fill patterns, and gradients (graduated color blends).

➤ The **Attributes** command lets you type notes that will appear as part of the PostScript code in the print file for the illustration, display the center point, reverse path direction, and set different printing resolutions for different elements.

➤ The **Join** command can be used to "fuse" two endpoints on an open path, or two endpoints of two paths, by adding a line segment to join them. The **Average** command moves two or more points to the same position.

➤ The Guides, Masks, Compound Paths, and Crop Marks submenus let you **Make** or **Release** guides (for positioning objects), masks (for "cropping" objects), compound paths (the appearance of "windows" in solid objects created by joining two objects), and crop marks (trim marks around selected objects).

➤ The Graphs submenu lists commands that let you create and format graphs—columns, lines, pie charts, area charts, or scatter diagrams—based on numerical data.

6.0 NEW FEATURE

The **Expand** command converts gradients and pattern fills to objects, the **Apply Knife** command lets you use a shape as a "cookie cutter," and the **Rasterize** command converts Illustrator artwork to bitmap images. All of these commands are described in later chapters, but the ***Paint Style*** command and palette are introduced briefly in the next steps.

Object Font Type F
Paint Style...   ⌘I
Custom Color...
Pattern...
Gradient...
Attributes...   ⌘⌃A
Join...   ⌘J
Average...   ⌘L
Expand
Apply Knife
Rasterize...
Guides   ▶
Masks   ▶
Compound Paths   ▶
Cropmarks   ▶
Graphs   ▶

Figure 2.31 The Object menu.

EXERCISE: USING THE PAINT STYLE PALETTE

There are several ways of changing the appearance of an object in Illustrator. You can use the Paint Style palette to change the color of an object. You can use other tools, such as the Paintbucket tool to color an object. Each of these methods, and the differences among them, are explained in detail elsewhere in this book. In the next step, we use the Paint palette to change the color of one of the rectangles you created earlier.

1. If the Paint Style palette is not already displayed on your screen, display it now by choosing **Window > Show Paint Style**, or **Object > Paint Style** (**Command+I**).

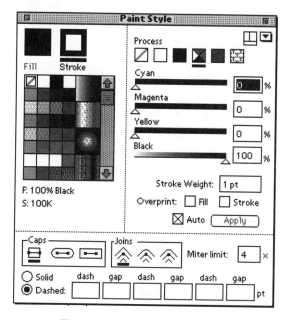

Figure 2.32 The Paint Style palette.

2. Click on one of the rectangles on the Artboard to select it if none is selected.

3. In the Paint Style palette, click on the top left square, labeled **Fill**.

4. Click on the first box in the second row of the paint palette—a gray box. When you click on a color in the Paint Style palette, it is automatically applied to the selected object.

If the rectangle is still not gray, make sure that *View > Preview* is selected, and that you have selected the *Fill* option in the Paint Style palette.

NOTE

5. In the Paint Style palette, click on the top left square, labeled **Stroke**.

6. Click on the black box in the first row of the paint palette.

7. Click on any empty area of the Artboard to deselect the rectangle and view the thin black border.

This last step is not necessary when **View > Hide Edges** is active, or when the stroke thickness is wider than the thin blue line that represents the path on selected objects in **Preview** mode when **Show Edges** is active.

NOTE

The Font Menu

The Font menu lists all the fonts installed on your system. The font you select is automatically applied to currently selected text, or to the next text typed at the text insertion point (if the text insertion point is active and blinking when the font is selected). Fonts families—i.e., fonts that come with separate printer fonts for roman, bold, italic, and bold-italic styles—are followed by an arrow (>) on the menu, and you can set the font name and style through this submenu.

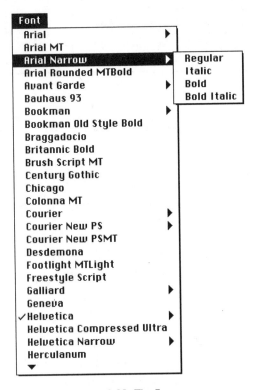

Figure 2.33 The Font menu.

NOTE

The commands on the Font and Type menus are described in Chapter 8.

The Type Menu

The commands in the Type menu affect text that you type in Illustrator.

➤ The **Size, Leading,** and **Alignment** commands all lead to submenus that let you select individual specifications quickly, or you can use the **Character** and **Paragraph** commands to display dialog boxes and set several characteristics at once.

➤ Illustrator incorporates sophisticated typographic controls such as letter and word spacing (**Tracking** and **Spacing** commands).

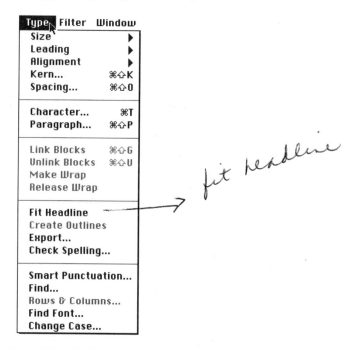

Figure 2.34 The Type menu.

➤ The **Link** and **Unlink Blocks** commands let you set up (or release) associations between one block of text and another, so that edits made in one block will cause text to flow from one block to another.

➤ The **Make** and **Release Wrap** commands let you control text wrap around a graphic object.

➤ The **Fit Headline** command lets you "force justify" text across the full width of a text path by automatically adjusting the weight of the font and the tracking values.

➤ The **Create Outlines** command lets you convert any text to graphic objects that can then be manipulated like any path drawn with Illustrator's graphics tools. This means you can create custom logos and special effects. You can also use this command to create files that will print without reference to printer fonts.

The last commands on the Type menu were moved from the **Filter > Text** submenu of version 5.5:

➤ **Export** lets you export text from Illustrator into a separate file, saved in one of 12 possible text formats—for compatibility with various word processing applications.

➤ **Check Spelling** checks words against a dictionary

➤ **Smart Punctuation** replaces straight keyboard text symbols with the special equivalents often used in publishing. This includes changing straight quote marks (") to opening and closing quote marks (" , ") as well as other options.

➤ **Find** finds and replaces specific strings of text that have been typed in Illustrator.

➤ **Rows & Columns** divides rectangles and text blocks into blocks of rows and columns.

➤ **Find Font** lists all the fonts used in a document, and lets you globally change all occurrences of one font to another. You can also save the font list as a text file.

➤ **Change Case** globally changes selected text to all uppercase, all lowercase, or caps and lower case (i.e., initial caps).

The Filter Menu

6.0 NEW FEATURE

The Filter menu commands each display a submenu listing the installed plug-in filters. Adobe supplies a variety of filters with Illustrator 6.0, and you can add (i.e., "plug in") more filters that you acquire from Adobe or other sources, or remove filters that you never use. Filters are arranged in submenus under the Filter menu: Colors, Create, Distort, Gallery Effects (new in 6.0), Ink Pen (also new), Objects, Pathfinder, Select, Stylize.

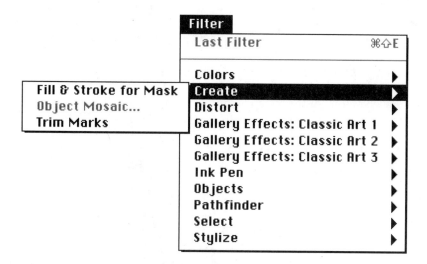

Figure 2.35 The Filter menu.

➤ The Colors filters adjust colors, intensify or diminish an object's color, or distribute colors among objects according to their orientation or stacking order.

➤ The Create filters create special effects such as multiple crop marks and mosaic tiling.

➤ The Distort filters create special effects by changing an object's shape and path directions.

➤ The new Gallery Effects filters let you apply special effects like those available in Adobe Photoshop.

➤ The Ink Pen filters let you define the effect created when you create objects with one of the Pen tools.

➤ The Objects filters add or remove anchor points and create copies of a path, and change stroked paths to filled objects.

➤ The Pathfinder filters combine, isolate, and subdivide paths, and build new paths formed by the intersection of objects.

➤ The Select filters select matching parts of an illustration by selecting objects with the same colors, paint styles, and stroke and fill weights.

➤ The Stylize filters let you add special elements to the artwork, such as arrows and drop shadows, as well as create calligraphic effects and rounded shapes.

EXERCISE: JUST FOR FUN

1. Click on one of the rectangles in your artwork to select it.

2. Choose **Filter > Distort > Zig Zag**.

3. Click **OK** or press **Return** to close the dialog box that displays.

4. If you've got the time, play with any of the other Distort filters.

Figure 2.36 Rectangle distorted by Zig Zag filter.

The Window Menu

The Window menu commands lets you show or hide the different palettes available with Illustrator. As you can open more than one Illustrator file at a time, or open more than one window on a single file, the Window menu also provides commands that open new windows or change the active window from one open window to another. The window that is active will have a check mark next to its name in the Window menu.

If your drawing is complex, you can open several windows containing different views of the same document (as set up by commands under the View menu). The Window menu provides an easy way to switch from one view to another. See "Custom Views" in Chapter 10.

SHORTCUT

The Window menu also includes commands for opening all of Illustrator's palettes. Some of these palettes are also opened from other menus and keyboard shortcuts, and you will find other references to the palettes throughout this book.

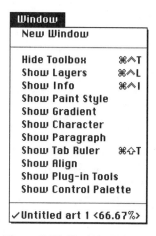

Figure 2.37 The Window menu.

NOTE

A quick overview of all the palettes concludes this chapter.

The Help Menu

6.0 NEW FEATURE

The **Show Shortcuts** command from the help menu displays the first of 12 help screens that show Illustrator's keyboard and mouse shortcuts. Other on-line help for Illustrator is available through the Help menu if you have installed the full help system from the Adobe Illustrator 6.0 deluxe CD-ROM.

EXERCISE: GET HELP

Choose **Show Shortcuts** from the Help menu (the question mark at the top right corner of the screen) to display the first of 12 shortcut lists. Click the **Forward** button if you want to view more.

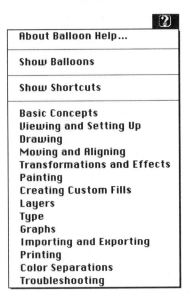

Figure 2.38 Help menu.

The Application Menu

System 7 allows you to run multiple software applications simultaneously—provided you have enough memory. For example, you can concurrently run Adobe Illustrator and Photoshop to create or edit bitmaps or PICT files as templates for Illustrator artwork, *and* you can run a page composition application (such as PageMaker or QuarkXPress) to place Illustrator artwork with text and graphics from other sources on a final page layout. Under System 7, you need not quit one application to start another.

When you are running under System 7, a list of all open applications appears under the Application menu—indicated as an icon at the far right on the menu bar. Choosing an application from the Application menu makes it the active application, displays that application's menu bar, and makes its most recently active window visible.

You cannot open the same document with more than one application at a time. For example, if you try to place an Illustrator document in a page composition application without first closing the document in Illustrator, you will get a message informing you that the file is busy.

WARNING

Examining the Palettes

In Macintosh terminology, a *palette* is a window that can remain open and active on the screen while you are working in a document window. It doesn't have to be closed before you can go on to the next step—as dialog boxes do. It doesn't render the document window inactive when you are working—which happens when you activate other applications or document windows.

The Toolbox is a palette that is normally open when you first start Illustrator (unless you change the defaults). Illustrator offers ten more palettes, including three that are new in version 6.0:

6.0 NEW FEATURE

> ➤ The Information palette (described later in this chapter)

> ➤ The Layers palette (described in Chapter 10)

> ➤ The Paint Style and Gradient palettes (described in Chapter 6)

> ➤ The Paragraph, Character, and Tab Ruler palettes (described in Chapter 8)

> ➤ The Align palette (new in version 6.0, described in Chapter 10)

> ➤ The Plug-in Tools palette (new in version 6.0, described in Chapter 4)

> ➤ The Control palette (new in version 6.0, described later in this chapter and throughout this book)

Basic techniques applicable to all palettes are described next, followed by descriptions of the Information and Control palettes. Other palettes are described in later chapters.

Displaying and Hiding Palettes

All of the commands for displaying or hiding the palettes are listed under the Window menu in Illustrator, and many of the palettes have other command alternatives as well as keyboard shortcuts, shown in Table 2.1.

If a palette is already displayed, you can choose **Window > Hide** (palette name) or use the keyboard shortcut (if applicable), but it's usually much easier to simply click the close box on the palette title bar.

SHORTCUT

Table 2.1 Methods of displaying and hiding palettes, shortcuts in bold.

To display or hide...	Actions
Toolbox	Window > Show/Hide Toolbox **Command+Control+T**
Layers palette	Window > Show/Hide Layers **Command+Control+L**
Information palette	Window > Show/Hide Info **Command+Control+I** Click Measure tool pointer on artwork
Paint Style palette	Window > Show/Hide Paint Style Object > Paint Style... **Command+I**
Gradient palette	Window > Show/Hide Gradient Object > Gradient **Double-Click Gradient Fill tool** Double-click a gradient fill name in the Paint Style palette
Character palette	Window > Show/Hide Character Type > Character **Command+T** Command+Shift+F Type > Tracking... or Kerning Command+Shift+K Type > Size > Other Command+Shift+S Type > Leading > Other
Paragraph palette	Window > Show/Hide Paragraph Type > Paragraph **Command+Shift+P** Type > Spacing Command+Shift+O
Tab Ruler palette	Window > Show/Hide Tab Ruler **Command+Shift+T**
Align palette	Window > Show/Hide Align
Plug-in Tools palette	Window > Show/Hide Plug-in Tools
Control palette	Window > Show/Hide Control Palette

Although you can have as many palettes open as you like while you are working, there are several good reasons for displaying only those palettes you need.

➤ One reason is space: palettes take up room on the screen and are always displayed on top of the document window, so they obscure part of your view of the artwork. The next section describes how to make the best of the situation.

➤ Another reason for limiting the number of open palettes is computer memory. Having more palettes open requires more computer memory, thus taking away from the amount of memory available for the artwork, and slowing performance while you work.

NOTE

Normally, Illustrator opens with all palettes displayed as you left them in the previous session, when you last quit Illustrator. To be sure you are opening Illustrator with minimal memory requirements, close palettes that you don't regularly use before quitting the program.

Positioning Palettes on the Screen

Palettes can be moved on the screen by dragging the title bar, just as you would to move any window. You can maximize your view of the artwork by dragging open palettes to the corners or edges of the screen display. You can even drag a palette off the edge of the display, so only a corner shows, and drag it back into view when you need it—but you might find it faster and more convenient to simply use the keyboard shortcuts to display and hide a palette as needed.

A palette will always display on top of all document windows, but the most recently used palette can appear on top of other palettes if there is overlap. You can bring any palette to the top by clicking on it.

SHORTCUT

If a palette is completely hidden under other palettes, you can move the other palettes or you can use the command under the Window menu to **Hide** and then **Show** the buried palette. Press the **Tab** key to close all palettes at once.

When you display a palette, it will appear in the same position and size on the screen as when you last closed it.

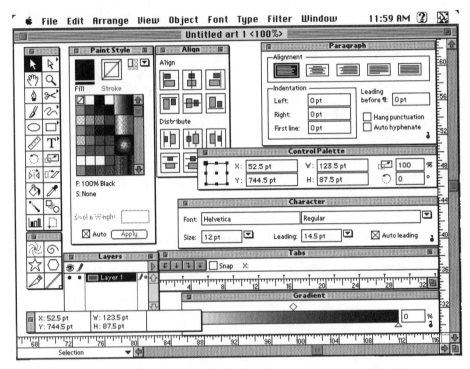

Figure 2.39 Screen display showing all palettes open in their most reduced views.

The Macintosh Interface

Windows and palettes can be moved and sized on the screen. You can have more than one document *window* open at a time, but the active document window will usually display *on top of* any other document windows (unless you have arranged them side-by-side). If you close a document window, you are closing the document. *Palettes*, on the other hand, are always displayed on top of the active window, and each palette is related to the active document only. You can close any palette without closing the active document.

Information Palette

The Information palette is a great productivity aid in precisely positioning and scaling selected objects. It displays information about the size and location of

70

selected objects, or the position of the cursor as you move it. You cannot make entries directly in the palette—changes in the palette reflect actions that you perform in the document window.

The **Window > Show Info** command (**Command+Control+I**) displays the Information palette. You can also display this palette by clicking once on the document window with the Measure tool selected.

If the palette is already displayed, the command on the menu changes to **Hide Info**. You can close it by choosing **Window > Hide Info** or use the keyboard shortcut **Command+Control+I**, but it's usually much easier to simply click the close box on the palette title bar.

Exercise: Display the Information Palette

1. If the Information palette is not already displayed on your screen, display it now by choosing **Window > Show Info**, or use the keyboard shortcut **Command+Control+I**.

2. Move the mouse and see how the numbers on the Information palette change to reflect the current position of the mouse pointer on the screen.

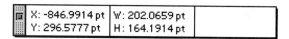

Figure 2.40 The Information palette.

The Information palette displays information that varies depending on the position of the cursor and what object is selected. This information will change dynamically as you move, scale, or otherwise change an active item. Variables that can be displayed in the Information palette include:

➤ X—The position of the cursor or lower left corner of the selected object relative to the zero point on the horizontal ruler.

➤ Y—The position of the cursor or lower left corner of the selected object relative to the zero point on the vertical ruler.

➤ W—The width of the selected object.

➤ H—The height of the selected object.

➤ D—The distance of the cursor or current anchor point from the last anchor point.

➤ r—The angle of the cursor or current anchor point from the last anchor point.

➤ If text is selected with the Selector tool, the Information palette displays the X-Y coordinates and height and width, but if the text is selected with the Type tool, the palette shows type size and font. If a range of text is selected with the I-beam, the palette shows tracking information; if the cursor is inserted between two characters the palette shows kerning information.

Measurements in the Information palette are given in the unit of measure specified through **File > Document Setup** or **File > Preferences > General**. The measurements on the Information palette reflect the mouse pointer's or selected object's position with respect to the **zero point** on the rulers, as described in Chapter 10.

NOTE

Control Palette

The Control palette, new in version 6.0, is also—like the Information palette—a productivity aid in precisely positioning, scaling, and rotating selected objects. Like the Information palette, it displays information about the size and location of selected objects (but not the position of the cursor)—and it adds controls for scaling and rotating selected objects. Unlike the Information palette, you *can* make entries directly in the Control palette—changes in the palette are reflected in the document window.

6.0 NEW FEATURE

The **Window > Show Control Palette** command displays the Control palette. If the palette is already displayed, the command on the menu changes to **Hide Control Palette**. You can close it by choosing **Window > Hide Control Palette**, but it's usually much easier to simply click the close box on the palette title bar.

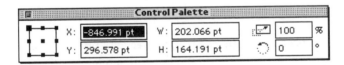

Figure 2.41 The Control palette.

The Control palette displays information about the location and size of a selected object. Unlike the Information palette, this information does not change dynamically as you move, scale, or otherwise change an active item—it changes when you have completed an action in the document window.

The Control palette also includes text-entry boxes that let you change the scale or angle of rotation of an object by making numerical entries.

Items displayed in the Control palette include:

➤ A *proxy* that represents the bounding box of the selected object. The proxy includes 9 *reference point options*—the largest represents the currently selected reference point.

➤ X—The position of the selected object's active reference point relative to the zero point on the horizontal ruler.

➤ Y—The position of the selected object's active reference point relative to the zero point on the vertical ruler.

➤ W—The width of the selected object.

➤ H—The height of the selected object.

➤ The percentage value by which the object has been scaled (enlarged or reduced), with the reference point as the point of origin.

➤ The angle of rotation of the selected object, with the reference point as the point of origin.

NOTE

Measurements in the Control palette are given in the unit of measure specified through *File > Document Setup* or *File > Preferences > General*. The measurements on the Control palette reflect the selected object's position with respect to the *zero point* on the rulers, as described in Chapter 10.

EXERCISE: USING THE CONTROL PALETTE

1. If the Control palette is not already displayed on your screen, display it now by choosing Window > Show Control Palette.

2. Click on one of the rectangles you created earlier to select it.

3. Double-click on the **W** (width) value in the Control palette to select it and type a new number.

4. Press **Enter** to apply the changed value to the selected rectangle.

5. Double-click on the rotation field (the bottom right entry area in the palette) to select it, and type an angle of rotation.

6. Press **Enter** to apply the changed value to the selected rectangle.

7. Choose **Edit > Undo** (**Command+Z**).

8. Click on the reference point of the proxy that is exactly opposite the current reference point in the Control palette. For example, if the top-left corner of the proxy is darker than all the others, click on the lower-right corner now.

9. Repeat steps 5 and 6, using the same rotation angle, and compare the different results.

NOTE

If you want to quit...you can stop going through this tutorial now by simply choosing **File > Close** (to close the file without quitting Illustrator) or **File > Quit** (to quit Illustrator), or you can go on with the exercise steps in the next chapter.

If other Illustrator artwork is open for other uses, be sure to save changes to artwork you want to keep.

In either case, if a dialog box asks if you want to save changes to the open Untitled document, click No—do not save changes.

Chapter Summary

This chapter took you through a tour of the document window and menus in Illustrator. Some of the commands and tools were used in exercises, and other commands and tools are described in more detail in later chapters. The next chapter picks up where this one leaves off, going on with a closer examination of some of the tools in the toolbox.

Chapter 3

Introduction to Tools

This chapter introduces some of the tools available in Adobe Illustrator as they appear in the Toolbox. You will find references to the tools throughout this book. The Toolbox in Illustrator 6.0 includes:

- ➤ Selection tools (described here)
- ➤ Hand tool (described here)
- ➤ Zoom tool (described here)
- ➤ Pen tool and Scissors tools (described in Chapter 4)
- ➤ Brush tool, Freehand and Trace tools (described in Chapter 4)
- ➤ Oval and Rectangle tools (described here)
- ➤ Measure tools (described in Chapter 10)
- ➤ Type tools (described here and in Chapter 8)
- ➤ Rotate tool (described here and in Chapter 5)
- ➤ Scale, Reflect, and Shear tools (described in Chapter 5)

➤ Paint Bucket and Eyedropper tools (described in Chapter 6)

➤ Gradient Vector and Blend tools (described in Chapter 6)

➤ Graph tool (described in Chapter 9)

➤ Page tool (described in Chapter 11)

In addition, Illustrator 6.0 adds a palette of Plug-in tools, described in Chapter 9.

Tutorial Results

In addition to examining the tools, you will learn more about the basic principles and terminology of Illustrator by creating a simple example of Illustrator artwork. The next sections take you through the steps in producing the artwork shown below. In the process, you will be introduced to some of the basic operations and vocabulary terms used throughout this book.

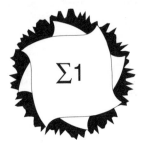

Figure 3.1 Artwork created in Illustrator.

Examining the Toolbox

Like other Macintosh graphics applications, the Illustrator toolbox is a palette, located vertically along the left side of the Illustrator screen, that contains icons for the various tools you use to create, select, and modify objects, and to adjust views of your files. The **Window > Show/Hide Toolbox** command (**Command+Control+T**) shows (or hides) the Toolbox palette, which normally appears along the left side of the Illustrator screen.

The tools are so essential that you will nearly always want them displayed. Adobe keeps the Toolbox small—so it won't interfere with your views of the artwork—by putting more than one tool in some slots and accessing them through pop-out menus. Here we describe some general features of the toolbox, before describing each tool in detail, in the sequence they are displayed in the Toolbox.

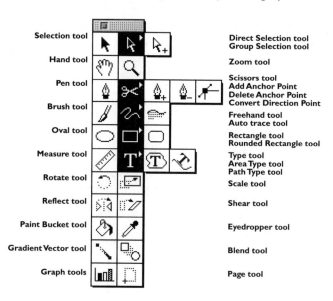

Figure 3.2 The Illustrator toolbox and normally displayed (left) and with all of the pop-out tool options (right).

You will often find yourself accessing the tools in Adobe Illustrator using a two-handed approach—with one hand on the mouse and the other on the keyboard. Becoming familiar with this two-handed approach is the key to attaining fluency in Illustrator, because many of the activities you perform in Illustrator require a combination of keyboard strokes and mouse movements. Although the number of combinations might at first seem daunting, you will find that there is a pattern to the way the keys combine with the various mouse tools. The result is an easy-to-learn set of powerful and flexible tools—once you learn how to activate and use one, you can readily apply the same or a similar technique to others.

NOTE

Hiding the toolbox lets you use the full screen for your drawing area. You can also move the toolbox around the screen by clicking on the top border of the toolbox window and dragging it with the mouse. (Note that you can choose the selection tools, the Hand tool, and the Zoom tools from the keyboard as well as from the toolbox. See descriptions of those tools in later in this chapter for details.)

EXERCISE: DISPLAY TOOL NAMES ON THE STATUS LINE

1. If you want to view the names of the tools as you choose them, and a tool name is not already displayed in the Status Line at the bottom left corner of the screen, then position the mouse over the arrow on the Status Line and hold the mouse button to display the pop-up menu, then keep holding the mouse button down as you drag to highlight **Current Tool** on the menu, then release the mouse button.

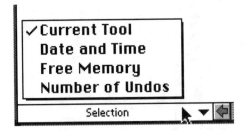

Figure 3.3 Status Line pop-up menu.

2. Display the toolbox by choosing **Window > Show Toolbox** (**Command+ Control+T**).

Selecting a Tool

To select any tool that is visible in the toolbox:

➤ Click on the icon for that tool in the toolbox using the mouse. This will highlight the tool, indicating it has been selected.

In addition to the default tools that appear in the toolbox when you start the program, most of the tools have alternates that appear as pop-up icons to the right of the toolbox. To access these:

1. Press the mouse button on a tool in the toolbox that shows the pop-out menu indicator (a right pointing arrow) until the pop-up icons appear.

2. Drag to the tool you want to use, and release the mouse button.

The alternate tools have functions that are closely related to the default tools from which they pop up. In most cases they can be accessed with a mouse-keystroke combination as well as from their pop-up icons.

When you choose a tool from a pop-up icon, it appears in the toolbox in place of the default tool with which it is associated. To reset a tool to its default, **Shift+double-click** that tool. To reset the whole toolbox to its defaults, **Command+Shift+double-click** any tool.

N O T E

Activating Tools with Keyboard Shortcuts

You can use the following shortcuts to activate many of the tools. For example, you can activate the Zoom-in tool from the keyboard using the **Command** key and the **Spacebar** (in combination with the mouse).

When using the keyboard to change tools, hold down the key(s) *before* you press the mouse button.

N O T E

> ➤ Holding down the **Command** key temporarily changes the current tool to whichever of the three selection tools currently appears in the toolbox, for selecting or moving objects on the page.

> ➤ Holding the **Spacebar** temporarily changes the current tool to the Hand tool for moving the page view in the window.

> ➤ Holding **Command+Spacebar** temporarily changes the current tool to the Zoom-in tool for enlarging.

> ➤ Holding **Command+Option+Spacebar** temporarily changes the current tool to the Zoom-out tool for reducing.

You will find these keystroke shortcuts useful when you are performing an action with one tool (for example, the Pen tool), and need to use another tool (for example, the Selection tool) to modify the action. In such cases, you will not have to divert your attention away from the drawing area of your screen, access the toolbox, select a new tool, and complete your activity. You simply hold down the appropriate key(s).

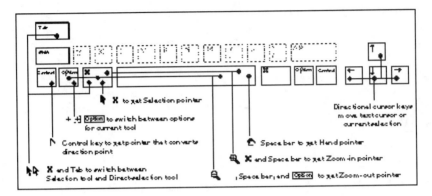

Figure 3.4 Keyboard shortcuts for the toolbox.

Interaction between Keyboard and Tools

The basic mouse operations used with the tools are *clicking* and *dragging*. The **Spacebar**, the **Command** key, the **Shift** key, the **Control** key, and the **Option** key all work interactively with the mouse. The **Shift** and **Option** keys are used to modify or constrain the action of mouse clicks, mouse drags, and the action of the **Command** key and the **Spacebar**.

➤ Pressing the **Shift** key after pressing the mouse button constrains the action of tools. For example, when you are drawing with the Pen tool, straight lines are constrained to 45° angles. When you are drawing with the Rectangle or the Oval tool, rectangles are constrained to squares, and ovals are constrained to perfect circles. Similarly, movements are constrained to 45° angles when you drag an object with the Selection tool.

➤ When you move or transform an object, **Option+clicking** on the Selection tool, or **Option+clicking** on the artwork after selecting the Rotate tool, Scale tool, Reflect tool, or Shear tool results in a dialog box that lets you enter numeric values for the action of the tool. This is a useful alternative to moving or transforming objects visually. Each of the transformation tools (Rotate, Scale, Reflect, and Shear) has an alternate pop-up tool that produces a dialog box, but you can always transform objects numerically without choosing the alternate tool by using the **Option+click** shortcut.

➤ When you move or transform an object, **Option+dragging** produces a copy of the selected object. This is a useful alternative to the **Copy** and **Paste** commands.

Using the Basic Shape Tools

Illustrator's toolbox includes six tools for drawing ovals and rectangles: the Oval tool and the Centered-oval tool, the Rectangle tool and the Centered-rectangle tool, and the Rounded-rectangle tool and the Centered-rounded-rectangle tool.

The Oval Tools

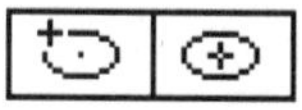

You use the oval tools to create elliptical objects or circles. The oval tools produce an object composed of two paths: an elliptical path, consisting of four curved segments joined by anchor points every 90°, and a single point in the center of the ellipse, which you can use to align the object with respect to other centered objects (text or graphics).

There are two oval tools, the Oval tool and the Centered-oval tool. In creating an ellipse with the Oval tool, you drag the mouse to define the opposite edges of the ellipse. You construct ellipses from center to edge (rather than from edge to edge), using the Centered-oval tool.

Clicking once selects the tool as currently displayed; double-clicking switches between the Oval tool and the Centered-oval tool (displayed with a + in the center). You can also switch between these tools by holding the **Option** key just before you click or hold down the mouse button to position the first point on the screen.

NOTE

Drawing an Oval Visually

1. Choose the Oval tool by clicking or double-clicking the icon in the toolbox.

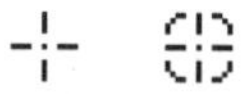

Figure 3.5 The mouse pointer changes to a + in the active window if the Oval tool is active, or to a + framed in four brackets if the Centered-oval tool is selected.

2. Position the + pointer at a corner or center of the ellipse (depending on the tool selection), then drag diagonally and release the mouse to complete the shape. The farther you drag from the starting point, the larger the object becomes.

NOTE

To constrain ellipses to perfect circles, press **Shift** while you drag the mouse (**Shift+drag**) in the desired direction. These techniques are shown in the following figure.

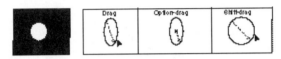

Figure 3.6 Three ways to use the oval tools: drag diagonally to draw an ellipse from edge to edge (left); hold down the Option key and drag diagonally to create an ellipse from center to edge (middle); hold down the Shift key and drag diagonally to create a perfect circle (right)

Creating an Oval Numerically

1. Choose the Oval tool by clicking or double-clicking the icon in the toolbox.

2. Click once in the active window. The point at which you click the tool on the screen defines either the upper left edge of the oval if the Oval tool is selected, or the center of the oval if the Centered-oval tool is selected or if you hold the **Option** key as you click.

3. The Oval dialog box appears, which you use to enter the width and height, up to 120 inches.

NOTE

You can enter values in the default unit of measurement, or enter a value followed by the abbreviation for any unit of measure: in (inches), pt (points), mm (millimeters), or cm (centimeters), (1 point = .0139 of an inch). You can also change the default unit of measure for Ruler units using the **File > Document Setup and File > Preferences > General** commands (see Chapter 10).

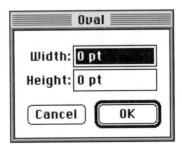

Figure 3.7 The Oval dialog box

EXERCISE: TO MAKE SURE YOU'RE IN SYNC...

If you have not been following this tutorial from the beginning of Chapter 2, and the rulers are not displayed on your screen, choose the following commands now, before you draw the circle in the next steps.

➤ Start Illustrator (if it is not already started).

➤ Choose **File > New** if a blank page is not already displayed. (Or you can continue using the file you started in Chapter 2.)

➤ Choose **View > Fit in Window** (**Command+M**).

➤ Choose **View > Preview** (**Command+Y**).

➤ Choose **Window > Show Toolbox** (**Command+Control+T**) if the Toolbox is not displayed.

➤ Choose **View > Show Rulers** (**Command+R**)

➤ You can also use the Information palette (**Window > Show Info**, or **Command+Control+I**) as a guide in positioning the pointer as described in the next steps.

EXERCISE: PLAYING AROUND

The next steps let you play with the Oval tool. If you don't have time for nonsense, you can skip to the next Exercise: Drawing a Serious Circle.

1. Select the **Oval** tool by clicking on it in the Toolbox.

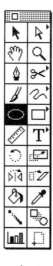

Figure 3.8 The Oval tool selected—no cross mark shows in the center.

NOTE

Be sure the Oval icon in the Toolbox is selected and *does not show* a cross mark in the center, as shown in the previous figure. If it does show a cross mark, then double-click on the Oval tool to remove it.

2. Position the mouse pointer on the page, so the cross bar cursor appears. Hold down the mouse button and drag the mouse diagonally—*do not release the mouse button until you go through this quick exercise:*

➤ As you drag with the mouse, an oval appears on the page, with a cross mark indicating the center of the oval—blue on a color monitor. The oval's edges extend between the starting and ending point of the drag.

➤ Notice that the Information palette changes to show the changing width and height of the oval.

➤ While still dragging with the mouse, hold down the **Shift** key—this forces the oval to be a perfect circle, regardless of where you drag the pointer.

➤ While still dragging the mouse, release the **Shift** key to see how the shape changes.

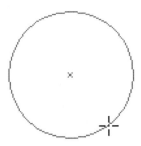

Figure 3.9 Oval shows cross mark in center as you drag the cursor.

3. Release the mouse button to complete the circle.

4. Drag the mouse on the screen again to create another oval. Continue playing with the Oval tool like this to see how it works. Notice that you can't change a finished oval as long as the Oval tool is still selected. You'll learn how to edit objects later in this tutorial.

5. When you are finished playing, simply choose **Edit > Select All** (**Command+A**) to select everything on the page, and then choose **Edit > Cut**, (**Command+X**) or press the Delete or Backspace key to remove all your experiments from the artwork (including those from Chapter 2, if you continued from there).

EXERCISE: DRAWING A SERIOUS CIRCLE

In the next steps, you will use the Oval and Rectangle tools to draw a circle and two squares, using the rulers and the Information palette as guides in determining the position and size of the squares.

1. Select the **Oval** tool by double-clicking on the Oval tool in the Toolbox. Notice that the cross bar cursor is now framed in brackets when you move the cursor onto the page.

Be sure the Oval icon in the Toolbox is selected and shows a cross mark in the center, as shown in Figure 3.10. If it does show a cross mark, then double-click on the Oval tool to display it.

NOTE

2. Position the crossbar pointer near the center of the page. The figure shows the pointer at the 306-point measure (4.25-inch mark) on the X axis or horizontal ruler (at the bottom of the window), and the 396-point measure (5.5-inch mark) on the Y axis or vertical ruler (the ruler on the right side of the window).

    It is not important that you draw the elements precisely as described here, but it is important to know that Illustrator offers you all the tools you need if you *want* to be precise in drawing.

3. Hold down the mouse button and drag the pointer. Hold down the **Shift** key and release the mouse button when the circle is approximately 360 points (5 inches) in diameter—as indicated by the W (width) and H (height) values on the Information palette.

Don't worry if you cannot get the mouse pointer to stop at exactly the measure you intend. You'll gain more proficiency with the tools as you gain experience (and you'll find it easier to work in finer increments in enlarged views).

NOTE

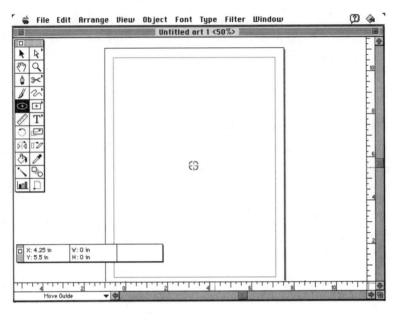

Figure 3.10 The Oval tool selected, and the pointer at the 396-point (5.5-inch) mark on the verti-cal ruler, and at the 306-point (4.25-inch) mark on the horizontal ruler.

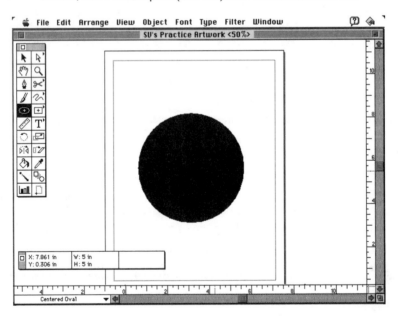

Figure 3.11 5-inch-diameter circle on the screen displays four "handles"—small blue squares at the top, bottom, and sides—indicating that it is *selected* or *active* on the screen.

The circle should appear as a thin blue line (on a color monitor) with black fill, but don't worry for now if the fill is not black—you'll learn how to correct this in the next steps.

Correcting Mistakes

If at any time during this tutorial you make a mistake that you want to correct right away, you can choose **File > Undo (Command+Z)** to reverse your last action(s). You can undo up to 200 of the last operations you performed, in reverse order, by repeated use of the **Undo** command. (You set the number of possible undo's through the **File > Preferences > General** command. If you followed the exercises steps in Chapter 2, you should have **20 Undo** levels.)

You can also press the **Delete** or **Backspace** key—or choose **Edit > Cut (Command+X)**—to remove an object immediately after creating it (i.e., while it is still framed in a blue outline or marked by handles).

Then simply resume at the appropriate step in this tutorial.

EXERCISE: USING THE PAINT STYLE PALETTE

There are several ways of changing the appearance of an object in Illustrator. You can use the Paint Style Palette to change the color of an object. You can use other tools, such as the Paint Bucket tool to color an object. Each of these methods, and the differences among them, are explained in detail elsewhere in this book. In the next step, we use the Paint Style palette to change the color of the circle.

1. If the Paint Style palette is not already displayed on your screen, display it now by choosing **Window > Show Paint Style**, or **Object > Paint Style (Command+I)**.

2. Make the Paint Style Palette smaller by positioning the mouse pointer over the down-pointing arrow in the top right corner of the palette and holding the mouse button down to display the pop-out list of palette display options, then drag the pointer to highlight the third option—to display only the upper left half of the palette. When you release the mouse button, the palette should become smaller, and you can drag it to the side of the artwork.

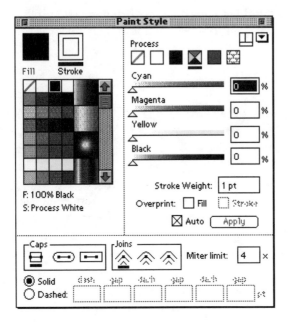
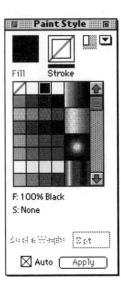

Figure 3.12 The Paint Style palette, full size and reduced.

3. In the Paint Style palette, click on the top left square, labeled **Fill**, then click on the 3rd box in the first row of the paint palette—a black box.

Whenever you make selections in a palette, they are automatically applied to whatever is selected. For this reason, you should always be sure that the object you wish to change is selected before making any entries in a palette.

N O T E

EXERCISE: TO MAKE SURE YOU'RE IN SYNC...

If the circle is still not black, click on the Selection tool in the Toolbox to select it, then select the circle by clicking on an edge so it displays four blue handles. Or, since the circle is the only object in your artwork, you can choose **Edit > Select All**, or use the keyboard shortcut **Command+A.** Then repeat step 2.

If the circle is *still* not black, make sure that **View > Preview** is selected, and that you have selected the **Fill** option in the Paint Style palette.

The Rectangle Tools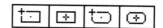

You use the rectangle tools to create rectangular objects or squares. The rectangle tools produce objects composed of two paths: a rectangular path, consisting of four straight-line segments joined at the corners, and a single point in the center of the rectangle, which you can use to align the rectangle relative to other centered objects (text or graphics).

There are four rectangle tools: the Rectangle tool, the Centered-rectangle tool, the Rounded-rectangle tool, and the Centered-rounded-rectangle tool.

➤ In creating a shape with the Rectangle tools, you drag the mouse to define the opposite corners of the rectangle.

➤ The Centered-rectangle and Centered-rounded-rectangle tools draw rectangles from center to edge rather than from corner to corner.

➤ The Rounded-rectangle and Centered-rounded-rectangle tools create rectangles with rounded corners of the radius specified in the General Preferences dialog box. (**File > Preferences > General.**)

You can draw a rectangle visually on the screen or create one with dimensions and rounded corners as specified numerically in a Rectangle dialog box.

Drawing a Rectangle Visually

1. Choose the Rectangle tool by clicking or double-clicking the icon in the Toolbox. To construct rectangles with rounded corners, choose the Rounded-rectangle or Centered-rounded-rectangle tool by holding the mouse button down on the Rectangle tool to display the pop-out menu.

Clicking once selects the tool as currently displayed; double-clicking switches between the Rectangle tools and the Centered-rectangle tools (displayed with a + in the center). You can also switch between these tools by holding the **Option** key just before you hold down the mouse button to position the first point on the screen.

NOTE

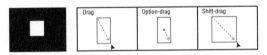

Figure 3.13 The mouse pointer changes to a + in the active window if the Rectangle or Rounded-rectangle tool is active, or to a + framed in four brackets if one of the Centered-rectangle tools is selected.

2. Position the + pointer at a corner or center of the rectangle (depending on the tool selection), then drag diagonally and release the mouse to complete the rectangle.

NOTE

To constrain a rectangle to a perfect square, press the **Shift** key while you drag the mouse (**Shift+drag**) diagonally.

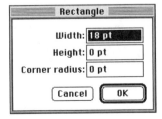

Figure 3.14 Three ways to use the rectangle tools: drag diagonally to draw a rectangle from corner to corner (left); hold down the **Option** key and drag diagonally to create a rectangle from center to edge (middle); hold down the **Shift** key and drag diagonally to create a perfect square (right).

Creating a Rectangle Numerically

1. Choose any of the rectangle tools, then click once in the active window.

   The point at which you click the tool on the screen defines either the upper left corner of the rectangle if one of the Rectangle tools is selected, or the center of the rectangle if the Centered-rectangle tool is selected. Hold the **Option** key as you click to change the current tool selection.

2. The Rectangle dialog box appears. Use the dialog box to enter specific dimensions for a rectangle, including width, height, and corner radius.

```
┌──────────── Rectangle ────────────┐
│                                    │
│        Width: [18 pt          ]    │
│       Height: [0 pt           ]    │
│ Corner radius: [0 pt          ]    │
│                                    │
│        ( Cancel )  (  OK  )        │
│                                    │
└────────────────────────────────────┘
```

Figure 3.15 The Rectangle dialog box.

Changing the Corner Radius Default

The default corner radius for the Rectangle and Centered-rectangle tools is 0 points. The default corner radius for the Rounded-rectangle and Centered-rounded-rectangle tools is 12 points. You can change the default radius using **File > Preferences > General**.

As you increase the value, the corner radius becomes more curved, approaching an oval shape as shown in Figure 3.16. The corner radius cannot exceed half the length of the short sides of the rectangle. If you enter a larger value, Illustrator will draw the largest oval that can fit into the rectangle. Setting the corner radius to 0 creates rectangles with squared corners.

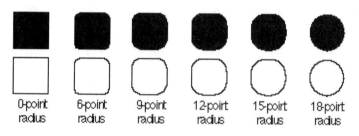

Figure 3.16 Examples of rounded corners on 36-point squares.

Using Filter > Stylize > Round Corners...

The Round Corners filter converts all corner points on any selected path—including rectangles—to smooth curves. To use this filter, follow these steps:

1. Select the path(s) that you want to affect.

2. Choose **Filter > Stylize > Round Corners** to display the Round Corners dialog box

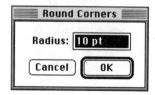

Figure 3.17 The Round Corners dialog box.

3. Enter a value in points in the radius box to determine the degree of roundness. The radius you enter here represents the radius of the circle that would fit exactly into the resulting rounded corners—a wider radius yields a more rounded curve.

4. Click **OK** to close the dialog box and view the effect.

WARNING

You cannot convert a round corner back to corner points, but you can use the **Undo** command if you do not like the effect. You can also use the **Convert Direction Point** tool to convert curve points to corner points—but you will need to move the converted point(s) back into the position where the original corner point was before you used the Rounded Corners filter.

EXERSISE: DRAWING A SQUARE

In the next steps you'll draw a square using a similar technique as you did for drawing a circle earlier.

1. Position the mouse pointer over the Rectangle tool in the Toolbox and hold down the mouse button to open up a pop-up display of a second tool. Select the square-cornered tool.

2. If a cross mark appears in the center of the Rectangle tool, then double-click on the Rectangle tool to simultaneously select it, and remove the cross mark. Otherwise, simply click once on the rectangle tool to select it.

   We wanted the cross mark to appear in the Oval tool for the previous steps, but this time we do not want to draw from the center—we want to draw from the corner of the rectangle—so we want the Rectangle icon in the Toolbox to be empty, as shown in Figure 3.18.

3. Position the crossbar pointer on the "north west" corner of the circle—at the 53-minute position if the circle were a clock face, or 315° point if the circle is 360°.

Figure 3.18 The Rectangle tool selected, and the pointer at the edge of the circle—the 53-minute position if the circle were a clock face, or 315° point if the circle is 360°

4. Hold down the mouse button and drag diagonally to draw the rectangle. Hold down the **Shift** key and release the mouse button when the square meets the opposite edge of the circle.

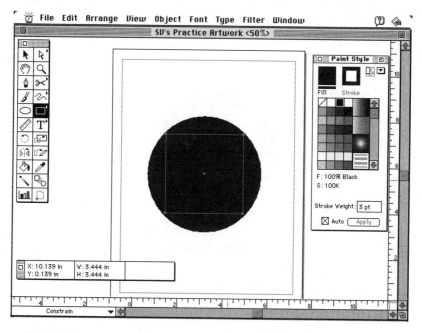

Figure 3.19 Perfect square inside the 5-inch circle on the screen displays four handles, indicating that it is *selected* or *active* on the screen, and the circle is no longer selected.

EXERCISE: OPTIONAL STEPS

You can play with the Rectangle tool(s) here, as you did with the Oval tool in earlier steps, but be sure to press **Delete** or **Backspace**, or choose **Edit > Cut (Command+X)**, or use the **Edit > Undo** command (**Command+Z**) as many times as necessary to remove all but rectangle created in the previous steps. Then select that rectangle with the Selection tool before going on to the next step.

EXERCISE: USING THE PAINT STYLE PALETTE AGAIN

In the next step, we use the Paint palette to change the color of the square.

1. If the Paint Style Palette is not already displayed on your screen, display it now by choosing **Window > Show Paint Style**, or **Object > Paint Style** (**Command+I**).

2. In the Paint Style palette, click on the top left square, labeled **Fill**, then click on the 2nd box in the first row of the paint palette—a white box.

NOTE

If the square does not become white, make sure it is selected, **View > Preview** is active, and you have selected the **Fill** option in the Paint Style palette.

Figure 3.20 The square becomes white when you click the **Fill** option and the white color in the Paint Style palette.

EXERCISE: TO MAKE SURE YOU'RE IN SYNC...

If the square did not turn white, click on the Selection tool in the Toolbox to select it, then select the square by clicking on the center of the circle—where the square is "hidden" since it is black on a black background—to display blue handles at each corner, and repeat Step 2.

Painting Order or Stacking Order

Notice that the rectangle appears on top of the circle. This is because it was drawn after the circle. Normally, objects drawn first appear *below* objects drawn later. You can change this painting, or stacking, order by using the **Arrange > Bring to Front** and **Arrange > Send to Back** commands. These commands rearrange objects that are on the same *layer*. Each layer in Illustrator has its own stacking order. See The Layers palette in Chapter 10 for more information on working in layers.

EXERCISE: SAVE OFTEN

If you have been working on artwork that has not yet been saved—indicated by the fact that the title bar shows it as "Untitled"—then the artwork is stored in the computer's memory, but not yet on a disk. If the power should fail suddenly, you would lose all of the work you have done so far. It's a good idea to save your documents often while you work.

1. Choose **File > Save** (**Command+S**). The first time you use this command, the Save document as dialog box is displayed. Type **Practice Artwork** (or whatever name you choose) in the dialog box. You can choose the drive and folder in which to store the document using the techniques described in Chapter 10 in the description of the **Save as** command. Format options are also described in Chapter 10.

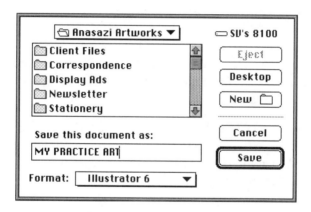

Figure 3.21 The Save document as dialog box.

2. Click **Save** or press **Return** to close the dialog box.

NOTE

Quitting and Resuming This Tutorial: At any time during this tutorial, you can choose **Quit** to exit Illustrator. You do not need to save your work unless you intend to resume the tutorial later.

If you start this tutorial, then save your work and quit Illustrator, you can later choose **Open** from the File menu (**File > Open**) to open the document you saved previously and continue where you left off. Pay attention to where (in what folder, on what disk) you are saving the exercise if you want to find it again!

Using the Selection Tools

The Selection tool—a black pointing arrow—is the default tool that is selected when Illustrator is first opened. It is also the most frequently used tool. In Illustrator, you must always select an object before you take action on it. Thus, you will probably use this and the other selection tools more than any others. You also use the selection tools to move objects, and to adjust curves by dragging curve segments, anchor points, or the direction lines that extend from smooth anchor points.

The Direct Selection tool is a hollow pointing arrow, next to the Selection tool in the toolbox. It shows a small black arrow in the top right corner, which indicates that this is a pop-out menu and that there are several tools in this category—the pop-out menu shows a hollow pointing arrow with a small plus sign beside it. There are actually three selection tools altogether: the Selection tool, the Direct Selection tool, and the Group Selection tool.

 Choose the Selection tool by clicking the solid black arrow icon in the Toolbox. When the Selection tool is active, the mouse pointer changes to a solid arrow.

 Choose the Direct Selection tool by selecting the hollow arrow icon from the Selection tool's pop-up menu and releasing the mouse button. When the Direct Selection tool is active, the pointer changes to a hollow arrow.

 Choose the Group Selection tool by selecting the hollow arrow with a plus sign iconfrom the Direct Selection tool's pop-up menu and releasing the mouse button *or* by pressing the **Option** key when the Selection tool is selected. When the Group Selection tool is active, the pointer changes to a solid arrow with a small plus sign beside it.

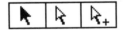

Figure 3.22 The Selection tools.

Selecting Objects

Objects that you create and manipulate in Illustrator include text objects, anchor points, line segments, direction lines, paths, and grouped objects. The two basic methods for selecting objects are to click on the object, or to drag a selection marquee around the object.

Using the Command Key

Holding down the **Command** key temporarily accesses the current selection tool, that is, the most recently active selection tool that appears in the Toolbox. When the **Command** key is pressed, you can toggle between the Selection and Direct Selection tool—or the Group Selection tool if that is displayed in the Toolbox—by pressing the **Tab** key.

Since the selection tools are used so frequently, always use the **Command** key to access the Selection pointer temporarily while using another tool. For example, draw a curve with the Pen tool, then hold down the **Command** key and use the Selection pointer to adjust it.

The only time you really need to click on a Selection tool icon in the Toolbox is when you want to move an object a specified distance (see "Moving Objects", later in this chapter).

Figure 3.23 Two methods of selecting objects.

Both of these methods are standard in many graphics applications and on the desktop of the Macintosh. Figure 3.23 shows both methods of selecting objects. If two or more objects overlap, clicking will select the topmost one, and dragging the selection marquee around the objects selects both (see "Selecting Multiple Objects" later in this chapter). (The selection marquee is a rectangle of dashed lines that appears when you drag the mouse on the screen without selecting any objects first.)

Differences between Selection Tools

The selection tools differ only in the kinds of objects they select. Objects that can be selected with the Selection tool are whole paths, grouped objects, and text objects. Selecting an anchor point also selects any segments that are connected to it, whereas selecting a segment does not select any anchor points.

The Direct Selection tool selects anchor points and line segments.

Clicking or dragging the Selection tool over a grouped object selects the entire group; using the Direct Selection tool allows you to select individual anchor points and line segments from a grouped object. Similarly, clicking or dragging the Selection tool over a path that contains text selects both the path and the type; using the Direct Selection tool allows you to select anchor points and line segments from the path without selecting the type.

The Group Selection tool selects incomplete paths (anchor points and their connecting line segments) or text objects that are part of a group. Clicking or dragging the Group Selection tool over part of a path selects the entire path. Holding down the **Option** key while the Selection tool is active accesses the Group Selection tool and vice versa.

Table 3.1 Selection methods

To select...	Action
An unfilled path	Click the path's outline.
A filled path	Click any part of the object in Preview mode, or the path outline in Artwork view.
More than one object	Shift+click each object, or drag the pointer to create a selection marquee.
All elements	Edit > Select (Command+A).
One object in a grouped set	Click to select the desired object with the Group Selection tool.

To deselect...	Action
One selected object	Edit > Select None (Command+Shift+A); or click an empty area; or Shift+click the object; or click another object to select it (and simultaneously deselect other objects).
All selected objects	Edit > Select None (Command+Shift+A); or click an empty area; or click another object to select it (and simultaneously deselect other objects).

One of several selected objects   Shift+click the object.

Selecting One Object

The most common method of selecting one object is to click it once with the arrow pointer. In Preview mode, you can select an object that has a fill color or pattern by clicking anywhere on the object—either the border or the fill area—if the **Area Select** option is active in the File > Preferences > General dialog box. To select a shape that has no fill, or to select *any* object in Artwork view, you must click on the border of the object.

When you click on a grouped object with the Selection tool, all objects within the group are selected. When you click on a grouped object with the Group Selection tool, only the objects you click within the group are selected. When you click on an ungrouped line or a path, the path displays anchor points.

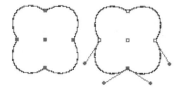

Figure 3.24 Selected objects show paths and anchor points with no handles (left); Direct Selected objects show anchor points (right).

Figure 3.25 To select a line segment without selecting the anchor point, click anywhere on the segment or drag the selection marquee over the segment.

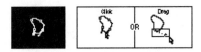

Figure 3.26 To select all of the anchor points and connecting line segments of an ungrouped path, click anywhere on the path with the Selection tool.

Selecting an Anchor Point

Use the Direct Selection tool to select anchor points. First click on any line segment of the object to select the segment and display the anchor points as hollow squares, then click on the anchor point you wish to select. Selected anchor points display as solid squares.

Figure 3.27 Direct Selected anchor points show direction lines and points.

Note that if you click on the fill of an object with the Direct Selection tool, you select the entire object—all segments and anchor points. To select a single anchor point, you can drag a selection marquee around the point. You can select a single *segment* in the same way or by clicking on the point.

There are times when you might find that one anchor point is sitting directly on top of another; this is why it is generally not a good practice to use the marquee selection technique when selecting anchors for joining or averaging. If an anchor point is sitting directly on top of another anchor point, simply select the top anchor point with the Direct Selection tool and move it slightly to one side. You can then work on either anchor point. You can also use the Layers palette to move the selected point/object to a different layer, and hide or lock objects on that layer.

When Joining or Averaging two anchor points, use the Direct Selection tool to select the first point. Press and hold down the shift key while you select the second the anchor point. If you try to use the marquee selection technique, you may accidentally select more than two anchor points and make a mistake.

NOTE

Selecting Text Objects

To select an entire text object, use any of the Selection tools to click on the baseline of the text, drag the selection marquee around the baseline of text, *or*, if the text has a path, click the path. If a text object contains multiple linked text blocks, use the Direct Selection tool to select a single text block by clicking on the baseline or dragging a selection marquee around the baseline of the text.

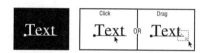

Figure 3.28 Two methods of selecting text.

When you click text using the Selection tool, *point* text is displayed as an anchor point and baseline below the text, *rectangular* text is displayed as text on a baseline surrounded by a rectangle, *area* text is displayed as text on a baseline inside the shape which defines it, and text on a *path* is displayed as text and the path to which it is attached. When text is not selected, you cannot see the baselines, rectangles or the paths to which the text is attached. Methods of associating text with a path are described in Chapter 8.

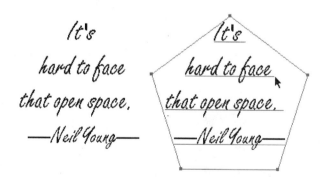

Figure 3.29 Selected text shows baselines and that path (if any) with which the text is associated.

When you click text using the Selection tool, any commands you choose will apply to all of the selected text. Methods of selecting a *range* of text (i.e., not the whole text block) are described in the "Type tool" section later in this chapter.

Selecting One Object that is Part of a Group

To select an entire path that is part of a grouped object, **Option+click** the path with the Direct Selection tool. Subsequent **Option+clicks** continue to add to the selection. If the grouped object consists of only one group, the second **Option+click** selects the entire group, but if the group is made up of objects that are also groups, **Option+clicking** adds those groups to the selection, one by one. This technique, called "up-selecting," is particularly useful when working with grouped objects, such as graphs, that contain many subgroups. (See "Customizing Illustrator's Charts" in Chapter 9.)

  Pressing the **Command** key and the **Tab** key toggles between the Selection tool and the Direct Selection tool or the group selection tool (whichever is displayed in the Toolbox). Holding the **Option** key toggles between the Direct Selection and Group Selection tools.

NOTE

Selecting Multiple Objects

To select more than one object, hold down the **Shift** key before you select each object, or drag the Selection marquee around several objects at once. To extend a selection to include a second object (after one object is selected) or to include additional objects that could not be encompassed by the selection marquee, **Shift+click** on the desired objects or hold down the **Shift** key and drag a selection marquee around the desired objects. The same action applies for deselecting individual objects in a group selection: select any number of objects, then **Shift+click** to deselect one or more.

 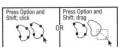

Figure 3.30 Shift+click to add objects to a selection.

Selecting Locked or Hidden Objects

You cannot select objects that have been locked through the **Arrange > Lock** command, unless you first choose **Arrange > Unlock All**. Similarly, you cannot select objects that have been hidden through the **Arrange > Hide** command, unless you first choose **Arrange > Show All**. You can also hide entire layers that have been created through the Layers palette, and you cannot select objects on hidden layers.

NOTE

See the description of the Layers palette in Chapter 10 for information about displaying and activating different layers.

Deselecting All Objects

To deselect all objects, click with the Selection tool on any blank area of the page or pasteboard, or choose **Edit > Select None** (**Command+Shift+A**). The **Undo** command sometimes deselects the current selection.

NOTE

It's a good practice to deselect objects as soon as you know you are finished working with the current selection. Otherwise, you might inadvertently send objects to another layer or apply a paint style when you had intended only to change layers or paint styles for the next action.

Using Filters to Select Objects

The Select filters select all objects that match the paint attributes of a single selected object. This is useful when you want to edit a number of objects in the same way. One of these filters finds stray single points in an illustration.

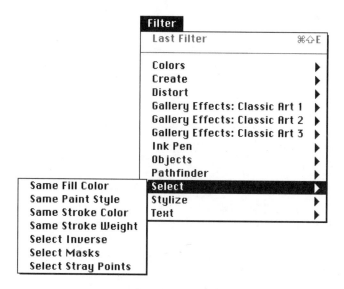

Figure 3.31 The Filter > Select submenu.

Filter > Select > Same Fill Color

To select all objects in the artwork that have the same fill:

1. Select one or more paths that share the same fill.
2. Choose **Filter > Select > Same Fill Color.**

Filter > Select > Same Paint Style

To select all objects in the artwork that have the same fill, stroke, and stroke weight:

1. Select one or more objects that share the same fill and stroke attributes (including stroke weight).
2. Choose **Filter > Select > Same Paint Style.**

Filter > Select > Same Stroke Color

To select all objects in the artwork that have the same stroke color:

1. Select one or more objects that share the same stroke color.
2. Choose **Filter > Select > Same Stroke Color.**

Filter > Select > Same Stroke Weight

To select all objects in the artwork that have the same stroke weight:

1. Select one or more objects that share the same stroke weight.
2. Choose **Filter > Select > Same Stroke Weight.**

Filter > Select > Select Inverse

To select all objects in the artwork that are not currently selected, and deselect the currently selected object(s):

1. Select one or more objects.
2. Choose **Filter > Select > Select Inverse.**

Filter > Select > Select Masks

To select all objects in the artwork that mask, choose **Filter > Select > Select Masks**.

Filter > Select > Select Stray Points

Stray points usually occur when you click the pen tool on the page and then switch to some other tool without creating a path, or if you delete ovals or rectangles without deleting their center points. They're hard to see because they have no fill or stroke, but they appear as little square's on the artboard when you select them. To select all stray points in the artwork—single points with no path, choose **Filter > Select > Select Stray Points**, then press the **Delete** key to remove all stray points.

Moving Objects

Here we describe the most basic method of moving objects using the Selection tool. There are a wide variety of other methods for moving objects—entering numeric values in a dialog box, using arrow keys, using the Control palette, using the **Move Each** command, and using the **Offset Path** command—all described under "Efficient Methods of Moving Objects" in Chapter 10.

To move a selected object visually on the screen, drag it using the Selection tool.

➤ **Shift+dragging** constrains the movement to a multiple of 45° angles—that is, you will be able to move the object only along one of eight angles: 0°, 45°, 90°, 135°, 180°, 225°, 270°, and 315°.

➤ **Option+dragging** moves a copy of the selected object and leaves the original in place.

NOTE

Using the **Option** key to toggle between the Group Selection tool and the Direct Selection tool is not the same as **Shift+dragging** or **Option+dragging**. To use the **Option** key to toggle between tools, you must hold down the key *before* pressing the mouse button. To **Shift+drag** or **Option+drag**, you must hold down the key *after* pressing the mouse button to select the object you want to drag.

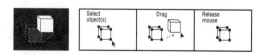

Figure 3.32 Moving objects.

EXERCISE: TO MAKE SURE YOU'RE IN SYNC...

In the next steps, you can click anywhere on the circle or square to select them because you are working in **Preview** mode, and the objects have a solid fill, and the **Area Select** option is on (File > Preferences > General). If you were working in Artwork view, or if the Fill were set to **None**, or if the **Area Select** option were off, you would have to click on an edge of the square to select it.

If Step 2 does not work for you as described below, be sure that **View > Preview** and **View > Show Edges** are selected, that the square has a solid white fill as applied in earlier steps, the circle has a solid black fill, and that the **Area Select** option is set on through File > Preferences > General.

EXERCISE: PLAY WITH THE SELECTION TOOLS

As long as the mouse pointer looks like a crossbar (as in the previous tutorial steps), every time you press the mouse button and drag you will start drawing another rectangle. To *change* a rectangle that you have already created, you must switch to a Selection tool.

1. Position the mouse pointer over the Selection tool—the black arrow—in the Toolbox and click.

2. Click alternately anywhere on the circle and then on the square and see how the values change in the Information palette. Notice that the currently selected object is displayed with a blue path (on a color monitor) and anchor points.

3. Hold the **Shift** key down as you click on both the circle and the square. By holding the shift key, you can select more than one object at a time. Notice that the Information palette changes to show the full dimensions of the selected items. The Paint palette shows a question mark in the Fill area, since there are different fills included in the selection.

4. Click away from the objects to deselect them, then position the pointer near the top left corner of the page and hold down the mouse button as you drag diagonally to surround both objects in a selection marquee—a dotted-line square on the screen. When both objects are surrounded by the marquee. Release the mouse button and see that both objects are selected.

5. Position the pointer on the square and hold down the mouse button and drag. As you drag with the mouse, notice that the Information palette changes to show the changing position of the rectangle as it moves. While

still dragging, hold down the **Shift** key to move the rectangle along a 45°
angle; then release the **Shift** key to see how the position changes.

6. When you release the mouse button, choose **Element > Undo move**
immediately (**Command+Z**).

Remember that you can use the **Undo** command to successively undo the most
recent previous actions—up to 200 previous steps, or as many as you specify through
the **Preferences** command (described in Chapter 10).

N O T E

7. Position the pointer on the square and hold down the **Option** key as you
drag the mouse to move the square—notice that you are actually dragging a copy of the square.

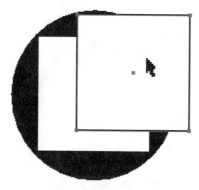

Figure 3.33 Hold the **Option** key to drag a copy of the square.

8. When you release the mouse button, choose **Edit > Undo** immediately
(**Command+Z**).

9. Position the pointer on a corner of the square and hold down the **Control**
key as you drag the mouse to move the corner—notice that you are only
dragging the corner of the square, and thereby changing its shape.

10. When you release the mouse button, choose **Edit > Undo** immediately
(**Command+Z**).

11. Position the pointer on a corner of the square and hold down the **Option**
and **Control** keys as you drag the mouse to move the corner—notice that
you are not only dragging the corner of the square, you are actually drag-

ging a copy of the corner point and its two adjacent anchor points, thereby creating a second, different shape.

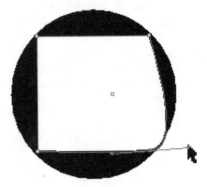

Figure 3.34 Hold the **Control** key to drag an anchor point.

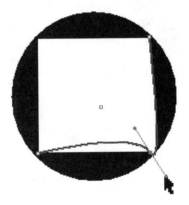

Figure 3.35 Hold the **Option** and **Control** keys to drag a copy of an anchor point and its two adjacent points.

12. When you release the mouse button, choose **Edit > Undo** immediately (**Command+Z**).

Using the Rotate Tool

There are two ways to rotate an object: numerically (as we do in the next step) or visually. Both methods are described in detail in Chapter 5.

EXERCISE: MAKE SURE YOU'RE IN SYNC...

Before going on to the next step, make sure that the artwork shows simply a white square on a black circle. If the square has been moved or copied, choose **Edit > Undo (Command+Z)** as many times as necessary to "back up" to the early stage.

EXERCISE: ROTATING VISUALLY

1. With the square selected (that is, with the handles displayed), click the Rotate tool in the Toolbox to select it.

2. Position the mouse pointer anywhere on the square and hold down the mouse button as you drag the mouse slowly in a circular motion. Notice that the square rotates around the point where you first positioned the mouse.

3. Release the mouse button to end the rotation. You can rotate objects visually like this on the screen, but there is another method that lets you control the angle of rotation numerically, used in the next steps.

4. Choose **Edit > Undo (Command+Z)** to undo the rotation.

EXERCISE: ROTATING NUMERICALLY

1. With the Rotate tool still selected, hold down the **Option** key and click once (i.e., **Option+click**) in the center of the square to display the Rotate dialog box.

2. Type **45** in the Angle edit box, as shown in the figure below.

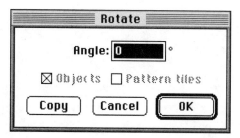

Figure 3.36 Rotate dialog box is displayed when you **Option+click** with the Rotate tool pointer on the screen.

3. Click **Copy** to close the dialog box. This creates and rotates a copy of the square.

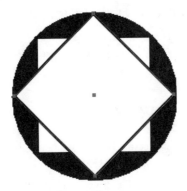

Figure 3.37 Rotated square.

NOTE

You've now learned how the Rotate tool works, and you can use similar techniques with the other transformation tools—the Scale, Reflect, and Shear tools.

EXERCISE: SAVE AGAIN

➤ Choose the **File > Save**, or use the keyboard shortcut **Command+S**.

Remember that when you used the **Save** command for the first time you got a dialog box that asked you to name the file and tell Illustrator where to save it. Subsequently, whenever you use the **Save** command Illustrator simply updates the same file. If you want to save the file again without overwriting the first file, you can use the **Save as** command, as described in Chapter 10.

If You Want to Quit...

Before quitting, you might want to skip ahead and try printing your work now.

Otherwise, you can stop going through this tutorial now by simply choosing **File > Close** (to close the file without quitting Illustrator) or **File > Quit** (to quit Illustrator).

If you want to resume this tutorial later, start Illustrator, then choose **File > Open** and locate the name of the file you used in the previous steps.

Using the Type Tool T

You can use the Type tool to type text in Illustrator, as shown in the next steps. The Type tools are described in detail in Chapter 8.

EXERCISE: TYPE TEXT

1. Click the Type tool in the Toolbox, then position the I-beam pointer in the center of the squares and click to position a blinking text cursor.

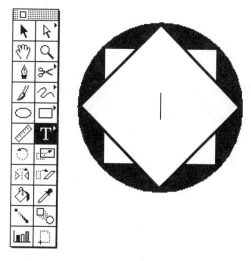

Figure 3.38 A blinking text cursor appears on the screen when you select the Type tool and click on the page.

2. Type your initials or any short word. It doesn't matter whether you type a period after each initial, or whether you type them in all caps—these are your own design decisions.

The text appears as a small gray bar in the center of the square. You can't read the type because you are viewing a 50% reduction of 12-point type. You'll make the text more visible in the next steps.

NOTE

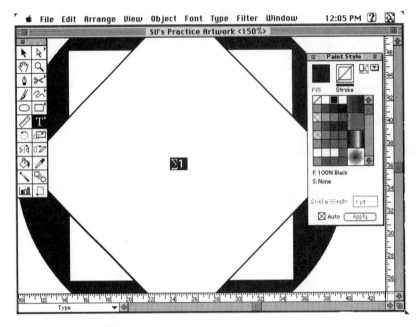

Figure 3.39 Type your initials

Using the Hand Tool

You can use the Hand tool as an alternative to the scroll bars to move the view of the artwork within the document window. The Hand tool can move the image of your artwork in the active window vertically, horizontally, and diagonally. It moves the whole page, not the selected objects on the page. Think of the Hand tool as your own hand and the image in the active window as a piece of paper sitting on your desk. Just as you place your hand on top of the paper and move it across your desk, so the Hand tool moves the image across the screen. By using the Hand tool, you can scroll diagonally with one movement instead of having to click on two scroll bars to accomplish the same movement. You can also use the Hand tool to go quickly to or Fit in Window view, as described here.

➤ Choose the **Hand** tool by clicking on its icon in the toolbox beside the Zoom tool, or hold down the **Spacebar** when a different tool is selected to activate the Hand tool temporarily. When you release the Spacebar, the previously selected tool will once again be active. When the Hand tool is active, the mouse pointer changes to a hand.

➤ To scroll with the Hand tool, position the hand on the active window, hold down the mouse button, and drag in the direction you wish to scroll.

➤ To change to **Fit In Window** view, double-click on the **Hand** tool icon in the toolbox as an alternative to using **View > Fit In Window (Command+M)**.

Double-clicking the **Hand** icon does not select the Hand tool, but leaves the currently selected tool still in effect.

NOTE

Figure 3.40 summarizes two ways of using the Hand tool to change views of your image in the active window.

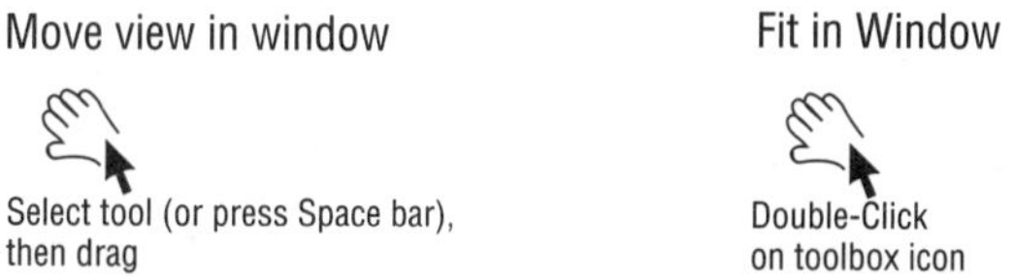

Move view in window   Fit in Window

Select tool (or press Space bar),   Double-Click
then drag   on toolbox icon

Figure 3.40   Three uses of the Hand tool icon in the toolbox.

Always use the **Spacebar** to access the Hand tool quickly while another tool is selected. The only time you need to click on the Hand tool icon in the toolbox is when you want to change to a Fit in Window view. When a Type tool is selected, hold down the **Command** key and then hold the Spacebar , then release the Command key to get the had tool.

SHORTCUT

Using the Zoom Tool ⚲

Use the Zoom tool to change the level of magnification at which you view your file. Illustrator provides nine levels of magnification, each increased or decreased by a factor of two. From actual size (100%), you can zoom in (magnify) to 200%, 400%, 800%, and 1600%, and zoom out (reduce) to 50%, 25%, 12.5%, and 6.25% of actual size.

There are several ways of activating magnifying and reducing the view:

➤ Choose the Zoom tool by clicking its icon in the toolbox.

➤ Change the Zoom from magnify to reduce by holding the **Option** key after the Zoom tool is selected.

➤ Hold **Command+Spacebar** to select the Zoom-in tool temporarily if you have another tool already selected. The mouse pointer changes to a magnifying glass with a **plus** sign in the center. When you release the **Command** key and **Spacebar**, the previously selected tool will once again be selected.

➤ Hold **Command+Option+Spacebar** to select the Zoom-out tool temporarily if you have another tool already selected. The mouse pointer changes to a magnifying glass with a **minus** sign in the center. When you release the **Command** and **Option** keys and the **Spacebar**, the previously selected tool will once again be selected.

➤ To zoom in to an actual size (100%) view of the center of the active window, double-click the Zoom tool icon in the Toolbox. Note that double-clicking does not select the Zoom tool, but leaves the currently selected tool in effect.

➤ To zoom out to a 6.25% view of the entire pasteboard, hold down the **Option** key and double-click the Zoom tool icon.

➤ You can also change views using commands under the View menu, described in Chapter 2. See also the description of the **View > New View** command in Chapter 10.

Figure 3.41 shows the various pointer shapes for the zoom tools: a plus sign enlarges the view, a minus sign reduces the view, and an empty Zoom icon indicates that you have enlarged or reduced to the limit.

$$\oplus \quad \ominus \quad Q$$

Figure 3.41 The appearances of the zoom tools: (1) A plus sign enlarges the view, (2) a minus sign reduces the view, (3) an empty Zoom icon indicates that you have enlarged (or reduced) to the limit.

Always use the **Command** key and **Spacebar** to magnify a detail of your drawing; this method is much faster than clicking the icon in the Toolbox.

NOTE

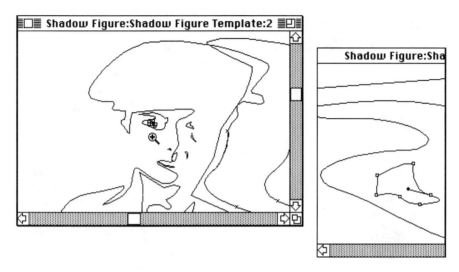

Figure 3.42 Reduced and enlarged views of the same detail.

EXERCISE: CHANGING VIEWS

Up until now you have been viewing the entire page on the screen. In the next steps, you'll zoom in to a closer view. You could click on the Zoom tool in the Toolbox to select it, or choose commands from the View menu to change views, but here we'll use a much faster method of changing the view.

1. Hold down the **Command** key and **Spacebar**—the mouse pointer changes to a magnifying glass with a plus sign in the middle—and click once on the center of the square. The screen view changes to an enlarged view of the artwork.

2. Hold the **Option** key along with the **Command** key and **Spacebar**—the mouse pointer changes to a magnifying glass with a minus sign in the middle—and click once on the center of the square. The view changes again to a reduced view.

3. Play with these keys a little until your view looks like the one in Figure 3.43—100% magnification (i.e., actual size).

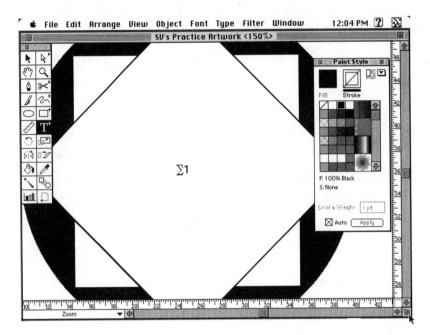

Figure 3.43 An enlarged view of the artwork.

NOTE

If the text is invisible, don't worry—go through the next steps to the next "Make Sure You're in Sync" step.

Selecting and Formatting Text

Notice that the blinking text cursor is still visible at the end of the text. This shows you where the next characters you type will appear. You could keep typing to add more text, but in order to change the text you have already typed you need to select it, as shown in the next steps.

EXERCISE: TO MAKE SURE YOU'RE IN SYNC...

Make sure that the blinking text cursor is still visible at the end of the text. If you don't see it, first make sure the Type tool is selected in the Toolbox, and click the I-beam anywhere on the text in the center of the square.

NOTE

If the text is invisible, it might have taken on the white fill and stroke settings in the Paint Styles palette. You can correct this after Step 1 or 2—while the text is selected—by clicking on the Fill icon at the top left corner of the Paint Style palette, and then clicking the black box on the top row of the color palette.

EXERCISE: FORMAT TEXT

1. Choose **Edit > Select All** (**Command+A**). The selected text becomes highlighted on the screen. The black text should appear white on a black bar when selected.

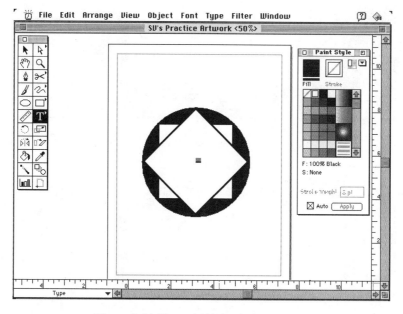

Figure 3.44 Text is highlighted when selected.

2. Make the text 72-pt by making choosing **Type > Size > 72** from the Size pop-up menu under the Type menu. Choose **Type > Alignment > Center**. Select any font you wish from the Font menu.

3. Click away from the text to deselect it.

SHORTCUT

As an alternative to making changes using the **Size**, **Alignment**, and **Font** commands, you could use the Character and Paragraph palettes or the Control palette, as described in Chapter 8. As a general rule, if you want to change only one type specification, you should use the menu command. If you want to change two or more variables, open the palettes.

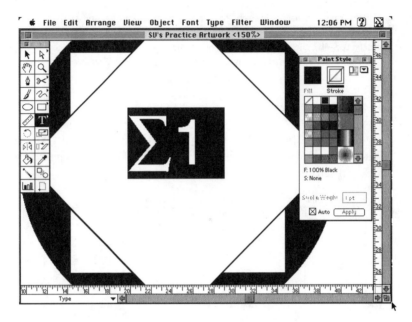

Figure 3.45 The enlarged text is still highlighted.

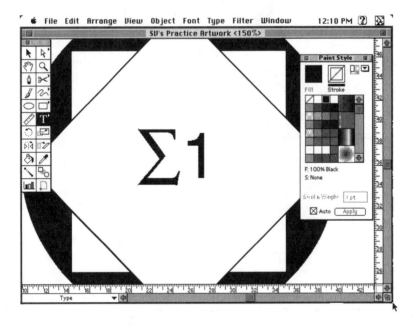

Figure 3.46 Larger, centered type.

EXERCISE: TEMPORARILY SELECTING THE SELECTION TOOL

So long as the Type tool is selected, you can type new text or edit existing text, but you cannot select other objects or select and move a text block *unless* you use the Selection tool.

1. With the Type tool still selected, hold down the **Command** key to get the Selection tool. Holding down the **Command** key, position the pointer on various parts of the text and click.

NOTE

You should notice that the text block becomes selected—the baseline appears as a blue line below the text, and the alignment point appears as an anchor point on the baseline—*only* when you click on the baseline with the pointer. Otherwise, when you click on any other part of the text, you actually select the square behind it.

2. Holding down the **Command** key, select the text and drag it to the center of the square (if it is not already centered).

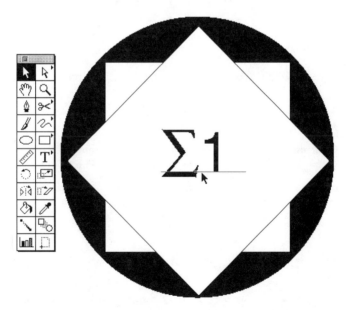

Figure 3.47 Roughly centered text.

3. When you release the **Command** key the Type tool is still selected.

Editing Text

Next you will edit the text that you have already typed. You edit text the same way you edit text on the desktop (such as file names and folder names) or in most Macintosh applications. Position the I-beam pointer within a line of text and:

➤ Click once to position the pointer for inserting text.

➤ Double-click a word to select the whole word.

➤ Drag the I-beam pointer over a range of characters to select them.

Type to insert text or replace the selection. The Type tool and the Text dialog box are explained in detail in Chapter 8.

EXERCISE: EDIT THE TEXT

➤ With the Type tool selected, click to position the blinking cursor just before your last initial, and type your middle initial (if you did not type it already) or press the **Delete** or **Backspace** key to remove it if you did type it.

EXERCISE: SAVE AGAIN

➤ Choose the **File > Save**, or use the keyboard shortcut **Command+S**.

N O T E

If You Want to Quit: Before quitting, you might want to skip ahead and try printing your work now.

Otherwise, you can stop going through this tutorial now by simply choosing **File > Close** (to close the file without quitting Illustrator) or **File > Quit** (to quit Illustrator).

If you want to resume this tutorial later, start Illustrator, then choose **File > Open** and locate the name of the file you used in the previous steps.

Using the Align Palette

N O T E

The next few steps are optional. You can learn a few more commands or features by going through them now, or you can skip ahead and try printing your work now.

6.0 NEW FEATURE

If you are very careful and work with the rulers displayed and the Information palette open, you might be able to center two or three objects by dragging them on the screen, but Illustrator offers a much quicker and precise method of aligning objects— the Align palette, added in Illustrator 6.0 and described in detail in Chapter 10.

1. Choose **View > Fit in Window** (**Command+M**) to view all of the artwork on the screen.

2. Hold down the **Command** key to get the Selection tool, and drag a selection marquee to surround all the objects and select them.

Figure 3.48 Dragging the pointer to select objects.

3. Choose **Window > Align** to display the Align palette, then click **Center** for both Horizontal and Vertical alignment as shown in Figure 3.49.

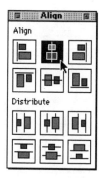
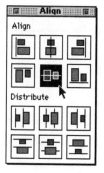

Figure 3.49 The Align palette set to align the centers of all elements.

Figure 3.50 All objects aligned to a common center point.

4. Click **OK** or press **Return** to close the dialog box.

Distorting

Illustrator offers several filters for quickly changing the shape of an object or group of objects. In the next steps you'll use the Roughen filter, but you can try similar steps with the other filters as well—as described in Chapter 5.

1. Choose **Edit > Select All** (**Command+A**) to select all the elements.

2. Choose **Filter > Distort > Roughen**.

3. Keep the default values in the dialog box for now.

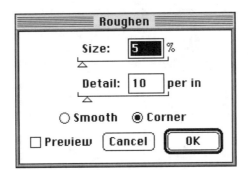

Figure 3.51 The Roughen dialog box.

4. Click **OK** to close the dialog box.

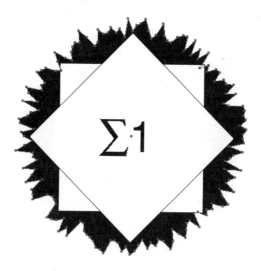

Figure 3.52 The changed objects.

If you want to try different values, or to try some of the other Distort filters on your own, press **Command+Z** to reverse the last step.

NOTE

Printing

If you have a printer hooked up to your system, choose the **File > Print** (**Command+P**) and then click **OK** or press **Return** to close the dialog box and accept all of the defaults for printing.

The **Print** command and all of the dialog box options are explained in detail in Chapter 11.

NOTE

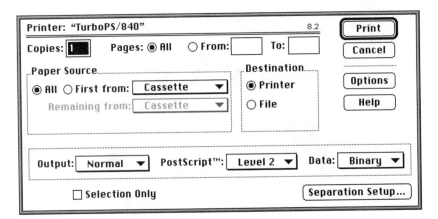

Figure 3.53 The Print dialog box.

Quitting

1. Whenever you want to stop using Illustrator, choose **File > Quit** (**Command+Q**). If you have not saved your work, Illustrator will prompt you to do so whenever you quit the program.

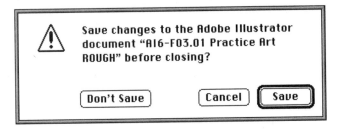

Figure 3.54 Prompting to save your latest changes.

2. Click **Save** to save the changes you have made since the last Save, or click **Don't Save**—do not save the latest changes to the artwork—if you want the cancel any changes you have made since you last saved the artwork. The previous version will still remain on disk.Click **Cancel** to cancel the **Quit** command

NOTE

If you click **Save**, Illustrator saves the file using the artwork name in the title bar or, if the window is named "Untitled art," Illustrator displays the Save as dialog box, prompting you to enter a new name for the file. Once you do this, Illustrator completes the **Quit** command, returning you to the desktop.

Summary

You should now be familiar with some of the basic concepts and terminology that you will encounter in learning Illustrator.

In addition to the Oval and Rectangle tools that you used in earlier steps of this tutorial, one of the most commonly used drawing tools in Illustrator is the Pen tool. If you are not already familiar with this tool, we recommend that you study the first few techniques described in the next chapter, before attempting some of the more advanced techniques described in Chapter 9.

Chapter 4

The Key to the Kingdom— Drawing Lines and Curves

Illustrator (like other PostScript-based drawing applications) calls any line or curve a *path*. Paths may be composed of both curved and straight line segments, connected by *anchor points*. Paths may be open (lines or curves) or closed (shapes). An *open* path has two endpoints; a *closed* path or solid shape has no endpoints—all points are connected to each other. The anchor points along curves usually have *direction handles*. Each of these elements is shown in the figure below.

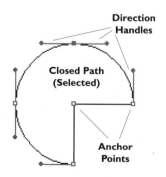

Direction Handles

Closed Path (Selected)

Anchor Points

Illustrator has several drawing tools that can be used to draw curves and lines. Many illustrators use the Pen tool more than any other tool to create paths, supplemented by the Freehand tool and the Autotrace tool. The Freehand tool and Pen tool and the types of paths they create are described in this chapter. Other tools that create paths include the Oval and Rectangle tools, used in the tutorial in Chapters 2 & 3, and the new plug-in tools in Illustrator 6 that create common shapes like spirals, stars, and polygons.

This chapter summarizes the basic steps in drawing a line or curve and then describes how to edit paths. Chapter 9 goes beyond these basics by describing how to create special effects related to the appearance of the line or *stroke* and the *fill*.

NOTE

In all of the techniques that follow, we assume that you are working in Preview mode (**View > Preview**, or **Command+Y**, or **View > Preview Selection**, **Command+Control+Y**). You can work in Artwork view, but you won't be able to see the results the way they are shown in the figures here unless you change to Preview mode.

About Paths, or Bezier Curves

All of the drawing tools in Illustrator create *Bezier curves*—paths composed of dots (anchor points) connected by lines (segments).

Paths may be composed of both curved and straight line segments, and may be open (lines) or closed (shapes). An *open* path has two endpoints; a *closed* path, or solid shape, has no endpoints—all points are connected to each other. The anchor points along curves usually have *direction handles*—direction lines with direction points on the end. Each of these elements is shown in the next figure, and you will learn how to create and modify them in the following tool descriptions.

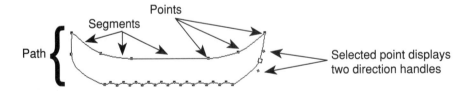

Figure 4.1 In PostScript, Bezier curves are paths composed of points that are joined by straight lines or curves defined by direction handles.

There are two types of points that can occur on a path:

➤ *Smooth* or *curve points* create a smooth curve between two other points. Smooth points display as hollow squares with two handles (direction lines and direction points) when the path they are on is selected, or as solid-filled squares with two handles when the anchor point is selected. The direction lines and direction points control the shape of a curve.

➤ *Corner points* cause an abrupt change in the direction of the curve or line. They join two straight lines, a straight line and a curve, or two curves which meet at a point. Like smooth points, they display as hollow squares when the path they are on is selected, or as filled squares when the point itself is selected. No handles are apparent if the point joins two straight lines, one handle shows if the point joins a straight line to a curve, and two handles are visible if the point joins two curved segments.

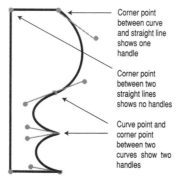

Corner point between curve and straight line shows one handle

Corner point between two straight lines shows no handles

Curve point and corner point between two curves show two handles

Figure 4.2 Examples of the various types of points.

Using the Freehand Tool

Use the Freehand tool to draw a continuous line of any shape freehand—that is, without clicking and dragging each anchor point (as required when using the Pen tool).

You choose the Freehand tool by clicking the icon in the Toolbox. The mouse pointer changes to a pencil icon in the active window. Hold down the mouse button and begin drawing your object by dragging the mouse along the path you wish to draw.

Dragging quickly results in fewer anchor points in a given distance than dragging slowly does. You can also force more or fewer anchor points per distance by adjusting the tolerance level through the General Preferences dialog box (see File

> Preferences > General in Chapter 10). A low tolerance value results in more anchor points per given distance than does a high tolerance value. The following figure shows the effects of different tolerance settings.

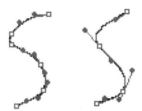

Figure 4.3 Set tolerance in the General Preferences dialog box to control the number of anchor points created by the Freehand tool: Line drawn with a tolerance value of 2 pixels (left); and with a tolerance value of 10 pixels (right).

N O T E

Use a high tolerance setting (in the General Preferences dialog box) and drag the Freehand tool quickly unless you need a lot of anchor points for fine adjustments; note that anchor points increase the amount of disk space required by an illustration. You can always add anchor points with the Scissors tool if you need more (see later in this chapter).

After you have drawn a path with the Freehand tool, you can adjust the line segments and anchor points as described under the Pen tool later in this chapter, and set Stroke and Fill patterns as described under the Paint Style palette in Chapter 6. You can also erase anchor points while you are drawing by holding down the **Command** key and backing up along the line you have just traced with the Freehand tool.

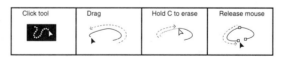

Figure 4.4 Using the Freehand tool.

SHORTCUT

You can temporarily change the Freehand tool to the Pen tool without returning to the tool palette by holding down the **Control** key.

Completing an Open Path

To complete an open path (with the Freehand tool, simply release the mouse button. To complete an open path with the Pen tool, you must click the or Pen tool icon in the toolbox or hold the **Command** key to change to the Selection tool and then click anywhere. The pointer changes from a + to an x, indicating that the Freehand or Pen tool is available to start a new path.

Using the Pen Tool

Other tools that also create paths are the Oval tool, the Rectangle tool, and the Freehand tool. A path is any line or shape drawn in Illustrator. Paths may be composed of both curved and straight line segments and may be open (straight or curved lines) or closed (shapes).

 In the next sections, we summarize the methods of drawing complex curves using the Pen tool, and then apply those methods in exercise steps to manually draw eight familiar symbols composed of simple lines and curves: the numbers 1 through 8.

Pen Tool Overview

Choose the Pen tool by clicking the icon in the toolbox. The mouse pointer changes to a pen (or an x if **Use Precise Cursors** is slected through **File>Preferences General**) in the active window. To use the Pen tool, position the pointer on the screen and click the mouse button. This positions an anchor point on the screen. Before releasing the mouse button, drag the pointer to set a direction line for the anchor. As you drag the pointer around the screen while holding down the mouse, the direction line for the anchor point changes. When you release the mouse button, the anchor point and direction lines are set and the pointer changes from an x to a +, ready to position the second anchor point along the path. Reposition the pointer and repeat for each new anchor point.

The direction lines do not print. They are tangent to the line of the curve and determine in which direction and how deep the curve will be drawn.

Drawing Straight Lines

To draw a straight line, follow these steps:

1. Click the mouse button once to position the first anchor point. Do not drag the mouse yet. If Use Precise Cursors is selected through File>Preferences> General, the mouse pointer changes to a +, indicating that the next point you click with the mouse will create another anchor point on the current path.

2. Move the mouse and click again to set the anchor point for the other end of the straight line. A straight line automatically appears on the screen, connecting the two anchor points. Holding the **Shift** key before clicking on the second point constrains the line to 45° angles.

The following figure shows how these steps combine to result in a straight line.

Figure 4.5 Drawing straight lines.

Exercises in Drawing Curves and Lines

The exercises steps in this chapter are not simply a lesson in creating your own numerals—you can use text more easily for that. It just so happens that the numbers offer a range of challenges in using the Pen tool: straight lines, curves, corner points, open paths, and closed paths. By following these steps, you should learn enough to be able to draw any shaped path you can imagine.

In all of these exercises steps, you can work at any scale you like, but choose a magnification such that the number you are creating fills as much as one-fourth of the screen—roughly centered.

EXERCISE: THE NUMBER 1: STRAIGHT LINES

The number 1 is the simplest to draw. In the next steps, you'll draw three versions.

1. Select the **Pen** tool (an ink pen nib in the Toolbox) and click the mouse once to position the bottom of a straight line.

2. Position the pointer where you want to position the top of the number and hold the **Shift** key as you click once again. By holding the **Shift** key, you can force the line to follow the closest 45° angle from the first point to the second point you click.—in this case, a vertical line.

NOTE

Notice that you do not drag the mouse with the button held down—you simply click to position a point when drawing a straight line. You will not see a line segment on the page until you position a second point. You'll learn how dragging the mouse creates curves in later steps.

3. To complete the object, click on the **Pen** tool in the Toolbox again. This frees the Pen tool for use in drawing the next object. Otherwise, if you click a third point you will add another line segment to the vertical line.

4. Press **Command+I** (**Object > Paint Styles** or **Window > Show Paint Styles**) to display the Paint Style palette if it is not already displayed.

5. Set the Fill to None and Stroke to Black (see Chapter 6 for a detailed description of the Paint Style palette). You can select any line width (stroke width) you wish. The figures here use a 2-point line weight.

EXERCISE: THE NUMBER ONE WITH A SERIF

If you want to be more formal, you can use the Pen tool to create a number 1 with a serif at the top (see next figure).

1. First select the **Pen** tool and click once on the page in the document window to position the endpoint of the serif.

2. Then release the mouse button and move the pointer up and to the right (diagonally) and click again to create the point at the top of the number.

3. Next, move the pointer down and click again to create the bottom of the number.

4. When you are finished, click the **Pen** tool in the Toolbox again to end the path. (Otherwise, the next point you position with the Pen tool will be connected to this endpoint.)

Drawing Straight Lines of a Specific Length

You can draw a straight line of an exact length by displaying the Information palette (**Command+Control+I**) and clicking the position of the first point, then watching the value of the distance field in the Information palette (D) change as you move the mouse to position it precisely before clicking the second point.

Another way to draw a line of exact length is to create one anchor point, then **Option+click** on the Selection tool to get the Move dialog box. Enter the desired length of the line in the Distance field, and enter the desired angle of the line, then click **Copy** to make a copy. Select both anchor points and use the **Join** command (**Command+J**) to draw a line connecting the two points (see **Object > Join** later in this chapter).

If the line is precisely vertical or horizontal, you can also adjust the length to an exact amount by first displaying the Control palette (**Window > Show Control Palette**). Then select an endpoint with the Direct-selection tool, and drag the point (or use the arrow keys to nudge it), watching the height (for vertical lines) or width (for horizontal lines) value change as the point moves.

EXERCISE: ADD A FOOT

The most formal number 1 includes a serif at the bottom of the number as well as the top (rightmost figure, above).

1. With the **Pen** tool still selected, click once to the left of the bottom point of the number.
2. Hold down the **Shift** key (to force the serif to be horizontal) as you click again to the right of the number.

3. This number 1 is now composed of two paths (if you ended the first path in step 4, earlier). If you want to be able to move them and transform them as a unit, you can use the Selection tool (solid black arrow) to select them both and then press **Command+G** (**Arrange > Group**).

Create a Grid

For the purposes of following these exercises, create a visible "grid" by following these steps:

1. Press **Command+H** (**View > Actual Size**) to enlarge your view of the page, and **Command+R** (**View > Show Rulers**) to display rulers at the right and bottom of the screen.

2. Create a "grid" of ruler guides by dragging guides from the rulers onto the page, aligning with numbered tic marks on the rulers, as shown in the figure below.

If you don't know how to create ruler guides, you can refer to View > Show/Hide Rulers in Chapter 10, or you can complete these steps without them.

By the way, it does not matter exactly what size numbers you create in this exercise, so it does not matter what magnification you are working in, or how far apart your grid lines are, so long as they are at even intervals and you have at least three going in each direction.

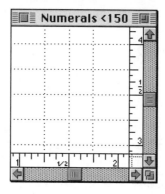

Figure 4.6 Grid created using ruler guides

EXERCISE: THE NUMBER 4: 45° ANGLES

The number 4 can be created as a single open path or as two open paths. The next steps take you through both variations, using the Shift key to force 45° lines as appropriate.

To create the number 4 as two open paths, the mouse follows the pattern of movement commonly used in printing the number 4 by hand.

1. Select the **Pen** tool and click once at the top of the 4.

2. Then move the pointer down and to the left and click again.

3. Next, hold down the **Shift** key (to force a horizontal line) and click to the right. This forms the "L" component of the number.

4. Click on the **Pen** tool in the Toolbox again to complete the path (Otherwise, the next point you position with the Pen tool will be connected to this endpoint.)

WARNING If you forget to click the **Pen** tool icon in the Toolbox to start a new path after completing an open path, you will end up with a line joining the last anchor point in the previous path to the first anchor point on your new path. If this happens, simply press **Delete** once to remove the new anchor point. Then click the **Pen** tool icon, or hold down the **Command** key to change the pointer to the **Selection** tool and click anywhere on the page to start a new path.

5. Then click the pointer at the top of the number.

6. Hold down the **Shift** key to force a vertical line as you click the bottom of the number.

EXERCISE: GROUP THE TWO ELEMENTS

1. To combine the two elements, first press **Command+Shift+A** (**Edit > Select None**) to deselect all points.

2. Hold down the **Command** key (to activate the Selection tool) and the **Shift** key (to multiple-select objects), and click each element of the number.

3. Then press **Command+G** (**Arrange > Group**).

EXERCISE: THE NUMBER FOUR AS A SINGLE PATH

If you want the number to be a single open path, follow these steps to create a new version.

1. Select the **Pen** tool in the Toolbox again to end the path previous and click once to position the bottom point.

2. Hold down the **Shift** key to force a vertical line and click to position the top point.

3. Hold down the **Shift** key to force a 45° line and click to the left of the middle of the vertical line.

4. Then hold down the **Shift** key to force a horizontal line and click to the right of the vertical line.

5. Press **Command+Shift+A** (**Edit > Select None**) to deselect all points.

EXERCISE: THE NUMBER 7: STRAIGHT OR CURVED

In the next steps, you will draw a number 7 as an open path, later in this chapter, you will duplicate it and join the end points to create a hollow closed path.

1. Select the **Pen** tool in the Toolbox.

2. To create the number 7 simply select the **Pen** tool and click three points. You can force 45° angles by holding down the **Shift** key as you click. You can give the number a curved back by dragging the bottom point instead of clicking.

3. Remember to click the **Pen** tool in the Toolbox to end the path before starting a new element.

All of the numbers we have created so far are composed of open paths—you can change the thickness, color, and line style of the paths but if you fill them with a color or pattern, you will get strange results. This number 7 is converted to a closed path later in this chapter, to allow separate fill and stroke attributes.

Drawing a Curve

Here are the basic steps in drawing a curve:

1. Hold down the mouse button to position the first anchor point, and *drag* to create a direction line, then release the mouse button. If **Use Precise Cursors** is slected through Filemouse pointer changes to a +, indicating that the next point you click or drag with the mouse will create another anchor point on the current path.

2. Position the pointer at the next anchor point and either click or drag:

   ➤ If you *click* the second anchor point, you complete a curve (the curved line automatically appears on the screen). You then have the option of continuing the current path with either a straight line (by clicking the third point) or with another curve (by dragging the third point).

   ➤ If you *drag* the second anchor point, you can continue drawing a smooth curved line (by clicking or dragging the third point).

3. Repeat the process to continue the path. The following figure illustrates the drawing of a curved line.

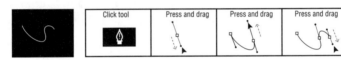

Figure 4.7 Drawing curved lines.

It will require practice with the Pen tool to learn where anchor points are best placed and how to drag direction lines. The following suggestions should help you understand the principles of drawing curves in Illustrator.

NOTE

Determining the Direction of the Curve

The direction of a curve is determined by the direction in which you drag as you position an anchor point. In dragging a direction handle after positioning an anchor point, drag in a direction that is tangent to the curve you intend to draw. A *tangent* is a straight line that touches a curve at only one point, as illustrated in the next figure.

Once you have positioned a point, the point is selected and you can see the direction handles. You can display any point's direction handles by selecting the point: click on the path to select it, then click on the point. Figure 4.9 shows a variety of curves created by dragging the mouse in a different direction when positioning the middle point. (The endpoints on each curve have vertical handles.)

Figure 4.8 A tangent is a straight line that touches a curve at only one point.

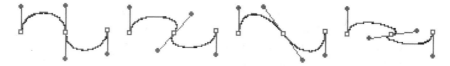

Figure 4.9 The direction handles are always tangent to the curve.

The handles of corner points are usually contracted to the point itself, and are therefore not visible until you drag them out as described later in this chapter.

NOTE

Determining the Depth of a Curve

The depth of a curve—the size of the hump—is determined by the length of the direction handles. When you first create a smooth or curve point, the distance you drag affects both the incoming and the outgoing line segment. One rule of thumb is to drag the direction handle a distance that is about one-third of the length of the curve between the current and the next anchor points. Later, you can select a point and drag individual direction handles to change the incoming and outgoing line segments separately.

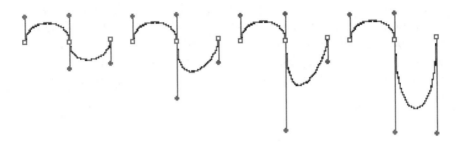

Figure 4.10 The length of the direction handles determines the size of the curve.

EXERCISE: THE NUMBER 6: A CONTINUOUS SMOOTH CURVE

The number 6 is a relatively simple continuous curve with no straight segments or corners.

1. Select the **Pen** tool and create the top point by positioning the pointer and dragging down and to the left at about a 45° angle. You can hold down the **Shift** key while dragging to force a 45° drag.

2. Position a second point directly below the first and drag to the right, holding down the **Shift** key to force a horizontal drag. Drag as far as you need to in order to get the backbone of the 6 shaped as you like.

3. Finally, position a third point just below the middle of the backbone and drag down and to the left, holding down the **Shift** key to force a 45° drag. Drag as far as you need to in order to get the bowl of the 6 shaped as you like.

Position as few points as possible in creating a path. This makes the path easier to edit, and takes up less disk space for storing the file.

SHORTCUT

4. Click on the **Pen** tool in the Toolbox again to end the path before going on to a new element.

Converting a Smooth Point to a Corner Point as You Draw

If you *drag* to position an anchor point, you can continue drawing a smooth curved line (by clicking or dragging the next point). The Option key lets you create corner points along a curve—points where the curve changes direction abruptly, not gradually. To create a corner point:

1. First click to set the anchor point and drag to set the direction line.
2. Then hold down the **Option** key, click on the anchor point you have just set.

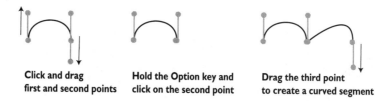

Click and drag
first and second points

Hold the Option key and
click on the second point

Drag the third point
to create a curved segment

Figure 4.11 Converting a point from a smooth point to a corner point as you draw.

Alternatively, you can add a straight line segment to a curved segment by following these steps:

1. First position the point and drag to shape the curved segment.
2. Then release the mouse button and click once on the anchor point you just created—this removes the direction handle that defines the next curve, making it a straight line.
3. Click on the next anchor point to create a straight line segment.

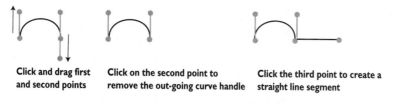

Click and drag first
and second points

Click on the second point to
remove the out-going curve handle

Click the third point to create a
straight line segment

Figure 4.12 Drawing paths composed of curved lines and straight lines.

Use combinations of the techniques that have been described up to now to create paths composed of curved and straight line segments.

NOTE

EXERCISE: THE NUMBER 2: MIXED CURVES AND STRAIGHT LINES

The number 2 is a curved line connected to a straight line. You can try drawing this number with the Freehand tool (curved line in the Toolbox), but you might find this difficult to control precisely (see the figure on the right). A better way is to use the Pen tool, as described in the next steps.

1. Select the **Pen** tool and position it on the page in the document window as you would if the pointer were truly a pen in your hand and you wanted to draw the number 2—at the top left end of the number. If you created a grid as suggested earlier, position it on an intersection of the grid of ruler guides.

2. Hold down the mouse button and drag the mouse straight up, to the next intersection point on the grid, then release the mouse button.

3. Next, position the pointer two grid intersection points to the right of the first point, then hold down the mouse button and drag down. As you drag, you will see a curved line segment forming between the two points. You can change the shape of the curve by changing the distance and direction of the drag—and you can experiment as much as you like so long as you are holding down the mouse button. You can see that you are also affecting two direction handles as you drag—the handle of the segment you can see changing as you drag is at the other end of a tangent line from the point you are dragging. The point you are dragging is the direction handle for the next segment you will create.

4. Release the mouse button when the pointer is approximately one grid intersection point below the curve point you are creating.

5. Next, position the pointer two grid intersection points below the first point and simply click—this creates a corner point at the base of the number.

NOTE A corner point can join two straight line segments, as it did at the top of the number 1, or a curve segment and a straight segment, as you are about to see, or two curve segments, as you will see in creating the number 3. The difference between a curve point and a corner point is that the direction handles for the two curves extending from a curve point are always at the end of a straight-line tangent to the curve point (and if you change the angle of one of the direction handles, the opposite handle also moves), whereas the two handles of a corner point can be moved independently of each other.

6. Finally, hold down the **Shift** key as you click two grid intersection points to the right of the last point. The **Shift** key forces a horizontal line. The figure on the right shows the path with black points where you positioned them. The last point is a filled square indicating that it is selected.

7. Click the **Pen** tool again in the Toolbox to end the path before going on to a new element.

EXERCISE: CREATE THE NUMBER 5

The simplest number 5 is composed of three corner points and two curve points. You can go through these steps quickly now, because they repeat what you have already learned.

1. Use the Pen tool to click the first point at the top right of the 5.

2. **Shift+click** the second and third points (to force a horizontal and a vertical line).

3. Drag down the fourth point, and drag up the last point.

4. Remember to click on the **Pen** tool in the Toolbox again to end the path before going on to draw a new element with the Pen tool.

NOTE When you click on a path to select it with the Selection tool (black arrow icon), all points along the path are displayed. When you click on a point or line segment with the Direct-selection tool (hollow arrow icon) to select it, the selected point shows direction handles. There are no handles for corner points that join straight line segments—you can think of them as hidden "inside" the anchor point, because they can be "pulled out" when you convert a corner point to a curve point. The figure on the previous page shows the resulting number 5 with the path selected with the Selection tool and with the Direct-selection tool (to show the anchor points and direction handles).

Holding Down the Shift Key while You Draw

Holding down the **Shift** key *before* positioning on an anchor point constrains the position of the point to 45° angles relative to the previously positioned point. Holding down the **Shift** key *as you drag* to create a new smooth point constrains the direction line to 45° angles.

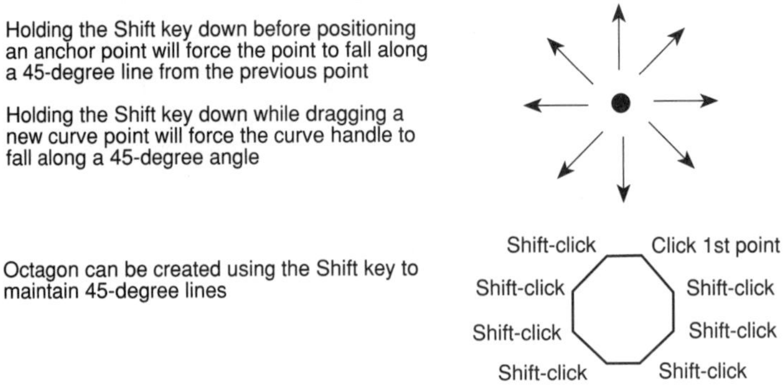

Holding the Shift key down before positioning an anchor point will force the point to fall along a 45-degree line from the previous point

Holding the Shift key down while dragging a new curve point will force the curve handle to fall along a 45-degree angle

Octagon can be created using the Shift key to maintain 45-degree lines

Shift-click   Click 1st point
Shift-click   Shift-click
Shift-click   Shift-click
Shift-click   Shift-click

Figure 4.13 Effects of the Shift key.

You've already seen how this works with straight line segments—when drawing the numbers 4 and 5. You can use the same techniques in drawing curves, as shown in the next exercise.

EXERCISE: THE NUMBER 3: TWO CURVES WITH A CORNER POINT

The number 3 is composed of two curve segments, joined by a corner point in the middle where the direction of the lines changes abruptly.

1. Begin this number as you did the number 2: Select the Pen tool and position it on the page in the document window at the top left end of the number. Hold down the mouse button and drag the mouse straight up one grid intersection point, then release the mouse button. (Again, it does not matter exactly how far you drag the mouse.)

2. Next, position the pointer two grid intersection points to the right of the first point, then hold down the mouse button and drag down one grid intersection point and release the mouse button. As you drag, you will see a curved line segment forming between the two points.

3. Next, position the pointer one grid intersection point down and to the left of the last point—halfway between the two first points and below them—and hold down the mouse button as you drag about one-half the distance between grid intersection points to the left.

4. Before clicking on the next point, hold the Option key down, to display a small convert-direction-point symbol next to the pen of the mouse cursor, and click once on the point you just created, to convert it from a curve point to a corner point. Notice that one handle disappears.

If you make any mistakes in these steps, you can simply click Undo any number of times to go back to a previous step, or delete what you've done and start again.

NOTE

5. Position the pointer on the fourth point of the number 3—two grid intersection points below the second point you positioned—and drag down one grid intersection point.

6. Finally, position the fifth and last point two grid intersection points to the left of the fourth and drag up one grid intersection point.

7. Click the **Pen** tool again in the Toolbox to end the path when you have completed the object.

Creating a Closed Path

Up until now you have been creating open paths—paths with two end points. In the next sections you'll learn how to create closed paths—paths in which all the anchor points are joined—with no end points. There are several different ways to create a closed path.

➤ You can create closed paths using the Pen tool.

➤ You can close open paths using the **Join** and **Average** commands.

➤ The Outline Stroked Path filter creates a closed path that outlines another path.

➤ You can create closed paths that look like brush strokes using the Brush tool, described later in this chapter.

➤ You can convert any stroke—of an open or closed path—into a closed path that emulates the stroke created by a calligrapher's pen, using the Calligraphy filter described later in this chapter.

➤ You can also create closed paths such as stars and polygons using the plug-in tools described later in this chapter.

➤ The Autotrace tool, described in Chapter 7, usually creates closed paths.

These first methods are described under the next headings. In addition:

➤ The Oval and Rectangle tools described in Chapter 3 create closed paths.

Drawing Paths Efficiently

The more efficiently you build your paths, the easier they will be to edit and the less editing they are likely to need. The goal is to build paths as efficiently as possible using the minimum number of anchor points. You will need to practice with the Pen tool to learn where anchor points are best placed and how to drag direction handles, but following is a tip about how efficient curves are constructed.

Anchor points along a curved path are best placed where the direction of the curve changes. Another way of saying this is that anchor points usually are not required in the middle of continuous curves, such as the peak of a hill or the bottom of a valley. This is sometimes called the "bump" rule—points should be positioned at either side of a bump, rather than at the peak.

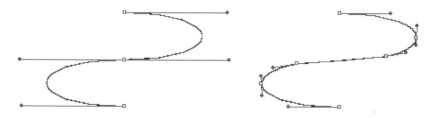

Figure 4.14 Efficient (left) vs. inefficient (right) paths.

You can think of the anchor points as the places along a winding mountain road where you would turn the wheels of the car from pointing right to pointing left, or vice versa. Remember that when you are driving around the hump of a curve you are holding the wheels in one direction, and an anchor point is not required. As you come out of the turn you let the steering wheel return to center, and you turn it in the opposite direction when you come to the next curve. It's at the moment that the steering wheel passes the center point that you position an anchor point.

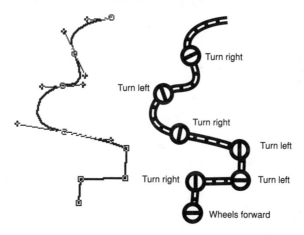

Figure 4.15 Anchor points placed where the direction of the wheels would change in driving around curves in a road.

By following this guide, you can create curves that are easy to control, and that can be edited with a minimum number of anchor points—two goals for efficiency and economy of disk space.

Closing a Path with the Pen Tool

Visually, there might not be much difference between an open path and a closed path—a straight line with a wide stroke might look like a filled rectangle, for example. However, there are some features that can be applied to closed paths only. Open paths cannot be made into masks, for example. So, unless you intend to draw only basic shapes such as ovals, rectangles, stars, and polygons, it's useful to know how to create a closed path with the Pen tool.

The principle is simple:

1. Use the **Pen** tool to click corner points—or click-and-drag curve points—along a path.

2. Close the path by clicking (or click-and-dragging) the last point exactly on top of the first point. The pointer changes from a + to an x, indicating that the Pen tool is available to start a new path.

NOTE

This works easiest if the Snap-to-point option is turned on in the File > Preferences > General dialog box. Snap-to-point causes two points to snap together when they are within two pixels of each other and moves objects in two-pixel increments.

If you want to close an open path after it has been created, you can follow these steps:

1. Select one end point with the Direct-selection tool.

2. Select the **Pen** tool in the Toolbox and click (or click and drag) on the selected point, to resume drawing at that point.

3. Then click (or click and drag) on the other end point of the open path, to create a line segment joining them.

EXERCISE: A CRAZY 8: A CLOSED PATH

Drawing the number 8 uses the same skills you learned in earlier steps, but we use the number 8 to demonstrate how to create a closed path.

1. Select the **Pen** tool, position the pointer at the center of the number 8 and drag to the left—holding down the **Shift** key to force a horizontal drag.

2. Position a second point at the top of the 8 and hold down the **Shift** key as you drag to the right.

3. Position the third point next to *but not on top of* the first point and hold down the **Shift** key as you drag to the left.

NOTE

If you position the third point on top of the first, you close the path prematurely. Press **Command+Z (Undo)** as many times as needed to delete all the points and start the number again, or see the description of editing techniques later in this chapter.

4. Position the next point at the bottom of the 8 and hold down the **Shift** key as you drag to the right.

5. Position the last point *on top of* the first point and hold down the **Shift** key as you drag to the left.

As soon as you complete the final point that closes the path, the number takes on the current fill pattern.

6. Next, select the number and choose a fill of None and a thick Black line weight from the Paint Style palette, such as the 6-point stroke in the figure at right.

Using the Join Command

Another way to close an open path after it has been created is to select the two end points with the Direct-selection tool, then press **Command+J** (**Object > Join**). The **Join** command connects two endpoints with a straight line segment or, if the two points you wish to join are on top of one another, replaces them with one point. In the latter case, the Join dialog box, shown allows you to choose a smooth point or a corner point.

NOTE

You can use the **Join** command to close an open path by joining the two endpoints, or to connect two endpoints of two separate open paths—thus merging two open paths into one open path. You must have only two endpoints selected when you use this command, and the endpoints must not belong to a grouped object.

To use the Join command:

1. Select two ungrouped endpoints with the Selection tool.

2. Choose **Object > Join** or press **Command+J**.

➤ If you select two points that are not already touching, the Join command creates a straight line that connects the two points. When the endpoints are joined, both endpoints and the straight line segment between them become selected.

Figure 4.16 Two endpoints, before and after using the Join command.

➤ If you select two points that are already within two pixels of each other (or the Snap-to-point setting in the Preferences dialog box is two pixels), using the **Join** command results in the Join dialog box, which allows you to determine whether the joined point will be a corner, or smooth, point.

WARNING

Some paths may appear closed until you try to use a command that requires that the path be closed. If you make this mistake, you will get an alert box with a message that the path is open. To find the endpoints along what looks like a closed path, select the path and choose **Filter > Stylize > Add Arrowheads**. Click **OK** to close the Add Arrowheads dialog box and accept the default style. An arrowhead should appear at one point along the path—an end point that probably overlaps another end point. Press **Command+Z** to Undo the arrowhead, then select the two overlapping points with the Direct-selection tool and choose **Object > Join (Command+J)** to close the path.

EXERCISE: JOIN TWO SEPARATE OPEN PATHS INTO ONE CLOSED PATH

The next steps join two open paths into one closed path. These steps start with the number seven that you created earlier in this chapter (if you were following the exercises), but you can use the same steps to join any two open paths.

1. Use the Selection tool (the black arrow) to select the number 7 figure created earlier.

2. Press **Command+Shift+M** (**Arrange > Move**) to get the Move dialog box.

3. Type **9 points** (**.25 inch**) in the Distance area, and **45** in the Degree area. The Horizontal and Vertical values are adjusted automatically.

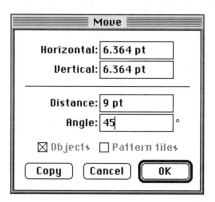

4. Click **Copy** to close the Move dialog box and simultaneously create a copy that is slightly offset from the first.

NOTE

You can instead use the **Filter > Objects > Offset Path** command to get a slightly different result. The figure at right shows both techniques.

5. Select the **Direct-selection** tool (the hollow arrow) and drag a selection marquee around the two top points of the two shapes to select them.

6. Press **Command+J** (**Object > Join**). A line segment automatically joins the two points.

7. With the Direct-selection tool still selected, drag a selection marquee around the two bottom points of the two shapes.

8. Press **Command+J** (**Object > Join**). A line segment automatically joins the second set of points, creating a closed path.

9. You can use the Paint Styles palette to set different Fill and Line attributes.

NOTE

You can create the same or a similar effect as accomplished in the previous steps by instead using the Outline Path filter, as described in the next exercise using the number 8.

Using the Average Command before Joining

The **Object > Average** command (**Command+L**) moves two or more selected anchor points to the average position of the selected points along the axis you specify: the horizontal axis, vertical axis, or both axes. You can average points— end points or any two anchor points—and text objects.

You can first use **Object >Average** to bring two end points to a common point between them, and then press **Command+J** to join the points, and specify that they be joined as a corner point or a smooth point.

The figure at right shows an open path (top), then the two points joined by a straight line segment (using the **Join** command), and then the two points averaged before they are joined as a corner point or a smooth point (bottom figure).

To use the **Average** command:

1. Select two or more anchor points or objects with the Selection tool, then choose **Object > Average** or press **Command+L**.

NOTE

If you don't properly select two or more anchor points, you will get an alert message asking you to "please select two or more points to average."

2. The Average dialog box offers the options of averaging along the horizontal axis, the vertical axis, or both (the default setting). If you average points along both axes, they move to the same location—that is, halfway between their original positions. If you average along one axis only, each point moves to the halfway point along that axis.

The following figure shows the effect of averaging two anchor points along both the horizontal and vertical axes.

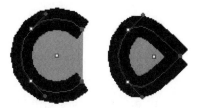

Figure 4.17 Two anchor points, before and after using the Average command.

NOTE

Averaging two or more anchor points enables you to maintain a curved path while bringing two points together before using the **Join** command (see **Object > Join**). Otherwise, the **Join** command creates a straight line between the two points.

Remember that averaging does not join anchor points. If you wish to join the points, you must use the **Join** command after averaging.

3. First, select the endpoints you wish to average with a selection tool (if they are not still selected after step 2).

4. Choose **Object > Join**, or press **Command+J**. The following figure illustrates how this is done.

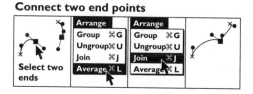

Figure 4.18 Connecting endpoints.

Using Outline Path

The Outline Path filter traces an outline of the selected stroked paths and substitutes a filled object of the identical width as the original stroked path. This is especially useful in preparing artwork for custom trapping in printing color separations, but you can also use it to convert a stroke to a shape that can have different fill and stroke attributes.

This filter requires a math coprocessor.

WARNING

To outline a stroked path, follow these steps:

1. Select the path(s) that you want to affect. The selection can contain both filled and stroked paths, but only stroked paths will be affected.

2. Choose **Filter > Objects > Outline Path**.

➤ If the selected object was a stroked path with no fill, then the stroked path is replaced by a compound path that outlines the original path.

➤ If the selected object was both stroked and filled, then the original path remains with the fill as specified, but a compound path is added that outlines the original path. The new object(s) appear above the originals in stacking order, and are selected.

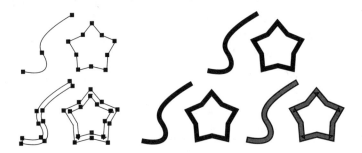

Figure 4.19 Objects before and after using the Outline Path filter.

It's a good idea to work in two views at the same time—one in Preview and one in Artwork mode—when using this filter, so you can see what's really happening in Artwork mode and see the effect in Preview mode.

NOTE

EXERCISE: OUTLINE THE PATH OF THE NUMBER 3—AN OPEN PATH

1. Use the Selection tool to select the number 3 created earlier in this chapter—or any open path.

2. In the Paint palette, set the stoke width to 12 points or some other wide width—this will make the effect of step 3 more evident.

NOTE

Make sure the fill is set to **None** and the stroke is black or some other visible attribute.

3. Choose Filters > Objects > Outline Path.

The results look the same as before you outlined the path, but in fact you have created a new object. When the object is selected, you can see that the path now *outlines* the shape that was previously a stroke. The stroke of the original path is replaced by a closed path with no stroke, but a fill that matches the original stroke color.

NOTE

If the original closed path has a fill of None, as in this example, the Outline Path filter traces the stroke only, and does not create a second object for the fill—as it does in the next example.

4. Now you can fill the compound path that outlines the original stroke with a gradient—an option not otherwise available for the stroke of a path.

EXERCISE: OUTLINE THE PATH OF THE NUMBER 8 —A CLOSED PATH

1. Use the Selection tool to selection then number 8 created earlier in this chapter—or any closed path.

2. In the Paint palette, set the stoke width to 12 points or some other wide width, and set the fill to a gray shade (or any color other than the stroke color.

3. Choose **Filters > Objects > Outline Path**.

Again, the results look the same as before you outlined the path, but this time you have created several objects. To see the results most clearly, press **Command+Shift+A** to deselect all objects, then use the Selection tool to drag the black figure 8 away from the gray fill.

As with the previous example, the results depend on the stroke and fill assigned to the original path. The stroke of the original path is replaced by a compound path with no stroke, but a fill that matches the original stroke color (leftmost figure). If the original number is filled with black or any color or tint, the Outline Path filter creates an additional path that outlines the original fill, and gives it a stroke of none, a fill to match the original fill (rightmost figure).

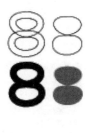

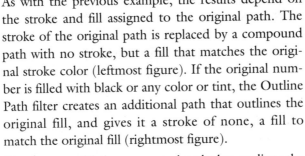

4. Now you can fill the compound path that outlines the original stroke with a gradient—an option not otherwise available for the stroke of a path.

Using the Brush Tool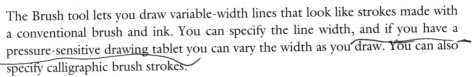

The Brush tool lets you draw variable-width lines that look like strokes made with a conventional brush and ink. You can specify the line width, and if you have a pressure-sensitive drawing tablet you can vary the width as you draw. You can also specify calligraphic brush strokes.

Using the Brush Tool with Default Settings

1. Select the **Brush** tool in the Toolbox. The pointer changes to a brush when positioned over the document window.

2. Position the brush pointer where you want to start, and hold down the mouse button as you drag the mouse—or press the stylus as you drag the pen on a tablet. You drag continuously, as you do when using the Freehand tool.

3. When you release the mouse button, the path you have followed is displayed as a closed path, with anchor points along the perimeter of the stroke.

Figure 4.20 Closed path created by the Brush tool.

You can edit the path as you would any closed path, as described earlier in this chapter. To change the width of the path, however, it's more efficient to change the Brush tool preferences before you begin drawing, as described next.

Setting the Brush Stroke Width

Before using the Brush tool as just described, you can change the brush width, line style, corner style, and end cap style (the shape of the end of the brush stroke). To do this, double-click on the **Brush** tool in the toolbox to display the Brush Preferences dialog box.

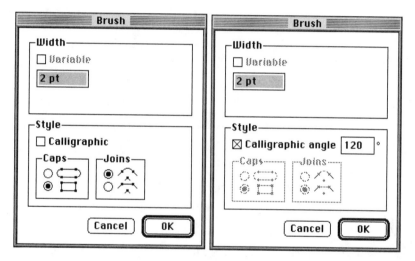

Figure 4.21 The Brush Preferences dialog box with and without Calligraphic options checked.

➤ The Variable Width option in the Brush Preferences dialog box applies only to pressure-sensitive drawing devices, as described in the next section. For any other drawing device, such as a mouse, you can set a single line width for the Brush tool.

➤ If you check the **Calligraphic Style** option, the line width varies depending on the angle at which you drag the brush and the angle you specify as the calligraphic angle, to simulate the effect of drawing with a wide, flat pen tip.

➤ Style options also include round or butt (squared) Caps and round or bevel Joins. These are the same options as can be set for any path through the Paint Styles palette, described in Chapter 6, and examples are shown in the next figures.

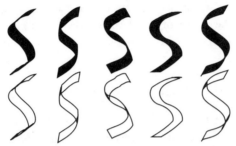

40 Degrees   80 Degrees   120 Degrees   180 Degrees   240 Degrees

Figure 4.22 Calligraphic strokes at various angles.

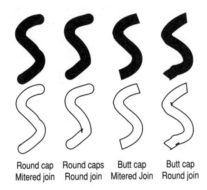

Round cap   Round caps   Butt cap   Butt cap
Mitered join Round join   Mitered Join Round join

Figure 4.23 Brush strokes with various Cap and Join settings.

Using a Drawing Tablet

If you have a pressure-sensitive drawing tablet, you can specify **Variable Width** in the Brush Preferences dialog box (described earlier), and create wider strokes by pressing harder and thinner strokes by releasing pressure as you draw.

Figure 4.24 Brush strokes drawn with a pressure-sensitive tablet.

Using the Calligraphy Filter

6.0 NEW FEATURE

Illustrator 6 introduces a Calligraphy filter that lets you convert any stroke—of an open or closed path—into a closed path that emulates the stroke created by a calligrapher's pen (or by the Brush tool when a Calligraphic angle is specified). To use this filter:

1. First select the path(s) to which you want the filter to affect.

2. Choose **Filter > Stylize > Calligraphy**.

3. In the Calligraphy dialog box, specify the pen width and angle you wish to emulate.

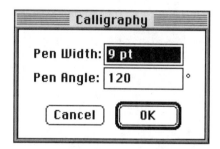

4. Click **OK** to view the effect.

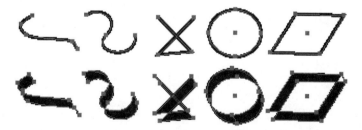

Figure 4.25 Selected paths before (above) and after (below) applying the Calligraphy filter.

SHORTCUT

Use the Brush tool if you want to see the calligraphic effect as you are drawing freehand. Use the Calligraphy filter if you want to apply the effect retroactively to strokes drawn with the Freehand or Autotrace tools, or if you want to start with the Pen tool to create a more controlled path.

Using Plug-in Tools

Illustrator 6 adds six plug-in tools that display in a Toolbox, just like the main Illustrator tools. You display the plug-in tools by choosing **Window > Show Plug-in Tools**. The default plug-in tools are shown in the figure. Additional plug-in tools can be added just as plug-in filters can be added—as released by Adobe or purchased from other vendors.

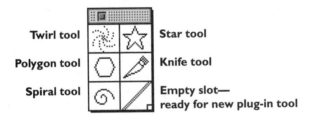

Twirl tool   **Star tool**

Polygon tool   **Knife tool**

Spiral tool   **Empty slot— ready for new plug-in tool**

Figure 4.26 The Plug-in Tools Toolbox.

You can rearrange the order of tools in the Plug-in Tools Toolbox by holding the **Control** key as you drag a tool from one location to another—other tools automatically shift to accommodate the new order.

The Star, Polygon, Spiral, and Twirl tools replace plug-in filters that performed the same functions in version 5.5.

Using the Polygon Tool

6.0 NEW FEATURE

The Polygon plug-in tool draws an object with a specified number of sides, each of equal length. You can create a polygon using numerical values, or visually—as described in the next sets of steps.

USING NUMERICAL VALUES

To create a polygon numerically, follow these steps:

1. Choose **Window > Show Plug-in Tools** to display the Plug-in Tools' Toolbox.

2. Click on the **Polygon** tool to select it.

3. Click once in the document window to display the Polygon dialog box.

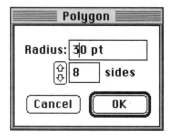

4. Type the number of sides and the radius (the distance of each side from the center point) of the object to be created.

5. Click **OK** to close the dialog box and create the object. The polygon appears centered over wherever you clicked the mouse in step 3.

Creating a Polygon Visually

To create a polygon visually on the screen:

1. Click on the **Polygon** tool to select it.

2. Position the pointer at the center of the area for the shape, and drag to create the object. The further you drag, the larger the polygon. You can drag in a circular motion to rotate the polygon as you create it. Holding different keys as you drag creates different effects:

➤ Hold the **Shift** key to constrain rotation to increments of 45°.

➤ Hold the **Spacebar** to move the position of the polygon as you drag.

➤ Press or hold the **up** or **down arrow** key to add or delete sides as you drag.

3. Release the mouse button when you have created a polygon of the size and angle you wish.

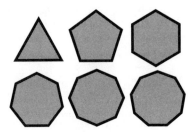

Figure 4.27 Polygons with 3, 5, 6, 7, 8, and 9 sides.

Once you have created a polygon, you can edit it using any of the techniques described in this chapter for editing paths, and you can change it using the transformation tools and filters described in Chapter 5. However, to change the number of sides, it will be easier to simply delete the shape and repeat these steps.

N O T E

Using the Star Tool

The Star plug-in tool creates a star-shaped object with the number of points you specify. You can create a star using numerical values, or visually—as described in the next sets of steps.

**6.0 NEW
FEATURE**

Using Numerical Values

To create a star shape using numerical values, follow these steps:

1. Choose **Window > Show Plug-in Tools** to display the Plug-in Tools' Toolbox.

2. Click on the **Star** tool to select it.

3. Click once in the document window to display the Star dialog box.

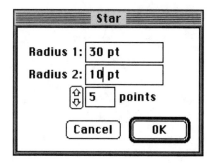

4. Type the number of points, the length of the First Radius (the distance of the outermost points from the center point), and the length of the Second Radius (the distance of the innermost points from the center point).

5. Click **OK** to close the dialog box. The star appears centered over wherever you clicked the mouse in step 3.

Creating a Star Visually

To create a star visually on the screen:

1. Click on the **Star** tool to select it.

2. Position the pointer at the center of the area for the shape, and drag to create the object. The further you drag, the larger the star. You can drag in a circular motion to rotate the star as you create it. Holding different keys as you drag creates different effects:

   ➤ Hold the **Shift** key to constrain rotation to increments of 45°.

   ➤ Hold the **Spacebar** to move the position of the star as you drag.

   ➤ Press or hold the **up** or **down arrow** key to add or delete sides (points) as you drag.

   ➤ Hold the **Option** key to make the slopes of every other side run parallel to each other.

   ➤ Hold the **Control** key to change the inner radius.

3. Release the mouse button when you have created a star of the size and angle you wish.

Figure 4.28 Stars.

NOTE

Once you have created a star, you can edit it using any of the techniques described in this chapter for editing paths, and you can change it using the transformation tools and filters described in Chapter 5. However, to change the number of points or distances of the points from the center, it will be easier to simply delete the star and repeat these steps.

Using the Spiral Tool

6.0 NEW FEATURE

The Spiral plug-in tool creates a spiral-shaped object of a given radius and number of winds (complete turns). You can create a spiral using numerical values, or visually—as described in the next sets of steps.

Using Numerical Values

To create a spiral numerically, follow these steps:

1. Choose **Window > Show Plug-in Tools** to display the Plug-in Tools' Toolbox.

2. Click on the **Spiral** tool to select it.

3. Click once in the document window to display the Spiral dialog box.

4. Type the number of segments (each full wind equals four segments), the radius (the distance of the farthest edge from the center point), the degree of Decay (relative size of each segment relative to the next), and click one of the radio buttons representing the direction of the spiral.

5. Click **OK** to close the dialog box and create the spiral.

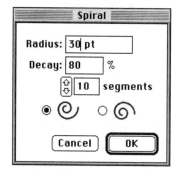

Figure 4.29 The Spiral dialog box.

Creating a Spiral Visually

To create a spiral visually on the screen, first go through the previous steps to specify the number of segments in the spiral and the degree of decay, but then:

1. Click on the **Spiral** tool to select it.

2. Position the pointer at the center of the area for the shape, and drag to create the object. The further you drag, the larger the spiral. You can drag in a circular motion to rotate the spiral as you create it. Holding different keys as you drag creates different effects:

    ➤ Hold the **Shift** key to constrain rotation to increments of 45°.

    ➤ Hold the **Spacebar** to move the position of the star as you drag.

    ➤ Press or hold the **up** or **down arrow** key to add or delete winds as you drag.

3. Release the mouse button when you have created a spiral of the size and angle you wish.

Figure 4.30 Spirals.

Editing a Path

Once you have completed a path, there are a variety of methods for editing it—changing the shape of it. (Editing the fill and stroke attributes, independent of the shape, is described in Chapter 6.)

➤ You can use the Selection tools to select and move individual line segments, anchor points, and direction handles.

➤ The Scissors tool opens a closed path or splits an open path into two paths.

➤ The Add-anchor-point tool adds anchor points along an already-drawn line segment.

➤ The Delete-anchor-point tool deletes anchor points from a path.

➤ The Convert-direction-point tool changes a corner point to a smooth point or vice versa. (See The Anchor Point Tools, described next.)

These techniques are described in the next sections. In addition, you can edit shapes using these techniques, described elsewhere in this book:

➤ You can close an open path by either selecting the two endpoints and using the **Object > Join** command (described earlier in this chapter).

➤ You can close a path by selecting one of the endpoints with the Pen tool and then clicking on the other endpoint to join them with a straight line, or dragging on the other endpoint to join them with a curved line segment.

➤ You can move anchor points by selecting them with the Direct-selection tool and then choosing **Object > Average**, described earlier in this chapter and in Chapter 10.

➤ You can merge two closed paths into one compound path by selecting the two paths and choosing **Object > Compound Path > Make**, described in Chapter 9.

Using the Direct-selection Tool

To edit a path, use the Direct-selection tool to move an anchor point, drag a curved line segment, or adjust direction lines. The following figure shows a path edited in each of these ways.

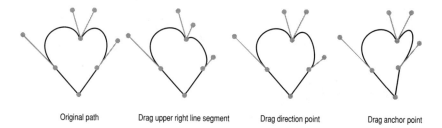

| Original path | Drag upper right line segment | Drag direction point | Drag anchor point |

Figure 4.31 Three methods of editing a path with the Direct-selection tool.

SHORTCUT

You will find that using the **Command** key shortcut to switch to the Direct-selection tool makes it easier to adjust curves while you draw. This way you don't need to end the path by going to the Toolbox to select the Direct-selection tool. You can resume adding points to the same path after adjusting part of the path. The only requirement is that you first select the **Direct-selection** tool in the Toolbox to activate it before switching to the **Pen** tool.

EXERCISE: EDIT THE PATH OF THE NUMBER 5 CREATED EARLIER

If you want to change the shape of a path, you can play with the number 5 created earlier in this chapter—or work with any shape you like.

1. Select one of its segments with the Direct-selection tool (to display the direction handles) and move the handle, the anchor point, or the segment.

2. Change the depth of the curve by extending or shortening the direction handles (i.e., the distance of the handle from the point).

3. Change the angle of the curve by changing the angle of the direction handles.

4. Move a handle from one side of the point to another, for the effect of twisting the two curve segments that extend from the point (see figure on the right).

To move the handles of a straight line segment, select the point with the Direct-selection tool, then:

5. Hold down the **Control** key to activate the Convert-Direction-Point tool and drag from the center of the point—converting the point to a curve point and dragging directions handles to change the shape of the curve.

Anchor Point Tools

The Scissors tool that is initially displayed on the Toolbox lets you cut a single open path into two paths, or open a closed path. The Scissors tool pop-out menu gives access to additional tools that let you add anchor points, delete anchor points, and convert direction points from corner points to smooth points or vice versa. All these tools are described in the next sections.

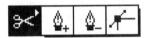

Figure 4.32 The Scissors tools pop-out menu.

The Scissors Tool

You use the Scissors tool to break a path into two or more separate objects. Splitting a closed path produces one open path. Splitting an open path produces two open paths. (See definitions of open and closed paths earlier in this chapter.)

Choose the **Scissors** tool by clicking the icon in the toolbox. The mouse pointer changes to a + in the active window. Click on a path at the point where you want to split the path. You can split a path anywhere except at the endpoints of an open path. The Scissors tool splits the path, producing two new endpoints which are selected, as shown in the top part of the following figure.

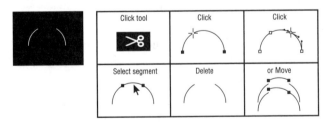

Figure 4.33 First click the **Selection** tool anywhere on a path, then select the **Scissors** tool and click on a line segment to cut the line (and create two endpoints).

NOTE

After splitting a path, you can use the Direct-selection tool to separate the new end-points of the two paths. Click the **Direct-selection** tool in any open space in the drawing window to deselect all objects. Click on the location of the two new endpoints. This selects the frontmost of the two endpoints, which you can then drag to separate the ends of the path(s).

The Add-anchor-point Tool

You use the Add-anchor-point tool to add a new anchor point to an existing path.

You can activate the Add-anchor-point tool by either of two methods:

➤ Drag to its pop-up icon next to the Scissors tool in the Toolbox and release the mouse button, or

➤ Hold down the **Option** key when the Scissors tool is active.

The mouse pointer changes to a + in the active window. Click on a path at the point where you want to add a new anchor point. The Add-anchor-point tool adds a new anchor point, which is selected, to the path at the point at which you clicked.

NOTE

This is different from the operation of the Scissors tool. The Scissors tool creates two new anchor points, one on top of the other, and splits the path. The Add-anchor-point tool adds only one new anchor point and does not split the path.

The Delete-anchor-point Tool

You can use the Delete-anchor-point tool to delete an anchor point from an existing path.

1. First click anywhere on the path from which you wish to delete the anchor point.

2. Then choose the **Delete-anchor-point** tool by dragging to its pop-up icon next to the Scissors tool in the toolbox and releasing the mouse button. The mouse pointer changes to a + in the active window.

3. Click on the anchor point you wish to delete. The anchor point is deleted and the remaining adjacent anchor points are joined by a new line segment.

NOTE

If you want to delete an anchor point and its adjoining line segments, for example to redraw a section of a path, do not use the Delete-anchor-point tool. Instead, use the Selection tool or the Direct-selection tool to select the anchor point, then press the **Delete** key. This removes the anchor point and the adjacent line segments, leaving the adjacent anchor points selected.

The Convert-direction-point Tool

You use the Convert-direction-point tool to convert an anchor point from a smooth point to a corner point or vice versa.

1. First choose the **Convert-direction-point** tool using either of three techniques:

   ➤ Drag to its pop-up icon next to the Scissors tool in the Toolbox and release the mouse button; it looks like a corner anchor point with direction handles.

   ➤ Alternatively you can hold down the **Control** key when any selection tool is active.

   ➤ When a Selection tool is not active, you can hold the **Control+ Option** keys.

   The mouse pointer changes to a the angled tip of an arrow in the active window.

2. To convert a smooth point to a corner point, simply click the point you wish to convert. To convert a corner point to a smooth point, place the pointer over the anchor point, then drag to create a direction point and change the shape of the curve.

SHORTCUT

The quickest way to access the Convert-direction-point tool is by using the **Control** key shortcut when a selection tool is active, or the **Control+Option** keys when any other tool is selected. When you release the keys, your previous tool selection will still be in effect.

Filter > Objects > Add Anchor Points

The Add Anchor Points filter adds a new anchor point between every two anchor points in the selected paths. This is a convenient alternative to using the Scissors tool to add anchor points manually when you want to change the shape of a path.

This tool is especially handy to use before using one of the Distort filters to change a shape—the more anchor points, the more distorted the effect.

NOTE

To add anchor points, select the path(s) in the Adobe Illustrator document that you want to affect. Then choose **Filter > Objects > Add Anchor Points**.

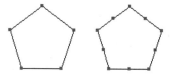

Figure 4.34 Object before (left) and after (right) adding anchor points.

Clean Up Artwork Filter

The Clean Up filter in Illustrator 6.0 expands the functionality the Select Stray Points filter of earlier versions. When you choose **Filter > Objects > Clean Up**, you get a dialog box offering three options:

**6.0 NEW
FEATURE**

> ➤ Delete Stray Points—to delete points not connected to any path and therefore having no fill or stroke attributes that would print. You might inadvertently create such points in the artwork by clicking the pen tool once without then clicking a second point to start a path.

> ➤ Delete Unpainted Objects—to delete any paths that have a fill and stroke attribute of None.

➤ Delete Empty Text Paths—to delete points that were created by clicking the Text tool on the page and then either not typing text, or later deleting text that was typed at that point.

Using the Knife Tool to Divide Paths

6.0 NEW FEATURE

Illustrator 6.0 introduces a Knife tool, found in the Plug-in tools Toolbox, that lets you slice any closed path or shape in pieces using a dragging motion. You could, for example, take a large solid shape and slice it into puzzle pieces. Here's how it works:

1. Choose **Window > Show Plug-in Tools** to display the Plug-in Tools' Toolbox.

2. Click on the **Knife** tool to select it.

3. Drag the Knife tool across any object you wish to slice—it doesn't matter if the paths are selected or not. As long as the Knife tool is selected, you can keep slicing objects. Each object becomes selected after you slice it—and a series of sliced objects all remain selected when you are finished.

4. You can assign different pieces different paint attributes, or drag them apart, as shown in the figure.

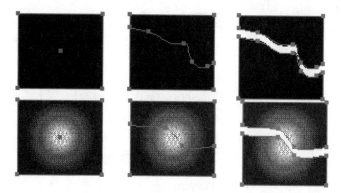

Figure 4.35 Closed paths before being sliced with the Knife tool (left), after being sliced (middle), and after being moved (right).

Using Commands to Merge or Divide Paths

The Pathfinder filters combine, isolate, and subdivide paths, and build new paths formed by the intersection of objects. This submenu also includes filters that let you blend overlapping colors and trap objects—filters that are described in Chapter 6.

The commands that merge and divide paths, described in this section, were originally designed for preparing artwork for color separations—before the newer trapping features were added in Illustrator 6.0—but they can also be used to simplify complex artwork and to create new shapes from a collection of different objects.

 Unless otherwise noted, all paths created by the Pathfinder filters are assigned the same paint style as the top path on the current layer's stack.

NOTE

Most of the Pathfinder filters create *compound paths*—groups of two or more paths that are painted such that overlapping areas appear transparent.

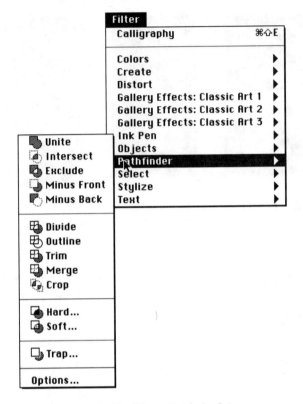

Figure 4.36 The Filter > Pathfinder Submenu.

WARNING

Applying the Pathfinder filters to very complex selections may fail due to memory limitations. You can avoid this problem by increasing the amount of memory allocated to the Illustrator program, as described in Chapter 10.

Defining Pathfinder Filter Options

The Pathfinder Options filter allows you to change the precision of pathfinder filters, remove redundant points created with other Pathfinder filters, and set the **Divide** and **Outline** commands to remove unpainted artwork.

1. Choose **Filter > Pathfinder > Options** to open the Pathfinder Options dialog box.

```
┌──────────────────────────────────────────────────────────┐
│ ═══════════════ Pathfinder Options ═══════════════         │
│                                                            │
│  Calculate results to a precision of [0.028] points   ( OK ) │
│  ☐ Remove redundant points                          (Cancel) │
│  ☒ Divide and Outline will extract unpainted artwork (Defaults)│
│                                                            │
└──────────────────────────────────────────────────────────┘
```

Figure 4.37 Pathfinder Options dialog box.

2. Make one or more of the following entries:

➤ Enter a precision value to be used by other pathfinder filters when calculating. Larger values yield more accurate drawings but take longer to execute.

➤ Click **Remove Redundant Points** to delete any coincident points that are created when using a pathfinder filter.

➤ Click **Divide and Outline will Extract Unpainted Artwork** to delete any unfilled objects remaining in the selected artwork when using the Divide filter or the Outline filter.

3. Click **OK** to close the dialog box.

Entries made in the Pathfinder options dialog box affect all subsequent uses of the affected Pathfinder filters—they have no affect on existing artwork.

NOTE

Using the Pathfinder Filters

To use any of the Pathfinder filters, follow these steps:

1. Select two or more objects that you want to affect.

2. Then choose a filter from the Filter > Pathfinder submenu and view the results.

➤ The Unite filter creates a single path that traces the outermost outline of all selected objects (see Figure 4.38). Objects that fall completely within the outermost edges are deleted.

➤ The Intersect filter traces the outline of all overlapping shapes in the selection, ignoring non-overlapping areas (see Figure 4.39). This filter works on only two objects at a time.

➤ The Exclude filter traces all non-overlapping areas of selected objects, making overlapping areas transparent (see Figure 4.40).

➤ The Minus Front filter subtracts the frontmost selected objects from the backmost selected path in the stacking order (see Figure 4.41).

➤ The Minus Back filter subtracts the backmost selected objects the frontmost selected path in the stacking order (see Figure 4.42).

➤ The Divide Fill filter divides selected objects into their components' faces—where face is any area undivided by a line segment. Each face of the original object becomes a separate object that can be manipulated as an independent object (see Figure 4.43). The faces are associated as a group. You can ungroup them or select and modify individual components using the Direct-select tool.

NOTE

If the Divide and Outline will Extract Unpainted Artwork option is set in the Pathfinder Options dialog box, described earlier, then any unfilled objects remaining in the selection will be deleted when these filters are used.

➤ The Outline filter (formerly the Divide Stroke filter) divides an image into its component line segments. Each edge takes on a Fill of None and a Stroke matching the Fill of the frontmost selected object (see Figure 4.44). The resulting line segments are grouped but they can be ungrouped and independently manipulated.

➤ The Trim and Merge filters both remove parts of selected objects that are "hidden" behind other objects, but the Merge filter merges any adjacent objects that are filled with the same color (see Figure 4.46), and the Trim filter removes hidden parts of objects but does not merge objects (see Figure 4.45).

➤ The Crop Fill filter divides the image into its component faces— areas that are undivided by line segments—and then deletes all the parts of the image that fall outside the boundary of the topmost object (see Figure 4.47).

Figure 4.38 Objects before and after using the Unite filter.

Figure 4.39 Objects before and after applying the Intersect filter.

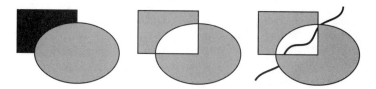

Figure 4.40 Objects before and after using the Exclude filter.

Figure 4.41 Objects before and after using the Minus Front filter.

Figure 4.42 Objects before and after using the Minus Back filter.

Figure 4.43 Objects before and after using the Divide filter.

Figure 4.44 Objects before and after using the Outline filter.

Figure 4.45 Objects before and after using the Trim filter.

Figure 4.46 Objects before and after using the Merge filter.

Figure 4.47 Objects before and after using the Crop filter.

Chapter Summary

This chapter described most of the methods for creating open and closed paths, editing them (changing their shapes), and creating or extracting specific paths or shapes using various commands and tools. Additional methods for working with paths to create special effects are detailed in Chapter 9.

The next chapter describes how to modify open or closed paths using the transformation tools and commands that specifically alter shapes. Chapter 6 describes how to change the paint attributes (stroke and fill) applied to paths.

Chapter 5

Using the Transformation Tools and Filters

This chapter describes Illustrator's transformation tools and filters, including:

➤ Scaling with the Scale tool, through the Control palette, and with the **Transform Each** command

➤ Rotating with the Rotate tool, through the Control palette, and with the **Transform Each** command

➤ Creating a mirror image with the Reflect tool

➤ Skewing the object with the Shear tool

➤ Filters under the Distort submenu—Free Distort, Punk and Bloat, Roughen, Scribble and Tweak, Twirl, and Zig Zag

➤ The Twirl tool—a new tool in the Plug-in Tools Toolbox that supplements the Twirl filter

➤ The Blend tool, which can create new objects that are a "blend" of two different shapes.

Each of these tools or commands represent automated methods of transforming objects as shown in Figure 5.1.

Figure 5.1 Original object (top left) scaled, rotated, reflected, and sheared (first row), punked, bloated, roughened, scribbled, twirled, and zig-zagged (second row), and blended with a second object (bottom right).

The Transformation Tools

Illustrator offers four functions that are often referred to as *transformations*. These functions include rotating, scaling, reflecting, and shearing.

Figure 5.2 The transformation tools in the Toolbox.

They all operate using very similar procedures:

➤ Select the object(s) to be transformed before using the tool.

➤ To transform visually on the screen, first select one or more objects, then click once on the tool, then click once on the screen to position the point of origin around which the transformation will occur, then drag the mouse to see the effect as you drag.

➤ To transform numerically, relative to the center of the selected object(s), or to rotate pattern tiles separately, double-click the tool and make entries in the dialog box.

➤ To transform numerically, relative to a point other than the center of the selected object(s), or to rotate pattern tiles separately, click the tool, then Option+click once on the screen to position the point of origin around which the transformation will occur, then and make entries in the dialog box.

These procedures are each described separately for each tool under the next headings.

Scaling Objects

Use the Scale tool to change the size of selected objects. Scaling an object stretches or compresses it horizontally, vertically, or both, relative to some fixed point you choose. You can scale objects visually on the screen or by an amount specified in the Scale dialog box or in the Control palette or in the Transform each dialog box.

Scaling Objects Visually on the Screen

1. First select the object(s) to be scaled.

2. Choose the **Scale** tool by clicking the icon in the Toolbox. The mouse pointer changes to a cross-hair (+) in the active window.

3. Click the + pointer on the screen to set a point of origin for the scaling transformation. This point functions like an anchor when you scale the object. When you click the mouse, the pointer changes to an arrowhead.

4. Position the arrowhead pointer away from the point of origin and drag away from the origin to enlarge the object or toward the origin to reduce the object.

   ➤ Shift+dragging the arrowhead constrains the direction of dragging to horizontal, vertical, or a 45° angle, resulting in horizontal, vertical, or proportional scaling respectively.

➤ Option+dragging the arrowhead leaves the original object unchanged and produces an enlarged or reduced scaled duplicate.

➤ Shift+Option+dragging produces a constrained duplicate.

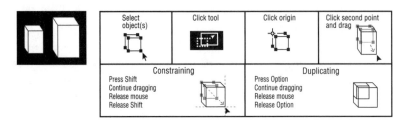

Figure 5.3 Scaling objects visually on the screen: (1) click the **Selection** tool anywhere on the path, then (2) select the **Scale** tool and click to establish an origin point, and (3) drag to scale the object relative to the origin. Use the **Shift** key to constrain scaling; use the **Option** key to produce a duplicate.

5. Release the mouse button when you have scaled as much as you want.

Scaling Objects by a Specified Percentage with Pattern Options

1. Select the object to be rotated.

2. Double-click the **Scale** tool to scale the object around its center point, or click once on the **Scale** tool to select it and then hold down the **Option** key when you click to set a point of origin for the scaling transformation.

3. The Scale dialog box appears as shown in the Figure 5.4. It allows you to specify Scale parameters, which include Uniform scale, Non-uniform scale, and whether to scale pattern tiles separately from the object, if the object is filled with a custom pattern (see the Paint Style palette and Object > Pattern commands in Chapter 6). The Scale dialog box also allows you to make a copy of the scaled object by clicking on **Copy**. If you select uniform scaling (that is, scaling equally in the x and y directions), you can also scale line weights.

4. When parameters are set as you wish, click on **OK**.

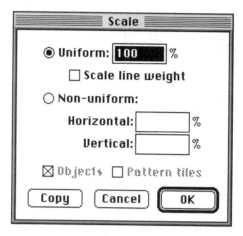

Figure 5.4 Option+click the origin point to enter scaling amounts through the Scale dialog box.

NOTE

You can create a set of concentric shapes by selecting a path, then using the Scale tool. Click at the center of the shape to set the origin of the transformation, then Option+drag to produce a transformed copy. Press **Command+D** (shortcut for **Arrange > Repeat Transform**) to produce a series of objects scaled to the same proportion. Draw the outer edge first and produce progressively smaller duplicates layered on top of the first object (see **Arrange > Repeat Transform** later in this chapter). Also see the Blend tool, later in this chapter, which can be used to create a series of concentric shapes, and the **File > Print** command in Chapter 11, which can be used to scale whole illustrations during printing.

Using Arrange > Transform Each to Scale

6.0 NEW FEATURE

If you select more than one object at a time and use the Scale tool, you scale all the objects at once as if they were a single object—scaling the bounding box that encompasses the objects. The **Transform Each** command offers the option of scaling each object in the selection without scaling the bounding box—the same way objects are rotated through Control palette (described next)—as well as scaling each object a different amount. (This command was formerly **Scale Each** on the Filter menu of version 5.5.)

To scale each object around its own center when several objects are selected, follow these steps:

1. Select the object(s) in the Adobe Illustrator document that you want to affect.

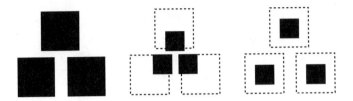

Figure 5.5 Three objects (left) scaled with the Scale
tool (middle) and with the **Transform Each** command (right).

2. Choose **Arrange > Transform Each**.

3. In the Transform Each dialog box, enter the horizontal and vertical scaling factors, and click **Random** if you want the filter to vary the scaling percentages for each object using your values as maximums.

4. Click **OK** or press **Return** to close the dialog box and view the effect.

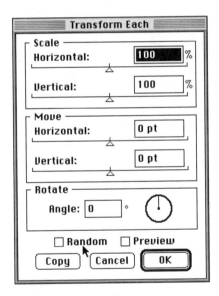

Using the Control Palette

**6.0 NEW
FEATURE**

Illustrator 6.0 introduces a Control palette through which you can scale an object and have the same effect as the Scaling options of the **Transform Each** command. Follow these steps:

1. Select the object(s) to be scaled.

2. Choose **Window > Show Control palette** (if it is not already displayed).

3. Click on a point in the proxy that represents the objects—at the left side of the Control palette—to select the point relative to which the scaling will occur.

4. Use the mouse or press the **Tab** key to highlight the value next to the scaling symbol in the upper-right corner of the palette.

5. Enter a scaling percentage.

6. Press **Enter** to apply the new value.

NOTE

Once the scaling is complete, the percentage value reverts to 100% in the Control palette—past scaling values are not stored. Also, notice that objects scaled through the Control palette are each scaled relative to their own proxy point, like using the **Transform Each** command (described earlier).

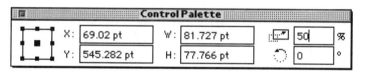

Figure 5.6 Control palette shows center point of Proxy is selected, and value of 50% is entered as the scaling value.

Figure 5.7 Object before and after entering scaling | percentage in the Control palette and pressing **Enter**.

Rotating Objects

Use the Rotate tool to rotate selected objects relative to a fixed point. You can rotate objects visually on the screen or by an amount specified in the Rotate dialog box. (You already used this tool in the exercises in Chapter 3, but it's explained in more detail here.)

Rotating Visually on the Screen

1. First select the object(s) to be rotated.

2. Choose the **Rotate** tool by clicking the icon in the Toolbox. The mouse pointer changes to a cross-hair (+) in the active window.

3. Click the + pointer on the screen to set a point of origin for the rotation. This point functions like an anchor when you rotate the object. When you click the mouse, the pointer changes to an arrowhead.

4. To make the object rotate, position the arrowhead pointer away from the point of origin, hold down the mouse button, and drag in the direction of the desired rotation.

    ➤ Shift+dragging the arrowhead (pressing the **Shift** key as you drag the mouse) constrains the rotation to multiples of 45° angles.

    ➤ Option+dragging the arrowhead (pressing **Option** when you release the mouse) leaves the original object unchanged and produces a rotated duplicate.

    ➤ Shift+Option+dragging produces a constrained duplicate.

5. Release the mouse button when you have rotated as much as you want.

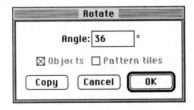

Figure 5.8 Rotating objects visually on the screen: (1) click the **Selection** tool anywhere on the path, then (2) select the **Rotate** tool and click to establish an origin point, and (3) drag to rotate the object relative to the origin. Use the **Shift** key to constrain rotation; use the **Option** key to produce a duplicate.

Rotating by a Specified Angle with Pattern Options

1. Select the object to be rotated.

2. Double-click the **Rotate** tool to rotate the object around its center point, or click once on the **Rotate** tool to select it and then hold down the **Option** key when you click to set a point of origin for the rotation transformation.

3. The Rotate dialog box appears, as shown in Figure 5.9, allowing you to specify the angle of rotation (in degrees) and whether to rotate pattern tiles separately from the object, if the object is filled with a custom pattern (see the Paint Style palette and **Object > Patterns** in Chapter 6). You can rotate a copy of the object by clicking the **Copy** button instead of the **OK** button.

NOTE

Angles are measured counterclockwise, with zero at three o'clock. You can rotate objects in a clockwise direction by entering a negative number.

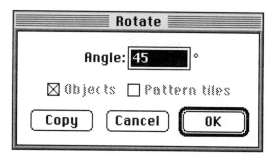

Figure 5.9 Option+click the origin point to enter the angle of rotation through the Rotate dialog box.

4. When parameters are set as you wish, click on **Copy** or **OK**.

SHORTCUT

If you hold the letter **P** key on the keyboard during any transformations, you transorm pattern fills only.

Using Arrange > Transform Each to Rotate

6.0 NEW FEATURE

If you select more than one object at a time and use the Rotate tool, you rotate *all* the objects around a single point at once—as if they were a group—and they maintain their positions and aspects relative to each other. The **Transform Each** command offers the option of rotating *each* object in the selection around its own center point—the same way objects are rotated through Control palette (described next). (This command was formerly **Rotate Each** on the Filter menu of version 5.5.)

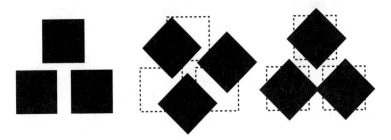

Figure 5.10 Three objects (left) rotated with the Rotate tool (middle) and with the **Transform Each** command (right).

To rotate each object around its own center when several objects are selected, follow these steps:

1. Select the object(s) in the Adobe Illustrator document that you want to affect.

2. Choose **Arrange > Transform Each**.

3. In the Transform Each dialog box, enter a rotation angle, or use the mouse to move the angle line in the "clock face" to the right of the angle text box, or click **Random** if you want the filter to pick different angles of rotating for each object.

NOTE

You can watch the angle line in the circle next to the angle-entry text box to see what effect your typed entry will have—or you can use the mouse to move the angle line itself and see the text entry change.

4. Click **OK** or press **Return** to close the dialog box and view the effect.

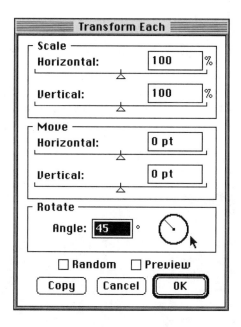

Using the Control Palette

6.0 NEW FEATURE

Illustrator 6.0 introduces a Control palette through which you can change the angle of rotation of an object and have the same effect as the Rotate options of the **Transform Each** command. Follow these steps:

1. Select the object(s) to be rotated.

2. Choose **Window > Show Control palette** (if it is not already displayed).

3. Click on a point in the proxy that represents the objects—at the left side of the Control palette—to select the point around which the rotation will occur.

4. Use the mouse or press the **Tab** key to highlight the value next to the rotation symbol in the lower-right corner of the palette.

5. Enter a rotation value.

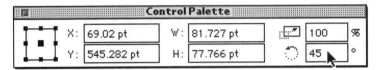

Figure 5.11 Control palette shows center point of Proxy is selected, and value of 45° is entered as the rotation value.

6. Press **Enter** to apply the new value.

Figure 5.12 Object before and after entering rotation angle in the Control palette and pressing **Enter**.

NOTE

Once the rotation is complete, the rotation angle reverts to zero in the Control palette—past rotation values are not stored. Also, notice that objects rotated through the Control palette each rotate relative to their own proxy point, like using the **Transform Each** command (described earlier).

Arrange > Repeat Transform

The **Repeat Transform** command (**Command+D**) repeats the most recent transformation. Transformations that can be repeated are those created using the Scale, Rotate, Reflect, and Shear tools. Moving of objects can also be repeated using **Repeat Transform**. If the last transformation also made a copy of the object, **Repeat Transform** will transform and make another copy.

After transforming an object, with the same or another object selected, choose **Arrange > Repeat Transform** or press **Command+D** to repeat the transformation. The last transformation will be repeated on the currently selected object.

There are numerous applications for **Repeat Transform**. The most common would be to transform one object and then repeat the same transformation on other objects using this one command, rather than repeatedly using the transformation tools and dialog boxes.

As another example, you can draw a single object, use the Rotate tool to rotate a copy around a central point, then press **Command+D** as many times as needed to make a radially symmetrical object. (See next sections in this chapter.)

You can intersperse other commands between uses of the **Repeat Transform** command, as long as only one of the commands is a transformation (Scale, Rotate, Reflect, Shear, or Move).

Each newly transformed copy will appear on the top in "painting order" on of the artwork. When creating a series of objects, always start with the one that you want to end up on the bottom.

NOTE

Creating Symmetrical Objects

The next exercises describe how to create objects that are symmetrical radially—around a center point. Remember that you can also use Illustrator's Oval, Rectangle, Spiral, Polygon, and Star tools to create symmetrical shapes.

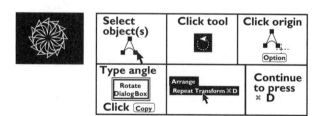

Figure 5.13 Radially symmetrical objects can be created with the Rotate tool—or the Rotate dialog tool, the Control palette, or the **Transform Each** command—and the **Transform Again** command.

EXERCISE: RADIAL SYMMETRY: METHOD I

Radial symmetry describes any object composed of a single shape that is repeated in a pattern around a central point. An example of radial symmetry is a flower, such as the one shown here in step 4. In this technique the Rotate tool is used to create simple patterns in which the shapes do not need to meet precisely at the edges—that is, they can overlap, or there can be gaps between them.

You can use this technique to create any radially symmetrical design that allows some gap or overlap between the units of the design.

1. Create an object that will become the basic unit of the radial design, using whatever tool is appropriate. In this example, use the Pen or Freehand tool to create a petal-shaped object, as in the figure at right.

2. Select the **Rotate** tool and Option+click on the point you want to use as the center of the design—in this case, the base of the petal.

3. In the Rotate dialog box, enter the number of degrees yielded by dividing 360 (degrees) by the number of repeated units. In this example you want ten units, so you type **36** as the number of degrees (360 divided by 10). Some other common values are shown in Table 5.1.

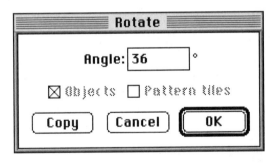

4. Click **Copy** to close the Rotate dialog box and make a rotated copy of the first object, then press **Command+D** (**Arrange > Repeat Transform**) until the circle is complete—eight more copies in this example.

5. Select all the elements with the Selection tool and press **Command+G** (**Arrange > Group**) to group the objects that make up your shape.

Table 5.1 Calculating degrees of rotation for symmetry

Number of repeated units in object	Degrees
2	180
3	120
4	90
5	72
6	60
7	51.43
8	45
9	40
10	36

NOTE Once you create a design, you can create many variations by scaling, overlaying, and/or shearing the object. The figure on the right shows three copies of the flower petals scaled progressively smaller, with variations in the fill and stroke for each group of petals in the object.

EXERCISE: RADIAL SYMMETRY: METHOD 2

This second technique for creating radially symmetrical designs is more controlled than the first, creating shapes that meet precisely at the edges, such as the one shown in the accompanying figure.

1. Use the Oval tool with the **Shift** key to draw a circle (as shown in the figure at right) whose center will be the center of the radial design and whose circumference will cross through the points you want the radial elements to touch or cross.

2. Select the **Pen** tool and click anywhere on the circumference of the circle to set an anchor point. In this example, the anchor point is just to the right of the top of the circle.

3. Select the **Rotate** tool and hold the **Option** key as you click on the center of the circle. The Rotate dialog box appears.

4. In the Angle field of the Rotate dialog box, type the number of degrees yielded by dividing 360 (degrees) by the number of repeated units. (See the table in Radial Symmetry: Method 1 for some common values.)

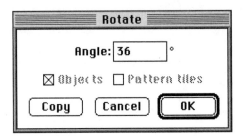

5. Click **Copy** to close the box and make a rotated copy of the anchor point.

6. Create an object that will become the basic unit of the radial design, using the two anchor points as guides for the edges of the shape. In this example, use the Pen or Freehand tool to draw an irregular polygon.

7. With the basic radial element selected, select the **Rotate** tool and Option+click the center of the circle, which happens to be the base of the polygon in this example. In the Angle field of the Rotate dialog box, type the number of degrees you used in step 2 (**36** degrees in this example), and click **Copy** to close the box and make a rotated copy of the object.

8. Press **Command+D** (**Arrange > Repeat Transform**) as many times as needed to complete the design.

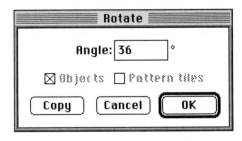

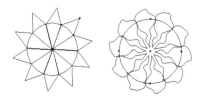

9. Select and delete the original circle and the two anchor points you used as guides.

10. Then select the remaining objects and press **Command+G** (**Arrange > Group**).

NOTE

The figure below shows the correct positioning of the basic radial unit with respect to the circle and anchor points for various other designs that can be created using this technique.

Reflecting Objects

You use the Reflect tools to transform an object into a mirror image of itself. You can reflect objects visually on the screen or at an angle specified in the Reflect dialog box.

Reflecting a Mirror Image Visually on the Screen

1. First select the object(s) to be transformed, then choose the **Reflect** tool by clicking the icon in the toolbox. The mouse pointer changes to a cross-hair (+) in the active window.

2. Click the + pointer at some point on the object to set a point on the axis of reflection. The pointer changes to an arrowhead.

3. Position the arrowhead pointer away from the first point of origin and hold down the mouse button to define a second point on the axis of reflection, then drag to rotate the axis and pivot the object around the axis visually.

   ➤ Shift+dragging the arrowhead (pressing **Shift** and dragging the mouse) constrains the reflection angle to multiples of 45°.

   ➤ Option+dragging the arrowhead (pressing **Option** before releasing the mouse) leaves the original object unchanged and produces a reflected copy.

   ➤ Shift+Option+dragging produces a constrained duplicate.

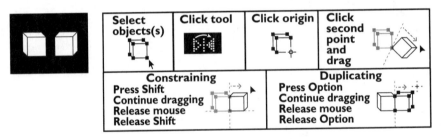

Figure 5.14 Reflecting objects visually on the screen (1) click the **Selection** tool anywhere on the path, then (2) select the **Reflect** tool and click to establish point on the axis of reflection; (3) click to establish a second point and thereby establish the axis of reflection; (4) drag to pivot the object around the axis. Use the **Shift** key to constrain the reflection axis; use the **Option** key to produce a duplicate.

4. Release the mouse button when you have rotated as much as you want.

The Reflect tool is one of the most difficult tools to control visually at first. The further you move away from the origin point to drag, the more incrementally, and therefore more slowly, the reflection will occur.

WARNING

To avoid unwanted effects, always group the object, then make a copy by holding down the **Option** key as you use the Reflect tool. If the copy is correct, delete the original. If the effect is not correct, you can delete the copy and try again.

NOTE

Specifying the Reflect Axis Numerically with Pattern Options

1. Select the object to be reflected.

2. Double-click the **Reflect** tool to reflect the object around its center point, or click once on the **Reflect** tool to select it and then hold down the **Option** key when you click to set a point of origin for the Reflect axis.

3. The Reflect dialog box appears, allowing you to specify which axis to reflect across: horizontal, vertical, or angled, and whether to reflect pattern tiles separately from the object, if the object is filled with a custom pattern (see the Paint Style palette and **Object > Patterns** in Chapter 6). You can make a copy of the object, reflected, by clicking on the **Copy** button instead of to clicking on **OK**.

The axis for reflection is specified by angles measured counterclockwise, with zero at three o'clock. You can reflect over an axis in a clockwise direction from three o'clock by entering a negative number.

N O T E

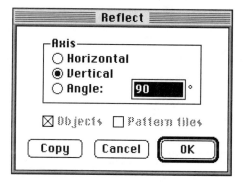

Figure 5.15 Option+click the origin point to enter the angle of rotation through the Reflect dialog box.

4. When parameters are set as you wish, click on **Copy** or **OK**.

EXERCISE: LINEAR SYMMETRY

Symmetrical shapes are common in man-made designs and in nature. The accompanying figure shows one common linearly symmetrical shape—a goblet or chalice. This technique can be used to create any linearly symmetrical object.

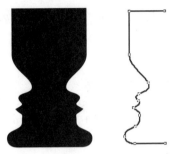

1. Create one half of the object—top or bottom, left or right. The figure above shows the left half of this object created with the Pen tool.

2. With the drawn elements selected, choose the **Reflect** tool and then hold down the **Option** key as you click on one of the two endpoints.

3. In the Reflect dialog box, select **Vertical axis reflection** and close the dialog box by clicking **Copy**. This creates a mirror image—in this case, the right half of the object.

NOTE

If the object you create in this step is not to your liking, delete one half and rework the other half, then go back to step 2.

4. With the Direct-selection tool, drag a selection marquee to select one pair of the common points where the two paths join. Press **Command+J** (**Object > Join**) to join the pair.

5. Repeat step 4 with the other pair of common points.

6. Use the Paint Style palette (**Command+I**) to set the stroke and fill you wish.

Shearing Objects

Use the Shear tools to change the angle between the axes of selected objects. (Normally the *x* and *y* axes are set at 90° angles.) Shearing is easy to picture if you think of it as describing the action of the blades of scissors; see Figure 5.16. (This is just a visual analogy—the Shear tool is unrelated to the Scissors tool.) You can shear objects visually on the screen or at an angle specified in the Shear dialog box.

Figure 5.16 In shearing, the change of the angle between the axes is similar to the movement of the blades of scissors.

Shearing Visually on the Screen

1. First select the object(s) to be sheared.

2. Choose the **Shear** tool by clicking the icon in the Toolbox. The mouse pointer changes to a cross-hair (+) in the active window.

3. Click the + pointer on the object to set a point of origin for the shear axis. When you release the mouse, the pointer changes to an arrowhead.

4. Position the arrowhead pointer away from the point of origin and drag.

➤ The direction in which you drag defines the axis of shear: if you drag left or right you change the angle of the vertical axis; if you drag up or down you change the angle of the horizontal axis.

➤ The distance you drag defines the angle of shear.

➤ Shift+dragging the arrowhead constrains the axis of shear to multiples of 45° angles.

➤ Option+dragging the arrowhead leaves the original object unchanged and produces a sheared copy.

➤ Shift+Option+dragging produces a constrained duplicate.

In Figure 5.17 the top boxes demonstrate the result of shearing an object visually, the lower-left illustration shows how Shift+dragging limits shearing to 45° increments, and the lower-right illustration shows how to create a sheared duplicate copy, leaving the original in place, using Option+drag.

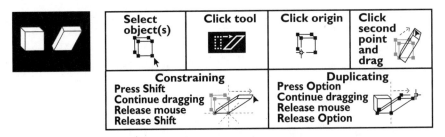

Figure 5.17 Shearing objects visually on the screen: (1) click the **Selection** tool anywhere on the path, then (2) select the **Shear** tool and click to establish an origin point, then (3) drag horizontally to change the angle of the y axis, or vertically to change the angle of the x axis. Use the **Shift** key to constrain shearing to 45° increments; use the **Option** key to create sheared copy.

5. Release the mouse button when you have the effect you want.

To avoid unwanted effects, always group the object, then make a copy by holding down the **Option** key as you use the Shear tool. If the copy is correct, delete the original. If the effect is not correct, you can delete the copy and try again.

NOTE

Shearing by a Specified Amount with Pattern Options

1. Select the object to be sheared.

2. Double-click the **Shear** tool to shear the object around its center point, or click once on the **Shear** tool to select it and then hold down the **Option** key when you click to set a point of origin for the shearing transformation.

3. The Shear dialog box appears, allowing you to specify the angle of shear, the axis to shear along, and whether to shear pattern tiles separately from the object, if the object is filled with a custom pattern (see the Paint Style palette and **Object > Patterns** in Chapter 6). You can also specify that a copy of the sheared object be made by clicking the **Copy** button before clicking **OK**. Figure 5.18 shows the Shear dialog box.

Figure 5.18 Option+click the origin point to enter the angle of shear through the Shear dialog box.

4. When parameters are set as you wish, click on **OK**.

Using Filters to Change Shapes

6.0 NEW FEATURE

The Distort filters create special effects by changing an object's shape or the directions of their paths. These commands in Illustrator 6.0 have been slightly modified from their version 5.5 counterparts, and some have been moved from the **Filter > Stylize** submenu.

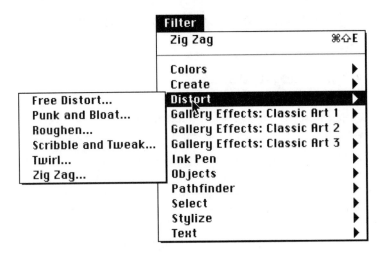

Filter > Distort > Free Distort...

The Free Distort filter lets you change the size and shape of an object by dragging the corner points of a Distort box. This offers an advantage over simply dragging individual anchor points, in that you can effectively distort several objects at once or affect many anchor points at once.

1. Select the object(s) in the Adobe Illustrator document that you want to affect.

2. Choose **Filter > Distort > Free Distort** to display the Free Distort dialog box.

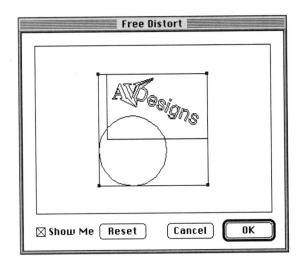

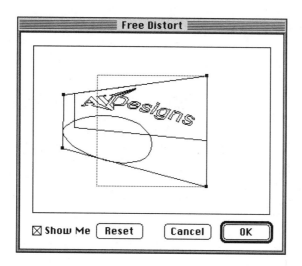

3. Distort the shape by dragging any of the four corner points.

4. Click **OK** or press **Return** to close the dialog box and view the effect.

Figure 5.19 Object before (left) and after (right) distorting.

Filter > Distort > Punk and Bloat

6.0 NEW FEATURE

The Punk and Bloat filter in Illustrator 6.0 combines two filters from Illustrator 5.5—**Filter > Stylize > Punk** and **Filter > Stylize > Bloat**.

The Punk filter curves paths inward from their anchor points to the degree determined by a negative Percent value.

The Bloat filter curves paths outward from their anchor points to a degree determined by a positive Percent value.

1. Select the path(s) in the Adobe Illustrator document that you want to affect.

2. Choose **Filter > Distort > Punk and Bloat** to display the Punk and Bloat dialog box.

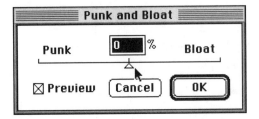

3. Drag the marker to the left or right, or enter a negative percentage as the degree of punking, or a positive percentage as the degree of bloating.

Click **Preview** to see the effect applied to the selected objects as you change the values, before applying the effect.

NOTE

4. Click **OK** to close the dialog box and view the effect.

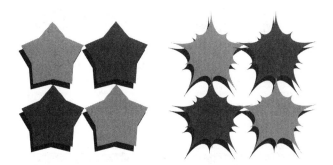

Figure 5.20 Object before and after the Punk effect has been applied.

Figure 5.21 Object before and after bloating.

Filter > Distort > Roughen...

The roughen filter moves anchor points in a jagged array from the original path, creating a rough edge on the object.

1. Select the path(s) in the Adobe Illustrator document that you want to affect.

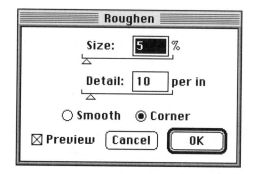

2. Choose **Filter > Distort > Roughen** to display the Roughen dialog box.

3. Enter the Size of each hump as a percentage of the size of the selected object(s), and, in the Detail field, the number of humps or segments per inch along the path. You can specify that the anchor points be **Smooth** (rounded) or **Corners** (jagged).

4. Click **OK** or press **Return** to close the dialog box and view the effect.

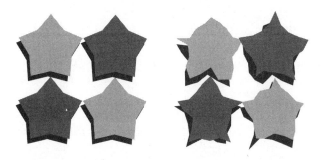

Figure 5.22 Object before and after the Roughen effect.

Filter > Distort > Scribble and Tweak

6.0 NEW FEATURE

The Scribble and Tweak filter in Illustrator 6.0 combines two filters from Illustrator 5.5—**Filter > Distort > Scribble** and **Filter > Distort > Tweak**.

The Scribble effect randomly moves anchor points away from the original path. The percentage you specify goes into the mysterious "scribble" formula and is an indicator of how similar the result will be to the original—0% being identical.

The Tweak also moves anchor points—but by a number of points you specify, instead of a percentage.

1. Select the path(s) in the Adobe Illustrator document that you want to affect.

2. Choose **Filter > Distort > Scribble and Tweak** to display the Scribble and Tweak dialog box.

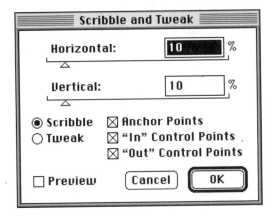

3. Enter the horizontal and vertical size of each hump as a percentage of the size of the selected object(s) when **Scribble** is selected, or as a numerical amount if **Tweak** is selected. You can specify that the humps be created by moving the current anchor points, and/or the "in" and "out" control points. (Again, these values are part of the scribble formula. "In" control points fall along the path that leads into an anchor point, "out" control points fall along the path leading out of an anchor point.)

4. Click **OK** or press **Return** to close the dialog box and view the effect.

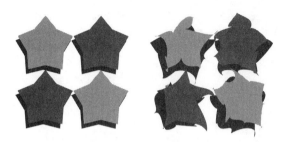

Figure 5.23 Object before and after the Scribble effect.

Filter > Distort > Twirl...

The Twirl filter rotates a selection more sharply in the center than at the edges.

1. Select the path(s) in the Adobe Illustrator document that you want to affect.

2. Choose **Filter > Distort > Twirl** to display the Twirl dialog box.

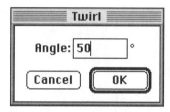

3. Enter a value between -999 and 999 for the twirl angle.

4. Click **OK** or press **Return** to close the dialog box and view the effect.

Figure 5.24 Object before and after Twirl filter.

NOTE

If you select only one path, the "center" around which all points are rotated is an average of all the anchor points in that path. If you select more than one path, the center is the average of all anchor points in all selected paths.

The Twirl Tool

6.0 NEW FEATURE

Illustrator 6.0 introduces a Twirl tool that has the same effect as the Twirl filter. Here's how it works:

1. Choose **Window > Show Plug-in Tools** to display the Plug-in Tools Toolbox, if it is not already displayed.

2. Use a selection tool to select the object(s) to be twirled.

3. Click on the **Twirl** tool to select it.

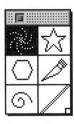

4. Position the pointer anywhere in the document window—usually the center of the selection(s), but this does not change the result—and drag the mouse pointer in a circular motion. You can see the object(s) change as you move the mouse.

5. Release the mouse button when you have achieved the effect you wish.

6.0 NEW FEATURE

As an alternative to step 4, you can Option-click in the document window to display a dialog box and enter a numeric value between -999 and 999 for the angle of the twirl.

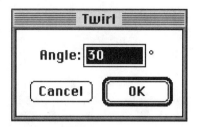

Filter > Distort > Zig Zag

The Zig Zag filter in Illustrator 6.0 creates a jagged path composed of either straight lines or curves between anchor points of the selected objects.

6.0 NEW FEATURE

1. Select the path(s) in the Adobe Illustrator document that you want to affect.

2. Choose **Filter > Distort > Zig Zag** to display the Zig Zag dialog box.

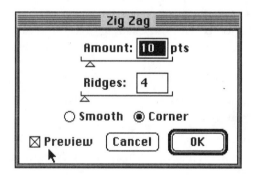

3. Enter the following values:

➤ Amount of Zig Zag effect in points indicates how far the current anchor points will be moved from their current positions. Anchor points are alternately moved toward or away from the center of the object.

➤ The number of Ridges is the number of anchor points that will be added between each adjacent pair of anchor points of the original object.

➤ You can specify that the anchor points be **Smooth** (rounded) or **Corners** (jagged).

4. Click **OK** or press **Return** to close the dialog box and view the effect.

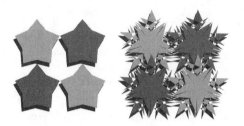

Figure 5.25 Object before and after the Zig Zag effect.

Using the Blend Tool to Change Shapes

Use the Blend tool to transform one object into another object in a series of steps. You create the starting object and the resulting object using Illustrator's tools. The intermediate objects are created automatically during the transformation process.

1. Create two objects. One object represents the beginning of the transformation series, and the second object represents the resulting object after the transformation series is completed.

2. Select one or more anchor points on each object. These will serve as corresponding reference points during the transformation.

3. Next, click the **Blend** tool in the Toolbox. This changes the mouse pointer to a cross-hair pointer.

4. Click the cross-hair pointer on one point of each of the two objects: these points will be the primary points of correspondence throughout the transformation.

5. When you click a point on the second object, the Blend dialog box appears as shown in the following figure. You can enter a number from **1** to **1296** to determine how many intermediate objects will be created by the blending process.

6. Click **OK** to close the dialog box and view the effect—the new objects fall between the original objects and are automatically grouped.

Figure 5.26 Example of shapes changed by using the Blend tool.

Both the starting object and the resulting object must be either closed or open paths; you cannot blend a closed path with an open path. (See Chapter 4 for definitions of open and closed paths.)

NOTE

Before using the Blend tool, select the points of the two objects in pairs; that is, hold down the **Shift** key, then click the **Selection** tool on a point on the first object, then click the **Selection** tool on the corresponding point on the second object. You can select more than one pair of points. Generally speaking, you select only one pair if the two objects and all blended results have the same shape. Select more than one pair of points if the two objects have very different shapes, or if you want the blended results to assume new shapes. Different sequences of pairs produce different results.

SHORTCUT

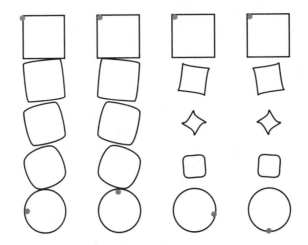

Figure 5.27 Selecting different pairs of anchor points produces different effects.

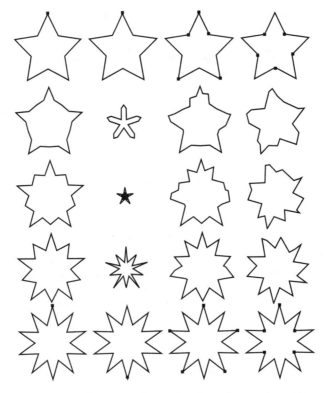

Figure 5.28 Selecting different paired sets of anchor points produces different effects.

You can use the Blend tool for a variety of effects: to create a series of gradual changes of color or pattern (see Chapter 6), to create a series of gradual changes from one shape to another (Figure 5.26), or to create special highlight effect (see figure in step 8 below).

EXERCISE: CREATE A CUSTOM HIGHLIGHT EFFECT

You can use the Gradient palette, described in Chapter 6, to create linear or radial gradient fills for three-dimensional effects that require a line or point of highlight. Use the Blend tool when the highlight is a curved line or irregular shape, as in this exercise.

1. Draw a shape—like the apple in this exercise.

2. Choose **Object > Paint Style** (**Command+I**) to display the Paint palette, if it is not already displayed, and assign a fill and no stroke to the shape—bright red, in this case.

3. Draw a custom highlight point—in this case a wide flat oval.

4. Assign a white fill and no stroke to the highlight point.

5. Select corresponding points on the two objects using the Direct-selection tool.

6. Click on the **Blend** tool to select it.

7. Click one point on the outer object, and then click the corresponding point on the highlight.

The first object you click after you select the Blend tool will fall on the bottom in the painting order of the blended series of objects; the second object will fall on the top.

NOTE

8. Type the number of steps in the Blend dialog box, and click **OK** to view the results.

Summary

This chapter built on Chapters 3 and 4, by showing you a variety of ways you can change the shape of objects created using Illustrator's drawing tools. You now know everything you need to know to create almost any shape you need in Illustrator. In addition, some more advanced techniques are described in Chapter 9.

The next chapter describes in detail how you can apply colors or patterns to the stoke (outline) and fill (area defined by the outline) of any object created using Illustrator's tools.

Chapter 6

Painting Objects

Up to this point, you have learned how to create objects in Illustrator, and edit or otherwise change their *shapes*. This chapter describes how to change the color or pattern that defines the stroke (outline) and fill (inside area) of any shape.

Any path—open or closed—can have a fill that is different from the stroke or border around it. You can create and assign fills through the Paint Style palette. You can also create fills through the **Object > Custom Color Pattern** and **Gradient** commands. You can access colors from other files by opening those documents, or by using the **File > Import Styles** command. In addition, the Blend tool and commands on the Filter > Colors submenu can be used to create new colors.

In this chapter, we describe these basic features and commands as well as some of the more difficult or unusual uses of these functions. Topics covered in this chapter include:

➤ Using the Paint Style palette to assign colors to the stroke and fill

➤ Applying the paint swatches in the palette

➤ Customizing the contents of the Paint Style palette

➤ Creating new colors

➤ Using Adobe's custom fills, including Default Custom Colors and Color Matching Systems

➤ Creating your own Custom Fill Sets, including Customizing the Startup File, Working with Multiple Start-up Files, Importing Custom Fill Sets, Opening a Paint Style Window

➤ Using color matching systems—like the PANTONE colors

➤ Working with Blends and Gradients, including Creating Optimal Blends, Blending to Create New Colors or Grays, Blending for Spot Color Separation

➤ Working with Patterns, including Transforming Existing Patterns, Creating a Linear Pattern, Creating Patterns of Discrete Objects, Creating Continuous Wavy Line Patterns, Creating Continuous Geometric Patterns, Creating Amorphous Patterns

➤ Using the Paintbucket and Eyedropper tools

➤ Using Color filters to adjust, blend, separate, invert, and mix colors, and convert custom colors to process colors

➤ Trapping colors before printing color separations

NOTE Illustrator displays colors and gradients best when the monitor is set to display millions of colors. If your monitor is set to 256 colors, screen redraw may be faster, but the colors and gradients you see on the page and in the Paint Style palette will not be as accurate as when they are printed in color. If you plan to rely on your monitor's display of colors in selecting colors from the Paint Style palette, it's a good idea to calibrate your monitor as described at the end of this chapter.

Introduction to the Paint Style Palette

The Paint Style palette lets you set the fill and stroke attributes of an object through a palette—a moveable window that can remain open while you work. You can display the palette through two commands: **Window > Show Paint Style** or **Object > Paint Style** (**Command+I**). If the Paint Style palette is already

displayed, you can choose **Window > Hide Paint Style**, but
easier to simply click the close box on the palette title bar, or
Command+I to close it.

The Paint Style palette lets you set attributes for existing objects or for new object
you create, including settings for how paths or text characters are filled and stroked.
Fills can be None (transparent), White, Black, Process Color, Custom Color, Pattern,
Gradient. Strokes can be dashed or solid lines, with a line weight of 0 to 1296 points,
in None (transparent), White, Black, Process Color, Custom Color, or Pattern.

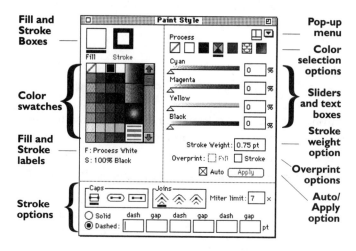

Figure 6.1 The Paint Style palette expanded to full size.

The Paint Style palette displays the current default paint attributes if no object is
selected, or the current selection's attributes if only one object is selected or if several selected objects share the same attributes. If more than one object is selected
and they do not share the same attributes, then attributes in common will be
clearly indicated in the Paint Style palette and attributes not shared will be indicated by question marks in the Fill or Stroke boxes at the top left in the palette.
Any changes you make to the Paint Style palette will affect all selected objects.

By default, all new objects you create in Illustrator automatically take on the current fill
and stroke attributes shown in the Paint Style palette. This applies whether the Paint
Style palette is actually displayed or not. You can change the defaults by changing the
palette values when no object is selected.

N O T E

When working in Preview mode (**View > Preview**, or **Command+Y**), you can see the paint style attributes of objects as you work without opening the Paint Style palette—but you must open the palette to change attributes (unless you use the Eyedropper and Paint Bucket tools, described later in this chapter). When working in Artwork view (**View > Artwork** or **Command+W**)—which yields faster screen display and easy selection of paths—the Paint Style palette is your only source of information about fill and stroke attributes.

NOTE

Work in Artwork view and keep the Paint Style palette open when editing complex illustrations. Use **View > Preview Selection** (**Command+Shift+Y**) if you want to see the preview of any selected objects.

To use the Paint Style palette, follow these steps:

1. Select one or more objects for which you wish to modify the Paint attributes, or de-select all objects if you want the new attributes to apply to the next objects you create.

2. Choose **Object > Paint Style**, or use the keyboard shortcut **Command+I**, to display or activate the Paint Style palette.

3. Select the **Auto** check box to automatically apply each change to all selected objects as you make entries. Deselect this box if you want to make several changes to the palette and then apply the palette settings manually by clicking **Apply**.

4. Make changes to the Paint Style palette by clicking on the appropriate option or by typing in the desired values. Specific entries are described in the next sections.

NOTE

The Paint Style palette takes up a lot of screen space in its expanded size, but you can make it smaller as described in the next section. You can also cluster all open palettes next to each other, added by the snap-to effect of the edges in Illustrator 6.0.

NOTE

Did you know you can close all open palettes at once simply by pressing **Tab** key? Press **Tab** and then **Command+I** to display only the Paint Style palette.

NOTE

Any changes you make to the Paint Style palette are automatically applied to whatever objects are currently selected on the Artboard. Be sure that only objects you wish to change are selected when you make entries in the palette.

Adjusting the Size and Position of the Paint Style Palette

You can move the Paint Style palette on the screen by dragging the title bar. The palette will always display on top of all document windows, but the most recently used palette can appear on top of this palette if there is overlap between palettes. You can bring any palette to the top by clicking on it.

You can change the size of the Paint Style palette by choosing from the palette display pop-out menu—activated by holding the mouse button down when the pointer is over the arrow at the top right of the palette. You can also change size by simply clicking on one of the panels in the icon left of the pop-up menu indicator. The choices on the menu are represented as icons to indicate the full palette, the top of the palette (i.e., minus options for Caps, Joins, Miters, and Dashed lines), the left of the palette (for setting fill and stroke attributes from swatches, minus options for selecting new colors, patterns, or gradients by name), or the right of the palette (for setting fill and stroke attributes by selecting percentages or names of colors, patterns, or gradients).

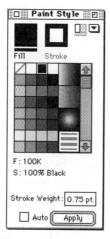
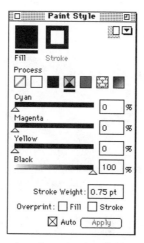

Figure 6.2 The Paint Style palette in two reduced views.

NOTE

Click the size box at the top right of the title bar to toggle between the two most recent views of the Paint Style palette.

Setting Current Default Paint Styles

By default, all new objects you create in Illustrator automatically take on the fill and stroke attributes shown in the Paint Style palette. This applies whether the Paint Style palette is actually displayed or not. You can change these attributes for selected objects by modifying the palette. You can change the attributes that apply to the next drawn object in one of the following ways:

➤ Click on an object with the Selection tool to display all of that object's paint style attributes in the Paint Style palette.

➤ Click on an object with the Eyedropper tool to change only those paint style attributes in the Paint Style palette that have been specified in the Paintbucket/Eyedropper Preferences dialog box (described later in this chapter).

➤ Click on one object with the Selection tool, or select several objects, then make changes to the Paint Style palette as described under the next headings to affect the selected objects as well as the next drawn objects.

➤ Click away from all artwork with the Selection tool, or choose **Edit > Select None** (**Command+Shift+A**), to deselect all objects, then make changes to the Paint Style palette as described under the next headings to affect the next drawn objects.

What's In The Paint Style Palette

The Paint Style palette displays lists of all colors, gradients, and patterns defined for all open documents. You can have access to colors, gradients, and patterns created in another file simply by opening the other file. As long as the other file is open, you will have access to all its patterns in the current file, but when the other file is closed the fill options that apply to that document only will not appear in the Paint Style palette. You can permanently add all the fill options from one file to another by using the **File > Import Styles** command, described later in this chapter.

All fill patterns defined for the startup document are automatically displayed on all palettes when you first start Illustrator—even if you start it by opening a document that does not use those fills. You can reduce the number on the list for the current session by opening a new document and then using the **Object > Custom Colors, Object > Gradients**, and **Object Patterns** commands to delete all these fills—then when you open a document only the fills used in that document will appear in the palettes. You can reduce the number on the list for the all sessions by changing the startup document, as described later in this chapter under Customizing the Illustrator Startup File.

Applying Colors to Fills and Strokes

You can change the fill or stroke attributes in the Paint Style palette when no object is selected, to affect only the next drawn object, or you can change the appearance of selected objects by changing these attributes. In either case, the procedure is the same.

NOTE

Steps 1 and 2 can be done in any order—step 2 can precede step 1.

1. Select the object(s) to be changed, or press **Command+Shift+A** to deselect all objects and affect only the next drawn object(s).

2. Display the Paint Style palette by choosing **Window > Show Paint Style** or **Object > Paint Style** (**Command+I**).

3. Click the **Fill** or **Stroke** box at the top left in the palette, to determine which element you wish to affect. The Fill affects the area enclosed by the path, the Stroke affects the path itself—line segments that outline the object.

4. Specify fill or stroke attributes as described under the next headings.

5. If the **Auto** option is checked in the palette, all selected paths and type take on the new attributes automatically. If the **Auto** option is not checked, you must apply the new attributers to the selected objects by:

   ➤ clicking the **Apply** button, or

   ➤ pressing the **Enter** key, or

   ➤ double-clicking the **Fill** or **Stroke** box.

6. The next objects you draw using Illustrator's tools will take on the latest attributes shown in the Paint Style palette—whether or not the palette is displayed.

Fill and Stroke attributes apply to whole paths—you cannot give one line segment along a path a different weight, for example, than all other line segments on the same path. To achieve the effect of different fills or strokes, you must create several objects.

NOTE

All characters of text selected with the Selection tool will take on the Paint Style attributes you specify in the Paint Style palette, but you can change the attributes of individual characters by selecting them with the Type tool (i.e., the I-beam pointer). (See Chapter 8.)

Working with Paint Swatches in the Palette

You can apply a color to a Fill or Stroke by clicking on a paint swatch in the left side of the Paint Style palette—or double-clicking if the Auto option is not checked. The current color selection for fill (F) and stroke (S) is described numerically beneath the scrolling window of color swatches. Process colors are indicated by CMYK percentages, custom colors are indicated by name.

When the Paint Style palette is fully open, you can see the category of color selected at the top of the right side of the palette—None, White, Black, Process, Gradient, or Pattern.

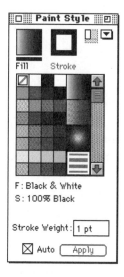

Figure 6.3 The current color selection for fill (F) and stroke (S) is described numerically beneath the scrolling window of color swatches.

Specifying a Color Not Included in Swatches

When the Paint Style palette is fully open, you can specify a color that is not a swatch by making entries directly to the right side of the palette (see Working with the Color Selection Options, later in this section). You can also create a new color by clicking on a swatch and then changing the percentages on the right side of the expanded palette.

Adding, Replacing, or Removing Color Swatches

If you have specified a color, pattern, or gradient fill not shown in the swatches—using techniques described later under Working with the Color Selection Options—you can add the color to the swatch selections using any of these techniques:

➤ Option+click on a swatch box. The swatch selection area includes white (unfilled) swatch boxes at the bottom of the scrolling display, and you can Option+click in one of these white boxes to add the current color (displayed on the right of the palette) without removing any from the swatch assortment. You can also Option+click on an existing swatch to remove it from the assortment of paint swatches, and replace it with the current color.

➤ Drag the current color, pattern, or gradient fill from the Fill or Stroke box, or drag the name of the fill from the scrolling list on the right side of the palette (see topics under the next heading, Working with the Color Selection Options) to the paint swatch you want to fill or replace.

➤ You can copy a swatch to a new location by holding down the **Option** key and dragging the swatch from one box to another.

NOTE The paint swatches you define are saved with the document, so you can create custom palettes. You can have up to 225 color swatches in the Paint Style palette, but you might find it more convenient to create a palette of only the colors you use. For some documents or publication groups, this might be only black and one or two custom colors—making it very simple to choose the color you want for each element.

To remove unused color swatches and simplify the Paint Style palette for the current document:

➤ Hold the **Command** key and click on the color swatch.

➤ Hold the **Command** key and drag over a group of swatches to clear several at once.

NOTE When deleting swatches, Illustrator displays a warning that you cannot use the **Undo** command to reverse the deletion (but you can always re-create the color as described earlier). The four top swatches—None, White, Black, and Process White—cannot be removed or replaced.

Working with the Color Selection Options

There are seven basic color options available in the Paint Style palette: None, White, Black, Process Color, Custom Color, Gradient, and Pattern. These are represented by the seven color selection boxes shown at the top right side of the Paint Style palette when it is fully open, and by various color swatches on the left side of the palette.

Figure 6.4 Color selection boxes at the top right side of the Paint Style palette represent None, White, Black, Process Color, Custom Color, Gradient, and Pattern.

Applying the "None" Attribute

The top-left swatch and the leftmost of the color selection boxes—a white box with a gray diagonal line—indicate None, or no color. If both the Fill and Stroke are set to **None**, then the object will not appear in Preview mode or printed artwork, but you can see the path in Artwork view.

NOTE

Both fill and stroke attributes are set to **None** automatically when you create a mask, a guide, or set up area text or text on a path.

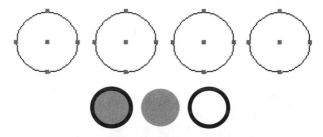

Figure 6.5 Artwork (top) and Preview (bottom) views of an object with black stroke and gray fill, no stroke and gray fill, black stroke and no fill, and no fill or stroke.

Using Black and White and Shades of Gray

The second and third boxes in the top row or swatches, and the second and third color selector boxes, indicate White and Black. These are the equivalent of process colors with a CMYK mix of 0% or 100%, respectively.

NOTE

The fourth color swatch represents Process White, which is not different from White but is a good choice when you want to create a new process color by setting percentages as described later in this section.

When **Black** is selected, you can make it a tint by sliding the indicator below the tint bar or specifying a percentage in the right side of the palette. You can also select tints of black from the color swatches.

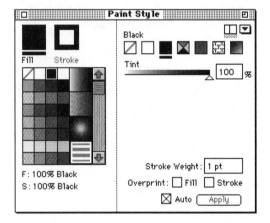

Figure 6.6 The Paint Style palette with **Black** selected, showing tint bar and percentage box on right.

The following figure shows examples of fill percentages, from 100% to 10% percent in increments of 10%.

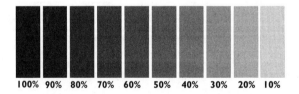

Figure 6.7 Examples of fills in various percentages.

Creating Process Color

The fourth color selector box and some of the color swatches indicate process color—colors produced by mixing various percentages of cyan, magenta, yellow, and black. When you select a process color, you can adjust the percentages of each color component—cyan, magenta, yellow, and black—by sliding the indicators below the color bars or specifying percentages in the right side of the palette. In either case, you can see the color change in the Fill or Stroke box as you create it.

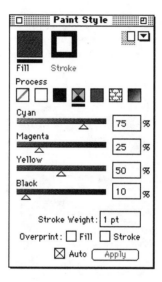

Figure 6.8 The Paint Style palette with a process color selected, showing color components.

NOTE

When you define a new process color by selecting the fourth color selector box and defining the percentages, the new color is automatically applied to the selected object(s) or to the next object you create. If no objects are selected, and if you select another object before creating a new one, your process color specifications are not saved. When you define a new process color that you intend to use more than once, it's a good idea to store the formula as a color swatch—by Option+clicking in one of the white boxes in the color swatch area of the palette to store the current color without removing any from the current swatch assortment.

Specifying a Custom Color, Gradient, or Pattern

The fifth, sixth, and seventh color selectors on the right side of the expanded Paint Style palette indicate custom (named) colors, gradients, and patterns, respectively. When any of these is selected, a scrolling list of named custom colors, gradients, or patterns appears on the right of the palette. You apply one of these by clicking on the name. Click **Apply** to apply the fill if the **Auto** option is not active.

When you choose a gradient fill, an Angle text box appears in the Paint Style palette and you can specify an angle for a linear fill. You can also change this angle later through the Paint Style palette, or by using the Gradient Vector tool as described later in this chapter.

NOTE

Gradients cannot be applied to strokes, but you can outline the stroke to create a fillable area using **Filter > Objects > Outline Path**, described in Chapter 4. To apply gradients or patterns to text you must first convert the text to outlines. See Type > Create Outlines in Chapter 8.

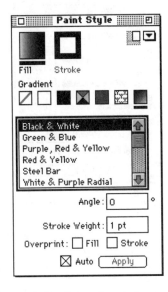

Figure 6.9 The Paint Style palette with **Gradient** selected, showing named gradients in a scrolling list.

NOTE

Whenever a scrolling list of custom colors, gradients, or patterns is displayed in the Paint Style palette, you can display a dialog box for changing or adding a new name by double-clicking on the one you want to change—or on any name if you want to create a new one. These are the same dialog boxes as displayed by the **Object > Custom Color**, **Object > Gradient**, and **Object > Pattern** commands described later in this chapter.

Specifying Stroke Attributes

The Stroke (border) of an object can have any of the attributes available for Fill except gradient, as well as a weight (thickness), miter limit, end cap, join style, and dashed pattern. These features are described here and in the next sections.

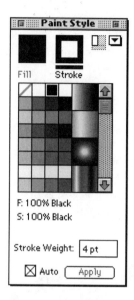

Figure 6.10 Stroke Weight option in the reduced Paint Style palette.

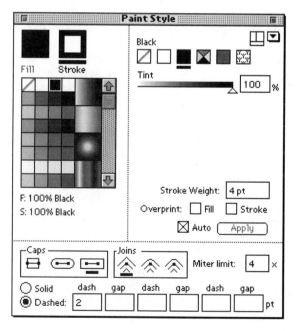

Figure 6.11 Stroke Weight and line style options plus end-cap styles, joins, miters, and dashed-line options in the fully expanded Paint Style palette.

NOTE

The Stroke Weight and line style options are available when the **Stroke** box is clicked in the top left of the Paint Style palette—grayed when the **Fill** box is clicked. In addition, options for defining end-cap styles, joins, miters, and dashed lines are available in the bottom of the Paint Style palette when it is fully open.

Stroke Weight (Line Thickness)

You can set the line weight of the stroke in points or decimal fractions of a point, from 0 to 1296 points in quarter-point increments, when Stroke is set to something other than None. This option is not available when Stroke is set to **None**. Lines are stroked from the center of the line that is displayed in Artwork view, outward in both directions.

Figure 6.12 Preview mode shows wide black stroke surrounding the actual path—which displays as a thin line with anchor points when the path is selected.

NOTE

A stroke weight of zero actually represents the thinnest line your printer is capable of printing—you must set the stroke color to **None** if you do not want it to print.

Overprint Option for Color Separations

Overprint results in the selected object overprinting colors and percentages of black on the objects below the selected object. The default is for no overprint. This creates a *knockout*, the traditional term for an overlay or color separation that deletes or "knocks out" the part of an image that is overlapped by another image of a different color. For example, in printing red type on a black background, the type is knocked out of the black color separation—leaving a white or blank space on the film and plate. Then the red ink of the type will—theoretically, at least—nestle perfectly in the space where the black ink does not print.

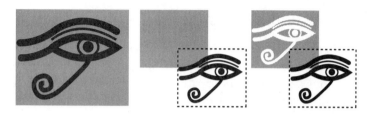

Figure 6.13 Black stroke backed by a color background (left) and the resulting color separations, when **Overprint** is on (middle) and off (right).

Problems arise when the registration is not perfect—white space might appear between the black and red areas. To reduce this possibility in our imperfect world, you can specify that the stroke and/or fill of one object *overprint*—literally print ink on top of—whatever object(s) fall below in stacking order.

Figure 6.14 Black stroke backed by a color background printed with Overprint off—with perfect registration (left) and with registration slightly off (right).

In our example of red type on a black background, you would want only the stroke to overprint—and give the type a stroke width greater than zero. Otherwise, if the fill overprints as well, you might not see the type at all—not many colors can successfully overprint on black and preserve their own identity! If the background is lighter than the foreground, however, you might choose to overprint the stroke and fill—as when printing black type on a color background.

See also Chapter 11, "Printing," for more on printing color separations.

NOTE

End Caps on Open Paths

You have a choice of three end caps for lines. This refers to the shape of each end of an open path. Butt caps (the default) are squared off perpendicular to the path; the cap does not extend beyond the path. Round caps end the line in a semicircular cap with a diameter equal to the line weight. Projecting caps have square ends that project half the line weight beyond the end of the path.

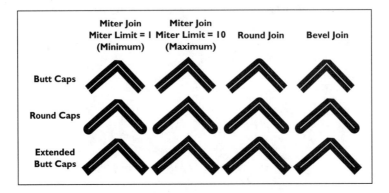

Figure 6.15 Examples of miter limit, end cap, and joins settings.

Joins between Line Segments

You have a choice of three joins for corner points. Miter joins (the default) extend the edges of two converging strokes until they meet. (See Miter Limit.) Round joins connect corners with a circular arc whose diameter is equal to the line weight. Bevel joins finish the converging lines with butt caps and fill the resulting notch with a triangle, giving the corner a squared-off appearance. (See Figure 6.15.)

Miter Limit at Sharp Angles

The miter limit determines the point at which, when two lines meet at a sharp angle, Illustrator switches from a miter (pointed) to a bevel (squared-off) join. You can set the miter limit only if you have specified a miter join; otherwise the option is disabled. The miter limit default value is **4**, which means that when the length of the spike formed by the miter join reaches 4 times the line weight, Illustrator switches from a miter to a bevel join. You can set the miter limit from 1 to 10. A value of **1** always creates a bevel join.

Dash Patterns

This option is enabled when Stroke is set to any color other than None. When stroke is set to **None**, the Dash pattern option is disabled.

You can set up custom dashed lines by clicking on **Dashed** and making entries in the boxes as follows:

➤ If you want an evenly dashed line with black dashes the same length as the white gaps, as shown in the first example in the following figure, enter one value (in points) for the interval in the first box provided.

➤ If you want two different measurements for the black and white portions of a line with a black stroke, which produces variations of dashed and/or dotted lines, enter the length of the black intervals in the first box and the length of the white intervals in the second box.

➤ You can create complex dashed lines by entering up to six values for intervals. The fourth example in the figure shows three values for intervals; the fifth example shows values entered in all six interval boxes.

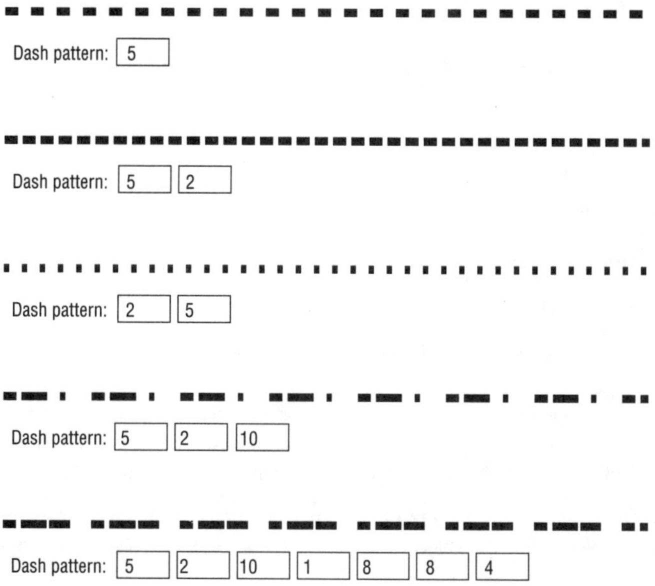

Figure 6.16 Examples of dashed line settings.

Applying Patterns to a Path

6.0 NEW FEATURE

Illustrator 6.0 introduces the ability to apply patterns to paths. (Formerly, patterns could be applied to fills only.) There are two ways to do this: directly through the Paint Style palette or using the **Filter > Stylize > Path Pattern** command. Both of these methods are described here.

To support this new feature, there are now two different types of pattern fills: those designed primarily as fill patterns and those designed primarily as stroke or path patterns. You can apply both types to either a Stroke or a Fill, but the results might not be what you expect, as shown in the next sections.

NOTE

Patterns work best when applied to relatively wide stroke widths, and some patterns are designed for specific stroke widths—as described in the next sections.

Using the Paint Style Palette

You can select any path and paint the Stroke with a pattern, just as you would for the fill:

1. Create or select the path to be stroked.

2. Click on the **Stroke** box in the expanded Paint Style palette.

3. Click on the **Pattern** color selection option.

4. Click on a pattern name in the list of available patterns.

5. Adjust the stroke width if necessary to achieve the effect you want.

NOTE

This technique works best in applying patterns that were designed to be fill patterns. Patterns that were designed to be path patterns should be applied through the **Filter > Stylize > Path Pattern** command, described in the next section

Strokes always appear gray on screen when patterns are applied through the Paint Style palette, but the selected pattern displays in the Stroke box in the palette and prints as a pattern.

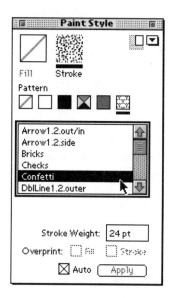

Figure 6.17 Paint Style palette with a pattern selected for a Stroke.

Figure 6.18 Examples of fill patterns applied to paths.

Figure 6.19 Examples of path patterns applied to paths through the Paint Style palette—results are better controlled using the Path Pattern filter.

Using the Path Pattern Filter

6.0 NEW FEATURE

The **Filter > Stylize > Path Pattern** command lets you outline objects with patterns to create decorative borders. The original Adobe Illustrator Startup file includes several patterns that were designed to be applied to paths, and the basic installation process adds two galleries of path patterns, stored in the Path Patterns folder (in the Sample Files folder in the Adobe Illustrator program folder). The Adobe Illustrator Deluxe CD-ROM includes even more path patterns.

When you apply a path pattern through the **Filter > Stylize > Path Pattern** command, you have these additional options that are not available when you use the Paint Style palette directly:

➤ You can select different patterns for the sides, outer corners, and inner corners of an object—and some path patterns have two or three variations designed to match these options.

➤ You can resize and flip the pattern.

➤ You can create different effects depending on whether the pattern is applied to a straight path or a curved path.

➤ When you use this command, you actually create a new object or set of objects that overlay the original path—the original path remains as a separate object. You can therefore create additional variations by applying a width and color to the path.

To outline a path with a pattern, follow these steps:

1. Create or select the object you want to outline.

2. Set the Fill and Stroke to **None**—unless you want to create special effects not intended by the path pattern designers.

3. If the pattern is not already listed in the Paint Style palette, open the gallery or file that includes the pattern you wish to use. This will add new patterns to the Paint Style palette temporarily. Then make your original artwork window active through the Window menu.

4. Choose **Filter > Stylize > Path Pattern** to display the Path Pattern dialog box.

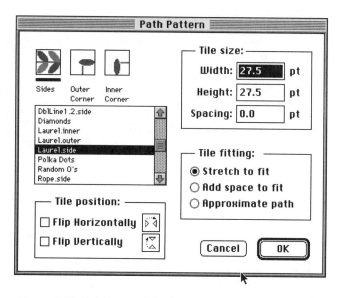

Figure 6.20 Path Pattern dialog box with the Sides option selected.

5. With the **Sides** option selected in the upper-left corner of the dialog box, choose a pattern for the sides of the object from the scrolling list of patterns. Patterns that have different designs for the sides and the corners have the word *side* appended to the name.

6. If the object has corners, select the **Outer Corner** option in the upper-left corner of the dialog box and choose a pattern. Patterns that have different designs for the corners have the word *Outer* or *In/Out* appended to the name.

Repeat the last step, selecting the **Inner Corner** option, if the object has inner corners.

You can apply the same pattern to the sides and the corners—but you must specify a pattern for each, if you want the object to be completely framed. You can also select **None** from the scrolling list to omit any pattern from the sides or the corners—and thereby create a border with sides or corners only.

NOTE

Figure 6.21 Objects with different patterns applied to the sides and corners.

7. To change the default size of the pattern by an amount you specify, enter a new width or height for the pattern tile. Adjusting the width or height automatically changes the opposite value proportionately. If you are applying both a side pattern and a corner pattern, adjust the height or width of both patterns by the same amount.

NOTE

If the path is a circle, specify a smaller width than the circle's radius for a donut effect, or match the tile width to the circle width for a solid fill.

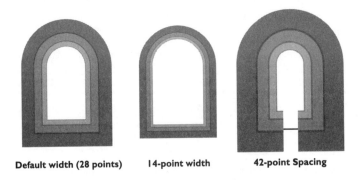

Default width (28 points)   14-point width   42-point Spacing

Figure 6.22 Objects with different tile widths.

8. Enter a value in the Tile Size Spacing text box if you want to add space between each tile.

9. To make sure the pattern evenly fits the length of the path, choose one of these options:

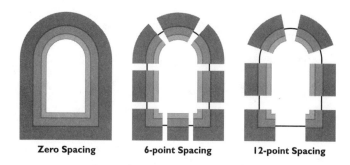

| Zero Spacing | 6-point Spacing | 12-point Spacing |

➤ **Stretch to Fit** lengthens or shortens the pattern tile to fit the length—but this can result in uneven tiling when different sides are different lengths.

➤ **Add Spacing to Fit** adds blank space between each pattern tile. You can let Illustrator calculate the space or specify the amount in the Tile Size Spacing text box.

➤ **Approximate Path** adjusts the pattern to be more inside or outside the path as needed to fit the path and achieve even tiling—rather than the default to center the pattern on the path. This option retains the default pattern tile size.

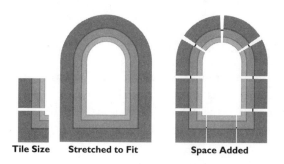

| Tile Size | Stretched to Fit | Space Added |

Figure 6.23 Pattern tiles adjusted to fit a path.

10. Flip the tiles horizontally or vertically or both to achieve different effects.

11. Click **OK** to close the dialog box and apply the pattern.

Some of the path patterns that come with Illustrator are shown in Figure 6.24.

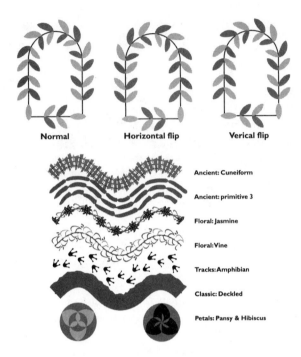

Figure 6.24 Examples of patterns applied to paths.

Editing a Path Pattern

Path patterns applied through the **Filter > Stylize > Path Patterns** command are composed of discrete objects that you can edit just as you would any artwork. For example, you can change the color, line, weights, and shapes of individual components of the pattern using normal editing techniques.

If you want to change a pattern for future uses, you can also edit any of the path patterns that come with Illustrator to create new patterns—using the same techniques described later in this chapter for editing fill patterns.

Figure 6.25 Color variations applied to path patterns.

Using the Paintbucket and Eyedropper Tools

You can use the Eyedropper tool to copy the paint attributes from an object to the Paint Style palette, and the Paintbucket tool to apply the current paint attributes to an object. You can view the paint attributes by displaying the Paint Style palette—but the palette does not have to be visible for these tools to work. Normally, the Paintbucket and Eyedropper tools affect all attributes of an object, but you can select which attributes are affected through the Paintbucket/Eyedropper Preferences dialog box. Each of these features is described in the next sections.

NOTE These tools can be used in conjunction with each other to copy paint attributes from one object to other objects in the same or different documents. This way you can selectively copy one paint style from one document to another—without actually copying the objects themselves between documents, and rather than importing all paint styles from one document to another through the **File > Import Styles** command.

Using the Paintbucket Tool

You can use the Paintbucket tool to apply the current paint attributes to an object. This is a handy alternative to displaying the Paint Style palette, or it can be a controlled method of applying attributes even when the Paint Style palette is open, because you can select which attributes are affected through the Paintbucket/Eyedropper Preferences dialog box.

To use the Paintbucket tool, follow these steps:

1. First make sure the current paint style settings are the ones you wish to apply to an object. There are several ways to do this:

   ➤ You can select an object that already has the paint style attributes you wish to copy.

   ➤ You can use the Eyedropper tool (described next) to click on an object that has the desired paint style to set that as the current paint style.

   ➤ You can choose **Window > Show Paint Style** (**Command+I**) to display the Paint Style palette and view the current settings if you do not know what they are.

2. Select the **Paintbucket** tool in the Toolbox.

3. Click on any object in the artwork to select the object and paint it with the attributes currently in the Paint Style palette.

Using the Eyedropper Tool

Use the Eyedropper tool to copy the paint attributes from an object to the Paint Style palette. Normally, the Eyedropper tool affects all attributes of an object, but you can select which attributes are affected through the Paintbucket/Eyedropper Preferences dialog box.

The Eyedropper tool updates the Paint Style palette whether or not it is open, and all new objects you create will also be painted with the current attributes until you modify the Paint Style palette or click another object with the Eyedropper tool.

Updating the Paint Style Palette

1. Select the **Eyedropper** tool in the toolbox.

2. Click on any object in the artwork to select the object and transfer the attributes to the Paint Style palette.

3. The next object(s) you create or click on with the Paintbucket tool, will take on the attributes of the object selected in step 2, until you modify the Paint Style palette.

You can choose **Window > Show Paint Style** (**Command+I**) to display the Paint Style palette and view the object's paint style settings if you do not know what they are.

NOTE

Sampling Colors from Other Open Documents

When more than one Illustrator document is open, you can use the Eyedropper tool to sample the color or set of attributes in one window and then apply those attributes to objects in another document's window.

1. Open the document window containing the object whose attributes you want to copy.

2. Select the **Eyedropper** tool in the Toolbox.

3. Click on any object in the artwork to select the object and transfer the attributes to the Paint Style palette.

4. Open the document window containing the object to which you want to copy the attributes.

5. Select the **Paintbucket** tool.

6. Click on the object(s) to be changed.

Changing All Selected Objects

1. Use a selection tool to select the object(s) you wish to change.

2. Select the **Eyedropper** tool in the Toolbox.

3. Double-click on any object in the artwork to transfer the attributes to the Paint Style palette and simultaneously apply those attributes to all selected objects.

Selecting Attributes that the Paintbucket and Eyedropper Tools Affect

Normally, the Paintbucket and Eyedropper tools affect all attributes of an object, but you can select which attributes are affected through the Paintbucket/Eyedropper Preferences dialog box. To do this, follow these steps:

1. Double-click the **Paintbucket** or **Eyedropper** tool in the Toolbox to display the Paintbucket/Eyedropper Preferences dialog box.

2. Click the check boxes beside each attribute that you wish the tool to affect.

3. Click **OK** to close the dialog box. The next application of the Paintbucket or Eyedropper tool will change only the attributes specified in the Paintbucket/Eyedropper Preferences dialog box.

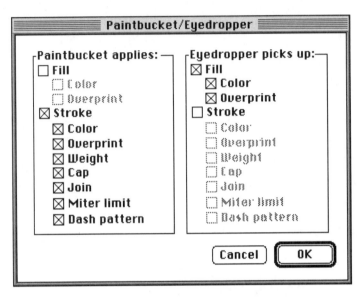

Figure 6.26 The Paintbucket/Eyedropper Preferences dialog box.

Using Custom Colors

When you choose the **Custom Color** option in the Paint Style palette, all the named custom colors that have been defined for all currently open Illustrator documents appear in a scrolling list in the palette. In addition, the **Object > Custom Color** command displays the Custom Color dialog box and lists the custom colors you have created and stored, or the PANTONE colors included on the Illustrator disks (if you have opened that document). It also lets you create new custom colors or change existing custom colors. Each of these options is described in the next sections.

My Fills

Why Name Custom Colors?

You may wonder why you need to create named custom colors when you can create any color you want and add it to the swatch area of the Paint

Style palette, or easily copy any color you want from one object to another in Illustrator. Here are some good reasons why:

➤ **Custom colors can be spot colors.** The print dialog box offers the option of printing custom colors for spot color. Otherwise, unnamed colors that you mix using CMYK values can be separated for four-color process printing only. See Chapter 11.

➤ **Named colors can be identical.** For example, you can create a color named "Sky" and another color named "Water" and give them both the exact same color composition. If you decide later to make all the water darker than the sky, you can simply edit the color named Water. This wouldn't be such an easy change if all the water and the sky were simply Blue.

➤ **Named colors can be different.** For example, you might have a color named "This Month's Color" that is blue in one document and red in another. You can easily change all the documents that use This Month's Color to use the same color by opening one of the documents first, editing This Month's Color, and then opening all the other documents that use that color—and save them if you want the color permanently changed, or just print them and don't save the changes.

You'll see that some of these wonderful benefits are flagged as Cautions in the steps that change colors—so you don't do so merely by accident!

NOTE

To view the process color components of any custom color, first make sure that no objects are selected in the artwork. Then click on the **Custom color selection** option at the top right in the Paint Style palette, select the custom color, and click on the **Process color selection** option.

Default Custom Colors

The list of custom colors that initially appears in the Paint Style palette includes more than 20 common color names that will be familiar to anyone who has used crayons, oil paints, or acrylics. When you apply any of these to an object in the artwork, you can print it as a separate spot-color separation or as four-process color separations (see Chapter 11, "Printing"). You can apply a tint of a custom color by typing a percentage or dragging the slider bar below the list of names.

If you print spot color separations, the film for each spot color shows the name of the color you used, but your commercial printer might ask you to select a color name from a swatchbook for one of the standard color matching systems that the printer uses. Adobe makes this process painless by providing a selection of color matching systems from which you can choose colors that the printer will know by name or number, as described next.

WARNING

If you intend to modify one of these colors, it's a good idea use the **New color** option in the Object > Custom Color dialog box (described later in this chapter) and type a new name for the changed color. Otherwise, the changed color specifications will apply only in the current open document(s), and new documents that you start later—when the current documents are not open—will use Adobe's default color specifications for the same color name. When you open two documents that use different color specifications for the same color name, the Paint Style palette reflects the specifications of the most recently opened document, and the paint style attributes of the files with different definitions for the same fill names can be affected.

Creating New Custom Colors

You can modify existing custom colors or create new ones by following these steps:

1. Choose **Object > Custom Color**, or double-click a color in the Paint Style palette. You do not have to select any objects to customize a color. The Custom Color dialog box appears, as shown in the following figure, allowing you either to create your own custom colors by naming a new color and then entering the percentages of cyan, magenta, yellow, and black, or to select an existing color and adjust the percentage mix of colors.

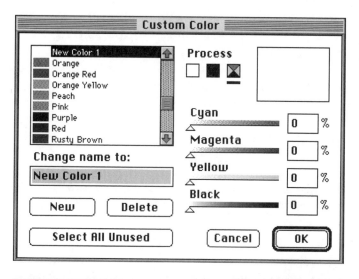

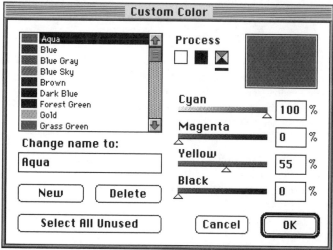

Figure 6.27 The Custom Color dialog box when a new color is being defined (top) and when a defined color is selected (bottom).

2. Make one of the following entries to create a new color. modify a color, or delete a color:

➤ To create a new custom color from scratch, click **New** and type a name in the text box below Change name to: (or you can use Illustrator's default naming convention, New Color 1). Click the **White** or **Black** option under the word Process at the top of the dialog box to choose a tint of white or black, or click the **Process color** box to specify a CMYK mix. Type percentage values for Cyan, Magenta, Yellow, and Black, or drag the triangles below each color bar to change the percentage. You can see the resulting color mix in the upper-right corner of the dialog box if you have a color monitor, but the best way to ensure a precise color match is to use the percentages from a process color swatch book (available in art supply stores). By clicking **New**, you can continue to add more custom colors.

WARNING

If you assign a custom color name that matches a color name used in any other open Illustrator file, the new specifications will automatically replace previous specifications in all open files that use the same color name.

➤ To create a new color based on an existing color, first click on the existing color name and make a note of the percentage values. Then click **New**, type a name for the new color, and enter percentage values that vary from those you noted for the existing color.

WARNING

If you select an existing color and change the name and percentage values *but do not click New*, the effect is to delete the previous color from the list and replace it with the new entry. Any objects that used the original color take on the new color. If you don't want this to happen, follow the procedure outlined above for creating a new color based on an existing color.

➤ To edit an existing color, click on the name of the color in the list at the top left of the dialog box, then change the percentage values and/or the name of the color.

NOTE

Changes made to an existing color will be reflected in the artwork wherever that color has been used.

➤ Click **Delete** to remove the selected name (and color) from the list. Objects that were filled with that color will revert to the default fill pattern (100% black).

➤ Click **Select All Unused** to select the names of all colors that are not currently used in the artwork. You can delete these colors to save memory and storage space.

3. Click **OK** to close the **Custom Color** dialog box.

The names of newly created colors appear in an alphabetical list in the Paint Style palette when you select its **Custom Color** button.

NOTE

If you want to create your own library of custom colors, save them all in a file created for this purpose. The file must include objects or Paint Style palette swatches that use each custom color. You can make any color available for use in a new file by simply opening the file that contains the desired color.

Working with Color Matching Systems

Adobe Illustrator comes with color palettes for the PANTONE Process Color System, TOYO Ink Electronic Color Finder 1050, the FOCOLTONE COLOUR SYSTEM, and the TRUMATCH color swatching system. This makes it easy to choose colors based on swatchbooks, rather than rely on the color displayed on your monitor (see "Calibrating Your Monitor" later in this chapter). It also makes it easy to specify spot colors exactly when you work with the same system that your commercial printer uses. When you apply any of these to an object in the artwork, you can print it as a separate spot-color separation or as four-process color separations (see Chapter 11, "Printing").

To use one of the Color Matching libraries that comes with Illustrator, follow these steps:

1. Choose **File > Import Styles**.

2. Select the **Color Systems** folder in the Utilities folder in the Adobe Illustrator program folder.

3. Choose from the list of color systems available—by clicking once on the name and clicking **Import**, or simply double-clicking on the set name. The system you choose will be listed in the Paint Style palette when you click the **Custom Color** box on the right of the palette.

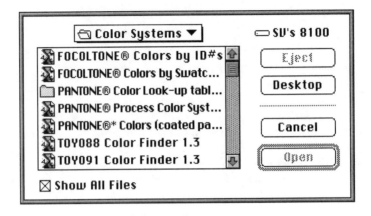

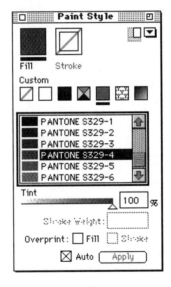

If you print spot-color separations (see Chapter 11), the names of the colors you choose will appear on the film for that color, making it easy for the commercial printer to know which inks to use. Process color separations based on these colors will be consistent with the formulas developed for each color system.

NOTE   Most of these color system lists are very long. If you normally use just a few of these colors, you can delete the unused colors from the list in the Paint Style palette to save memory and storage space. Choose **Object > Custom Colors** and click **Select All Unused** in the Custom Color dialog box, then click **Delete**. You can also modify the Startup file to display colors you use in the default Paint Style palette, or create your own importable "Custom Fill Sets" as described later in this chapter.

If you want to add back colors that you deleted during the current work session, you can use **File > Import Styles** again to import the whole color system, or import the original default fills by importing from the file named *Adobe Illustrator Startup* in the Plug-Ins folder in the Adobe Illustrator program folder.

WARNING

You can use one of the PANTONE color files as a basis for creating custom colors by opening the file along with your artwork. However, you should avoid modifying the PAN-TONE color file itself: Always close the PANTONE color file without saving any changes.

If you intend to modify one of these colors, it's a good idea use the **New color** option in the Object > Custom Color dialog box and type a new name for the changed color. Otherwise, besides the drawbacks described earlier for modifying any custom color, you will be losing the benefits of working with a standard system of names for specific colors.

Working with Gradients

A *gradient fill* is a blend between colors. It can be a blend between only two colors, or consist of multiple intermediate blends between a number of colors. A gradient fill can be linear, with color bands following a linear axis, or radial, with a center point around which the colors blend outward in concentric bands.

Illustrator comes with a number of pre-defined gradient fills that have already been set up for you. Some of these are automatically displayed in the Paint Style palette when you first install Illustrator, and there are others you can load using the **File > Open** or **File > Import Styles** command (described later in this chapter).

Gradients are handled through several options in Illustrator:

➤ New Gradients can be defined through the Gradient palette.

➤ Gradients that have already been defined can be applied through the Paint Style palette and adjusted with the Gradient Vector tool.

➤ The Blend tool can also be used to create gradations from one color or shade to another.

➤ Compatible Gradient Printing, an option that appears in the Document Setup dialog box, improves printing quality for gradient fills.

Each of these features is described in the next sections.

NOTE

If you apply gradient fills to graph objects, changing graph styles can cause unexpected results. To prevent this, use the Direct-selection tool to select each object and paint those objects with black, then reapply the original gradient.

Working with Adobe's Gradient Fills

Before you jump into the relatively advanced task of creating your own gradient fills, familiarize yourself with the gradients that Adobe has already created for you and included with Illustrator 6.0. These include eight gradients that are part of the default Startup file, plus three "galleries" of gradient fills that you can open and use.

The basic startup set of gradients is shown in the next figure. To add more gradients to the list, choose **File > Open** and locate the list of gradient galleries in the Gradients folder which is in the Sample Files folder in the Adobe Illustrator program folder—if you elected the **Easy Install** option during installation. (Figures 6.20 through 6.23 are also shown on the color pages of this book.)

NOTE

If you cannot find the Gradients folder on your disk, you can selectively install it from the original master disks or CD-ROM.

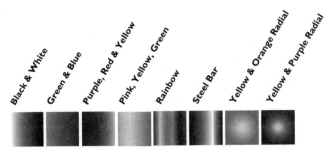

Figure 6.28 Default Startup Gradient Fills set.

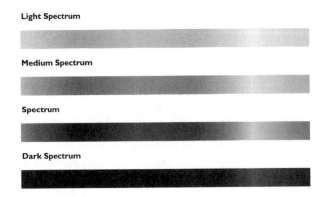

Figure 6.29 Color Spectrums file in Gradients folder.

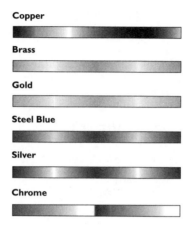

Copper

Brass

Gold

Steel Blue

Silver

Chrome

Figure 6.30 Metal Gradients file in Gradients folder.

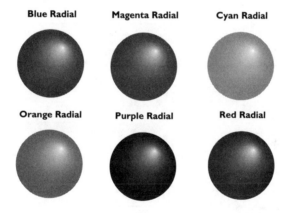

Blue Radial **Magenta Radial** **Cyan Radial**

Orange Radial **Purple Radial** **Red Radial**

Figure 6.31 Simple Radial Gradients file in Gradients folder.

You can create other exciting gradients by starting with one supplied by Adobe and modifying it using the techniques described in later sections—by changing the angle of the gradients or editing them.

NOTE

Creating New Fills through the Gradient Palette

You use the Gradient Fill palette to edit existing gradient fills or create new ones, and to delete fills from the Paint Style palette for the document. Like custom colors and patterns, gradient fills are saved with the document.

Fills created through this palette can be applied using the Paint Style palette as described earlier in this chapter, and the relative position of the gradient within an object can be adjusted using the Gradient Vector tool as described later in this chapter. Chapter 9 also includes examples of working with gradient fills to create three-dimensional shading.

Displaying the Gradient Palette

To display the Gradient palette, simply double-click the **Gradient Vector** tool in the Toolbox, or choose **Window > Show Gradient** or **Object > Gradient**. You can also display the palette by double-clicking a gradient fill name in the Paint Style palette, or double-clicking the **Gradient Vector** tool. If the Gradient palette is already displayed, you can choose **Window > Hide Gradient**, but it's usually easier to click the close box on the palette title bar.

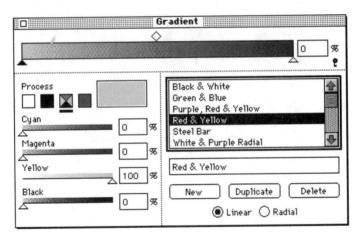

Figure 6.32 The Gradient palette displays a list of all gradient fills defined for the currently open document(s).

Adjusting the Size and Position of the Gradient Palette

You can move the Gradient palette on the screen by dragging the title bar. The palette will always display on top of all document windows, but the most recently used palette can appear on top of this one if there is overlap between palettes. You can bring any palette to the top by clicking on it. If a palette is completely hidden under other palettes, you can move the other palettes or you can use the command under the Window menu to Hide and then Show the buried palette.

You can toggle between two sizes of the Gradient palette by clicking on the "latch" icon just below the gradient bar and percent box at the top of the palette. In the reduced view, you can adjust the starting, ending, and midpoints of a fill, but you can't add colors without expanding the palette.

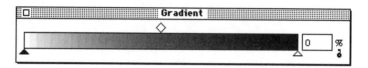

Figure 6.33 The Gradient palette in reduced view.

Creating New Gradient Fills

To create a new gradient fill, follow these steps:

1. Display the Gradient Fill palette, using any of these methods:

   ➤ Double-click the **Gradient Vector** tool in the toolbox

   ➤ Choose **Window > Show Gradient**

   ➤ Choose **Object > Gradient**

   ➤ Double-click a gradient fill name in the Paint Style palette

   ➤ Double-click the **Gradient Vector** tool

2. You can create a new gradient using either of two methods:

   ➤ To create a new blend from scratch, click the **New** button in the palette. The name *New gradient*, followed by a number, is displayed in the name area on the palette, and the default linear white-to-black blend is displayed in the gradient bar at the top of the palette with the midpoint—the point at which each color is 50%—in the center of the band.

   ➤ To create a new blend based on an existing fill, click once on the fill name and then click the **Duplicate** button in the palette.

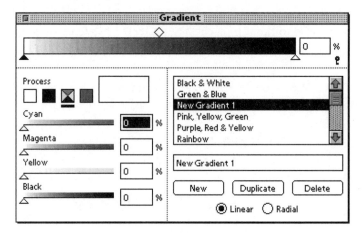

Figure 6.34 The Gradient palette when **New** is clicked.

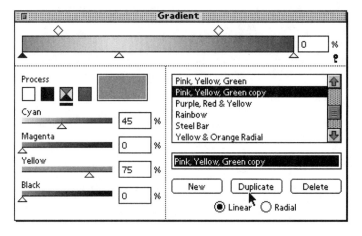

Figure 6.35 The Gradient palette when **Duplicate** is clicked.

3. Type the new gradient name in the text box beneath the list of fills, and press **Return** to add it to the list in the palettes.

Be sure to use a unique name that is not already used by any open file or any file you are likely to have open at the same time as the current file. If another gradient fill of the same name exists in an open file, the new specifications you make will automatically be applied in the open file.

WARNING

4. Click the **left triangle** below the gradient bar to select it, so its hollow fill turns to black, then using the procedures described next, under the heading Specifying a Color, specify the starting color in the bottom left area of the fully open palette.

5. Click the **right triangle** below the gradient bar to select it, so its hollow fill turns to black, then using the procedures described next, under the heading Specifying a Color, specify the ending color in the bottom left area of the fully open palette.

6. Click the **Linear** or **Radial** option.

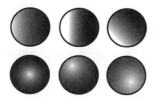

Figure 6.36 Linear (top row) and radial (bottom row) gradient fills.

7. Drag the triangles below the gradient bar to adjust the starting or ending point of the gradient fill—i.e., the point at which one color is 100% and the other is 0%. Drag the diamond above the gradient bar to adjust the midpoint of the gradient fill—i.e., the point at which each color is 50%.

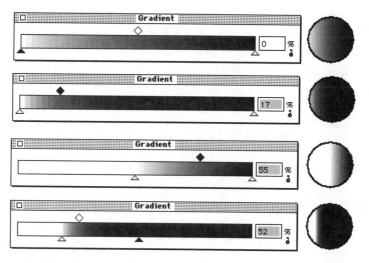

Figure 6.37 The Gradient palette with various starting, ending, and midpoints.

➤ You can transpose the starting and ending colors by dragging the triangles below the gradient bar to their opposite's position.

➤ You can add intermediate colors between the starting and ending colors by clicking below the gradient bar to add another triangle, then selecting another color as described next, under the heading Specifying a Color.

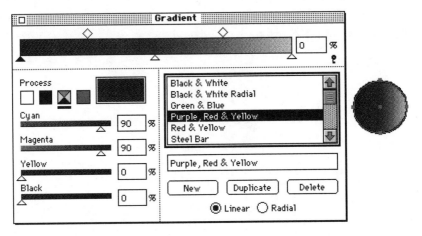

Figure 6.38 The Gradient palette with intermediate colors.

➤ To copy a color from one point to another along a gradient fill, hold down the **Option** key and drag the desired color to another location. By dragging it to an empty spot you add a new intermediate band or 100%; by dragging it onto another triangle you replace that triangle's color.

8. After using the Gradient palette to set up a new gradient, use the Paint Style palette to apply the gradient to selected objects.

Specifying a Color

Four color options—White, Black, Process Color, and Custom Color—are represented by the color selection boxes shown at the left side of the Gradient palette when it is fully open.

➤ When you select **White** or **Black**, you can adjust the percentage tint by sliding the indicators below the tint bar or specifying a percentage at the right of the bar.

➤ When you select a process color, you can adjust the percentages of each color component—cyan, magenta, yellow, and black—by sliding the indicators below the color bars or specifying percentages at the right side of the bars.

➤ When **Custom Color** is selected, a scrolling list of named custom colors, appears on the left in the palette. You apply one of these by clicking on the name. You can apply a tint of a custom color by typing a percentage or dragging the slider bar below the list of names. You can display a dialog box for changing or adding a new name by double-clicking on the one you want to change—or on any name if you want to create a new one. This is the same dialog box as displayed by the **Object > Custom Color** command described earlier in this chapter.

Whether specifying a tint, process color, or custom color, you can see the color change in the color box in the Gradient palette as you create it.

Editing Gradient Fills

You can modify an existing gradient fill by clicking once on the gradient name in the Gradient palette and then making changes, using the same techniques as described earlier. All objects in the current document and any other documents that use gradients of the same name will be changed to match your modifications.

Removing Gradient Fills

To remove a gradient fill from the Gradient palette by clicking once on the gradient name and then clicking the **Delete** button. All objects in the current document and any other documents that use gradients of the same name will be changed to have a black fill.

N O T E   All fill patterns defined for the startup document are automatically displayed on all palettes when you first start Illustrator—even if you start it by opening a document that does not use those fills. You can reduce the number on the list for the current session by opening a new document and then using the **Object > Custom Colors**, **Object > Gradients**, and **Object Patterns** commands to delete all these fills—then when you open a document only the fills used in that document will appear in the palettes. You can reduce the number on the list for the all sessions by changing the startup document, as described under "Customizing the Illustrator Startup File" later in this chapter.

Using Custom Colors in Gradient Fills

If you use custom colors in creating gradient fills, then custom color steps will be printed as separate plates when color separations are printed—unless **Convert to Process** is specified in the Separation Setup dialog box. The custom color in the gradient is printed as a series of graduated tints from 100% to 0%.

For example, if you create a gradient that blends between Aqua and Dark Blue, and print custom colors, objects that have that fill will print on two separate sheets—one labeled **Aqua**, with the color fading from 100% to 0% (or whatever percentages you assigned to the gradient), and one labeled **Dark Blue**, with the color fading in the opposite direction.

If you create a gradient between a custom color and a process color, the filled areas will print on five separate sheets: black, cyan, magenta, yellow, and the custom color.

To ensure that you print only four color separation plates, always choose **Convert to Process** in the Separations Setup dialog box.

If you do create a gradient fill between two custom colors that you intend to print as spot color rather than as process color, be sure to assign different screen angles to the colors in the Separation Setup dialog box (see Chapter 11, "Printing").

WARNING

Importing Gradient Fills

As mentioned earlier, the Gradient palette displays lists of all colors and gradients, defined for all open documents. There are three ways to import a gradient fill from one document to another.

➤ You can have access to custom colors and gradients created in another file simply by opening the other file. This will add the gradients to the Paint Style and Gradient palettes so long as the other file is open, but they will disappear from the palettes when you quit Illustrator, unless you use one of the following methods to add the gradients permanently to the current document.

➤ You can permanently add any gradient fill option to the current document's Paint Style and Gradient palettes by applying a gradient fill from another open document to an object in the current document.

➤ You can permanently add *all* the fill options from one file to another by using the **File > Import Styles** command, described later in this chapter.

Using the Gradient Vector Tool

Use the Gradient Vector tool to modify gradient fills that have already been applied to objects in the artwork through the Paint Style palette. This tool lets you adjust the gradient fill along a line you create by dragging. Using this technique you can change the angle or direction of a gradient fill, change the starting and ending point of a gradient, and apply the gradient across multiple objects.

1. Use the Selection tool to select the object(s) in the artwork whose gradient fill you want to modify.

2. Select the **Gradient Vector** tool in the Toolbox.

3. Position the pointer where you want to define the starting point of the gradient, and drag across the object in the direction you want the gradient to be painted. Release the mouse button where you want to set the ending point of the gradient.

You can constrain the angle of the fill to 45° increments by holding the **Shift** key as you drag. Also, the starting and ending points set with the **Gradient Vector** tool need not be the edges of the object.

NOTE

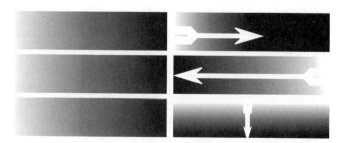

Figure 6.39 Object before (left) and after (right) adjusting gradient fill; arrows show angle and length of drag.

NOTE

If you drag across more than one selected object, the gradient will start in the first object and end in the last object you cross. (This is a way of assigning a single gradient across multiple objects that are *not* made into a compound path. If you make several objects into a compound path, a single gradient fill automatically paints all the elements.)

Figure 6.40 Multiple objects painted with a single gradient fill.

When working with radial gradient fills, the starting point of the fill determines the highlight area and the ending point determines the shadow area.

Figure 6.41 Radial gradient fill with changed starting point.

Activating Compatible Gradient Printing

Gradient fills in Illustrator are tuned for the least possible banding—so the changes from one color or shade to the next appear smooth or gradual rather than abruptly defined in visible bands.

If you are having trouble printing gradient fills, choose **File > Document Setup** (**Command+Shift+D**) to display the Document Setup dialog box, and select the **Compatible Gradient Printing** option. Click **OK** to close the dialog box.

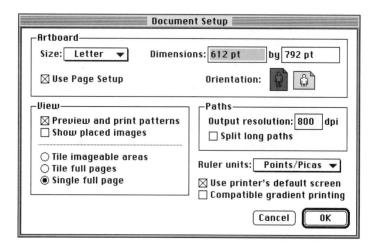

Figure 6.42 The Document Setup dialog box with the
Compatible Gradient Printing option selected.

Converting Gradients to Objects

You can convert a gradient fill into separate objects using the **Object > Expand** command.

1. Select an object with a gradient fill.

2. Choose **Object > Expand** to display the Expand dialog box.

3. Enter the number of separate objects you want the gradient divided into. The higher the number of objects, the less banding will occur—but more objects will make the document larger.

4. Click **OK** to close the dialog box and convert the gradient into objects.

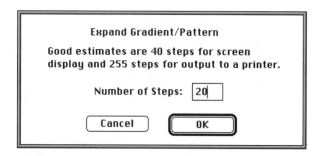

Figure 6.43 The Expand dialog box.

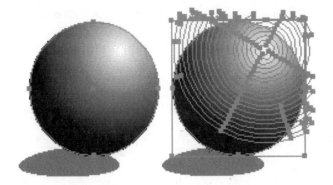

Figure 6.44 Gradient fill (left) converted to separate objects (right).

Working with Blends as Gradients

You can use the Blend tool for a variety of effects: to create a series of gradual changes from one shape to another (as described in Chapter 5), or to create a series of graduated colors as part of the artwork—as an alternative to specifying a gradient fill through the Paint Style palette. In this usage, you want to create blends that have smooth blends between colors—without the distinct "bands" of color that can result when you specify too few steps in the Blend dialog box. At the same time, you don't want to create so many blend steps that you increase the file size without improving the result.

The figure at left shows a rectangle created using the Black & White gradient fill (top) and the same area created as a blend composed of ten rectangles (bottom).

NOTE

As a general rule, it's a good idea to use gradient fills instead of blends where possible. When you must use blends to create an airbrush effect—when you want the shades of color to meet along a curved edge rather than the straight bands created by graduated fills, for example—calculate the optimum number of steps in the blend using one of the two formulas presented in the next steps.

Using the Blend Tool to Create Gradients

The following figures illustrate examples of blending to change colors.

The first object you click after you select the **Blend** tool will fall on the bottom layer of the blended series of objects; the second object will fall on the top layer.

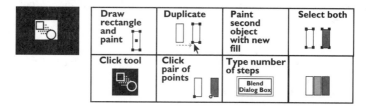

Figure 6.45 Blending to create gradual changes in color or shading.

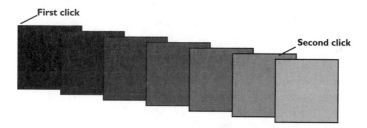

Figure 6.46 Stacking order when leftmost rectangle is clicked first and rightmost rectangle is clicked second.

NOTE

You can instead use the Gradient Vector tool or the blend commands under the **Filters > Colors** submenu (described later in this chapter) to blend colors across several objects. Use the Blend tool when you also want to *create* the intermediate objects between two different shapes, as shown in the next figures.

For example, you can use the Gradient palette to create linear or radial gradient fills for three-dimensional effects that require a line or point of highlight. Use the Blend tool when the highlight is a curved line or irregular shape.

Figure 6.47 Blending to create a three-dimensional appearance.

Both the starting object and the resulting object must be either closed or open paths; you cannot blend a closed path with an open path. (See Chapter 4 for definitions of open and closed paths.)

NOTE

Creating Optimal Blends

In using the Blend tool to produce smooth gradations of color, two factors influence whether and to what extent color banding will occur: the number of steps required in the blend, and the screen frequency used in the final output. In some cases, banding is inevitable in color blends, but the techniques explained here will minimize banding in color blends. (Color banding is the appearance of distinct bands of different colors or shades, an effect that is usually undesirable, as opposed to a perfectly smooth graduation from one color or shade to the next.) Banding is more evident with only 10 blends (next figure) than with 256 blends (right).

When you are using the Blend tool to create blends and printing on a 300-dpi laser printer, 25 blends are usually adequate for creating a gradual transition from white to black. On a 600-dpi printer, 45 blends are usually adequate. On a 1270-dpi phototypesetter, you need approximately 200 blends; on a 2540-dpi phototypesetter, use at least 448 blends. Using too few blends may create "banding"; that is, the colors may not transition smoothly.

NOTE

Follow these steps to create optimal blending with minimal banding:

1. The first step in preventing banding is to make sure that the imagesetter can produce 256 levels of gray at the screen frequency you specify. You need 256 levels of gray at the imagesetter even if your blend has fewer steps.

2. The second step in preventing banding is to determine the correct number of steps in the blend. The PostScript language allows a maximum of 256 color gradations in a blend. Illustrator will let you use a higher number, and this is useful for blending shapes, but using more than 256 steps for blending colors simply complicates the file unnecessarily. (See "Calculating shades of Gray.")

3. Whether you see a smooth blend or one that has visible breaks of color shades (banding) is determined by the length of each usable step, referred to as the *Step Length*. (See "Calculating shades of Gray.")

Blending to Create New Colors or Grays

You may want a color that is exactly halfway between two PMS colors, two process colors, or two gray fills. This technique uses the Blend tool to generate the color automatically. The result of the example you create here appears as shades of gray in the accompanying figure.

This is a good alternative to defining a new color numerically or visually through the Paint Style palette or the **Object > Custom Color** command, especially if you do not have a color monitor. Another alternative is to use the **Filter > Colors > Blend filters** described later in this chapter.

1. Draw two objects (closed paths) and use the Paint Style palette (**Command+I**) to assign them the two Fill colors (or grays) you wish to blend. In the figure on the left, the two rectangles are assigned different percentages of black fill. If you are using color, you must already know the cyan, magenta, yellow, and black percentages of the two starting colors, or use custom colors that have already been created (either your own custom colors or the custom colors provided by Adobe).

2. Select both objects with the Selection tool, then select the **Blend** tool in the Toolbox and click on two corresponding points on each of the objects, to display the Blend dialog box. Specify one step of blending between your two colors.

By leaving the defaults, the first blend to 50%, and the last blend to 50% , you will produce a new color that is exactly halfway along the spectrum between the two starting colors. This same procedure can be used to create automatically colors that are one-third, one-fourth, one-fifth, or even one-four hundredth of each other simply by increasing the number of steps or by adjusting the percentages entered in the Blend dialog box.

3. Click **OK** in the Blend dialog box. The Blend tool will produce the midway color and fill a new object with that color automatically in the active window.

4. Select the new object using the Selection tool, and view the cyan, magenta, yellow, and black percentage attributes of the new color fill in the Paint Style palette.

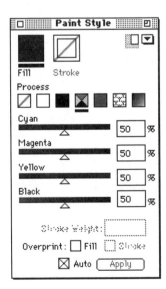

5. You can apply the color shown in the Paint Style palette to any existing object by clicking on the object with the Paintbucket tool. Also, whatever new object(s) you create will automatically take on the attributes shown in the palette.

WARNING

Remember that objects must be ungrouped in order to be blended.

Calculating Shades of Gray

To calculate how many shades of gray your printer or imagesetter can physically produce, you need to know both the resolution of the printer, expressed as *dots per inch* (dpi) and its line screen frequency, expressed as *lines per inch* (lpi). The maximum Number of Grays can be figured by this formula:

Number of Grays = [resolution (dpi)/line screen (lpi)]^2 up to a maximum value of 256.

You can determine the maximum line screen that a given imagesetter can use and still produce 256 levels of gray by dividing the imagesetter resolution (in dots per inch) by 16 (the square root of 256). For example, an imagesetter with a resolution of 2400 dpi can use a 150 line-per-inch screen and still produce 256 levels of gray, whereas a 1200 dpi imagesetter can do so only at a 75 line-per-inch screen, or lower.

For example:

Apple LaserWriter IINTX = [300 dpi/53 lpi]^2 = 32 Grays.

Medium resolution Image Setter: = [1270 dpi/100 lpi]^2 = 161 Grays.

High resolution Image Setter = [2540 dpi/150 lpi]^2 = 256 Grays. (The calculated value gives 286 but the maximum Number of Grays is 256 for any device.)

Bear in mind that the imagesetter usually substitutes its closest line screen for the one requested—the actual screen frequency can vary from your specification by 10 lines per inch or more. If you use a screen frequency that limits the imagesetter to 240 levels of gray rather than 256, you will not necessarily see banding, but in general you should use a resolution and screen frequency that comes as close as possible to producing 256 levels of gray.

Calculating Number of Blend Steps

To calculate the correct number of steps, you must first look at the percentage of the colors being blended.

A blend across the entire spectrum from 0% (white) to 100% (black) requires 256 steps. To blend between other shades, you should use the percentage difference between the two shades. For example, a blend from 30% to 90% should use 60% (the difference between 30% and 90%) of 256, or 154 steps. These rules apply to gray, but are also valid for the dark colors, cyan and magenta. To blend from 50% cyan to 40% magenta should be treated as a blend from 50% cyan to 0% cyan, plus a blend from 0% magenta to 40% magenta. Use the color with the greatest percentage difference, in this case cyan (0% to 50%). This blend would require 50% of 256, or 128 steps.

Banding with light colors (yellow) is normally almost imperceptible when these colors are used alone. However, when they are combined with dark colors, the results can be hard to predict. In general, the more colors used in the blend, the more likely banding will result. For this reason, you should use 256 steps when your blend contains several colors.

Calculating Step Length

To calculate Step Length, divide the length of your blend (going from one color or shade to another) by the total number of Usable Steps.

Step Length = Blend Length / Number of Usable Steps.

If your Step Length is less than 0.03 inches (or 2.16 points), your blend will usually appear smooth. Whether a blend appears smooth or banded is a question of visual perception by the eye. While Step Length is the predominant factor, such perception is also influenced by the actual colors of the blend, the dot shape created by the output devices, the paper upon which the image is printed, lighting, and other factors. Therefore, the 0.03 inch value is provided merely as a guideline. In general, the smaller the step length the smoother the blend is perceived.

Using the 0.03 inches figure above, you can calculate an approximate maximum length for a smooth blend once you know the number of Usable Steps for a given situation. Multiply the usable steps by 0.03 inches.

For example, in creating a 0% black to 100% black blend on a high resolution image setter:

256 (Usable Steps) × 0.03 inches = 7.7 inches.

In creating a 0% black to 100% black blend on an Apple LaserWriter IINTX:

32 (Usable Steps) × 0.03 inches = 0.96 inches.

Blending for Spot Color Separation

The Blend tool always creates *process* colors when two objects of different color are blended—even if spot colors were assigned to the original objects. It's a good idea to specify process colors for the original elements (and any other elements in artwork that contains color blends) so you can print only four color separations. Otherwise, you will need to print four color separations plus a separation for each spot color used. If you want to blend colors for spot-color printing, use the technique described here.

1. Create two objects that overlap to the extent you wish the two spot colors to blend or overlap. The figure at left shows two hearts with partial overlap.

2. Put the object(s) on different layers—one for each spot color. This is not essential to the result, but it will simplify your work tremendously. (The figure at left shows the two layers side by side—even though the objects actually overlap in the artwork, as shown in step 1.)

3. Assign each object a gradient fill. Specify each gradient from a spot color to a light *tint* of the same color, or to white. The darker end of the gradient of the first spot color should be the light end of the gradient for the second spot color, as shown in the figures below.

4. Print spot color separations. (See Chapter 11 for a detailed description.)

NOTE

You will not be able to print accurate color proofs or composites, because the "white" end of the graduated fill is not transparent. See color plates in this book for results of these steps.

Working with Patterns

The nuances of a repeating pattern can be difficult to visualize. Until you can see the result of a simple graphic repeat, you are not sure it is what you want. With traditional pen-and-ink methods, creating a pattern repeat is a costly and time-consuming exercise, often producing unusable results. Adobe Illustrator automatically generates repeating tiles of a pattern for you to see. The program does the tough work and all you have to do is decide if you like the results.

Besides creating your own custom fill patterns for charts or graphs or any shape, you can use Illustrator's pattern feature in designing fabrics or wallpapers.

Page Viewing Options

Choose **File > Document Setup (Command-Shift+D)** and click **Preview** and **Print Patterns** to view and print patterns fully. When **Preview** and **Print**

Patterns is off, the screen refreshes faster because you have instructed Illustrator not to preview the patterns, which take more time to draw. Also, when the setting is off, the illustrations print as drafts without patterns, which will print faster than if printing with patterns.

Working with Adobe's Patterns

Before you jump into the relatively advanced task of creating your own patterns, you should familiarize yourself with the patterns that Adobe has already created for you and included with Illustrator 6.0. These include 15 patterns that are part of the default Startup file, plus four "galleries" of pattern fills (shown in next figures) and two galleries of path patterns (see earlier in this chapter) that you can open and use.

The basic startup set of patterns is shown in the next figure. To add more patterns to the list, choose **File > Open** and locate the list of pattern galleries in the Fill Patterns or Path Patterns folders which are in the Sample Files folder in the Adobe Illustrator program folder—if you elected the **Easy Install** option during installation.

NOTE

If you cannot find the Patterns folders on your disk, you can selectively install it from the original master disks or CD-ROM which includes even more patterns in the Adobe Collector's Edition Folder, which is in the Illustrator Goodies folder.

Patterns (fill)

Patterns (path)

Figure 6.48 Default Startup Pattern Fills set.

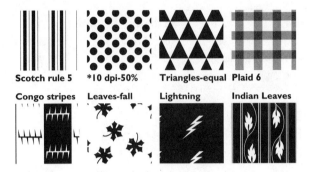

Figure 6.49 Fill Pattern Gallery 1.

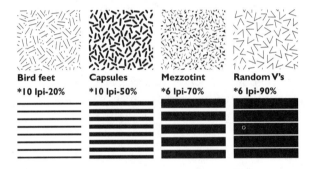

Figure 6.50 Fill Pattern Gallery 2.

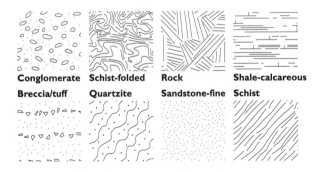

Figure 6.51 Fill Pattern Gallery 3.

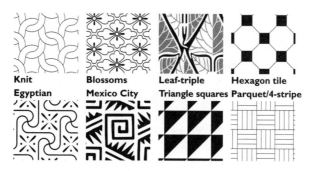

Figure 6.52 Fill Pattern Gallery 4.

 You can create other exciting patterns by starting with one supplied by Adobe and modifying it using the techniques described in later sections—by transforming the patterns or editing them. By the way, Illustrator 6.0 does not require a bounding box or tiling rectangle in defining a pattern—but the following exercises use one to control spacing.

N O T E

Creating a New Pattern

1. Draw a pattern shape or design and color it.

2. If the objects in the design extend beyond the intended "tile" size, or don't fill the intended tile area, use the Rectangle tool to draw a rectangle around your art defining the tiling element. Set the Fill and Stroke to none.

3. Select both the design and the tiling rectangle.

4. Then choose **Object > Pattern** to display the Pattern dialog box, which allows you to create a new pattern or delete, paste, or change the name of an existing pattern. The scrolling list displays all existing patterns.

5. Click **New** to display the selected pattern in the upper right area of the dialog box and name the pattern by entering the name in the text box.

6. Click **OK** to close the dialog box and record the changes.

When you close this dialog box, the pattern will then be available in the Paint Style Palette. You can apply patterns listed in this dialog box to selected objects by clicking the **Pattern** button in the Paint Style palette (see **Object > Paint Style**).

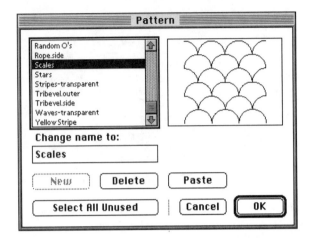

Figure 6.53 The Pattern dialog box if nothing was selected in the artwork, and an existing pattern is selected, showing one pattern tile.

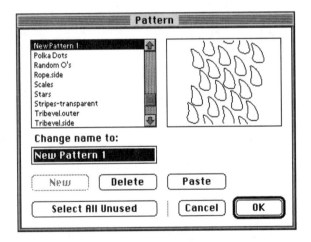

Figure 6.54 The Pattern dialog box with the selected objects shown.

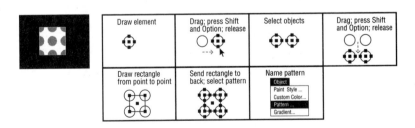

Figure 6.55 Procedure for creating a pattern.

EXERCISE: CREATING A LINEAR PATTERN

The simplest patterns to create consist of straight horizontal and/or vertical lines. These patterns are very common in creating shading effects—such as the stippling effects described in Chapter 4.

1. Draw one line by selecting the Pen tool and clicking once to position one end point, then holding the **Shift** key as you click the second point at a 90-degree angle—above or below the first point. Use the Paint Style palette (**Command+I**) to set the stroke you wish. Fill can be set to **None**.

2. Select the line with the Selection tool, and press **Command+Shift+M** (**Arrange > Move**). In the Move dialog box, enter the distance you wish between lines, in the axis that is perpendicular to the line. For example, move a horizontal line along a vertical axis.

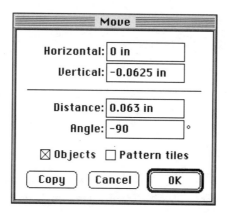

3. Click **Copy** to close the Move dialog box and create a duplicate of the line, slightly offset from the original. Press **Command+D** (**Arrange > Repeat Transform**) as many times as needed to fill a small area. Make them different widths or colors if you like.

4. Using the Rectangle tool, draw a rectangle around your art defining the tiling element. The rectangle should fall completely within the lines—so the

the lines meet or extend beyond the edges of the rectangle. To create a completely even pattern, the top edge of the rectangle should be positioned at the edge of the top line in the series as the bottom edge is below the bottom line, a distance equal to the desired space between lines. Otherwise, the linear pattern will show one pair of lines with a different distance between them than all the others.

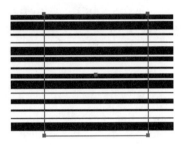

5. Select the rectangle and press **Command+hyphen** (**Arrange > Send To Back**) to position it behind the lines. You can set a fill for the rectangle, but make the outline of the rectangle invisible by setting the Stroke to **None** in the Paint Style palette. (Otherwise, the pattern will include the box border, and display as a series of grid lines.)

6. Select all the lines and the rectangle. Then choose **Object > Pattern** to display the Pattern dialog box. Click **New** to display the selected pattern in the top right area of the dialog box and name the pattern by entering the name in the text box.

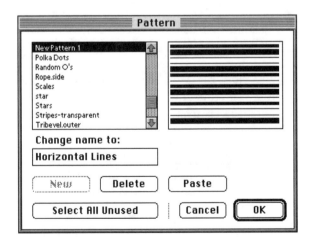

7. Click **OK** to close the dialog box and record the changes. When you close this dialog box, the pattern will then be available in the Paint Style palette.

8. Draw any shape to outline the area of the artwork you want to shade with the pattern.

9. In the Paint Style palette, click the pattern box to display the list of patterns, now showing the new pattern name.

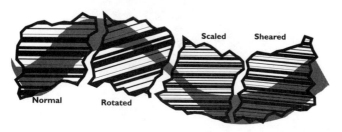

This technique can be adapted to create stippled shading effects, but if you use curved lines rather than straight, you'll find it tricky to get the pattern tiles to align seamlessly—as described in the exercise Creating Continuous Wavy Line Patterns, later in this chapter.

N O T E

EXERCISE: CREATING PATTERNS OF DISCRETE OBJECTS

Here is one example of how to build a simple pattern of geometric shapes. You can use this same technique to create any pattern of discrete, nonoverlapping objects.

1. Build a basic shape with one of the drawing tools. The figure below shows a circle shape customized in a particular color and stroke. This is the shape that will be repeated in a pattern.

2. Repeat the shape by Option+dragging to make copies. Arrange a small area as the basic tile that you want repeated as a fill pattern.

3. Using either the Rectangle tool or the Centered-rectangle tool, draw a nonstroked rectangle over the area you would like to serve as a pattern fill. To have the repeat line up well, position your rectangle (called the *tiling rectangle*) to surround all of the graphics, without letting any graphic cross the border of the rectangle, and with the space between the rectangle and the graphics roughly half the space you intend between graphics when the pattern is used to fill a shape. (See the next technique for a description of how to create tiles with cross-over patterns.)

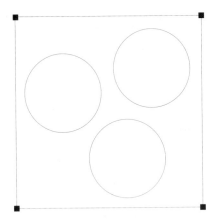

4. Send the tiling rectangle to the back by selecting it and typing **Command+hyphen** (**Arrange > Send To Back**).

5. Select all the geometric shapes and the tiling rectangle by dragging the selection marquee over them (see The Selection Tools in Chapter 3).

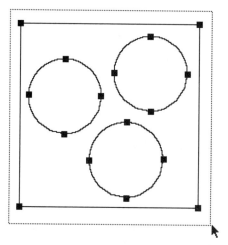

6. Choose **Object > Pattern** and click **New** to define the new pattern in the Pattern dialog box. You can use Illustrator's default pattern name (New Pattern 1), or type a name that you will recognize as describing this particular design. Click **OK** to close the dialog box and save the pattern.

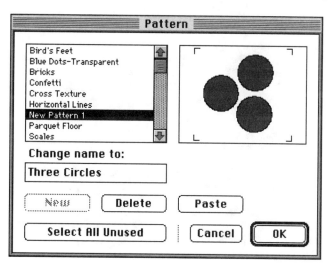

7. Now that you have created the pattern, you can fill any new shape with it using the Paint Style palette (**Command+I**). The new pattern name should appear in the scrolling window when you click the **Pattern** selection option.

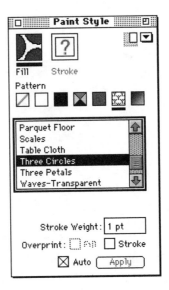

8. You can create variations by changing the artwork that you used originally to create the first pattern tile. Use the techniques described here to create another version with a different name.

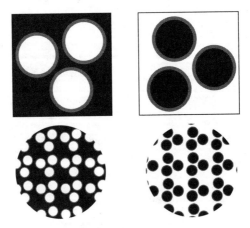

9. When you are satisfied with the pattern design, you can delete the tile artwork; the pattern will remain stored with the current file. If you want to edit the tile later, you can retrieve it by choosing **Object > Pattern**, select-

ing the pattern name from the list, and clicking **Paste**. This creates a copy of the original tile artwork, which you can edit to create a new variation.

10. Use the **Object > Pattern** command to delete any unwanted variations.

EXERCISE: CREATING CONTINUOUS WAVY LINE PATTERNS

The continuous wavy line patterns you can create with this technique offer one challenge not encountered by the two previous techniques: the lines must cross each border at the same position on opposite sides of the tiling rectangle. The first figure below shows a pattern that follows this rule; the second figure below shows a pattern that violates this rule.

1. Draw one wavy line by selecting the **Pen** tool and clicking then dragging to position each point, as described under the Pen tool in Chapter 4. Use the Paint Style palette (**Command+I**) to set the stroke you wish. Fill can be set to **None**.

One trick to apply in this step is to position the ending anchor points along the same horizontal or vertical axis. You can do this by displaying the rulers (**Command+R**) and dragging a guide onto the artwork that you use for positioning each end point.

NOTE

2. Select the line with the Selection tool, and press **Command+Shift+M** (**Arrange > Move**). In the Move dialog box, enter the distance you wish between lines, in the axis that is perpendicular to the line. For example, move a horizontal line along a vertical axis.

Vertical: 0.025 in

Copy

3. Click **Copy** to close the Move dialog box and create a duplicate of the line, slightly offset from the original. Press **Command+D** (**Arrange > Repeat Transform**) as many times as needed to fill the area spanned by the highest and lowest points on the middle wave.

4. Using the Rectangle tool, draw a rectangle around your art defining the tiling element. The rectangle should meet the end points of the lines. In addition, the wave crests should cross the top edges of the rectangle at exactly the same point on the horizontal ruler as the waves that cross the bottom edge of the rectangle. You can use ruler guides to make sure this is the case, and adjust the size of the rectangle as needed to make it happen.

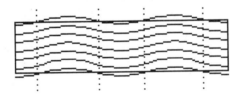

5. Select the rectangle and press **Command+hyphen** (**Arrange > Send To Back**) to position it behind the lines. You can set a fill for the rectangle, but make the outline of the rectangle invisible by setting the Stroke to **None** in the Paint Style palette. (Otherwise, the pattern will include the box border, and display as a series of grid lines.)

6. Select all the lines and the rectangle. Then choose **Object > Pattern** to display the Pattern dialog box. Click **New** to display the selected pattern in the top-right area of the dialog box and name the pattern by entering the name in the text box.

7. Click **OK** to close the dialog box and record the changes. When you close this dialog box, the pattern will then be available in the Paint Style box.

8. Draw any shape to outline the area of the artwork you want to shade with the new pattern.

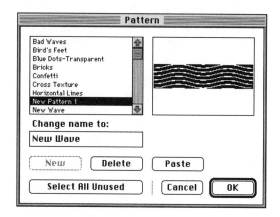

9. In the Paint Style palette, click the **Pattern** box to display the list of patterns. To make the outline of the shape invisible, set the Stroke to **None**.

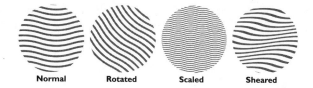

Normal   Rotated   Scaled   Sheared

EXERCISE: CREATING CONTINUOUS GEOMETRIC PATTERNS

The previous technique was used to create a simple pattern that is not continuous. In other words, the graphics of the pattern did not overlap the edges of the tiling rectangle. The process is a bit more complicated if you want to create continuous patterns, requiring that the graphics flow in a continuous connection from one tile to another. The technique described here can be used to create tiles that form a continuous, symmetrical pattern.

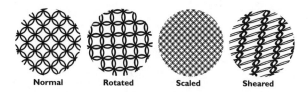

Normal   Rotated   Scaled   Sheared

1. Create a symmetrical design with one of the drawing tools. A symmetrical design is one in which the top half is a mirror image of the bottom half,

and the left half is a mirror image of the right half. The figure below shows a symmetrical design composed of five interlocking circles.

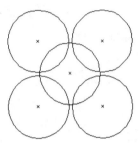

2. Using the Rectangle tool, draw a nonstroked rectangle over the area you would like to create as a pattern fill. To have the design cross over from one tile to another and line up well, position your rectangle so that its center point precisely matches the center of the symmetrical design. Send the tiling rectangle to the back by selecting it and typing **Command+hyphen** (**Arrange > Send To Back**).

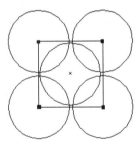

3. Select all the geometric shapes and the tiling rectangle by dragging the marquee over them.

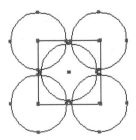

4. Choose **Object > Pattern** and click **New** to define the new pattern in the Pattern dialog box. You can use Illustrator's default pattern name (New Pattern 1), or type a name that you will recognize as describing this particular design. Click **OK** to close the dialog box and save the pattern.

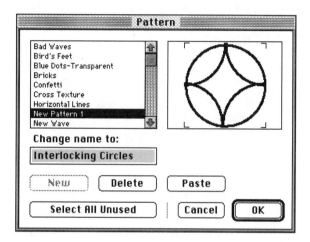

5. Now that you have created the pattern, you can fill any new shape with it using the Paint Style palette (**Command+I**). The new pattern name should appear in the scrolling window when you click the **Pattern** selection option.

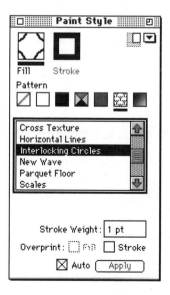

6. You can create variations by changing the artwork that you used originally to create the first pattern tile, using techniques described here to create another version with a different name.

NOTE

Notice that you can achieve different results in the overall pattern by changing the size of the rectangle. The figure at left shows three variations in the size of the rectangle and the resulting patterns.

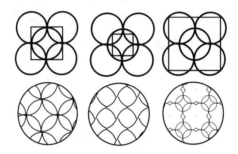

NOTE

Create more intricate symmetrical designs by drawing one quadrant of the design and using the Reflect tool to create the other four quadrants.

7. When you are satisfied with the pattern design, you can delete the tile artwork; the pattern will remain stored with the current file. If you want to edit the tile later, you can retrieve it by choosing **Object > Pattern**, selecting the pattern name from the list, and clicking **Paste**. This creates a copy of the original tile artwork, which you can edit to create a new variation.

8. Use the **Object > Pattern** command to delete any unwanted variations.

EXERCISE: CREATING AMORPHOUS PATTERNS

The previous technique was used to create a continuous, symmetrical pattern. The technique described here can be used to create a continuous pattern from any pattern—symmetrical as well as asymmetrical or amorphous designs.

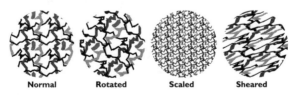

Normal   Rotated   Scaled   Sheared

1. Create a design with one of the drawing tools. The figure below step 2 shows a design composed of an series of open paths and two closed paths.

2. Using the Rectangle tool, draw a nonstroked rectangle over the area you would like to serve as a pattern fill. Send the tiling rectangle to the back by selecting it and typing **Command+hyphen** (**Arrange > Send To Back**).

NOTE
One important rule in this step is to make sure that the same number of lines cross the top of the tiling rectangle as cross the bottom, and that the same number of line segments cross the left edge of the tiling rectangle as cross the right edge. In other words, if the design crosses the top edge at three points, you want the bottom of the rectangle to be crossed at three points also.

➤ Additional precautions are required if all the design elements do not share the same stroke and fill. For example, if three lines cross the top border and use three different strokes, then the three lines that cross the bottom border must have the same sequence of strokes.

➤ If any fill colors will be used, then the edges of any filled shape must cross over a border an even number of times and cross the same number of times on the opposing sides of the tiling rectangle.

3. Next, make the lines that cross the left edge of the rectangle to match the vertical position of lines that cross the right edge, and lines that cross the top edge of the rectangle to match the horizontal position of lines that cross the bottom edge. To make this adjustment easiest, work in Artwork view (**Command+E**), and choose **View > Show Rulers** (**Command+R**) and drag ruler guides across the tile as guides for adjusting corresponding points.

NOTE

If the lines don't cross at a perpendicular angle to the edges of the rectangle, it's a good idea to use rounded caps rather than butt caps—set through the Paint Style palette.

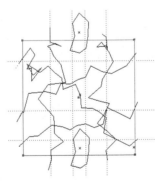

4. Regardless of which method is used in step 3, it is a good idea to check your tiles visually by selecting the whole design and the tiling rectangle, and following steps 5 through 7 using "dummy" pattern names (that you later delete), to check the alignment of adjacent tiles and to preview the pattern. Besides verifying that the design lines up across tiles, you want to be sure that the fill patterns and strokes assigned to crossing lines match up. Note any bad breaks and reshape the paths in original pattern art to eliminate problems.

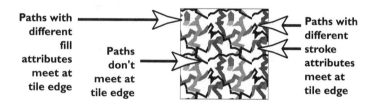

Paths with different fill attributes meet at tile edge

Paths don't meet at tile edge

Paths with different stroke attributes meet at tile edge

5. When you have achieved the effect you want, then select all the geometric shapes and the tiling rectangle by dragging the marquee over them.

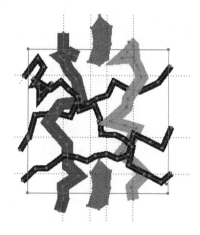

6. Choose **Object > Pattern** and click **New** to define the new pattern in the Pattern dialog box. You can use Illustrator's default pattern name (New Pattern 1), or type a name that you will recognize as describing this particular design. Click **OK** to close the dialog box and save the pattern.

7. Now that you have created the pattern, you can fill any new shape with it using the Paint Style palette (**Command+I**). The new pattern name should appear in the scrolling window when you click the **Pattern** selection option.

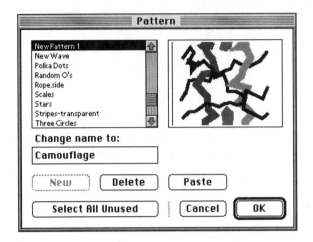

8. You can create variations by changing the artwork that you used originally to create the first pattern tile, using techniques described here to create another version with a different name.

9. When you are satisfied with the pattern design, you can delete the tile artwork; the pattern will remain stored with the current file. If you want to edit the tile later, you can retrieve it by choosing **Object > Pattern**, selecting the pattern name from the list, and clicking **Paste**. This creates a copy of the original tile artwork, which you can edit to create a new variation.

10. Use the **Object > Pattern** command to delete any unwanted variations.

Converting Patterns to Objects

Once you have created a pattern, you can convert it back to objects on the Artboard by following these steps:

1. Choose **Object > Pattern** to display the Pattern dialog box, as shown below.

2. Click on the pattern name in the scrolling list to select it.

3. Click **Paste** to paste a copy of the original tiling element artwork on the page.

4. Close the dialog box. The original pattern objects are now objects on the Artboard.

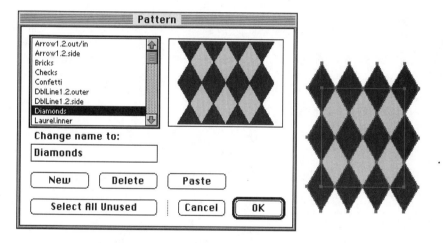

Figure 6.56 Pattern (left) converted to objects (right).

Editing an Existing Pattern

Once you have created a pattern, you can edit it by following these steps:

1. Choose **Object > Pattern** to display the Pattern dialog box, as shown above.

2. Click on the pattern name in the scrolling list to select it.

3. Click **Paste** to paste a copy of the original tiling element artwork on the page.

4. Close the dialog box, edit the pattern artwork, select it, and choose **Pattern** again to display the Pattern dialog box again. You can store the changed pattern under a new name, or you can delete the old name and then add it back as a new name.

5. Click **OK** to close the dialog box and record the changes, or click **Cancel** to close the dialog box without recording any changes.

Transforming Existing Patterns

Once you have filled an object with a pattern, you can use the transformation tools to scale, reflect, shear, or rotate the pattern—whether or not you transform the *shape* of the object at the same time.

NOTE

This is handy for creating custom effects if you are too proud to use the patterns that come with Illustrator, but too pressed for time to create your own. You can transform patterns through a dialog box, as in the next steps, or transform them by holding the **P** key as you use techniques described in Chapter 5 for transforming visually.

1. Draw any shape to outline the area of the artwork you want to shade with a pattern.

2. With the shape selected, select the **Fill** icon in the Paint Style palette, and click on the pattern box.

3. Click on a pattern name in the scrolling list to select it.

4. Select any of the transformation tools and Option+click on the shading object to display a dialog box. Uncheck the **Objects** option, check the **Patterns** option. The figures at left show the basic pattern (above), then scaled (lower left), and skewed (lower right).

Deleting a Pattern

You can delete a pattern from the Paint Style palette following these steps:

1. Choose **Object > Pattern** to display the Pattern dialog box, as shown an earlier figure under this heading.

2. Click on the pattern name in the scrolling list to select it, or click **Select All Unused** to select the names of all patterns that are not currently used in the artwork. You can delete these patterns to save memory and storage space.

3. Click **Delete** to remove the selected name (and pattern) from the list.

4. Click **OK** to close the dialog box. Objects that were filled with that pattern will revert to the default fill pattern (100% black).

NOTE

If you frequently use custom patterns, save them in a file created for this purpose. Opening the file will make your previously created patterns available, allowing you to use them in other Illustrator files. You can make any pattern available for use in a new file by simply opening the file that contains the desired pattern.

NOTE If you want a set of patterns to be available automatically whenever you use Illustrator, create an Illustrator file containing all the patterns you want, then name it Adobe Illustrator Startup, and place it in the folder containing the Illustrator application. You can also include custom colors, fonts, and graph designs in the Adobe Illustrator Startup document. These elements will automatically be available whenever you use Illustrator.

Working with Custom Fill Sets

My Fills

You can assemble collections of custom colors, patterns, and gradients and save them as custom fill sets using the techniques described here. You can also save subsets of custom fills as the startup file, so that the Paint Style palette shows only the colors and fills you use most frequently when you start the program or open a new document. You can still easily add more fills or colors during a work session using **File > Import Styles** or **Object > Custom Color, Pattern**, or Gradient, as described earlier in this chapter.

Importing Styles from Other Artwork

There are two methods of adding new colors, patterns, gradients, and graph designs to a document or template. The first way—the hard way—is to create them using the Paint Styles and Gradient palettes and the **Paint Style**, **Custom Color**, **Pattern**, **Gradient**, and **Graph** commands under the Object menu. The easier way, if you have already used the above methods to set up another Illustrator document or template, is to import the styles from one document to another using the **File > Import Styles** command described here. This adds the new custom colors, patterns, gradients, and graph designs to the current document's palettes and dialog box scrolling lists.

To import styles from another Illustrator document or template into the current document, follow these steps.

1. Choose **File > Import Styles** to display the Import Styles dialog box.

2. Find the document or template name from which you want to import the styles. Use the same techniques for finding a file here as described under the **File > Open** command earlier in Chapter 10.

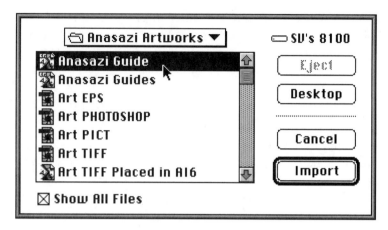

Figure 6.57 The Import Styles dialog box with a file name selected.

3. Double-click the file name—or use the slower method of clicking once on the file name to highlight it and then click **Open** or press **Return**.

The new custom colors, patterns, gradients, and graph designs will automatically be added to the current document's palettes and dialog box scrolling lists

Any new custom color, pattern, or gradient that has the same name as an existing paint style will overwrite the existing version, and objects painted with those colors, patterns, and gradients will change in the artwork.

WARNING

You can replace or modify the Adobe Illustrator start-up file so that these elements are automatically part of any new document you start. See Customizing the Startup File later in this chapter.

NOTE

Using Adobe's Custom Fills

Illustrator comes with a number of custom colors, custom gradients, and custom patterns that are automatically available in the Paint Style palette whenever you start Illustrator (unless you modify the Startup file as described later in this chapter). In addition, you can access other collections of colors, gradi-

Color Systems

ents, and patterns by choosing **File > Open** or **File > Import Styles** and opening the Color Systems or Gradients and Patterns folders that are automatically installed in the Adobe Illustrator program folder when you install Illustrator. These fill patterns were shown earlier in this chapter.

Creating Your Own Custom Fill Sets

Besides working with paint styles that have been created for other specific Adobe Illustrator artwork, you can create custom files designed specifically to contain custom collections of fill sets. These can by imported to any document using **File > Open** or **File > Import Styles**. Similarly, you can import the styles from the *Adobe Illustrator Startup* file or any one of the startup files you saved under other names.

1. Use the **File > New** command to start a custom files from scratch, or the **Open** command to open the file that you have already created that uses some of the paint styles you wish to include in the custom set.

2. Before you make any changes to this file, choose **File > Save** as and give it another name, such as *Project Z Custom Styles*—so existing artwork will not be replaced.

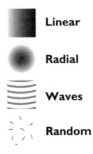

Linear

Radial

Waves

Random

3. Use the **File > Import Styles** command to import styles that you have already created in other files, that you want to become part of the startup file.

4. Use the **Object > Custom Colors**, **Gradients**, and **Patterns** commands to set up new custom colors, patterns, and gradients you want—and delete those you do not want. (Or wait until step 8 to delete all unused fills at the end of these steps.)

You can also use the **File > Document Setup** and **Page Setup** commands to set the default options you want, and set the zoom level and window size as you would like them to appear when you start Illustrator or open a new document.

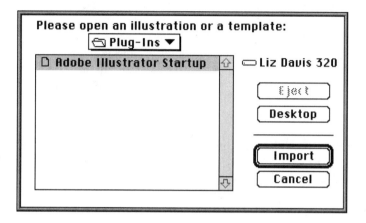

WARNING

Fills that you *create* are automatically saved as part of the document, but fills that are *imported*, or that were part of the initial startup file, or that appear when you open additional documents, are not saved as part of the current document unless they are actually applied to objects or added to the paint swatch area on the left side of the Paint Style palette, as described in the next two steps.

5. Delete the existing artwork, and create a layout of rectangles and apply to each one a different custom pattern, gradient, paint swatch, and custom color.

NOTE

The artwork could be simple rectangles, as described here, or it can be actual finished art that you have created for a specific use. In the latter case, it's still a good idea to add the name of each fill used (step 6) next to or below the object that uses the fill, or with arrows pointing to the object from the fill labels.

6. You can add text under the rectangles that describe the custom patterns and gradients in each.

My Fill Set I

Linear	Radial	Waves	Random
Black & White	**Purple & White**	**Aqua**	**Black**

NOTE

The advantage of showing names for each pattern or gradient is that you can print the artwork as a reference sheet for use in a large production department. Otherwise, if you don't have a color printer or can't find the reference sheet when you need it, you can open the artwork and click on any box to view the fill name in the Paint Style palette.

You can create a custom startup file without including any objects by simply applying the fills you want to keep to Paint swatches in the Paint Style palette, and then deleting the objects before you save the file—but you miss the advantage of being able to print a custom fill test sheet or reference sheet, and you cannot easily re-activate the same custom set if you later replace the startup file with new settings. You would have to repeat all the steps described here!

7. Delete all the fills you don't want by using the **Select all Unused** options under the **Object > Custom Color** and **Patterns** commands. This is also a good way to check that you *have* used all the fills on those lists, if that is your intention.

NOTE

You can delete unwanted fills through the Gradient palette (**Object > Gradient**) one by one, and if any are used in the artwork you will get a warning message.

NOTE

You can go on to create as many custom fill files as you want, each with a different name or number.

8. Print a proof sheet or reference sheet on a color printer. This is a good idea if several people will be sharing the same custom fill palette, or if you will be using many different custom fill palettes.

For a reference sheet, it is helpful to add a heading on the page that identifies the fill set name, and to add text labels next to each custom filled object, identifying the name of the custom fill and (if desired) the composition.

N O T E

Opening a Paint Style Window

If you know that you will be using certain attributes—such as colors, fills, or stroke combinations—repeatedly in a drawing, it is useful to create a small area on the pasteboard containing objects that use the basic styles. This way, you can apply the paint attributes with three clicks: click on the object in the pasteboard area to load the Paint Style palette with its attributes, click on the **Paintbucket** tool, then click on the object(s) to which you want to apply the paint style.

This is useful when you are creating artwork that repeatedly uses several sets of paint attributes—to affect both the stroke and fill of objects at the same time.

1. Draw a series of objects—or Option+drag copies of objects from the Artboard—and line them up off to the side of your drawing. Paint each object with the paint attributes you want using the Paint Style palette (**Command+I**). Optionally, you can label each object using the Type tool.

2. To apply the paint style attributes from one of the pasteboard objects to an object on the Artboard in Fit in Window view (**Command+M**), simply click on the object in the pasteboard area with any selection tool to load the Paint Style palette with its attributes, click on the **Paintbucket** tool, then click on the object(s) to which you want to apply the paint style.

To set up the attributes of the next object you draw, simply click on the object in the pasteboard area to load the Paint Style palette with its attributes (or Command+click if a selection tool is not already active). The next object you draw will have the attributes of the chosen palette oval.

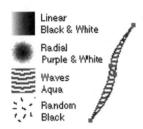

3. When working in close-up views of the artwork, you can keep the palette visible in a second open window. To do this, choose **Window > New Window**. Size the windows so they do not overlap. The palette window can be small and show a reduced view of the palette artwork.

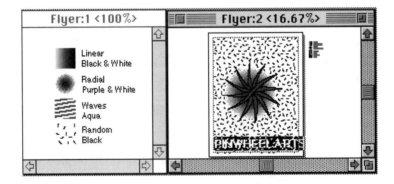

Customizing the Startup File

You can create a custom start-up file that contains only the custom colors, patterns, and gradients that you use. These options will be displayed in the Paint Style palette for any new document that you create. You can also set up specific graph design, Document Setup, Page Setup, zoom level, window size, and cursor location options as part of the startup file. To create a custom start-up file, follow these steps.

NOTE

It's a good idea to save the original default settings. One advantage is that you can return to them whenever you want. But there's another tremendous advantage: when you rename the original default startup file and open the renamed file, you get a complete page of artwork that shows all the custom fills and palette settings, as used in the next steps.

1. Use the **File > Open** command to open the file named *Adobe Illustrator Startup* inside the Plug-ins folder in the Adobe Illustrator program folder.

    When you open a startup file, you can see any artwork that was saved as a part of it. In this case, Adobe has created a nice layout of rectangles that show all custom patterns, gradients, paint swatches, and custom colors.

    You will use this file as a starting point for creating a custom startup file. Notice that by opening it all the original default custom fills are added to the Paint Style palette—even if you deleted some before this step.

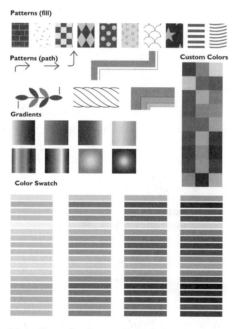

Figure 6.58 Adobe Illustrator Startup file includes objects painted with custom fills.

2. Before you make any changes to this file, choose **File > Save as** and give it another name, such as *Original Startup Defaults* or *Adobe Illustrator Startup 1*—so it will not be replaced when you create new startup files later. The use **File > Save as** again to save the file under a yet another name—such as *Adobe Illustrator 2*.

Adobe Illustrator Startup1

Adobe Illustrator Startup 2

NOTE

The advantage of simply adding a number to the end of the file name is that it will appear adjacent to similar names in an alphabetical list—though other naming standards can be more descriptive. Unfortunately, you can't add much description to the *end* of the starting name *Adobe Illustrator Startup*—which uses up 26 characters of the Macintosh's 31-character limit for file names, and only 27 characters are displayed in lists of file names under the Finder.

3. Use the **File > Import Styles** command to import styles that you have already created in other files, that you want to become part of the startup file.

4. Use the **Object > Custom Colors**, **Gradients**, and **Patterns** commands to set up new custom colors, patterns, and gradients you want—and to delete those you do not want. (Or wait until step 8 to delete all unused fills at the end of these steps.)

```
Object
  Paint Style...      ⌘I
  Custom Color...
  Pattern...
  Gradient...
```

You can also use the File > Document Setup and Page Setup commands to set the default options you want, and set the zoom level and window size as you would like them to appear when you start Illustrator or open a new document.

WARNING Fills that you *create* are automatically saved as part of the document, but fills that are *imported*, or that were part of the initial startup file, or that appear when you open additional documents, are not saved as part of the current document unless they are actually applied to objects or added to the paint swatch area on the left side of the Paint Style palette, as described in the next two steps.

5. Customize the paint swatch area on the left side of the Paint Style palette. Click the **Custom color** selection option and, one by one, drag each named custom color that you want to keep in the Startup file onto a paint swatch. Repeat this step for Patterns and Gradients.

NOTE The techniques for adding, deleting, and re-arranging the swatches were described in detail earlier in this chapter.

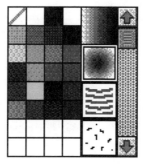

NOTE Even if you don't delete any default custom fills or add any new ones, you might want to customize the paint swatch area this way and save the file as described in step 8. The paint swatch area is not affected by the File > Import Styles command, but it does change to match the last-saved Paint Style palette for the active document window.

6. Using the boxes already created by Adobe in the original startup file—the currently open document—update the boxes under the paint swatch area of the artwork to reflect your custom paint swatch setting in the Paint Style palette. You can update the text under the boxes that describe the custom patterns and gradients if you change those fills in the artwork, or you can use or create un-named boxes for new fills—like the set of custom fills at the bottom.

NOTE

If your file is to have more custom fills than Adobe's original startup file, you might have to delete some of the large boxes that show patterns and gradients, and copy some of the smaller, unnamed boxes from the paint swatch or custom color area of the artwork.

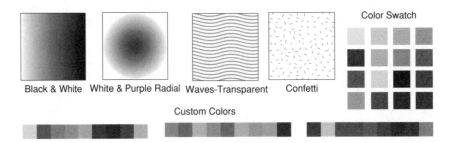

Black & White   White & Purple Radial   Waves-Transparent   Confetti

Color Swatch

Custom Colors

NOTE

The advantage of showing names for each pattern or gradient is that you can print the artwork as a reference sheet for use in a large production department. Otherwise, if you don't have a color printer or can't find the reference sheet when you need it, you can open the artwork and click on any box to view the fill name in the Paint Style palette.

You can create a custom startup file, without including any objects, by simply applying the fills you want to keep and then deleting the objects before you save the file—but you miss the advantage of being able to print a custom fill test sheet or reference sheet, and you cannot easily re-activate the same custom set if you later replace the startup file with new settings. You would have to repeat all the steps described here!

WARNING

Usually you go to this trouble to *shorten* the lists in the Paint Style palette, rather than lengthen them. Large startup files can affect the speed of starting Illustrator. If you simply want easy access to your own custom lists of fills, you can use the technique described later in this section for Working with Multiple Start-up Files and Creating Custom Color Sets.

7. If you didn't already delete all the fills you don't want in Step 5, you can easily delete them now using the **Select all Unused** options under the **Object > Custom Color** and **Patterns** commands. This is also a good way to check that you *have* used all the fills on those lists, if that is your intention.

NOTE

You can delete unwanted fills through the Gradient palette (**Object > Gradient**) one by one, and if any are used in the artwork you will get a warning message.

8. Save the file again as *Adobe Illustrator Startup 2* (or whatever name you chose in Step 2), the use File > Save as to save it as *Adobe Illustrator Startup* inside the Plug-ins folder in the Adobe Illustrator program folder.

9. When you quit and restart Illustrator, the new lists of custom fills will automatically appear in the Paint Style palette.

You can go on to create as many startup files as you want, each with a different name or number, and work with multiple startup files as described next.

NOTE

Working with Multiple Startup Files

You can use the technique described here to create any number of files, saving them under different names in the Plug-Ins folder—such as *Adobe Illustrator*

Startup 1, Adobe Illustrator Startup 2, etc. When you want to change the defaults that you are working with, you could Quit Illustrator, then delete (or rename) the current *Adobe Illustrator Startup* file in the Plug-Ins folder, and rename the file you want to use as the new *Adobe Illustrator Startup* —or duplicate it and name the copy *Adobe Illustrator Startup*. Then restart Illustrator.

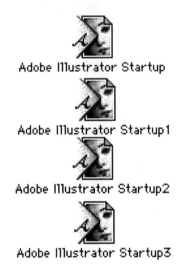

You can accomplish all this without actually going through the desktop (except in the first step, performed once) by following the next steps whenever you want to create and use a new startup file or switch from one startup file to another.

1. First, from the System 7 desktop, locate the icon for the Adobe Illustrator program and click once to select it, then choose **File > Make Alias**. Move this alias into the Apple Menu Items folder in the System Folder under System 7. This way, you can easily start Illustrator from the Apple menu at any time.

2. Start Illustrator, if it is not already started, by choosing **Adobe Illustrator alias** from the Apple menu.

3. Open one of the files you created using the techniques described in the previous section, such as *Adobe Illustrator Startup 2*, then use **File > Save as** to save the file as *Adobe Illustrator Startup* inside the Plug-ins folder in the Adobe Illustrator program folder—if you want this to be the next startup file you use.

   Otherwise, if you want to modify this file first, use the techniques described earlier and then use **File > Save as** to save the file as *Adobe Illustrator Startup* in the Plug-Ins folder in the Adobe Illustrator program folder, and **Save as** again under a second name—such as *Adobe Illustrator 3*—so it will not be replaced when you create new startup files later.

4. Choose **File > Quit**, then restart Illustrator by choosing **Adobe Illustrator alias** from the Apple menu.

Object > Attributes...

The **Attributes** command lets you add notes that will appear as part of the PostScript code when the artwork is saved in EPS format, display the center point, reverse path directions, or set the output resolution of selected objects.

Select the object you wish to annotate or affect, then choose **Object > Attributes**, or press **Command+Control+A**, to display the Attributes dialog box. Make entries as desired under the following categories:

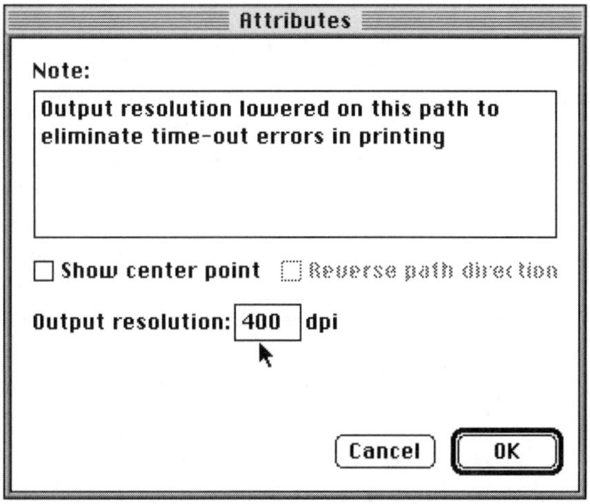

Figure 6.59 The Attributes dialog box with and example of Note text.

➤ You can type descriptive notes about a particular object as shown in the Note area of the dialog box. These notes do not print out, but you can use them as production aids or descriptions of when the specified Paint attributes are to be used. They appear as comments in the generated PostScript code, so you can also use the Note area for comments that will help you find specific portions of code if you are modifying the PostScript code directly.

➤ Click **Show Center Point** if you want to see the center point of the selected object, or turn this option off for objects that already show a center point—such as rectangles and ovals drawn with Illustrator's basic shape tools.

➤ The **Reverse Path Direction** option is dimmed unless a compound path is selected. (When a compound path is created, the **Reverse** option is automatically applied to the foreground objects in a compound path where they overlap the background object. The result is that the foreground objects create a "hole" in the background object. If you combine compound paths into a single compound path, the objects keep their Reverse options. Illustrator reverses objects only when they first become part of a compound path.) Click **Reverse Path Direction** to reverse the points that Illustrator regards as the beginning and end of an open path. (See Object > Compound Path > Make.)

➤ Illustrator's default resolution setting of 800 dpi (dots per inch) usually yields optimal printing quality and speed. You can raise the resolution for selected objects to improve print quality, or (more likely) lower the resolution of very long paths to avoid limitcheck errors in printing.

WARNING

When you change the output resolution of a selected object, you automatically change the flatness setting for that object. This determines the precision with which Illustrator calculates curves. Illustrator constructs curves by linking anchor points with a series of very short straight line segments (though the resulting curves appear smooth to the naked eye). A low flatness value (i.e., high-resolution setting) causes Illustrator to use a greater number of short line segments to create a more accurate curve.

NOTE

Note that resolutions are device-dependent. A resolution setting that works with a laser printer may not work with a Linotronic typesetter. You can also use a low-resolution value while working to speed up screen redrawing, then change it back to a high value for final printing.

NOTE

See also File > Document Setup for information about changing the resolution of objects as you create them.

Using Color Filters

The Colors filters adjust colors, intensify or diminish an object's color, or distribute colors among objects according to their orientation or stacking order.

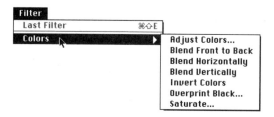

Filter > Colors > Adjust...

Use the Adjust Colors filter to change the percentage of CMYK color in a selected object by some percentage. This is an alternative to entering an absolute percentage in the Paint Style palette, and a way of setting up a command that you can repeat on different selections. The objects must be have process colors applied as the fill, and must be defined by paths. You cannot apply this filter to imported graphics or to text (unless the text has been converted to outlines using **Type > Create Outlines**).

1. Select the path(s) in the Adobe Illustrator document that you want to affect. The objects need not have the same paint styles.

2. Choose **Filter > Colors > Adjust** to display the Adjust Colors dialog box.

3. Type positive numbers in the boxes next to Cyan, Magenta, Yellow, and/or Black. Click either **Fill** or **Stroke** or both to specify which attributes are to change. Click **Custom to Process** to converta all custom colors in the selection to CMYK componiednts. Click B & W to process to convert all tints of black to Process Black tints.

NOTE

The value(s) you enter in the dialog box represent an absolute percentage screen for the color. For example, if you enter **20** for the Cyan value, and the currently selected object has a 60% Cyan screen, then the screen will change by 20%, thereby becoming 80%.

```
┌─────────────────────────────────────────────┐
│            Adjust Colors                      │
│  ┌─ Selection: ──────────────────────┐       │
│     Cyan:                    [ 0    ] │       │
│              ──────△────────          │       │
│     Magenta:                 [ 0   ]  │       │
│              ──────△────────          │       │
│     Yellow:                  [ 0   ]  │       │
│              ──────△────────          │       │
│     Black:                   [ 0   ]  │       │
│              ──────△────────          │       │
│  └──────────────────────────────────┘        │
│  ┌─ Convert: ────────────────────────┐       │
│    ☒ Fill      ☐ Custom To Process    │       │
│    ☒ Stroke    ☐ B&W To Process       │       │
│  └──────────────────────────────────┘        │
│                                               │
│    ☐ Preview    (Cancel)  (  OK  )            │
└─────────────────────────────────────────────┘
```

4. Click **Preview** to view the effects of your entries on the screen if you want the option of adjusting your values before closing the dialog box.

5. Finally, click **OK** to set the new values and close the dialog box, or click **Cancel** to close the dialog box without applying any changes.

Filter > Colors > Blend Filters

The Blend filters create a series of intermediate colors between a range of selected objects, based on the stacking order or orientation on the page.

1. Create two objects in the Adobe Illustrator document that you want to use as bases for the new colors. Create additional objects that you want Illustrator to color for you, and position them in one of the following ways:

   ➤ between the first two objects in stacking order

   ➤ between the first two objects relative to the horizontal ruler

   ➤ between the first two objects relative to the vertical ruler

2. Select all the objects created in step 1.

3. Choose one of the options from the **Filter > Colors** submenu.

➤ **Blend Back to Front** uses the objects on the top and bottom in the stacking order as the bases for creating the new colors, and paints all objects in between with the intermediate colors it creates.

➤ **Blend Horizontally** uses the objects farthest left and right in the selection as the bases for creating the new colors, and paints all objects in between with the intermediate colors.

➤ **Blend Vertically** uses the objects nearest the top and bottom in the selection as the bases for creating the new colors, and paints all objects in between with the intermediate colors.

Figure 6.60 Monochromatic objects before and after applying Blend filter (see also color plates).

Filter > Colors > Invert Colors

The Invert Colors filter creates a color negative of the selected object(s). For example, a 0% color would become 100%, 20% becomes 80%, and so on. Select the path(s) in the Adobe Illustrator document that you want to affect. Then choose **Filter > Colors > Invert**.

Figure 6.61 Monochromatic illustration before and after inversion.

Filter > Colors > Saturate

The Saturate color filter increases or decreases the color intensity of the selected object(s) by changing the percentages of CMYK color values.

1. Select the path(s) in the Adobe Illustrator document that you want to affect.

315

2. Choose Filter > Colors > Saturate.

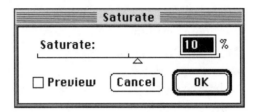

3. Enter a percentage in the Saturate dialog box—or change the percentage by dragging the slider bar. Positive values saturate the colors, negative values desaturate the colors.

Figure 6.62 Monochromatic illustration before (left) and after (right) desaturation.

Figure 6.63 Monochromatic illustration before (left) and after (right) saturation (see also color plates).

NOTE

It's a good idea to keep the paint Style palette open when you use these filters and monitor the CMYK values before and after using these filters. You can make minor adjustments as desired. Remember that most PostScript processors will print faster if the CMYK values are set in even increments of 5.

Filter > Pathfinder > Hard...

The Pathfinder filters combine, isolate, and subdivide paths, and build new paths formed by the intersection of objects—filters that are described in Chapter 5. This submenu also includes filters that let you blend overlapping colors and trap objects as described here and in the next sections.

The Hard filter mixes two or more colors from overlapping objects to create a color that represents how colors will overprint. The mix color is created by combining the highest CMYK value from each color in the selection. For example if one object has a 30% Cyan value, and another color has a 60% Cyan value, the new color will have a 60% Cyan value. This filter actually divides the image into its component faces—areas undivided by line segments—and combines them into a group.

1. Select two or more overlapping objects in the Adobe Illustrator document that you want to affect.

2. Choose **Filter > Pathfinder > Hard** to display the Hard dialog box.

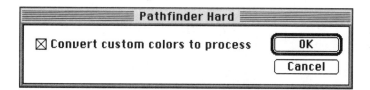

3. In the dialog box, select or deselect the option to convert custom colors to process colors, then click **OK**.

Figure 6.64 Objects before and after using the Hard filter.

Filter > Pathfinder > Soft...

The Soft filter creates a transparent effect on overlapping colors in the image, and divides the image into its component faces—areas undivided by line segments—and combines them into a group.

1. Select two or more overlapping objects in the Adobe Illustrator document that you want to affect.

2. Choose **Filter > Pathfinder > Soft** to display the Soft dialog box.

3. Enter a value between 0 and 100 to set the percentage of transparency you want in the overlapping colors. A higher value produces a higher degree of transparency.

4. In the dialog box, select or deselect the option to convert custom colors to process colors.

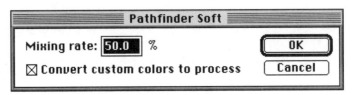

5. Click **OK** or press **Return** to close the dialog box and view the effects.

Figure 6.65 Objects before and after using the Soft filter.

Color Trapping

Once you get into the process of producing color separations on film, you will become aware of the many issues that were formerly handled by the commercial printer—issues that the "artist" never worried about. Now, with the miracle of computer illustration, the artist can—an sometimes must—participate in making certain technical adjustments to the artwork in order to get the best printing results. This section describes some of the issues involved in *trapping*—controlling the behavior of two adjacent or overlapping colors in the artwork in order to compensate for slight misregistration problems.

NOTE

The overprinting and knock-out effects described in the next sections do not appear in Preview mode on the screen but will print correctly when the Separation option is selected in the Print dialog box.

Using the Trap Filter

Adobe Illustrator includes a Trap filter for color *trapping*—creating a small area of overlap between two adjacent colors. This technique has been used traditionally to compensate for potential gaps between adjacent colors when color artwork is printed from color separations. Gaps result when two color plates are not precisely aligned or registered.

Figure 6.66 Adjacent colors can show gaps when two color plates are printed slightly "off register."

The Trap filter automatically determines the lighter of the two adjacent colors and creates an extension of the lighter color beneath the darker color. If the trap color chosen by the filter is not satisfactory, you can use the **Reverse Trap** option to force the darker color to spread rather than the lighter one.

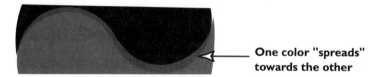

One color "spreads" towards the other

Figure 6.67 Trapping "spreads" one color to create an overlap with an adjacent color.

The Trapping plug-in filter supports a variety of trapping options including both process and custom colors and "enriched black" traps. Because Pathfinder trapping is object-based, it can create traps comparable in quality to those generated by high-end, stand-alone trapping programs that cost thousands of dollars.

This feature is tremendously useful, eliminating the need to export the artwork to another application for trapping. When Adobe Illustrator is used in conjunction with Adobe Acrobat programs to import PDF files (as described in Chapter 7), you can use this feature to trap artwork created in virtually any Macintosh program such as QuarkXPress, Adobe PageMaker, and Claris MacDraw.

WARNING

The trapping feature will not work on gradient fills, placed art, strokes, or patterns.

1. Select two or more adjacent objects with different fill colors and choose **Filter > Pathfinder > Trap** to display the Trap dialog box.

```
┌──────────────────────────────────────────────┐
│ ══════════════ Pathfinder Trap ══════════════ │
│                                                │
│  Thickness:     [0.25]  points    ( OK     )   │
│  Height/width:  [100.0]  %        ( Cancel )   │
│  Tint reduction:[40.0]  %         ( Defaults)  │
│  ☐ Convert custom colors to process            │
│  ☐ Reverse traps                               │
│                                                │
└──────────────────────────────────────────────┘
```

2. Enter the next values as recommended by your print shop for the trap, based on the maximum amount of misregistration and paper stretch that can be expected:

➤ Enter the thickness you desire for the trap. In general, the trap should be between 0.3 and 1.0 point.

➤ Enter a value in the Height/width percentage box to change the width of the trap on horizontal lines versus that on vertical lines, to compensate for paper stretch. To increase the thickness on horizontal lines without changing the vertical trap value, enter a value greater than 100%. Values less than 100% decrease the trap thickness on horizontal lines without changing the vertical trap value.

➤ Enter a Tint reduction under 100% to create a trap that is less than 100% of the CMYK values of the lighter trapped color. The CMYK value of the darker color remains at 100% regardless of the value entered here.

➤ Select **Convert custom colors to process** when trapping custom colors, if you want to convert the trap into equivalent process colors instead of creating a new custom color.

➤ Select **Reverse traps** to create a spread trap that traps darker colors into lighter colors. (This option does not work with "enriched black" colors that contain additional CMY colors to enrich 100% black values.)

3. Click **OK** to create trap on the selected objects, or click Default to return to the default trapping values.

NOTE

To use the Trap filter with text you first need to convert the text to outlines. See Type > Create Outlines in Chapter 8.

WARNING

Once you have trapped an object, the amount of trap will change if you scale the object. For example, if you create a .5-point trap for an object, then scale it up 200% (in Illustrator or in any other application) the trap will also increase 200%, to 2 points—much larger than recommended.

Overprinting Black

The **Overprint Black** option allows you to set all black fill or black stroked lines to overprint or to remove overprinting commands from black fill or black stroked lines. You can specify a specific percentage of black to be affected, or specify overprinting for custom colors with a specific percentage of black.

1. Use a selection tool to select one or more objects to be affected, then choose **Filter > Colors > Overprint Black** to display the Overprint Black dialog box.

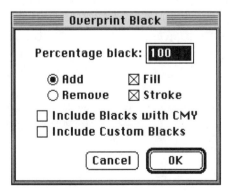

2. Enter the percentage of Black for which you would like to add or remove overprinting, then click one or more of the following options:

   ➤ **Add** or **Remove**—to either add or remove overprinting for the percentage black specified.

   ➤ **Fill**, **Stroke**, or **Both**—to apply overprinting to filled paths, stroked paths, or both.

   ➤ **Include Blacks with CMY**—to apply overprinting to paths painted with Cyan, Magenta, or Yellow as well as a Black component of the specified percentage.

   ➤ **Include Custom Blacks**—to apply overprinting to custom colors that include black at the specified percentage.

3. Click **OK** to close the dialog box. The results are apparent in printing color separations—they do not appear in the on-screen artwork.

You can apply or remove overprinting from all black in the entire document through the File > Separation Setup dialog box.

NOTE

Trapping Black Ink

If your color artwork includes black elements—as almost all artwork does—you can choose a black that is simply 100% black (0% cyan, magenta, and yellow), or you can choose a process black that is 100% of all four colors. Each alternative has specific benefits and drawbacks.

   ➤ Printing a simple 100% black that butts against other colors can result in the other colors showing through at the black edges when **Overprint** is selected in the Paint Style palette. The color is represented as gray dots in the next figure, representing a magnified view of four-color process printing.

When you choose **Black** in the Paint Style palette, you need not specify **Overprint** each time—instead, you can set Black to overprint automatically when printing color separations, through the File > Separation Setup dialog box.

NOTE

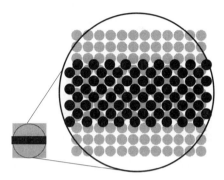

➤ If you deselect **Overprint** in the Paint Style palette—i.e., knock out any color elements that fall below the black object—you may end up with a thin white gap between the black and the color if the registration is not perfect when the final artwork is mass-produced by the commercial printer.

➤ If you select the option to overprint black in the File > Separation Setup dialog box, you can set up black as a process color and apply the process black to objects that you want to have knocked out. Even specifying as little as .1% of each of the other colors—cyan, magenta, and yellow—will override the overprint default. However, you still run the risk of a thin white gap with misregistration.

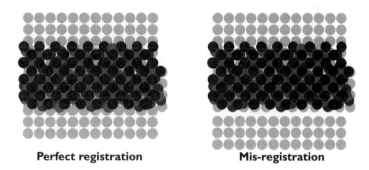

Perfect registration   **Mis-registration**

The solution to these problems is to use true four-color process black, with higher percentage components of each of the four process colors, and set the Overprint option in the Paint Style palette. Ask your commercial printer for recommended percentages, or use at least 20% cyan, 15% magenta, and 15% yellow.

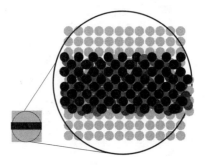

Trapping Solid Colors and Tints

Setting a filled or stroked shape to overprint can result in a transparent effect—the creation of an unintended color mix where the two colors overlap. This is the same effect as described earlier for printing black, but the effect is usually more obvious when printing lighter colors or tints than when printing black or dark colors.

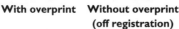

**With overprint   Without overprint
(off registration)**

The solution is to give the top object(s) a stroke of at least .5 points width, set to overprint. The stroke can be the same color as the object—or .1% shading of colors that are set to 0% for the fill—and setting the stroke to overprint. If the top object(s) already have a stroke that is a different color from the fill, you can simply set the stroke to overprint.

An alternative solution is to make a copy (**Command+C**) of the object(s), and paste it on top (**Command+F**) of the original object(s). Then choose **Filter > Pathfinder > Divide Stroke**. This automatically gives the new path(s) a fill of None and a stroke that is the same as the original object(s) fill. (The stroke is shown black in the next figure for illustrative purposes.)

Next, delete the portions of the divided stroke that do not overlap between two colors, and assign the remaining pieces an intermediate color between the two adjacent or overlapping colors. (The new strokes are shown wider in the next figure for illustrative purposes—in reality you would use a much thinner stroke.)

Objects duplicated pasted in Front | **Divide Stroke (stroke shown black)** | **Paint adjacent strokes (stroke shown wide)**

Trapping Custom Colors

When trapping custom colors be sure to stroke or spread the object of lighter color into the darker color. If the two colors are similar, an outline will appear as in the example below, and you should reduce the trap stroke weight or set the trap to an intermediate tint. (The effect is exaggerated in the figure below.)

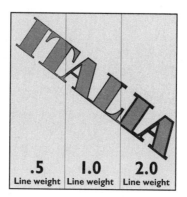

.5 Line weight | 1.0 Line weight | 2.0 Line weight

Trapping Lines

When trapping lines, you can run into two problems if the registration is slightly off when printing: a white gap will appear where the line prints off the knock out, and the line itself may become lost or muddy where it overlaps other colors if there is misregistration or if the ink bleeds in the paper.

The solution is to create two lines on top of each other. The top line should be the desired line weight with no overprint. The bottom line should be a heavier line weight, set to overprint. The trap will be one half the difference between the line weights.

The followiing figure at left shows a 2-point top line (the highway) with no overprint, over a 3-point line with overprint, both set to the color represented as light gray, butted against a color represented as black here.

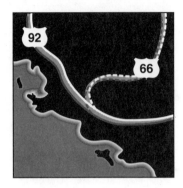

(By the way, the water's edge is created by blending two overlapping lines—a top thin line set to a 10% tint of the water color, and the bottom, thicker line set to a 90% tint—to create a series of 9 overlapping lines with gradual changes in stroke weight and tint percentage. This is for visual effect only, unrelated to trapping.)

Trapping Text

The best treatment for text depends on what color it is. The next headings describe color trapping for black text, white text, and color text.

Black Text

It's a good idea to force black text to overprint background colors—especially text in small point sizes. You do this by checking **Overprint** for the Fill in Paint Style palette (**Command+I**). Examples of text printed with and without this option (with a deliberate misregistration of one point) are shown in the text figures.

```
Stroke Weight: │1 pt        │
    Overprint: ☒ Fill  ☒ Stroke
```

For example, in the next figure 12-point Times text is set in a rectangle that is filled with a 40% Black tint. Overprint is checked in the Fill and Stroke dialog box.

**LA ILLAHA
ILLA'LLA
HU**

In the second figure, 12-point Times text is set in a rectangle that is filled with a 40% Black tint, but **Overprint** is *not* checked in the Paint Style palette. In printing, the two plates were off register by 1 point.

(Since we expected perfect registration in printing this book, we simulated this effect here by setting the same type in white under the black type, then moved the black type one point diagonally along a 45° angle.)

**LA ILLAHA
ILLA'LLA
HU**

White Text

When white text is placed on a four-color black background it can be difficult to hold registration on the press. Stroking the text with .1% of cyan, magenta, and yellow, and setting the stroke to Overprint, will push the color away from the edges, so there will not be any dot show-through. The fill, of course, must knock out the background (i.e., not overprint).

Color Text

Handle color text the same as white text, adding a stroke set to the same color as the text—or .1% shading of colors that are set to 0% for the fill—and setting the stroke to overprint.

Trapping Shadows

Misregistration can cause a white gap to appear between a foreground color and a knocked out drop shadow. To solve this problem, place a stroked line at the intersection of the two shapes, or stroke the foreground shape with one of the two colors (or, better yet, a blend of the two colors) and set it to Overprint.

With trap   **Without trap**

Calibrating Your Monitor

You can calibrate the color displayed on your color monitor to more closely match the inks you will use in printing by making adjustments through the Color Matching Preferences dialog box. When you use this option with a sample progressive color bar provided by Adobe or your printer, you can adjust your monitor and screen colors for current lighting situations. This allows you to customize your monitor without mechanically altering internal settings.

1. Choose **File > Preferences > Color Matching** to display the Color Matching dialog box, shown in the next figure.

2. Select **CIE color calibration** (developed by the Centre International d'Eclairage to convert images between RGB and CMYK color models) if you are using Illustrator with Adobe Photoshop and want to calibrate the color display between the two applications. When you click this option in the Color Matching dialog box, you can select from the following options:

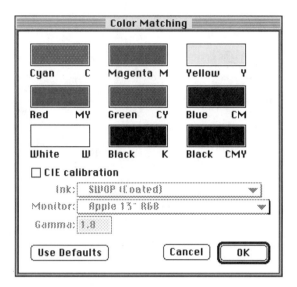

Figure 6.68 The Color Matching dialog box.

➤ The type of ink you are using from a pop-out list of inks, and select the type of monitor you are using from a pop-out list of monitors. In identifying ink types, the abbreviation SWOP indicates *standard web offset printing.*

➤ Paper types are also listed for various ink types, in order to achieve the closest equivalent to how your final printed piece will look.

➤ In the Gamma field, enter the same value as you used in Adobe Photoshop. (You can check this by choosing **Control Panel** from the Apple menu, and double-clicking the **Gamma** icon to get the Adobe Photoshop Gamma Control Panel.) By making these selections your monitor is automatically calibrated for you.

3. Click **OK** if the colors on the screen now match your printed color swatch, or go on to the next step.

4. As an alternative, or if the colors on the screen still do not match the colors on the printed color swatch you are using as a reference, you can double-click on a color swatch in the Color Matching dialog box to display the Apple Color Picker, which allows you to choose from a palette of more than sixteen million colors.

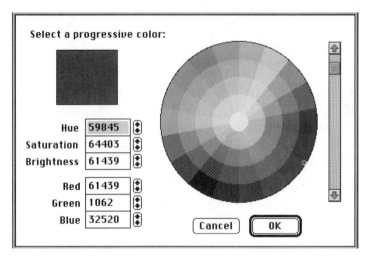

Figure 6.69 The Apple Color Picker.

5. Adjust the color in the Apple Color Picker dialog box by dragging the circle in the middle of the main color field, by dragging the slider on the luminosity bar on the right side of the box, or by entering new values in the Hue, Saturation, and Luminosity fields or the Red, Green, and Blue fields.

6. Click **OK** when the color matches your printed color swatch. Repeat steps 4 and 5 to adjust each color individually.

➤ Click **Use Defaults** in the Color Matching dialog box to cancel any custom color calibration settings.

Chapter Summary

This chapter described almost everything you need to know about painting fills and strokes of objects drawn with Illustrator's tools. The next chapter describes how to import and export graphics from or to other applications, including some additional considerations that can affect color and line weights. Chapter 8 adds a few notes about applying Paint Style attributes to text, and Chapter 9 includes more examples of special effects that can be achieved using different Paint Style attributes. Chapter 11, "Printing," describes how color is handled in printing composites or color separations.

Chapter 7

Working with Graphics from Other Applications

6.0 NEW FEATURE

Illustrator 6 lets you use artwork and text created with other applications with much more flexibility than earlier versions. It also adds the ability to save Illustrator files in a variety of formats, so you can use artwork created with Illustrator in other applications that were not formerly supported.

You can use (open or import) artwork created by many different applications in an Illustrator document—determined only by whether the originating application can save artwork in any of the following common graphic file formats:

- ➤ Illustrator file formats (including those for previous versions)
- ➤ Encapsulated PostScript format (EPS)
- ➤ Macintosh Picture format (PICT)

➤ Tagged Image File format (TIFF)

➤ Adobe Photoshop 2.0 format (PSD)

➤ Acrobat Portable Document format (PDF)

➤ Photo CD format

➤ PostScript language print file format

➤ PC Paintbrush format (PCX)

NOTE

From applications that can save artwork in two or more file formats supported by Illustrator, choose the format that preserves the most detail—usually EPS format.

There are six ways of incorporating artwork created by other applications into Illustrator documents:

➤ You can use the clipboard to copy text from another application and paste the text into an Illustrator document.

➤ You can drag-and-drop objects from Adobe Photoshop into Illustrator (and vice versa).

➤ With certain other Adobe applications, such as Adobe Photoshop and Adobe Dimensions, you can also use the clipboard to copy selected paths into an Illustrator document.

➤ You can use **File > Open** to open a document created by another application, creating a new Adobe Illustrator document.

➤ You can use **File > Place** to incorporate the contents of a document created by another application into an Illustrator document. The imported file remains separate from the Illustrator document, but is linked to it.

➤ You can use **Edit > Publishing > Subscribe** to subscribe to a document created by an application that supports the Macintosh Publish and Subscribe facility.

You can also open Illustrator artwork in other applications by saving a document in one of these formats through the File > Save dialog box:

➤ Acrobat (PDF 1.1)

➤ Amiga IFF format

➤ BMP format

➤ Earlier versions of Illustrator (back to 1.0)

➤ Illustrator EPS

➤ PCX format

➤ Photoshop JPEG format

➤ Pixar format

➤ Targa format

Each of these ways of working between Illustrator and other applications is described in this chapter, including a description of the differences between file formats.

Some Significant Differences between Versions 5 and 6

Illustrator 6 introduces the ability to either **Open** or **Place** a wide variety of graphics file formats not supported by earlier versions. Two points in particular are worth noting:

➤ Formerly, the **File > Place Art** command changed to the **Import Text** command when a Type tool was selected and the text cursor positioned in the artwork. Now, the **Place** and **Import Text** commands hold two separate positions on the File menu—but the **Import Text** command is grayed unless a Type tool is selected and the text cursor positioned in the artwork.

➤ Some non-Illustrator graphics files can only be opened, some only placed (imported), and some either opened or placed. Whether it is best to open or place artwork created by another application depends on how you plan to use the artwork—see sidebar later in this chapter.

Types of Graphics Supported by Illustrator

Illustrator imports two basic kinds of graphics from other programs: *object-oriented* or *vector graphics* and *bitmap graphics*. Some graphic file formats contain only vector drawings or only bitmap images, but many can include both in the same file.

Figure 7.1 Example of a vector graphic (left) and a bitmap graphic (right).

The next sections describe the differences between these types of graphics. All of the graphics that you create with Illustrator's tools are of the first type. You can also create graphics of either type using other applications and import them into Illustrator.

NOTE

You cannot import true three-dimensional or animated graphics into Illustrator, but you can use applications such as Adobe Dimensions to create a three-dimensional look, and import the resulting artwork into Illustrator. Adobe Dimensions can also add a three-dimensional look to Illustrator-originated artwork—so you might move artwork from Illustrator into Dimensions and then back again.

There are a variety of sources of graphics outside Illustrator, each suited to particular types of graphics:

➤ Scanners can digitize photographs or line drawings that can be manipulated using software like Adobe Photoshop and PaintBrush. Scanned images can also be saved in a variety of formats that can be opened or placed in Illustrator.

➤ Paint-type programs such as Adobe Photoshop and Fractal Design Painter are best suited for working with digitized images and for creating "fine art" illustration—original artwork that is never modified or edited.

➤ PostScript-type drawing packages, like Adobe Illustrator, are best suited to line art and technical illustrations. These types of programs can also be used to create original artwork or trace existing digitized images.

Object-Oriented Graphics

Object-oriented graphics are stored as PICT or Encapsulated PostScript (EPS) formats and are composed of separate objects such as boxes, lines, and ellipses. Illustrator's built-in graphics are object-oriented graphics, and you can import object-oriented graphics from other programs. Object-oriented graphics are sometimes called *vector graphics* because the lines and patterns that you see are actually stored as mathematical formulas for the vectors composing the image. A *vector*, shown in the next figure, is a line defined by a starting point, a directional angle, and a length.

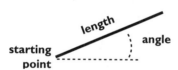

Figure 7.2 Example of a vector.

You can create object-oriented graphics in Illustrator or with drafting, draw, and spreadsheet programs. Programs that produce object-oriented graphics that can be placed in Illustrator include Adobe Illustrator, Macromedia FreeHand, Adobe Dimensions, ClarisDraw, or any application that creates PICT or Encapsulated PostScript (EPS) formats.

You can easily edit object-oriented graphics because you can change or move individual elements in the application that created them. (You cannot edit or move individual elements in imported graphics in Illustrator.) Because these vector graphics are defined mathematically, software can perform such operations as scaling and rotating without changing the quality of the artwork, and the program composes the graphic to match output resolution during the printing process, creating crisp line art and optimized gradient fill patterns. Most users, therefore, consider vector graphics better-quality images for line art and text than bitmap graphics.

PICT Format Graphics

Illustrator can open and import PICT files. PICT graphics can be opened as part of the artwork or as nonprinting templates that can then be traced with the Autotrace tool automatically (or traced manually with Illustrator's other drawing tools). You can also convert selected elements from an Illustrator document into PICT format and store them in the Clipboard by holding the **Option** key as you choose **Edit > Copy**—enabling you to **Paste** them into other applications that support PICT but not Illustrator's EPS format.

PICT is one of the most common graphic interchange formats for Macintosh applications. The first version of the PICT format, PICT 1, represents black-and-white vector and bitmap images with a fixed resolution of 72 dpi—the resolution of most Macintosh monitors.

The second and current version of the PICT file format, PICT 2, supports color vector and bitmap graphics that can have arbitrary resolutions and a bit depth of 1 or 8.

NOTE Illustrator cannot convert RGB bitmap images to CYMK images during printing. If you plan to separate your Illustrator document and you are using a PICT file that contains an RGB bitmap image, you must convert the RGB image to a CYMK image before you open or import the PICT file. If you receive a placed color image that only separates a black plate, it was probably saved in RGB mode and needs to be converted to CYMK.

NOTE If the entire PICT graphic is already a bitmap, you can convert to CYMK TIFF in Illustrator using the **Object > Rasterize** command, as described later in this chapter. You can also use this command on imported vector graphics, but it may change the quality of any embedded text and curved edges.

Figure 7.3 Graphics applications that create PICT file formats are usually restricted to geometrical shapes like ovals and rectangles, and they might offer a free-style drawing tool—but they don't offer the smooth Bezier curves available with PostScript language applications like Illustrator.

Encapsulated PostScript Format (EPS or EPSF)

Illustrator can open and place Encapsulated PostScript Format (EPS or EPSF) files. You can also save any Illustrator document in EPS format.

Encapsulated PostScript format files are a special variety of object-oriented graphics, designed to transfer PostScript language artwork between applications. Typically, EPS files represent single illustrations or tables that are placed on a host page, but an EPS file can also represent a complete page. Because they are based on the PostScript language, EPS files can contain both vector and bitmap graphics. And, like PostScript language files, early versions of EPS files contain only grayscale vector bitmap graphics while later versions support color graphics and compressed bitmap images.

Figure 7.4 Graphics applications that create EPS file formats usually offer the ability to draw smooth, editable Bezier curves of any shape.

In addition to the PostScript language representation of the graphics to be placed, many EPS files contain a preview bitmap representation of the graphic that an application can display. This preview bitmap is platform-specific. EPS files intended to be used by Macintosh applications, for example, contain PICT images for screen preview; those intended for use by Windows applications contain either TIFF or Windows Metafile bitmap images. Not all applications that create EPS files create preview images, however.

You can create Encapsulated PostScript (EPS) format files using drawing programs or by direct coding in the PostScript programming language. You can also create EPS versions of individual pages from page-layout applications such as PageMaker and QuarkXPress.

NOTE

You can use drawing applications on a PC to create graphics and save them in Encapsulated PostScript format. You can then transfer that EPS file as text from the PC to the Macintosh and place the graphics in Illustrator.

Other PostScript Language Files

Illustrator can open and import PostScript level 1 files created by any application running on any platform, and you can generate a PostScript language file from almost any application if you have a PostScript printer driver installed, by going through the Chooser as described in this section. Illustrator does not save PostScript files directly, but if you are using a PostScript printer, you can use the Print-to-file print option as described here to create a PostScript file.

NOTE

The first version of the PostScript file format, PostScript level 1, represents both grayscale vector graphics and grayscale bitmap images. The second version, PostScript level 2, represents color as well as grayscale vector and bitmap images, and supports RGB, CYMK, and CIE-based color models for both vector and bitmap graphics. (Some PostScript level 1 files also represent color with extensions to the PostScript language that were generalized in PostScript level 2.) PostScript level 2 also supports a number of compression techniques for bitmap images, including LZW, CCITT, and JPEG methods.

PostScript is a page-description language that is built into many desktop printers and virtually all high-end printing systems. Because it is built into so many printers, most Macintosh, Windows, and UNIX applications can create PostScript files for printing. Adobe recommends that you create PostScript files with the Apple LaserWriter 8 or Adobe PostScript printer driver. The following instructions assume you are using one of these printer drivers. Illustrator's Print dialog box is used in the example, but other applications that support PostScript printing should offer similar options.

To create a PostScript file that you can open or import with Illustrator:

1. Open the Chooser from the Apple menu, and choose a PostScript printer.

2. Open the document containing the page you want to open or import.

3. Choose **File > Print**.

4. If you are using an application that creates multi-page documents, enter the number of the page you want to use in both the From and To boxes.

5. Select **File** as the destination.

6. Select from the three pop-up menu options:

   ➤ **Output**—Composite or Separation. The **Separation** option requires Separation Setup, accessed through the option button in the lower-right corner of the Print dialog box.

   ➤ **Level 1 or Level 2 PostScript** (see earlier descriptions).

   ➤ **ASCII or Binary format**. Data-encoding affects size—a binary image file is half the size of an ASCII image file and takes half the time to transmit, if you are printing through a network. Both AppleTalk and Ethernet support binary transmissions, but check with your service bureau to see what their system will support—many PC systems do not support binary data transmissions.

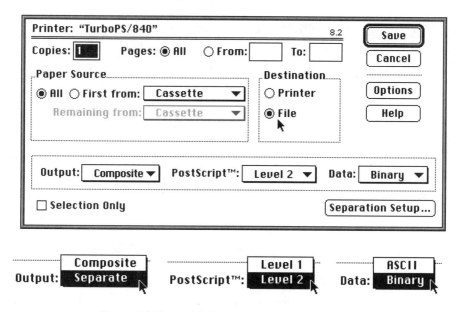

Figure 7.5 Illustrator's Print dialog box with **File** selected.

7. Click **Save** to display the Save PostScript file dialog box.

8. Select the disk and folder where you want to save the PostScript file and enter a name for the file. Conventionally, PostScript filenames end with **.ps** (for example, **Logo.ps**).

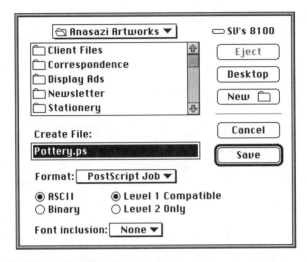

Figure 7.6 Illustrator's PostScript file dialog box offers additional Format and Font Inclusion options.

9. Select from the following options:

➤ Format options—If you will be opening and printing an Illustrator file containing placed images exclusively from Adobe Illustrator, you can save the file in **PostScript Job** format. This gives you the most compact file format. If you will be opening or printing an Illustrator file with placed images at some other time within another application, you should save the Illustrator file with one of the following Format options: **EPS No Preview**, **EPS Mac Standard Preview**, or **EPS Mac Enhanced Preview**. (Using the first option will give you no preview in the other application but the all color and other information will still be embedded in the document.)

➤ Select the **Level 1 Compatible** option for maximum flexibility.

➤ Font Inclusion—Select **None, All, All But Standard 13**, or **All But Fonts in PPD File**, depending on whether you will be using this file on the same or a similar system or sending it to another system that might not have the required fonts.

10. Click **Save**.

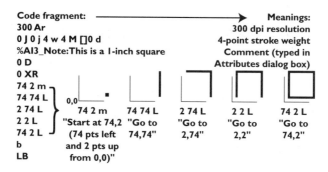

Figure 7.7 An example of PostScript codes that draw a rectangle.

See Chapter 11 for more information on creating a PostScript file specifically for printing.

PDF FILE FORMAT

Illustrator can open and import any page in a PDF file, including vector artwork and bitmap images. You can save any Illustrator document as a PDF file. You can also use Illustrator to make changes to individual PDF pages of PDF files.

The PDF file format is the Acrobat document format. Based on the PostScript level 2 language, PDF can represent both vector and bitmap graphics in both color and grayscale. For the purposes of representing pages, PDF pages are identical to PostScript pages, but PDF files also contain electronic document search and navigation features; for example, PDF files can contain hypertext links and an electronic table of contents.

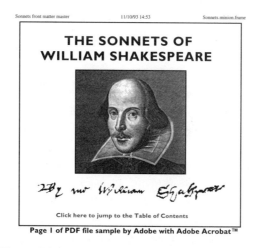

Figure 7.8 An example of a page from a PDF document.

Displaying Vector Graphics

Computer displays and printers are called *raster devices* because they present information with a *raster*, or grid of dots. The raster is a sequence of lines, and each line is a row of dots called *pixels* (picture elements). Raster devices can be characterized by their resolution in dots-per-inch (dpi). Many Macintosh monitors, for example, display information at 72 dpi, while most laser printers print information at 300 or 600 dpi.

Because vector artwork is represented mathematically as lines and shapes, software must convert vector artwork to pixels to display the artwork on a monitor or to print the artwork on a printer. Converting vector artwork to pixels is called *rasterizing* the artwork.

When software rasterizes vector artwork, it uses the resolution of the display or printer for the output raster. This means that higher-resolution devices, which have more dots per inch than lower resolution devices, produce finer artwork. A small vector circle that appears rough and jagged on a 72-dpi monitor, for example, appears smooth when printed on a 600-dpi printer.

Bitmap Graphics

Bitmap graphics are composed of a pattern of dots, or *pixels*, rather than separate *objects*—though your eye might see boxes and circles, the program sees only dots. This type of graphic comes from paint-type programs, such as ClarisWorks, MacPaint, Fractal Design Painter, and Photoshop. Figure 7.9 shows a bitmap graphic drawn with Fractal Design Painter.

Because bitmap images consist of dots rather than whole objects, you cannot easily break bitmap images into separate elements like boxes, circles, and lines. Bitmap formats do not usually *layer* objects one above the other as Illustrator does. When you draw a circle on top of a square, for example, intersecting dots that compose the circle actually *replace* the dots that composed the square.

Bitmap images are not smooth like vector graphics when printed. Bitmap graphics, therefore, are generally considered inferior to vector graphics for most line art and any text. Bitmap images, however, are superior for scanned images and for fine art images that call for air-brush effects.

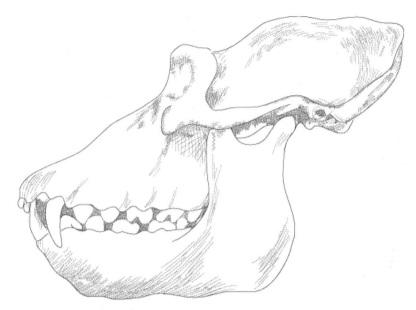

Figure 7.9 A bitmap image drawn with Fractal Design Painter.

N O T E

Use object-oriented graphics rather than bitmap graphics for line art whenever possible. Bitmap graphics have a jagged appearance and take much longer to print. When bitmap graphics are required, do not include text in the file in the paint program. Place the graphic portion in Illustrator and use Illustrator's Type tool to add captions and labels.

Some bitmap graphics may seem distorted on-screen, but they print well if the original graphic was not distorted.

PC PAINTBRUSH FILE FORMAT (PCX)

Illustrator can open and import PCX files. You can also save an Illustrator document as a PCX file.

PCX is a bitmap image file format that is supported by many Windows applications. PCX supports the RLE compression method. Images can have a bit depth of 1, 4, 8, or 24. Version 5 PCX files support a custom color palette, but version 3 PCX files do not. When you open or import a version 3 PCX file, Illustrator uses the VGA color palette.

N O T E

Because PCX files contain RGB images, you cannot use a PCX image in a document that you plan to separate. You can, however, use a program such as Adobe Photoshop to convert the PCX image to a CYMK TIFF or EPS image that can be separated. You can also use the **Object > Rasterize** command in Illustrator 6 to create a CYMK TIFF of any graphic.

343

A Bit of Information...

A 500K 1-bit graphic becomes a 4MB graphic when converted to grayscale! Why? Bitmap graphics are characterized by their *bit depth*—how many bits per pixel they store.

A 1-bit (per pixel) graphic is also called *black-and-white*. A pixel (dot) is either black or white (empty). One-bit bitmap graphics are transparent in Illustrator—you can see through the "white" areas to whatever is below them. You can work this to your advantage by saving or converting imported bitmaps to 1-bit black-and-white images if you want the transparent effect, or you can convert the images to grayscale and eliminate the transparency.

Grayscale images have depths of both 4 and 8. Four-bit (per pixel) bitmaps can produce up to 16 shades of gray—each bit can be either on or off, so the number of possibilities is 2 X 2 X 2 X 2. This is a simple formula to a statistician, but you can list the possibilities yourself: 0000, 0001, 0010, 0011, 0100, 0101, 0110, 0111, 1000, 1001, 1010, 1011, 1100, 1101, 1110, 1111. There are 16 ways of storing 4 on-off bits!

An 8-bit (per pixel) bitmap can produce up to 256 shades of gray (2 X 2 X 2 X 2 X 2 X 2 X 2 X 2).

Color images can have bit depths of 4, 8, 16, and 24. A 4-bit color image has 16 colors, an 8-bit image has 256 colors, a 16-bit image has thousands of colors, and a 24-bit image has millions of colors. You can try listing the possibilities yourself, starting with 00000000...

These formulas might help you see why some bitmap graphics take up so much more space than others that might print at the same size. If there are 72 pixels per inch (an average monitor's resolution), a one-inch square 1-bit (per pixel) bitmap image will require only 5K of storage (72 X 72 = 5,184), but the same image will require 20K if saved or scanned with 16 shades of gray, or 40K with 256 shades of gray, or 120K in 24-bit color.

Because bitmap images can require so much storage, many techniques have been developed for compressing image data to reduce storage requirements, and they are distinguished by whether they remove detail from the image.

WINDOW BITMAP FILE FORMAT (BMP)

You can save an Illustrator document as a BMP file, and you can save selected portions of an Illustrator document as a BMP file. BMP is a bitmap image file format that is supported by many Windows applications, and it supports the RLE compression method. Images can have a bit depth of 1, 4, 8, or 24.

When you save a BMP file, you must specify whether the file is saved in the Windows or OS/2 format, and whether the image is saved with a bit depth of 1 or 24.

COMPUSERVE GRAPHICS INTERCHANGE FORMAT (GIF)

The CompuServe GIF format is a bitmap image file format that is used extensively on both the CompuServe network and the World Wide Web. GIF images can have a bit depth from 1 to 8. The GIF format supports LZW compression. When you save a GIF file, you must specify a bit depth of from 1 to 8.

Illustrator cannot open or import GIF files.

TIFF IMAGES

Illustrator can open and import any version of a TIFF (tagged image file format) image. The TIFF format is bitmapped but enables higher resolutions than most other bitmap formats.

TIFF is a flexible bitmap image format that is supported by virtually all paint, image-editing, and page-layout applications. Also, virtually all desktop scanners can produce TIFF images. Early versions of the TIFF format supported only uncompressed black-and-white images, but the most recent version supports up to 24-bit RGB, CYMK, and YCbCr color images, and both the LZW and JPEG compression methods. The latest version also supports multi-page images, although such images are rare.

SCANNED IMAGES

Scanned images are also bitmap images, but the latest scanning applications enable you to store images in your choice of graphic format. These can include formats supported by Illustrator: PICT, EPS, or TIFF.

You can edit images in a paint program or in a program that enables you to edit scanned image files before inserting the files into Illustrator. You also can use Adobe Photoshop for adjusting gray and color values in scanned images saved as

TIFFs, and for creating special effects. In addition, some of Photoshop's effects are now available directly in Illustrator, as described later in this chapter.

You can scan line art, such as a graphic logo, and save it in PICT or EPS format. These are object-oriented formats, but the scanned image is not stored as layered elements or as separate, editable objects as they would be if you created the logo from scratch (using an object-oriented drawing application).

You can scan continuous-tone images, such as photographs or artwork created with brushes or charcoals, and save them in TIFF or PICT or EPS format. Good-quality scanned photographs can look like halftones when printed, even though the images may look coarse on your low-resolution screen or draft printer.

Most scanning software lets you choose between *line art*, *halftone*, and *grayscale*. It's a good idea to choose **Line Art** (for black-and-white images) or **Grayscale** (for images with shades of gray). Halftone scanning sets up halftone dots at scan time, so they often create moiré patterns when scaled.

NOTE

Figure 7.10 A scanned image saved as (left to right): a PICT file, an EPS, black-and-white line art, a halftone, and a TIFF image.

If the placed image was created in a bitmapped or pixel-based application like Adobe Photoshop, the resolution set in the original application will stay with the image. You will not have the resolution-independent scaling you get with Illustrator's vector-based images. Consequently, scaling up artwork will result in bitmapped, and possibly jagged, placed images.

NOTE

Choosing Scanning Settings (Grayscales, Resolution, and Size)

You can save 1-bit black-and-white line art in TIFF format at the highest resolution you like—usually the same as the resolution of the final printer. One-bit graphics files are usually small (and will stay small so long as you don't change them to grayscale images).

You can conserve disk storage space and shorten printing time by saving grayscale images at fewer levels of gray, lower resolutions, and cropping and reducing them at the scanning stage rather than scaling them in Illustrator. For example, an image saved at 72 dpi can offer acceptable results when printed on a 300 dpi printer. Using higher resolutions will not provide better printed results and may result in longer printing times. For high-resolution imagesetters, you need to save the image at 100 dpi or more when printing at 1200 dpi, or 300 or more when printing at 2400 dpi or more.

The number of resolutions and gray levels you have to choose from will be limited by the scanning device and printer you are using, but you can use two formulas to determine roughly what to look for, then choose the option that equals your target or higher.

The optimum number of *gray levels* needed can be determined by the formula:

(Printer resolution (dpi)/Final Screen Frequency (lpi))^2

Resolution on a scanner refers to the number of data "samples" taken per inch (spi) or pixels per inch (ppi), but these measures are not related not the number of dots per inch (dpi) set for the printer. The optimum *scanning resolution* is determined by the screen frequency you'll use for the final reproduction of your document. A good formula to use is:

Scanning Resolution (spi) = 2 X Final Screen Frequency (lpi)

The image may seem rough on low-resolution screens but should look better when printed (see Figure 7.11). Line screens for a 300 dpi desktop printer are typically set at 53–60 lpi; line screens for high-resolution imagesetters are usually between 90 and 150 lpi. This means that you should scan at about 100 spi or ppi

(2×50) if your final printer will be at 300 dpi resolution, or at 300 spi (2×150) if your final masters will be imageset.

It's a good idea to test this yourself by saving a sample scan at various resolutions and printing it on the final printer before doing all the scans for a heavily illustrated publication.

Figure 7.11 Scanned images at 72 and 300 dots per inch.

If you are only proofing to a 300 dpi printer, and will later be printing to a higher lpi device, use the resolution appropriate for the higher device.

NOTE

Pasting from Other Applications

You can use the standard Macintosh **Copy** and **Paste** commands and go through the clipboard to copy some graphics and most text formats from other applications into Illustrator. Special considerations in using these commands are described under the next headings.

Pasting Graphics from Other Applications

You can copy selected paths from Adobe Photoshop, Adobe Streamline, Adobe Dimensions, and Adobe Premiere to an Illustrator document.

1. Open the Adobe Photoshop, Adobe Streamline, Adobe Dimensions, or Adobe Premiere document containing the artwork you want to copy and select the vector artwork.

2. Choose **Edit > Copy**.

3. Open the Adobe Illustrator document into which you want to copy the artwork.

4. Choose **Edit > Paste**.

NOTE

Some file formats that cannot be pasted through the Clipboard can instead be opened or placed as described later in this chapter.

PostScript and the Clipboard

When you cut or copy a selection, the selection is placed onto the Clipboard. You can use the Clipboard to copy a selection as either a PostScript language description or as a bitmap PICT image. You can paste PostScript language descriptions in many Adobe applications, such as Adobe Photoshop and Adobe Dimensions. You can paste bitmap PICT images in most Macintosh applications.

To copy a PostScript language description to the Clipboard:

1. Select the object or objects you want to copy in Illustrator.

2. Choose **Edit > Copy**.

To copy Illustrator artwork as a bitmap PICT image to the Clipboard:

1. Select the object or objects you want to copy in Illustrator.

2. Press the **Option** key and choose **Edit > Copy**.

Copying Text through the Clipboard

You can use the clipboard to copy text from any application that creates text.

1. Use any text-handling application to open the document containing the text you want to copy, and select the text using the methods of that application.

2. Choose **Edit > Copy**.

3. Open the Adobe Illustrator document into which you want to copy the text.

4. Select a Type tool and either create a new text block or place the insertion cursor in an existing text block, on a path (for Path text), or inside a graphic (for Area text).

5. Choose **Edit > Paste**.

The text is imported, but special formatting may be lost.

NOTE

Drag and Drop from Photoshop

Illustrator 6.0 supports the drag-and-drop feature between Illustrator and Photoshop: you can select a Photoshop image, or part of it, in Photoshop and simply drag it across to an open Illustrator window. This has the same result as if you imported the file with the **Place** command. You can do this with the Photoshop file in any format.

Pasting vs. Opening vs. Placing Art into Illustrator

Some graphics applications may afford the options of either Pasting, Opening, or Placing the artwork they create into Illustrator. Here are some of the considerations that can help you decide which option to use.

➤ When copying/pasting or using the drag-and-drop feature, you can select only a portion of a graphic document and bring it into Illustrator. The **Open** and **Place** commands force you to use the entire graphic document.

> ➤ When you use the **File > Open** command, the opened document actually becomes a new Illustrator document. You can add more artwork through Illustrator. Any changes you make to the opened artwork will affect the original source, unless you use the **File > Save As** command to save it under a new name.

> ➤ When you use the **File > Place** command, the graphic is added to the open Illustrator document. Non-EPS formats are included as part of the Illustrator file, but EPS graphics remain linked to the original file. Placed EPS documents remain separate files and any changes you make to the placed document are automatically reflected in the Illustrator document.

Notice that the originating application for any given graphics format can vary. For example, scans, as well as files from Photoshop, FreeHand, Cricket Draw, PageMaker, Pixel Paint, and other applications, may be saved in formats supported by Illustrator.

Opening Graphic Files as Illustrator Artwork

6.0 NEW FEATURE

Adobe Illustrator 6 introduces the ability to import graphics files in a wide variety of format files—such as those created or saved in ClarisDraw, Canvas, MacPaint, Photoshop, or scanning applications—and convert them to Encapsulated PostScript Format (EPSF) images. When you open a document created by another application, you create a new untitled Adobe Illustrator document. Graphic elements in the document you open are converted to Illustrator objects that (in some cases) you can manipulate and modify with Illustrator tools.

To open artwork created by another application:

1. Choose **File > Open** (**Command+O**) from the Illustrator menu.

2. Click **Show All Files** if you want all file names to be listed, or deselect this option to see only the names of files that can be imported into Illustrator.

N O T E

If you don't see the name of the file you want to open when Show All Files is dese-lected, the file might be stored in a format that Illustrator cannot open.

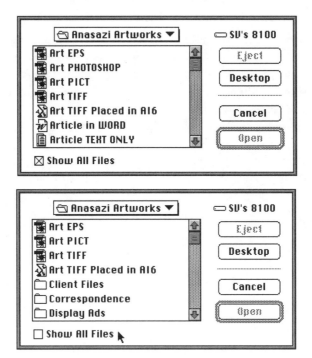

Figure 7.12 Open dialog box showing all files (top) and Illustrator-compatible files only (bottom).

3. Locate and select the document you want to open.

4. Click **Open**.

➤ If the selected file is in PICT format, a second dialog box is displayed asking if you want to open the file as an Illustrator template (i.e., an image that can be seen on-screen and traced but not printed or manipulated), or as a PICT file (converted to PostScript format).

➤ If the selected file is not already an Illustrator document, the artwork is converted to the Adobe Illustrator Format and appears in a new window. Additional dialog boxes may be displayed, depending on the file type (see next headings).

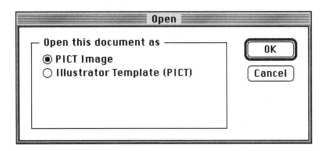

Figure 7.13 Second dialog box displayed when you open a PICT file format.

NOTE

Illustrator cannot convert RGB bitmap images to CYMK images during printing. If you plan to separate your Illustrator document and you are using EPS or PICT or TIFF files that contain an RGB bitmap image, you must convert the RGB image to a CYMK image before you open or import the PICT file.

NOTE

If the RGB image is already a bitmap, you can convert to a CYMK TIFF in Illustrator using the **Object > Rasterize** command, as described later in this chapter. You can also use this command on imported vector graphics, but it may change the quality of any embedded text and curved edges.

Trapping Placed Images

When an image is placed within Illustrator it acts like a filled object. Placed images will always knock out objects or colors layered beneath them. You can create a choke trap against a placed image by creating a rectangle around the placed image. Paint the rectangle with a Fill of None and stroke with the color you want to trap. If your placed image is a halftone or has blends and/or is placed above a halftone or blend, you should probably place a keyline around the image instead of trapping.

Opening or Importing EPS Files

➤ When you open or import an EPS file, spot colors are converted to process color. Also the overprint attribute is lost.

➤ When you open, import, or place an EPS file created by another application that uses fonts not installed in your system, Adobe Illustrator gives no indication that the fonts are not available. Unless you are using SuperATM, Courier will be used for the missing fonts when you print. If you are using SuperATM, it will create substitutes for the missing fonts when you print.

➤ When you place an EPS file without a preview image, or with a TIFF or Windows Metafile preview image, Illustrator displays a box with an **X** to represent the EPS artwork.

➤ You can also choose not to display EPS preview images in Artwork view by clearing the Show Placed EPS option in the Document Setup dialog box. When this option is cleared, EPS images are also displayed as a boxes with an **X**.

Opening or Importing Other PostScript Language Files

➤ Illustrator can open and import PostScript level 1 files created by any application running on any platform. If you open or import a multi-page PostScript file, however, Illustrator opens or imports only the first page.

➤ When you open or import a PostScript file, spot colors are converted to process color. Also, the overprint attribute is lost.

Opening or Importing PICT Files

➤ When you open or import a PICT file that contains vector artwork, the elements of the artwork are converted to Illustrator objects. You can then use the Illustrator tools to modify the converted artwork.

Opening and Importing TIFF Files

➤ If you open or import, a black-and-white (i.e., 1-bit) TIFF image, you can change all the black pixels to a color by choosing a color for the Fill attribute through the Paint Style palette. You cannot change the colors of grayscale or color TIFFs.

Ohwl as an eps file

Figure 7.14 Imported black-and-white TIFF (left), changed to a lighter color in Illustrator (right).

➤ If you open or import a multi-page TIFF image, Illustrator opens or imports only the first page.

➤ You can save an Illustrator document as a TIFF file.

PC Paintbrush file format (PCX)

➤ When you open or import a version 3 PCX file, Illustrator uses the VGA color palette.

➤ Because PCX files contain RGB images, you cannot use a PCX image in a document that you plan to separate unless you use a program such as Adobe Photoshop to convert the PCX image to a CYMK TIFF image that can be separated.

You can convert to CYMK TIFF in Illustrator using the **Object > Rasterize** command, as described later in this chapter.

NOTE

Importing PDF Files

➤ When you open or import a PDF file, you must specify which page you want to use.

Importing Photoshop Files

➤ You can open or import a file saved in native Photoshop 2.5 (or later) format, but native Photoshop-format files from earlier versions cannot be opened or placed.

Importing Documents from Other Applications

The **File > Place** command imports any graphics file saved in the wide variety of formats supported by Illustrator 6. This includes most of the formats described at the beginning of this chapter and in the previous sections.

NOTE

If you don't see the name of the file you want to open when Show All Files is deselected, the file might be stored in a format that Illustrator cannot import—including native Illustrator files that can be *opened* but not *placed*.

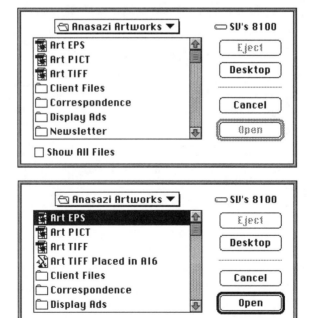

Figure 7.15 Files listed in Place dialog box (top) may differ from those in Open dialog box (bottom) when Show All Files is not selected.

When you place any graphics file, you create a link between the Illustrator document and the separate file. You can position the placed artwork anywhere on the page, and you can apply transformation attributes, such as scaling and rotating, but you cannot otherwise change the placed artwork. It remains a separate file that is owned by the application that created it. Whenever a placed EPS graphics file is modified by the application that created it, those changes are automatically reflected in the Illustrator document.

To place a graphics file into an Illustrator document:

1. Open the Illustrator document into which you want to place the graphics file.

2. Choose **File > Place** to display the Place dialog box, which lists all files on the selected disk that are in formats supported by Illustrator, as shown in Figure 7.16.

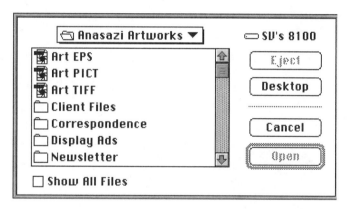

Figure 7.16 The Place dialog box.

3. To select a file, scroll through the file list to locate the desired file name, click on the name, and then click the **Place** button, or double-click on the file name.

An outlined box appears. If it is an EPS graphic, the box shows diagonal lines crossing from corner to corner. This box defines the artwork's dimensions. The box is placed into the center of the active window, in front of all other artwork on the active layer in your document, and is selected.

It's a good idea to select the layer onto which you wish to place the imported art, either in this step or after importing the art. See the description of the Layers palette in Chapter 10.

N O T E

357

4. You can move or manipulate imported graphics as single objects with any of Illustrator's transformation tools (Scale, Rotate, Reflect, or Shear), but you cannot change the strokes of lines or of fill patterns or otherwise make detailed edits to the graphic. You cannot adjust any of its anchor points, segments, or paths or use the Object or Type menu commands. The image box always remains a parallelogram, even if you transform it. Imported graphics can be masked, but they cannot be made into patterns.

5. If a placed EPS file has a preview image, you can see it in Preview view. You can also control how imported images display in Artwork mode using the **Show Placed EPS** option in the File > Document Setup dialog box. When this option is turned off, imported EPS images display as a box with an **x** in the center in Artwork view, but they Preview correctly. When **Show Placed EPS** is turned on, a preview image appears inside the box in Artwork view as well as in Preview mode.

NOTE

Displaying preview images of placed EPS files in the Artwork view slows the display of your Illustrator document.

 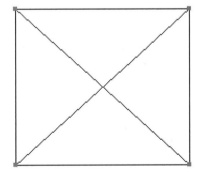

Figure 7.17 Imported EPS graphic in Artwork view with Show Placed EPS on (left), and off (right).

WARNING

Illustrator will need to refer to the original EPS files whenever you open or print the document. Selecting the Include placed images option in the File > Save As dialog box affects only saved as EPS files that are brought into another application for printing—Illustrator will still look for the placed EPS graphics when you open the file. Placed images cannot be edited in detail, so it's usually a good idea to keep a copy of the original EPS file in the same folder with your artwork.

Editing Imported EPS Graphics

When you make changes to a placed EPS file, the changes are automatically applied to the Illustrator documents that contain the placed file.

To edit a placed EPS file:

1. Start the application that originally created the placed EPS file and open the original artwork file.

2. Edit the image. When you have finished, save the document as an EPS file. Save the file with the same name and in the same location as the placed EPS file you want to replace.

3. Start Adobe Illustrator and open the document containing the placed EPS file. The Illustrator document now contains the edited artwork.

Replacing Imported EPS Graphics That Have Been Transformed

If your document contains a placed EPS file to which you have applied transformation attributes (such as scaling, rotating, reflecting, or shearing), you can replace that EPS file with another EPS file and automatically apply the transformation attributes to the new placed file. For example, if a placed EPS file has been scaled by 50%, you can replace it with another EPS file and the new EPS file is automatically scaled at 50%.

To replace placed artwork and apply transformation attributes:

1. Select the placed artwork that you want to replace.

2. Choose **File > Place EPS**.

3. Select a new EPS file, and click **Place**. A dialog box appears asking if you want to replace the currently selected image.

Figure 7.18 Dialog box asking if you want to replace the selected graphic.

4. Click **Replace**. The new EPS file appears in the Illustrator document with the same transformation attributes as the original.

If the dimensions of new EPS file are larger or smaller than the original, the new EPS file might need to be resized to fit your illustration.

N O T E

Finding the Disk Location of Placed EPS Artwork

Before you can move or edit a placed EPS file, you have to know where the file is located. If you don't know, you can use the **Attributes** command to display the location of a single placed EPS file. You can also produce a report that lists the locations of all the placed files in an Illustrator document.

To determine the location of a placed EPS file:

1. Select the placed artwork.

2. Choose **Object > Attributes** or **File > Selection Info**.

3. Use the Location of Placed Art pop-up menu to display the location of the placed image.

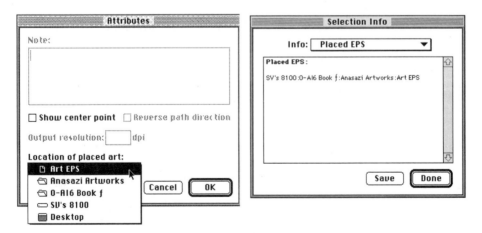

Figure 7.19 Location of imported EPS image shows in pop-up menu of Attributes dialog box (left), or in Selection Info dialog box (right).

To determine the location of all the placed files in an Illustrator document:

1. Click away from all artwork to deselect it.

2. Choose **File > Document Info**.

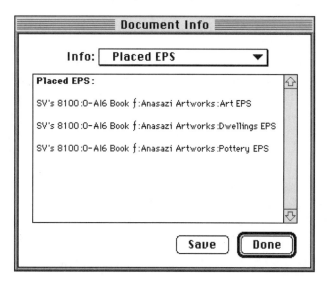

Figure 7.20 Document Info dialog box shows location of all imported EPS graphics.

3. If you want to save the information as text, click **Save**.

4. Select a folder and name for the Document Info text file and click **Save**.

5. You can import the Document Info text file into Illustrator as text, or open it with TeachText or any word processing program. The Placed Art section lists the locations of all the placed EPS files.

Moving Adobe Illustrator Documents Containing Imported EPS Artwork

When you move an Illustrator document that contains placed EPS artwork, you must either move the files containing the placed artwork, or re-link the placed artwork the next time you open the Illustrator document.

If you plan on moving an Adobe Illustrator document that contains placed EPS artwork, it is usually a good idea to store the document and the placed artwork files in the same folder. You can then move the document by moving the folder and Illustrator won't ask you to locate the placed EPS files when you open the document.

Exporting Illustrator Documents Containing Imported EPS Artwork

If you will be opening or printing an Illustrator file containing placed images exclusively from Adobe Illustrator, you can save the file in native Illustrator format (with your choice of version compatibility). This gives you the most compact file format. If you will be opening or printing an Illustrator file with placed EPS images at some other time within another application, you should save the Illustrator file in EPS format. When you choose this option, an **Include Placed EPS Images** check box will become available.

When you use an Illustrator document that contains placed EPS artwork in another application, such as a page layout program, you must embed the placed artwork in the Illustrator document. Unless the placed artwork is included in the Illustrator document, the other application cannot print the placed artwork.

To include placed EPS artwork in an Illustrator document:

1. Open the Illustrator document containing placed artwork.

2. Choose **File > Save As**.

3. Choose **EPS** from the Format pop-up menu, and click **Save**.

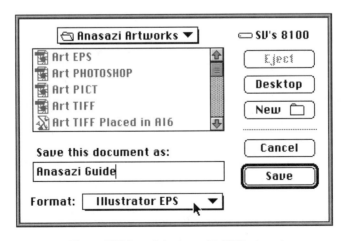

Figure 7.21 Save dialog box with **EPS** selected.

4. In the EPS Format dialog box, select the **Include Placed EPS Files** option, as well as any other options you want to use:

➤ Save EPS files with older Illustrator version-compatibility if you will be importing the EPS file into applications that do not support Illustrator 6.0 features. Choosing older versions may disable some editing features if you reopen the file using version 6.0.

➤ In the Preview options, None will give you no preview in the other application but all color and other information will still be embedded in the document. One-bit options will give you black-and-white preview, and the 8-bit options will give you color and grayscale options.

➤ Select **Include Document Thumbnails** if you want to be able to preview the artwork before you open it from applications that support the preview feature.

➤ Enter Fetch Information for easy retrieval using Fetch's search features.

5. Click **Save**. The file is saved with your Adobe Illustrator artwork.

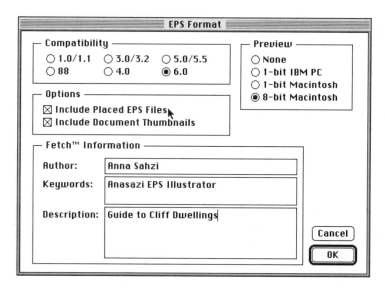

Figure 7.22 EPS Format options.

NOTE **Include Placed EPS Files** is for the benefit of other applications only. If you will be reopening a file with placed images in Illustrator, you must still have the original source files for placed images available regardless of whether **Include Placed EPS Files** is checked. When you open an Illustrator document that was saved with placed artwork included, Illustrator asks you to re-link the placed EPS files.

Importing Text

You can import formatted text from many different applications. Adobe Illustrator uses the Claris XTND document format translators to import text from word processor and page layout applications. You can import text from any document type for which an XTND translator has been installed. The Adobe Illustrator includes translators for MacWrite, Microsoft Word, WordPerfect, Microsoft Rich Text Format (RTF), and Write Now.

To import text with the **Import** command:

1. Select a Type tool and either create a new text block or place the insertion cursor in an existing text block where you want to import the text.

2. Choose **File > Import Text**.

3. Locate and select the document containing the text you want to import.

NOTE

If you don't see the name of the file you want to import in the folder where it is stored, the file is stored in a format for which you do not have an XTND translator.

4. Click **Import**.

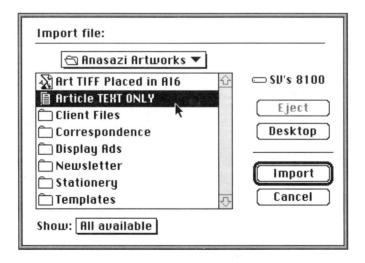

Figure 7.23 Import Text dialog box.

Using the Publish and Subscribe Features of System 7

In addition to using the **Cut, Copy**, and **Paste** commands or the **Open** or **Place** commands to include elements from other applications in Illustrator documents, you can use System 7's Publish and Subscribe features, accessed through the commands on the **Edit > Publishing** submenu in Illustrator.

➤ The **Create Publisher** command lets you create or *publish* objects that other applications can import or *subscribe* to. The material in the publisher is actually saved as a separate file called an *edition*.

➤ The **Subscribe to** command imports such objects—editions—created by Illustrator or by other applications.

The advantage of using System 7's Publisher/Subscriber feature is that objects imported through this option are automatically updated in the Illustrator document when they are updated by the originating application. Similarly, Illustrator graphics that are created as *editions* through the **Create Publisher** command will be automatically updated in other applications that subscribe to that edition when the original artwork is updated through Illustrator.

NOTE

This feature is especially useful when you intend to use the same artwork in several documents, and update it through one document. The updates will carry through a whole network when the publisher edition is stored on the network and the subscribing documents are on the network or on local workstations.

Figure 7.24 The Edit > Publishing submenu.

NOTE

Automatic updating is available only in applications that support this feature of System 7, by including **Publisher** and **Subscriber** commands such as those described here.

Publishing an Illustrator Document

The **Edit > Publishing > Create Publisher** command copies selected objects into a special document called an *edition* that is updated whenever the original is changed.

1. Create and select the object(s) you want to make into a publisher.

2. Choose **Edit > Publishing > Create Publisher** to display the Create Publisher dialog box.

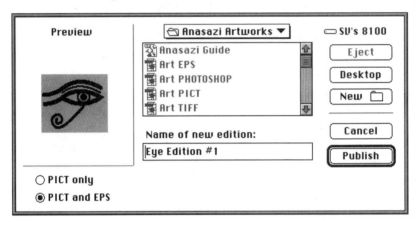

Figure 7.25 The Create Publisher dialog box.

3. Select the file format in which you want to save your artwork, either **PICT only**, or **PICT and EPS**.

NOTE You can publish your artwork as a PICT file, containing a PostScript language resource for printing, or as a combination PICT and EPS file. If the file is being subscribed to by an application that is compatible with the EPS format, such as Adobe Illustrator, save the file as PICT and EPS. If the subscribing application is not EPS compatible, save the file as PICT only.

4. Type the name for the edition that you wish to create. Locate the target disk and directory using the same techniques as described for the Open dialog box under **File > Open**, in Chapter 10.

5. Click **Publish** or press **Return** to close the dialog box and save the edition.

6. To use the edition in another Illustrator document or in another application, open the target document and use the **Subscribe to** command as described next (or its equivalent in another application that supports this feature).

Whenever you modify the artwork that was saved as an edition, it will be updated automatically in all other documents that subscribe to it (unless the automatic update option has been turned off in the subscriber document).

The edition becomes a file on the desktop. If you want to update the edition, you can open it by double-clicking the icon to display a window that shows the contents of the edition and offers the option of opening the publisher—the Illustrator document, in this case. You also automatically update the edition whenever you update the original artwork directly through Illustrator.

Subscribing to an Edition

The **Edit > Publishing > Subscribe to** command displays a dialog box that lets you select and insert an edition in the Illustrator artwork.

1. Create an edition as described under **Edit > Publishing > Create Publisher** (or using a similar command in another application).

2. Open the Illustrator document into which you wish to insert the edition, and select the layer onto which you wish to insert the edition.

NOTE

It's a good idea to select the layer onto which you wish to place the imported edition, either in this step or after importing the object. See the description of the Layers palette in Chapter 10.

3. Choose **Edit > Publishing > Subscribe to** to display the Subscribe to dialog box.

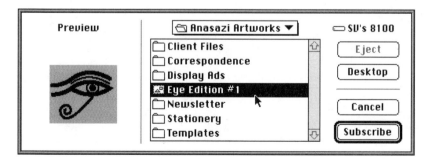

Figure 7.26 The Subscribe to dialog box.

4. Use the techniques described for the Open dialog box (under **File > Open**, in Chapter 10) to locate the edition you want, and click once on the name to display it in the preview window before clicking **Subscribe**, or simply double-click to import it without previewing it.

5. Position the imported object where you want it in the artwork.

6. With the imported edition selected, you can modify the Publisher Options as described next.

Setting Publisher Options

The **Edit > Publishing > Publisher Options** command lets you select timing of updates, locate files, modify files, and cancel updating options for publishers and subscribers created by the two preceding commands (or similar commands in other applications).

1. Select the Illustrator object(s) that have been made into a publisher (using **Edit > Publishing > Create Publisher**), or an object that has been imported into Illustrator using **Edit > Publishing > Subscribe to**.

2. Choose **Edit > Publishing > Publisher Options** to display the Publisher Options dialog box (if you have selected original artwork in Illustrator that was made into a publisher) or the Subscriber Options dialog box (if you have selected an imported edition).

3. If the Publisher Options dialog box is displayed, make the entries described in this step as appropriate. Other wise, go to Step 4.

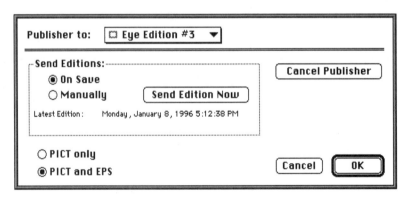

Figure 7.27 The Publisher Options dialog box.

➤ Verify that the edition name shown at the top of the dialog box is the one you intend to affect. A pop-up list shows the disk and directory where the edition is stored. A line below the **Send Edition Now** button shows the date and time the edition was last modified or saved.

➤ You can set the edition to always be sent (updated) **On Save**—whenever you save the Illustrator artwork—or **Manually**. If you select the manual option, then you need to open this dialog box and click **Send Edition Now** whenever you change the artwork and want to update the edition.

➤ Select the file format in which to update the edition, either **PICT only** or **PICT and EPS**.

➤ Click **Cancel Publisher** to remove the object's designation as a publisher. Changes made to the artwork will no longer be reflected in other documents that have subscribed to it, but the original artwork will remain in the subscriber documents.

4. If the Subscriber Options dialog box is displayed, make the entries described in this step as appropriate.

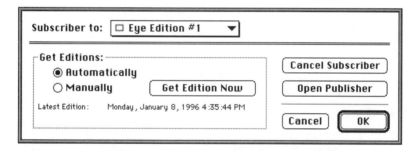

Figure 7.28 The Subscriber Options dialog box.

➤ Verify that the edition name shown at the top of the dialog box is the one you intend to affect. A pop-up list shows the disk and directory where the edition is stored. A line below the **Get Edition Now** button shows the date and time the edition was last modified or saved.

➤ You can set the edition to always be gotten (updated) **Automatically**—whenever the original artwork is changed—or **Manually**. If you select the manual option, then you need to open this dialog box and click **Get Edition Now** whenever you change the artwork and want to update the subscribing document.

➤ Click **Cancel Publisher** to remove the object's designation as a publisher. Changes made to the original artwork will no longer be reflected in this document.

➤ Click **Open Publisher** to open the originating application and modify the object.

5. Click **OK** to close the dialog box and effect the changes.

Showing or Hiding Edition Borders

Objects that have been made into publishers (editions) using **Edit > Publishing > Create Publisher** are framed in a nonprinting gray border if **Edit > Publishing > Show Borders** has been selected. You can hide this gray frame by choosing **Hide Borders**.

➤ Use **Show Borders** when you want to edit and update editions, or simply see what parts of the artwork have been published as editions.

➤ Choose **Hide Borders** when you want to see what the artwork would look like when printed.

These commands have no immediate effect if no elements have been published as editions from this artwork, and they do not effect the way the artwork prints.

Figure 7.29 Edition appearance with **Show Borders** (left) and **Hide Borders** (right) selected.

NOTE

Hide Borders has no effect on the gray border that frames editions that you have *subscribed to* in the artwork using **Edit > Publishing > Subscribe to**.

Modifying a Page within a PDF File

You can use Illustrator to make changes to individual PDF pages of PDF files. To modify a page within a PDF file, follow these steps:

1. Choose **File > Open**.
2. In the Open dialog box, locate and double-click the PDF file name.
3. In the second dialog box, select the page you wish to modify by scrolling through the thumbnails, then click **OK**.

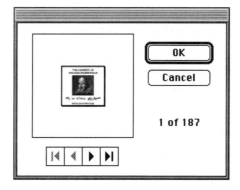

Figure 7.30 Dialog box displayed when opening a PDF file.

4. Make changes in Illustrator.
5. Choose **File > Save** to save the modified PDF file. The modified page is restored to its original position in the PDF file.

NOTE

You can instead choose **File > Save As** and give the saved document a different name, and (optionally) a different format—but the updates will not be reflected in the original PDF document.

Converting Illustrator Artwork to Bitmaps

6.0 NEW FEATURE

Illustrator 6.0 includes a command for changing selected vector graphics and imported graphics within an Illustrator document to rasterized (bitmap) objects. There are a number of ways in which this feature can really simplify creating effects that were difficult or impossible previously, for example:

➤ The most obvious use is that you can draw an object in Illustrator and then make it look like it is a bitmap with rough curves. Why would you want to? Well, the next possibilities might make this more interesting.

➤ If you copy the object first, the rough version could become a background shadow to the vector version.

➤ If you rasterize an imported graphic as a 1-bit black-and-white bitmap, you can apply a single color to it (see Figure 7.14).

➤ If you rasterize an object as a grayscale or RGB bitmap, you can apply Photoshop effects to it, including halftone screens.

➤ You can rasterize all of the artwork in a document and then save the file as a rasterized EPS artwork, for import into other applications that require rasterized images.

NOTE

You can use **Object > Rasterize** to convert imported bitmap graphics from RGB to CYMK TIFF, or from color to black-and-white bitmap or grayscale.

To rasterize an object:

1. Select it with a Selection tool.

2. Choose **Object > Rasterize** to display the Rasterize dialog box.

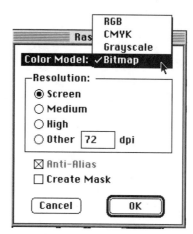

Figure 7.31 Rasterize dialog box and Color Model options.

3. Make selections from the following options:

➤ Choose a Color Model from the pop-up menu—**RGB**, **CYMK**, **Grayscale** (8-bit black-and-white), or **Bitmap** (1-bit black-and-white).

➤ Choose a Resolution—**Screen** (72 dpi), **Medium** (150 dpi), **High** (300 dpi), or any value you enter in the Other text box.

➤ Select **Anti-alias** if you want soften imported graphics that aren't already anti-aliased. This filter blends pixels together so that high-contrast areas, including the "jaggies" along angled lines or curves, appear smoother.

➤ Select **Create Mask** if you want the bounding box that surrounds a non-rectangular object to be see-through, so other objects show behind the edges of the object. Otherwise, the bounding box becomes an opaque rectangular background to the object.

NOTE   You can apply single colors or fill attributes to objects that have been rasterized as 1-bit black-and-white bitmaps, you can apply Photoshop effects to objects that have been rasterized as grayscale or RGB images. You cannot colorize grayscale or RGB objects, and you can neither colorize nor apply Photoshop effects to CYMK objects. Remember that Illustrator cannot color-separate RGB objects.

NOTE   You can also save Illustrator documents in bitmap formats, as described later in this chapter.

Figure 7.32 Illustrator graphics (left), converted to 72-dpi rasterized objects (second), or converted to 150-dpi objects (third). Grain Gallery Effect was applied to fourth image.

Tracing Template Graphics

You can create closed paths by using the Autotrace tool to trace bitmapped or PICT images that have been opened as templates. You use the Autotrace tool to trace automatically the path around any solid object that is part of a template. This is faster and easier than the alternative of tracing a template with the Freehand tool or the Pen tool. It works best if the template is composed of distinct areas of solid black or solid outlines with curved edges. The Autotrace tool always creates rounded joins and is therefore not used to trace objects with pointed corners and straight lines.

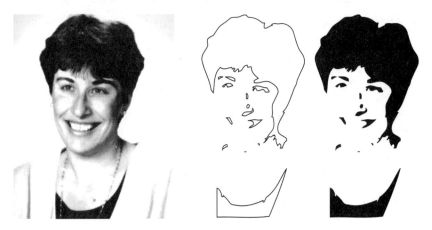

Figure 7.33 Examples of a traced bitmap.

To use the Autotrace tool, follow these steps:

1. Use one of two methods to open a new document with a template:

➤ Press **Command+Option+N** to open a new Illustrator document with a PICT template. This displays a dialog box, listing all of the bitmapped and PICT format files available on the disk.

➤ Choose **File > Open** (**Command+O**) to display the Open dialog box.

2. In either dialog box, select the a PICT format file you want to use as a tracing template and click **Open**. If you used the **Open** command to display the dialog box, a second dialog box is displayed offering the option of opening the PICT file as a template or as part of the artwork. Choose **Illustrator Template (PICT)**.

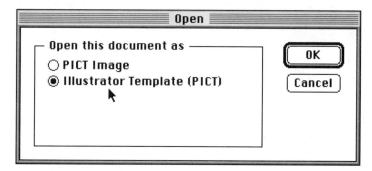

Figure 7.34 Dialog box entry for opening a template.

Illustrator opens a file and assigns it the name Untitled art in the title bar, followed by a colon (:) and the name of the PICT template file.

Figure 7.35 PICT is grayed as template (left)—and only traced objects will print (right).

3. Choose the **Autotrace** tool by dragging to its pop-up icon beside the Freehand tool in the Toolbox and releasing the mouse button. The mouse pointer changes to a cross-hair (+).

4. Use one of three techniques to trace the template:

➤ Position the pointer and click on the edge of a solid object in the template layer to trace a path around that object.

NOTE

You can adjust the sensitivity of the Autotrace tool in the File > General Preferences dialog box. With the Autotrace gap distance set at **0** in the Preferences dialog box, the Autotrace will read every pixel in the template. If the gap distance is set at **1**, the Autotrace jumps across one-pixel gaps and connects them. If it is set at **2**, the Autotrace jumps across two-pixel gaps and connects them. This can be useful if your template is very sketchy.

Figure 7.36 Creating a path with the Autotrace tool.

➤ To trace only part of a shape, click on the **Autotrace** tool and position the cross-hair pointer on the edge of the template at the point where you wish the tracing to begin. Instead of clicking, drag the cursor to the second point where you wish the tracing to end, then release the mouse button. Only the distance between those two points is traced.

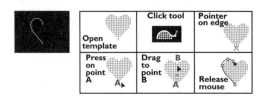

Figure 7.37 Tracing part of a shape.

NOTE

To trace hollow shapes, use Autotrace to trace the outer edge of the shape first. Then trace the inside edges. This way, the inside shape will always be on a layer above the outer shape, and you can set the hollow shape to have a White fill pattern.

5. Once you have drawn a path with the Autotrace tool, you can adjust the line segments and anchor points as described under the Pen tool, and set Stroke and Fill patterns as described under the Paint Style palette in Chapter 6.

NOTE

As a rule, use the Autotrace tool on shapes with relatively smooth curved edges. Use the Freehand tool to trace edges that are extremely ragged or irregular (see The Freehand Tool). Do not use the Autotrace tool to trace shapes made up of straight lines or rectangles, because the Autotrace tool may introduce curves. Use the Pen or Rectangle tools to draw straight lines or rectangular shapes.

Changing Imported Objects in Illustrator

Once you have imported a graphic into an Illustrator file or opened a graphic from another source using Illustrator, you may be able to manipulate in different ways, depending on the type of graphic.

➤ Template graphics cannot be moved or changed in any way—they can only be traced, and the resulting paths can be manipulated like any graphic drawn in Illustrator.

➤ Any graphics that were brought into Illustrator using **File > Open** or **File > Place** can be moved and transformed using any transformation tool: scaled, rotated, reflected, and sheared.

➤ Any graphics that were brought into Illustrator using **File > Open** or **File > Place** can be rasterized using **Object > Rasterize**. You can use this command to convert imported graphics from RGB to CYMK, or from color to black-and-white bitmap or grayscale.

➤ PDF file formats and some EPS file formats can be edited like any graphic drawn in Illustrator.

➤ Any imported bitmap image or any object that has been rasterized using Illustrator's **Object > Rasterize** command, can be converted to a mosaic pattern using the **Filter > Create > Object Mosaic** command (see Figure 7.39).

➤ One-bit (black-and-white) bitmap formats can be assigned any Fill through Illustrator's Paint Style palette—changing the black pixels to any color or tint. (Pattern and Gradient fills have no effect.)

➤ Eight-bit (or higher) grayscale and RGB graphics can be changed by applying Photoshop effects through the **Filter > Gallery Effects** submenu (see Figure 7.40).

Creating a Mosaic Object

The **Filter > Create > Mosaic** filter creates sharp definition in an imported bitmap image (such as those created in Adobe Photoshop) by clustering pixels of similar color values together into individual tiles. You can control the tile size, the spacing between tiles, the total number of tiles, and the ratio of horizontal to vertical tiles.

1. Select an imported bitmap image in the Illustrator file.

2. Choose **Filter > Create > Object Mosaic** to display the Mosaic dialog box.

   The Mosaic dialog box shows the dimensions of the image file shown at the top, and optimum levels for Tile Spacing, New Size, and Number of Tiles automatically filled in by the filter.

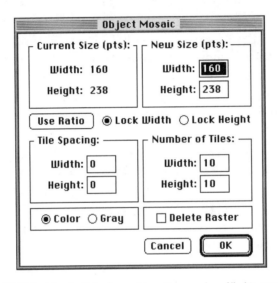

Figure 7.38 The Mosaic dialog box with optimum values filled in automatically.

3. You can accept the optimum values or make changes to the values for Tile Spacing, New Size, and Number of Tiles. If you change the New Size values, you can click **Use Ratio** if you want Illustrator to automatically calculate the proportional ration of tiles for the Size indicated—locking either the width or height value to allow the other value to change as needed.

4. You can also opt to convert a color graphic file to a black-and-white grayscale image.

5. Select **Delete raster** if you want the original graphic to be removed from the artwork. Otherwise, the Mosaic result will overlay the original.

6. Click **OK** to close the dialog box and import the PICT file.

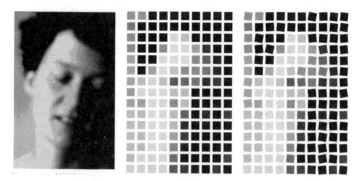

Figure 7.39 PICT file (left) and mosaic effect (middle), then each
tile rotated with the **Arrange > Transform Each** command (right).

Applying Photoshop Effects

**6.0 NEW
FEATURE**

Illustrator 6.0 introduces the ability to apply selected Photoshop effects to imported
or rasterized grayscale and color objects in Illustrator. The Photoshop commands are
accessed through the **Filter > Gallery Effects** submenus. Some of the effects that
come with Illustrator 6.0 are shown in Figure 7.40, and you can add other effects from
Adobe Photoshop by dragging them into the Gallery Effects folder in the Plug-ins
folder in the Adobe Illustrator program folder.

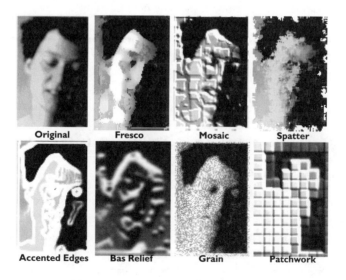

Figure 7.40 Examples of Photoshop effects.

379

Using Illustrator 6.0 Artwork in Other Applications

To use an Adobe Illustrator document in another application, you must save the document in a graphics file format that the other application can use.

➤ The most common way of making Illustrator artwork available to other applications is to save the artwork as an EPS file. Virtually all page-layout and word-processing applications can import or place EPS files.

➤ You can also save Illustrator documents in a number of other graphic formats, including Acrobat (PDF 1.1), and bitmap formats such as Amiga IFF, BMP, PCX, Pixar, and Targa formats. However, using a format other than EPS or PDF often results in a loss of quality, and you will not be able to edit the artwork in Illustrator again.

➤ You can save artwork in previous versions of Illustrator, so it can be opened and edited using an earlier version. Sometimes this is also necessary when importing Illustrator artwork into applications that do not recognize the latest version's formats.

Each of these options is described under the next headings.

Always keep the original version of the Illustrator artwork. When you are saving a document in a bitmap format, or in an older version's format, use **File > Save As** and give it a different name.

NOTE

Saving Documents in Previous Versions of Adobe Illustrator

Some applications can import Illustrator's EPS-format files directly. You might find, however, that older applications cannot import the current version of the Illustrator file format. (If you want to use the Windows version of the Illustrator program to change a document, for example, you must save the document in Illustrator 4 file format.) If this is the case, you can save documents in any previous version of Illustrator file format.

NOTE

Before you save a document in a previous version of the Illustrator file format, save a copy of the document with the current version first. Some features available with the current version of the Illustrator file format are lost when a document is saved as a previous version. Bitmap graphics are removed, for example.

To save a document in previous versions of Illustrator file format:

1. Choose **File > Save** and save the document in Illustrator 6 format.

2. Choose **File > Save As**.

3. Select the folder where you want to save the new document and enter a document name.

4. Choose the version of the Illustrator file format you want to use from the Format pop-up menu.

5. Click **Save**.

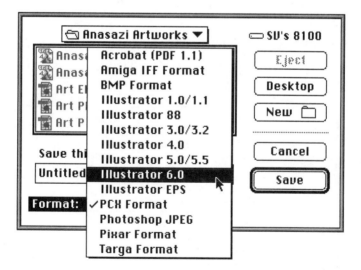

Figure 7.41 Format options in saving Illustrator documents.

Saving Documents in EPS Format

The most common way of sharing Illustrator artwork is to save the artwork as an EPS file. Virtually all page-layout, word-processing, and graphic applications accept placed EPS files. And unlike many other graphic file formats, EPS files preserve all of the graphic elements you can create with Adobe Illustrator.

Illustrator documents saved as EPS files remain Illustrator documents. You can double-click an Illustrator EPS file to start Illustrator and open the document.

NOTE

Most applications cannot display EPS artwork directly but they can display a review image saved as part of the EPS file. Working with other applications, you can use the preview image to locate and size the EPS artwork. See "Encapsulated PostScript (EPS) File Format" earlier in this chapter for a description of the preview options.

To save a document as an EPS file:

1. Choose **File > Save As**.

2. Select the folder where you want to save the EPS file and enter a name for the file.

3. Choose **EPS** from the Format pop-up menu.

4. Click **Save**. The EPS Format dialog box appears.

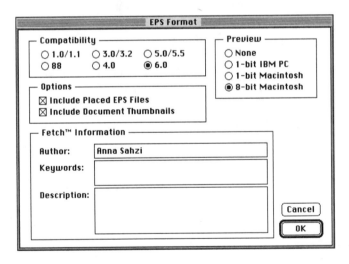

Figure 7.42 EPS Format dialog box.

5. Select the kind of preview image you want to save with the EPS file.

6. Select the Adobe Illustrator compatibility option you want to use. If you plan to change the EPS file with the Windows version of Adobe Illustrator, for example, select the **Illustrator 3/4** option. Remember, however, that features such as gradients, layers, and bitmap elementsare not supported by earlier versions of the Illustrator file format.

7. If the Illustrator document contains placed EPS artwork and you are creating an EPS file for use with another application, select the **Include Place EPS files** option to include the placed artwork in the EPS file.

8. If you want to be able to see a thumbnail of the EPS artwork in the illustrator Open dialog box, select the **Include Document Thumbnail** option.

9. If you plan to manage the EPS file with Adobe Fetch, enter the Information field values.

10. Click **Save**.

Saving in Acrobat PDF and Bitmap Formats

You can save Illustrator documents in the Acrobat Portable Document Format (PDF), and in bitmap image formats, including Amiga IFF, BMP, PCX, JPEG, Pixar, and Targa formats.

NOTE

Illustrator uses the Adobe Photoshop plug-in mechanism to convert Illustrator documents to different graphic file formats. This means that you may be able to acquire third-party plug-in modules that let you save Illustrator documents in graphic file formats not supported by Illustrator as shipped by Adobe.

To save a document as a PDF or bitmap image graphic format file:

1. Choose **File > Save As**.

2. Select the folder where you want to save the file and enter a name for the file.

3. Select the file format you want to use from the Format pop-up menu.

4. Click **Save**. Depending on the format you choose, a dialog box may appear with format options for the new file.

5. If a format options dialog box has appeared, select the options you want to use and click **Save**.

See the descriptions of the individual graphic file formats at the beginning of this chapter for considerations of saving Illustrator documents in different file formats.

Figure 7.43 Example of Illustrator art (bird, woman, Anubis) incorp
orated into a Photoshop image. (see color plates).

NOTE

Saving an Illustrator document in Acrobat (PDF) format does not embed fonts used in the document in the PDF files. To embed fonts in the PDF files, save the Illustrator document in EPS file format, then convert the Illustrator EPS file to a PDF file using Adobe Acrobat Distiller.

Chapter 8

Typing, Editing, and Formatting Text

Adobe Illustrator enables you to set type with precise typographical controls. Besides controlling the spacing between letters, words, and lines, you can use Illustrator's transformation tools to scale, rotate, reflect, stretch, and shrink text just as you can any other graphic element. You can also create special effects using Illustrator's commands for text formatting or by converting the text to outlines and manipulating the fill and line characteristics.

The tools and menu commands that control text are described in this chapter, including techniques that combine different tools and commands to achieve specific results with text.

Techniques covered in this chapter include:

➤ Typing, selecting, and formatting text

➤ Filling an existing path with text

➤ Creating type along a path

➤ Working with text on a circle

➤ Importing text from other sources

➤ Creating columns of text

➤ Wrapping text around graphics

➤ Linking graphics as text containers for a continuous flow

➤ Globally editing text, including using the spelling checker, converting punctuation, and searching for specific words

➤ Creating the effect of inline type

➤ Creating nonprinting text—or "hidden" notes

➤ Converting text characters to editable paths

➤ Exporting text

Besides using the techniques described here, you can use most of the techniques for transforming text described in Chapter 5 and the techniques for painting text described in Chapter 6.

Using the Type Tools   T ⟨T⟩ ↷

You use the type tools to create text objects (into which you will type or import text), or to edit existing text. There are three type tools: the Type tool, the Area-type tool, and the Path-type tool.

➤ Use the Type tool to create text at an alignment point for a text object of any width (*point* text) or to define a rectangle into which you type text that wraps at the defined edges (*rectangular* text). When you choose the **Type** tool by clicking the icon in the Toolbox, the mouse pointer changes to an I-beam surrounded by a dotted box in the active window.

➤ Use the Area-type tool to fill an existing path of any shape with text. The path may be open or closed. When you choose the **Area-type** tool by dragging to its pop-up icon in the Toolbox and releasing the mouse button, the pointer changes to an I-beam surrounded by dotted parentheses in the active window.

➤ Use the Path-type tool to type text along a path. When you choose the **Path-type** tool by dragging to its pop-up icon in the Toolbox and releasing the mouse button, the pointer changes to an I-beam intersected by a dotted wavy line in the active window.

Creating Point Text

Point text is a text object that takes on whatever width is required to fit the text that you type. The text object will become larger if you make the text larger by increasing the point size, leading, tracking, or spacing—or smaller if you decrease these values. You can force lines to end as you type by pressing the **Return** key.

1. Choose the **Type** tool by clicking the icon in the Toolbox. The mouse pointer changes to an I-beam surrounded by a dotted box in the active window.

2. Choose type specifications from the Font or Type menu, or from the Character and Paragraph palettes.

3. Click on the Artboard or pasteboard to position an alignment point for point text. .The crossbar on the I-beam sets the baseline and anchor point for the text.

4. Begin typing. The text you type forms one continuous line unless you break it by inserting a **Return** character.

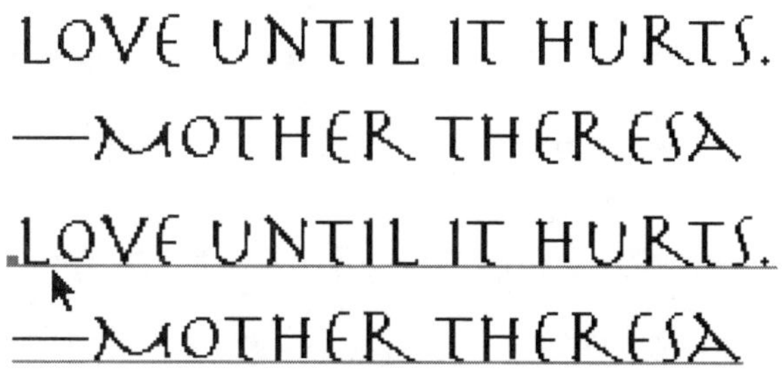

LOVE UNTIL IT HURTS.

—MOTHER THERESA

LOVE UNTIL IT HURTS.

—MOTHER THERESA

Figure 8.1 Point text shows anchor point and baseline when selected with a selection tool.

5. Click the **Type** tool again to stop typing in the current text string, and click or drag the I-beam at another location on the Artboard to begin another text object.

WARNING

Be careful when creating text objects near a path or an object. For a normal text object (point text or rectangular text) the type I-beam will have a set of square dotted brackets around it. If your I-beam touches or is too close to a path, the square brackets will disappear and be replaced by a slanted line crossing the I-beam. This is the Text on a Path I-beam. If you start to type at this point, you'll get text on a path. Similarly, if you're too close to an object or closed path, the I-beam squared brackets will be replaced by rounded brackets indicating text within an object. If you need a text object near or aligned to a path, create it elsewhere and then position it near the path.

Typing Special Characters

Some special characters that are available with most fonts are not shown on the keys of the keyboard, but they can be typed using the **Option** key, as shown here. See also "Using Smart Punctuation," later in this chapter, for a method of automatically changing quotes and ligatures.

Example	Description	Keys
"	typographer's open quotation marks	Option+[
"	typographer's close quotation marks	Option+~SH+[
'	typographer's single open quotation marks	Option+]
'	typographer's single close quotation marks	Option+~SH+]
•	bullet	Option+8
™	trademark symbol	Option+2
®	registered trademark symbol	Option+R
©	copyright mark	Option+G
¶	paragraph symbol	Option+7
§	section symbol	Option+6

Example	Description	Keys
...	ellipsis (nonbreaking)	Option+;
°	degree	Option+~Shift+8
π	pi	Option+P
¢	cent	Option+4
£	English pound	Option+3
¥	Japanese yen	Option+y
fi	f and i ligature	Option+Shift+5
fl	f and l ligature	Option+Shift+6
—	em dash	Option+Shift+(hyphen)
–	en dash	Option+(hyphen)

Creating Rectangular Text

Rectangular text is a text object that takes on whatever width and length you define by dragging the mouse diagonally between two points. The text wraps automatically when it reaches the edge of the rectangle as you type. The text will fit itself into the same rectangle by wrapping differently if you make the text larger by increasing the point size, leading, tracking, or spacing—or smaller if you decrease these values. If the typed text does not fit within the rectangle, it will seem to disappear, but you can display the overflow by enlarging the rectangle or by creating a linked rectangle as described in the next steps. As with point text, you can still force lines to end as you type by pressing the **Return** key.

1. Choose the **Type** tool by clicking the icon in the Toolbox. The mouse pointer changes to an I-beam surrounded by a dotted box in the active window.

2. Choose type specifications from the Font or Type menu or from the Character and Paragraph palettes.

3. Drag to define a rectangular area on the Artboard or pasteboard. A blinking insertion point appears in the rectangle.

4. Begin typing. Text typed into a rectangle wraps automatically to fit inside the rectangle.

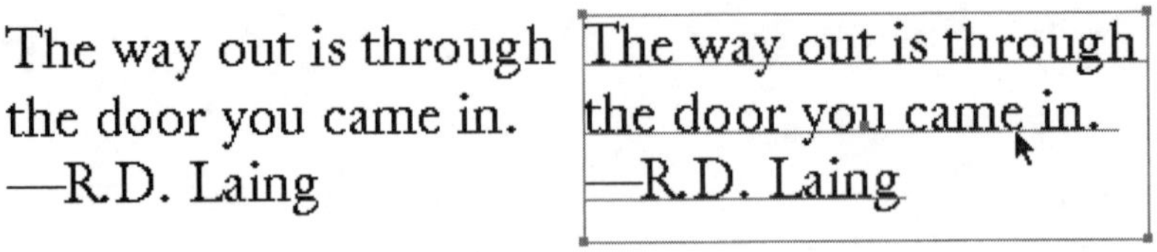

The way out is through the door you came in. —R.D. Laing

The way out is through the door you came in. —R.D. Laing

Figure 8.2 Rectangular text shows baseline and rectangle when selected with a selection tool.

5. If there is too much text to fit inside the rectangle you formed by dragging the I-beam, a small plus sign appears at the end of the text. To display the overflow text, you can either:

➤ enlarge the rectangle using the Direct-selection tool or

➤ duplicate the rectangle by Option+clicking on it with the Direct-selection tool, then Option+dragging to create a duplicate. The overflow text flows into the second rectangle, and the two rectangles form a single text object.

WARNING

You must first Option+click on the text rectangle to select it with the Direct-selection tool before Option+dragging to create a duplicate. The text rectangle cannot already be selected when you Option+click. Otherwise, Option+dragging will create an unlinked duplicate with the same text, and the same text overflow problem.

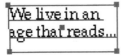

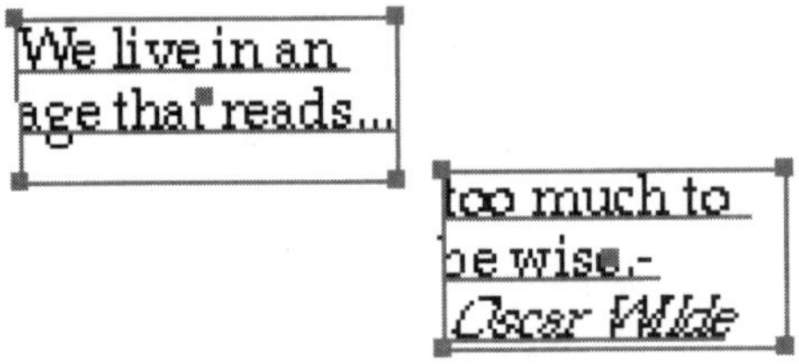

We live in an age that reads...

too much to be wise.— Oscar Wilde

6. Click the **Type** tool again to stop typing in the current text string, and click or drag the I-beam at another location on the Artboard to begin another text object.

NOTE

Rectangles created with the Type tool are unpainted paths (their Fill and Stroke are both set to **None**), but you can assign them a Fill and Stroke by selecting the rectangle only with the Direct Selection tool and using the Paint Style palette as described in Chapter 6.

Filling an Existing Path with Text

Area text is like rectangular text in most respects. The main difference is that you create the shape of the area to be filled by drawing a path using any of Illustrator's drawing tools first, before choosing the Area-text tool and typing. The path can be any shape, and may be either open or closed. As with rectangular text, the text wraps to fit inside the path, and the presence of overflow text is indicated by a small plus sign at the end of the text.

1. Create a path using any drawing tool in Illustrator—the Pen tool, Freehand tool, Autotrace tool, Rectangle or Oval tools, or one of the plug-in tools to create a polygon or star.

2. Choose the **Area-type** tool by dragging to its pop-up icon in the Toolbox and releasing the mouse button. The pointer changes to an I-beam surrounded by dotted parentheses in the active window.

3. Click on the path you want to fill with text. A blinking insertion point appears in the path, and its Paint attributes change to a Fill and Stroke of **None**.

Clicking on a path with the Area-type tool or Path tool changes its Paint attributes to a Fill and Stroke of **None**. If you want the path to be visible, select it with the Direct-select tool after typing the text, and set the Fill and Stroke attributes in the Paint Style palette as described in Chapter 6.

N O T E

4. Begin typing. As with rectangular text, the text wraps to fit inside the path, and the presence of overflow text is indicated by a small plus sign at the end of the text.

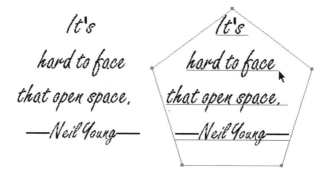

Figure 8.3 Area text shows baseline and area border when selected with a selection tool.

NOTE

To flow text through several paths, use the Area-type tool to click on the first path, then type the text or choose **File > Import Text** (described later in this chapter). Next, use the **Selection** tool to select the text-filled path and the other paths into which the text should flow, then use the **Type > Link Blocks** command. The text flows into the paths according to the paths' stacking order, from back to front. The text flows into the backmost path first and the frontmost path last.

Creating Type along a Path

You can type text to follow the shape of the path—following along the edges of the path rather than filling the area enclosed by the path. The path may be open or closed.

1. Create a path using any drawing tool in Illustrator—the Pen tool, Freehand tool, Autotrace tool, Rectangle or Oval tools, or one of the plug-in tools to create a polygon or star.

NOTE

When putting text on a path that is large or complicated, it is advisable that you create a copy of the original path before putting text on it. Once you place text on a path, you cannot make that path regular artwork again; it will always be a text path. You can modify the path itself by using the direct-selection tool to pick out the anchor point(s) you want to manipulate. If you need just a regular path again and you have not made a copy of it beforehand, you can use the direct-selection tool to make a copy of just the path (be sure to click only on the path and not the text), then paste the path back into your document and delete the text path.

2. Choose the **Path-type** tool by dragging to its pop-up icon in the Toolbox and releasing the mouse button.

3. Click on the path along which you want to place the text—at the point where you want the text to be aligned. A blinking insertion point appears where you click on the path.

NOTE

Once you click on the path, you cannot change the position of the insertion point by simply clicking again—but you can reposition the insertion point using the techniques described in step 6.

4. Begin typing. The text you type follows the shape of the path.

NOTE

Clicking on a path with the Path-type tool changes its Paint attributes to a Fill and Stroke of **None**, but you can select it later (after step 4) with the Direct-selection tool and change the Paint Style attributes (see earlier Note).

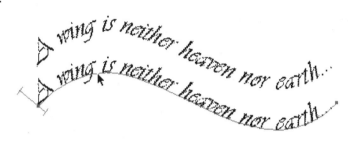

Figure 8.4 Path text shows path only when selected with a selection tool.

5. You can select all or part of the text with the I-beam and format it as you would any text.

NOTE

If the text seems to disappear off one or the other end of the path, you can either make it a smaller font (step 5), reposition the text (step 6), or lengthen the path itself (Chapter 4).

6. There are several ways to change the position of type along a path:

   ➤ You can choose alternative alignments from the Type menu or Paragraph palette. These commands align the text relative to the point you initially clicked on the path.

   ➤ You can adjust the baseline of the text to move it above or below the current position on the path.

   ➤ Select the type with the Selection tool to display an I-beam that represents the alignment point of the text—the point you initially clicked on the path. (Note that this is a display icon—not the mouse cursor or the Type tool.) Then:

   ➤ You can drag the I-beam left or right along the path to move the text sideways.

   ➤ Double-click on the I-beam with the Selection tool to flip the text across the path.

Some of these options are demonstrated in the next exercise.

EXERCISE: WORKING WITH TEXT ON A CIRCLE

In this section you will learn to set text along the boundary of a circle, as shown in the figure. But you can apply the technique to a path of any shape.

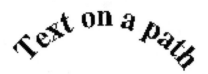

This technique is especially useful for logos, labels, maps, and other applications that require text to follow an arbitrary path.

1. First create a circle with the oval tool. The curvature of the circle can be adjusted now or changed at any time by selecting points with the Direct-selection tool.

2. Next, select the **Text on a Path** tool, and with most of the I-beam placed above the circle, click on the top anchor point of the circle.

3. Type text along the circle.

4. Choose **Type > Alignment > Center** (**Command+Shift+C**) to center the text around the top point of the circle, where you first clicked.

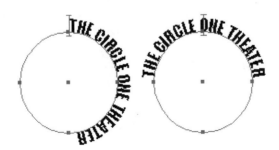

5. Once you have typed the text you can edit the contents or type specifications by selecting it with the I-beam pointer.

6. To move text to the inside of the circle, choose the **Selection** tool and double click on the I-beam that marks where you first clicked on the outside of the circle. This will flip the text to inside the circle and running in a counterclockwise direction.

NOTE

Text will always type clockwise when on the outside of the circle and counterclockwise on the inside of the circle.

7. You can then drag the text to the bottom of the circle to make it right side up.

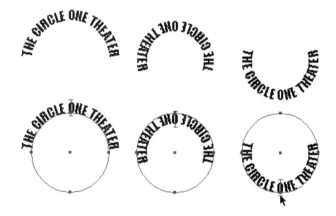

Figure 8.5 Text on a circle shows path only in Artwork view, or when selected with the selection tool in Preview mode (bottom row).

8. You can vertically shift the text down so that it appears outside if so desired. In the expanded Character palette (**Command+T**) enter a negative number equal to the type point size in the Baseline Shift box. This will force the text below the baseline, making it appear on the outside of the circle.

Importing Text

You can import text that has been created by another application, such as a word processor, using the Import Text commands as described in the next steps.

1. Choose any one of the Type tools and position it as described under the previous headings—to begin point text, rectangular text, area text, or text on a path.

2. Choose **File > Import Text** to display a dialog box.

The **Import Text** command is available on the File menu only when the **Type** tool is selected and the I-beam is positioned on the Artboard or pasteboard.

N O T E

File	Edit	Arrange	View
New			⌘N
Open...			⌘O
Close			⌘W
Save			⌘S
Save As...			
Revert to Saved			
Place...			
Import Styles...			
Import Text...			

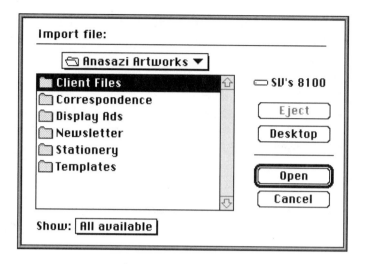

3. Double-click the name of the text file you want to import.

4. To flow Area text through additional paths, use the **Selection** tool to select the text-filled path and the other paths into which the text should flow, then use the **Type > Link Blocks** command. The text flows into the paths according to the paths' stacking order, from back to front. The text flows into the backmost path first and the frontmost path last.

5. Some of the formatting done in the original application may still hold when it is imported to Illustrator, but you can use the techniques described next to edit any imported text or text you have typed.

N O T E

To quickly incorporate formatted text in a columnar layout into your artwork, first type and format the text using a word-processing application. Then drag the Type tool to create a text rectangle and use the **File > Import Text** command to import the text into the rectangle. Most of the text's formatting is retained. To accommodate overflow text, duplicate the text rectangle by Option+dragging it with the Direct-selection tool.

Selecting and Editing Text

All of the methods and options for formatting and editing text described in the rest of this chapter require that you first select the text to be affected. There are three methods for selecting text, each with a different effect or purpose:

➤ To modify all the text in a text object, use the Selection tool to select the entire text object.

➤ To modify a single block in a text object, or to change a text path without changing the text itself, use the Direct-selection tool.

When text is selected with a Selection tool, you can use any commands or tools to affect its position, shape, and format—but you cannot edit individual characters (formatting commands apply to the entire selection).

NOTE

➤ Use any of the type tools to select part of the text in a text object. When you move any of the type tools over existing text, the pointer changes to an I-beam.

When text is selected with a Type tool, you can edit the content or change the format of individual selected characters or words, but some commands and tools that affect its position and shape will not be available.

NOTE

Illustrator follows standard Macintosh text-editing conventions when text is selected with the I-beam:

➤ Click the I-beam to create an insertion point at which you can enter text by typing; delete text using the **Delete** key.

➤ Drag the I-beam to select a range of characters.

➤ Double-click to select a complete word and triple-click to select a complete paragraph.

➤ Use any of the above techniques to select some part of text, then choose **Edit > Select All** (**Command+A**) to select all of the text in the current text object and any linked text containers.

Once text is selected with the I-beam, you can use standard Macintosh text-editing conventions:

➤ Begin typing to replace the selected text.

➤ Use commands from the Edit menu to **Cut, Copy, Clear,** and **Paste** the text.

➤ Additional commands for globally editing text include **Find Font**, **Check Spelling**, **Smart Punctuation**, and **Change Case**—all described later in this chapter.

➤ You can change any of the Paint or Type attributes of text selected using the type tools without affecting the rest of the text in the text object.

When working with paragraph formatting options, you need not select all the text in a paragraph:

➤ To select a single paragraph, click the **Type** tool to make an insertion point anywhere in the paragraph, or drag to make a selection anywhere in the paragraph.

➤ To select several paragraphs, drag the Type tool to select them.

NOTE Since text is almost always intended to print on top of all other objects in the artwork, you can use Illustrator's Layers palette, described in Chapter 10, to position all the text on one layer and put that layer on top of all others. This way, you can also make the text layer invisible on the screen when you want to work with the artwork only, or you can make all the other layers invisible when you want to work with the text only.

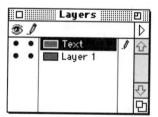

Figure 8.6 Text layer in Layers palette.

Setting Character Attributes

The commands in the Type menu affect text that you type in Illustrator. The **Size**, **Leading**, and **Alignment** commands all lead to submenus that let you select individual specifications quickly, or you can use the **Character** and **Paragraph** commands to display palettes and set several characteristics at once. The **Alignment** command lets you justify text as well as set it to align left, right, or centered.

Illustrator incorporates sophisticated typographic controls such as letter and word spacing (**Tracking** and **Spacing** commands), and baseline shift (for creating superscripts and subscripts).

SHORTCUT The most efficient way to format text is to use keyboard shortcuts—available for most options. For those of us who can't remember all the shortcuts, the next most efficient method is to display the Character and Paragraph palettes, described in the next sections. This way you have immediate access to most formatting options, without going to the menu bar or opening other submenus or dialog boxes.

Displaying the Character Palette

The Character palette lets you set the attributes of text characters—font, style, size, leading, baseline shift, horizontal scale, and tracking or kerning—through a palette that can remain open while you work. This palette can be accessed through a number of commands from the Type menu. Additional text attributes that apply to whole paragraphs are set through the Paragraph palette, described later in this chapter.

To display the Character palette, simply use the keyboard shortcut **Command+T**, or choose **Window > Show Character, Type > Character (Command+Shift+F), Type > Tracking...** or **Kerning (Command+Shift+K), Type > Size > Other,** or **Type > Leading > Other (Command+Shift+S)**. If the Character palette is already displayed, you can choose **Window > Hide Character**, but it's usually much easier to simply click the close box on the palette title bar.

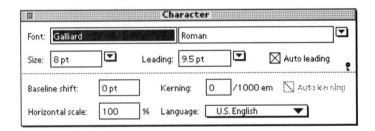

Figure 8.7 The Character palette, maximized.

SHORTCUT The four keyboard shortcuts for displaying the Character palette are easy to remember if you know that **Command+T** displayed the Type Style dialog box in earlier versions, **Command+Shift+F** displayed the Font dialog box, and **Command+Shift+S** displayed the Size dialog box. Now the information from all three dialog boxes is combined in the Character palette. **Command+Shift+K** is the keyboard shortcut for the **Tracking/Kerning** command. This command always opens the expanded Character palette—the other three commands open the palette in whatever view it was last closed.

Grapes are ellipses with a radial gradient fill, clustered and grouped

Bezier curves can take any shape

Type on an invisible ellipse, converted to paths, roughened, distorted, and masked by itself to create custom inline effects

Type on an invisible ellipse

Imported scanned EPS image (saved as a brown monotone in Photoshop) masked by a diamond shape

Rectangle filled with a gradient fill, overlayed by a rectangle filled with a small diamond pattern

Wine label designed by Susan Equitz

This wine label designed by Susan Equitz illustrates a variety of Illustrator's features. See Chapter 1 for more details.

Learn how to create three-dimensional package designs in Chapter 9.

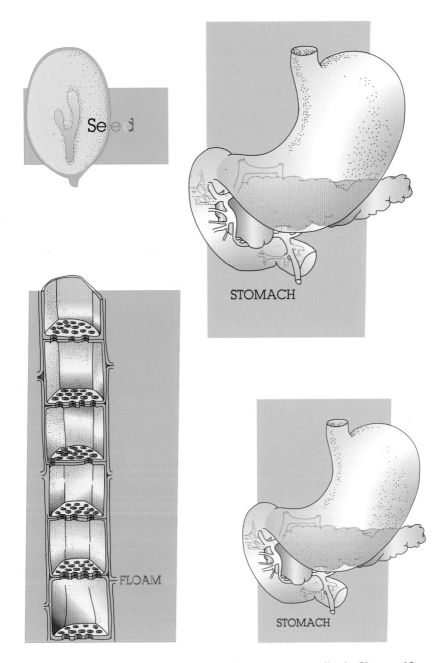

Se d

STOMACH

FLOAM

STOMACH

Sue Sellar's anatomical illustrations are case studies in Chapter 12.

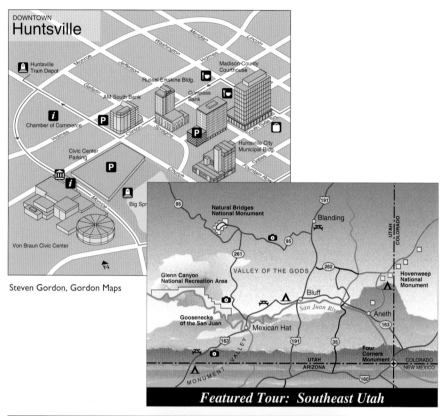

Steven Gordon, Gordon Maps

Featured Tour: Southeast Utah

DHeinlein Park Avenue: Puzzle #2 from "The Virtual Erector Set: The E-Force Rescue"
©1995 Imagination Pilots Entertainment

**Steven Gordon's maps and Doug Heinlein's bird's-eye view
of Park Avenue are case studies in Chapter 12.**

Scott Crouse's technical illustrations for Scotty's Inc. are case studies in Chapter 12. (Look for the tip on wrapping text around a cylinder!)

© Marina Thompson 1995

© 1995 Arthur J. Saarinen, AVID

**Marina Thompson's Beach Scene and Arthur Saarinen's
illustration for AVID are case studies in Chapter 12.**

With perfect registration colors meet but do not overlap (except black, which usually overprints all other colors).	When registration is off slightly, gaps show as white lines and overlapping colors yield a darker, muddy line.

LA
ILLAHA
ILLA'LLA
HU

LA
ILLAHA
ILLA'LLA
HU

LA
ILLAHA
ILLA'LLA
HU

Text in
Spot Color 1
set with
Overprint off

Background
with knockout
in Spot Color 2

Composite
makes text slightly
darker where it
overlaps at edges

LA
ILLAHA
ILLA'LLA
HU

Text in
Spot Color 1
with Overprint on

Background
with no knockout
in Spot Color 2

Composite
makes text slightly
darker all over

Overprinting colors is one solution to the possibility
of mis-registration. See Chapters 6 and 11 for details.

Screens for cyan, magenta, yellow, and black are normally rotated relative to each other to prevent moiré patterns in printing process colors.

Magnified views of spot (left square in each pair) and process (right) versions of black, blue, green, and red

Black **Blue** **Green** **Red**

Spot color overlays (right) and four-color process separations (below) yield same colors in final printing (far right). Bottom row shows actual colors separated.

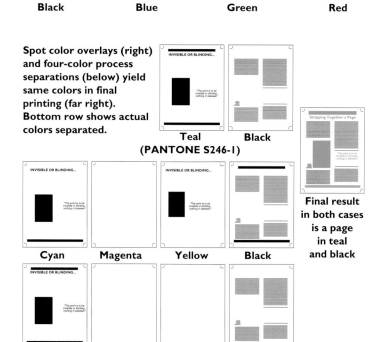

Teal
(PANTONE S246-1)   Black

Cyan   Magenta   Yellow   Black

Final result in both cases is a page in teal and black

You can print spot color or four-color process separations directly from Illustrator. See Chapter 11 for details..

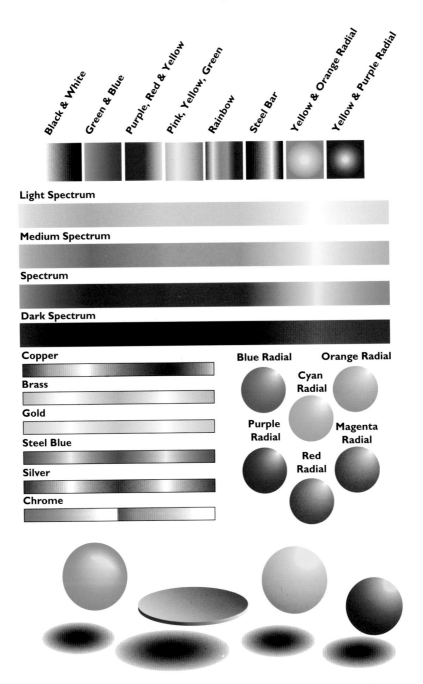

Learn how to use color gradients and path patterns (facing page) in Chapters 6 and 9, and how to create blends as an alternative to gradient fills.

Patterns (fill)

Patterns (path)

Multilines 1.4
side   outer

Arrows 1.2
side   outer/inner

Multilines 1.3
side   outer/inner

Arrows 1.4
side   outer/inner

Arrows 1.5
side/outer/inner

Multilines 1.5
side   outer

Braids
side

Radius: 90
Width: default

Victorian
side   outer

Marjoram
side   outer   inner

Vine
side   outer   inner

Rough
side   outer/inner

Double Lines 1.5
side   outer

I started with one of my wife's stained glass patterns (small version at the right). Then, I applied KPT ShatterBox [radial 8 segments; no offset or disruption] to add panes to the window. (If you look closely, you'll see that the impact wasn't quite centered horizontally.)

Next I made a copy of the window in a separate layer, and set the fill to black. Then I applied KPT Neon [50%, 8pt] to create the "lead" lines.

This outlined each piece individually, which looked funny because they overlapped. (See example.) To create continuous lines, I first used Outline Path to convert the lead to filled shapes. Then, I repeatedly selected one shape, and did Select Same Paint Style, Unite, and Hide, until all individual shapes were merged. (Let me know if you think of a better way to do this!) The example at the top right shows the before and after effect.

Larry Rosenstein

LarryR9@aol.com
lsr@taligent.com

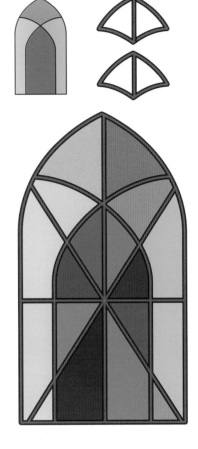

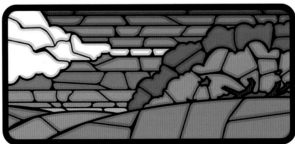

Larry Rosenstein and Rob Marquardt take two very different approaches in producing these stained glass effects, described in case studies in Chapter 12.

**Ian Shou's whimsical penguin Lucian and political cartoon
Shakedown are case studies in Chapter 12.**

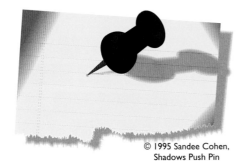

© 1995 Sandee Cohen,
Shadows Push Pin

Sandee Cohen's Shadows Push Pin (made three-dimensional in Adobe Dimensions), Eve Elberg's After the Shower, Marina Thompson's winter scene cover illustration for Workforce Diversity Magazine, and Garry Allen's Cyberwoman are case studies in Chapter 12.

Eve Elberg, After the Shower

© Marina Thompson 1995

© 1995 Gary Allen Smith, Commercial use prohibited
without author's consent. (garyallen@aol.com)

Copyright © 1994, Lester Yocum

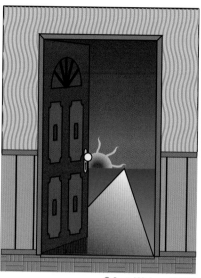

© Scott Winkowski 1994

Gary Symington

Ray Villarosa

Lester Yocum's Santa, Scott Winkowski's Doorway, Gary Symington's Furnace and Ray Villarosa's Domestic Violence are case studies in Chapter 12.

© 1995 OOMM Studios, Stephen Czapiewski, Nephthys

© 1995 Robin Bort

In this design by Stephen Czapiewski, the swan, the woman (Nephthys) and the god Anubis were drawn in Illustrator, then exported to Photoshop and arranged in the clouds. This and Robin Bort's Peruvian musician are case studies in Chapter 12.

YOU CAN TEACH AN OLD DOG

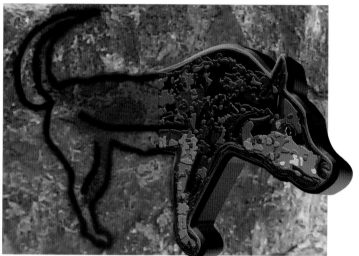

drzox@aol.com

NEW TRICKS

© 1995 Ben Gorman

Dr. Zoc used Illustrator to get a rise out of a 5,000 year old dog, and Ben Gorman uses Illustrator to rough out his designs for silver jewelry. See case studies in Chapter 12.

Blend

Saturate

Invert

Mix Hard and Soft

Create the effect of interlocking objects by cutting paths or by using the Outline Paths and Divide filters.

Overlap gradients blends of two custom colors to get a third color.

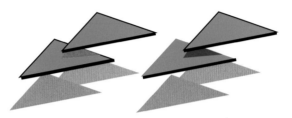

Mix colors Hard to color shadow on lower triangle.

Apply one custom color (above) and then change the components to get different effects in artwork composed of many strokes and fills. Examples here also show embossing (above) and beveled edges (below).

Create a gradient fill for a shadow that fades into a background color (left).

When the Character palette is displayed on the screen, you can view the type specifications of selected text, and change them by making entries in the palette. If you choose **Type > Character** when text is selected, the character attribute currently applied to the text is displayed in the palette. If you choose **Type > Character** when no text is selected, then the Character palette shows the defaults that would apply to the next text typed. You can change the defaults by changing the palette values when no text is selected.

Any changes you make to the Character palette are automatically applied to whatever text is currently selected on the Artboard. Be sure that only text you wish to change is selected when you make entries in the palette.

WARNING

Adjusting the Size and Position of the Character Palette

You can move the Character palette on the screen by dragging the title bar. The palette will always display on top of all document windows, but the most recently used palette can appear on top of this palette if there is overlap between palettes. You can bring any palette to the top by clicking on it. If a palette is completely hidden under other palettes, you can move the other palettes or you can use the command under the Window menu to **Hide** and then **Show** the buried palette.

You can toggle between two sizes of the Character palette by clicking on the "latch" icon to the right of the **Auto Leading** option. You can change the font, style, size, and leading between lines through the reduced palette, or click the "latch" symbol in the lower-right corner to expand the palette and set baseline shift, horizontal scaling, kerning and tracking options as well.

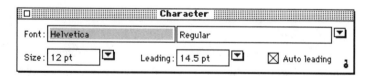

Figure 8.8 The Character palette, minimized.

Since the Character and Paragraph palettes take up space on the screen, you might want to group your activities in Illustrator in this way. First, draw the artwork—or as much of it as you can before seeing the text with it. Then add all the text, keeping the Character and Paragraph palettes open for formatting. Close the palettes when you are finished with the text, and reopen the Paint Style palette (If you had to close it to make room on the screen).

NOTE

Setting Character Attributes on the Palette

You can change the character attributes in the Character palette when no text is selected, to affect only the next text typed, or you can change the appearance of selected text by changing these attributes. In either case, the procedure is the same.

Note that steps I and 2 can be done in any order—step 2 can precede step I.

N O T E

1. Display the Character palette by using the keyboard shortcut **Command+T**, or choose **Window > Show Character, Type > Character (Command+ Shift+F), Type > Tracking...** or **Kerning (Command+Shift+K), Type > Size > Other**, or **Type > Leading > Other (Command+Shift+S)**.

2. Use the Selection tool (pointer) to select the text object(s) to be changed, or use the Type tool (I-beam) to select a range of characters within a text object and change only those characters, or press **Command+Shift+A** to deselect all objects and affect only the next text typed.

Figure 8.9 Select point text, area text, or text on a path with the Selection tool, or a range of characters with the Type tool.

3. Make entries in the Character palette. If you make entries in the Character palette when more than one text object is selected, you will globally change type attributes for all selected text objects.

4. Whenever you change values in the Character palette, press the **Tab** or **Enter** key to apply them, or click in another field in the palette, or click outside of the palette.

The Character palette lets you set the character-level type specifications described under the following sections.

Changing the Font

The Font pop-up menu on the Character palette is identical to the Font menu, which lists all the fonts installed on your system. Font families—i.e., fonts that come with separate printer fonts for roman, bold, italic, and bold-italic styles—are followed by an arrow, and you can set the font name and style through this submenu.

➤ When you choose a font from the Font menu, the choice you make applies immediately to any selected text, or to the next text typed if no text is currently selected.

➤ When you choose a font from the Character palette, the choice you make applies to any selected text when you press **Tab** or **Enter**, or to the next text typed if no text is currently selected.

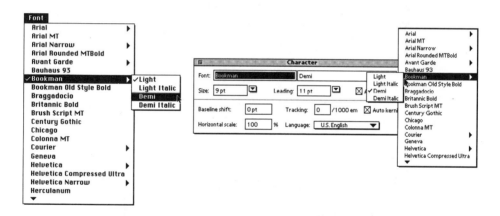

Figure 8.10 The Font menu and the Character palette's pop-out menu.

In the Character palette, you can simply type the first letter or two of the font or style you want at the beginning of the Font or Style text box. Illustrator fills in the full name of the font or the style beginning with the letter(s) you type.

NOTE

You can also use **Type** > **Find Font** to change fonts, as described under "Globally Finding and Changing Fonts," later in this chapter.

Changing Type Size

The **Type** > **Size** submenu lets you specify the font size of selected text. Font size is measured in points. The Size submenu offers a choice of 11 preset font sizes, and the **Other** command, which lets you specify sizes that do not appear on the submenu. The keyboard shortcut for the **Other** command is **Command+Shift+S**, which displays the Character palette.

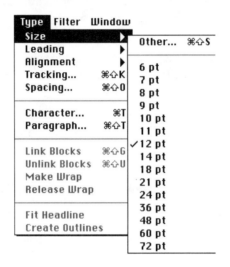

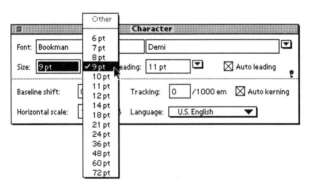

Figure 8.11 The Type > Size submenu and the Character palette's pop-out menu.

The Size field in the Character palette lets you enter a font size, in points, for the selected text, or choose from the list of sizes in the pop-up menu. You can enter any size, including decimal increments to an accuracy of one one-hundredth of a point; you are not limited to the sizes in the list.

See also "Changing the Horizontal Scale" later in this chapter.

The fastest way to change size is by using the keyboard shortcuts—**Command+Shift+>** to increase size, and **Command+Shift+<** to decrease size. The size changes by the increment specified for the **Keyboard Increments-Size/Leading** option in the File > Preferences > General dialog box.

NOTE

Changing the Space between Lines (Leading)

Leading (rhymes with heading) is a measure of the vertical distance between base-lines of type for rectangular or area text (see the description of these under the Type tool earlier in this chapter). For example, 12-point type with 14-point leading would have 14 points of space between the baselines. Leading is measured in points. If a line of type contains characters with different leading specifications, the line uses the largest leading value.

Figure 8.12 Examples of the same text with different leading.

The **Type > Leading** submenu and the Character palette let you specify the leading of selected text. The Leading submenu offers a choice of 11 preset leading values, plus Auto leading, which sets the leading at 120%t of the font size, and the **Other** command (**Command+Shift+S**), which displays the Character palette and lets you specify leading values that do not appear on the submenu, to an accuracy of one one-hundredth of a point.

Select **Auto Leading** if you want Illustrator to set the leading for you, calculated as 120% of font size. With this option checked, the leading will automatically be adjusted whenever you change the type size.

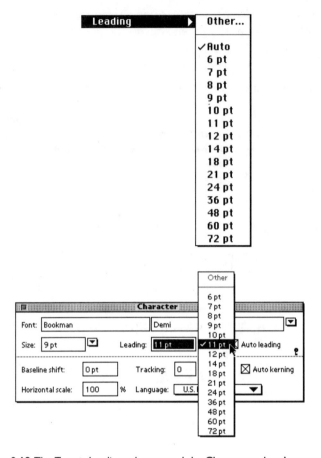

Figure 8.13 The Type > Leading submenu and the Character palette's pop-out menu.

NOTE

You can also increase the leading by holding down the **Option** key while pressing the **down arrow** key or decrease leading by holding down the **Option** key while pressing the **up arrow** key. The leading changes by the increment specified for the **Keyboard Increments-Size/Leading** option in the File > Preferences > General dialog box.

Adjusting the Baseline Shift

The Baseline shift field in the Character palette lets you shift the selected text above or below the baseline. You can do this to create superscripts and subscripts or to create your own custom effects. The units used are those you specified in the Indent/shift Units field in the General Preferences dialog box (see **File > General > Preferences** in Chapter 10). Positive increments shift the type above the baseline; negative increments shift it below the baseline.

$$H^20 \qquad _A{}^V{}A \qquad a^2{=}b^2{+}c^2$$

Figure 8.14 Examples of baseline shift.

See also the earlier example of using baseline shift on text on a path.

SHORTCUT

You can adjust the baseline shift through the keyboard: to move selected characters up above the baseline, press **Option+Shift+up arrow**. To move lower, press **Option+Shift+down arrow**.

Changing the Horizontal Scale

The Horizontal scale field in the expanded Character palette lets you condense or expand the selected type by entering a percentage. Unscaled type is 100%. Percentages greater than 100 expand the type; percentages less than 100 condense it. Scaling is different from tracking: with tracking, only the *space between* the characters is adjusted, while with scaling, the vertical and horizontal proportions of the letterforms themselves are changed.

The Rose Garden　　**The Rose Garden**　　The Rose Garden

Figure 8.15 Examples of horizontal scaling.

NOTE

You can also affect horizontal scaling by using the Scale tool and entering nonuniform scaling values.

Adjusting the Space between Letters (Tracking / Kerning)

Tracking and kerning both affect the spacing between letters, but they work in two different ways. When you *track* the space between letters in a selected range of text, Illustrator changes the spacing based on a table of values that is part of each font's definition. For example, the tracking table's values might always adjust the spaces between the capital letters *A* and *V* to be tighter than the space between *N* and *E* in order to achieve a consistent overall look. When you select a group of letters such as **NEW WAVE** and adjust the tracking value, the relative space between *A* and *V* will still be tighter than the other spaces. Tracking is a good way to force text to fit or fill a confined space if you don't want to change the type size.

You can override the tracking table values by manually *kerning* the space between two letters, to make any two letters as close together or as far apart as you wish. This might be to compensate for your personal dissatisfaction with how the tracking table is handling the spacing—but more likely you'll only use manual kerning to create special effects or custom looks.

The **Type > Tracking/Kerning** command (**Command+Shift+K**) opens the expanded Character palette which includes the Tracking/Kerning field, where you can enter a tracking value for the selected text in units of 1/1000 of an em space. (An *em space* is the same width as an uppercase *M*.) Positive values increase the space between characters; negative values reduce the space between characters.

You can also change the space between characters through the keyboard. Place an insertion point between two characters, or select a range, then:

NOTE

Press **Option+left arrow** key to move them closer together

Press **Option+right arrow** key to move them apart

The characters move by the increment specified in the File > Preferences > General dialog box. Press **Command+Option+left arrow** or **Command+Option+right arrow** to move characters by 5 times this increment.

THE NEW WAVE
THE NEW WAVE
THE NEWWAVE

Figure 8.16 Examples of kerned letters.

The label on the menu and in the Character palette changes according to what is selected. If you place an insertion point between two characters, the command or label is **Kern**. If a range of text or an entire text object is selected, the command or label is **Tracking**.

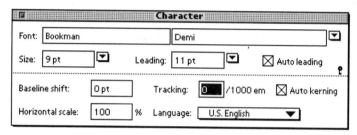

Figure 8.17 The Character palette with the Tracking option.

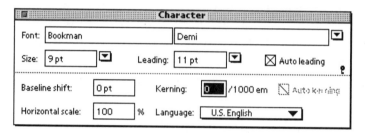

Figure 8.18 The Character palette with the Kerning option.

NOTE

You can view the assigned kerning value between two characters by clicking the I-beam to insert the cursor between them with the expanded Character palette displayed. You can view the assigned tracking value by dragging to select two or more characters. You cannot, however, view both the kerning value and the tracking value at the same time. If you change the tracking value and the space between characters doesn't seem to change, check to see that a kerning value hasn't also been assigned (and vice versa).

Setting Auto Kerning

Turning **Auto kerning** on causes Illustrator to use the pair-kerning tables built into the font. Any manual kerning values you set override auto-kerning values.

NOTE

See also how spacing is controlled in justified text, later in this chapter.

Forcing Text to Fit a Width

The **Type > Fit Headline** command lets you "force justify" text across the full width of the text path by automatically adjusting the tracking values and (for Adobe multiple master fonts) the weight of the font. Here's how it works:

➤ This command works on rectangular text and area text only—it does not affect text on an open path or point text.

➤ It forces the currently selected paragraph(s)—all of the text up to a forced line break—to fit the width of the text container. (This is not the same as justifying text, where the space between letters is adjusted within the limits you specify and text is allowed to wrap at the edge of the text area.)

➤ If the paragraph is shorter than the container width, space is added between letters. If the paragraph is longer than would fit on one line, space is removed between letters. There are no limits to how tight or wide the spaces can be.

➤ If you edit or change the format of the text after applying this command, you must reapply this command to recalculate the spacing.

To force a paragraph to fit a given width:

1. Use the Type tool to create a text rectangle the width you want and then type the text, or create a closed path the width you want and use the Area-type tool to enter the text.

2. Use any type tool to insert a cursor in the paragraph you want to affect—or drag the I-beam to select more than one paragraph.

3. Choose **Type > Fit Headline**.

Figure 8.19 Text before and after applying Fit Headline.

Globally Finding and Changing Fonts

The **Type > Find Font** command lists all the fonts used in a document and lets you globally change all occurrences of one font to another. You can also save the font list as a text file.

1. Choose **Type > Find Font** to display the Find Font dialog box, listing all fonts used in the current document. By clicking the options below the lists, you can display **Multiple Master** fonts, **Standard** fonts (Courier, Helvetica, Symbol, and Times), **Type 1** (PostScript) fonts, or **TrueType** fonts—or any combination. You can also opt to display as replacement fonts only the fonts already being used in the document or all fonts installed on the system.

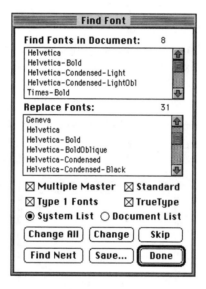

2. Click on a font name in the top list—the fonts found in the document—to find the next occurrence of that font in your document. Then choose one of these options:

   ➤ To replace the font of the selected text, click on the new font name in the second list—the Replace Fonts list—then click **Change** (to change this occurrence only) or **Change All** (to change all occurrences).

   ➤ Click **Find Next** to skip the current instance and find the next.

   ➤ Click **Skip** to skip this font search entirely and search for the next font on the first list.

   ➤ To save a list of all fonts found in the document, click **Save**. A dialog box will prompt you to enter a name and location for the text file. You can import the text to Illustrator to print it, or open, edit, and print it from any text editor or word processor.

3. Click **Done** to end the search process.

NOTE

See also the description of the **File > Document Info** command in Chapter 10, which also lists fonts used in a document. Both of these commands are useful when moving a document from one system to another—because you can verify that the other system has the needed fonts. Otherwise, if you can't install the missing fonts on the new system, and if the document is final, you can convert the missing fonts to outlines before transferring the document. The **Type > Create Outlines** command is described later in this chapter.

Globally Changing Case

The **Type > Change Case** command globally changes selected text to all uppercase, all lowercase, or mixed caps and lowercase (i.e., initial caps).

1. Use a text tool to select the text to be changed.

2. Choose **Type > Change Case** to display a dialog box of options.

3. Select the desired option and click **OK**.

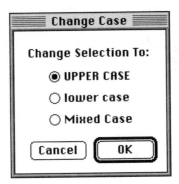

Setting Paragraph Attributes

Commands in the Type menu and options in the Paragraph palette affect the appearance or relationship between whole paragraphs. Alignment options affect whole paragraphs, for example, and you can set limits for the automatic adjustment of spacing between words and letters in justified text. You can also set values for indenting paragraphs, and turn hyphenation on or off for selected paragraphs.

NOTE To apply alignment and other paragraph-level formatting options such as indents, it is not necessary to select the entire paragraph or paragraphs to which you wish to apply the format. Selecting any part of the paragraph, or placing an insertion point in the case of a single paragraph, is all that is required. See also the earlier section on selecting text.

Displaying the Paragraph Palette

The Paragraph palette lets you set the attributes of paragraphs of text—indentation, alignment, and spacing—through a palette that can remain open while you work. This palette can be accessed through a number of commands. (Additional text attributes that apply to individual characters of text are set through the Character palette, described earlier in this chapter.)

To display the Paragraph palette, simply use the keyboard shortcut **Command+Shift+T**, or choose **Window > Show Paragraph**, **Type > Paragraph**, or **Type > Spacing** (**Command+Shift+O**). If the Paragraph palette is already displayed, you can choose **Window > Hide Paragraph** to close it, but it's usually much easier to simply click the close box on the palette title bar.

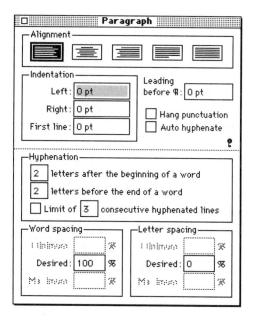

Figure 8.20 The Paragraph palette, maximized.

When the Paragraph palette is displayed on the screen, you can view the type specifications of selected text, and change them by making entries in the palette. If you choose **Type > Paragraph** when text is selected, the paragraph attribute currently applied to the text is displayed in the palette. If you choose **Type > Paragraph** when no text is selected, then the Paragraph palette shows the defaults that would apply to the next text typed. You can change the defaults by changing the palette values when no text is selected.

You can change the alignment, indentation, and spacing between paragraphs through the reduced palette, or click the "latch" symbol in the lower-right corner to expand the palette and set hyphenation and spacing options as well.

Any changes you make to the Paragraph palette are automatically applied to whatever text is currently selected on the Artboard. Be sure that only text you wish to change is selected when you make entries in the palette.

WARNING

Adjusting the Size and Position of the Paragraph Palette

You can move the Paragraph palette on the screen by dragging the title bar. The palette will always display on top of all document windows, but the most recently used palette will appear on top of this palette if there is overlap between palettes. You can bring any palette to the top by clicking on it. If a palette is completely hidden under other palettes, you can move the other palettes or you can use the command under the Window menu to **Hide** and then **Show** the buried palette.

You can toggle between two sizes of the Paragraph palette by clicking on the "latch" icon just below the **Auto hyphenate** option.

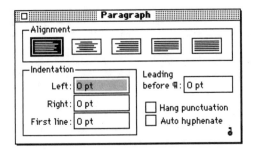

Figure 8.21 The Paragraph palette, minimized.

Setting Paragraph Attributes

You can change the character attributes in the Paragraph palette when no text is selected, to affect only the next text typed, or you can change the appearance of selected text by changing these attributes. In either case, the procedure is the same.

Note that steps 1 and 2 can be done in any order—step 2 can precede step 1.

NOTE

1. Display the Paragraph palette by using the keyboard shortcut **Command+Shift+T**, or choose **Window > Show Paragraph**, **Type > Paragraph**, or **Type > Spacing** (**Command+Shift+O**).

2. Use the Selection tool (pointer) to select the text object(s) to be changed, or use the Type tool (I-beam) to select a range of paragraphs within a text object and change only those paragraphs, or press **Command+Shift+A** to deselect all objects and affect only the next text typed.

Figure 8.22 Select point text, area text, or text on a path with the Selection tool, or a range of paragraphs with the Type tool.

3. Make entries in the Paragraph palette. If you make entries in the Paragraph palette when more than one text object is selected, you will globally change type attributes for all selected text objects.

4. Whenever you change values in the Paragraph palette, press the **Tab** or **Enter** key to apply them, or click in another field in the palette, or click outside of the palette.

The Paragraph palette lets you set the paragraph-level type specifications described under the following headings.

Setting Paragraph Alignment

You can specify **Left**, **Right**, **Centered**, or **Justified** alignment by choosing from the **Type > Alignment** submenu or by clicking on one of the alignment icons at the top of the Paragraph palette. If you specify **Justified** alignment, you have the option of whether or not to justify the last line in a paragraph. If you choose to justify the last line it stretches the full width of the paragraph.

Alignment options have keyboard equivalents: **Command+Shift+L** to set alignment left, **Command+Shift+C** to center each line, **Command+Shift+R** to set alignment right, **Command+Shift+J** to justify paragraphs, **Command+Shift+B** to justify last line.

SHORTCUT

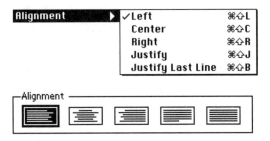

Figure 8.23 The Type > Alignment submenu and symbols from the Paragraph palette.

Figure 8.24 Text aligned left, centered, right, justified, and last-line justified.

Setting Indentation

You can enter left, right, and first line indent values in the Paragraph palette.

➤ The Left indent value indents the left edge of the paragraph from the left side of the text container by the specified amount.

➤ The Right indent value indents the right edge of the paragraph from the right side of the text containerby the specified amount.

➤ The First Line indent value indents the beginning of the first line of the paragraph from the left edge of the paragraph. Negative values result in hanging indents.

NOTE

The units used are those you specified in the **Type Units** option in the File > Preferences > General dialog box.

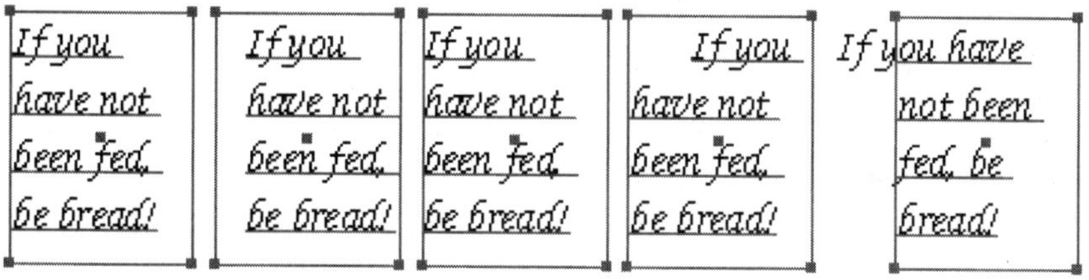

Figure 8.25 Rectangular text with no indents, left indent, right indent, and first-line indents set to +12 points and -12 points.

Spacing between Paragraphs

The Leading before ¶ value in the Paragraph palette adds points for extra leading (vertical space) before paragraphs. Spacing is added between paragraphs, but not at the top of a text container. You can enter negative leading values to force paragraphs to overlap.

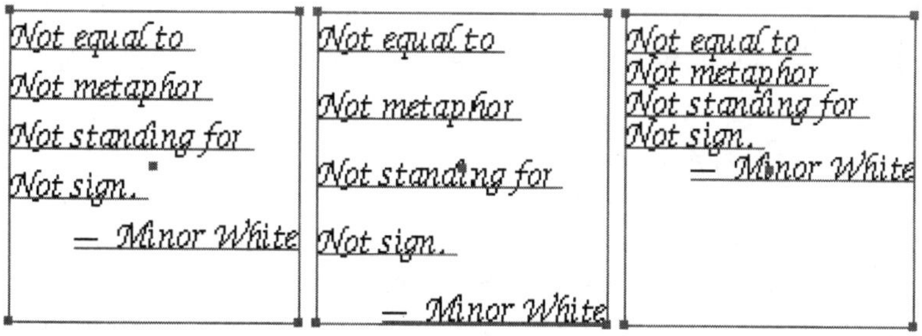

Figure 8.26 Paragraphs with leading before set to 0, 4, and -4 points.

Hanging Punctuation

Turning the **Hang Punctuate** option on places punctuation marks that fall at the ends of lines outside the paragraph margins of rectangular or area text—it has no effect on point text or text along a path.

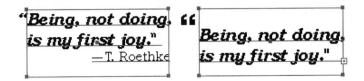

Figure 8.27 Paragraphs with hanging punctuation.

Hyphenating Text

Check the **Auto hyphenate** box in the Paragraph palette to let Illustrator hyphenate words in a selected paragraph for you. When this feature is active, the options you enter under the next headings will control the hyphenation that occurs. You can also specify the way a specific word can be hyphenated, or exclude a word from being hyphenated, using **File > Preferences > Hyphenation**.

Hyphenation Options

If **Auto hyphenate** is active in the Paragraph palette, you can specify the minimum number of letters from the beginning or end of a word a hyphen can appear, and limit the number of consecutive hyphens in a row. You can also specify the way specific words will be hyphenated using **File > Preferences > Hyphenation Options**, as described in the next sections.

Spacing Options

The **Spacing** options in the expanded Paragraph palette let you specify the amount of space between words and between characters in selected text. Spacing options apply to entire paragraphs of text. The values are expressed as percentages of the width of a space.

Word Spacing options control the amount of white space between words. For justified type, you can set minimum, desired, and maximum values for word spacing. The default values are 100% minimum, 100% desired, and 150% maximum. At 100%, no additional space is added between words. With nonjustified type, you can specify the desired value only.

Letter Spacing controls the amount of white space between letters. For justified type, you can specify minimum, desired, and maximum values. The default values are 0% minimum, 0% desired, and 25% maximum. At 0%, no extra space is added between letters. (The actual amount of space is built into each font by the font's designers.) You can enter negative amounts to reduce letter spacing. With nonjustified type, you can specify the desired value only.

These spacing options apply to entire paragraphs. If you want to adjust the spacing in a smaller amount of text, use the **Tracking/Kerning** option instead, described earlier under the Character palette.

NOTE

Selecting and Editing the Hyphenation Dictionary

Besides controlling hyphenation options through the Paragraph palette, you can use the **File > Preferences > Hyphenation** command to select a default language dictionary for all new documents and define specific words. The hyphenation dictionary can be changed for the current document through the Character palette.

To select the default hyphenation dictionary or hyphenate specific words:

1. Choose **File > Preferences > Hyphenation** to display the Hyphenation Options dialog box.

2. Select the language in which the rules will apply from the Language pop-out list. This selection becomes the default dictionary for all new documents, and it appears in the Character palette.

3. In the Entry field, type a word.

➤ If you enter the word with no hyphens and click **Add**, then Illustrator will never hyphenate the word.

➤ If you type the word with hyphens inserted and click **Add**, then Illustrator will only hyphenate the word at those places where you typed hyphens.

➤ If you type a word and click **Delete**, the word will be removed from the hyphenation list.

4. Click **Done** when you are finished adding or deleting words.

5. To hyphenate words in the artwork, select the paragraphs in which they appear and make sure that the hyphenation is set on the Paragraph palette.

6. To select a different language dictionary for hyphenating the current document only, choose a dictionary in the expanded Character palette.

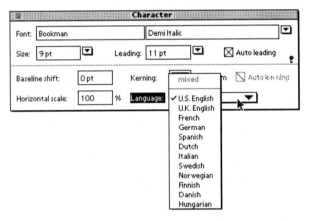

Figure 8.28 Override the default hyphenation dictionary for the current document through the Character palette.

Globally Editing Text

Illustrator includes text-handling capabilities found in no other graphics program: tabs, automatic rows and columns, a full-featured spell checker, automatic "smart" quotes and dashes, and search-and-replace by font or case. A Tabs palette makes applying tabs quick and easy, including graphic tabs that use graphic elements such as lines and arcs as tab stops.

These next sections describe the text-editing commands that appear under the Type menu in Adobe Illustrator 6.0. They include: **Check Spelling**, **Smart Punctuation**, and **Find**.

Checking Spelling

The **Type > Check Spelling** command compiles a list of misspelled words in your document, and offers a list of alternatives. You can skip individual words without changing them, or add them to the dictionary list (the AI User Dictionary in the Text folder in the Plug-ins folder). You can also edit the AI User Dictionary directly using any text editor.

To check spelling in the current document, follow these steps:

1. Choose **Type > Check Spelling**. This displays the Check Spelling dialog box, where words that are not found in the AI User Dictionary are shown in the Misspelled Words list.

2. Click the **Case Sensitive** option if you want words to be listed separately that are misspelled the same but are in different cases.

3. Click **Language** to select a specific language dictionary if you have installed more than one. Adobe Illustrator includes a U.S. English dictionary and a U.K. English dictionary, and other language dictionaries are available from Adobe.

4. To obtain a list of alternatives for a misspelled word, click on the word in the Misspelled Words list. The first instance of that word in your document is highlighted, and any alternatives are shown in the Suggested Corrections list.

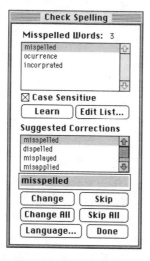

Figure 8.29 The Check Spelling dialog box with Suggested Corrections list for a selected misspelled word.

5. You have three options in handling a misspelled word: change the spelling, skip the word (leave it unchanged), or add it to the dictionary.

   ➤ To change the spelling of the word in the document, either click on the correct spelling in the Suggested Corrections list or type the correct word in the text box below the list. Then click **Change** to change only the first instance of the misspelled word, or click **Change All** to change all instances of the misspelled word in the document.

   ➤ Click **Skip** to leave the current instance of the word unchanged, or click **Skip All** to leave all instances of the word unchanged.

   ➤ Click **Learn** to add the word to the dictionary.

6. To edit the current dictionary list, click **Edit List....** The Learned Words dialog box lists all words added to the AI User Dictionary in the Text folder in the Plug-ins folder.

   ➤ To change a word in the dictionary, select a word in the list then type the replacement word or new spelling in the text box below the list and click **Change** (to replace the selected word) or **Add** (to add the entry as a new word or alternative spelling).

   ➤ To remove a word from the dictionary, select it and click **Remove**.

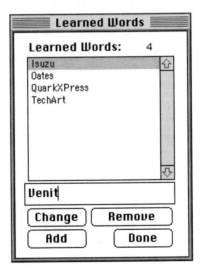

Figure 8.30 Learned Words dialog box.

7. Click **Done** when you are finished spell checking the document.

NOTE

You can also edit the AI User Dictionary directly using any text editor. This is convenient if you want to add a long list of words quickly. Using a text editor, you can easily select and copy words you have entered in other user dictionaries and paste them into the AI User Dictionary.

Using Smart Punctuation

The **Type > Smart Punctuation** command replaces straight keyboard text symbols with the special equivalents often used in publishing. This includes changing straight quote marks (") to opening and closing quote marks ("") as well as other options described in the next steps. You can select the types of symbols to be replaced, and search the entire document or only the selected text.

1. Select text to be searched if you do not want to search the entire document, then choose **Type > Smart Punctuation** from the filter menu to display the Smart Punctuation dialog box.

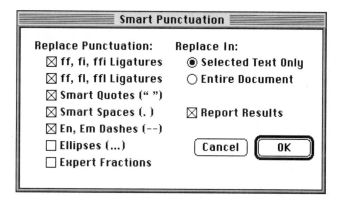

2. Click one or more of the replacement options:

➤ **ff, fi, ffi Ligatures**—replaces these two- and three-character combinations with single "characters" in which the components are kerned to touch: fi.

➤ **Smart Quotes**—replaces straight keyboard quote marks (", ') with opening and closing quote marks (", ", ', ').

➤ **Smart Spaces**—replaces multiple spaces after a period with a single space.

➤ **En, Em Dashes**—replaces a double keyboard dash (--) with an en dash (–) and a triple dash (---) with an em dash (—).

➤ **Ellipses**—replaces three periods (...) with a single-character ellipsis (…).

➤ **Expert fractions**—replaces separate characters used to represent fractions (1/2) with their single-character equivalents (if available for the font).

3. Click **Selected Text Only** or **Entire Document** to specify the extent of the search. Click **Report Results** if you want to view a list of the number of symbols replaced. Click **OK** to search for and replace the selected options.

NOTE

You can also enter most of these punctuation marks and symbols directly while typing in most fonts—see the sidebar near the beginning of this chapter.

WARNING

This filter does not prompt you for each individual instance of change, so be careful not to replace all straight quotes with curly quotes if some are intended as the symbols for feet and inches, where straight marks are appropriate.

Finding and Replacing Characters

The **Type > Find** command finds and replaces specific strings of text that have been typed in Illustrator.

1. Choose **Type > Find** to display the Find Text dialog box.

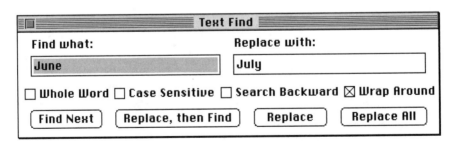

2. Type the text you wish to find in the Find what box, and the replacement text in the Replace with box, if you want not only to find it but to replace it with new text.

3. Choose from four options:

➤ Click **Whole Word** to find only whole words that match the search text—to find *axiom* but not *axiomatic*, for example.

➤ Click **Case Sensitive** to find text that matches exactly the capitalization you entered in the text search area.

➤ Click **Search Backwards** to search from the current position of the selection cursor toward the top or beginning of the document.

➤ Click **Wrap Around** to search from the current position of the selection cursor to the end of the document and then from the front of the document to the place where the search started.

4. Click **Find** or **Replace All**. If you click **Find**, then on each found occurrence you can click **Replace** or **Replace, then Find**.

Creating Columns of Text

There are several ways to create and work with tabular text in Illustrator:

➤ You can use the Tab Ruler palette to set tabs for selected paragraphs.

➤ You can use the **Rows and Columns** command to break a text container (rectangular text or area text) into separate but linked blocks, arranged as rows and columns.

These features are described under the next headings.

Using the Tab Ruler Palette

The Tab Ruler palette lets you set left, right, center, and decimal tabs in text. The keyboard shortcut **Command+Shift+T** quickly displays or hides the palette, which you can position over the text you want to tab. Units of measure on the tab ruler match the unit of measure on the page rulers, as defined in the File > Document Setup dialog box.

Follow these steps to set tabs:

1. Select any text object using a selection tool or a range of text using the text tool.

2. Select **Window > Show Tab Ruler,** or press **Command+Shift+T** to display the Tab Ruler palette. It's a good idea to make the following adjustments before setting tabs:

➤ Click the **Alignment** box in the top-right corner of the palette to automatically align the tab ruler with the selected text. This is much quicker and more precise than simply dragging the palette into position—which is also an option.

➤ Drag the **Extend Tab Ruler** button at the bottom right in the palette to make the ruler wider if necessary to match the text width.

➤ Click the **Snap** option box (right of the four tab icons) if you want the tabs to snap to increments shown on the ruler as you position them. Hold the **Option** key while positioning a tab to reverse the effect of this option.

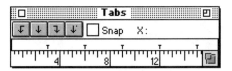

Figure 8.31 Tab Ruler palette.

3. To set a tab, click a **Tab Style** button (one of four icons at the top left in the palette) for the tab you wish to set (left, right, center, or decimal) then click on the tab ruler in the position where you want the tab—or click and drag to display a visual guide as you move and position the tab. The guide disappears when you release the mouse button, but whether you click or drag to position the tab, the Tab position is shown in numeric value in the top center area of the palette.

Repeat step 3 to position other tabs.

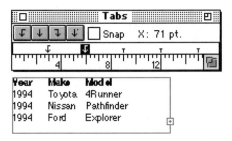

Figure 8.32 Tab Ruler palette with text showing tab settings.

4. You can edit existing tabs using one of these procedures:

   ➤ To change a tab style for an existing tab, click on the tab mark on the ruler to highlight it, then click on one of the **Tab Style** buttons.

   ➤ To move a tab, click on it, and drag it to a new position.

   ➤ To remove a tab, click on it, and drag it off the top or the left side of the palette.

Breaking a Text Container into Rows and Columns

The **Type > Rows and Columns** command divides rectangles and text containers of any shape into rows and columns or rectangles. You can precisely adjust the height, width, and gutter size between rows and columns. You can also use this filter to change the way text flows (from left to right or up and down).

This command is a handy alternative to using the link command (described next) to flow text through several text containers, especially when you want to create columnar text where each column is the same width and height.

1. Use a selection tool to select a graphic rectangle or a text container of any shape.

2. Choose **Type > Rows and Columns** to display the Rows and Columns dialog box.

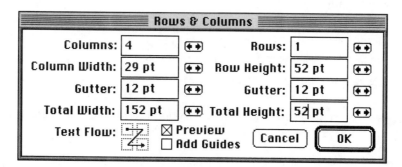

3. Type the number of Columns and Rows you want, or use the control buttons at the side of the Columns and Rows text boxes to change the values.

4. Click the **Preview** option to view the effect. The filter automatically adjusts the columns' width and row height to fit the selected rectangle.

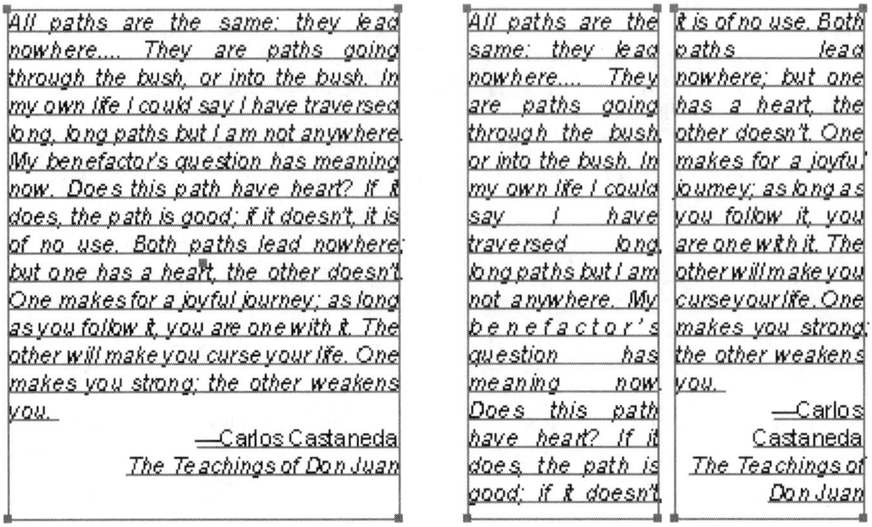

All paths are the same: they lead nowhere.... They are paths going through the bush, or into the bush. In my own life I could say I have traversed long, long paths but I am not anywhere. My benefactor's question has meaning now. Does this path have heart? If it does, the path is good; if it doesn't, it is of no use. Both paths lead nowhere; but one has a heart, the other doesn't. One makes for a joyful journey; as long as you follow it, you are one with it. The other will make you curse your life. One makes you strong; the other weakens you.

—Carlos Castaneda
The Teachings of Don Juan

All paths are the same: they lead nowhere.... They are paths going through the bush, or into the bush. In my own life I could say I have traversed long, long paths but I am not anywhere. My benefactor's question has meaning now. Does this path have heart? If it does, the path is good; if it doesn't,

it is of no use. Both paths lead nowhere; but one has a heart, the other doesn't. One makes for a joyful journey; as long as you follow it, you are one with it. The other will make you curse your life. One makes you strong; the other weakens you.

—Carlos Castaneda
The Teachings of Don Juan

Figure 8.33 Text in a rectangular text box changed from one row, one column, to one row, two columns.

5. Adjust the column width, row height, column gutter, row gutter, and overall height and width of the rectangle as desired. Click **Add Guides** to add guide paths along the row and edges.

6. Click **OK** to close the dialog box. The selected rectangle is broken into several linked rectangles. The rows and columns are grouped and the guide paths are grouped.

7. So long as both groups are selected, you can drag the rows and columns by dragging the guides, or use the guides to align the rows and columns against other elements of the artwork.

8. Delete the guide paths when you are finished.

You can change the direction of text flow from left to right, or from top to bottom, by clicking the **Text Flow** icon at the lower left in the dialog box.

NOTE

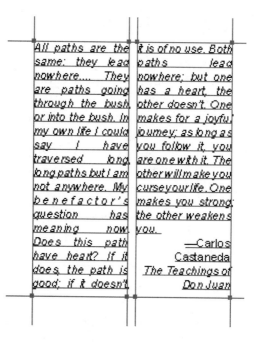

Figure 8.34 Rows and Columns of text with guide paths.

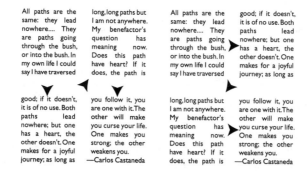

Figure 8.35 Four rows and four columns with left-right text flow (left in figure) changed to top-down text flow (right).

Linking Text Containers

The **Link** and **Unlink Blocks** commands let you set up (or release) associations between one block of text and another, so that edits made in one block will cause text to flow from one block to another.

Use the **Type > Link Blocks** (**Command+Shift+G**) command to link a text object with another path or paths, which are automatically converted to text paths. The linked objects become a single text object. To link a series of paths:

1. Select the text object and the path or paths you want to link.

Figure 8.36 One text object and several paths selected.

2. Choose **Type > Link Blocks** or press **Command+Shift+G**. If the original text object contains overflow text, that text flows into the linked path or paths in the order in which they were created. It is not necessary to change the linked paths to text paths—the **Link** command automatically does this.

Figure 8.37 Text flows from first object into others after linking.

NOTE

You can change the order before linking by using the **Send To Back** and **Bring To Front** or **Paste In Front** and **Paste In Back** commands—the frontmost object is always last in the flow. If you want to change the flow order after linking the objects, you must unlink them again.

3. You can replace one of the linked paths with a different one without unlinking. To do so:

➤ Use the Direct-selection tool to select the path you want to remove and choose **Edit > Clear** or press the **Delete** or **Backspace** key. The path disappears, and the text it contained flows into the remaining path. If there is too much text to fit, a plus sign appears at the lower-right corner of the path.

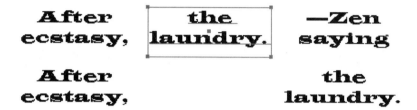

Figure 8.38 Text Middle object selected (top) and deleted (bottom).

➤ Then create or select the path into which you want the text to flow, extend the selection to include the text object, and choose **Link** once more.

Figure 8.39 New path added (top) and linked (bottom).

SHORTCUT

If you are working with text in columns, you can quickly produce a series of linked columns with identical dimensions, without using the **Link** command. Create the first column by dragging a rectangle with the Type tool and type or import the text. To create additional linked columns, select the text rectangle by Option+clicking with the Direct-selection tool, then Option+drag to create an exact duplicate. Any overflow text flows into the duplicate rectangle, and the two rectangles form a single text object.

WARNING

You must first Option+click on the text rectangle to select it with the Direct-selection tool before Option+dragging to create a duplicate. The text rectangle cannot already be selected when you Option+click. Otherwise, Option+dragging will create an unlinked duplicate with the same text, and the same text overflow problem.

431

NOTE

See also the **Rows and Columns** command described earlier in this chapter.

4. If you don't like the result, or change your mind for some other reason, the **Type > Unlink Blocks** command (**Command+Shift+U**) unlinks linked text paths that make up a selected text object.

All the component text paths in the text object are unlinked and selected. The text remains in the individual text paths, but no longer flows from one path to the next. You cannot unlink only one text path from a text object that contains multiple paths. All the paths in the text object become separate unlinked text objects when you choose **Unlink**.

Wrapping Text around Graphics

The **Type > Make Wrap** command makes type in an area wrap around another path or paths. It is used primarily to run text around a graphic object. You can make one or more text objects wrap around a path. The path around which you want the text to wrap must be in front of the text object.

1. Create the text object or objects that you want to wrap and the graphic object around which you want them to wrap.

NOTE

The object that the text is going to wrap around has to be in the front of the text container(s). If the object is behind the text just use the **Bring To Front** command under the Arrange menu to adjust the layer of the object.

2. Select the text object or objects and the graphic object using the Selection tool.

3. Choose **Type > Make Wrap**. The text then wraps around the graphic object, and the text object and the graphic object around which the text wraps are grouped.

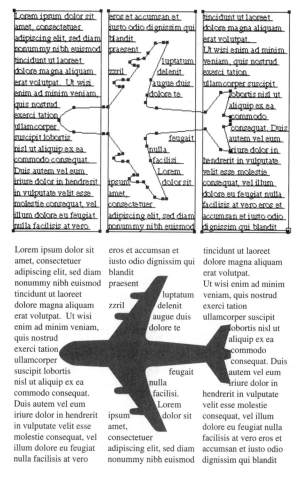

Figure 8.40 Text wrapped around a graphic in Artwork view (top) and Preview (bottom).

4. If you don't like the result, or change your mind for some other reason, the **Type > Release Wrap** command releases the text wrap from selected objects and ungroups the text object from the graphic object around which the text wraps. Both the text object and the graphic object are left selected.

Sometimes the text wrap results in text butting right against an object. You can control text wrapping precisely by creating an unstroked, unfilled path that you place over the graphic object around which you want the text to wrap. Adjust the text wrap by adjusting the unpainted object to achieve the desired text wrap.

N O T E

Transforming Text

You can use the transformation tools to scale, rotate, shear, and reflect a text object just as you would any graphic object in Illustrator, as described in Chapter 5. The only proviso is that you must select the text object(s) with the Selection tool—not with a Type tool. You cannot transform individual characters, separate from the rest of the text object of which they are a part.

In transforming text on a path or area or rectangle text, you also have these options:

➤ To transform the entire text object—including all linked text containers—select the text object with the Selection tool.

➤ To transform one type container that is part of a linked series, use the Direct-selection tool to select only those type containers you want to transform. Make sure the text baselines also appear if you want to transform the text along with the container. Otherwise:

➤ To transform the type path or type container without also transforming the text itself, use the Group-selection tool to select only the path—make sure the baselines of the type do *not* appear.

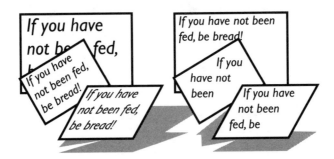

Figure 8.41 Transforming the containers with the type (left),
and transforming the containers only (right).

Transforming type may change its point size. After the transformation, you can select the type and set it to an exact point size if you wish.

NOTE

1. Create a type block with the text you wish to use. Select the **Type** tool and click it in the active window. Type the text you wish to use for the inline type. Then select it with the Selection tool and use the Paint Style palette (**Command+I**) to set Fill and Stroke to **100% Black**, and a wide Stroke Weight, such as **8 points** for 72-point type.

Inline Type
Inline Type

NOTE

The important aspect of this step is that you must set a stroke weight. Variations result by choosing different weights and shades for the stroke. If you use a wide stroke at a small point size, the type will appear compressed. Add a few points to the desired letter spacing in the Tracking Options area of the Paragraph palette.

Inline Type
Inline Type
Inline Type
Inline Type

2. Press **Command+C** and **Command+F** (**Edit > Copy** and **Edit > Paste in Front**) to copy the type block and paste the copy in front of the original, then set Fill to **100% Black**, Stroke to **White**, and Weight to **5** points.

NOTE

The important aspect of this step is that the stroke weight must be less than that used in step 1. Variations result by choosing different weights and shades for the stroke and different Fill settings. You can create shadow effects by offsetting each text object slightly.

3. Always make a test print of the effect, using **File > Print**, because the Preview image of stroked type is not always accurate.

N O T E

Because the two text objects that compose the inline type overlap precisely, it can be tricky to select and edit the lower text objects' fill and stroke attributes. To select the top text object only, click the **Selection** tool on the top block's anchor point. To select both text objects, use the Selection tool to drag a marquee over the overlapping anchor points of the text objects. To select the bottom text object only, select both blocks, then hold down the **Shift** key and click on the anchor point of the top block to deselect it.

Converting Text to Paths

The **Create Outlines** command converts an entire selected text object into a compound path composed of editable path outlines which you can then manipulate by moving anchor points and direction points, just as you would any other path. This means you can create custom logos and special effects other than those available through the Type menu. You can also use this command to create files that will print without reference to printer fonts.

The **Create Outlines** command retains all the formatting and paint attributes of the selected type. However, once a text object has been converted to outlines, it becomes a set of graphic objects rather than text, so it can no longer be edited or formatted using type tools or commands.

WARNING

Adobe Type Manager software, which is included in the Adobe Illustrator package, must be installed in your system to use the **Create Outlines** command. If you do not have ATM version 2.0 or later, the **Type > Create Outlines** command is grayed, indicating that it is not available. In addition, the Type 1 outline fonts (printer fonts) must be available in your System Folder for the text you wish to convert to outlines, including the printer fonts that might also be installed in your printer—such as the PostScript fonts that come built into the Apple LaserWriter series.

1. Use the Selection tool to select the text object you want to convert to a compound path.

NOTE

You can only convert an entire text object to outlines. The command is grayed on the menu when a Type tool is selected. If you want to convert a single character, such as a drop cap, create a separate text object containing only that character.

2. Choose **Type > Create Outlines**. The figure below shows text before (above) and after (below) using the **Create Outlines** command.

Figure 8.42 Text before and after creating outlines.

NOTE

Each character is converted to a compound path. This means that the bowls in the characters will be holes through which you can see elements below.

3. It's a good idea to use the **Arrange > Group** command (**Command+G**) immediately after converting text to outlines, so the character forms retain the spatial relationships set up by the font tables.

4. You can apply colors to the line and fill through the Paint Styles palette to text converted to paths, just as you can apply colors to the fill of normal text. You can also use commands not normally available for text objects—from the Objects menu, or from the Paint Styles palette—to change the appearance of the text that has been converted to paths.

➤ You can apply gradient fills.

➤ You can use the text shapes as masks, filling the text with graphics or with other text. The next figure shows an abstract design composed using Illustrator's drawing tools (above) masked by the text shapes (below).

NOTE Individual letters are compounded automatically when you create outlines so that the centers of letters like Os will knock out but it is still necessary to compound the entire word or phrase together if you want to use an entire text object as a mask (a word or a phrase): select the text outlines using the selection arrow, and select **Object > Compound > Make** to allow all letters to act as a single mask. (See Masks in Chapter 9. See the description of the Wine Label in Chapter 1 for an example of using text as a mask to create custom inline type.)

➤ If you want to manipulate individual characters, you can subselect them with the Direct-selection tool. Once you have selected an individual character, with the Direct-selection tool, you can change the shape of the path by moving the points or direction handles (see Chapter 4).

NOTE

Text converted to paths is no longer a font, and you can no longer edit it as text or apply commands under the Type menu. You can deliberately convert text to paths so you can take the artwork from one system to another and print it easily without worrying about what fonts are installed on each system. This is a good idea if the artwork includes very few words in a rarely available font, but it will increase the file size in direct proportion to the amount of text.

Figure 8.43 Text outlines modified to create special effects.

Exporting Text

The Type > Export filter lets you export text from Illustrator into a separate file, saved in one of 12 possible text formats, for compatibility with various word processing applications. Text formatting (bold, italic, etc.) is preserved if supported by the target word processor.

1. Use the Text selection tool to select the text in the Adobe Illustrator document that you want to export.

2. Choose **Filter > Text > Export** to display the Export Text dialog box.

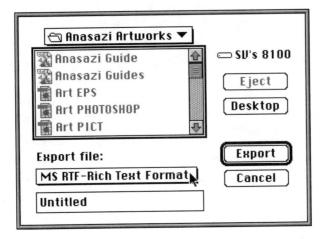

3. Select the desired file format for the exported text from the pop-out menu above the file name, and type the file name in the text box at the bottom of the dialog box. Use the techniques described for the File > Open dialog box (see Chapter 10) to specify the directory into which you want to export the text.

4. You can open the text in any application that supports the file format you selected.

Chapter Summary

In this chapter you learned *almost* everything there is to know about text in Adobe Illustrator. Besides using the techniques described here, you can also use most of the techniques for transforming text described in Chapter 5, and the techniques for painting text described in Chapter 6. Additional special effects using text are described in Chapter 9.

Chapter 9

Examples of Common Objects and Techniques

This chapter combines most of the commands and tools presented in earlier chapters, describing techniques for creating some common objects or effects that you can use to create similar objects or effects of your own.

Techniques described in this chapter include:

➤ Dashed and Dotted Lines, including special uses such as text background, grid elements, and design elements

➤ Stippling Effects

➤ Overlapping Lines, including overlapping dashed lines, and parallel curves

➤ Arrowheads

➤ Hand-drawn Looks (Uneven Line Widths)

➤ Photoshop Effects

- ➤ Shared Borders (Puzzle Pieces)
- ➤ Compound Paths (the Donut-Hole Effect)
- ➤ Working with Masks
- ➤ Drop Shadows
- ➤ Cast Shadows
- ➤ Cubes, including package design
- ➤ Three-Dimensional Polygons
- ➤ Shading on Cylinders
- ➤ Highlights on Spheres
- ➤ Interlocking Objects
- ➤ Coils and Springs
- ➤ Graphs

Dashed and Dotted Lines

Illustrator allows you to make dashed and dotted lines easily, but the next sections demonstrate some tricks you might not have thought about. Dashed lines are useful for architectural and schematic drawings, and they provide a great way to indicate movement or sequential steps of a process. Dashed lines can also be used to add tab leaders to tabular text formats.

You can make dashed or dotted strokes around closed paths, using the same techniques described here for open paths.

You can simplify your artwork and save disk space by using dashed lines instead of rectangles or ellipses. This is useful when you want the effect of shaded bands of color as a background to text or graphics. The only limitation is that strokes cannot be wider than 1800 points, and dashed segments cannot be wider than 1000 points. The next headings show some examples.

NOTE

Perfect Circles and Squares along a Path

In the next steps you'll learn how to make lines of perfect circles or perfect squares, in any specific size and with any specific spacing you like.

1. Before beginning to draw, make sure the Paint Style palette is displayed on the screen, opened to its fullest view: press **Command+I (Object > Paint Style** or **Windows > Show Paint Styles)** to display the Paint Style palette, and click on the bottom section of the display icon at the top left of the palette, or select the top icon from the pop-out menu.

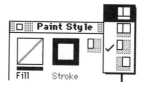

2. Draw a line or shape using one of the drawing tools (the Pen tool, the Freehand tool, or the Autotrace tool). The figure below shows a curved line drawn with the Pen tool.

3. With the line still selected, in the Paint Style palette set Fill to **None,** Stroke to any percentage of black or a color, and Weight to a point size equal to the width measurement of the squares or dots you wish to create. In this example, we use a weight of 6 points.

4. Click the second choice under Caps (the round ends) for a line of dots, or the third choice (the extended blunt ends) for a line of squares.

5. Click **Dashed** in the Dash pattern box located at the bottom of the Paint Style palette. In the first box type the number **0**, which creates either perfect circles or squares. Tab to the second box and type the number of points you want as space between dots. In this case, we type **12**.

NOTE

Typing **0** in the first Dash pattern box, setting Round or Extended Blunt end caps, and clicking **None** in the Fill box are the only three constants you must remember to enter for this special effect to work. If you type a number of greater value in the first Dash pattern box, you will get ellipses and rectangles instead of circles and squares.

6. You can create variations by changing the following values:

   ➤ Try changing the stroke weight and the gap measurement (the second box under Dash pattern) for different effects. For example, in step 3, you can change the size of the dot or square by specifying a thicker or thinner weight.

   ➤ In step 5, changing the gap measurement will decrease or increase the distance between the dots or squares. If the gap measurement equals the stroke weight measurement, the dots or squares will just touch.

   ➤ You can create other effects by varying the dash and gap sizes. Some examples of lines and their gaps are shown next to an example of each dash pattern applied to a 2-point line in the figure on the next page.

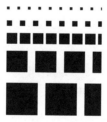

➤ If you select the first Cap option in the Paint Style palette (blunt ends, instead of extended blunt ends), you can make lines of perfect squares by making the stroke weight equal to the dash pattern. The figure below shows examples ranging from 2 to 24 points stroke weight with matching dash sizes and a 6-point gap.

WARNING

If the gap size is equal to the stroke weight, you create a string of pearls in which each dot touches the next. Smaller gap sizes result in overlapping dots. If you type a number of greater value than zero in the first box, you will get oblong circles and rectangles instead of circles and squares.

Dashed Lines as Text Background

You can use a dashed line as a decorative background for a text. In lists that are printed in a small font, the alternating gray/white lines can actually serve as a reading aid.

In the following example, the text is set in 10-point Times and the dashed vertical line is set in 30% gray with 260 points weight (the width of the background for the text). The dash and gap distance are each set at 10 points (so the dashes and gaps coincide with the lines of 10-point text). (See Aligning Text in Chapter 10.)

Time	Events	Room
8:00 am	Registration	Lobby
9:00 am	Session 1: *Crisis in Education*	Room A
10:15 am	Break with Coffee and Pastry	Room B
10:45 am	Session 2: *Solutions in the Schools*	Room A
12:00 pm	Lunch with Keynote Speaker	Room C
2:00 pm	Session 3: *Solutions through Media*	Room A
3:15 pm	Break with Beverage Service	Room B
3:45 pm	Session 4: *Solutions at Home*	Room B
5:00 pm	Social Hour	Lobby

Dashed Lines as Grid Elements

In the calendar template shown below, each week is composed of two overlaid dashed lines. Both strokes are set at 72-point weight, with 72-point dashes, and 12-point gaps. The lower stroke is tinted 80% gray, the top stroke 30% gray.

Month

X X X X X X X
X X X X X X X
X X X X X X X
X X X X X X X
X X X X X X X

The only other elements in the template are text: one text block for the month, plus seven text blocks for the days of the week. A close-up of two cells is shown below.

Dotted Lines as Design Elements

You can create design elements composed of large squares or circles. The only difference here is that you must think big. The figure below shows two overlapping 72-point dashed strokes with rounded end caps, 1-point dashes, and 90-point gaps.

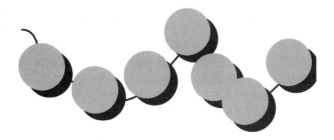

Stippling Effects

The previous sections mentioned some of the special uses for dotted and dashed lines. The next techniques describe a special use of dotted and tinted strokes in places that would normally be solid strokes in artwork—of any color or weight—to yield a softer, more irregular effect, such as a stippled effect or a sketched or brushed ink look.

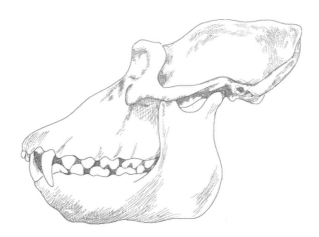

There are countless variations on the suggestions listed here. You are encouraged to experiment with them.

Stippling One Line

1. Draw a line using one of the drawing tools (the Pen tool, Freehand tool, or Autotrace tool). The figure below shows a curved line drawn with the Pen tool.

2. In the Paint Style palette (**Command+I**), set Fill to **None**. Set Stroke to a percentage of black less than 50 (or choose a muted color). Set a fairly thin stroke weight. For this example, enter **30%** black and type in **.5** points Weight.

Figure 9.1 Black stroke (left) changed to thin gray, ready for stippling.

3. Experiment with other paint settings. **Option**+drag multiple copies away and set Stroke to different percentages of black to change the stroke weights. Type in random values for the dash pattern and gaps, such as **1, 5, 0, 5, 2, 0**. Dash values of 2 points or more will create short strokes. A dash value of 0 will create single dots.

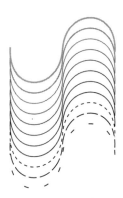

NOTE

Using different percentages of black (or muted color) and different random dash patterns can create lines in your final output resembling the etching effect created with a traditional tool called a *roulette wheel.* You will find that thinner strokes generally create subtler effects. Subtle line effects are difficult to preview on-screen. You probably will want to print a proof on a laser printer, or even an imagesetter, to fine-tune the effect. In either case, you can shorten the cycle of experimentation by setting up a variety of lines on one page and printing them all at once. Then decide which one you will use or modify for use in the final artwork.

Creating Multiple Lines Using the Copy Command

You can draw a series of lines and apply the technique just described to create a shaded area on a drawing, such as the one shown below. Here is the first of several approaches to using multiple lines to stipple (shade) an area in a drawing.

1. Draw one line or curve and set it to the stippling effect you want, using the steps from the previous technique.

2. Select the path with the Selection tool, and press **Command+Shift+M** (**Arrange > Move**). In the Move dialog box, enter the distance you wish between lines—usually very small for a stippling effect. Enter an offset angle if you want.

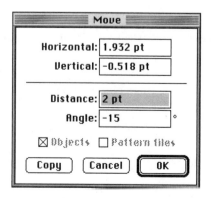

WARNING

If the stroke is very wide and dark, making copies can result in the appearance of rows and columns of dots.

3. Click **Copy** to close the Move dialog box and create a duplicate of the line, slightly offset from the original. Press **Command+D** (**Arrange > Repeat Transform**) as many times as needed to fill the area.

Figure 9.2 Black line (left), copied many times (right).

4. It's a good idea to select all the lines and press **Command+G** (**Arrange > Group**), since you do not want to inadvertently select and move individual lines in the set when you are using them as shading in various parts of the artwork. Use the Direct-selection tool in a magnified view to adjust the lengths or position of lines against an irregular border, if necessary.

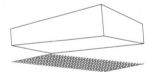

Creating Multiple Lines with the Blend Tool

This next technique for creating multiple lines adds the ability to change the size of the lines in the set. You can also get a more random effect by setting up the two starting lines as dashed strokes with different dash/gap patterns—the Blend tool will create intermediate strokes with different dash/gap values.

1. Draw one line or curve and set it to the stippling effect you want, using the steps from the first stippling technique. Make it as long as the widest span for the area you desire to stipple, and position it at the widest stretch.

2. Select the line with the Selection tool, hold the **Option** key as you drag the line to create a copy, and move it to the next narrow point in the area you wish to shade.

3. Use the Direct-selection tool to select and move, or remove, the end-point(s) to shorten the second line.

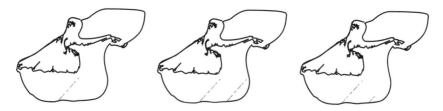

Figure 9.3 Skull with a thin stippled line (left), copied (middle), and shortened (right).

4. Select both strokes with the Selection tool, then click on the **Blend** tool to select it and click on the lowest endpoint of each stroke.

5. In the Blend dialog box, enter the number of lines you wish to create between these two lines. Usually this will be a high number for a stippling effect.

6. You will probably need to experiment to get the effect you want. Try these variations:

➤ If the first blend attempt does not yield the results you want, delete the blended strokes—which are automatically grouped—and repeat step 5, entering a different number of steps.

➤ If the area you wish to shade includes several "wide" and "narrow" bands, repeat steps 2 through 5 to drag additional lines from one of the first two you created, modify them to the desired length, and use the Blend tool to fill in the spaces between them. (But it might be faster to use the next technique instead.)

NOTE

You can create a more random effect by applying the **Filter > Distort > Roughen** or **Scribble** filters to the lines.

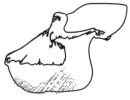

Figure 9.4 Stippled lines (left) can be roughened (middle), or scribbled (right).

Using Photoshop Effects to Stipple Lines

6.0 NEW FEATURE

Illustrator 6.0 introduces the ability to convert graphics drawn with Illustrator's tools to rasterized objects to which Photoshop effects can be applied. You can use these new features to create custom stippling or shading effects.

1. Draw the lines you wish to use as shading or stippling. You can apply any of the attributes mentioned in the earlier sections here, such as dashed patterns and gray tints.

2. Select the lines and choose **Object > Rasterize.**

3. In the Rasterize dialog box, choose a low resolution (screen resolution is 72 dpi), and choose a grayscale or RGB color model if you want to apply Photoshop effects. Click **OK** to close the dialog box and rasterize the selection.

4. With the rasterized object selected, choose an effect from one of the Filter > Gallery Effects submenus. Figure 9.5 shows some examples of effects that work well for shading.

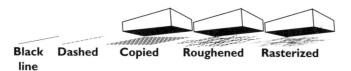

Black line **Dashed** **Copied** **Roughened** **Rasterized**

Figure 9.5 Paths in Illustrator (top left), rasterized, and then with Photoshop effects applied.

5. If you selected **RGB** so you could apply Photoshop effects, but if you intend to print color separations, select the rasterized object and choose **Object > Rasterize** again, but this time choose the **CMYK** model.

Creating a Mask Around Stippled Lines

If the area you want to shade is a very amorphous shape, here's a fast way to create a stippled area of any shape:

1. Use the technique described earlier, under Creating Multiple Lines with the Copy Feature, to create a series of stippled lines that completely cover the area you wish to shade.

2. Draw the shape you want the stippling effect to cover, and position it on top of the lines you created in step 1.

3. Select both the mask and the stippled lines.

4. Choose **Object > Mask > Make**. The mask itself is automatically assigned a Fill and Stroke of **None**.

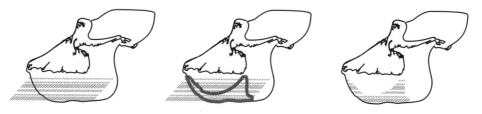

Figure 9.6 Copied series of stippled lines (left) framed by a path that outlines desired shading area (middle), then masked (right).

NOTE

There are other masking examples later in this chapter.

Applying Ink Pen Effects

Illustrator offers an Ink Pen filter that will fill any path with a pattern that looks like hand-inked stippling or brushing. What the filter actually does is described in the next steps.

1. Create a path to which you want to apply Ink Pen effects.

2. Select the path and choose **Filter > Ink Pen > Effects**.

3. In the Ink Pen Effects dialog box, you can choose an effect from the drop-down menu and make a variety of custom adjustments to suit your needs. As you make entries in the dialog box, a preview of the result shows in the preview window if you have selected the **Preview** option.

➤ Select an Ink Pen effect basic pattern from the Settings drop-down menu. Adobe supplies 25 basic patterns, and you can add, modify, or delete patterns as you like.

➤ Under Style, you can select from seven variations for a Hatch pattern, change the original color, opt to retain the background color of the selected area, or change the entire fill to the **Hatch Only**. Then you can select a Fade of **None**, **Fade to White**, **Fade to Black**, or set a gradient. You can also set a fade angle.

➤ Set a density percentage (by typing a number or dragging the slider bar) to determine the number of Ink Pen pattern elements to fill the selected area.

➤ Set Dispersion, Thickness, Rotation, and/or Scale to **None**, **Constant**, **Linear**, **Reflect**, **Symmetry**, or **Random**; in each option you can set the Range, Percentage, and Angle. On the slider bars under each option, the left marker changes the Range value and the right marker changes the Percentage value—or you can type numeric values.

With all these variables, you can create an almost infinite number of variations!

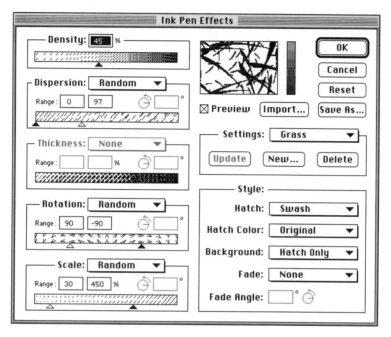

Figure 9.7 Ink Pen Effects dialog box.

4. Click **OK** to close the dialog box and create the effect.

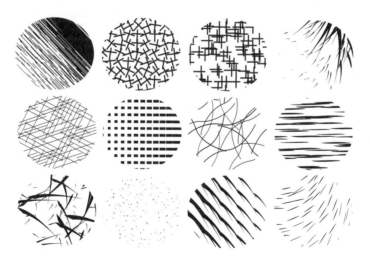

Figure 9.8 Ink pen effects offered with Illustrator's Ink Pen filter.

What Illustrator actually does in creating Ink Pen effects is:

➤ Insert the selected pattern as paths behind the selected path, and

➤ Change the selected path to a mask, assigning a Fill and Stroke of **None**.

NOTE

Be prudent in applying Ink Pen effects, since they can add significantly to the size and complexity of an illustration.

You can create your own Ink Pen effects or edit those that come with Illustrator, much the same way you create or edit patterns, as described in Chapter 6. To create a new effect, start with step 1 here; to edit an existing pattern, start with step 3:

1. Draw the effect you want using Illustrator's drawing tools.

2. Select the objects and press **Command+C** (**Edit > Copy**).

3. Choose **Filter > Ink Pen > Edit** to display the Ink Pen Edit dialog box.

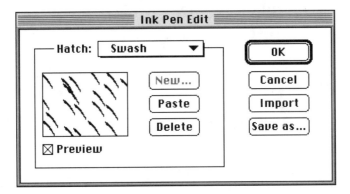

Figure 9.9 Ink Pen Edit dialog box.

4. In the Ink Pen Edit dialog box, choose one or more options:

➤ Choose from the Hatch pop-out menu if you want to edit an existing hatch pattern.

➤ Click **New** to create a new effect composed of the artwork you selected and copied before opening the dialog box (steps 1 and 2). The artwork automatically appears in the Preview window (if **Preview** is selected).

➤ Click **Paste** to paste a copy of the current pattern selection onto the Artboard, for editing.

➤ Click **Delete** to remove the current pattern from the list.

➤ Click **Import** to open a batch from another location.

➤ Click **Save As** to save the current pattern under another name.

Overlapping Lines

The overlapping lines described in this section consist of two identical paths with different stroke attributes: a black or colored stroke on the bottom layer, and a slightly thinner, lighter-colored stroke on top. The effect created by this technique can appear to be one line with a fill color or pattern that is different from the line color at the outer edge of the line—such as the effects shown in the following figures.

The steps listed here create an element composed of a solid black stroke with a thinner, dashed white stroke on top, as illustrated in the figure, but you can use the same technique to create a variety of effects.

You can use these types of lines in maps to represent roads or trails or railway lines. You can also use them in line graphs, floor plans, and other schematic drawings. You can apply the same technique to the borders (strokes) of closed paths (such as rectangles, circles, polygons, or any shape).

Overlapping Lines

This technique can be used to create a path of any shape, open or closed.

1. Use the Pen tool to draw the whole path (such as a train line on a map), then use the Paint Style palette (**Command+I**) to set the attributes of the lower stroke. The bottom layer in this example has the attributes of 100% black stroke color, no fill, and 8-point weight.

2. With the path still selected press **Command+C**, **Command+F** (**Edit > Copy**, then **Edit > Paste In Front**) to make a duplicate of the line, layered on top of the first. Set the top stroke's attributes in the Paint Style palette. The weight should be smaller than the bottom stroke. In this example we use white stroke color and 4-point stroke weight. Use the techniques described earlier under Dotted and Dashed Lines to create a custom dashed line. Figure 9.10 shows 12-point dashes and gaps.

Figure 9.10 First path with 8-point weight (left) copied and
pasted in front and assigned a dash pattern (right).

3. You can group the layered strokes by selecting them and pressing
Command+G (Arrange > Group).

Create and print a test sheet to determine what attribute combinations look best in
the size you will use in the final artwork. In the following figure, the top stroke was
created with 2-point dashes, the bottom stroke with 12-point dashes, and the variations between were created with the Blend tool.

NOTE

Editing Overlapping Lines

You can make adjustments to the stroke weights if necessary to get the look you
want. Because the two paths overlap precisely, use the following techniques to
select and edit strokes.

Selecting Individual Ungrouped Strokes

➤ If the two paths are grouped, then click on any part of them with the
Selection tool and press **Command+U (Arrange > Ungroup)**.

➤ To select the top stroke only, click with the Selection tool on the top stroke.

➤ To select both strokes, use the Selection tool to drag a selection marquee
over any part of them.

➤ To select the bottom stroke only, use the technique just described to select both paths, then hold down the **Shift** key and click the top stroke to deselect it.

Selecting Individual Strokes in a Group

➤ To select the top stroke only, hold down the **Option** key and click with the Direct-selection tool on the top stroke.

➤ To select both strokes, click the **Selection** tool on any part of them.

➤ To select the bottom stroke only, drag the **Group-selection** tool over any part of them to select both paths, then hold down the **Shift** key and click the top stroke to deselect it.

Changing the Shape of an Overlapping Line

If you want to add, delete, or move part of a path, you can use the Direct-selection tool to drag a selection marquee over the segment or anchor point that you want to move and drag the selection to change the shape of both paths at once. If you move a direction handle, however, you will affect the top line only.

If you want to have more flexibility in editing the paths—by moving direction handles or adding new segments or anchor points—then go through the following steps:

1. First select the top line only and press **Command+Shift+M** (**Arrange > Move**) to move it a specific distance away from the bottom layer. Then edit the bottom layer.

2. After changing the shape of a bottom path, select it and press **Command+C**, **Command+F** (**Edit > Copy**, then **Edit > Paste In Front**) to make a duplicate of the line, layered on top of the first.

3. Next, select the **Eyedropper** tool in the Toolbox and click on the previous version of the top line—the line you moved at the beginning of this step. This loads the paint style attributes of that line into the Paint Style palette. Then select the **Paint bucket** tool in the Toolbox and click on the new top line.

4. Finally, select the original top line and delete it.

Overlapping Dashed Lines

If you combine what you learned about dashed and dotted lines at the beginning of this chapter with the overlapping stroke technique, you can create fairly complex line patterns such as those shown in the figures that follow. Rather than go through step-by-step instructions here, I will give you the dash and gap specifications used to create the examples shown, and you can get the steps from the previous two techniques.

As you can imagine, there are millions of variations you can create by overlaying strokes of different dash patterns and colors, and by overlaying three or more strokes at a time. The next examples are just a start.

OVERLAPPING DASHED LINE #1

The result of the following specifications appears to be a dotted stroke with 4-point white dots bordered by a 1-point black circle, as shown below.

➤ Bottom Stroke: Black dashed 6-point stroke with rounded end caps (second Cap option) and a dash size of 1 point and a gap of 20 points.

➤ Top Stroke: White dashed 4-point stroke with rounded end caps and a dash size of 1 point and a gap of 20 points.

As long as the dots on each line are spaced the same distance apart, the apparent border size will be one-half of the difference between the stroke weights of the two lines. In this case, the 2-point difference in dot size yields the effect of a 1-point border. If you wanted a 2-point border, you would need a 4-point difference in stroke weights, as shown below when the bottom stroke is 8 points wide.

OVERLAPPING DASHED LINE #2

The result of the next specifications is a dotted line with a drop-shadow effect, as shown below.

➤ Bottom Stroke: Black dashed 8-point stroke with rounded end caps (second Cap option) and a dash size of 1 point and a gap of 20 points.

➤ Top Stroke: White dashed 8-point stroke with rounded end caps and a dash size of 1 point and a gap of 20 points, cloned from the first stroke and then moved up and left 2 pixels. The stroke was moved by pressing the **Up Arrow** key twice and the **Left Arrow** key twice in 100% magnification.

OVERLAPPING DASHED LINE #3

The following attributes yield a line of waves, as shown below.

➤ Bottom Stroke: Black dashed 8-point stroke with rounded end caps and a dash size of 2 points and a gap of 8 points.

➤ Top Stroke: White dashed 8-point stroke with rounded end caps and a dash size of 2 points and a gap of 8 points, cloned from the first stroke and moved up 3 pixels.

OVERLAPPING DASHED LINE #4

The next attributes yield what appears to be a line of 6-point white dots on black squares, as shown below.

➤ Bottom Stroke: Black dashed 6-point stroke with extended butt end caps (third Cap option) and a dash size of 1 point and a gap of 20 points.

➤ Top Stroke: White dashed 6-point stroke with rounded end caps and a dash size of 1 point and a gap of 20 points.

OVERLAPPING DASHED LINE #5

The next specifications produce a line of 4-point white lines with rounded ends, framed by a 1-point black border, as shown below.

➤ Bottom Stroke: Black dashed 6-point stroke with rounded end caps and a dash size of 25 points and a gap of 11 points.

➤ Top Stroke: White dashed 4-point stroke with rounded end caps and a dash size of 25 points and a gap of 11 points.

Overlapping Dashed Line #6

The first example below shows a 2-point dotted line, the second example uses a 6-point line. In both examples, the following attributes were applied:

➤ Bottom Stroke: Black dashed stroke with rounded end caps, a dash of 1 point, and a gap of 29 points.

➤ Top Stroke: Black 2-point dashed stroke with butt end caps (first Cap option), a dash of 20 points, and a gap of 10 points. This stroke is cloned from the first line and then moved 5 points to the right using **Arrange > Move** (**Command+Shift+M**).

The key to creating strokes that overlap but use different dash/gap settings is that the sum of the dash length plus the gap length is the same for both strokes—30 in this case. The offset distance is half the gap size of the stroke that you move.

NOTE

The Look of Parallel Curves

Often you will need two parallel lines separated by a specific distance. If there are no curves in the line, you can draw one line and then drag away a copy. Trying to create curved parallel lines using this method poses a problem; the original line and the copy will not run parallel at the curves—instead you get the same effect as using the Brush tool with the **Calligraphic** option (described in Chapter 4). Moreover, it is very difficult to place a small, precise distance between each line. The technique just described for overlapping strokes provides the solution—and you can make the lines as curved as you like.

To set the stroke weight for the parallel lines, use a formula, as follows:

➤ Decide which "apparent" line weight you want for each parallel line and how many points of space you want between the parallel lines. Double your desired line weight and add in the number of points you want between the parallel lines. For example:

2	pts	Line weight for each line	
x	2	lines	Times 2
4	pts	Line weight doubled	
+	1.5	pts	Space between lines
5.5	pts	Total entered as stroke weight	

➤ Enter the total in the Stroke width box in the Paint Styles palette for the bottom stroke—**5.5** points in this case.

➤ Set Stroke of the top line to **White** and Weight to the number of points you want to separate the parallel lines—**1.5** points in this case.

Adding Arrowheads to Open Paths

The **Filter > Stylize > Add Arrowhead** filter makes it easy to add arrowheads or arrow tails to selected open paths.

1. Select the open path(s) in the Adobe Illustrator document that you want to effect.

2. Choose **Filter > Stylize > Add Arrowheads** to display the Add Arrowheads dialog box.

➤ Select different styles of arrowheads or tails by clicking the **forward** or **back** icons below the arrow box, where the current selection is displayed.

➤ Click **Start** to apply the style to the beginning of the path—the first point you clicked in drawing it.

➤ Click **End** to apply it to the last point along the path.

➤ Click **Start and End** to apply the style to both ends of the path. The arrowhead is automatically adjusted to match the stroke weight of the selected path(s)—wider stroke widths get larger arrows or tails—but you can enter a percentage value in the scale box to customize the scaling.

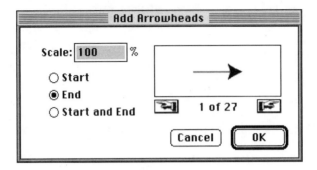

3. Click **OK** to close the dialog box and apply the arrowheads.

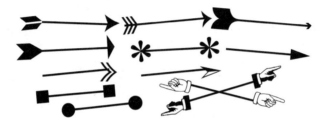

Figure 9.11 Examples of different arrowheads and tails.

Hand-Drawn Looks

You may want a line that has an uneven, hand-drawn look—one that seems to go from thick to thin, a line you might describe as *calligraphic*. You can create this effect with Illustrator's Brush tool and have even more options if you have a pressure-sensitive stylus. Here you'll learn how to create your own custom hand-drawn looks using the Pen tool. You have complete control of the thickness of the line even after you have drawn it.

Applying Calligraphic Effects to Existing Lines

The **Filter > Stylize > Calligraphy** filter adds a calligraphic effect to a filled or stroked path. Unlike the **Calligraphy** option in the Brush tool dialog box (see The Brush Tool in Chapter 4), this filter can be applied to a path drawn with the Pen tool and creates a compound path.

NOTE

The filter does not effect text, but calligraphic fonts exist for text if you want to create a hand-lettered look.

1. Select the filled or stroked path(s) to which you want to apply the calligraphic effect.

2. Choose **Filter > Stylize > Calligraphy** to display the Calligraphy dialog box.

3. Enter values in the Pen Width and Pen Angle fields to create the effect you want.

4. Click **OK** to close the dialog box and view the effect.

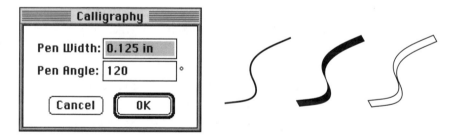

Figure 9.12 The Calligraphy dialog box, and a stroked path before and after applying the **Calligraphy** filter (fill is set to **None** at far right).

WARNING

Selecting more than one path at a time may cause unexpected results.

5. You can exaggerate the effect using the **Filter > Distort > Roughen** filter, setting low values and applying the **Smooth** option.

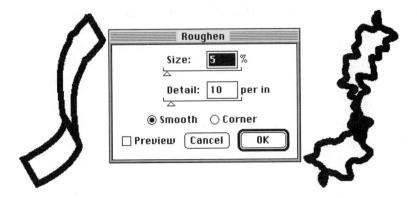

Figure 9.13 The Roughen dialog box with **Smooth** selected, and the resulting path.

Uneven Borders around Solid Shapes

You can use this first technique to create the effect of a hand-drawn or brush-stroked border around any solid shape (such as a closed path). In this example, you will draw an uneven black line on a white background.

1. Using the Pen tool or Freehand tool, draw a closed shape, such as the heart shape shown. The fewer points you click with the Pen tool, the smoother the line will be; the more points you click, the more uneven the line will be.

2. Using the Pen tool, draw a similar but slightly different shape that is smaller than the first. If you prefer, use one of the Scale tools from the Toolbox and scale a copy. Then adjust the curves and anchor points to change the second shape slightly. Select the second shape and drag it on top of the first shape.

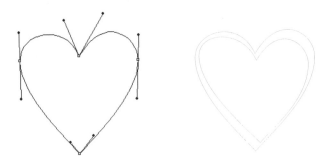

3. With the inside shape still selected, use the Paint Style palette (**Command+I**) to set Fill to **White** (to match your paper color or background). For this effect to work, always match the fill color of the smaller, inner shape to the desired background color. For this demonstration, assume you are drawing on a white page.

4. Select the larger, outer shape and set the Fill to the percentage of black or color that you want for the hand-drawn line; set Stroke to **None**. Here you have created a shape that can be filled with any color or pattern—it does not really have to match the background. The figure shows the outer heart-shaped path with black fill.

5. Refine the unevenness of the visible black line using the **Filter > Distort > Roughen** filer, to allow less or more of the black to show. You can also use the Direct-selection tool to move the curves or anchor points and direction handles. Use the Add-anchor-point tool or the Scissors tool while you press down the **Option** key to add anchor points if you need them to refine the curves.

6. You can make the center a transparent "hole" by selecting both objects and choosing **Object > Compound Paths > Make**.

Uneven Open Paths

In the preceding technique, you drew lines with a hand-drawn look around a solid shape. In this example, you will use a different technique to create the appearance of hand-drawn lines as open paths.

The illustration on the next page is composed entirely of elements created using the technique described here. The steps are shown for creating one of the S-shaped highlights near the top of the wing (see next page), using the Pen tool.

NOTE

You can get a similar result using the Brush tool with a pressure-sensitive tablet.

1. Double-click the **Brush** tool to get the Brush dialog box, and set a narrow width (**1** point in this case), round caps, and round joins. Click **OK** to close the dialog box.

NOTE

A 1-point brush produces the appearance of a 2-point line, because it creates two parallel 1-point strokes with no fill. You change the fill to match the stroke in the next steps.

2. Using the Brush tool, draw the lines you want to represent as brush strokes.

3. With the shape or some part of it still selected, use the Paint Style palette (**Command+I**) to set the Fill and Stroke to the percentage of black or color you wish the line to be.

4. Refine the unevenness of the hand-drawn lines, using any method you like:

➤ You can select all of the lines at once and use the **Filter > Distort Roughen** filter, setting low values for percent and number of details per inch and selecting smooth corners.

➤ You can select all the lines at once and use the **Filter > Scribble and Tweak** filter, setting low percentage values for horizontal and vertical.

➤ With time and patience, you can use the Direct-selection tool to move the curves or anchor points and direction handles. Use the Add-anchor-point tool or the Scissors tool while you press down the **Option** key to add anchor points if you need to refine the curves.

Figure 9.14 Paths drawn with a 1-point Brush tool (left),
then roughened (middle), or scribbled (right).

5. For a water-color effect where the color fades from dark (where the brush stroke starts) to light (where the stroke ends), set the Stroke to **None** and choose a gradient fill.

Applying Photoshop Effects

Illustrator 6.0 introduces two new features that can be combined to create special effects directly in Illustrator that were previously possible only by importing bitmap graphics from Photoshop and other applications that worked with rasterized images.

6.0 NEW FEATURE

➤ The **Object > Rasterize** command turns selected objects that were created using Illustrator's drawing tools into rasterized (bitmap) images.

➤ The Filter menu now includes three Gallery Effects submenus that let you apply Photoshop effects to imported bitmaps or rasterized images in Illustrator.

Photoshop effects were applied to imported bitmaps in Chapter 7. The next steps show how to rasterize and apply Photoshop effects to graphics drawn using Illustrator's tools.

1. Create artwork using Illustrator's tools.

2. Select the object(s) to be rasterized.

3. Choose **Object > Rasterize**.

4. In the Rasterize dialog box, choose a color model and resolution. Select **Make mask** if the selected objects form a nonrectangular shape and you want to be able to see background objects behind them.

5. Click **OK** to rasterize the selection. If more than one object was selected, they all become part of one bitmap image.

6. With the rasterized art selected, choose any of the Gallery effects from the Filter menu.

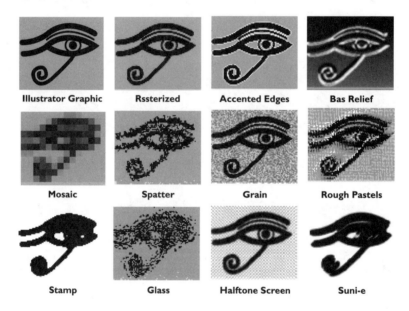

Figure 9.15 Original art (top left), rasterized, then modified with Photoshop effects.

Creating Shared Borders

Separate shapes that share common irregular edges—shapes that must fit together like jigsaw puzzle pieces—are a common drawing situation. Individual countries, states, or counties on a map are a typical example. In Illustrator, there are two easy ways to handle this drawing situation, described in the next sections. (A third way—the old-fashioned manual method of copying a part of an existing path and then building on it—was made obsolete by the Knife tool and the Divide filter.)

Perfect for map work, this technique also proves useful for illustration styles that simulate dimension by using shapes of various gray fills.

Using the Knife Tool

6.0 NEW FEATURE

Illustrator 6.0 introduces a new Knife tool in the Plug-in Tools palette that makes the task of cutting a shape into puzzle pieces "a piece of cake."

1. Using the Pen or Freehand or Autotrace tool, create a path that outlines the entire area that you will be cutting into pieces—the entire country that you want to divide into states or provinces, for example. Give the shape a Fill other than None.

WARNING

The Knife tool does not work on shapes with Fill of **None**—if you slice such objects, they disappear. Otherwise, it cuts everything beneath its path—not just selected objects—so be careful not to cut objects that overlap other objects that you do not mean to cut.

2. Choose **Window > Show Plug-in Tools** (if that palette is not already displayed), and select the **Knife** tool.

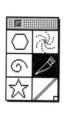

3. Drag the Knife tool along a path that will cut the original shape in two. Continue using the Knife tool to cut the shape into as many pieces as you need.

NOTE

If you are working with a template and you traced the first outline with the Autotrace or Freehand tool, then work in Artwork View (**Command+E**), to hide the Fill and trace the inside shapes with the Knife tool.

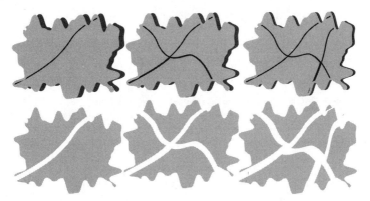

Figure 9.16 Original shape cut in two (left), then second slice, then third. Bottom row shows pieces burst apart.

Using the Apply Knife Command

Illustrator's **Object > Apply Knife** command makes this second technique a perfect solution when you already have a shape with an irregular border that you want to share with an adjacent shape. It's also a good alternative if you would rather trace the puzzle cuts with the Freehand or Autotrace tool—or simply draw more controlled cuts with the Pen tool—than cut with the Knife tool as in the previous technique.

1. Using the Pen or Freehand tool, draw the path that starts and ends at two points along another path's irregular border, then click on the first point to close the path. In this case we begin with an amorphous puzzle shape.

2. Select the original object with the Selection tool and press **Command+C**, **Command+F, Command+=** (Copy, Paste in Front, Bring to Front).

3. Choose **Object > Apply Knife.**

Figure 9.17 Original shape (left), overlapped by new shape, then original shape copied and brought to the front, then changed by the Apply Knife filter. Second row shows pieces burst apart.

4. Delete the unwanted parts of the cut object.

NOTE

If you start with the outline of the entire area, and then trace puzzle cuts with the Freehand or Autotrace tool—or simply draw more controlled cuts with the Pen tool—you can use the Divide filter to separate the artwork into closed-path pieces of the puzzle.

Figure 9.18 Original shape (left), criss-crossed with paths drawn with the Freehand tool (middle), then changed by the Divide filter. Rightmost figure shows pieces burst apart.

Creating Compound Paths

A *compound path* is a group of two or more overlapping paths combined into a single compound object. The most common use of compound objects is to create a hole in an object so that you can see through it. When the paths making up a compound object overlap, a hole appears where they overlap. You can control which areas become transparent using the **Reverse Path Direction** option in the Attributes dialog box.

You can associate as many different paths as you like into one compound path, have as many different compound paths as you like in the artwork, or use compound paths as clipping paths (masks). You can select two or more existing compound paths and combine them into a single compound path. You can use the Blend tool to create a blend between two components of a compound path, but you cannot create a blend between one entire compound path and another.

Figure 9.19 Objects before (left) and after (right) being made a compound path.

Compound paths may cause printing problems if they become very complicated.

WARNING

1. Draw the elements you wish to associate as a compound path. You can also type text and convert it to paths using **Type > Make Outlines**. Make sure that the backmost object in the stack has the paint attributes you wish to assign to the final compound path, and that any paths you want to see through (the counters) are in front of the paths that make up the outer boundaries.

2. Select all the objects.

3. Choose **Object > Compound Paths > Make**. The keyboard shortcut is **Command+8**.

It's a good idea to work in Preview mode when creating compound paths, so you can see the effect as you create it, or undo the command immediately if the effect is not what you wish.

N O T E

All objects in the compound path take on the paint attributes of the back-most object in the stacking order.

Compound paths have the same properties as grouped objects—you must use the Direct-selection tool to select and modify individual elements. If you copy part of a compound path by **Option**+dragging with the Direct-selection tool, the copy becomes part of the compound path. You can add elements to the masked set by drawing the new object, then using the **Cut** command, selecting an element within the mask with the Direct-selection tool, and then using the **Paste In Back** and **Paste In Front** commands from the Arrange menu.

4. Since the advantage of creating compound paths is to see through "holes" in the objects, you will usually want to position the compound path on top of other objects in the artwork.

NOTE

If an area you expected to become a hole does not appear transparent, you may need to change the winding direction of the hole's path. Normally, you do not need to concern yourself with a path's winding direction. However in certain situations such as files converted by Adobe Streamline or hand-drawn shapes with multiple overlaps, you may need to reverse a path's direction. Generally, for a hole to appear transparent, its path must wind in the opposite direction of the compound object's outer path.

5. To change the way holes are created in a compound path, use the Group-selection tool to select the part of the compound path that you want to affect, then choose **Object > Attributes** to display the Attributes dialog box. Click **Reversed Path Direction** and then click **OK** to close the dialog box and view the effect.

NOTE

If the Reversed check box is filled with gray, this indicates that you have a mixed selection; that is, some of the objects in the selection are reversed and others are not.

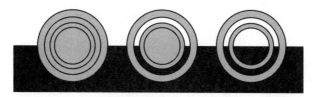

Figure 9.20 Concentric circles before (left) and after making compound paths (middle), then reversing the path direction of the center circle (right).

WARNING

Turning the **Reversed Path Direction** option on does not necessarily make the object appear either filled or transparent—the effect is based on how Illustrator fills compound paths.

6. To release a compound path, select the path and choose **Object > Compound Paths > Release**. The keyboard shortcut is **Command+9**.

WARNING

All objects in the compound path take on the paint attributes of the backmost object in the stacking order, and releasing the compound path does not restore the previous paint attributes. If you want to preserve the original paint attributes, make a copy of the objects and store it on the Pasteboard before using the **Make Compound Paths** command.

Working with Masks

Masking is a way to crop illustrations, type, or patterns with a specific shape. Masking can prove useful in many graphic art applications, such as packaging and logo design. Here we describe how to create a simple mask and then add a few more twists to the basic steps.

Figure 9.21 Example of a letter shape masking a mountain scene.

Using the Mask Command

You can make selected objects into a mask through which only parts of an object or objects are visible in your drawing. For example, you might have a drawing of a mountain reflected in a lake with a man in a boat on the lake. You could draw a rectangle (or any shape) around the man in the boat and make it a mask, so only the man in the boat appear on the artwork and in printing—the larger lake and mountain would be hidden, or *masked*. In PostScript programming this is called *clipping*.

You can view your drawing through any shape you draw—a single path or a compound path—but compound paths may cause printing problems when used as masks.

WARNING

1. Draw the objects you wish to mask.

2. Draw the shape you want to use as a mask, and position it on top of the objects you want to mask, framing the objects as you wish. The mask need not be in the same layer as the objects you wish to mask.

3. Select both the mask and the objects to be masked.

4. Choose **Object > Mask > Make**.

Figure 9.22 Background (left), overlaid by masking shape (middle), and masked (right).

➤ The mask itself is automatically assigned a Fill and Stroke of **None**. If you want to give the mask a border (or a background shade or color), you can copy the mask shape and paste it on top of the mask (or below all the masked objects), then set the fill and stroke through the Object > Paint Styles palette, or use the filter that automates this common procedure: **Filter > Create > Fill & Stroke for Mask** (see next section).

➤ Masked artwork has the same properties as grouped objects—you must use the Direct-selection tool to select and modify individual elements. You can add elements to the masked set by drawing the new object, then using the **Cut** command, selecting an element within the mask with the Direct-selection tool, and then using the **Paste In Back** and **Paste In Front** commands from the Arrange menu.

5. To release the masking effect, select the mask and choose **Object > Masks > Release**. Remember that the mask itself retains a Fill and Stroke of None unless you change those attributes after releasing the mask.

NOTE

To find out what objects are part of a mask, activate the Group-selection tool, click once on the mask itself, then click once again to select all the masked objects.

WARNING

If you use complex shapes or compound paths as masks, have several masks in one file, or create masks within masks, you may have problems printing. You may need to eliminate some masks to simplify the artwork.

Creating a Fill and Stroke for a Mask

When you create a mask, the mask outline automatically takes on a Fill and Stroke of **None**. Since it is often desirable to have a border around a mask, the **Object > Create > Fill & Stroke for Mask** filter creates one for you by copying the mask and applying the Fill and Stroke you specify.

1. Create a mask as described in the previous section.

2. Select the mask and choose **Object > Paint Style** to display the Paint Style palette (if it is not already displayed). Set the Fill and Stroke you want.

3. Choose **Filter > Create > Fill and Stroke for Mask**.

NOTE

The filter automatically makes two copies of the mask, one positioned on top of the stack with the Stroke specified in the Paint Style palette, and a second copy behind all the masked objects with the Fill you specified. The original mask shape remains with a Fill and Stroke of **None**.

Figure 9.23 Mask before and after applying Fill and Stroke for Mask.

Using Type as a Mask

Besides using objects drawn with Illustrator's drawing tools as masks, you can use type to crop or mask an area. Here's a technique for masking with type. This technique is useful in many graphic art applications, such as packaging and logo design.

1. Create the artwork to be masked, such as the scene shown below.

2. Use the Type tool to type the word you want to use as a mask, and use commands under the Font and Type menus—or the Character palette—to set it in the font and size you want. It should be large and bold to yield the best results.

If you want to be able to manipulate the shapes of the letters, follow steps 3 and 4. Otherwise (if you want to keep the letterforms exactly as the are) you can skip to step 5.

NOTE

3. Select the word with the Selection tool, then choose **Type > Create Outlines**. This converts each character of the text to a compound path that can be handled like any object drawn with one of the drawing tools. You can change the shapes as desired.

After this step, you cannot edit the text with the Type tool or apply changes using commands under the Type or Font menu. If you don't like the effect at the end of these steps, you can change the outlines using any of the methods applicable to graphic objects, but if you want to change the word(s) or the font, you have to go back to step 2.

WARNING

4. If the text consists of more than one character, select all the outlines and choose **Object > Compound > Make**, to make the whole phrase into a compound path.

Figure 9.24 Type before and after being changed to outlines and a compound path.

5. Position the text object or outlines over the artwork to be masked.
6. Select the outlines and all of the elements to be masked and choose **Object > Masks > Make**.

Figure 9.25 Outlines over artwork, before and after being changed to a mask.

7. The mask itself is automatically assigned a Fill and Stroke of **None**. If you want to give the mask a border, you can copy the mask shape and paste it on top of the mask, then set the Fill and Stroke through the Object > Paint Styles palette, or use the filter that automates this common procedure: **Filter > Create > Fill and Stroke for Mask**, described earlier.

Masking to Change Fills

Besides using masks to give artwork a special border or shape, as in the previous technique, you can use a mask to create the effect of changing fills in an object that crosses over different background shades. In this example, text overlaps black and white areas. The masking technique is used to put white text over the black background, black text over the white background.

1. Type text and position it to partly overlap a background of the same color. The figure below shows black type that has been rotated and skewed and positioned to overlap a black palm tree.

2. Select the text and press **Command+C, Command+F** (**Edit > Copy, Edit > Paste iIn Front**). Make the copied text white in the Paint Styles palette.

3. Select the background object (the tree in this case) and press **Command+C** (**Edit > Copy**), then select the white text and press **Command+F** (**Edit > Paste In Front**). You now have four stacked objects: a black tree on the bottom, then black text, then white text, then another black tree.

4. Select both the white text and the topmost black tree, and choose **Object > Masks > Make**. The result is text that appears to change from black to white as it crosses different background shades.

Figure 9.26 Black text over black tree (left), copy of text painted white (middle), and final masked white text with black tree and text also visible (right).

Masking to Create Highlights

You can use a mask to make an object appear to change fill or stroke color and thereby create shadows or highlights. In this example a ray of moonlight is highlighted in water.

1. Begin with the basic, unhighlighted elements—in this case, a moon over a mountain lake.

2. Select the object(s) to be highlighted (the wavy water lines in this case) and press **Command+G, Command+C, Command+F** (**Arrange > Group, Edit > Copy, Edit > Paste In Front**).

3. Use the Paint Styles palette (**Command+I**) to change the attributes of the copied object(s)—making them darker to create a shadow effect or lighter to make a highlight.

In this case, the **Filter > Colors > Saturate** command was applied several times with a negative value to lighten the selection.

NOTE

Figure 9.27 Lake elements are duplicated and lightened and positioned on top of the darker version.

4. Use one of the drawing tools to outline the area you wish to highlight or shadow. In this case the Pen tool is used to draw a polygon in the shape that moonlight might appear reflected on water.

5. Select the highlight outline and the changed copy of the water waves, and choose **Object > Masks > Make**.

Figure 9.28 Lightened lake elements are overlaid with a shape that represents the moon's reflection on water (left), and then masked (right).

Selecting All Masks

The **Filter > Select > Select Masks** filter finds any mask you have created using **Objects > Mask > Make**. This is useful in distinguishing individual objects from masked sets of objects, since part of the masked Artwork is made invisible in Preview mode, and in Artwork mode masks are not easily distinguished from grouped paths. You can then select individual masks and their components more easily.

Simply choose **Filter > Select > Select Masks**. All masks become selected and you can find the one you want to modify.

Creating Three-Dimensional Effects

This section describes techniques that simulate three-dimensional objects. Three-dimensional effects can be achieved through use of perspective and shading.

The three-dimensional objects you can create with Adobe Illustrator are not truly three-dimensional; you cannot rotate a drawing of a house to see a front view and a back view. But you can create a "third dimension" visually using the techniques described here.

NOTE

Drop Shadows

The simplest method of creating a three-dimensional effect is to create a "shadow" of a shape. That is, a copy of the shape is placed behind the shape, offset slightly, and given a dark fill. This effect is commonly referred to as a *drop shadow* in graphic design. A more realistic cast shadow effect is demonstrated later in this section.

This technique is frequently used to add dimension or visual interest to conceptual illustrations such as bar charts and organization charts. You can add special effects to any illustration by using this three-dimensional technique on text, borders, and other two-dimensional objects.

Illustrator offers an automated command to create this effect, or you can do it manually. Both techniques are described here.

THE EASY WAY

The **Filter > Stylize > Drop Shadow** filter adds a three-dimensional effect called a drop shadow to two sides of the selected object(s).

1. Select the path(s) in the Adobe Illustrator document that you want to affect.

2. Display the Drop Shadow dialog box.

3. Make entries as appropriate in the dialog box:

➤ Enter the distance in points that you want the shadow to be offset along the X (horizontal) and Y (vertical) axis—positive values position the shadow to the right and down from the selected object(s), negative values position the shadow left and up.

➤ Click **Group Shadows** if you want the resulting drop shadow to be grouped with the selected object.

➤ Enter the percent screen for darkness of the shadow. If the object is in color, the resulting shadow will be a tint of the color.

4. Click **OK** or press **Return** to close the dialog box and view the effect.

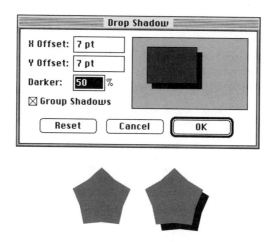

Figure 9.29 The Drop Shadow dialog box, and object before and after applying the Drop Shadow filter.

THE HARD WAY

1. Create an object using whatever tool is appropriate. In this example, use the Pen tool or the **Filter > Create > Polygon** command to draw a polygon.

2. Use the Selection tool to select the object, then drag the object diagonally a short distance, still holding the **Option** key to create a copy of it.

3. Use the Paint Style palette (Command+I) to give the second or top object a White fill and the first or lower object a Black or dark fill to create a shadow effect.

Figure 9.30 Object (left), copied (middle), and each filled to create drop-shadow look (right).

Embossing

You can create an embossed look by creating two drop shadows the hard way, as described in the next steps. The one additional requirement is that the embossed object must be on a shaded background.

1. Create a shaded background—here we use a 30% gray fill.

NOTE

It's a good idea to lock the background object (**Command+ I**), or switch to Artwork view (**Command+E**) before going on to the next steps.

NOTE

If you apply shades of a custom color in this step, you can easily play with the final result by changing the color components of the custom color (see Figure 9.31). If you don't want to affect other objects that use the same custom color, create a new one before you start this step. You can always convert it to process colors in printing.

2. Create the object(s) to be embossed, and give it the same fill as the background and a Stroke of **None**.

3. Select the object(s) to be embossed, then press **Command+G, Command+C, Command+B** (**Arrange > Group, Edit > Copy, Edit > Paste In Back**). (The **Group** command is not necessary if the selection is a single object.)

4. With the copy still selected, press the **right** and **down arrow** keys a few times each to offset the copy from the original slightly.

5. With the copy still selected, assign a stroke of **None** and a dark fill through the Paint Style palette.

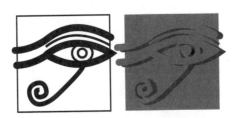

6. With the copy still selected, press **Command+C, Command+B** (**Edit > Copy, Edit > Paste In Back**).

7. With the new copy still selected, press the **left** and **up arrow** keys a few times each to offset the new copy from the original slightly. (Press the keys twice as many times as you did in step 4.)

8. With the copy still selected, assign a Stroke of **None** and a white or light Fill through the Paint Style palette.

 You can achieve special effects by applying a pattern fill to the background and top objects. You can also select each of the objects one by one—the embossed components and the background—and choose **Object > Rasterize** to convert them to bitmap objects that can be changed using Photoshop effects from the Filter > Gallery effects submenus—including the **GE Bas Relief** and **GE Accented Edges**.

N O T E

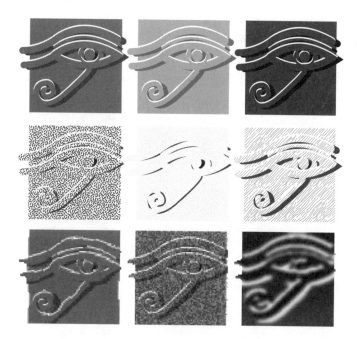

Figure 9.31 Variations created using different values of a custom color (top row), pattern fills (middle row), and Photoshop effects (last row).

Beveling

Beveling is another way of making an object appear to lift off the page. There are two ways to create a bevel effect, described under the next headings.

BEVELING ROUNDED OBJECTS

This first technique is best for rounded objects, but you can also use it as a lazy method of beveling objects with pointed corners.

1. Create the object to be beveled.

2. With the object selected, choose **Filter > Objects > Offset Path**.

3. In the Offset Path dialog box:

   ➤ Enter a distance equal to the width of the beveled edges.

   ➤ Select **Miter** from the Line Join pop-up menu if the object includes any pointed corners.

   ➤ You can play with the Miter limit for different effects on pointed corners, but this doesn't affect rounded edges.

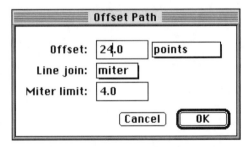

Figure 9.32 Offset Path dialog box.

4. Click **OK** to create a duplicate, slightly larger object.

NOTE

If the object has pointed corners and the Offset Path filter created weird results, see the next section—Beveling Pointed Objects—for solutions.

5. To position the new, larger object behind the original, do one of two things:

➤ If there are no other objects below these, press **Command+hyphen** to send the new object to the bottom layer.

➤ If there are other objects below these, press **Command+X** (**Edit > Cut**), then select the original object and press **Command+B** (**Edit > Paste In Back**).

6. With the larger object still selected, apply a gradient Fill and a Stroke of **None** from the Paint Style palette.

Figure 9.33 Various rounded shapes with a gradient-filled background object.

BEVELING POINTED OBJECTS

Creating realistic bevels around objects with pointed corners is a little trickier, as you'll see in these next steps. The first four steps are the same:

1. Create the object to be beveled.

2. With the object selected, choose **Filter > Objects > Offset Path**.

3. In the Offset Path dialog box:

➤ Enter a distance equal to the width of the beveled edges.

➤ Select **Miter** from the Line Join pop-up menu.

➤ Play with the Miter limit for different effects (see step 5).

4. Click **OK** to create a duplicate, slightly larger object. Now the toil and trouble begins.

5. Press **Command+E** to switch to Artwork view and assess the results of the last step:

➤ If the outer points are squared instead of mitered (see next figure), press **Command+Z** (**Edit > Undo**), then choose **Filter > Objects > Offset Path** again and set a higher miter limit in the Offset Path dialog box.

➤ If the inner points overlap (see next figure), choose **Filter > Pathfinder > Minus Front**.

Figure 9.34 Desired result (left) vs. squared corners (middle) vs. overlapping inner points (right).

6. Select the **Pen** tool from the Toolbox, and for each point around the edges:

➤ Click once on a point on the outer object.

➤ Click once on the corresponding point of the inner object.

➤ **Command**-click away from the line to deselect it.

This step works best if the **Snap to Point** option is selected in the File > Preferences > General dialog box.

N O T E

7. Select all the objects—the two closed paths plus all the line segments you just created, and choose **Filter > Pathfinder > Divide** to convert the "faces" of the bevel to separate, closed paths.

8. Press **Command+Y** to switch back to Preview and apply different shades to each face of the bevel, each with a stroke of **None**.

If you apply shades of a custom color in this step, you can easily play with the final result by changing the color components of the custom color (see second figure following). If you don't want to affect other objects that use the same custom color, create a new one before you start this step. You can always convert it to process colors in printing.

N O T E

Figure 9.35 Two objects with line segments joining each pair of points (left) become separate closed paths after the Divide filter (middle, burst apart to show result), that can be shaded with different fills (right).

9. You can adjust the angle of the bevel by dragging over each outer corner with the Direct-selection tool and pulling it further out.

Figure 9.36 Examples of different bevel depths—each example also affected by changing the color components of the custom color (see also color plates).

Casting Shadows

Cast shadows are a bit more realistic than simple drop shadows. Whereas drop shadows can make it appear that an object is lifted off the paper, cast shadows make it appear as if the object is standing with its "feet" or base on the paper and light is hitting it from the side.

There are two techniques for casting shadows, depending on whether you want the light to be coming from *in front of* or *behind* the object.

LIGHTED FROM THE FRONT

To cast a shadow as if by a light source in front of the object, follow these steps:

1. Create the object to be shadowed.

2. Make a duplicate by pressing **Command+C**, **Command+B**, and, if the original object is composed of more than one element, **Command+G** (**Edit > Copy**, **Edit > Paste In Back**, **Arrange > Group**).

NOTE

If the shadow is composed of more than one element, you can use **Filter > Pathfinder > Unite** to make them all one object instead of grouping them in this step.

3. With the shadow object still selected, select the **Shear** tool, then click on a base corner to position the focal point, move the pointer away from the focal point and drag to cast the shadow at an angle.

4. With the shadow still selected, make entries in the Paint Style palette to give it true shadow coloring:

➤ Set the Stroke to **None**.

➤ Assign a linear gradient fill if you want the shadow to appear to fade.

➤ Use the gradient tool to drag from the base to the top of the shadow if necessary to put the dark end of the gradient nearest the base.

Figure 9.37 Original object, sheared copy with gray fill, and linear gradient fill.

5. If the shadow falls against a color background and you want the gradient to actually fade to the color of the background:

➤ Double-click the gradient name in the Paint Style palette to display the Gradient palette.

➤ Click **New** to set up a new gradient if you don't want to change the current gradient's attributes, and type a new gradient name.

➤ Click the triangle below the light end of the gradient to select it.

➤ Select the **Eyedropper** tool in the Toolbox.

➤ Hold down the **Control** key and click the background behind the shadow.

NOTE

Control+clicking with the Eyedropper tool copies the color to the selected slider in the Gradient palette and updates the gradient to fade to that color.

6. For true perspective and to make the light source appear closer to the object, with the shadow still selected choose **Filter > Distort > Free Distort** and pull each of the top two corners slightly away from each other.

Figure 9.38 Sheared shadow (left) distorted to varying degrees (see also color plates).

LIGHTED FROM THE BACK

To cast a shadow as if by a light source from behind of the object, follow these steps:

1. Create the object to be shadowed, and select it with the Selection tool.

2. Select the **Reflect** tool and click once on one corner of the base of the object, then **Option**+click on the other base corner to reflect a copy of the original object.

3. With the shadow still selected, choose **Arrange > Group or Filter > Pathfinder Unite** (see previous steps).

4. With the shadow object still selected, select the **Shear** tool, then click on a base corner to position the focal point, move the pointer away from the focal point and drag to cast the shadow at an angle.

5. Apply Paint Style attributes as in steps 3–5 for **Lighted from the Front**.

6. For true perspective, and to make the light source appear closer to the object, with the shadow still selected choose **Filter > Distort > Free**

Distort and pull each of the bottom two corners slightly away from each other.

Figure 9.39 Sheared shadow (left) distorted to varying degrees.

SHADOWS ON COLORED BACKGROUNDS

When a shadow falls on a colored object or background, the shadow should actually take on some of those color values in order to be realistic. A shadow might appear black or gray on a white background, for example, but it would realistically appear reddish if it fell on a red background.

You can give a shadow a color manually—and this might be easy if the entire shadow falls on one solid color background. If the shadow falls against two differently colored objects, however, these next steps should be taken:

1. Create the object(s) to cast shadows, and the background object(s) or colors.

2. Create the shadows using any of the techniques just described.

3. Select the shadows and the background objects and choose **Filter > Pathfinder > Hard**. This displays a dialog box offering the option to convert custom colors to process colors in the new mix—generally a good idea.

4. Click **OK** to change the shadow color to a combination of its original color or tint and the background colors. (This filter also has the effect of dividing the selection into parts, much like the Divide filter.)

Figure 9.40 Shadow cast onto lower triangle (left) mixed hard to blend
shadow with background color (right). See also color plates.

Creating Three-Dimensional Cubes

The next three techniques describe approaches to drawing a cube with perspective. You can use these techniques to create any three-dimensional objects with rectangular sides, like the drawing in the accompanying figure. For related information, see also Using a Grid for Perspective, later in this chapter.

➤ The first method is good if you want to see the shape change as you work, and decide the perspective as you go along.

➤ The second method is good if you already have some idea of the perspective you want.

➤ The third method is the most complicated but the most versatile, in that you can create three-dimensional package designs, with complex artwork on each "face" of the cube.

CUBES: METHOD 1

The first method uses a simple, visual approach to build a six-sided wire-frame cube.

1. Use the Rectangle tool to draw a rectangle or square like the one in the figure below. (Recall that holding down the **Shift** key with a Rectangle tool forces a perfect square.)

2. Click with the Selection tool to select the square, and **Shift+Option**+drag a copy of it away from the original. Position the copy against the first square so they share a border.

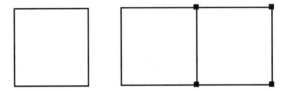

Figure 9.41 Rectangle (left) with copy aligned to one edge (right).

3. Use the Direct-selection tool to select the two leftmost anchor points on the left square and drag them up slightly at a diagonal.

4. Use the Selection tool to select the object you just changed into a parallelogram. Holding the **Option** key to make a copy, drag the copy into position to meet the opposite edge of the first square.

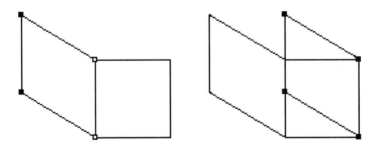

Figure 9.42 One side changed to a parallelogram (left) then copied to opposite side (right).

5. Use the Pen tool to draw a polygon that matches the top side of the cube formed by the three sides you just created, by clicking on each anchor point that marks the top corners.

6. You can then delete the "hidden" side if you like (since only three sides would be visible if the object were solid). This is easier in Artwork view if the rectangles have solid fills.

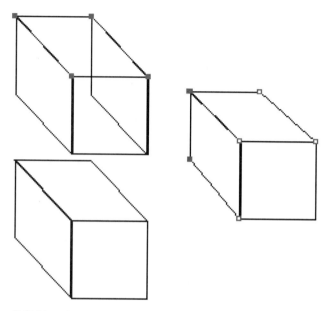

Figure 9.43 New shape drawn as top face (left) then "hidden" side deleted (right).

7. Shade each of the three "visible" sides with a different percentage of black.

8. To create true perspective, use the Direct-selection tool to select the two anchor points at the upper, backmost edges of the cube and hold down the **Shift** key as you drag them down slightly. Then select the two left-most anchor points and drag them slightly to the right.

9. When the cube is complete, drag the Selection tool to select the entire cube, and press **Command+G** (**Arrange > Group**) to make it a single object.

CUBES: METHOD 2

Here is a second approach to the same goal of producing a three-dimensional-looking cube.

1. Use the Rectangle tool to draw a rectangle.

2. Select the **Scale** tool and make one smaller copy of the rectangle. In this case we **Option**+clicked on the rectangle to open the Scale dialog box, clicked on **Uniform** scale, entered **75%**, and then clicked **Copy**.

3. With the copy selected, position it so it overlaps the first rectangle.

NOTE

The size and positioning of the smaller rectangle in steps 2 and 3 will determine the apparent length of the box as well as the viewer's perspective. For example, if you position the smaller rectangle above the larger one, the cube will appear deep and will be viewed from an overhead perspective; if you position the smaller rectangle to overlap the larger rectangle, as in this example, the perspective will be nearly head-on.

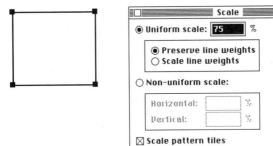

Figure 9.44 Rectangle and Scale dialog box.

4. Select the **Pen** tool and draw polygons that match the two new "visible" sides of the cube that would be formed with the first two rectangles at front and back. (The backmost rectangle becomes "hidden" when the visible sides are filled.)

5. Use the Paint Style palette (**Command+I**) to set a gray fill (that is, some percentage of black) to shade each side.

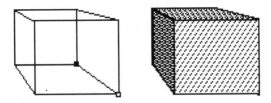

Figure 9.45 Top and side drawn with Pen tool using large and small rectangles as guides (left) then sides and front shaded differently (right).

6. When the cube is complete, use the Selection tool to select the entire object, and type **Command+G** (**Arrange > Group**) to make it a single object.

Three-Dimensional Polygons

Besides adding dimensions to create representation of solid objects such as boxes, buildings, and books, you can add special effects to any illustration by using this three-dimensional technique on text, borders, and other two-dimensional objects.

1. Create an object using whatever tool is appropriate. In this example, use the Pen tool or the Polygon tool to draw a polygon.

2. Use the Selection tool to select the object. Holding down the **Option** key, drag the object diagonally a short distance to create a copy of it.

3. With the copied object still selected, select the **Scale** tool from the Toolbox and scale the object slightly smaller than the original object (see step 2 in the previous example).

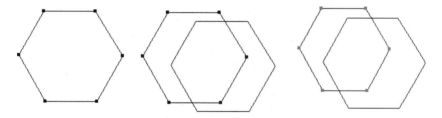

Figure 9.46 Polygon (left), copied (middle), then copy scaled smaller (right).

4. Using the Pen tool, draw polygons to connect each set of corresponding anchor points that form the side faces of the object, as shown in the figure below.

5. Delete the small polygon, which would be the "invisible" face when the other faces are shaded.

6. Use the Paint Style palette (**Command+I**) to add shading to the three-dimensional faces of the object. In the figure below, we used a fill of 100% black for the bottom face, 70% black for the middle face, and 40% black for the top face.

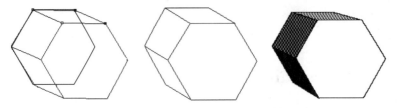

Figure 9.47 Three sides drawn with Pen tool using two polygons as guides (left), "hidden" face deleted (middle), then sides and front shaded differently (right).

Package Design

Box-packaging design often calls for accurate three-dimensional, perspective views of rectangular-sided objects such as boxes. This technique lets you create accurate 3-D perspectives for several common engineering views by creating the sides of the box as rectangular objects, then scaling, shearing, and rotating them into place around a common point.

For this technique to work correctly, it is essential that the scaling, shearing, and rotating transformations be applied in precisely the order given here. It is also important that all the elements comprising a face of the cube be grouped before starting the transformation.

WARNING

1. Create the side, front, and bottom faces of the package as rectangular objects that surround the artwork of the package faces. As each face is completed, select all elements that compose it and type **Command+G** (**Arrange > Group**) to group all the elements on each face, so that you have three grouped objects, one for each face.

Use rounded caps and joins for the stroke of each rectangle to avoid "spikes" at the corners of the finished package.

NOTE

2. Arrange the faces with their long sides touching, as if the package were flattened.

3. Use the Selection tool to select all three faces, then select the **Scale** tool and **Option**+click at the point where all three faces touch. This point of mutual intersection is the origin point for all the transformations used in this technique.

4. In the Scale dialog box, click **Non-uniform scale**, then enter scaling values of **100%** horizontal and **86.602%** vertical and click **OK**.

Figure 9.48 Three sides at their actual size (left), scaled non-proportionately (right).

5. Select the group that comprises the side of the package, then select the **Shear** tool and **Option**+click at the point of mutual intersection, and enter a shear value of **30** degrees along the horizontal axis.

6. Select the **Rotate** tool and **Option**+click at the same point and rotate the side surface 90 degrees.

In the next steps you will repeat the process of shearing and rotating the two remaining surfaces, using the values in the table on page 505.

NOTE

7. Select the group that comprises the front of the box, then select the **Shear** tool and **Option**+click at the point of mutual intersection. In the Shear dialog box, enter a shear value of **−30** degrees along the horizontal axis and click **OK**.

8. Select the **Rotate** tool and **Option**+click at the point of mutual intersection, enter a rotation value of **30** degrees, and click **OK**.

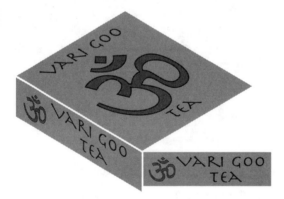

9. Select the group that comprises the bottom of the box, then select the **Shear** tool and **Option**+click at the point of mutual intersection, enter a shear value of **30** degrees along the horizontal axis, and click **OK**.

10. Finally, select the **Rotate** tool and **Option**+click at the point of mutual intersection, enter a rotation value of **30** degrees, and click **OK**.

The transformation values given here produce an isometric view. The values for some other common views are listed in the table that follows. Note that, while an isometric view uses the same vertical scaling percentage for each face, some of the other views require different scaling percentages for the different faces.

Transformation values for common engineering views					
View		Face	Vertical Scale	Shear	Rotate
	Axonometric	Side	70.711%	45°	90°
		Front	100%	0°	45°
		Bottom	70.711%	45°	45°
	Isometric	Side	86.602%	30°	90°
		Front	86.602%	-30°	30°
		Bottom	86.602%	30°	30°
	Dimetric	Side	96.592%	15°	90°
		Front	96.592%	-15°	60°
		Bottom	50%	60°	60°
	Trimetric	Side	96.592%	15°	90°
		Front	86.602%	-30°	45°
		Bottom	70.711%	45°	45°
	Trimetric	Side	96.592%	15°	90°
		Front	70.711%	-45°	30°
		Bottom	86.602%	30°	30°

Using a Grid for Perspective

If you are creating a series of objects that are all to have a three-dimensional look with the same reference point or vanishing point, you can create a grid that shows perspective, like the one shown in the accompanying figure. You can use this grid as a template for any illustrations that show three-dimensional perspective of single objects, or for several objects that will appear to be standing beside each other.

NOTE

Adobe provides one such grid as a part of the Illustrator package—which you can access by opening the file named 1-point Perspective Grid in the Templates folder, in the Sample Files folder, in the Adobe Illustrator program folder.

1. Use the Rectangle tool to draw a rectangle the size of the finished illustration. In Figure 9.49, the size of the rectangle is the size of the page.

2. Select the **Scale** tool and **Option**+click on the center of the first rectangle to display the Scale dialog box and make one smaller copy of the rectangle.

3. Use the Selection tool to position the smaller rectangle inside the first rectangle.

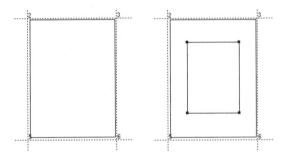

Figure 9.49 Rectangle (left) and scaled copy (right).

NOTE

The positioning of the smaller rectangle will determine the viewer's perspective—identified by the grid lines that are closest to horizontal. Also, the smaller the rectangle you make in step 2, the deeper the perspective will seem. The extreme version—where all the lines converge at a point (i.e., the smallest possible rectangle)—demonstrates why this is called *one-point perspective*. The point at which the lines converge is called the *vanishing point*.

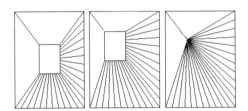

4. Select the **Pen** tool and click on one corner of the large rectangle, then on the corresponding corner of the smaller rectangle to connect the two corners with straight lines, as shown in Figure 9.50. Reselect the **Pen** tool and repeat this step for each of the four corners.

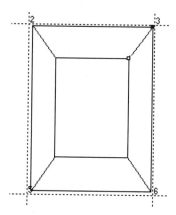

Figure 9.50 Corresponding corners of two rectangles joined using the Pen tool.

5. Use the Blend tool to add more grid lines for depth. First use the Selection tool to select the two lines that join the corners at the top and bottom of the left side of the rectangles, then select the **Blend** tool and click once on the outer anchor point of each line to display the Blend dialog box and enter a number of blends.

Repeat this step for the two lines that join the corners at the bottom of the rectangles.

To keep the grid as simple as possible, add grid lines only to two sides, such as the bottom and right sides of the field, as shown in the figure below.

N O T E

6. Press **Command+A** (**Edit > Select All**) and choose **Object > Guides > Make Guide** (**Command+5**).

7. In drawing three-dimensional objects, use the diagonal depth lines as guides in drawing the side walls of the object, but maintain horizontal and vertical lines for the front face of the object. For example, in the figure

below, the front and back faces are normal rectangles, but the side walls follow diagonal grid lines.

Figure 9.51 Additional guides created using the blend tool (left), and objects drawn following the guides (right).

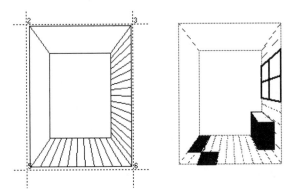

 You can use the same technique to create two-point perspective using two vanishing points. The vanishing points can extend into the pasteboard area, as shown in the figures below. The two vanishing points usually fall along the same horizontal line. As with one-point perspective, the viewer's perspective is identified by the grid lines that are closest to horizontal.

N O T E

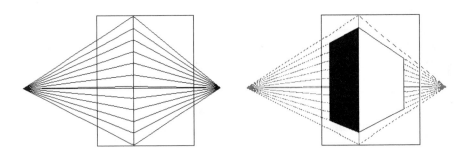

Scaling Objects down a Corridor or Straight Road

The next steps demonstrate a technique that is particular to creating perspective along a *corridor* or *straight road* or *pathway*—though you can later rearrange the objects to create nonlinear effects. It uses a single vanishing point, similar to the previous example, but the grid is much simpler.

1. Use the rectangle tool to create the outer frame for the artwork, and use the Pen tool to draw a horizon line. Draw straight lines from each corner of the rectangle, intersecting at a vanishing point along the horizon.

2. Select all the objects and choose **Object > Guides > Make**.

3. Draw the object(s) that frame the foreground and will be repeated along the corridor or road.

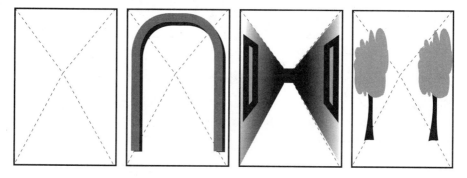

Figure 9.52 Guides converging at vanishing point (left), and objects drawn in the foreground (right).

4. Select the foreground objects with the Selection tool, then select the **Scale** tool and **Option**+click on the vanishing point to display the Scale dialog box. Enter a value (**75%** in this case) and click **Copy**.

5. Press **Command+D** (**Arrange > Repeat Transform**) as many times as needed to create the effect you want.

6. You can rearrange the objects to create nonlinear effects.

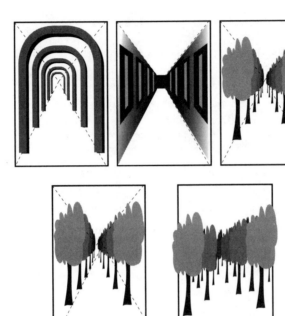

Perspective and Shading on Cylinders

This technique uses a gradient fill to create realistic highlights on curved surfaces. The example used here is a cylinder, but you can adapt this technique to produce shading on any curved surface.

1. First use the Oval tool to draw an ellipse that will form the face of the cylinder. How you draw it depends on the perspective view you want to achieve.

   ➤ For a horizontal cylinder, make the ellipse taller than it is wide.

   ➤ For a vertical cylinder, make the ellipse wider than it is tall.

If the end of the cylinder is to be a face with a design, like a jar lid or drum face, you can create the design in a circle and then select the whole design and scale it non-proportionally.

NOTE

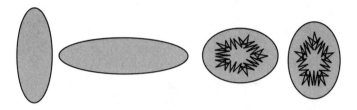

2. Next, use the Direct-selection tool to select an anchor point of the ellipse, and press **Command+C, Command+F** (**Edit > Copy, Edit > Paste In Front**). Drag the copy a distance equal to the length of the cylinder you want to create.

   ➤ For a horizontal cylinder, drag the left or right anchor point.

   ➤ For a vertical cylinder, drag the top or bottom anchor point.

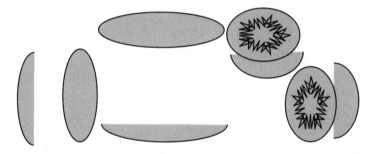

3. Use the Scale tool to scale the copy slightly smaller.

4. Use the Pen tool to connect the corresponding points of the ellipse with the two ends of the copied arc.

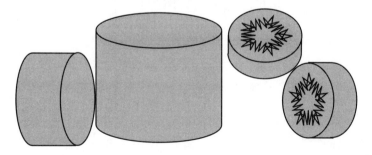

5. Type **Command+hyphen** (**Arrange > Send to back**) to position the cylinder shape behind the elliptical face.

6. Use the Paint Style palette to give the ellipse a stroke of **None** and a **Gradient** Fill, and the shaft a fine black stroke and Steel Bar gradient fill (available in the Adobe Illustrator default startup set of fills).

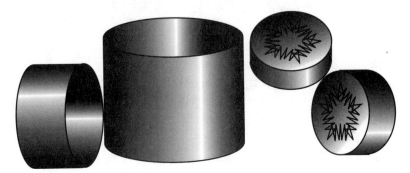

7. Select the **Gradient** tool, and drag it across the width of the cylinder shaft to change the angle, or if you know the angle, you can type it in the Paint Style palette—in this case **45** degrees.

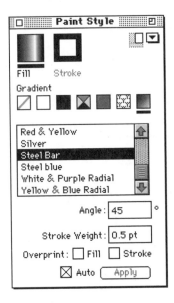

8. Finally, drag a selection marquee around the entire cylinder, and press **Command+G** to group it.

Highlights on Spheres

Highlights are not always the same shape as the object being highlighted, nor are they always linear or radial. Shapes like spheres can be shaded with a radial gradient fill, or you can use the technique described here, using the Blend tool. Remember that the Blend tool blends not only different paint attributes, but different shapes as well. This allows you to blend and highlight gradations smoothly between disparate shapes to create more realistic three-dimensional shading effects.

1. The object to be shaded is a perfect circle, shown in the figure below. To create your circle, choose the **Oval** tool from the Toolbox. In the active window, the pointer becomes a cross. Hold down the **Shift** key as you draw the object to be highlighted. Recall that using the Oval tool with the **Shift** key constrains the object to a perfect circle.

2. Now you will draw the shape of the highlight that would appear if the object were truly three-dimensional and lighted from a single source. Choose the **Pen** or **Freehand** tool to draw a crescent shape, which is the natural highlight for a sphere. Position it inside the circle, off center.

3. Use the Paint Style palette (**Command+I**) to paint the circle a deep color or a deep gray, and the crescent shape fill to a lighter shade of the same color, such as 20%.

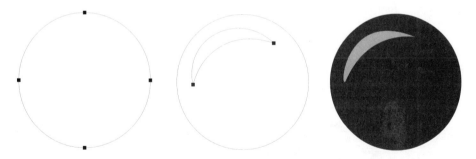

Figure 9.53 Circle (left), with shaped highlight (middle), given two fills (right).

4. Use the Selection tool to drag a selection marquee over the circle and the crescent, and display the anchor points along the path of each object.

5. Select the **Blend** tool from the Toolbox and click on an anchor point of the sphere, then **Shift**+click on a corresponding point of the highlight. These act as reference points for the blend.

WARNING

Whenever you are blending two different shapes, you can get different effects depending on which two points are clicked (see the Blend tool in Chapter 5). Here we checked the leftmost points on both shapes.

6. After you click the second object, the Blend dialog box appears. Type in the number of blend steps you would like the transformation to use. The more steps you request—up to 1296—the smoother the visual illusion. After selecting the number of blend steps, click **OK**.

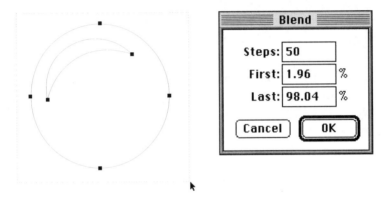

Figure 9.54 Objects selected (left), and entries in Blend dialog box (right).

SHORTCUT

The more blend steps you use, the larger and slower the file will be. Usually no more than thirty blends are needed to yield a smooth transition on a laser printer, and fewer blends are needed when the objects are small.

Figure 9.55 Blend results in Artwork view (left), and printed result (right).

7. You may need to try a couple of different blends to create the most effective visual illusion and highlight. Experiment by choosing different points to blend. Do not forget that blending is affected by the pairs of reference points you choose initially. Successful illusion blending happens when you choose two points that have a smooth and direct transition path.

Interlocking Objects

Interlocking objects is a wonderful effect that is relatively easy to do with Illustrator's tools. Two methods are presented here:

➤ If the interlocking objects need to have (or appear to have) a fill that is different from the stroke color, you have to create them as overlapping paths and use Illustrator's stacking and layering features to produce series of interlocking objects.

➤ If each object is a single color or pattern, you can use the Divide command to break the artwork into pieces that can be filled with appropriate colors to create the effect.

The next examples show two techniques that happen to represent interlocking circles and a interlocking triangles—but you can adapt these techniques to any shape, including type converted to paths. You can also adapt these techniques to make objects appear to come through the "holes" in compound paths.

INTERLOCKING OBJECTS THAT APPEAR TO BE OUTLINED BY STROKES

This first example shows how to create a series of interlocking circles that appear to have a black stroke with a white fill. In fact the circles are composed of two overlapping paths, a thick black stroke below a thinner white stroke.

NOTE You could adapt this technique to interlocking any paths—but if the path does not need to appear "outlined" it is much easier to use the second technique, described after this. This technique requires more steps than the next one: you have to break the objects into two halves, and then work with the **Send To Back** command, as in the next steps.

1. Select the **Oval** tool and hold the **Option** key as you click on the Artboard to display the Oval dialog box and enter values to create a circle 36 points (.5 inch) in diameter. Then use the Paint Style palette (**Command+I**) to give it a black 6-point stroke and no fill.

2. Press **Command+Shift+M** (**Arrange > Move**) to display the Move dialog box and move a copy 18 points (.25 inch) horizontally. Click **Copy** to close the dialog box.

3. Select the first circle you drew, **Command+C, Command+F** (**Edit > Copy, Edit > Paste In Front**) to make a copy, and give the copy a 4-point white stroke and no fill. With the Selection tool, drag a selection marquee around these two overlapping circles then press **Command+G** to group them.

Figure 9.56 Circle (left), duplicated and moved (middle),
then duplicated and given white stroke overlapping a wider black stroke (right).

4. Use the Scissors tool to cut the second circle at the left and right anchor points, then press **Command+Shift+A** (**Edit > Select None**) to deselect everything.

5. Select both segments of the right circle, then press **Command+C, Command+F** (**Edit > Copy, Edit > Paste In Front**) to make a copy, and give the copies a 4-point white stroke and no fill.

6. With the Selection tool, drag a selection marquee around the two upper overlapping half-circles then press **Command+G** to group them. Then drag a selection marquee around the two lower overlapping half-circles and press **Command+G** to group them.

7. With the two lower half-circles still selected, press **Command+hyphen** (**Arrange > Send To Back**) You now have two interlocking circles.

N O T E If there is additional artwork below the elements that you want to interlock, you might need to use **Command+X** (**Edit > Cut**) on the selected elements in this step, then select the object(s) that you want them to appear behind, and then use **Command+B** (**Paste In Back**) to paste it behind selected objects only. It would be better to construct your interwoven elements away from all other artwork, and then move them into place.

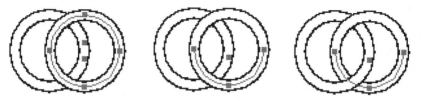

Figure 9.57 Second circle cut in half with scissors tool, duplicated, and given white stroke overlapping a wider black stroke (left), the bottom halves selected (middle), and sent to the back layer (right).

8. If you want to produce additional circles, first determine how many additional circles you want to make. Then use the Selection tool to select all four half-circles—two upper and two bottom halves— and type **Command+Shift+M** (**Arrange > Move**) to display the Move dialog box. Move a copy 20 points horizontally. Type **Command+D** (**Arrange > Repeat Transform**) to produce the desired number of additional copies.

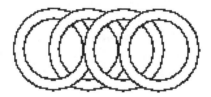

9. Starting at the third circle from the left, select the group that comprises the lower half of the circle and press **Command+hyphen** to send it to the back of the layer. Then repeat for the lower halves of the remaining new circles, working from left to right.

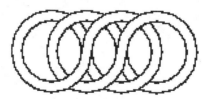

INTERLOCKING OBJECTS THAT HAVE NO STROKE

This second technique works for interlocking objects that have no Stroke (or the Stroke and Fill are the same).

1. Create the objects that compose the artwork to be interlocked or interwoven—they must be closed paths with a Fill but no Stroke (or have a stroke the same as the path).

NOTE

If the objects are composed of paths with no fill, you must convert them to objects that have a Fill but no Stroke using the **Filter > Objects > Outline Stroke** command.

2. Select all the objects and choose **Filter > Pathfinder > Divide.**

Figure 9.58 Paths before and after using the Divide filter.

3. Hold down the **Shift** key and use the Direct-selection tool to select all of the intersections that you want to change, and assign them the second fill color or pattern through the Paint Style palette.

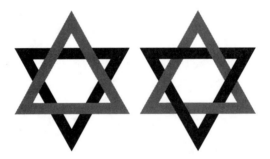

Figure 9.59 Artwork before and after changing selected intersections to the second color.

Coils and Springs

Coils and springs are common parts of mechanical devices and appear in many technical drawings, but they can be difficult to create unless you know the right techniques. Using the technique described here, you will draw a coil like the one pictured below.

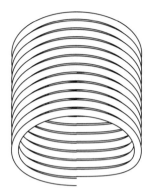

1. Use one of the Oval tools to draw an ellipse.

2. Press **Command+Control+A** to display the Object > Attributes dialog box, and deselect Show Center Point, then click **OK** to close the dialog box.

3. Use the Scissors tool to cut the ellipse at its lowest anchor point.

4. With the Direct-selection tool, select one of the two anchor points created by the cut, and drag it slightly up or down, holding the **Shift** key as you release the mouse button to constrain the movement to precisely vertical.

5. You can refine the shape by dragging the next anchor point (along the line from the lower of the two severed points) down about half the distance of the first movement.

Figure 9.60 Ellipse (left), cut with scissors tool (middle), and with anchor points moved (right).

6. Use the Paint Style palette (**Command+I**) to set the Stroke of the ellipse to **100%** Black with a Weight of 10 points (or any thickness you desire) for the coil. Fill is set to **None**.

7. With the figure selected, type **Command+C, Command+F** (**Edit > Copy, Edit > Paste In Front**). With the copy selected, use the Paint Style palette to change the copy to an 8-point White Stroke (or two points less than the weight selected in step 4).

8. Select the composite figure, then type **Command+G** (**Arrange > Group**). With the Selection tool, **Shift+Option**+drag a copy of the figure up (if you want the viewing perspective to be from the top of the coil) or down (if you want the viewing perspective to be from the bottom) to meet the first coil. Be sure to hold down the **Shift** key and the **Option** key as you release the mouse button. Type **Command+D** (**Arrange > Repeat Transform**) to create as many additional loops of the coil as you wish.

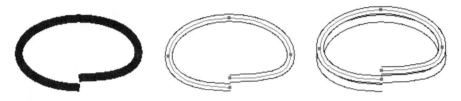

Figure 9.61 Cut ellipse with black stroke (left), duplicated and given a thinner white stroke over the black original (middle), both paths duplicated and moved (right).

Using the Graph Tools

You can create graphs in Illustrator based on numeric data that you type in or import from another source, such as a spreadsheet application. You can customize graphs using any of the commands and tools that are normally available for coloring and transforming any other object created in Illustrator.

You use the graph tools to create graphs from numeric data. There are six graph tools: the Grouped-column graph tool, the Stacked-column graph tool, the Line graph tool, the Pie graph tool, the Area graph tool, and the Scatter graph tool. They differ only in the kind of graph each creates. The default graph tool is the Grouped-column graph tool. Graphs are created as grouped objects, but you can modify individual elements by selecting them with the Direct-selection or Group-selection tools.

If you ungroup them, you will be unable to change the graph's style or modify the graph's data.

WARNING

Starting a Graph

To start building a graph, follow these steps:

1. Choose the graph tool corresponding to the kind of graph you wish to create:

   ➤ Click the current Graph tool icon in the Toolbox, if it displays the type of graph you wish to create, and go on to step 3, or

   ➤ Double-click on the graph icon in the toolbox to display a dialog box that lets you choose another graph type, or

   ➤ Choose **Object Graphs Style** (**Command+Shift+Option+S**) to display the same dialog box.

2. Make entries in the Graph Style dialog box as described in the next section and click **OK** to close the dialog box.

3. The mouse pointer changes to a + in the active window. You can either:

   ➤ Drag the cross-hair pointer on the artwork to define the area of the graph, or

   ➤ Click the pointer on the screen to display the Graph dialog box and enter dimensions numerically.

   An empty graph of the shape and dimensions you defined appears, and the Graph Data window opens.

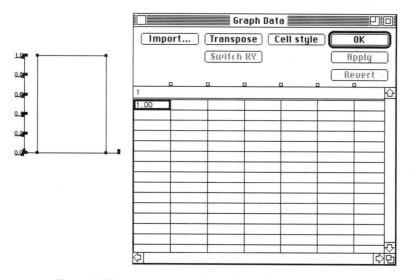

Figure 9.62 An empty graph with the Graph Data window open.

NOTE

Holding the **Option** key when clicking or dragging makes the first position of the pointer the center of the graph rather than a corner.

4. Use the commands described next to define the graph.

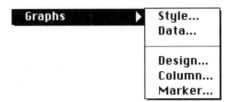

NOTE

Its a good idea to select the layer onto which you wish to position the graph, either as the first step or after creating the graph. See the description of the Layers palette in Chapter 10.

Creating a Graph with Numerically Specified Dimensions

When you click one of the graph tools in the drawing window at the upper left corner of the area in which you want to create the graph, or hold down the **Option** key and click the center of the area in which you want to create the graph, the Graph dialog box appears, containing fields in which you enter the desired measurements for the graph's width and height.

NOTE

You can enter values in the default unit of measurement, or enter a value followed by the abbreviation for any unit of measure: in (inches), pt (points i.e., 1/72nd of an inch), mm (millimeters), or cm (centimeters), You can also change the default unit of measure for Ruler units using the **File > Document Setup** and **File > Preferences > General commands**.

When you click **OK** to close the Graph dialog box, a graph with the dimensions you defined appears, and the Graph Data window opens.

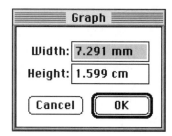

Figure 9.63 Graph dialog box for entering dimensions.

Entering Data

The Graph Data window opens automatically when you start a new graph, or you can open it any time using the **Object > Graph > Data** command (**Command+Shift+ Option+D**). This command is dimmed unless a graph is selected. Use the Graph Data command to open the Graph Data window for an existing, selected graph in order to modify the data and update the graph to reflect the changes you have made.

The Graph Data window, unlike most dialog boxes, is a true window with a close box and title bar. You can move it around the screen and leave it open as you continue to work on your graph. The lower part of the Graph Data window contains an area similar to a spreadsheet where you enter or import the data you wish to graph.

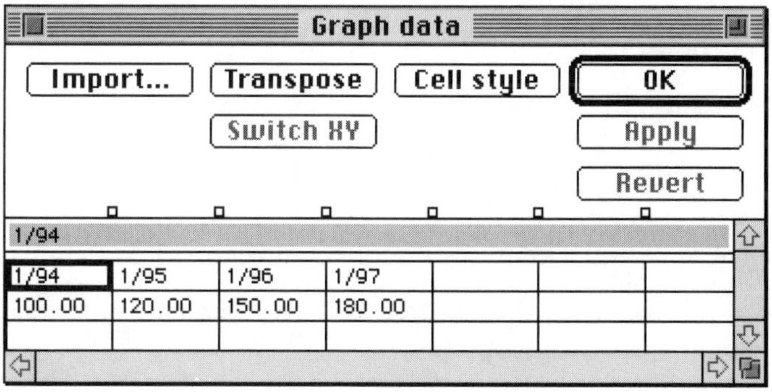

Figure 9.64 The Graph Data window.

The lower part of the window is a data entry area similar to a spreadsheet. The data entry area contains *cells* arranged in rows and columns. You enter *data series* in the worksheet columns and *categories* in the rows. Labels entered at the top of columns label a data series, and are known as *legends*. Different data series are depicted in graphs by using a different fill for each—the legends appear as a key to the different fills. Categories appear as labels on the *x* axis in column, line, and area graphs. Pie graphs have only one category. Scatter graphs are unique in that they plot data points as paired sets of coordinates along the *x* and *y* axes, with both axes measuring values. Scatter graphs also lack categories.

➤ You enter each label or value in a separate cell.

➤ Labels are words or numbers used to describe a row or column—normally, you enter these in the first row or column.

➤ To use numbers as labels, you must put them in quotes, otherwise Illustrator will interpret them as values.

➤ If you want a label to have multiple lines, use the vertical line character (|) to indicate line breaks.

➤ You can type data directly into the data entry window, you can paste it from another Graph Data window or from a spreadsheet application, or you can import it from a disk file by clicking the **Import** button in the Graph Data window. Imported data must be in Tab-delimited text-only format (cell values separated by Tabs).

➤ You can move from cell to cell using the mouse, the **Tab** and **Return** keys, or the **Arrow** keys. Tab moves the current selection one cell to the right, and **Return** moves it one cell down.

➤ You can specify the number of decimal places used in each cell and the width of the columns in the Graph Data window by clicking the **Cell style** button and entering the appropriate values in the dialog box that appears. Note that the column width value has no effect on the width of the columns in the graph itself, only in the Graph Data window.

➤ Once you have entered the data, you can click **OK** to close the window and apply the data to your graph.

➤ If you click **Apply**, the data is applied to the graph and the Graph Data window remains open.

The upper part of the Graph Data window contains seven control buttons: **Import, Transpose, Cell Style, Switch XY, OK, Apply,** and **Revert**. A description of each follows.

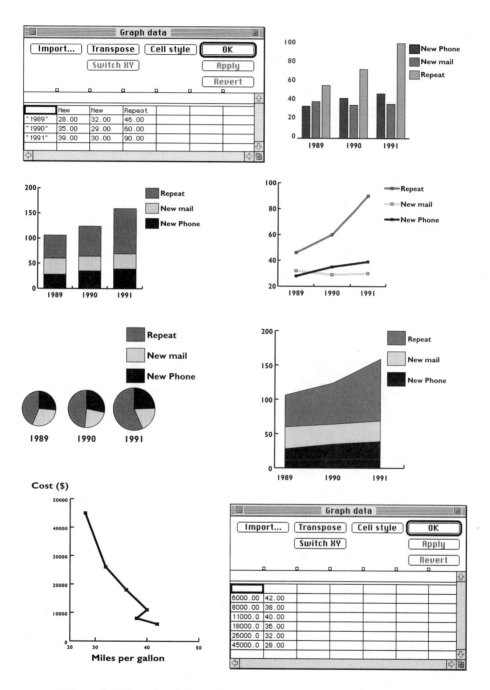

Figure 9.65 Examples of data and the resulting graphs, one for each graph type.

IMPORT...

Clicking this button presents an Open dialog box, containing a list of all files on the current disk or in the current folder. Click the name of the file you want to import, then click **Open** or double-click the file name. The data is imported and entered into the worksheet in the Graph Data window.

Note that although the file list shows all files, the only files that can be successfully imported into the Graph Data window are those in Tab-delimited text-only format. (This is the format used by most databases and spreadsheets when you choose **Save As Text**. In the case of spreadsheets, each column is separated by a tab and each row is separated by a carriage return.)

TRANSPOSE

If you accidentally enter graph data backwards (in rows instead of columns or vice versa) you can use the **Transpose** button to convert your columns to rows and rows to columns.

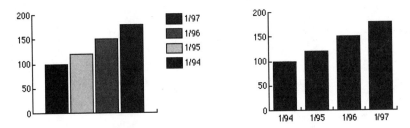

Figure 9.66 Grouped column graph and data before and after transposing.

CELL STYLE

You can specify the number of decimal places (from 0 to 10) used in each cell and the width of the columns (from 3 to 20) in the Graph Data window by clicking the **Cell Style** button and entering the appropriate values in the dialog box that appears. Note that the column width value has no effect on the width of columns in the graph itself, only in the Graph Data window.

SWITCH XY

This option is available only for scatter graphs. It transposes the x and y axes.

OK

Clicking this button closes the window and applies the data to your graph.

APPLY

Clicking this button applies the data to the graph so you can see the changes on the screen but leaves the Graph Data window open. (You might need to move the Graph Data window in order to see the changed graph.)

REVERT

Clicking this button returns your data to the state it was in when you last applied it to your graph. If you change your data without applying it to the graph, close the Graph Data window by clicking its close box; a message appears asking if you want to apply the changes to the graph.

Editing Graphs

Once a graph has been created, you can change it as described under the next headings.

WARNING

Graphs are created as grouped objects. If you ungroup a graph, you will no longer be able to update it with new data. Instead of ungrouping to modify individual elements in a graph, select them using the Direct-selection tool, as described later in this chapter.

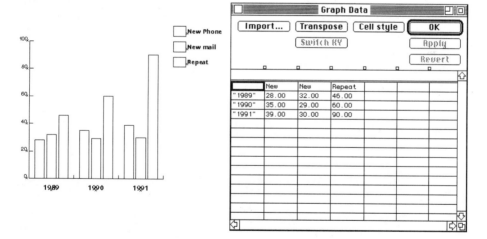

Figure 9.67 A grouped-column graph and the associated Graph Data window.

CHANGING THE GRAPH STYLE

The **Object > Graph > Style** command (**Command+Shift+Option+S**) opens the Graph Style dialog box, where you can choose between six different graph types: grouped column, stacked column, line, pie, area, or scatter. You can also combine different graph types into one graph. Use this command to change an existing, selected graph from one type to another or to customize the options associated with a particular graph type.

All graph types except the area graph have options. Grouped column and stacked column graphs share the same options, as do line and scatter graphs. Some options are only available when the entire graph is selected, while others can be applied to parts of graphs. Each option is described under the next headings.

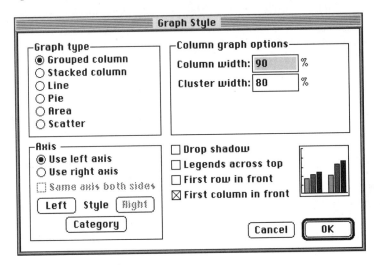

Figure 9.68 The Graph Style dialog box.

Selecting a Graph Type

Each graph type is suited to illustrate particular types of data. For a given set of data, one graph type is usually more appropriate than the others.

➤ Grouped column graphs are best for comparing one item to another or for comparing several items over time.

➤ Stacked column graphs are best for comparing a group of variables over time or for showing the relationship of parts to the whole.

➤ Line graphs show the trend of one or more items over time. The *y* axis represents values while the *x* axis represents time.

> ➤ Pie graphs show percentages of a total.

> ➤ Area graphs, like line graphs, show fluctuations over time, but also emphasize totals.

> ➤ Scatter graphs are unique in that each axis measures a value. Data points are plotted as paired sets of coordinates along the x and y axes.

If you are unsure which kind of graph best illustrates your data, experiment with the different graph types.

Each graph that you create has its own Graph Data window but you can quickly create a series of graphs based on the same data by pasting the data from one Graph Data window to another.

> ➤ First, select all the data in the Graph Data window associated with your existing graph and choose **Copy**.

> ➤ Then choose a different graph tool and create a new graph.

> ➤ Finally, select the upper-left cell in the new Graph Data window, choose **Paste**, and click **Apply** in the Graph Data window.

The new graph is updated to reflect the data you paste. You can repeat this procedure to create as many different kinds of graph as you wish. You can also use the **Object > Graph > Style** command to change a graph.

GRAPH TYPE

The Graph type area at the upper left of the dialog box has six radio buttons, allowing you to choose among different types of graphs. The choices are: **Grouped Column, Stacked Column, Line, Pie, Area**, or **Scatter**. Depending on which graph type you select, options in the top right of the dialog box change.

The options at the top right in the dialog box vary according to the type of graph. There are no additional options for area graphs. The options for the other graph types are described here.

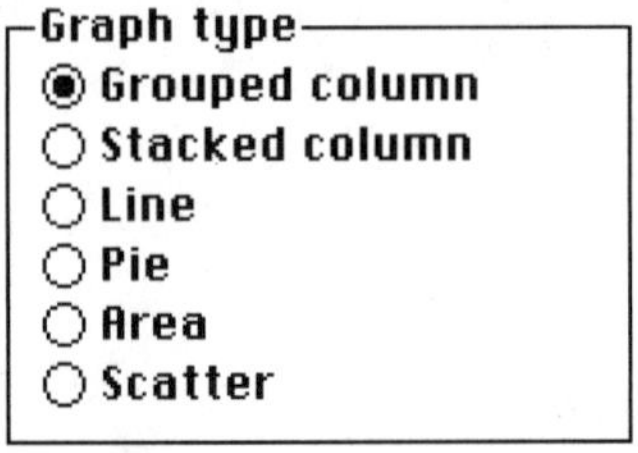

```
┌─Graph type─────────────┐
│ ◉ Grouped column       │
│ ○ Stacked column       │
│ ○ Line                 │
│ ○ Pie                  │
│ ○ Area                 │
│ ○ Scatter              │
└────────────────────────┘
```

Figure 9.69 A detail of the Graph Style dialog box—detail: Graph type.

GROUPED-COLUMN AND STACKED-COLUMN GRAPHS

For grouped-column and stacked-column graphs, the options are **Column width** and **Cluster width**. Both are expressed as percentages.

A *cluster* is a group of columns corresponding to a row in the worksheet. The default values are 90% for column width and 80% for cluster width. This leaves space between both the columns and the clusters. Setting the values to 100% makes both the columns and the cluster fit flush against each other. Values above 100% make the columns overlap. For stacked-column graphs, set the cluster width to **100%** and use only the column width option to adjust the width of the columns. The entire graph must be selected to use these options.

LINE AND SCATTER GRAPHS

The options for line and scatter graphs are **Mark data points, Connect data points, Fill lines,** and **Edge-to-edge lines.**

➤ **Mark data points** places square markers at each data point.

➤ **Connect data points** draws lines that connect the data points and makes the **Fill lines** option available. This option creates a line of a width that you specify and fills it with the appropriate fill for the data series.

➤ **Edge-to-edge** lines extends the lines beyond the first and last data points to the full width of the graph. This option is not available for scatter graphs.

PIE GRAPHS

The pie graph options are **Standard Legends, Legends in Wedges,** and **No Legends.**

➤ The **Standard Legends** option places the worksheet column labels outside the graph.

➤ The **Legends in Wedges** option places the label for each worksheet column in the corresponding wedge of the pie.

➤ The **No Legends** option omits the labels entirely.

AXIS

The axis options at the lower left of the dialog box control the axis attributes of your graph. You can specify whether to display the *y* axis on the left side, on the right side, or on both sides of the graph.

➤ The default is **Use Left Axis**.

➤ The **Same Axis Both Sides** option is dimmed unless the entire graph is selected. If you select the **Same Axis Both Sides** option, you can select either **Use Left Axis** or **Use Right Axis**. However, if you have manually set axis attributes for an axis, you should select that axis if you want those attributes to be used.

➤ Pie graphs have no axis, so these options are dimmed when a pie chart is selected.

Figure 9.70 A detail of the Graph Style dialog box showing the Axis options.

The **Left**, **Right**, and **Category** buttons open the Graph Axis Style dialog box, where you can specify tick mark options for each axis. (*Tick marks* are lines placed perpendicular to the axes to mark the units of measurement or the divisions between categories.) You must select the entire graph to use these options.

The Axis label and tick line values options apply only to axes that show values. In all types except for pie and scatter graphs this is the *y*, or vertical, axis. In a scatter graph, both axes measure values, and the **Category** button is relabeled to read **Bottom**.

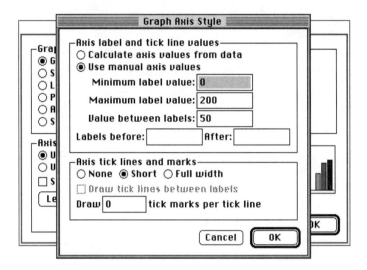

Figure 9.71 The Graph Axis Style dialog box.

CALCULATE AXIS VALUES FROM DATA

The default option automatically assigns tick marks and value labels to the axis.

USE MANUAL AXIS VALUES

Lets you specify a minimum and maximum label value and the value between labels. If you do not want any labels to appear on the axis, enter zero in the Value Between Labels field.

PUT ON LABELS BEFORE/AFTER

This option lets you add information to value labels. For example, you may want to add a dollar sign before dollar values or percentage or degree signs after values that reflect these measurements.

The Axis tick lines and marks options apply to all axes. You can specify **no tick marks**, **short tick marks**, or **full width tick marks** that stretch the full width of the graph. Tick lines are placed at value labels. You can also specify a number of intermediate tick marks, which are then spaced evenly between the tick lines, according to the number of tick marks per tick line you specify. The **Draw tick lines between labels** option applies only to the category, or x, axis. It is dimmed when a value, or axis is selected.

MORE OPTIONS

A third set of four options is at the lower right of the dialog box.

> ➤ The **Drop Shadow** option places a drop shadow behind the graph elements. This option is more effective with column and pie charts than with line graphs.

> ➤ The **Legends Across Top** option places the legends in a horizontal row across the top of the graph, rather than as a vertical list at the right. This option is only available when the entire graph is selected.

The two remaining options in the set, **First Column in Front** and **First Row in Front**, apply mainly to grouped column graphs when the columns overlap one another.

> ➤ **First Column in Front**, the default option, places the first column of data in the worksheet as the frontmost object in the graph. (For area graphs, you must select this option, otherwise some data may not be displayed.)

> ➤ The **First Row in Front** option places the first row of data in the worksheet frontmost in the graph.

Click **OK** to close the Graph Style dialog box and view the results.

CHANGING THE GRAPH DESIGN

The **Object > Graph > Design** command (**Command+Shift+Option+G**) displays the Define Graph Design dialog box, which allows you to create a new graph design or delete, paste, or change the name of an existing graph design. The scrolling list displays all existing graph designs.

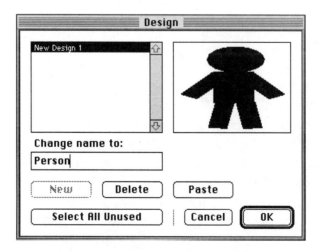

Figure 9.72 The Define Graph Design dialog box.

1. Draw a graph design shape or design and color it.

2. Using the Rectangle tool, draw a rectangle around your art defining the "tiling element."

3. Select the rectangle and use the **Send To Back** command to position it behind the design.

4. Select both the design and the rectangle.

5. Then choose **Object > Graph > Design**. The Define Graph Design dialog box appears, as shown in the preceding figure.

6. Click **New** to display the selected graph design in the bottom right area of the dialog box and name the graph design by entering the name in the text box.

7. When you close this dialog box, the graph design will then be available in the Use Column Design and Use Marker Design dialog boxes.

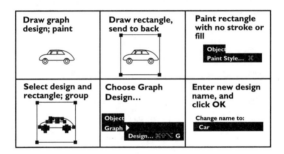

Figure 9.73 Procedure for creating a graph design.

To create a sliding graph design, you must add a horizontal guide to indicate where the design will be stretched or compressed.

1. Follow the procedure for creating a graph design until you have the design in front of the rectangle, then:

2. Use the Pen tool to draw a horizontal line at the point where you want the design to be stretched or compressed.

3. Select all parts of the design including the horizontal line, then choose **Arrange > Group** or **Command+G**.

4. Use the Direct-selection tool to select only the horizontal line, then choose **Object > Guides > Make** or press **Command+5**.

5. Use the Selection tool (not the Direct-selection tool) to select the entire design, then choose **Define Graph Design** and follow the procedure for naming a new graph design.

➤ Click **New** to store the graph design under a new name.

➤ Click **Delete** to remove the selected name (and graph design) from the list. Graphs that used that graph design will revert to the default graph design.

➤ Click **Select All Unused** to select the names of all graph designs that are not currently used in the artwork. You can delete these graph designs to save memory and storage space.

➤ Click **Paste** to paste a copy of the graph design on the page if you want to edit the design, then close the dialog box, edit the design artwork, select it, and choose **Define Graph Design** again to store the changed design under the same name or a new name.

➤ If you save the changed design using the same name, Illustrator offers you two options: **Redefine and Recreate** changes the graph design definition and recreates graphs using the design so that they use the changed design, while **Redefine Only** updates the graph design for future use, but leaves existing graphs that use the design unchanged.

6. Click **OK** to close the dialog box and record the changes, or click Cancel to close the dialog box without recording any changes.

NOTE   If you frequently use custom graph designs, save them in a file created for this purpose. Opening the file will make your previously created graph designs available in other open Illustrator files.

If you want a set of graph designs to be available automatically whenever you use Illustrator, create an Illustrator file containing all the graph designs you want, then name it **Adobe Illustrator Startup**, and place it in the folder containing the Illustrator application. (If you keep the application on the desktop, place the Adobe Illustrator Startup file in your startup disk's disk window.) You can also include patterns, colors, and fonts in the Adobe Illustrator Startup document. These elements will automatically be available whenever you use Illustrator.

DESIGNING A COLUMN GRAPH

The **Object > Graph > Column** command lets you use any graph design created with the **Object > Graph > Design** command in a column graph. This command is only available if a graph design has been defined in an open document *and* one or more columns in a column graph are currently selected.

1. Select the entire column graph using the Selection tool, or select those columns and legends for which you want to substitute the design using the Direct-selection tool.

2. Then choose **Object > Graph > Column**. The Graph Column Design dialog box appears as shown below.

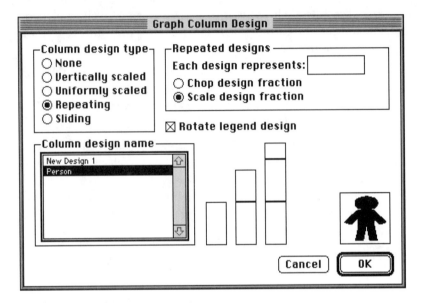

Figure 9.74 The Graph Column Design dialog box.

The Graph Column Design dialog box lets you control how graph designs appear in your graph. The Column design type options are as follows:

NONE

Click **None** to convert a graph or column that uses a graph design back to regular columns.

VERTICALLY SCALED

Click this button to scale the graph design vertically to the height of the selected column or columns.

UNIFORMLY SCALED

Click this button to scale the graph design uniformly to the height of the selected column or columns.

REPEATING

Click this button to create columns of repeating graph designs. If you use this option, you must also enter a value in the Each design represents field, and click either the **Chop design fraction** or **Scale design fraction** button under the **Repeated designs** options. These options are dimmed unless you choose the **Repeating** option from Column design type. **Chop design fraction** places a truncated design at the top of columns where the column value is not an exact multiple of the unit specified in the Each design represents field. **Scale design fraction** uses a vertically scaled design instead.

SLIDING

Click this button to use sliding column designs. To use this option, the graph design you choose must contain a guide that indicates the sliding point. (See **Object > Graph > Design**.)

ROTATE LEGEND DESIGN

Click this option to rotate the design that appears in the legend 90 degrees.

COLUMN DESIGN

The Column design name area shows a scrolling list of all available graph designs. You can make any graph design available by opening a document that contains the design.

NOTE If you want a set of graph designs to be available automatically whenever you use Illustrator, create an Illustrator file containing all the graph designs you want, then name it **Adobe Illustrator Startup**, and place it in the folder containing the Illustrator application. (If you keep the application on the desktop, place the Adobe Illustrator Startup file in your startup disk's disk window.) You can also include custom colors, fonts, and patterns in the Adobe Illustrator Startup document. These elements will automatically be available whenever you use Illustrator.

DESIGNING MARKERS

The **Object > Graph > Marker** command (**Command+Shift+Option+M**) lets you use any graph design created with the **Object > Graph > Design** command in a line or scatter graph. This command is only available if a graph design has been defined in an open document *and* one or more data points in a line or scatter graph are currently selected.

1. Select the entire graph using the Selection tool or select those data points and legends for which you want to substitute the design using the Direct-selection tool.

2. Then choose **Object > Graph > Marker** or press **Command+Shift+ Option+M**. The Graph Marker Design dialog box appears.

3. The Graph Marker Design dialog box lets you control how graph designs appear in your graph.

   ➤ Click **None** to convert an existing data point that uses a marker design back to the default square marker design.

   ➤ Click on data point to replace the selected data point markers and legends with a graph design.

   ➤ Choose the graph design from the scrolling list under Marker design name.

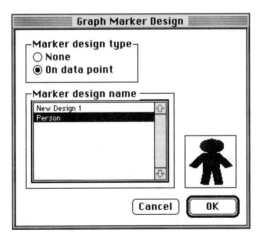

Figure 9.75 The Graph Marker Design dialog box

Customizing Illustrator's Charts

Illustrator's graph tools let you quickly create various types of charts and graphs directly from numeric data. However, the default colors and patterns assigned by the program are often not the ones desired in the final artwork. This section describes a technique that lets you select related elements of the graph without first ungrouping it.

This example used in the next steps is a grouped-column graph, but it can be applied to any other graph types generated by the graph tools.

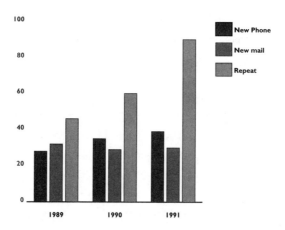

Unless you have compelling reasons to ungroup a graph, you should avoid doing so. Once a graph has been ungrouped, you can no longer update it to reflect changes in the underlying numeric data.

WARNING

1. Create a grouped-column graph using the Grouped-column graph tool, then either import or type the data into the Graph Data Window, and click **OK**. The resulting graph is a grouped object, and default fills and strokes are assigned to the various components.

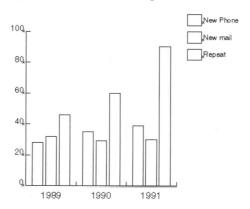

NOTE

You can use the Direct-selection tool to select individual components of the group. However, you can also use the Direct-selection tool to automatically select related elements, to which you can then assign the desired stroke and fill, or in the case of labels, type attributes. In each case, the technique involves **Option**+clicking the Direct-selection tool twice.

The first time you click, the object you clicked becomes selected.

The second time you click, all the related elements in the graph also become selected.

Clicking a third time selects the entire graph.

2. To change the paint attributes for the legend and all the columns in a data series, **Option**+click the Direct-selection tool twice on the legend.

➤ The first time you click, the legend is selected.

➤ The second time you click, all the columns in the data series are also selected.

3. You can now use the Paint Style palette (**Command+I**) to change the stroke and fill for the entire data series at once. You can repeat the process for the other data series.

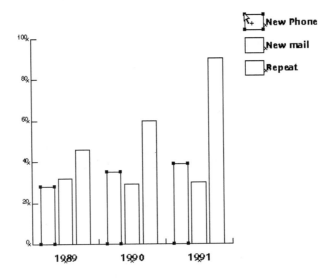

4. To change the paint or type attributes for all the legend labels, **Option**+click the Direct-selection tool twice on any legend label.

➤ The first time you click, the label is selected.

➤ The second time you click, all the legend labels are selected.

5. You can now modify the paint and type attributes for all the legend labels.

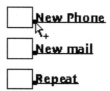

6. To change the paint or type attributes for all the category labels, **Option**+click the Direct-selection tool twice on any category label.

➤ The first time you click, the label is selected.

➤ The second time you click, all the category labels are selected.

7. You can now modify the paint and type attributes for all the category labels.

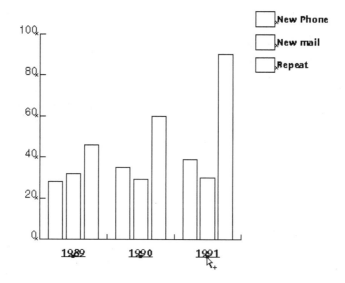

8. To change the paint or type attributes for all the value axis labels, **Option**+click the Direct-selection tool twice on any value axis label.

➤ The first time you click, the label is selected.

➤ The second time you click, all the value axis labels are selected.

9. You can now modify the paint and type attributes for all the value axis labels.

10. To change the paint attributes for all the tick marks on an axis, **Option**+click the Direct-selection tool twice on any tick mark.

➤ The first time you click, the tick mark is selected.

➤ The second time you click, all the tick marks are selected.

11. You can now modify the paint attributes for all the tick marks on the axis. You can hide the tick marks by setting their Stroke to **None**.

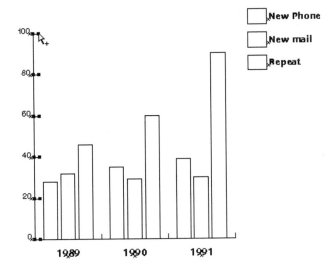

12. To select an entire axis, **Option**+click the Direct-selection tool twice on the axis.

➤ The first time you click, only the axis is selected.

➤ The second time you click, both the axis and the tick marks are selected.

NOTE

In the case of the value axis, the axis labels are also selected, but in the case of the category axis, the labels are not selected.

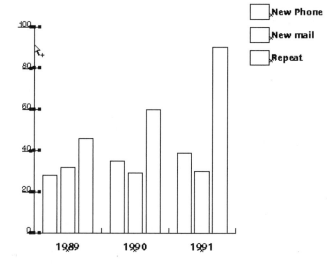

NOTE

You can hide an entire axis by setting the Stroke and Fill to **None**. This solution is better than simply deleting the axis, because to delete the axis you must ungroup the graph. Ungrouping the graph not only makes it impossible to update the data, but also disables the automatic selection features described here.

Chapter 10

Design and Production

This chapter presents some topics you may find very basic and others you might think too pedantic, but they all relate to improving your productivity, not just in Illustrator but in project management. Believe me, it's worth a skim!

Topics in this chapter include:

➤ Setting up to begin a new project

➤ Basic design principles, including efficiency tips

➤ Efficient methods of moving objects

➤ Other tips on alignment and spacing

➤ Creating custom grids

✝ ➤ Managing overlapping objects, including coincident identical paths

➤ Working in named layers, including layering overhead transparencies, and layering different type specifications

➤ Creating custom views and working in multiple windows

➤ Handling the Real World challenges of space and time—how to make things smaller and go faster

NOTE

Items of special interest in this chapter include how to add, delete, or change the template (traceable PICT) associated with an Illustrator file.

Getting Off to a Good Start

The File menu has commands that affect whole documents. It includes commands that are common to most Macintosh applications, such as **New**, **Open**, **Close**, **Save**, **Save as**, **Page Setup**, **Print**, and **Quit**. The Preferences submenu displays four preferences categories—**General**, **Color Matching**, **Hyphenation Options**, and **Plug-ins**—that let you change how Illustrator displays elements on the screen.

This section offers some production tips in working with some of these basic commands, as well as tips on what to do *before* you start a new document or project.

Organizing Your Files and Folders

➤ If you are starting a new project that will involve using or creating more than one file, it's a good idea to begin by creating a folder in which all files related to that project will be stored.

➤ If some files already exist, move or copy them into that folder.

➤ Decide in advance what format all Illustrator files are to be saved in— native Illustrator format creates the smallest files, but you must save the files in EPS format if they are to be placed in other applications like PageMaker or QuarkXPress. And will they *all* be saved in Illustrator 6.0 format, or should you save some of them in Illustrator 5 format for compatibility with others on the project. (Remember, Illustrator 6.0 requires a lot more memory than earlier versions, and some users might not be able to or want to upgrade right away!)

➤ Decide on naming conventions for the files and name all files consistently. For example, a large design and production shop might assign each client or project a number, and each document name will start with that number.

➤ If an Illustrator document will include imported EPS files, it's a good idea to give the Illustrator document and the imported EPS similar enough names that you know they belong together. For example, the Illustrator file might be named **House Ad #1 AI6**, and the imported EPS might be named **House Ad #1.eps**. If the Illustrator file itself is also saved in EPS format, it might be named **House Ad #1 AI6.eps**. This way, all the files related to the same document will sort together when the project folder is viewed By Name on the Desktop.

➤ If the files will be taken to another system, for further editing or for printing, you might include a copy of the required fonts in the folder, so you can take them to the new system or let the service bureau know what they are.

➤ If the files will be taken to a Windows-based PC system, develop naming conventions that will work on both systems. For PC systems, this still means keeping the name to only eight characters (ouch!), followed by a period and a three-character file-type indicator. (Windows 95 promised to change this, but the transition isn't as smooth as we might have wished.)

NOTE You can give a Macintosh Illustrator file a name up to 30 characters long (including spaces), but the list of files displayed in the Open dialog box will display only the first 20 characters. It is a good idea to name related files with the same initial characters (so they will be grouped together in an alphabetical list), but be sure to differentiate among the names within the first 20 characters.

Adding Elements from the Deluxe Edition

The Adobe Illustrator 6.0 package includes Adobe Illustrator Deluxe Edition, a CD-ROM that contains:

➤ All the files required to install Adobe Illustrator on your hard disk.

➤ Adobe Gallery Effects, which can be added to Illustrator as plug-ins as well as to other applications that use Adobe Photoshop-compatible plug-ins—like Adobe Photoshop, Adobe Premiere, Adobe After Effects, Fractal Design Painter, PixelPaint Professional, and Strata Vision 3D.

➤ A folder called *Illustrator Goodies* that includes a plethora of patterns, textures, and shapes from Adobe Collector's edition, including more path patterns, plus 35 more templates or pre-defined grid systems for setting up business cards, envelopes, letterhead, mailing labels, and other common forms. Patterns and templates can be used as-is or modified to suit your needs.

➤ Disk versions of the Adobe Illustrator and Adobe Acrobat manuals and PDF tech notes for advanced users written by Adobe staff.

In addition to these files that work directly with Illustrator, the CD-ROM includes:

➤ Adobe Acrobat Reader, for reading PDF files.
➤ Adobe Dimensions 2.0 for creating three-dimensional art that you can import into Illustrator, or for giving three-dimensional shading to Illustrator objects.
➤ Adobe Fetch for easily cataloging and retrieving graphic images.
➤ Adobe ScreenReady, which streamlines the production of graphics intended for on-screen display, combining functions that can otherwise require several different applications and many production steps. You can use it to anti-alias, or smooth, the edges of type and graphics, and to optimize the color palette of a graphic to meet the requirements of multimedia, video, and online publishing projects. Adobe ScreenReady saves the graphic into a PICT image, ready to import into a screen-oriented project.
➤ Demonstration versions of other Adobe products, including After Effects, Phototshop, Premiere, and Streamline.
➤ Guides to Adobe's educational services.
➤ The PSPrinter 8.3 printer driver (recommended for use with Illustrator 6.0).
➤ 220 Type I fonts—the same 40 fonts available on the disks, plus 54 additional Type I font families.
➤ Apple Extensions QuickTime 2.1 and Sound Manager 3.1, required for running some of the product demos.
➤ Adobe Connect software for hooking up to the Adobe Bulletin Board via modem.

It also includes products or samples from third parties, including:

➤ A PDF document listing sources of plug-ins that can be added to Illustrator
➤ Plug-in samples, demos, and catalogs from CD-Q, Cytopia Socket Sets, Draw Tools, Infinite FX/1, KaraFonts, KPT Vector Effects, Letraset Envelopes, and MAPublisher
➤ Photoshop plug-ins from Andromedia Software, Cytopia, Intellihance, MetaTools, and XAOS Tools

➤ Stock photos and textures from Artbeats, CLASSIC PIO, ColorBytes, Digital Media, Digital Stock, Image VAULT, PhotoDisc, and PhotoGear

➤ Hundreds of pieces of third-party clip art and/or catalogs from Aridi Computer Graphics, DigitArt, Instant Icons, MapArt, MIM, MoonlightPress Studio, One Mile Up, Oswego Company, and Ultimate Symbol, Inc., including discount offers from vendors on clip art libraries

NOTE It's a good idea to familiarize yourself with the contents of the CD-ROM as soon as you get Illustrator 6.0, so you can take advantage of some of the extra plug-ins and other aids that will make your work easier. Rather than working directly off the CD-ROM, you should copy the files you want (or install them) into the Adobe Illustrator 6.0 program folder on your hard drive.

Managing Plug-in Filters

The Filter menu contains a number of submenus that give you access to Illustrator's plug-in filters. Adobe supplies a variety of filters with Illustrator, and you can add (i.e., "plug in") more filters that you acquire from Adobe or other sources, or remove filters that you never use. The list on the menu and submenus reflects only those plug-in filters that are installed in the Plug-in folder within the Adobe Illustrator 6.0 folder, or whatever folder is specified through the **File > Preferences > Plug-ins** command.

Filter Window 4:07:32 PM
Last Filter ⌘⇧E
Colors ▶
Create ▶
Distort ▶
Gallery Effects: Classic Art 1 ▶
Gallery Effects: Classic Art 2 ▶
Gallery Effects: Classic Art 3 ▶
Ink Pen ▶
Objects ▶
Other ▶
Pathfinder ▶
Select ▶
Stylize ▶

Figure 10.1 The Filter menu showing the categories of filters that come with Illustrator 6.0.

Filters that come with Illustrator 6.0 are arranged in submenus under the Filter menu: Colors, Create, Distort, Gallery Effects, Ink Pen, Objects, Pathfinder, Select, and Stylize:

➤ The Colors filters adjust colors, intensify or diminish an object's color, or distribute colors among objects according to their orientation or stacking order.

➤ The Create filters create special effects such as adding a Fill and Stroke to a mask, multiple crop marks, and mosaic tiling.

➤ The Distort filters create special effects by changing an object's shape and path directions.

➤ The Gallery Effects submenus let you apply Photoshop effects to bitmaps.

➤ The Ink Pen filter lets you create and apply special "patterns" as fills.

➤ The Objects filters add anchor points to a path, delete stray points, create copies of a path, and change stroked paths to filled objects.

➤ The Pathfinder filters combine, isolate, and subdivide paths, and build new paths formed by the intersection of objects.

➤ The Select filters select matching parts of an illustration by selecting objects with the same colors, paint styles, and stroke and fill weights.

➤ The Stylize filters let you add special elements to the artwork, such as arrows and drop shadows, as well as create calligraphic effects and rounded shapes. In Illustrator 6.0, you use this submenu to apply patterns to strokes (path patterns).

You can add more filters, and these will show up on one of the existing submenus or will add a submenu of their own. You can reduce Illustrator's memory requirements by removing filters you do not use, as described under the next headings.

SHORTCUT

ADDING FILTERS

To install new plug-in filters, either from the Adobe Illustrator 6.0 Deluxe CD-ROM, from third-party sources, or to restore filters you previously removed, follow these steps:

1. Drag the plug-in filter icon into the Plug-in folder in the Adobe Illustrator 6.0 folder—or whatever folder you name through the **File > Preferences > Plug-ins** command.

2. To display the new filters on the Filters menu, **Quit** and restart the Adobe Illustrator program.

REMOVING FILTERS

The more filters you have installed, the longer it takes to start Illustrator and the more memory it requires. You can save time and space by removing filters you don't use. (See also the next section on creating and selecting different filter sets.)

1. From the desktop, open the Plug-ins folder in the Adobe Illustrator 6.0 folder—or whatever folder you named through the **File > Preferences > Plug-ins** command.

2. Drag the icons for the filters you wish to remove out of the folder.

3. To display the new filters on the Filters menu, **Quit** and restart the Adobe Illustrator program.

If you are short on disk space, you can always drag some filters into the Trash and re-install them when you need them from the Adobe Illustrator installation disks. If disk space is no problem, it's a good idea to create a folder called "Unused Filters" (or something similar) for storage of filters that you rarely use, rather than drag them into the Trash.

NOTE

CHANGING THE PLUG-IN SET

Normally, the Filters menu displays the list of filters that are currently installed in the Plug-ins Filters folder stored in the Adobe Illustrator 6.0 folder. You can use the **File > Preferences > Plug-ins** command to specify a different folder as the source of plug-ins on the list.

By creating several different folders with different combinations of filters, you can create custom Filter menus that include only those filters used in a specific project, and change the menu by selecting a different folder rather than moving or removing the filters in each folder.

NOTE

To specify a different plug-in filter:

1. Create a folder with the plug-in filters you wish.

2. Choose **File > Preferences > Plug-ins** to display the Plug-ins Preferences dialog box.

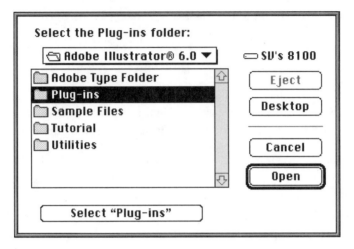

Figure 10.2 The Plug-ins Preferences dialog box.

3. Select a folder for the new set of plug-ins filters, using the same techniques to locate the folder as described for the Open dialog box, under **File > Open**, later in this chapter. Then click **Select** to close the dialog box.

4. **Quit** and restart the Adobe Illustrator program to install the new set of filters on the menu (and remove the old set of filters).

USING PLUG-IN FILTERS

Steps in using individual plug-in filters are described throughout this book, but here's a summary of how to use any filter:

1. Select the object(s) in the Adobe Illustrator document that you want to affect.

2. Choose a filter from the Filters menu.

To re-apply the same effect:

1. Select the object(s) in the Adobe Illustrator document that you want to affect.

2. Press **Command+Shift+E**, or select the last-used filter name from the top of the Filters menu.

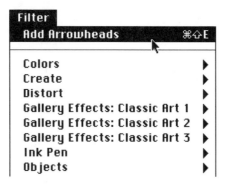

Figure 10.3 The last filter used is displayed at the top of the Filters menu.

Setting General Preferences

The **File > Preferences > General** command (**Command+K**) lets you change settings that affect how various commands and tools in Illustrator work.

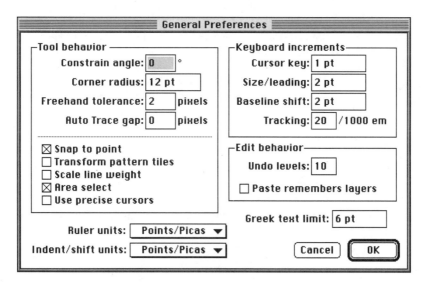

Figure 10.4 The General Preferences dialog box.

When you choose **File > Preferences > General** or press **Command+K**, Illustrator displays the Preferences dialog box, shown in the figure, which lets you set the preferences described in the following paragraphs by either clicking the appropriate checkbox or button or typing in desired values.

➤ Options in the top-left corner of the dialog box affect how various tools behave: Constrain angle, Corner radius, Freehand tolerance, Autotrace gap, Snap to point, Transform pattern tiles, Scale line weights, Area select, and Use precise cursors.

➤ Two options in the bottom left corner of the dialog box affect how measurements are displayed: Ruler Units and Type Units.

➤ Options in the top right of the General Preferences dialog box affect how objects move incrementally in response to keyboard commands: Cursor Key, Size/Leading, Baseline Shift, and Tracking.

➤ You can also set the number of Undo levels, through two options in the General Preferences dialog box: Undo Levels and Paste Remembers Layers.

➤ The last option in the dialog box, Greek text limit, affects screen redraw time.

See also "Customizing the Illustrator Startup File" in Chapter 6.

NOTE Preference settings cannot be reversed with the **Undo** command. The most current Preference settings are stored as part of the Adobe Illustrator startup file so that these settings are automatically part of any new document you start. They are *not* stored differently for each document. Before changing these values, make a note of the original settings in case you wish to revert. (Preference settings do not affect the artwork.)

CONSTRAIN ANGLE

When set to **0** degrees (default setting), this constrains all objects to the normal horizontal and vertical positioning. However, by changing this value, you can rotate the x and y axes of the artwork so that objects will draw at the angle specified. The x and y axes remain at right angles to one another, but are no longer vertical and horizontal. All transformation, constraining, and moving operations are performed relative to the x and y axes—if these are rotated from the vertical and horizontal, the operations will be translated by the same angle.

CORNER RADIUS

When set to **0** points (the default), this results in rectangles with square corners. Adding points to this setting changes the square corners to curved corners. Corner radius values must be between 0 and 1296 points, but cannot exceed half the length of the short sides of the rectangle. If you enter a larger value, Illustrator will draw the largest oval that can fit into the rectangle. (See "The Rectangle Tool" in Chapter 3 for examples of different corner radius settings.)

FREEHAND TOLERANCE

This sensitizes the mouse movement and determines the number of anchor points that will be created when you use the Freehand tool to draw an object. When you enter a higher number, fewer anchor points occur along a path and the mouse becomes less sensitive. When the tolerance is set higher, using the Autotrace tool also yields fewer anchor points (see "The Autotrace Tool" in Chapter 7). When you enter a lower value, more anchor points occur along a path because the mouse becomes more sensitive to movement. You can set the tolerance from **1** to **10** pixels. If you set tolerance beyond this range, an alert box appears. (See "The Freehand Tool" in Chapter 4 for examples of different tolerance settings.)

AUTOTRACE GAP

This determines the number of pixels Illustrator reads when the Autotrace tool is in use. With Autotrace over gap set at **0** (the default setting), the Autotrace tool will read every pixel in the template. With the setting at **2**, Autotrace will jump across two-pixel gaps and connect the pixels on either side of the gap, which is useful if your template is very sketchy. With the setting at **1**, Autotrace connects across one-pixel gaps.

SNAP TO POINT

This turns the Snap to point feature on or off. The normal default setting of Snap to point is on. Snap to point causes two points to snap together when they are within two pixels of each other and moves objects in two-pixel increments. With Snap to point off, you can move objects one pixel at a time. Snap to point is very useful for aligning objects, but you can turn this feature off when you are positioning objects very close to each other but do not want them to touch.

TRANSFORM PATTERN TILES

When turned on, this causes patterns within objects to be changed along with the path of the object when any transformation tool is used. (Transformation tools include the Scale, Rotate, Reflect, and Shear tools; see Chapter 5.) Otherwise, with Transform pattern tiles off (the default setting), only the path is transformed, not the pattern.

SCALE LINE WEIGHT

When turned on, this causes line weights to be scaled when you are scaling an object by dragging the Scale tool. Otherwise, only the path is scaled, and the line weights retain their original value when scaling visually on the screen.

NOTE

You can still opt to transform patterns or scale line weights or not by **Option**-clicking the Scale tool on the Artboard to display the Scale dialog box.

AREA SELECT

Make sure the Area select option is set on if you want to be able to select a filled object in Preview mode by clicking anywhere within the area. Otherwise, if this option is off, you must click on a path segment or anchor point to select an object.

USE PRECISE CURSORS

The painting and editing tools (Pen tool, Brush tool, Freehand tool, Paint Bucket tool, and Eyedropper tool) usually have pointers that look like the tool (a pen, a brush, a pencil, a paint bucket, or an eyedropper). You can change the pointer for all these tools to a cross-hair for more precise positioning by choosing **Use Precise Cursors** in the General Preferences dialog box.

SHORTCUT

Whether Use Precise Cursors option is selected or not, you can toggle between the current cursor appearance and its alternative by pressing the **Caps Lock** key. For example, if the Brush tool currently shows a brush pointer, press the **Caps Lock** key to change it to a cross-hair; if it currently shows a cross-hair, press the **Caps Lock** key to change it to a brush.

RULER UNITS AND TYPE UNITS

These options, displayed in a box in the lower-right portion of the dialog box, determine the units of measure displayed on the ruler and used for paragraph indents and baseline shifting. You can select **Centimeters**, **Inches**, or **Picas/Points** (the default).

NOTE

The units you select do not affect the units for font size, leading, or leading before paragraphs, which are always measured in points.

CURSOR KEY

This determines the distance a selected object or group of objects will move when you press one of the arrow keys. You can enter a value from 1 to 1296 points (or decimal equivalents in other units of measure).

SIZE/LEADING, BASELINE SHIFT, AND TRACKING

You can also set the increments by which font size, leading, baseline (vertical) shift, and tracking/kerning change when you use keyboard shortcuts. The default values are **2** points for size and leading, **2** points for vertical shift, and **0.02** ems for tracking and kerning.

UNDO LEVELS AND PASTE REMEMBERS LAYERS

Illustrator lets you set up to 200 levels of Undo and Redo. This means that you can undo (and redo) up to 200 of the last operations you performed, in reverse order, by repeatedly choosing the **Undo** (or **Redo**) command. The default Undo level is set to **5**, but you can enter any number from **0** to **200**, through the **File > Preferences > General** command.

Select the **Paste Remembers Layers** option if you want the exact layer accessed in a **Paste** command to be remembered and applied in using the **Undo** and **Redo** commands.

The higher the number of Undo levels, the more memory Illustrator will require while you are working. Lower this number if you run into memory limitation problems.

WARNING

GREEK TEXT LIMIT

Enter a value in Greek Text Limit to control the minimum size at which text is displayed as type. Type that is smaller than the size you enter appears on the screen as gray bars that show the line length and spacing. This is known as *greeked* type. Greeking type speeds up screen redrawing. For example, if you enter a value of **10** in the Greek type below box, 12-point text will display normally when viewed at actual size. If you change the view to 50% size, 12-point text appears as 6-point text, hence it will appear greeked. Greeking only affects screen display. The type will print normally at all sizes.

Starting a New Document

The **File > New** command creates a new Illustrator artwork file. The keyboard shortcut is **Command+N** or **Command+Option+N** to open a template.

It's a good idea to decide ahead of time if you will be using a template or not, but if you don't know or want to change or remove the template later, you can use the technique described a little later in this chapter.

NOTE

➤ To open a new document without a template, press **Command+N** or choose **File > New**. Illustrator opens a new untitled document without displaying a dialog box.

➤ Press **Command+Option+N** to open a template—a bitmap or PICT file that you can trace or use as a background. Template elements do not print out as part of the Illustrator artwork. Illustrator displays a dialog box, in the next figure, listing all of the bit-mapped and PICT format files available on the disk. You can select one of these bitmap or PICT files as a template file and use it as the background from which to trace new artwork. If you do not want to use a template, click the **None** button. If you click the **None** button, Illustrator presents an untitled, blank page. You can cancel the entire command by clicking the **Cancel** button or by using the keyboard shortcut, **Command+period**.

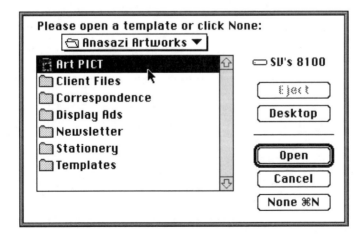

Figure 10.5 The New dialog box for opening a template.

➤ You can also open a template through the **Open** command (see next heading). If you choose **File > Open** and select a PICT file format, Illustrator displays a dialog box asking whether you want to open the PICT as part of the artwork or as a template.

NOTE

As with other Macintosh applications, Illustrator opens a file and assigns it the name "Untitled art" in the title bar. You can change the name of the file by choosing **File > Save** or **File > Save As**. You can also name the file when you close it by clicking the file's close box or by choosing **File > Close**. If you close the file using either of these methods and you have unsaved work on the screen, Illustrator displays an alert box asking if you want to save changes. If you click the **Yes** button, Illustrator displays the Save As dialog box (see **File > Save As**).

Opening an Existing Document

6.0 NEW FEATURE

The **File > Open** command (**Command+O**) opens an existing Illustrator file or a template file or a graphics file in any of the formats supported by Illustrator 6.0 (see list in Chapter 7). The number of files you can have open simultaneously is limited by available memory (RAM). You can switch between windows by selecting one of the open windows listed under the Window menu.

When you choose **File > Open** or press **Command+O**, Illustrator displays the Open dialog box, as shown in the following figure, listing all Illustrator files, supported graphic file formats, and template files on the selected disk.

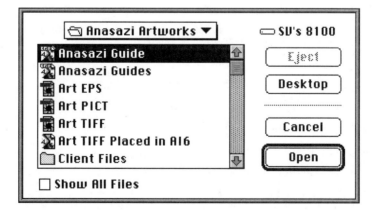

Figure 10.6 The Open dialog box lists all files with formats supported by Illustrator 6.0.

➤ Click the **Desktop** button to view the list of drives and view the files from another disk.

➤ Click the **Eject** button to change disks.

➤ To select a file, scroll through the file list to locate your desired file, click its name, and then click the **Open** button, or double-click on the file name. You can select an existing Illustrator file, or open a graphics file in any format supported by Illustrator 6.0 (see Chapter 7), or open a bitmap or PICT format as a template for a new file.

Illustrator opens a new window displaying both the artwork and its template, if there is one. The window's title bar has a name in the form *Artwork:template*, where *Artwork* is the name of the Illustrator file and *template* is the name of the template file.

If you are creating a new Illustrator file based on an existing template file, and have selected a bitmap or PICT format as the template file from the Open dialog box, Illustrator opens a new window with the name *Untitled art:template* in the title bar, where *template* is the template file name. You can change the Illustrator file name from *Untitled art* to something more meaningful when you save the Illustrator file.

Adding a New Template to Existing Artwork

You can force Illustrator to prompt you for a template file whenever you open an existing Illustrator artwork file by holding down the **Option** key when you choose **File > Open**.

1. If you want to change the template in the current document, or add one to the current document if it has none, save it and close it first.

2. Hold the **Option** key as you choose **File > Open**, or press **Command+Option+O**.

3. In the first dialog box that is displayed, highlight the Illustrator document and hold the **Option** key as you click **Open**.

4. In the second dialog box, you can either:

➤ Double-click a PICT file name to include it as a new or different template in existing artwork, or

➤ Click **None** to remove the current template form the existing artwork.

Saving Your Work

The **File > Save** command (**Command+S**) saves the latest version of the active Illustrator file. The **Save As** command lets you save the file in the active window under a new name or on a different disk or in a different format—such as a preview format that will display the artwork when it is imported into a page layout application. There is no keyboard shortcut for the **Save As** command.

➤ When you choose **File > Save** or press **Command+S**, Illustrator saves the file that is in the active window using the same name as shown in the artwork portion of the title bar.

➤ If the Illustrator file name is Untitled art, Illustrator displays the Save As dialog box, prompting you to provide a new artwork file name. (See **File > Save As**, described next).

➤ Choose **File > Save As**. Illustrator displays a dialog box, shown in Figure 10.7, into which you enter the name for the file you wish to save and from which you specify the disk and file folder in which you wish the file to be saved. Illustrator saves the file and leaves the active file window on the screen so that you can continue working on it.

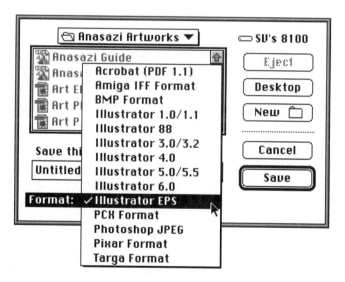

Figure 10.7 The Save As dialog box with format options shown in pop-up menu.

➤ There are a variety of compatibility modes (six different versions of Adobe Illustrator) and file formats that you can specify through the Save As dialog box. To save a file under more than one of these formats, you must save it under a different name for each format. Chapter 7 describes these formats in detail.

Illustrator saves the file on the current disk and leaves the active file window on the screen. If there is not enough room on the disk, Illustrator notifies you that you do not have enough room with an alert dialog box, and you can then choose **File > Save As** to save the file on another disk.

WARNING

You should save frequently to prevent losing the work you have completed. At the very least, always save your work before you print. This is recommended because, when printing, the application accesses the AppleTalk network, thus becoming slightly more vulnerable to failure than when working locally on your Macintosh. And although system crashes may be rare, you can bet that the one system crash you experience per year will happen when you did not save your file and you have a critical deadline to meet. It is much easier to press **Command+S** frequently than to redraw your work.

Choose **File > Revert to Saved** to cancel all changes that you have made since the last time you saved the document.

ILLUSTRATOR FORMAT OPTIONS

You can save your work in formats that can be opened by earlier versions of Illustrator, but some elements or attributes that are not supported by the earlier versions may be lost. If you are unsure about what attributes are supported by the earlier version, it's a good idea to save the work twice: first in version 6.0 format, then in the earlier format. Give each file a different name (ending in AI6 and AI5, for example).

EPS FORMAT OPTIONS

If you choose to save a document in EPS format, a second dialog box is displayed offering more format options.

Select **Adobe Illustrator 6.0** from the Compatibility list in the dialog box to save the file in a format that can only be edited by Adobe Illustrator 6.0. Earlier versions of the Illustrator program cannot open documents saved in this format. However, if any of the preview options other than **None (Omit EPS Header)** have been used, you can place a file of this format in page layout applications such as PageMaker or QuarkXPress.

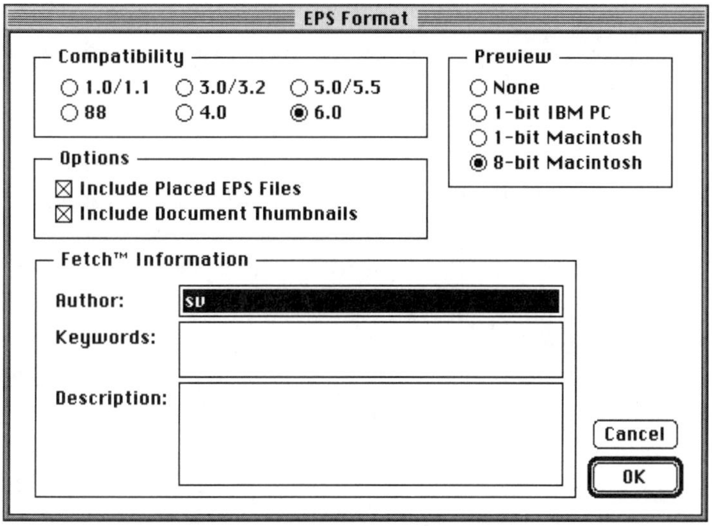

Figure 10.8 The EPS Format dialog box.

Select **Adobe Illustrator 5.0/5.5, 4.0 (Windows), 3.0/3.2, 88,** or **1.1** to save the file in a format that can be opened and edited using earlier versions of Illustrator or Macromedia FreeHand. If you choose one of these modes, however, some new features in version 6.0 will not be available, and some elements may be lost or modified. For example, in version 88 format, compound paths, guide objects, and most text objects are saved in a modified form. In version 1.1 format, custom colors are converted to process colors, masking is not in effect (though all objects in the mask are present), and patterns and placed images are removed. If any of the preview options other than **None (Omit EPS Header)** have been used, you can place a file of this format in page layout applications such as PageMaker or QuarkXPress.

Preview modes affect how the illustration will be displayed on the screen when placed in other applications like PageMaker or QuarkXPress but do not affect how the illustration will print.

➤ Select **None** to save the file as a complete PostScript language program with an EPSF Header. You can use this format if you want to open the document with the Adobe Separator program. When placed in other Macintosh applications, such as PageMaker or QuarkXPress, a file saved in this format displays as a gray box, but prints correctly. This format takes up more disk space than the native Illustrator (non-EPS) formats, but less than any other EPS preview format. If you know how to program in the PostScript language, you can open and edit the PostScript code of documents saved in this format with a word processor or text editor. You may need to change the file type to TEXT in order to do so.

➤ Select **1-bit IBM PC** to save the file in an EPS format that you can transfer to an MS-DOS system and place in MS-DOS applications, such as PageMaker and QuarkXPress for Windows. The artwork will be displayed on the screen either as artwork or as a place-holding box, depending on the application. Both PageMaker and QuarkXPress for the PC display the actual artwork.

➤ Select a **1-bit Macintosh** mode to save a simple black-and-white preview image (PICT preview). This format is designed to be used in conjunction with page layout applications that support the EPS format, allowing you to see a preview image of your artwork after it has been imported into the page layout application. You cannot edit documents saved in this format with word processors or text editors. When placed in other Macintosh applications, such as PageMaker or QuarkXPress, a file saved in this format displays a black-and-white preview image. However, any color information in the document is preserved for printing. This format takes up considerably more disk space than no preview image, but takes up less space than those saved with an 8-bit preview image.

➤ Select **8-bit Macintosh** to save the file in an EPS format with a grayscale or color preview image in Macintosh QuickDraw PICT format. The preview image is limited to 256 colors, but the image will print with as many colors as used in its creation. This format is designed to be used in conjunction with page layout applications that support the EPS format, allowing you to see a preview image of your artwork after it has been imported into the page layout application. You cannot edit documents saved in this format with word processors or text editors. When placed in other Macintosh applications, such as PageMaker or QuarkXPress, a file saved in this format displays a grayscale or color preview image. You should use this format when you know that you will use a color monitor, and that you will import the file into a page layout application such as PageMaker or QuarkXPress.

If your artwork contains placed EPS images, the **Include Placed EPS Files** check box is enabled. Clicking this option saves a copy of any EPS files you placed using the **Place Art** command within your document. To select this option, click in the check box or anywhere on the label. Using this option means that Illustrator no longer requires a copy of the original placed image, but it results in a larger file. Also, placed images cannot be edited in any detail, so it's generally a good idea to keep the placed image file separately. You should always use the **Include Placed Images** option when you intend to place your artwork in another application such as a page composition application, but you should generally wait until you are sure that the artwork is finalized before you do so.

Choosing the Include Placed Images option includes the placed image as part of the file, but Illustrator will still prompt you to find the image in order to display it correctly when the file is opened in Illustrator. This option is designed for files that will be placed in other applications—so you don't have to provide the imported EPS files

NOTE when printing from those other applications.

Select **Include Document Thumbnails** if you want to be able to preview the illustration in a Thumbnail window before opening or selecting the file through applications that support Thumbnails, such as Adobe Fetch. You can also enter Fetch Information that can be searched for: Author, Keywords, and Description.

SAVING ILLUSTRATOR ARTWORK IN OTHER FORMATS

Saving Illustrator artwork in any of the other formats is described in Chapter 7. Note that Illustrator artwork saved in any format other than a native Illustrator format, EPS format, or PDF format cannot be re-opened and edited as Illustrator artwork. If you plan to save an illustration in one of these other formats, it's a good idea to save it in Illustrator format first, and then under another name in the other format.

Sources of Useful Information

Commands under the Help menu are always useful when you are stuck on a problem or can't quite remember a shortcut—and the Adobe Deluxe CD-ROM includes additional help files you can access through the **Help** command.

In addition, there are three commands that you'll find useful in solving problems: the **Document Information** command, the **About Illustrator** command, and the **About Plug-in** command. Each of these is described under the next headings.

GETTING INFORMATION ABOUT A DOCUMENT OR A SELECTED ITEM

The **File> Document Info** command displays a dialog box that lists the number and names of custom colors, patterns, gradients, fonts, and placed art, as well as general document information and object characteristics. You can list information for the whole document, or only for selected objects.

1. Use a selection tool to select one or more objects about which you want information, or click on an empty area to deselect all objects if you want information about the entire document.

2. Choose **Filter > Other > Document Info** to display the Document Info dialog box. (The command becomes **Selection Information** if an object is selected.)

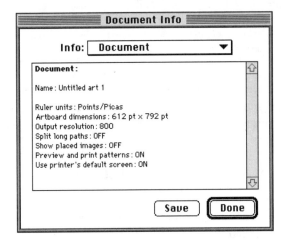

Figure 10.9 The Document Info dialog box.

3. Choose from the eight information screens listed in the Info pop-up menu:

➤ General lists the document name, file format, settings in the Document Setup dialog box, and the modification status of the file.

➤ Objects lists the number of paths, masks, compound paths, custom colors, patterns, gradients, fonts, and placed art contained in the selection or document.

➤ Custom Colors lists the names of any custom colors in the selection or document.

➤ Patterns lists the names of any patterns used in the selection or document.

➤ Gradients lists the names and types of gradients in the selection or document.

➤ Fonts lists the names and fonts styles used in the selection or document.

➤ Placed Art lists the name and path of any placed EPS art in the selection or document.

➤ Raster Art lists the name and attributes of any placed bitmap images.

Figure 10.10 Objects information option in the Document Info dialog box.

4. Click **Save** in the Document Info dialog box to save all the information to a text file. The text can then be imported into Illustrator (see **File > Import Text** in Chapter 8) or opened by any text editor and printed.

GETTING INFORMATION ABOUT ILLUSTRATOR

Choosing **About Illustrator** from the Apple menu displays a dialog box that shows the version of Illustrator you're using, the authors of Illustrator, and a copyright notice. If you wait a few seconds, the information at the bottom of the screen will begin scrolling to reveal additional details. Click anywhere to close the dialog box.

GETTING INFORMATION ABOUT PLUG-INS

The About Plug-ins submenu on the Apple menu lists plug-in filters for which there is information available—usually about the version number and copyright information. Click anywhere to close the dialog box.

Figure 10.11 The About Illustrator dialog box.

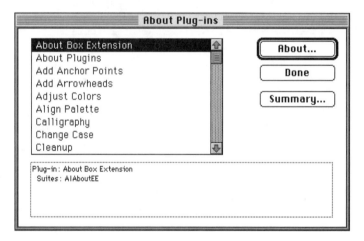

Figure 10.12 The About Plug-ins submenu.

Principles of Good Design

No book of rules and laws should ever limit your creativity, spontaneity, and inventiveness in developing a design, but before you deliberately violate some of the common practices of good graphic design, you should be familiar with what those practices are. Here is a simple list of suggestions gathered from a variety of sources:

General Design Guidelines

➤ Don't be afraid of white space.

➤ Be sure that the space between text and graphics is the same for all figures, and the space between adjacent text blocks is uniform.

➤ Use only one or two different typefaces in a document.

➤ Use all capitals (uppercase text) as a deliberate design strategy rather than as a method for emphasizing text or indicating a heading.

➤ Use running heads and running feet to help readers find topics in multiple-page documents.

➤ Text on each page should bottom out to the grid margin.

Promotional and Presentation Material Design

You are likely to find more exceptions to the rules when designing fliers, ads, and logos than in any other type of publication. Some of the common exceptions are described in the next bullets to give you an idea of how and why fliers and ads can break the rules.

➤ The choice of font sets the tone of the piece.

➤ Keep text to a minimum.

➤ Try to limit the text on an overhead transparency or slide to no more than 25 words, five or fewer bullet points, eight or fewer lines.

➤ For images that will be projected as slides or overhead transparencies, use large point sizes for the text. Printouts for overhead transparencies should be readable at 10 feet; printouts for slides should be readable at seven feet.

➤ For overhead transparencies, use black type on white or a light background; for slides, use white or light type on a dark background.

➤ For overhead transparencies, fit all images into a 7-by-9-inch area.

➤ If you use a laser printer for the final output, use a gray screen rather than solid black areas for the best projection image.

➤ For materials to be made into slides, set all images within an area of approximately 3:2 proportions.

➤ Give graphs short but descriptive, meaningful titles.

➤ Counteract the Curls!—The heat that is applied to acetate sheets when they run through a laser printer tends to make them curl up toward the toner side. If you select all the artwork and use the Reflect tool to flip the entire image along its vertical axis before printing, they still curl toward the toner, but the text will be readable on the non-toner side. When you place them on the overhead projector, they will tend to curl down, but this effect will be counteracted to some extent by the weight of the acetate.

Design and Production Aids

➤ Use a grid system (described later in this chapter).

➤ Treat all figures within a document consistently in the fonts, line weights, and fill patterns you use.

➤ Let the same graphic elements carry the theme throughout the document.

➤ If possible, design all the images in a series to use the same page orientation.

➤ Build a master boilerplate for all figures or for related figures in a publication or project (see next heading).

Designing Boilerplates

Build a master boilerplate for all figures or for related figures in a publication or project. The boilerplate could include:

➤ Ruler guides to define the maximum size of an illustration (described later in this chapter)

➤ Custom colors and patterns, including customized swatches in the Paint Style palette (see Chapter 6)

➤ Predefined layers, with names that clearly suggest contents of each (described later in this chapter)

➤ Dummy text in place on the page, or on the pasteboard to be cloned and used for captions and headings (see Chapter 8)

➤ Dummy paths with predefined Fill and Stroke attributes that can be copied to new objects using the Eyedropper and Paint Bucket tools (see Chapter 6)

NOTE

You can set up a separate text object on the pasteboard that describes the attributes or the objects to which they belong, and then *apply the actual attributes to the text objects*, so the attributes can be copied to new elements on the Artboard using the Eyedropper and Paint Bucket tools.

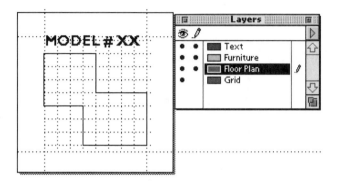

Figure 10.13 Boilerplate with guides, dummy text, and a custom Layers palette.

To use the boilerplate, simply open it when you want to start a new illustration for the project and immediately save it under a different name.

WARNING

If you will be placing the illustrations in other applications, like PageMaker or QuarkXPress, it's a good idea to delete all elements from the Pasteboard surrounding the actual artwork before you save the final version. EPS files saved from Illustrator include everything in the document—whether on the Artboard or on the Pasteboard.

Efficient Methods of Moving Objects

Chapter 3 described methods of moving objects using the Selection tools. Here you will learn a variety of other methods that offer some special advantages.

SHORTCUT

You can create step-and-repeat designs rapidly using the **Move** and **Repeat Transform** commands. Create the repeating element of your design using any of Illustrator's tools, then select the element, move a copy the desired distance using the **Move** command, and produce subsequent copies by choosing **Arrange > Repeat Transform** or pressing **Command+D**.

Using the Move Dialog Box

The Move dialog box allows you to specify the distance and direction of the move, whether to move pattern tiles, and whether to move the selected object or a copy of it. To use this feature, first select the object with the Selection tool, then choose any of these options:

➤ **Option**+click the Selection tool icon in the toolbox, or

➤ Choose **Arrange > Move**, or

➤ Use the keyboard shortcut, **Command+Shift+M**.

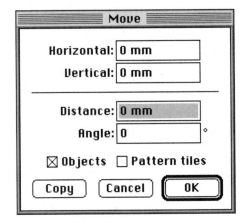

Figure 10.14 **Option**+click the Selection tool icon in the Toolbox and,
in the Move dialog box, enter the distance and angle you want selected objects to move.

NOTE You can see the distance and angle of a move by first moving an object visually on the screen and then **Option**+clicking on the Selection tool to see the numeric values in the Move dialog box. This can be useful if you want to duplicate the same movement later. You can also use the **Arrange > Repeat Transform** command (**Command+D**) to repeat the last movement on any selected object(s).

The Distance field is already selected when you call up the Move dialog box. The Direction defaults to the angle of the previous move. If you do not want the Direction to be the same as the previous one, select the value in the text box next to the direction you want—**Horizontal, Vertical, Distance,** or **Angle**—and simply type the new distance you wish to move the object.

➤ To move an object horizontally or vertically, enter the desired distance in the Horizontal or Vertical field. The unit of measurement used is that specified in the File > General Preferences dialog box. (See **File > Preferences**.) Positive numbers move the object toward the right and top of the page; negative numbers move the object toward the left and bottom of the page.

➤ To move an object diagonally, you can specify either horizontal and vertical distances or a distance and an angle for the move. Directions of angled moves can be specified in degrees, with horizontal as 0° and angles measured counterclockwise for positive values, clockwise for negative values.

➤ If you enter horizontal and vertical distances, the diagonal distance and angle are automatically displayed in the other fields. Conversely, if you enter a diagonal distance and angle, Illustrator calculates and displays the horizontal and vertical distances.

You can enter values in the default unit of measurement, or enter a value followed by the abbreviation for any unit of measure: in (inches), pt (points, i.e., 1/72nd of an inch), mm (millimeters), or cm (centimeters). You can also change the default unit of measure for Ruler units using the **File > Document Setup** and **File > Preferences > General** commands.

NOTE

➤ If you want to move pattern tiles, click **Pattern tiles** in the Move dialog box.

➤ When you have specified all your choices for the move, click either the **OK** button to move the selected object or the **Copy** button to move a copy of the selected object. The dialog box closes, and a copy of the selected object appears offset from the original at the distance you specified.

The distance and direction specified in the Move dialog box are relative to the x and y axes, which are normally, but not necessarily, parallel to the edges of the window. The value entered in the Constrain angle field in the File > Preferences > General dialog box determines the orientation of the x and y axes. If the axes are rotated, moves are made relative to the rotated axes.

WARNING

Using the Control Palette

Illustrator 6.0 introduces a Control palette that not only displays information about a selected object (like the Information palette), but lets you make entries in the palette that change the selected objects). The X and Y position values in the Control palette indicate the position of the current reference point on the Proxy at the left side of the palette. You can move a selected object a precise horizontal and vertical distance by changing the X and Y values.

6.0 NEW FEATURE

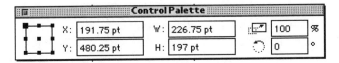

Figure 10.15 The X and Y options in the Control palette indicate
the position of the current reference point on the selected object.

Using the Arrow Keys for Small Movements

You can also move selected objects by pressing the arrow keys (available on most keyboards). The increment of movement per keystroke can be set in the File > General Preferences dialog box.

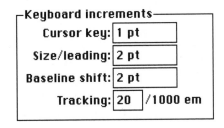

Figure 10.16 Cursor key distance in the General Preferences dialog box
determines the increments for movement with the arrow keys.

Using the Move Each Feature for Multiple Objects

If you select more than one object at a time and use the **Arrange > Move** command you move all the objects the same distance and direction at once. The **Arrange > Transform Each** command offers the option of moving each object in the selection a different amount.

1. Select the object(s) in the Adobe Illustrator document that you want to affect.

2. Choose **Arrange > Transform Each** to display the Transform Each dialog box with the Move Each options.

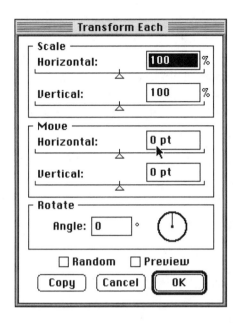

Figure 10.17 The Move Each options in the Transform Each dialog box.

3. Enter the horizontal and vertical distance, and click **Random** if you want the filter to move each object a different amount using your values as maxiumums, then click **OK** or press **Return** to close the dialog box and view the effect.

Figure 10.18 Objects before (above) and after (below) applying the Move Each options.

Using the Offset Path Filter

The Offset Path filter creates a duplicate of a path, set off from the selected path by the distance you specify. This is useful when you want to create concentric shapes or make many replicas of a path at regular intervals. If the original path is open, the duplicates are positioned in one direction away from the original. If the original path is closed, the duplicates are positioned outside the original.

1. Select the path(s) in the Adobe Illustrator document that you want to affect.

2. Choose **Filter > Objects > Offset Path** to display the Offset Path dialog box.

3. Enter a value for Offset Distance, Line Join Type, and Miter Limit.

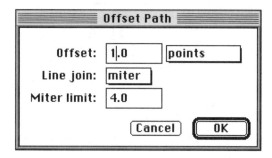

Figure 10.19 The Offset Path dialog box.

4. Click **OK** or press **Return** to close the dialog box and view the results.

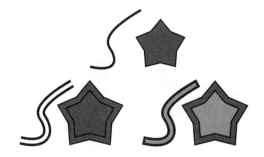

Figure 10.20 The original path and resulting duplicates.

Alignment and Spacing

Traditionally, the process of making sure that all elements lined up properly required a lot of time spent in developing a complex illustration. The alignment of objects had to be carefully thought out before pen or brush touched paper. With Adobe Illustrator, you can think through the alignment requirements before you start an illustration, or you can simply begin illustrating and move objects into alignment later. This is one of the outstanding advantages of using a computer.

Illustrator offers several aids in aligning objects to each other or to an axis, including the Information palette (which shows position of objects as you create or move them), the rulers, ruler guides, and the Align palette. This chapter offers some suggestions on using Illustrator's alignment aids, and adds a few additional methods of aligning objects.

Alignment methods covered include:

➤ using the Align palette to align or distribute objects evenly

➤ using the Snap-to effect of ruler guides

➤ using the Measure tool to measure the distance between objects

➤ aligning objects as you create them

➤ dividing an object into equal parts—either as goal in itself or to create a movable custom ruler with tick marks

The next major heading will describe using grids for page layout.

Using the Align Palette

6.0 NEW FEATURE

The Align palette aligns selected objects horizontally and/or vertically, using the center or edge of the objects as a reference point. This is usually a much faster method of aligning objects than by dragging them individually, and visually aligning them against a ruler line or guide. With this option, you can create or copy elements quickly into an area without paying much attention to their alignment, then select them all and use this palette.

1. Create the objects using whatever tool is appropriate, positioning them roughly where you want them on the screen. The next figure shows four separate rectangles that are not exactly aligned.

2. Select all of the objects using the Selection tool.

3. With all of the text blocks selected, choose **Window > Align palette**. In the Align palette:

   ➤ Click one of the Horizontal axis options (left edges, centers, or right edges) if the text blocks are already arranged beside each other.

   ➤ Click one of the Vertical axis options (tops, center, or bottom edges) if the text blocks are already arranged one above the other.

   ➤ Click one or two distribution options to evenly space the objects.

NOTE

Changes take place immediately when you click an option in the Align palette. If you make a mistake or don't like the result, press **Command+Z** to undo the change.

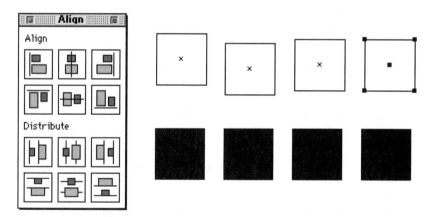

Figure 10.21 Objects before and after using the Align palette.

NOTE

If you want to distribute the elements along an axis, it's a good idea to position an object at each extreme of the distance you want covered, before using this palette to align them.

Using Rulers and Guides

Illustrator lets you create nonprinting guidelines on the page that help you align objects: If Snap to Point is selected in the File > Preferences > General dialog box, the ruler guides have a snap-to effect on objects and the cursor when they come within two pixels of the guide.

You can position ruler guides on a page before you create objects, and use the snap-to effect of the rulers to help position the pointer when you start a new element. You can also position ruler guides at any time and use them as guides for dragging existing elements into alignment, as described in the next steps.

You can also use ruler guides to help align the Scissors tool when you are cutting a path.

NOTE

1. Create the objects using whatever tools are appropriate, positioning them roughly where you wish them to be on the screen. The figure here shows four squares created with the Rectangle tool, not exactly aligned.

2. Press **Command+R** (**View > Show Rulers**) to display the rulers (if they are not already displayed), then position the mouse pointer over the horizontal ruler at the top of the page and drag a horizontal ruler guide onto the page. (It does not matter what tool is selected.)

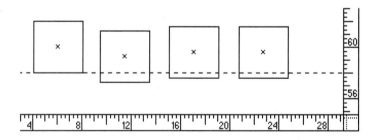

3. Press the **Command** key to get the Selection tool if it is not already selected, and drag each object to touch the alignment guide. The snap-to effect will help you align the objects against the ruler guide in any magnification. However, it might help to first select the Zoom tool (or hold down the **Command** key and the **Spacebar**) and click on the objects you wish to align, to invoke a magnified view.

4. Once you have positioned all of the objects, you can select them all and press **Command+G** (**Arrange > Group**) to group them and thereby keep them in alignment when you want to move them as a unit.

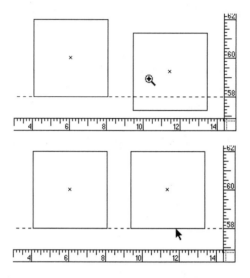

You can use ruler guides to create a complete grid system before starting an illustration, and save a document with the ruler guides only as a template for creating a series of related illustrations.

SHORTCUT

Using the Measure Tool

You can use the Measure tool to measure the distance and angle relative to the *x* axis between any two locations on the page. Simply select the **Measure** tool, then click on two points. The points do not have to be anchor points. This displays the Information palette, shown in the following figure, which shows the distance and angle between the two points you have clicked.

X: 12.183 cm	W: 3.881 cm	D: 3.881 cm
Y: 15.24 cm	H: 0 cm	∠ 0°

Figure 10.22 The Information palette shows the distance between two points you click with the Measure tool.

To ensure that the distance being measured is a straight horizontal or vertical line between two points, and not slightly angled, hold the **Shift** key before clicking the second measuring point. This provides for accurate measurement of an object without an accidental angled move of the mouse.

NOTE

When you use the Measure tool to measure a distance, the Move dialog box is automatically updated to reflect the distance and angle you just measured. To move an object a measured distance, you can measure the distance with the Measure tool, then choose **Move** and click **OK**.

SHORTCUT

Aligning Objects as You Create Them

Another good strategy in aligning objects is to drag the original object while holding both the **Shift** key (to force alignment along the horizontal or vertical axis) and the **Option** key (to create a copy of the object). You may then edit the copied object if you desire.

1. Create the first object using whatever tool is appropriate (Freehand tool, Autotrace tool, Pen tool, Type tools, Rectangle tools, or Oval tools). For example, use a Rectangle tool to create a rectangular object, as shown in the figure below.

2. If subsequent objects are to be identical, drag the first object to the new position, and hold the **Shift** and **Option** keys to align and copy the object as you release the mouse button.

3. Press **Command+D** (**Arrange > Repeat Transform**) to align another copy of the object the same relative distance apart. Press **Command+D** for each additional copy you wish to make.

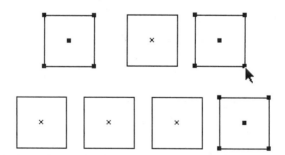

Figure 10.23 One object (top left), copied (second two figures in top row), then duplicate with **Repeat Transform**.

4. Modify the copied objects as appropriate *after* you have used the **Repeat Transform** command.

5. Once you have positioned all the objects, you can select them all and press **Command+G** (**Arrange > Group**) to group them and thereby keep them in alignment when you want to move them as a unit.

Dividing Equally

You may find that it is necessary to divide a shape or a line into a specific number of segments. Even dividing something in half can be difficult if you rely on the rulers or the Measure tool as your only aids. With the following technique, you do not need to actually calculate the divisions; Illustrator does it for you.

Common applications for this technique include dividing lines and shapes for technical or architectural drawings or creating grids and guidelines for templates and artwork. This is also an easy way to create forms.

1. For this demonstration, first use the Pen tool with the **Shift** key to draw a horizontal line of any length. This is the line you will divide into equal segments.

2. Select the **Pen** tool and draw a short vertical line.

3. With the **Snap to Point** option turned on (in the File > Preferences > General dialog box), snap this vertical line to one endpoint of the horizontal line.

4. Hold down the **Command** key to get the Selection tool and drag this vertical line to the opposite endpoint of the horizontal line and snap once again, holding down both the **Shift** key (to align the second tick relative to the first tick along the horizontal axis) and the **Option** key (to create a copy) as you release the mouse button.

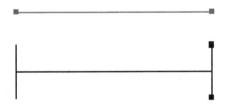

Figure 10.24 Horizontal line framed by two vertical lines.

5. Using the Selection tool, **Shift**+click both vertical lines to select both lines and their anchor points.

6. Choose the **Blend** tool and click once on the top point of each of the vertical lines.

7. When the Blend dialog box appears, type in a number that is one less than the number of parts you would like. For example, if you would like to divide the line into six equal parts, type in **5** for number of steps.

8. Click **OK**. In this example, five dividers are added at six equal intervals between the two end lines.

NOTE

This procedure adds dividers but does not actually break the horizontal line into segments. If you want to break up the horizontal line into separate parts, you can use the Scissors tool. You can use the same steps to divide a rectangle (or any closed path) into equal parts, and then use the Divide filter to break it into separate objects.

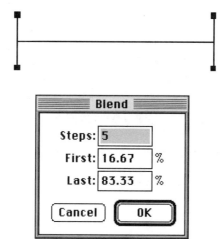

Figure 10.25 Additional markers are created by blending.

9. If the divisions look correct, and you want to use the objects as a movable "ruler" on the screen, drag the Selection tool to display the selection marquee over all of the lines and press **Command+G** (**Arrange > Group**). This way the dividers will retain their relative positions if you move them later.

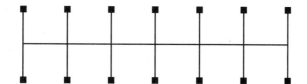

Creating Custom Grids

The next sections show you how to make custom guides and then suggest two types of boilerplates you can make using custom guides as grids.

Creating Custom Guides

The Guides submenu lists commands that let you **Make**, **Release**, and **Lock** guides—nonprinting lines that you position on the Artwork to help you align printing objects.

The **Make Guide** command (**Command+5**) converts a selected object or objects into guide objects. Guide objects appear as dotted lines in the artwork window, but they do not print. If the Snap to point option is turned on in the Preferences dialog box, objects will snap to the guide object whenever they are within two pixels of the guide object.

The **Release** command (**Command+6**) converts selected guide objects to paths.

TO MAKE A GUIDE OBJECT

1. Use Illustrator's drawing tools to create the object(s) you wish to use as guides.

2. Select the objects, then choose **Object > Guides > Make** or press **Command+5**. The selected objects become a guide object and appear as dotted lines in the artwork view.

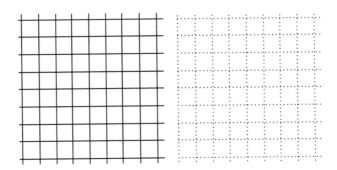

Figure 10.26 Objects (left) converted to guides (right).

3. To select a guide object, hold down the **Shift** and **Control** keys while clicking the object with a selection tool. To convert a guide object back into a path, hold down the **Shift** and **Control** keys while double-clicking the object with a selection tool. To delete a guide object, first convert it back to a path or paths, then press **Delete**.

NOTE

Guide objects are particularly useful for setting up perspective grids (see Chapter 9).

TO RELEASE A GUIDE

Select the guide object to be released, then choose **Object > Guides > Release**, or press **Command+6**. All selected guide objects are converted to paths and are selected.

Because **Release All Guides** leaves the newly converted guide objects selected, you can quickly delete all guide objects from your artwork when you no longer require them by choosing **Release All Guides** from the Object menu, then immediately pressing the **Delete** key.

NOTE

If you cannot select the guide objects, then the **Lock** option on the Guides submenu is active (checked). You must first choose **Object > Guides > Lock**, or press **Command+7**, to unlock all guides before you can select them. After you have released selected guides, it's a good idea to press **Command+7** again to lock the guides.

LOCK GUIDES

The **Lock Guides** command locks or unlocks all guide objects in the artwork. Guide objects should normally be locked so they cannot be selected or moved, but they must be unlocked if you want to select them and then delete or modify them.

Choose **Object > Guides Lock**, or press **Command+7**, to unlock all guide objects when this option is checked on the menu, or to lock all guide objects when this option is not already checked.

Creating Quadrille Rules

This technique shows you how to create a visible grid of squared rules that is a part of the artwork. You can use this type of grid as a design element or as an integral part of a technical drawing such as a floor plan.

1. Select the **Pen** tool and click once near a corner of the Artboard, then hold down the **Shift** key as you click the pointer on the opposite corner to draw a straight line along one of the sides of the page or drawing area—an 11-inch line along the left edge of an 8.5-inch-wide page is shown in the figure below.

NOTE

Note that in steps 1 and 3, the drawing area can be the entire page or a small area on the page. For large pages, perform steps 1 and 3 in the Fit in window view (**Command+M**).

2. Hold down the **Command** key to get the Selection tool, and click on the line to select the entire path. Press **Command+Shift+M** (**Arrange > Move**) to get the Move dialog box. Enter a value in the Horizontal Distance box that matches your desired grid size—for example, **72** points (one inch). Click **OK** to close the dialog box and make a copy of the first line.

3. Press **Command+D** (**Arrange > Repeat Transform**) as many times as you need to fill the image area with grid lines. If the image area is rectangular, make enough copies to fill the longest dimension. In this example, we only need eight lines to span the image area, but we make 11 copies—enough to fill the page in step 6, as you'll see.

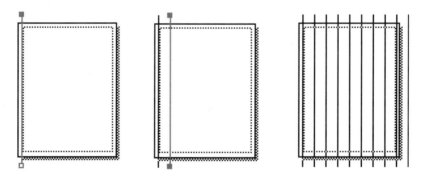

Figure 10.27 Lines drawn (left), copied (middle), then duplicated with **Repeat Transform**.

4. Press Command+A and Command+G (Edit > Select All and Arrange > Group).

5. Select the **Rotate** tool in the Toolbox and **Option**+click on the center of the grid to get the Rotate dialog box. Type **90** (degrees) in the Angle

box, and click **Copy** to close the box and rotate a copy of the horizontal lines to create a vertical grid.

6. While the vertical grid lines are still selected, use the Scale tool to stretch them to the 11-inch height of the page, and move them if necessary to center over the horizontal grid lines. Use the Direct-selection tool to select and delete extra lines that fall beyond the Artboard edges, if you like.

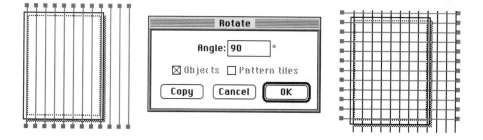

Figure 10.28 Copy of grouped lines rotated 90 degrees.

7. Select both grid sets—horizontal and vertical—and use one of the following command options:

➤ If you do not want the grid to appear on printed versions, choose **Object > Guides > Make** (**Command+5**). This converts the grid lines to guides that appear on the screen but do not print out and cannot be selected (so long as **Object > Guides > Lock** is active). They will not be unlocked by the **Arrange > Unlock All** command. They can be hidden through the **View > Hide Guides** command.

➤ If you want the grid to appear on printed versions of the artwork, set the Stroke to very thin and/or a light tint. It's a good idea to place it on a layer of its own (see Layer palette later in this chapter) and lock the grid (**Arrange > Lock**).

8. Save the grid as a boilerplate document that you can use repeatedly.

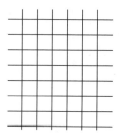

9. When you open the boilerplate to start a new document, use the **Save As** command (from the File menu) to give it a new name so the original grid boilerplate document will remain unchanged.

Using the grid as part of the artwork will give you more precision in positioning objects relative to the grid, but it will also increase the overall size of files. You can reduce file size by deleting the grid when the artwork is finished.

NOTE

Creating Grids for Page Layout

Often you will want to have an accurate grid or guidelines to follow in an illustration. Adobe provides several such grids as a part of the Illustrator package—which you can access by opening the files in the Templates folder, in the Sample Files folder, which is in the Adobe Illustrator program folder. But if you have your own custom grid for your overheads or newsletter, you can use the technique described here to create it in Illustrator.

You can use a grid like the one shown in the next figure in creating a series of illustrations that must all conform to the same page layout specifications. Then use this grid as a template for creating each document. With this technique create any template system for consistent page layout, such as in a series of ads, overheads or slides, or charts.

If you have a drawing of the grid or guidelines and you have a scanner, you can scan the printed grid and use the scanned template as a background while you work. But you may find the lines on a scanned template are too coarse for your needs. Using the grid as the template also precludes using other images as the template.

NOTE

1. Determine the basic grid of the page layout and sketch it with the Pen tool and/or the Rectangle tool.

2. Press **Command+A** (**Edit > Select All**) to select the entire grid and choose **Object > Guides > Make** (**Command+5**).

3. Add ruled lines and standing text that are intended to print on every page. Press **Command+A, Command+1** (**Edit > Select All** and **Arrange > Lock**) to lock the objects in place so they will not be selected or moved as you work.

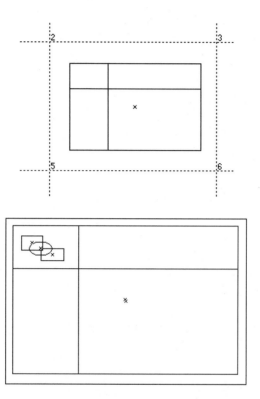

4. Add dummy text blocks that will change on each page and move them into their fixed positions. The figure here shows dummy text blocks.

   The content of the dummy text blocks will be altered for each page, but their positioning will not.

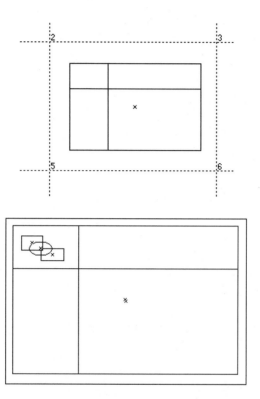

5. Save the grid as a boilerplate document that you can use repeatedly.

6. When you open the boilerplate to start a new document, immediately use **File > Save As** to give it a new name so that the original grid boilerplate document will remain unchanged.

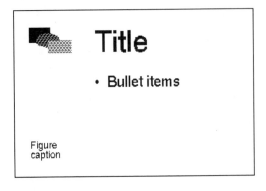

Managing Overlapping Objects

Most artwork designed in Illustrator is composed of an assortment of objects, some of which overlap others. If the artwork becomes very complicated, it can be a challenge to select or change an object that falls below others. The next headings present some methods of handling complex artwork, including:

➤ Grouping Objects

➤ Locking Objects

➤ Hiding Objects

➤ Rearranging Overlapping Objects

➤ Managing Overlapping, Identical Objects

The next major heading, Working In Named Layers, will describe the ultimate solution for any complex illustration.

Grouping Objects

The **Arrange > Group** command (**Command+G**) combines selected objects into a group. Objects that are grouped can be selected with a single click of the Selection tool, making this command especially useful in maintaining control of multiple layers and selections in a complex drawing.

1. Select an ungrouped path, or any group of objects, using any of the techniques described in "The Selection Tools" in Chapter 3.

2. Choose **Arrange > Group** or press **Command+G**.

If you select some but not all of the anchor points in a path, this command adds the entire path to the group.

Some of the characteristics of groups are:

➤ A group itself can be composed of subgroups. Select a set of elements and group them, then select additional elements, including the grouped set, and group again. You need to invoke the **Ungroup** command twice to ungroup both sets in this instance (see **Arrange > Ungroup**).

➤ You can modify grouped paths using any commands or tools. To modify grouped paths by moving individual line segments, anchor points, or direction lines, you must use the Direct-selection tool. Rectangles and ovals drawn with the Rectangle or Oval tool are automatically grouped when you draw them.

➤ You can select whole paths that are part of a group by using the Group-selection tool.

➤ You can transform and move grouped objects as a whole, but grouped objects retain their individual paint and type attributes. If you select a group of objects with different paint attributes, the Paint Style palette (**Object > Paint Style**) will display only those selections that are common to all elements in the group. If you make no entries in the Paint Style palette, all ele ments of the group retain their different attributes. If you change the paint or type attributes for a group, all the objects in the group will be changed to the new attributes. (See the tip under **Select All** for grouping objects that share the same attributes. See also the Paint Style palette in Chapter 6.)

➤ The **Arrange > Ungroup** command (**Command+U**) breaks a group into independent objects, ungrouped paths, or subgroups (if a group has grouped objects within it). Select a grouped path or a group of objects with the Selection tool and choose **Arrange > Ungroup** or press **Command+U**. If a group consists of other grouped objects, you must ungroup the subgroups repeatedly to reduce them into individual objects.

Clicking on objects with the Selection tool tells you whether objects are grouped or ungrouped. When you click on an ungrouped object, only the paths and anchor points that are part of that object are selected. When you click on an object that is part of a group, all the paths and anchor points that are part of that group are selected.

N O T E

Locking Objects

The **Arrange > Lock** command (**Command+1**) locks selected objects so you cannot select, move, or modify them until you unlock them. This command protects parts of your illustration from accidental changes.

Use **Arrange > Lock** when you create complex artwork. Locked objects can be seen but not selected, thus enabling you to work easily with adjacent objects without affecting the locked objects. See the tip under **Select All** for locking all elements except the group you are currently working on.

N O T E

Locked objects remain locked until you use the **Unlock** command. The locked attribute is stored with the document when you close it and remains with the document when it is reopened until the **Unlock** command is used.

Some things you should know about locking and unlocking:

➤ Holding down the **Option** key while choosing **Arrange > Lock**, or pressing **Command+Option+1**, locks all *unselected* objects.

➤ To unlock an object, choose **Arrange > Unlock All** or press **Command+2**. This action unlocks all locked objects and automatically selects them. Previously selected objects are deselected. If you have not locked any objects, **Unlock All** has no effect.

➤ If you inadvertently select the **Unlock All** command, immediately select **Lock** again. Since invoking **Unlock All** results in all locked objects being selected, this quick recovery makes it easy to restore the locked status of the selected objects.

➤ If you want to unlock only some objects, you can put those objects on a different layer than the others *before* locking them, then lock them and make that layer invisible before using the **Unlock All** command. Note that you must position the objects on different layers while they can still be selected—*before* locking them.

Hiding Objects

The **Arrange > Hide** command (**Command+3**) hides all selected objects from view in both Artwork and Preview modes and in the printed artwork. Hidden objects do not display in Preview mode, nor do they appear on printed versions.

This command is extremely useful for complex drawings. You can hide parts of the illustration, making the artwork less complex and reducing the time it takes Illustrator to refresh the screen in Preview mode. You can also hide parts of drawings as you complete them, leaving only incomplete objects visible on the screen. (See also **Arrange > Lock**.)

➤ Holding down the **Option** key while choosing **Arrange > Hide**, or pressing **Command+Option+3**, hides all unselected objects.

➤ You lose the Hide attribute when you quit or save the document.

➤ You can redisplay all hidden objects by choosing the **Arrange > Show All** command (**Command+4**). When you choose this command, all hidden objects display and are automatically selected. Previously selected objects are deselected. If you have not hidden any objects, choosing **Show All** has no effect.

➤ You can also hide objects by putting them on a separate layer and making that layer invisible (as described later in this chapter).

NOTE To glimpse all hidden elements and then hide them again, choose **Show All** (or press **Command+4**), then choose **Hide** (**Command+3**) while the previously hidden objects are still selected, before clicking any other selections. To add a group of elements to a hidden set, first group the new elements, then choose **Show All**, **Shift**+click on the new group to add it to the selection, then choose **Hide/Arrange > Hide**.

Rearranging Overlapping Objects

These next techniques are useful whenever you need to rearrange the sequence of three or more overlapping elements that are all on the same named layer, like the three stars shown in the next figure.

When you want to position a selected object as the frontmost or backmost object relative to selected objects of an illustration, you can use the **Paste In Front** or **Paste In Back** command (**Command+F** or **Command+B**), respectively. Otherwise, when you want to move a selected object to a different position in the painting order, use Illustrator's "smart pasting" ability, described next.

PASTING IN FRONT OF OR BEHIND A SELECTED OBJECT

This technique is useful whenever you need to rearrange the pointing order of three or more objects, like the three layers of star shapes shown in the previous figure.

The **Paste In Front** and **Paste In Back** commands are especially useful for pasting objects between other objects. If you want to paste in front of all objects in your artwork—not in front of selected objects only—you can use the **Paste** command. Another difference between **Paste** and **Paste In Front** is that **Paste** brings the objects to the center of the window, whereas **Paste In Front** positions the objects over their last location.

N O T E If you are moving one object to the front or back of the painting order, simply select the object and press **Command+hyphen (Arrange > Send To Back)** to move a selected object to fall behind all other objects on the same layer, and press **Command+= (Arrange > Bring To Front)** to move a selected object to become the topmost object. If you want to re-sequence the stacking order of a single object, use the **Paste In Front** or **Paste In Back** command, described here. If you want to rearrange a series of objects, use **Arrange > Send to Back**, described next.

1. Assuming you have a series of objects stacked on top of one another, select the Selection tool and click on the object you want to move, such as the middle star as shown in the figure on the next page, and press **Command+X** (**Edit > Cut**). The selected object is cut to the Clipboard for pasting later.

2. Now choose the object you would like to paste behind or in front of and click on it. This selection now acts as a "reference object" for the pasting function. The bottom star is selected in this example.

3. Then press **Command+F** or **Command+B** (**Edit > Paste In Front** or **Edit > Paste In Back**). The cut object is pasted in front or in back of the object you selected as a reference object in step 2. (If you do not choose a reference object before pasting, **Paste In Front** or **Paste In Back** will simply paste the object as the frontmost or backmost item in the painting order.)

Figure 10.29 Bottom object selected and pasted in front of top object.

USING THE SEND TO BACK AND BRING TO FRONT COMMANDS

This alternative is useful when four or more overlapping objects are seriously out of order. In the next steps, we'll convert the painting order from the leftmost figure to the rightmost figure. Here we use the **Send To Back** command (**Command+hyphen**). You could instead use the **Bring To Front** command, or **Command+=** , to rearrange objects by moving selected objects to the top of the stack in the active layer in the artwork—but then they'd be in the way of selecting the next object!

1. Select the object that you want to end up on top of all the others and press **Command+hyphen** (**Arrange > Send To Back**).

2. Select the object that you want just below the top and press **Command+hyphen** again.

3. Continue selecting objects in the top-down order you intend and typing **Command+hyphen**. The last object you select should be the one you intend to be below all the others. The end result should be the intended sequence of levels.

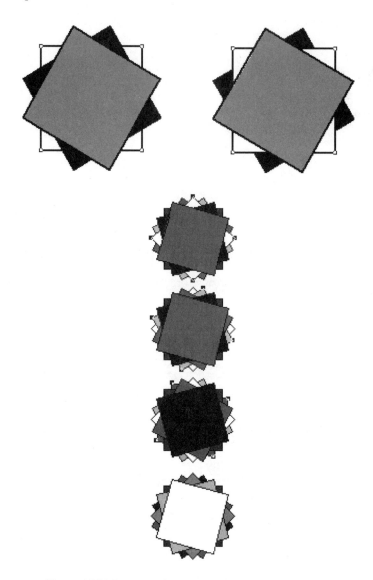

Figure 10.30 Painting order rearranged one element at a time.

Managing Overlapping, Identical Objects

You can overlap different objects within one named layer. Usually when objects overlap, you can select the objects below other objects by finding an exposed edge of the box you wish to select. If the overlapping objects are identical paths—such as a mask overlapped by a stroked identical path, or compound lines such as described in Chapter 4 and shown in the next figure—then there is no exposed edge. Besides, even if only one of the objects is selected, it's difficult to know which object since the path and handles all look the same.

Here are two handy techniques for managing overlapping, identical objects.

CHANGING THE PAINT ATTRIBUTES OF THE LOWER OF TWO OBJECTS

If there are only two identical overlapping objects, you can easily select and modify the top object by clicking on it. To modify the object below it, drag the Selection tool over both paths to select them, then **Shift**+click on the top object to de-select it. You can make your modifications while the object is more or less hidden by the top object, or you can use the next steps to be more certain of what object is selected and to see the changes more clearly.

WARNING

> These next steps work only if you are working in an area where the two overlapping identical objects do not also overlap other objects in the artwork, and you are changing the paint attributes but not the shape of either path. Also, if you're working with masks with overlapping stroked paths, see the next technique instead.

1. Select the top object as described in the previous paragraph, then press **Command+hyphen** (**Arrange > Send to Back**). The appearance of the overlapping objects before and after this rearrangement is shown in the next figure.

2. Click away from the objects (or press **Command+Shift+A**) to deselect everything, then click again on the overlapping objects to select the one that is now on top, and make your modifications. In this case, the line is changed from black to gray.

3. Select the top object by clicking on it (if it is not still selected after the previous step), then press **Command+hyphen** (**Arrange > Send To Back**). The final appearance of the overlapping objects is shown in Figure 10.31.

Figure 10.31 Two overlapping lines (top), re-ordered to change the bottom path (middle), then returned to original order (bottom).

WHEN THERE ARE THREE OR MORE OBJECTS

The problem is more complicated when there are three or more identical overlapping objects, such as the three-part line shown in the next figure (a solid black line, a dotted white line with round caps, and a dashed white line with butt caps). These next steps make it easy to select and modify each object.

Figure 10.32 Solid black line below a dotted white line and a dashed white line.

1. Select the top object by clicking on it, then press **Command+Shift+M** (**Arrange > Move**) and enter a number that is easy to remember—such as **10**. Select the direction that will most clearly separate the objects— **Horizontal** if the objects are vertical lines, **Vertical** if the objects are horizontal lines. If you move at an angle, you will need to remember the number of degrees you used. Click **OK** to close the dialog box and move the object.

NOTE

If you are moving objects with White stroke and no fill—or vice versa—you might want to create a temporary black background rectangle against which you can see the moved objects. Another alternative is to change the paint attributes to a more visible color before moving them, then change them back to White after replacing all the objects in step 4.

2. Select the second object by clicking on it, and repeat step 1, but this time *double* the numeric value you entered in step 1. Repeat this for each object in the stack except the last one—keep the object on the lowest level in its original position.

3. Now that the objects are separated, you can easily select and modify each one.

4. When you are finished, select the top object and press **Command+ Shift+M** (**Arrange > Move**). This time, enter the *negative* of the number you entered in step 1 to return it to its former position. Repeat this step for each item you moved.

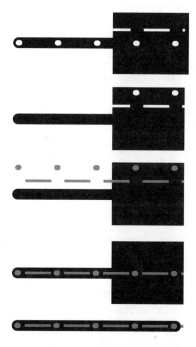

Figure 10.33 Lines separated (top), modified (middle), and re-positioned (bottom).

CHANGING THE SHAPE OF OVERLAPPING, IDENTICAL OBJECTS

The two previous techniques work well if you are simply selecting objects to change the paint attributes, but if you want to change the shape of overlapping identical objects—such as the shape of a mask and its overlapping stroked path—the following technique is helpful.

If you want to add, delete, or move part of two or more overlapping paths, you can use the Direct-selection tool to drag a selection marquee over the segment or anchor point that you want to move, and drag the selection to change the shape of both paths at once. If you move a direction handle, however, you will affect the top line only.

If you want to have more flexibility in editing the paths—by moving direction handles or adding new segments or anchor points—go through the following steps:

1. First select the top object only and press **Command+Shift+M** (**Arrange > Move**) to move it a specific distance away from the bottom layer. Then edit the bottom layer.

2. After changing the shape of a bottom path that is not a mask, select it and press **Command+C**, **Command+F** (**Edit > Copy**, then **Edit > Paste In Front**) to make a duplicate of the line, layered on top of the first. If the bottom path is a mask, choose **Filter > Objects > Outline Path**.

3. Next, select the **Eyedropper** tool in the Toolbox and click on the previous version of the top line—the line you moved at the beginning of this step. This loads the paint style attributes of that line into the Paint Style palette. Then select the **Paintbucket** tool in the Toolbox and click on the new top line.

4. Finally, select the original top line and delete it.

Working in Named Layers

In Illustrator, as in all object-oriented drawing applications, you can make one object overlap another, and you can rearrange this "painting order" sequence using the **Send To Back** and **Bring To Front** commands. In addition, Illustrator lets you create named layers within the artwork and manipulate them through the Layers palette. This is a tremendous productivity tool in working with complex illustrations. Individual layers can be locked, hidden, printed, and rearranged.

The **Window > Show Layers** command (**Command+Control+L**) displays the Layers palette. If the palette is already displayed, the command on the menu changes to **Hide Layers**.

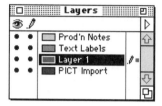

Figure 10.34 The Layers palette with several named layers.

Layering is not the same as stacking order or painting order. Each layer named in the Layers palette has its own stacking order or painting order for objects on that layer. (In this book, we have used the word *layers* to describe the named layers listing in the Layers palette, and the phrase *painting order* to describe the overlapping sequence of objects within one named layer.)

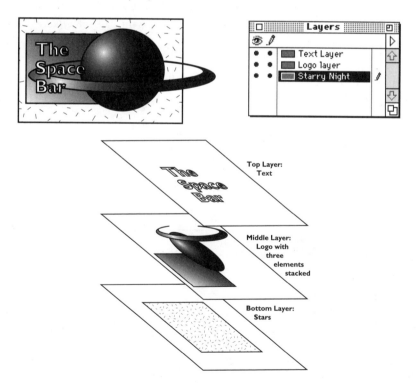

Figure 10.35 Stacking order within layers.

Why Bother?

You could work without ever opening the Layers palette or knowing that it exists, but once you use it you will wonder how you ever lived without it. There are many reasons for working in multiple layers. A few uses are suggested here, with specific uses demonstrated in the following techniques.

PROTECT ELEMENTS FROM CHANGES

You can set individual layers to be visible but not editable, so there's no danger of inadvertently selecting or moving finished elements. This also simplifies editing complex illustrations.

SAVE SCREEN REDRAW TIME

By dividing complex illustrations into layers, you can save screen re-draw time while you are working by making one or more layers invisible. Objects that make especially good candidates for invisible layers include imported images, objects with pattern fills, and masks with complex contents. Using layers to hide objects is more flexible than using **Arrange > Hide**, since you can selectively "unhide" individual layers instead of revealing everything with the **Arrange > Show All** command.

You hide a layer by clicking the dot left of the layer name, beneath the eye icon in the Layers palette.

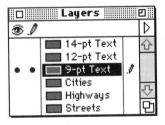

Figure 10.36 Layers palette shows some layers are hidden.

SAVE PRINTING TIME

You can save printing time when printing drafts of complex illustrations by printing only the new or changed elements that need to be proofed—putting the approved or unchanging elements (such as placed images, masks, or patterns) on layers that you set not to print.

Turn the **Print** option on or off for individual layers by clicking on the layer name in the Layers palette to highlight it, then choose **Layer Options for (Layer Name)** from the Layer options pop-out menu. The Layer Options dialog box is displayed as shown and described in the next sections. Set the **Print** option on for layers you wish to print and off for those you do not wish to print.

This option can be also used to print multiple versions of the artwork, as demonstrated later in this chapter. (See Figure 10.47.)

REARRANGE LAYERS EASILY

You can move finished layers to the bottom of the artwork while you work on other layers, then rearrange layers at any time as needed.

Working with the Layers Palette

To display the Layers palette, simply use the keyboard shortcut **Command+ Control+L**, or choose **Window > Show Layers**. If the Layers palette is already displayed, you can choose **Window > Hide Layers** or use the keyboard shortcut **Command+Control+L**, but it's usually easier to click the close box on the palette title bar.

When the Layers palette is displayed on the screen, you can view the layer position of selected objects, move them to other layers, rearrange whole layers relative to each other, and change the display and printing attributes of each layer.

THE DEFAULT PALETTE

When the Layers palette is first displayed, it shows only one layer, named *Layer 1*. You can work entirely on this layer and never use the Layers palette—but then you would be missing out on the wonderful benefits listed earlier in this section!

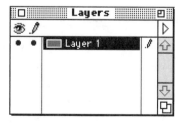

Figure 10.37 The default Layers palette.

CREATING A NEW LAYER

You can create any number of layers in a document—subject only to the limitations imposed by your computer's memory. Each new layer adds some memory requirements for Illustrator's internal "layer management" functions, in addition to the space requirements of the actual artwork on that layer. To create a new layer, follow these steps:

1. Choose **Window > Show Layers** (**Command+Control+L**) to display the Layers palette.

2. Position the mouse pointer over the arrow at the top-right corner of the Layers palette and hold down the mouse button to display the Layers palette pop-out menu, and drag to select the **New Layer** command.

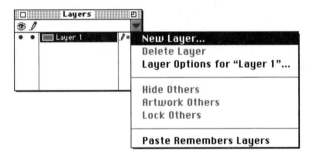

Figure 10.38 The Layers palette pop-out menu with **New Layer** selected.

3. In the Layer Options dialog box, type the name of the new layer (or accept Illustrator's numerical layer name).

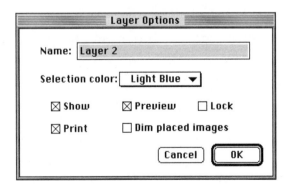

Figure 10.39 The Layer Options dialog box.

➤ You can select the color you want to indicate selections on that layer by choosing from the Selection color drop-down list or let Illustrator assign one for you. By specifying a different selection color for each layer you can easily see what layer objects are on when you select them—even when the Layers palette is closed.

➤ For each layer, you can also activate or de-activate options to **Show** (i.e., display or hide on screen), **Preview** (vs. Artwork view), **Lock** (i.e., prevent objects on that layer from being selected), **Print**, or **Dim Placed Images**. These options are described under the next headings.

4. Click **OK** or press **Return** to close the dialog box and view the new layer name in the Layers palette.

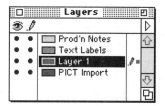

Figure 10.40 The Layers palette with several named layers.

SELECTING THE ACTIVE LAYER

New objects that you add to the artwork are automatically positioned on the layer that is currently active in the Layers palette. You can determine the layer for a new object by clicking on the layer name in the Layers palette, or, if the palette is not displayed, you can activate a layer by selecting any object on that layer. If any object is selected in the artwork, a colored dot appears to the right of the layer name in the palette.

MOVING ELEMENTS FROM ONE LAYER TO ANOTHER

Once an object is in position on a layer, you can move it to another layer using either of two methods:

➤ If the Layers palette is displayed, you can select the object(s) you want to move from one layer—a colored dot will appear to the right of the layer name. Then, with the object(s) still selected, drag the colored dot to the layer on which you want the object.

605

➤ Whether or not the Layers palette is displayed, you can also move objects from one layer to another using the **Paste** commands.

Whenever the **Cut** or **Copy** command is used to put objects in the Clipboard, the **Paste** command behaves as follows—*unless* the **Paste Remembers Layers** option is checked in the File > Preferences > General dialog box (see note, below):

➤ If the objects in the Clipboard were on several different layers when cut or copied and you do nothing more to specify the target layer, then the **Paste** command inserts the Clipboard contents on the top of the top-most layer from which the objects were selected.

➤ If you make a specific layer active before using the **Paste** command—by selecting any object on the layer or by selecting the layer in the Layers palette—then the **Paste** command inserts the Clipboard contents on the top of the selected layer.

➤ If any object is selected before using the **Paste** command, you can use the **Paste In Front** or **Paste In Back** command to position the Clipboard contents within the stacking order of the selected layer. If the selected objects are grouped, the pasted objects become part of the group.

NOTE

If the **Paste Remembers Layers** option is checked in the File > Preferences > General dialog box, then the **Paste** commands always position the pasted object(s) on the same layers from which they were cut or copied. You can still move objects from one layer to another through the Layers palette, however.

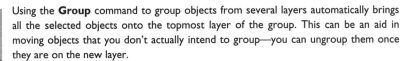

SHORTCUT

Using the **Group** command to group objects from several layers automatically brings all the selected objects onto the topmost layer of the group. This can be an aid in moving objects that you don't actually intend to group—you can ungroup them once they are on the new layer.

REMOVING LAYERS

To delete a layer from the artwork, click on the layer name in the Layers palette to highlight it, then choose **Delete Layer** from the Layer options pop-out menu. All objects on that layer are also deleted from the artwork.

REARRANGING LAYERS

You can rearrange the order of layers by dragging the layer names in the Layers palette from one position to another. The layer listed at the top of the list in the palette is always the topmost layer in the artwork, and objects on that layer will view and print on top of objects on other layers.

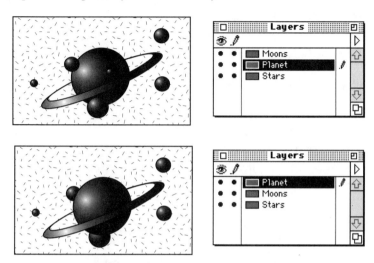

Figure 10.41 Layers before and after rearranging.

ADJUSTING THE SIZE AND POSITION OF THE LAYERS PALETTE

You can move the Layers palette on the screen by dragging the title bar. The palette will always display on top of all document windows, but the most recently used palette can appear on top of this palette if there is overlap between palettes. You can bring any palette to the top by clicking on it. If a palette is completely hidden under other palettes, you can move the other palettes or you can use the command under the Window menu to **Hide** and then **Show** the buried palette.

You can adjust the size of the Layers palette by dragging the sizing square in the lower-right corner of the palette. If there are more layer names than can be displayed in the smallest window, then the scroll bars right of the layer names become active for scrolling through the list.

You can also click the sizing box at the top right of the title bar to toggle between two sizes.

Changing Layer Attributes

To change the name of a layer, or modify any of the attributes you specified when creating the layer, simply double-click on the layer name, or use the slower method of clicking once on the layer name in the Layers palette to highlight it, then choosing **Layer Options for (Layer Name)** from the Layer options pop-out menu. The Layer Options dialog box is displayed as shown and described earlier, and you can make changes as desired.

You can also change some attribute without opening the Layer Options dialog box, as described under the next headings.

MAKING LAYERS VISIBLE OR INVISIBLE

You can turn the **Show** option on and off (i.e., display or hide a layer), by clicking the dot beneath the eye icon to the left of the layer name in the Layers palette. This is faster than opening the Layer Options dialog box as described in the previous section. You can hide layers one by one this way, or you can hide all layers *except* one, as described next.

To hide all layers except those you select, click on the name of the layer (and **Shift**+click on additional names) you want to be visible in the Layers palette to highlight it, then choose **Hide Others** from the Layer options pop-out menu.

Hiding a layer has a similar effect to choosing **Arrange > Hide**, except that one hides whole layers while the other hides selected objects. Hidden layers, like hidden objects, cannot be viewed or edited, but they will print unless the **Print** attribute is also turned off for the layer.

Hide layers with masks, patterns, imported images, or other complex elements before closing a file to reduce the time for screen display when you reopen the file.

N O T E

SETTING LAYERS TO PREVIEW OR ARTWORK VIEWS

To display all layers in Artwork mode except those you select, click on the name of the layer (and **Shift**+click on additional names) you want to display in Preview in the Layers palette to highlight it, then choose **Artwork Others** from the Layer options pop-out menu.

You can toggle between Preview and Artwork views of each layer by **Option**+clicking the dot beneath the eye icon to the left of the layer name in the Layers palette. This is faster than opening the Layer Options dialog box as described in earlier sections.

SHORTCUT

LOCKING LAYERS

You can turn the **Lock** option on and off by clicking the dot beneath the pencil icon to the left of the layer name in the Layers palette. This is faster than opening the Layer Options dialog box as described in earlier sections. You can lock layers one by one this way, or you can lock all layers *except* one, as described next.

To lock all layers except those you select, click on the name of the layer (and **Shift**+click on additional names) you want to lock in the Layers palette to highlight it, then choose **Lock Others** from the Layer options pop-out menu.

Locking a layer has a similar effect to choosing **Arrange > Lock**, except that one locks whole layers while the other locks selected objects. Locked layers, like locked objects, cannot be selected or edited.

SELECTIVELY PRINTING LAYERS

Turn the **Print** option on or off for individual layers by clicking on the layer name in the Layers palette to highlight it, then choose **Layer Options for (Layer Name)** from the Layer options pop-out menu. The Layer Options dialog box is displayed as shown and described earlier.

Set the **Print** option on for layers you wish to print and off for those you do not wish to print. This can be used to print only those elements that need to be proofed, to save printing time by not printing placed images, masks, or patterns. This also facilitates printing multiple versions of the artwork.

DIMMING PLACED IMAGES

Turn the **Dim Placed Images** option on or off for individual layers by clicking on the layer name in the Layers palette to highlight it, then choose **Layer Options for (Layer Name)** from the Layer options pop-out menu. The Layer Options dialog box is displayed as shown and described earlier.

Set the **Dim Placed Images** option to "screen," or "gray" placed images, to make it easier to see and edit objects on top of the image.

EXAMPLE: LAYERING OVERHEAD TRANSPARENCIES

Since each layer can be printed separately, we'll present these next steps as being specifically useful for creating a series of images that will be printed as one image for handouts during a presentation, and then printed separately and projected during the presentation as overlaid transparencies. You can use the same steps in handling any artwork.

1. Draw the artwork that will compose the bottom layer—the first transparency when additional transparencies are overlaid during a presentation. Use the Paint Style palette (**Command+I**) to set the Fill and Stroke of each elements, including different colors if you wish.

Layer I

2. To ensure that you don't change the artwork on the first layer as you are creating the second layer, press **Command+Control+L** (**Window > Show Layers**) to display the Layers palette, and click the dot beneath the pencil icon to the left of the layer name in the Layers palette to lock all the elements on this first layer.

3. Position the mouse pointer over the arrow at the top-right corner of the Layers palette and hold down the mouse button to display the Layers palette pop-out menu, and drag to select the **New Layer** command. In the Layers options dialog box, type the name of the new layer (or accept Illustrator's numerical layer name). Set other options as described for the Layers palette in the next sections. Click **OK** or press **Return** to close the dialog box and view the new layer name in the Layers palette.

4. Draw the artwork that will compose the second layer—the second transparency when the two transparencies are overlaid during a presentation. Click the dot to the left of the first layer name, beneath the eye icon in the Layers palette, to hide the first layer and verify that the second layer includes all the elements you need.

5. If a third overlay is called for, repeat steps 2 and 3 to lock all the elements on the second layer and create a third named layer.

6. Then draw the artwork that will compose the third transparency overlay. Click the dot next to the first and second layer names, beneath the eye

icon in the Layers palette, to hide the first two layers and verify that the third layer includes all the elements you need. Repeat these steps for each additional overlay.

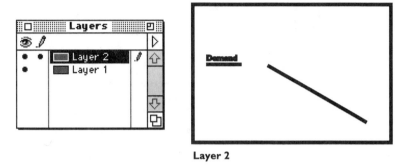

Layer 2

Figure 10.42 Layers palette shows second layer name.

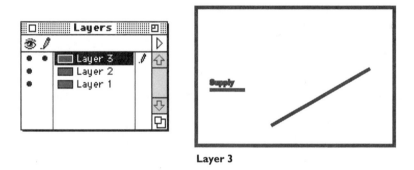

Layer 3

Figure 10.43 Layers palette with third layer added.

7. Print the artwork with all layers showing, then print each overlay on a separate sheet by setting the **Print** option off for each layer, one by one. To do this, click on a Layer name in the Layers palette to highlight it, then choose **Layer Options for (Layer Name)** from the Layer options pop-out menu. The Layer Options dialog box is displayed as shown and described in earlier. Set the **Print** option on for layers you wish to print and off for those you do not wish to print.

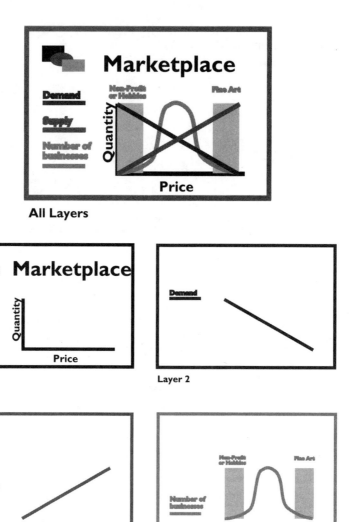

Figure 10.44 Composite (above) of individual layers (bottom row).

Examples: Simplify Complex Artwork

Layering can help simplify complex illustrations. By putting different collections of objects on different layers, you can make layers invisible so you can easily work on one portion of the artwork at a time.

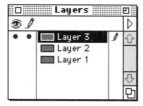

You can set one layer to be the unlocked layer, so you can make changes to it while other layers are locked (i.e., visible but not active). Objects on locked layers are unselectable. This reduces the chances of making the common mistake of selecting the wrong element when many elements overlap. It also enables you to use the selection marquee to select elements on unlocked layers only—elements on locked layers will not be selected, even if included in the selection marquee.

The ability to rearrange layers easily means that even when you want to see all layers, you can bring the layer you want to work on to the top, then move it back to its proper place when you have finished working on it.

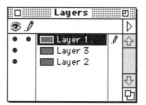

Layers can be set up for related groups of elements, or you could maintain two layers: one layer with all of the finished art, and a "working" layer where you create new elements while the other layer is made hidden or locked. When you're finished creating an object, you would move the elements from the "working" layer to the "finished" layer.

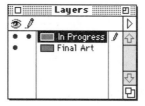

You can also simplify complex artwork by putting all the elements that share the same type or paint attributes on one layer, thereby making global changes a snap, as demonstrated in the next technique.

EXAMPLE: LAYERING DIFFERENT TYPE SPECIFICATIONS

If you put text that shares the same type specifications on one layer, you can easily select all of the text at once and change the font, size, style, color, or other type specifications.

This technique is especially useful if you are working with large volumes of text, as in maps and technical illustrations. This technique can also be used to layer other types of elements that share paint attributes—such as lines that represent highways or shapes that represent water or land.

1. Use the techniques described earlier in this section to create one new layer for each different type specification (i.e., each unique combination of choices from the commands under the Type menu, or set in the Character and Paragraph palettes).

2. If you have already added text to the artwork, select all of the text objects that share one set of specifications, then drag the dot to the right of the layer name in the Layers palette to the new layer with that specification name. Repeat this step for each set of like text objects.

As you add new text objects, click on the layer named for the new object's type specifications.

Figure 10.45 Layers separate different type elements.

3. To view and edit text elements have been assigned a set of common type specifications, make all of the other layers invisible by clicking on the dot next to their names, below the eye icon in the Layers palette—leaving only one layer visible at a time. Click on the name of the layer that contains the objects you want to edit, then press **Command+A** (**Edit > Select All**) and use commands under the Type menu or the Character and Paragraph palettes to change the specifications.

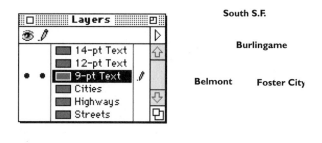

Figure 10.46 All layers hidden but one.

EXAMPLE: USING ONE LAYER FOR NONPRINTING ELEMENTS

You can use one layer to store elements that are aids in your work—elements that you never need to print. For example, the custom grids described in Chapters 3, 6, and 8 might be positioned on the lowermost layer.

EXAMPLE: CREATE DIFFERENT VERSIONS OF ARTWORK

Working in layers, you can create multiple versions of an illustration. For example, the lowermost layer might contain a complex floor plan. You can create a separate layer for a schematic of emergency evacuation routes, another layer for the names of people in each unit or room, another layer for an equipment and furniture inventory of each room, etc. In printing, you always print the lowermost layer plus only *one* of the other layers.

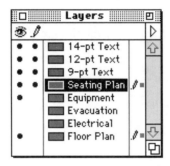

Figure 10.47 Layers palette set up to print different floor schematics.

EXAMPLE: DIVIDING LAYERED ARTWORK INTO SEPARATE DOCUMENTS

Use this technique in storing the elements that are to appear on each layer in a separate document. This can be a productivity aid when each overlay—or the final composite image—is so complicated or so large that the work is shared between several artists until the final stages (when it is all merged into one document).

1. Create only as much of the artwork as you will need for a grid or guide to create subsequent layers. Create each layer name and save the new document under a descriptive name such as "Monster Art Boilerplate."

2. To work on each layer, open the Monster Art Boilerplate and add the elements for one or more layers. Save each working file under a different name.

3. When all the layers are ready, open the most complicated or largest file of the set and save it as "Monster Art Final." Then open each separate working document, select all the elements on one of the layers that changed in that document, press **Command+C** (**Edit > Copy**), then activate that layer in Monster Art Final and press **Command+V** (**Edit > Paste**). Repeat this step for each layer in each separate working document.

Working with Custom Views

The **View > New Views** command (**Command+Control+V**) lets you create up to 25 "custom" views of your document: zoom level, layer options, and viewing mode (i.e., Preview or Artwork). These settings are saved and named so they can be activated at any time. Named views appear at the bottom of the View menu, with automatically assigned keyboard shortcuts.

To create a new view:

1. Set the screen display to the magnification and mode you want (i.e., Preview or Artwork).

2. Choose **View > New View** to display the New View dialog box.

3. Type the name of the view.

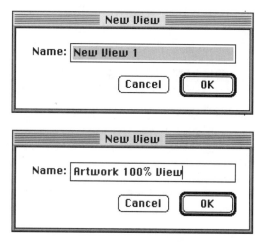

Figure 10.48 The New View dialog box when first displayed, and with custom view name.

4. Click **OK** or press **Return** to close the dialog box and save the view settings.

5. Continue working, changing the screen display as needed. Whenever you want to return to the saved settings, choose the custom view name from the bottom of the View menu.

It's a good idea to use consistent naming conventions. For example, "100% view" and "200% view" will appear in numeric order on the View menu, but "25%" will appear below the two unless you follow the three-digit number convention and use the name "025%."

NOTE

View Object Font Type Filt
✓Preview   ⌘Y
Artwork   ⌘E
Preview Selection   ⌘⌥Y
Hide Template   ⌘⇧W
Hide Rulers   ⌘R
Hide Page Tiling
Hide Edges   ⌘⇧H
Hide Guides
Zoom In   ⌘]
Zoom Out   ⌘[
Actual Size   ⌘H
Fit In Window   ⌘M
New View...   ⌘⌃V
Edit Views...
400% Artwork view ⌘⌃1
Fit in Window Preview ⌘⌃2

Figure 10.49 Custom views appear by name at the bottom of the View menu.

Editing Saved Views

Once you've used the **View > New Views** command to create a custom view, you can change the name or delete it using the **View > Edit Views** command.

To change a view name or delete it:

1. Choose **View > Edit Views** to display the Edit Views dialog box.

2. Click on a view name to select it.

3. Choose one of two options:

➤ Type a new name for the view then click **OK** or press **Return** to close the dialog box and save the view name, or

➤ Click **Delete** to delete the custom view name from the View menu.

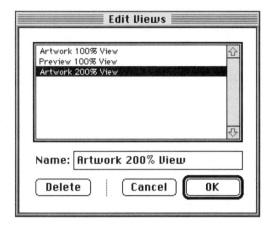

Figure 10.50 The Edit Views dialog box with a view name highlighted.

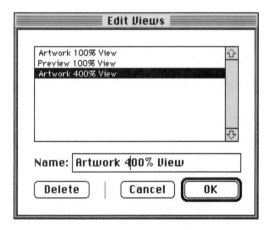

Figure 10.51 The Edit Views dialog box with a new name typed.

Opening the Same Document in More than One Window

The **Window > New Window** command creates a duplicate window of the active file. The original window and its duplicate are linked, so that changes to artwork in one window are duplicated in the second window. You can view one window in Preview mode and the other in Artwork mode and zoom in one window independently of the other.

➤ When you choose **New Window** from the Window menu, the duplicate window appears slightly offset from the original window. The newly created view becomes the active window, which you can move, resize, or close just like any Macintosh window.

➤ When two or more views of the same file are on the desktop, Illustrator assigns each a number that appears in the window's title bar: Untitled art:1, Untitled art:2, and so on. When you close a window from a set of multiple views, Illustrator renumbers the remaining windows accordingly.

➤ You can work in full views or overlapping views, and you can change the active window by choosing from the Window menu.

EXAMPLE: ARTWORK AND PREVIEW

Work in two views of the same illustration, one in Artwork view and one in Preview. This way, you can see the results of changes in real time as you work in the Artwork view on the wireframe image. Working in this way is especially good for making the final touches on artwork.

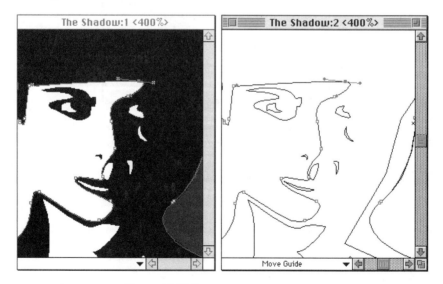

Figure 10.52 Preview and Artwork views.

EXAMPLE: ACTUAL SIZE AND CLOSE-UP

Work in two different magnifications: an actual size (or smaller) view of the entire artwork, and an enlarged view of the detail on which you are working. This allows you to see extended sections of long paths in the smaller view and to pinpoint anchor points easily in the enlarged view.

The reduced view can be in either Artwork or Preview mode.

Figure 10.53 Two magnifications of wireframe artwork.

EXAMPLE: ARTWORK AND PAINT PALETTE

View the artwork of the illustration in one window and a palette of Paint settings in another window.

EXAMPLE: MULTIPLE ILLUSTRATIONS

You can view two or more illustrations at once. This is useful when you want to compare images, overlay images, or copy elements from one document to another.

Working with windows open in the Preview mode may slow down the system if the illustration is complex, because the Preview mode constantly refreshes the screen. It may not be practical to work this way for long periods on complex drawings.

WARNING

Choosing the Active Window

If you can see part of a window behind the active window, you can activate it by clicking on it on the screen. Otherwise, the last section of the Window menu contains a list of all currently open windows—selecting a window name from this menu places a check mark beside its name in the Window menu and makes that window the active window.

Real-World Challenges: Time and Space

The old adage "bigger is better" can be reversed when applied to computer files. Many of us have expanded our computer systems' hard disk space and memory to run full-featured applications like Illustrator more efficiently, but we still run into the limits of disk space, memory space, screen redraw time, and printing time when working with large, complicated illustrations.

Here are a few suggestions for overcoming these limitations. Most of these concepts are covered elsewhere in this book—in Tips or scattered throughout the command and tool descriptions. We collect them here for easy reference.

Getting Faster Screen Redraw

The screen image is re-created every time you open an existing illustration file, scroll on the page, change the magnification of the page, close certain dialog boxes or windows that cover the artwork, or change large portions of the artwork in a single step. If you find that you are waiting what seems like a long time for the screen to redraw, or if you are planning a change to the artwork that will result in a long wait for the screen to refresh, try one or more of these solutions *before* you make the next change:

> ➤ Work in Artwork view (**Command+E**), or **View > Preview Selection** (**Command+Option+Y**). You can change between these and full Preview mode (**Command+Y**) as often as you like while working. Also, if you save the file in Artwork view, it will open a lot faster the next time.

➤ If the artwork uses patterns, turn off the **Preview and Print Patterns** option in the File > Document Setup dialog box. Also, when the setting is off, the illustrations print as drafts without patterns, which will print faster than if printed with patterns.

➤ If the artwork includes placed images, turn off the **Show Placed Images** option in the File > Document Setup dialog box. The image will print correctly, but it appears as a box in Artwork view and is invisible in Preview view.

➤ Put masks and other complex elements on layers of their own and make these layers invisible until you need them.

➤ Use the Monitors Macintosh Control Panel (under the Apple menu) to turn color off or reduce the number of colors displayed on your monitor. For example, a screen that takes 20 seconds to display in 256 colors requires only 17 seconds to display in 256 shades of gray. Display time can be further shortened by choosing fewer colors or shades of gray. (See later section in this chapter.)

➤ Before starting Illustrator under System 7.0 or later, select the **Illustrator** program icon on the Macintosh desktop and choose **File > Get Info** (**Command+I**) to increase the memory allocation for Illustrator.

Getting Files to Print Faster

Illustrations that take a long time to print can be handled by planning to print the files during lunch breaks, during meetings, or at the end of the day. Unfortunately, these solutions are not always practical when you have deadlines to meet or when you share the printer with others who might want to print their own files while you are at lunch. Here are some suggestions for decreasing the time it takes to print your artwork:

➤ Set a page size close to the size of the artwork. Do not create small illustrations surrounded by white space in a page size that happens to match the paper size in your printer. The amount of printer RAM required in printing a page is directly related to the size of the page specified in the Document Setup dialog box. In one test, a simple 4-inch by 4-inch image required 14 seconds to print on a Linotronic 300 when letter-size paper was specified, but only 8 seconds when a 4-inch by 4-inch page size was specified.

➤ Use duplicated objects rather than tiled fills. Tiled fills take longer to print, and very complex tiled fills might not print at all.

➤ Use blends rather than gradient or radial fills. This will speed printing time but increase the file size. (You can use the **Object > Expand** command to convert gradients to separate components.)

➤ If your printer allows different printing resolutions, or if you have a choice of printers with different printing resolutions, choose a lower printing resolution when printing drafts. You can do this through the Print dialog box in Illustrator, described in Chapter 11.

➤ Decrease the screen ruling setting in Separations Setup Halftone dialog box pop-up menu or through the EPSF Riders file as described in Chapter 11.

➤ Use the **Object > Attributes** command to change the output resolution of selected elements in your artwork. When you change the output resolution of a selected object, you automatically change the flatness setting for that object. This determines the precision with which Illustrator calculates curves. Illustrator constructs curves by linking anchor points with a series of very short straight line segments (though the resulting curves appear smooth to the naked eye). A low flatness value (i.e., high-resolution setting) causes Illustrator to use a greater number of short line segments to create a more accurate curve.

➤ While you can scale placed images once inside Illustrator, it is best to complete the size, orientation, and other attributes of the image beforehand in its original source application. Scaling, shearing, and especially rotating placed images will lengthen printing times.

Decreasing the output resolution (increasing the flatness settings) for long paths can also eliminate *limitcheck* errors in printing.

NOTE

Keeping Files Small

Many of the problems you may have with screen redraw time, printing time, and memory limitations are caused by large files. You do not want to limit your creativity or restrict your artwork simply to save time and space, but here are some suggestions for minimizing file size:

➤ Draw efficiently. This means drawing curved paths with as few anchor points as possible. See Chapter 4 for tips on placing anchor points efficiently.

➤ Use gradient fills instead of blends where possible. (This will decrease the file size but is likely to increase printing time.) Otherwise, in blending, use as few blends as necessary to get the best effect. See Chapter 9 for suggestions and examples.

➤ If the artwork is very large or complicated or includes imported images, plan on printing the final directly from Illustrator rather than exporting it as an EPS (Encapsulated PostScript) file with preview options. EPS files with preview options are always larger than the source artwork in Illustrator, sometimes dramatically so.

Setting the RAM Cache

Choose the **General** command from the Control Panel submenu on the Apple menu to gain access to the RAM cache controls. If you are running Illustrator on a Macintosh equipped with a limited amount of RAM, you should turn the RAM cache off. If you have larger amounts of RAM available, you may wish to use the RAM cache; although Illustrator will not benefit from it, other applications may.

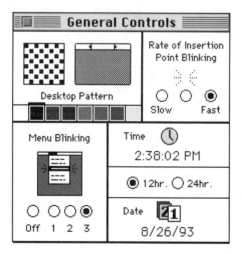

Figure 10.54 The General Control Panel.

Setting the Number of Colors the Monitor Displays

If you are using a Macintosh with a color monitor and you wish to use Illustrator's color preview features, you can set the monitor to 16, 256, thousands, or millions colors, depending on how much memory you have installed on your video card. To do this, choose the **Monitors** command from the Control Panel submenu under the Apple menu and make the appropriate selections by scrolling through the Colors scroll box and then clicking on the desired number of colors, as shown in the following figure.

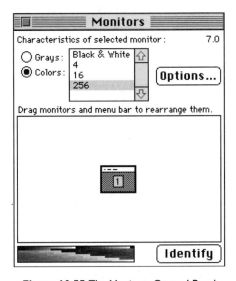

Figure 10.55 The Monitors Control Panel.

SHORTCUT If you do not need to display color, you can have quicker screen response and save memory by selecting two colors and changing to black-and-white mode. Displaying colors can slow screen redrawing. If you need to work with millions of colors on a regular basis, you may want to install an accelerated video card. Working in 256-color mode is a good compromise for most situations.

Memory Management

Some of the suggestions under "To Decrease Screen Redraw Time" will also reduce the amount of memory required by Illustrator—such as turning off the display options for patterns and imported images and increasing the point size for on-screen Greek type, turning color off, and turning Preview off. Here are some other ways to reduce the amount of memory required by Illustrator:

➤ You can decrease the amount of memory allocated to the program under System 7.0 or later through the **Get Info** command in the Finder's File menu, but this can slow the speed of some operations and might prevent you from opening large files. See "Changing Memory Allocation."

➤ Decrease the number of undos allowed through the **File > Preferences > General** command.

OUT OF MEMORY MESSAGES

Messages relating to memory may occur while opening Adobe Illustrator, opening a specific Adobe Illustrator document, or performing a specific operation in Adobe Illustrator. Following are some reasons why the messages may be appearing and what you can do to address memory problems.

Depending on the version of Illustrator you are running, the exact wording of the messages you get may vary slightly from the examples.

NOTE

➤ "Cannot open the Illustration. Out of memory or missing resource" ID = -192 or -43, occasionally -37, -38 or -39: When Adobe Illustrator opens, it checks the system to determine what type of output device is used so it can display the correct page size and imageable area. The output device is specified by selecting it in the Chooser. If you have recently reinstalled your system or printing software, the device may not be selected in the Chooser and the System cannot provide the needed information. Similarly, if you've just reinstalled Illustrator, the previous link to the System may be broken. In these cases, the "missing resource" referred to in the error message is the Chooser device. To solve the problem, select **Chooser** from the Apple menu and click on the appropriate device icon (**LaserWriter**, for example).

➤ Message appears while opening a specific Adobe Illustrator document stating that there is not enough memory to open the document: When you open an illustration, Adobe Illustrator loads the artwork information into RAM. The amount of RAM available depends on how much total RAM your computer has, your System software configuration, and how much RAM has been allocated to Adobe Illustrator. To allocate more memory to Adobe Illustrator, see "Changing Memory Allocation" in the next section.

➤ Message appears while performing a specific operation in Adobe Illustrator stating "nearly out of memory" or that there is not enough memory to perform the operation requested: This also indicates a limitation of available RAM. Adobe Illustrator must store a duplicate of the selected artwork in RAM to revert to if you choose **Undo**. Since Illustrator only has to duplicate the objects being edited, you may be able to work on individual objects or smaller groups of objects. Editing many objects simultaneously may be too much information for the available memory. To solve this problem, close other documents, select a smaller number of objects to modify, reduce the number of undos, or allocate more memory to Adobe Illustrator. See "Changing Memory Allocation" in the next section.

➤ Message appears while saving an Illustration with a preview stating that Adobe Illustrator "Cannot save preview but all other information was saved successfully": When you select a preview option other than "None" in the EPS Format dialog box, when saving artwork in EPS format, Adobe Illustrator must create a picture of the file as it appears on your screen and attach it to the EPS file. The amount of memory required is directly related to the physical dimensions of the image. The larger the image, the more RAM required to create the picture. Additionally, more memory is required to create a color preview than a black-and-white preview. To solve the problem:

➤ Allocate more memory to Adobe Illustrator. See "Changing Memory Allocation."

➤ Try saving the file with Preview set to **1-Bit Macintosh**. The file will appear black-and-white on screen but will retain all color information and print properly to a Postscript printer.

➤ Try saving the file with Preview set to **None**. The file will appear as a gray box on screen when placed in other applications like PageMaker and QuarkXPress, but will retain all color information and print properly to a PostScript output device.

CHANGING MEMORY ALLOCATION

You can change the amount of memory allocated to Illustrator through the following steps:

1. Press **Command+Q** to quit Adobe Illustrator.

2. From the desktop, select **Adobe Illustrator** by highlighting the program icon. (Make sure you have the Illustrator program selected and not the folder.)

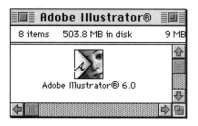

3. Select **File > Get Info** (**Command+I**).

4. Enter the desired amount of memory in the Current Size field in the Get Info dialog box. If you are running System 7.1 (or higher) enter this amount in the Preferred Size field. Try increasing the amount by 1000K. More can be added later if necessary.

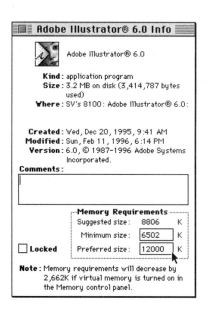

5. Close the Get Info dialog box. Adobe Illustrator will now request the amount of memory you specified whenever you open it.

Chapter 11

Printing

6.0 NEW FEATURE

Illustrator 6.0 lets you print four-color process separations or custom (spot) color separations directly through Illustrator's **File > Print** command, instead of using a separating program such as Adobe Separator, as required by earlier versions. This chapter describes how to set up a document for printing, how to print composites and color separations, how to adjust the line screen and measure the dot density of printed film, and how to solve some common printing problems. Topics include:

➤ Using the Chooser to select a printer and driver

➤ Using the **Page Setup** and **Document Setup** commands to define your pages

➤ Using the Page tool to define tiling

➤ Using the **Separation Setup** command to define color separation parameters

➤ Using the **Print** command

➤ Editing linescreen information in a PPD file

➤ Editing the EPSF Riders file

➤ Dot Density Calibration

➤ Solving printing problems

Installing a Printer Driver

6.0 NEW FEATURE

If you are already using your system and have been printing documents from Illustrator or any other application, you can assume that your printer driver is already set up and running. If you have just installed Illustrator 6.0, however, you should know that Adobe recommends also installing the Adobe PostScript Driver 8.3, which comes on the Adobe Illustrator 6.0 Deluxe CD-ROM.

The Adobe printer driver offers the following features:

➤ Full support for all your printer's features, including multiple input paper trays or output bins, duplex (two-sided) printing, and other print enhancement technologies, specified by PostScript Printer Description (PPD) files

➤ Capability of saving PostScript files in a variety of portable formats

➤ Maintenance of separate printer settings for each PostScript printer, making it easy to use two or more PostScript printers with the same computer

➤ Automatic configuration for PostScript printers that support it

➤ Setup and configuration of disconnected printers and the capability of saving PostScript files for archiving until your computer is connected to a printer (via the Virtual Printer feature)

➤ Capability of defining and printing custom media sizes from most applications to printers that support this feature

➤ Capability of saving unique printer-specific settings as Adobe printer driver software defaults for each printer you use

➤ Support for all PostScript Level 1 and Level 2 printers, imagesetters, and film recorders

The Adobe printer driver is an operating system program that lets application programs communicate with printers. The Adobe printer driver translates your application's documents into the PostScript language and sends the PostScript document descriptions to your printer. The driver also provides information about your printer, such as available paper sizes and memory, resolution, and so on.

The Adobe printer driver supports PostScript Type 1 fonts (including multiple master fonts), TrueType fonts, and Apple QuickDraw GX fonts, and can automatically download fonts to your printer. You can use the Adobe printer driver to save your documents as PostScript files to send to a service bureau. You can also create Encapsulated PostScript (EPS) files so that graphic images you create with one application and place into the documents of another application print with the greatest quality possible.

Several steps are involved in installing a new driver. You may perform them manually or let the installation program that came with the printer or the driver handle it all for you:

➤ If the driver is simply an icon—that is, a Chooser Extension file—on a disk that came with your new printer, you can simply drag it into the System folder. System 7 will prompt you to let it put it in the Extensions folder, where it belongs.

➤ If the driver also comes with PPDs (PostScript Printer Description files), you should select the ones that match printers on your system and drag them into the Printer Descriptions folder in the Extensions folder in your System folder.

To install the Adobe PostScript Printer Driver version 8.3, follow these steps:

1. Insert the Adobe Illustrator 6.0 Deluxe CD-ROM into the CD-ROM drive on your computer.

2. Open the PSPrinter 8.3 folder on the CD-ROM and double-click the **Installer** icon.

3. Follow the prompts to select the hard drive.

4. Select **Custom** installation unless you really want to install a PPD for every printer Adobe had the forethought or permission to include on the CD-ROM.

5. On the Custom Install screen, opt to install the driver, the Readme file, and the PPDs that you want.

6. The installation program will prompt you for any missing information.

7. When the installation is complete, restart your computer and select the driver through the Chooser, as described in the next section.

Choosing a Printer

Since the AppleTalk network lets you connect up to 30 devices on a single network, you can have more than one printer available to any Macintosh. The AppleShare network also allows more than one file server to be accessed. The

Chooser lets you select which printer you will use to print your artwork or which file server you wish to access.

The following steps are required only if you have more than one printer hooked up to your system and you want to change from the last one you used or if you have installed a new driver or a new printer and this is the first time you are using it:

1. Select **Chooser** from the Apple menu.

2. Click on a printer driver icon or the AppleShare icon. The screen changes to display a list of all available devices (printers or file servers) that are currently connected and active (Figure 11.1). The dialog box displays only those devices for which the power switch is on. If the full list of printers on your network is not displayed, it may be due to a loose cable connection between your machine and the printer.

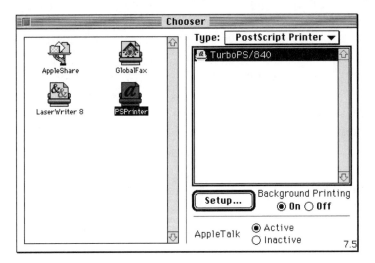

Figure 11.1 The Chooser dialog box.

3. Select the zone in which your printer resides by clicking its name in the lower-left scroll pane of the Chooser. You may need to scroll through the list of zones and printers to find the one that you want to use.

4. Click the name of the printer you want to use in the list in the upper-right scroll pane of the Chooser. A message appears reminding you to click **Setup** to assign a PPD after selecting the printer. If you wish to be reminded to click **Setup** each time you select a printer, click **OK** in this message box. To avoid viewing this message every time you select a printer, deselect the option to be reminded, and then click **OK**.

5. You can turn on Background printing by clicking the **Background Printing Active** radio button.

Background printing lets you work while a document is printing, but it requires additional disk space (to store temporary print files) and memory and can severely degrade the performance of the foreground application.

WARNING

6. Click **Setup**. For most printers, the Adobe printer driver searches for a PPD file that matches the model of the selected PostScript printer and automatically configures the driver to match the printer.

7. If the Adobe printer driver finds a match and the PPD file supports automatic configuration, you have completed the setup of the driver. An icon appears to the left of the printer name in the Chooser to show that the driver is set up to work with that printer. If the Adobe printer driver cannot automatically set up the driver, it requests one of the following actions:

➤ If the Adobe printer driver discovers no PPD files that match the selected printer, you must choose a PPD file manually. The Adobe printer driver displays a complete list of the PPD files now available on your hard disk.

➤ If the list of Printer Descriptions in the following dialog box does not contain the desired PPD, you can use the **Generic PPD** or install the desired PPD from the PSPrinter 1 or PSPrinter 2 diskette. Install only the desired PPDs; do not reinstall the Adobe printer driver. Once you have installed the desired PPDs, begin this procedure again.

➤ For information on the selected printer, click **Info**. To select the **Generic PPD**, click **Use Generic**. To select another PPD file, click the PPD name, and then click **Select**. If the selected PPD does not support automatic configuration, the driver displays a Configure dialog box.

➤ The Configure dialog box shows the installable options for the selected PPD file. If more than four are available, scroll through the list of pop-up menu items. Press the down arrow for each option that you want to configure, and then release on the value you want to assign to that option. When you are satisfied with the values, click **OK**.

➤ If the Adobe printer driver finds more than one PPD file that matches the selected printer, choose from the matching subset of all available PPD files. The Adobe printer driver displays a dialog box with the following options:

➤ Click the name of the PPD file to use, and then click **Select**. For information on the currently selected printer, click **Info**. If you want to view all available PPD files, click **Other**, and a complete list of the available PPDs will appear. Click the name of the PPD file you want to use, and then click **Select**.

➤ If the Adobe printer driver finds a match, but the PPD file does not support automatic configuration, manually configure the printer. A Configure dialog box appears. Assign values to the installable options, as described earlier in this list.

5. Click **Close** when you are done.

Once you have selected a PPD file, you can change it later following the steps described next or change it through the Illustrator Print dialog box (see the section describing the **Print** command, "Printing Composites and One-Color Documents," later in this chapter).

NOTE

Changing the Current PPD File

Use the **Setup** option in the Chooser dialog box to change the current PPD file for a selected printer after the initial setup.

To change the selected PPD file:

1. Select **Chooser** from the Apple menu, and click the **PSPrinter** icon. You may need to scroll down to locate the PSPrinter icon.

2. In the upper-right scroll pane of the Chooser, double-click the name of the PostScript printer for which you want to change the PPD file. Optionally, select the name of the printer, and then click **Setup**. The Setup dialog box appears.

3. Choose one of two options:

➤ To let the Adobe printer driver automatically select a new PPD file, click **Auto Setup** in the Setup dialog box. If the Adobe printer driver cannot automatically set up the printer, you must manually set it up. For more information, see the preceding section.

➤ To select a specific PPD file, click **Select PPD**. The Adobe printer driver displays a dialog box showing the PPD files that exist in the Printer Descriptions folder in the Extensions folder. Click the name of the PPD file that you want to use, and then click **Select**. If none of the PPD files seem to match your printer model, you can use the generic PPD, use a PPD file for another printer similar to yours, or cancel the operation. To use the generic PPD, click **Use Generic**. To select a similar printer's PPD file, click the name from the PPD files listed, and click **Select**. To cancel and return to the Setup dialog box, click **Cancel**.

Selecting a PPD for a Printer on Another System

You may wish to set up the driver to work with a printer that is turned off or not currently connected to the computer you are using, either directly or over the network. This feature, called Virtual Printer, can be handy if you are working on a portable computer, for example, and need to adjust the margins associated with the Page Size value or view a document via Print Preview or Page Layout. This feature is called *virtual* because it associates the document with the attributes of a specific printer, rather than with the physical device itself.

To select a PPD file when your computer is not connected to the desired printer:

1. Select **Chooser** from the Apple menu and click the **PSPrinter** icon. You may need to scroll down to locate the PSPrinter icon.

2. From the Type menu above the list of printers in the Chooser, choose **Virtual Printer**. The Adobe Virtual Printer Driver screen appears. When you first set up the Virtual Printer, the selected printer type is **Generic**.

3. Click **Setup**. The Setup dialog box appears.

4. Click **Select PPD**. The Adobe printer driver displays a dialog box showing the PPD files that exist in the Printer Descriptions folder in the Extensions folder. If you do not select a PPD, the Adobe printer driver uses the generic PPD.

5. Click the name of the PPD file that you want to use, and then click **Select**. If required, the driver displays a Configure dialog box that shows the installable options.

6. Manually configure Virtual Printer by scrolling through the list of pop-up menu items and pressing the down arrow for each option you want to configure. Release on the value you want to assign to that option. When you are satisfied with the values, click **OK**.

7. In the Setup dialog box, click **OK**, and then close the Chooser.

NOTE If Virtual Printer is unavailable in the Type menu in the Chooser, the correct version of the Chooser is probably not installed on the computer or is not being used. To set up a virtual printer, you must be running Chooser version 7.3 or higher. Make sure the correct version of the Chooser is installed in the Apple Menu Items folder of the System Folder. If the correct version is not installed, copy it from the installation disk.

Also, if you will be using the Virtual Printer feature to create and save PostScript files, Adobe suggests that you remove "Assistant Tool Box" from your Extensions and Preferences folders. If Assistant Tool Box is present and you choose to save a PostScript file, the message "This document cannot be printed at the current time on the printer "Virtual Printer" because the printer is not available on the Apple Talk network" will be displayed. However, pressing the **Print Later** button will allow your document to be saved.

Configuring Options in the PPD File

Some printers support additional installation options for which you can configure your printer. For information on configuring your printer, see your printer documentation. If you do change the configuration of your printer, you should notify the Adobe Printer Driver of the current set of installed options. To do so, use the **Configure** option.

To notify the Adobe printer driver of the installed options:

1. Select **Chooser** from the Apple menu and click the **PSPrinter** icon. You may need to scroll down to locate the PSPrinter icon.

2. In the upper-right scroll pane of the Chooser, double-click the name of the PostScript printer for which you want to change the PPD file. Optionally, select the name of the printer, and then click **Setup**. The Setup dialog box appears.

3. Click **Configure** in the Setup dialog box. The installable options for the selected PPD file appear. For example, for some printers, the amount of memory installed in the printer is configurable and can be upgraded (see step 4).

4. Select the value for the option to configure. If more than four options are available, scroll through the list of pop-up menu items, press the **down arrow** for each option that you want to configure, and then release on the value that you want to assign to that option.

5. When you have finished configuring the installable options, click **OK**. The Setup dialog box reappears.

6. Click **OK** to close the dialog box, then click the close box on the Chooser dialog box.

Changing the Page Setup

Illustrator's **File > Page Setup** command controls the page settings that determine how an artwork file will be printed. The **Page Setup** command lets you select the paper size, the reduction or enlargement percentage, the page orientation (tall or wide), and special printer effects, such as font substitution, smoothing, and faster bitmap printing. This command affects the printing of each page for the file in the active window. Here's how it works:

1. Choose **File > Page Setup** to display the Page Setup dialog box, which is specific to the printer driver you select with the Chooser. Figure 11.2 shows the Page Setup dialog box for the Adobe PostScript printer driver, which is used by most PostScript laser printers.

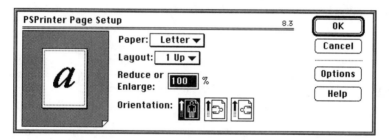

Figure 11.2 The Page Setup dialog box for the Adobe PostScript Printer 8.3 driver, recommended for use with Illustrator 6.0.

2. Make the following entries as needed:

➤ Select a size from the Paper drop-down menu to match the paper tray loaded in the printer. If your printer supports custom paper sizes, the **Custom** option is available in the Paper pop-up menu. If you select **Custom**, you can edit the dimensions of the page.

If you reconfigure the Adobe printer driver with a new printer that does not support the previously selected paper size or the **Custom** feature, the item **Other** is added to the Paper menu and selected as the default. Do not leave **Other** selected; select another Paper value, and click **OK**.

NOTE

➤ The page image option shows the size, arrangement, and appearance of the printed results. The page image changes to reflect the layout options chosen. The outer, solid rectangle represents the edge of the physical paper. The inner, dotted rectangle represents the boundaries of the area in which the Adobe printer driver will print and is called the *imageable area*.

For a listing of the dimensions of this image, click anywhere within the page image icon (see Figure 11.2). Dimensions include height and width of the paper size and the imageable area for the top, left, bottom, and right margins. Click a second time to view the values in alternate units (inches or millimeters). Click a third time to return to the page image.

➤ If the selected PPD allows you to select **Custom** as the Paper value and you do, you can edit the image values to reflect the size of your paper. Click the page image anywhere to display the numerical values of the default dimensions. Use the **Tab** key to move through the dimensions and select the field that you want to edit. Enter the new value in millimeters or inches. For more information, see the preceding section, "Paper."

NOTE

Although you can specify custom dimensions in millimeters or inches, the Adobe printer driver stores these values internally in points (one point equals 1/72 of an inch). You may notice a difference in reported dimensions because of the driver's internal conversion from millimeters or inches to points.

If you have selected **Custom** as a Paper value, two types of paper devices are possible: roll-fed or cut-sheet. The default dimensions of the paper image vary according to the type of paper device.

➤ For roll-fed devices, no margin dimensions are necessary because the imageable area is the same as the requested page size, and the margins are fixed at zero. Four numerical dimensions are possible: width, height, width offset, and height offset. The width shows the size of the page perpendicular to the direction of the paper device feed. The height is measured parallel to the direction of the paper device feed. The offsets are measured from the bottom-left edge of the device.

➤ For cut-sheet devices, the page image icon lets you set width, height, and the left, top, right, and bottom margins.

➤ The Layout pop-up menu offers choices of printing multiple pages or tiles 1-up, 2-up, 4-up, 6-up, 9-up, or 16-up (if the tiling option yields this many pages). For Illustrator documents, these options apply if the Artboard is larger than the paper size specified in the Page Setup dialog box and if **Tile Imageable Area** is selected in the Document Setup dialog box, as described later in this chapter. The Adobe printer driver adjusts the orientation of the physical page to best fit the orientation of the logical pages selected for printing. With the 2-up and 6-up options, the orientation of the physical page is opposite from the orientation of the logical page. In all modes but 1-up, lines appear around each document page arranged on the page of paper. Once you select a Layout value, the page image changes to reflect your selection.

➤ The **Reduce** or **Enlarge** setting lets you specify a percentage reduction or enlargement from 25 to 400%. If pages in the document are larger than the printer paper size, for example, a complete image is not printed. The Adobe printer driver does not automatically tile the print image—that is, the driver does not print an image over several pages.

➤ The **Orientation** setting lets you choose whether your artwork will be printed vertically (tall) or horizontally (wide) on the page. Different printer manufacturers may have different preferred rotation directions for landscape orientation. The PPD file of the selected printer usually specifies the direction in which pages are automatically rotated from portrait to landscape orientation. The two landscape buttons in the Page Setup dialog box indicate in which direction the Adobe printer driver will rotate portrait pages to a landscape position—clockwise or counterclockwise. The **counterclockwise** orientation option is usually the best choice if you want hole punches to appear at the top of your landscape page. You should print a test page to verify that the selected landscape option and the position of the three-holed paper in the printer's paper tray produce the desired results. If they do not, change the landscape option accordingly.

3. The **Options** button, when clicked, displays the Options dialog box, shown in Figure 11.3. Make entries as appropriate.

Visual Effects options let you:

➤ Flip the image vertically or horizontally, to print mirror images of the document.

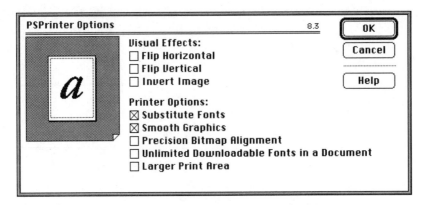

Figure 11.3 The Page Setup Options dialog box.

NOTE

If you have specified a layout value other than 1-up and an orientation value of landscape or alternate landscape, you cannot use the **Flip Horizontal** or **Flip Vertical** options of the Options dialog box. Also, to print a document upside down, turn on both the **Flip Horizontal** and **Flip Vertical** checkboxes.

➤ Invert, or reverse, the image (i.e., print a negative).

➤ The Printer Options—Font Substitution, and Smooth Graphics—have no effect on Illustrator files. You can leave them all checked, which are their default settings.

➤ The **Precision Bitmap Alignment** option aligns screen-resolution bitmap printing more precisely by way of a 4% reduction.

➤ The option of using unlimited downloadable fonts in a document is not recommended when printing Illustrator documents. It is normally applicable when you use a large number of fonts in a document and want them sent to the printer as needed to print, but your printer has limited memory installed.

➤ The option of using a larger print area than normal (which will reduce the allowable number of downloadable fonts) has no effect on Illustrator files. The availability of this option depends on the PPD and paper type that you select and whether the selected printer supports the larger print area.

4. You can also choose **Help** from the Page Setup dialog box. Click on the **Help** button to get details on how Page Setup options affect printing.

NOTE

To save the settings you specify in the Options dialog box as default values, when exiting the dialog box click **OK** while holding down the **Option** key.

Changing the Document Setup

The **File > Document Setup** command lets you define the size and orientation of the Artboard—which might be different from the paper size defined in the Page Setup dialog box as just described—opt to print patterns (or not), set tiling options, and set output options that can affect how paths and gradients are sent to the printer.

NOTE

You can accept Illustrator's default for these options every time you start a new document, or you can change the defaults by opening the Illustrator Startup file, which is in the Plug-ins folder in the Illustrator 6.0 program folder, changing the settings, and then saving the file under the same name. See additional tips in Chapter 6 on changing the startup file.

To define the Document Setup options, follow these steps:

1. Open the Illustrator document you wish to affect, start a new document, or open the Illustrator Startup file if you intend to change the defaults for all new documents in the future.

2. Choose **File > Document Setup** (see Figure 11.4).

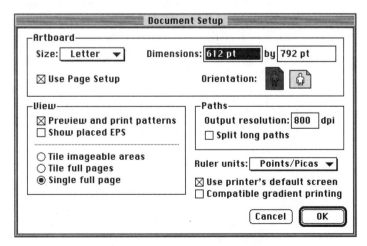

Figure 11.4 The Document Setup dialog box.

3. In the Document Setup dialog box, select the desired options:

➤ Choose an Artboard size from the pop-up menu, enter your own custom dimensions, or click **Use Page Setup** to copy the current Page Setup specifications.

SHORTCUT

In this dialog box—or any option that let you enter numerical values—you can simply type numbers that correspond with the currently shown measurement system, or you can override the current measurement system and enter values using any measurement system you like by adding the measurement abbreviations after the numeric values: *pt* for points, *in* for inches, or *mm* for millimeters.

➤ Select **Tall** or **Wide** orientation by clicking on the appropriate icon. This does not change the paper orientation selection in the Page Setup dialog box—it only affects how the Artboard is oriented on the screen. You could print a business card using wide orientation (252 points wide by 144 points tall) on letter paper that prints tall from the printer (612 points wide and 792 points tall).

The View options affect how the page is displayed on the screen, and some of these options also affect how it prints:

➤ Select **Preview and Print Patterns** if you want patterns to display on the screen in Preview modes and print out. When this option is not selected, patterns display as gray fills on the screen and in draft printings.

If the Document Setup dimensions differ from the Page Setup dimensions, you can set the tiling options to view and print parts of pages. Tiling options include **Tile Imageable Areas**, **Tile Full Pages**, and **Single Full Page**:

➤ The **Tile Imageable Areas** option partitions the Artboard into printable areas without page margins. The entire image will print in tiles, with no part "lost" in the printer's nonimageable margins.

➤ The **Tile Full Pages** option displays the page boundaries as they would print in tiles to cover the entire Artboard area. Inside each page boundary a second outline indicates the printable image boundary, as determined by the limitations of the selected output device. Elements that appear in the margin will not print.

➤ Select **Single Full Page** to view the dotted outline of exactly one printable page—the size specified in the Page Setup dialog box—to be displayed on the Artboard one at a time.

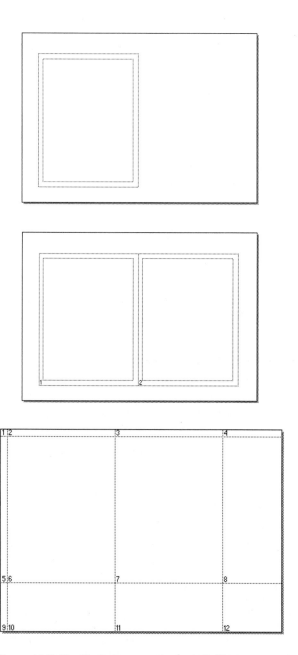

Figure 11.5 The **Single Page** option (top), **Full Pages** option
(middle), and **Tile Imageable Area** option (bottom).

NOTE

To make the tiling guides visible or invisible on the screen, choose **View > Show Page Tiling** or **View > Hide Page Tiling**.

➤ You can set the output resolution assigned to paths. This doesn't actually change the output resolution of the printer, but it affects how much smoothing Illustrator imposes on a path during printing. The default output resolution is set at **800 dpi** (dots per inch) for optimal print quality and speed. Changing the Output resolution is one way to change the flatness of a curve—the lower the output resolution, the greater the flatness. Changing flatness through the Riders file is described later in this chapter.

NOTE

The Output Resolution value you enter in the Document Setup dialog box affects any new objects you add to the artwork, but the output resolution of existing objects is not affected (although you can change any object's output resolution through the **Object > Attributes** command).

➤ Turn the **Split Long Paths** option on only if you experience problems printing a document containing long, complicated paths. The default setting for this option is off. If you use this option, you should also enter the value for your printer's output resolution in the Output resolution field (described earlier). When this option is turned on, Illustrator checks the path length every time you save or print an image. If the path length exceeds the capabilities of your printer's memory, Illustrator breaks the path into pieces. This option does not affect stroked paths, compound paths, or masks.

WARNING

Note that splitting paths changes your artwork. Once the paths have been split, you must either work with the separate shapes or rejoin the paths manually. For this reason, you should always keep a copy of your original artwork if you plan to use the **Split Long Paths** option. When you save the document, make sure you save a copy with the **Split Long Paths** option turned off.

➤ You can select a unit of measure to be displayed on the rulers and in dialog boxes by choosing **Points and Picas**, **Inches**, or **Millimeters** from the drop-down menu.

➤ Normally, Illustrator ignores the default screen for low-resolution printers (less than 600 dpi) and uses Adobe Screens to enhance the output of gradients. If you know you want to keep the printer's default screen (e.g., if the printer uses special screening such as stochastic screening) you can select **Use Printer's Default Screen** to have Illustrator extract any line screen values from the PPD selected through the Print dialog box.

➤ If you are printing to an older PostScript Level 1 imagesetter that has trouble printing gradients, select **Compatible Gradient Printing** to speed up printing or enable printing gradients that otherwise fail to print. If your printer or imagesetter does not have trouble with gradients, do *not* select this option—it can actually slow printing on Level 2 imagesetters.

4. Click **OK** to close the dialog box and implement the changes, or click **Cancel** to close the dialog box without making any changes.

NOTE

If you change the Artboard size after starting the artwork, you may have to select and move all the existing artwork to match the new Artboard boundaries. Illustrator maintains the center of the Artboard as the constant and aligns the print area (defined by the Page Setup paper selection) to the top-left corner of the Artboard. See Figure 11.6.

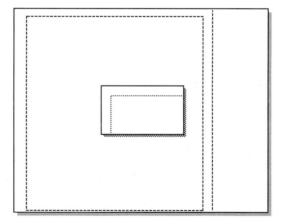

Figure 11.6 Document Setup changed from letter size, wide orientation (outer drop-shadowed rectangle), to business-card size, also wide orientation (inner drop-shadowed rectangle). Dotted lines show Illustrator's automatic indicators for the limits of the print area in both cases, with Page Setup set to **Tall** orientation.

Changing the Print Area

The Illustrator drawing area is a square measuring up to 120 by 120 inches. When you print a file, Illustrator tiles, or subdivides, it into pages that match the paper size used in your printer. Normally, the top-left corner of the paper's printable area is automatically positioned just inside the top-left corner of the Artboard, but the Page tool lets you change this and specify where the pages break. You also use the Page tool to control the tiling of an Illustrator file that is too big for one sheet of paper onto several printed pages.

Here's how it works:

1. Choose the **Page** tool by clicking its icon in the Toolbox.

2. The mouse pointer changes to a + in the active window. When you hold down the mouse button a dotted rectangle appears, marking the area that can be printed on a single 8.5-by-11-inch page.

3. Use the mouse to drag the rectangle to define where you wish the pages to break, as shown in Figure 11.7.

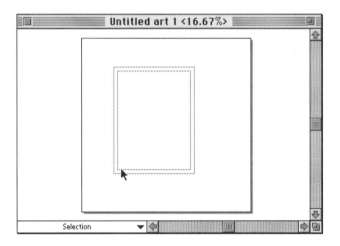

Figure 11.7 Drag the dotted rectangle to set page breaks.

The Page tool is easiest to use in Fit In Window view (choose **View > Fit In Window** or press **Command+M**). If the **Tile Imageable Areas** option is selected in the Document Setup dialog box, Illustrator displays page numbers at the lower-left corner of each page boundary on the screen.

N O T E

Creating Custom Crop Marks

If you select the **Use Default Marks** option in the Separations Setup dialog box, described later in this chapter, Illustrator will automatically print *crop marks* — printer's marks that show how a page is to be trimmed—that mark the edges of the artwork's invisible, nonprinting *bounding box*. You can define your own crop marks to define a trim size that is different from the artwork size or to define crop marks around several different images on a page that might be printed in one run (to save time, paper, film, or service bureau charges).

To print crop marks that match the edges of the artwork's bounding box, select **Use Default Marks** in the Separations Setup dialog box as described later in this chapter. The next two sections describe using the **Object > Crop Marks** submenu and using the **Filter > Create > Trim Marks** filter.

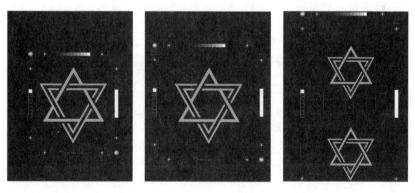

Figure 11.8 A color separation printed with crop marks: (a) generated through the Separation Setup dialog box marking the artwork's bounding box edges; (b) created using **Object > Crop Marks** with a custom rectangle to extend the crop marks; (c) created using the trim marks filter to add crop marks around several objects, in addition to the normal default marks.

Defining a Custom Trim Area

You use the **Object > Crop marks** command when you want to change the bounding box that defines where crop marks and other printer's marks will be printed. You use this option when:

➤ You want the crop marks to be further from the edges of the actual artwork than the normal position defined by the bounding box that frames the artwork exactly. For example, you have created artwork that fits in a

5-by-8-inch bounding box for an ad that is to be trimmed to 5.5-by-8.5 inches.

➤ You want the crop marks to match a page size, regardless of how the artwork itself is positioned on the page. For example, you want the final page trimmed to letter size, but you will be printing on a 12-inch-wide roll of film.

➤ You want to create crop marks that will be visible when you print a composite for one-color printing. (Additional printer's marks are usually only available when printing color separations.)

To define custom crop marks that match the Page Setup specifications (not the Artboard) or to define your own rectangular trim area, follow these steps:

1. Define the trim area in either of two ways:

➤ If the trim area is to be the same as the imageable area derived from the File > Page Setup dialog box entries, you have selected the **Single Full Page** option in the File > Document Setup dialog box, and you will be printing the final version on paper that is actually larger than the current page setup size (for example, printing letter-size sheets on rolls of film in an imagesetter), you can use the **Object > Crop Marks > Make** command without first drawing a bounding rectangle. If you have selected **Tile Full Pages** or **Tile Imageable Areas**, the **Object > Crop Marks > Make** command is unavailable unless a rectangle is selected (see next bullet).

➤ If the trim size is not related to the Page Setup specifications, draw a rectangle to define the boundary of your artwork or the trim area.

2. With the rectangle selected, choose **Object > Crop Marks > Make**. Crop marks then replace the selected rectangle.

3. Once you have set crop marks, you cannot select them. However, you can:

➤ Delete existing crop marks by choosing **Object > Crop Marks > Release**. This converts crop marks back to a rectangle that defines the bounding area of your artwork.

➤ Replace crop marks by drawing a new bounding rectangle and choosing **Object > Crop Marks > Make** again.

4. When printing color separations, choose **Use Default Marks** in the Separations Setup dialog box to print printer's marks that match the newly defined crop marks. The crop marks will also be printed when you print a composite of the artwork. Note, however, that if you print separations and do not choose **Use Default Marks**, the crop marks will not be printed.

Using the Trim Marks Filter

The **Filter > Create > Trim Marks** command creates lines to indicate where a printed image should be trimmed. The marks can be created around a single object or around multiple objects. The trim marks created by this filter do not replace crop markss created with the **Object > Crop Marks > Make** command, nor do they affect the bounding box (or printable image area) around the artwork or replace the bounding box crop marks created through the Separations Setup dialog box.

This filter is useful when you want to create a number of crop-marked objects on one page, as when you are creating a sheet of business cards to be printed and trimmed.

1. Select the object or set of objects in the Illustrator document you want to be marked with a single set of trim marks.

2. Choose **Filter > Create > Trim Marks** to create trim marks based on the smallest rectangular shape that could frame the imageable area of the selected object(s).

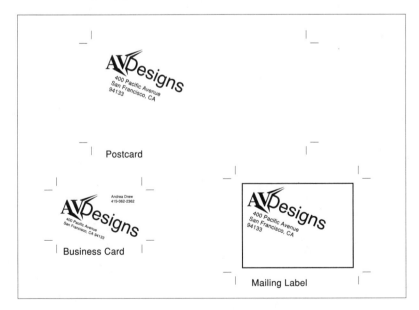

Figure 11.9 Trim marks created by **Filter > Create > Trim Marks**.

NOTE

If you want the object(s) to "bleed" beyond the trim marks, draw a rectangle that marks the area you want to trim to and select only that rectangle before choosing **Filter > Create > Trim Marks**. You can then delete the rectangle or set the fill and stroke to **None**.

Also, it's a good idea to select the layer onto which you wish to position the trim marks after creating them. See the description of the Layers palette in Chapter 10.

Printing Composites and One-Color Documents

The **File > Print** command (**Command+P**) prints the artwork in the active window to the printer that has been designated by the Chooser (see **Apple > Chooser** command):

1. Choose **File > Print** to display the Print dialog box, which is specific to the printer you select with the Chooser. Figure 11.10 shows the Print dialog box for a PostScript printer.

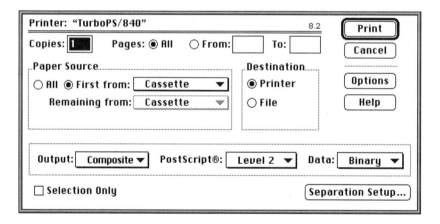

Figure 11.10 The Print dialog box for a PostScript printer.

2. Make entries as desired:

➤ The Copies setting lets you specify the number of copies you wish to print.

➤ The Pages settings let you print all pages (by selecting **All**) or a range of pages (by selecting **From** and **To** and specifying the range; for example, from **1** to **3**). When **Tile Imageable Area** is selected in the Document Setup dialog box, the page numbers are shown at the corners of pages bordered with dotted lines on the screen display of the artwork, as shown in Figure 11.11.

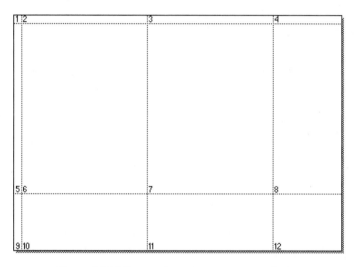

Figure 11.11 Page numbers shown on screen display.

➤ The Paper Source settings let you choose paper cassette or manual feed. By clicking on the **Paper Cassette** option, you choose to use the paper source in the printer's paper tray. If you click on the **Manual Feed** option, the system will prompt you to feed paper to the printer one page at a time. You can also opt to print only the first page from one source (for example, to manually feed special paper as the first sheet and all the other pages from another source, such as the cassette tray).

➤ The Output drop-down menu lets you choose to print a composite—a single sheet with all color elements printed as one image—or create separations. (The **Separations** option is available only if you have already set up for color separations by clicking the **Separations Setup** button in the Print dialog box or by choosing **File > Separations Setup** as described later in this chapter.)

➤ You can choose **PostScript Level 1** or **Level 2** from the PostScript drop-down menu (see descriptions in Chapter 7).

➤ You can choose to send binary or ASCII data to the printer. Choose **Binary** if you are printing from a Macintosh (see "Printing a Document to Disk" later in this chapter).

➤ Choose **Selection Only** if you want to print only the objects that were selected on the Artboard before you chose the **Print** command.

➤ If you select **Printer** as the destination, the document will be queued to print on the printer currently selected through the Chooser. If you select **File** as the destination, a second dialog box is displayed, and you can set more options to create a printable PostScript file on disk (described later in this chapter).

NOTE

The default value is normally **Printer**. If you choose a different destination, once that print job is complete the value is restored to **Printer**. If you are setting up a virtual printer, however, the value is always **File**.

3. Making one of the following choices yields another dialog box:

➤ Click **Print** to start printing the document to the printer. A dialog box will be displayed indicating the progress of the printing—either to the printer itself or to the PrintMonitor (if Background Printing is active).

➤ The **Print** button changes to **Save** if you select **File** as the destination. Clicking **Save** results in a dialog box for selecting the destination of the file, along with additional options, described later in this chapter.

➤ Click the **Options** button to displays a second dialog box for setting printing options (described next).

➤ Click **Separation Setup** if you want to print color separations or if you want to set up printer's marks and other options described later in this chapter.

➤ You can also choose **Help** from the Print dialog box. Click on the **Help** button to get more information on printer settings and options that affect your printed output. Help will display only if the Help files are loaded on your system.

➤ Click **Cancel** to close the dialog box without printing.

Selecting Additional Printing Options

The Print Options dialog box, accessed by clicking the **Options** button in the File > Print dialog box, offers the following additional options in printing:

Some options that you can set in the Print Options dialog box vary from printer to printer. These differences include duplex printing, printer resolution settings, image enhancement functions, and so on. The availability of these options depends on the selected printer model and the way in which the driver is configured for that printer.

NOTE

Print Options   8.2   [**OK**]

Cover Page: ● None   ○ Before   ○ After Document   [**Cancel**]

Print: [Color/Grayscale ▼]

PostScript™ Errors: [Print Detailed Report ▼]   [**Help**]

   IET: [Printer's default ▼]

Resolution: [Printer's default ▼]   [**Save**]

Figure 11.12 The Print Options dialog box.

➤ You can choose to print a cover page as either the first or last page. The cover page will contain the user name (that you have entered in the Chooser), the application you used to print the document, the document name, the date and time of printing, printer name, and number of pages in the job. You will find this feature useful in identifying your printouts when several computers share the same printer over an AppleTalk network.

➤ The Print drop-down menu lets you specify whether and how to print the document in color:

➤ The **Color/Grayscale** option (the default) provides for color printing and, for monochrome printers, maps colors to equivalent PostScript grayscale shades. Color/Grayscale imaging generally produces better results than does black-and-white, even on monochrome printers.

➤ The **Black and White** option limits printing to monochrome only. Use this option if you want the same output as you used to obtain using the Apple LaserWriter 7.x printer driver with black-and-white printers. Most users will not use this option, which is provided only for historical purposes.

➤ The **Calibrated Color/Grayscale** option matches as closely as possible the colors on the printed page to the colors on your monitor screen. This feature uses the device-independent color capabilities built into each Adobe PostScript Level 2 printer and is available only on Level 2 printers. Use this option if you need more precise color than Color/Grayscale can provide.

➤ The PostScript Errors drop-down menu lets you specify the level of error reporting for PostScript errors that may occur during the course of printing:

➤ The **No Special Reporting** option (the default) provides no detailed information about the PostScript error.

➤ The **Summarize on Screen** option displays a message describing on the screen the nature of the PostScript error. This feature is available only when background printing is turned off.

➤ The **Print Detailed Report** option prints a report describing the PostScript error to the printer.

➤ The Printer's default value for the printer-specific values IET and resolution tells the driver to use the values that have been manually set on the printer's front panel.

NOTE The settings for Cover Page, Print (Color/Grayscale), and PostScript Errors remain intact from document to document. The values for printer-specific settings—those that appear below the dotted line in the Print Options dialog box—can be saved as Adobe printer driver software defaults. To save these values as defaults, click the **Save** button on the Print Options dialog box. Each time you print to this printer, the Adobe printer driver returns to the default settings.

➤ Click **OK** to close this dialog box and return to the Print dialog box.

➤ You can also choose **Help** from the Print dialog box. Click on the **Help** button to get more information on printer settings and options that affect your printed output. Help will display only if the Help files are loaded on your system.

➤ Click **Cancel** to close the dialog box without printing.

Printing Color Separations

6.0 NEW FEATURE Illustrator 6.0 introduces the ability to print color separations directly through Illustrator's **File > Print** command. (Earlier versions required you to go through Adobe Separator, a separate application that Adobe packaged with earlier versions of Adobe Illustrator.) This section describes how to print color separations from Illustrator.

1. First, create an Illustrator document that uses more than one color—tints of the same color can still be printed on composites and do not require color separations.

   ➤ If you will be printing spot color separations, make sure the document uses only the spot colors you intend to print and no process colors that are defined only by their CMYK values. The document cannot contain any gradient blends between colors, only gradients from a custom color to white or black.

   ➤ If you will be printing four-color process separations, the document can include custom colors, but you must select **Convert Custom to Process** in the Separations Setup dialog box, described next.

   ➤ If you will be printing on a five- or six-color press, you can include two custom colors plus any number of CMYK process colors. Do *not* select **Convert Custom to Process** in the Separations Setup dialog box.

2. Display the Separations Setup dialog box, either by choosing **File > Separations Setup** or by choosing **File > Print** and clicking **Separations Setup** in the Print dialog box.

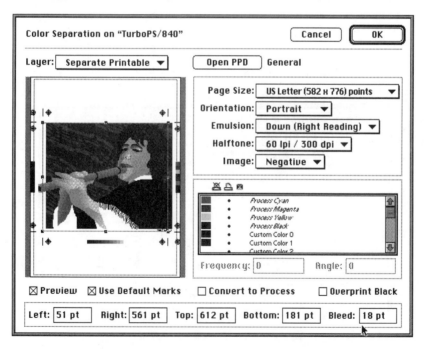

Figure 11.13 The Separations Setup dialog box.

3. In the Separations Setup dialog box, it's a good idea to select the appropriate PPD before making any other entries, since that selection could affect some of the available options. This is usually only necessary if you are setting up to print color separations from a printer other than the one currently selected through the Chooser (for example, if you are preparing a document to be sent to a service bureau).

➤ Click **Open PPD** to display a dialog box that lets you choose a PostScript Printer Description (PPD) file for the printer you are using. PPD files contain information about the printer's dot resolution, the available page sizes, whether the printer supports color output, and the acceptable screen settings. Find the PPD folder and double-click on that name in the dialog box. The name of the printer file is a cryptic abbreviation of the full name and model number of the printer.

➤ These files are usually stored in the Printer Description folder, in the Extensions folder, which in turn is in the System folder under System 7.

➤ Additional PPD files are stored in the Sample PPD folder, which is created when you install Adobe Illustrator 6.0 and stored in the Utilities folder in the Adobe Illustrator 6.0 program folder.

Once you have chosen a PPD file, Adobe Illustrator continues to use that PPD file unless you specify a new one.

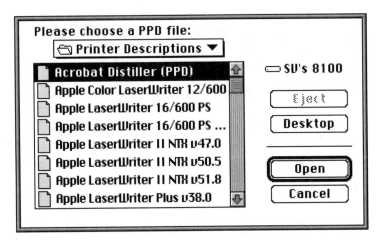

Figure 11.14 Dialog box asking for a printer description file.

4. After you choose the PPD file that matches the printer you are using, the Separation Setup dialog box returns. You can accept the default settings to print all four process color separations or you can choose different options as described in the following steps. The following options are available in the Separation Setup dialog box:

➤ The top line displays the name of the printer that is currently selected in the Chooser. To change printers, choose **Chooser** from the Apple menu and select the appropriate printer from the list in the Chooser window.

➤ The **Layer** drop-down menu lets you control which layers will be printed. If you set up layers in the document (see Chapter 10) and assigned some layers to be invisible or not to print, then in the Separations Setup dialog box you can opt to separate the printable layers only, separate the visible layers only, or separate all the layers.

➤ The **Page Size** drop-down menu lists page sizes available for the selected printer (as identified in the PPD file) you have chosen. The dimensions of the printable area are shown next to each page size on the menu, and these dimensions include the limits for the registration marks, color labels, and crop marks that are printed.

```
Custom

A4 (564 x 822) points
B5 (479 x 705) points
A4 Small (540 x 780) points
US Legal (582 x 992) points
Page Size: ✓US Letter (582 x 776) points
US Letter Small (552 x 730) points
```

NOTE

If your printer allows variable page sizes, a custom page size option will be displayed on the page size menu as **Other**, and you will be able to enter custom dimensions and offset. You will also be able to print the page transversely (rotated 90 degrees). You can use the last two options to avoid wasting film on phototypesetters.

➤ There are two orientation options. In **Portrait** mode, the top of the image is printed parallel to the short edge of the paper. In **Landscape** mode, the top of the image is printed parallel to the long edge of the paper.

NOTE

Note that orientation affects the position of the image on the page (as defined by the Page tool), whereas the **Transverse** option available on some printers through the **Page Size** option affects the orientation of that page (as defined in the Illustrator document) on the printout paper (as defined through the **Page Size** option).

➤ There are two emulsion options. **Emulsion Up (Right Reading)** means that any text in the image is readable when the printed paper or the chemical-treated side of the film is facing you. **Emulsion Down (Right Reading)** means that the text is readable when the paper or film is facing away from you. Normally you would choose **Emulsion Down (Right Reading)** only when printing to a transparent film. When printing to clear film, the emulsion side is dull; the shiny side is the base.

| Up (Right Reading) |
| ✓Down (Right Reading) |

➤ The **Halftone** drop-down menu shows the screen ruling of the halftone pattern used to print the separations, in halftone dots per inch, stated as lines per inch (lpi). The available choices vary depending on the PPD file you have opened. If you are printing to a high-resolution device, the screen angles for the four process colors and the custom color are listed in parentheses on the pop-up menu in the following order: cyan, magenta, yellow, black, and custom color.

NOTE

Note that as the screen ruling increases, the halftone dots are less noticeable, but there is a trade-off between screen ruling and the available number of gray shades. The number of gray shades per screen ruling is determined by the resolution of your printer.

| 75 lpi / 635 dpi |
| 90 lpi / 635 dpi |
| 90 lpi / 1270 dpi |
| 90 lpi / 2540 dpi |
| 112 lpi / 1270 dpi |
| 112 lpi / 2540 dpi |
| 120 lpi / 2540 dpi |
| 128 lpi / 1270 dpi |
| 128 lpi / 2540 dpi |
| ✓150 lpi / 2540 dpi |

➤ There are two image options: **Positive** or **Negative**. Positive images print exactly as shown in preview on the screen. Negative images reverse dark and light areas. You can save a step in offset printing by printing negative separations directly to film.

➤ A scrolling list of possible color separations lets you choose the type of separations to be printed. When you print individual separations, the color, screen frequency, and angle are appended to the file name on the separation negative. Choose options in any of the following ways:

➤ To select individual process color separations, click in the second column (under the Printer icon) to display a black dot next to the appropriate process color.

➤ To choose *not* to print a selected color separation, click in the first column (below the No Print icon) to display a black dot next to the color name.

➤ To select individual custom color separations, make sure **Convert to Process** is *not* selected and then click in the second column (under the Printer icon) to display a black dot next to the appropriate custom color in the scrolling list of custom colors.

➤ To convert an individual custom color to process color, click below the third column (under the CMYK symbol) to display a black dot next to the custom color name.

➤ Select **Convert to Process** to convert all custom colors to process color separations. The custom color names then appears in gray to indicate that it will be converted to process colors.

➤ When a specific color is selected, the frequency and angle set up for that separation is displayed below the scrolling list. You can change these values if you like, but it's not recommended unless you know exactly what you're doing.

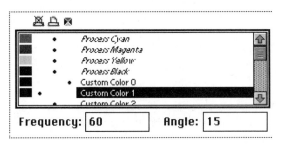

➤ If the **Preview** option is selected, you can see the artwork in the preview image area at the left of the dialog box. You can manually position the image within the print area by dragging the image.

➤ If **Use Default Marks** is selected, trim marks automatically snap to the corners of the bounding box. In addition, eight registration marks are printed to help align the plates, plus two star targets, a progressive color bar, a black overprint color bar, a gradient tint bar, a set of trim marks, and a label on each separation, in their default positions. These are guides for the commercial printer.

➤ Click **Convert to Process** if the document includes custom colors and you intend to print only four-color process separations. All custom colors will be printed in their CMYK components. It does not actually change the color assignments in the artwork itself.

➤ Click **Overprint Black** to force all nonprocess black elements to overprint, thereby eliminating knockout under black elements.

➤ The bottom line in the Separations Setup dialog box shows the positions of the edges of the bounding box relative to the zero point of the print area—that is, the lower-left corner of the paper or film—and the distance allowed for bleed beyond the edges as defined by the default crop marks. Changing these values causes the default marks to move toward or away from the zero point, but it does not move the art, *per se*. You might change these values to force a bleed or to get an exact dimension, if it is not the same as the dimensions set up in the Document Setup dialog box.

5. Click **OK** to close the dialog box and define the separations. If you came to the Separations Setup dialog box from the Print dialog box, the Print dialog box will be displayed again, ready for your next entries as described next.

6. Choose **File > Print** if the Print dialog box is not already displayed, and choose **Separations** from the Output drop-down menu if you want to print separations. If you choose **Composite**, the default marks will be printed if the paper size is smaller than the area required by the printer's marks.

Separating Illustrator Documents from Other Applications

Although it's no longer necessary, you might still choose to print color separations from another application, instead of directly from Illustrator. If that's the case, follow these steps:

1. Use Adobe Illustrator to create an illustration and apply one or more colors (other than black and white).

2. Save the file in EPS format.

3. From the Macintosh desktop, double-click on the **Adobe Separator 5.0** application icon to start it (or whatever application you are using for the separations).

Adobe Separator™ 5.0

4. In the dialog box that appears next, find and double-click the name of the document you wish to print.

Printing a Document to a Disk File

As an alternative to printing your document on your printer, you can save a PostScript language description of your document as a disk file. PostScript language descriptions of your documents can be useful for creating document archives or printing documents without using the application that created them (at a service bureau, for example).

PostScript is a page description language that is built into many desktop printers and virtually all high-end printing systems. Because it is built into so many printers, most Macintosh, Windows, and UNIX applications can create PostScript files for printing. Adobe recommends that you create PostScript files with the Apple LaserWriter 8 or Adobe PostScript printer driver. The Adobe Illustrator 6.0 Deluxe CD-ROM includes the Adobe PostScript 8.3 driver, which is recommended for printing from Illustrator 6.0.

The following instructions assume you are using one of these printer drivers. Chapter 7 included the steps for creating a printable PostScript file from any application on a Macintosh. These next steps and tips are specific to creating printable PostScript files from Illustrator documents.

To create a PostScript file that you can print by downloading the code to the printer (that is, without needing Illustrator):

1. Open the Chooser from the Apple menu, and choose a PostScript printer.

2. Open the Illustrator document you want to print to disk.

3. Choose **File > Print**.

4. If you selected **Tile Imageable Area** in the Document Setup dialog box and have created a multipage document, but you don't want to print every page, enter the number of the page you want to print in both the **From** and **To** boxes.

5. Select **File** as the destination.

6. Select from the three pop-up menu options:

   ➤ **Output > Composite** or **Separation**. The **Separation** option requires Separation Setup, accessed through the **Option** button in the lower-right corner of the Print dialog box.

   ➤ **Level 1** or **Level 2 PostScript** (see descriptions in Chapter 7). Select the **Level 1 Compatible** option for maximum flexibility. The **Level 2 Only** option specifies compatibility with Level 2 printers and speeds printing. However, PostScript files created with this option will most likely not print correctly on a PostScript Level 1 printer. Use this setting for all Level 2 printers.

   ➤ **ASCII** or **Binary** format. Data encoding affects size—a binary image file is half the size of an ASCII image file and takes half the time to transmit if you are printing through a network. Both AppleTalk and Ethernet support binary transmissions, but check with your service bureau to see what their system will support. Many PC systems do not support binary data transmissions.

7. Click **Save** to display the Save PostScript file dialog box (Figure 11.16).

8. Select the disk and folder where you want to save the PostScript file and enter a name for the file. By convention, PostScript filenames end with .ps (for example, Logo.ps), but this extension will change depending on the formatting option you choose in the next step.

9. Select from the following options:

   ➤ Format options. If you will be opening and printing an Illustrator file containing placed images exclusively from Adobe Illustrator, you can save the file in **PostScript Job** format. This yields Adobe printer driver's PostScript output exactly as it would have been sent to the output device and gives you the most compact file format. The **PJL Job** format is available only when you select a printer that supports PJL. This option lets you save the document in the HP Printer Job Language. If you save the document in PJL, it will print correctly only on a printer that supports PJL.

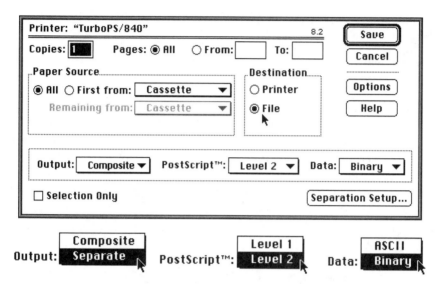

Figure 11.15 Illustrator's Print dialog box with **File** selected.

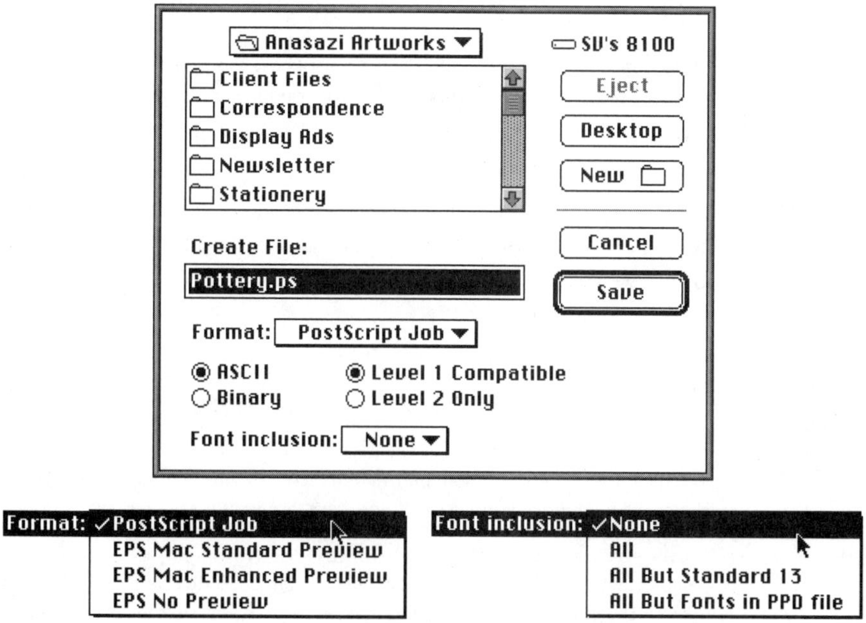

Figure 11.16 Illustrator's PostScript file dialog box
offers additional Format and Font Inclusion options.

NOTE

The other three options—**EPS No Preview, EPS Mac Standard Preview**, and **EPS Mac Enhanced Preview**—are mainly applicable when saving documents from other applications into EPS format so they can be viewed when placed in other documents as EPS artwork. These options are available for Illustrator documents, too, but it's usually more convenient to save Illustrator documents in EPS formats using the **File > Save** command options.

➤ Font Inclusion. Select **None, All** (that is, all fonts that are used in the document and are available on the host Macintosh), **All But Standard 13** (that is, all the fonts except the core set of 13 standard fonts that most PostScript printers support—Courier, Symbol, Helvetica, Times Roman, and their variations, such as bold and oblique), **All But Standard 35** (that is, all the fonts except the set of 35 standard fonts that many PostScript printers support—the standard 13 fonts and Avant Garde, Bookman, Helvetica Narrow, New Century Schoolbook, Palatino, Zapf Chancery, Zapf Dingbats, and their variations), or **All But Fonts in PPD File** (if you set up a PPD file for a printer, one of the things it does is read the fonts in the printer). If you always print to the same printer from the same system with the same PPD file set up for it, you could use the last option to make the file smaller.

NOTE

PPD File option is recommended. If you do not know the printer on which the document will be printed, the **All But Standard 13** option is recommended.

10. Click **Save**. The file is saved to the specified file and file folder, and you are returned to your application. All save options return to the default values every time you select **Save**.

NOTE

Including fonts in a printable file will increase the file size significantly. You might find it more efficient to simply install the needed fonts on the system and download them before printing the file.

No cover page or error handler information is saved with the PostScript language description of your document, even if you have previously selected these print and page setup options.

Also, when printing an Illustrator 6.0 document from an earlier version of Illustrator, you might lose some of the printing and text enhancements built in to Illustrator 6.0. To avoid this, either prepare a printable PostScript file as described here or use the **File > Save** command to save the file in EPS format, and then use **File > Place** to *import* it into the earlier version for printing.

Editing Linescreen Information in a PPD File

PostScript Printer Description (PPD) files contain specific information on the capabilities and characteristics of PostScript printers. This information includes the page sizes that a given device can output and some of the screen angles and frequencies the printer supports. Adobe Illustrator uses the information in PPD files in the printing process. In certain situations you may want to edit a PPD file to add or modify halftone screen angle and frequency information.

WARNING   It's not likely you will need to change this information unless the commercial printer you use on a regular basis requests specific linescreen values that are different from the defaults for your imagesetter. Remember that for individual documents you can set the frequency and screen angle for individual colors through the Separation Setup dialog box, but even this is discouraged unless you know what you're doing.

Many PPD files are included with Adobe Illustrator 6.0. PPD files are normally stored in the PPDs folder, located in the Utilities folder in the Illustrator program folder. If you do not find one that corresponds to your printing device, contact your printer manufacturer.

NOTE   Be sure you update the correct PPD file. If you are using Adobe Illustrator with the Adobe PS Printer 8.0 printer driver or the Apple LaserWriter 8.0 driver, Illustrator will automatically set its default folder to the Printer Descriptions folder that these drivers automatically create within the System 7 Extensions folder (which is in the System folder). If this folder does not exist, Illustrator will default to the PPD folder within the Illustrator 6.0 folder.

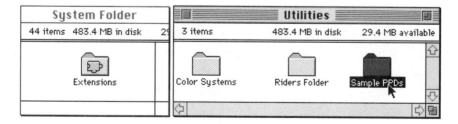

To edit an existing set of linescreen information in a PPD file:

1. Using a text editor, open the PPD file that corresponds to your printing device.

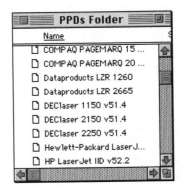

2. Search for groups of lines near the end of the file that are similar to the following:

```
*% For 132 lpi / 2540 dpi

*ColorSepScreenAngle ProcessBlack.132lpi.2540dpi/132 lpi / 2540 dpi: "45.0"

*ColorSepScreenAngle CustomColor.132lpi.2540dpi/132 lpi / 2540 dpi: "45.0"

*ColorSepScreenAngle ProcessCyan.132lpi.2540dpi/132 lpi / 2540 dpi: "18.4349"

*ColorSepScreenAngle ProcessMagenta.132lpi.2540dpi/132 lpi / 2540 dpi: "71.565"

*ColorSepScreenAngle ProcessYellow.132lpi.2540dpi/132 lpi / 2540 dpi: "0.0"

*ColorSepScreenFreq ProcessBlack.132lpi.2540dpi/132 lpi / 2540 dpi: "119.737"

*ColorSepScreenFreq CustomColor.132lpi.2540dpi/132 lpi / 2540 dpi: "119.737"

*ColorSepScreenFreq ProcessCyan.132lpi.2540dpi/132 lpi / 2540 dpi: "133.871"

*ColorSepScreenFreq ProcessMagenta.132lpi.2540dpi/132 lpi / 2540 dpi: "133.871"

*ColorSepScreenFreq ProcessYellow.132lpi.2540dpi/132 lpi / 2540 dpi: "127.0"
```

There will be several groups of lines such as these. Each group will correspond to a particular linescreen frequency and printer resolution combination in the Adobe Illustrator Halftone pop-up menu.

3. Locate the linescreen information that matches the linescreen frequency and printer resolution combination you wish to modify.

4. Change the screen angles at the end of each line starting with ***ColorSep ScreenAngle**. Only edit the values within quotation marks. Be sure to follow whole numbers with a decimal point and a zero. For example, to enter 45 degrees, type **45.0**.

5. Change the screen frequencies at the end of each line starting with ***Color SepScreenFreq**. These values are in lines per inch. Again, only edit the values within the quotation marks.

6. Save your new PPD file as a text file using a different name to prevent overwriting your original PPD file.

7. When you use this new PPD file with Adobe Illustrator, you will find the same choices available in the Halftone pop-up menu as before. However, when you select and print using the linescreen frequency/printer resolution combination matching the set you edited, Adobe Illustrator will use your new angles and frequencies.

NOTE

You can use the **Screen** function in the Adobe Photoshop Page Setup dialog box to compute angle and frequency combinations. These combinations may then be entered into the appropriate PPD file using this technique.

Creating and Editing the EPSF Riders File

After normal installation of Adobe Illustrator 6.0, you will find a folder called the Riders folder in the Utilities folder in the Adobe Illustrator application folder. The content of this folder is a filter called *Riders* that you can use to create and customize an EPSF Riders file. The EPSF Riders file is PostScript code that affects Adobe Illustrator 6.0 documents during the printing process or whenever you save a document with an EPSF header either by using **File > Save** to save a file in EPS format or by using **File > Print** to save printable PostScript code to disk.

You can use the plug-in described later in this section to adjust the code in the EPSF Riders file to:

➤ Add text or graphics that will print out on all pages you print from Illustrator

➤ Set the default flatness for your print job

➤ Set the default screen frequency and angle

➤ Define your own halftone cell spot function

➤ Add code that affects the setup or trailer sections of the PostScript code used in printing the Adobe Illustrator document

Modifications to the Riders file will not be seen in the on-screen preview of any document but will appear in the printout.

Using the Riders Plug-in Filter to Create a Riders File

To use the Riders Plug-in filter that comes with Illustrator 6.0, move it from the Riders folder in the Utilities folder to the Plug-ins folder in the Adobe Illustrator 6.0 program folder (Figure 11.17).

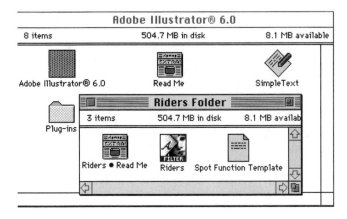

Figure 11.17 Mover the Riders filter from the Riders folder to the Plug-ins folder and restart Illustrator.

1. Copy or move the Riders filter from the Utilities folder in the Adobe Illustrator 6.0 program folder into the Plug-ins folder (that is, out of the folder called Riders Files).

2. Quit and restart Illustrator. A new **Other** submenu will appear on the Filter menu in Illustrator.

The **Filter > Other** submenu lists two options for making a Riders file with the Riders filter, **Make Riders** and **Delete Riders**. Both of these commands is described under the next headings.

MAKE EPSF RIDERS

The **Make Riders** option allows you to make an EPSF Riders file through the Riders filter.

1. Choose **Filter > Other > Make Riders**.

2. The Make Riders dialog box allows you to select the items you wish to include and set the appropriate settings. To include or adjust any of the settings described next, simply select a value from the drop-down menu.

If a menu offers additional choices such as **Other…** or **Setup…**, a second dialog box will appear, and you can type in the value you wish the Illustrator document to print with. Make the following entries as desired:

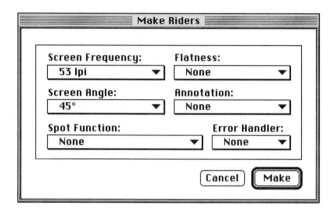

Figure 11.18 The Make Riders dialog box.

➤ **Screen Frequency**. If you look closely at a printed document from Illustrator, you will notice that any object that is not painted with 100% black is made up of small dots. Because printers cannot have an infinite number of gray inks to print with, they use a process called *halftoning* to simulate levels of gray. The farther the dots are placed from one another, the lighter the level of gray looks.

The screen frequency, also called the *linescreen*, designates the actual size of the halftone dots. A low number, called a *coarse screen*, designates a large dot, and a large number, called a *fine screen*, designates a small dot. The smaller the halftone dot, the less obtrusive it looks to the eye, resulting in a more realistic representation of gray.

The screen frequency can be set to **None** (for black-and-white line art with no tints) or any value between 1.0000 and 999.0000, but the drop-down menu lists common settings: **10**, **30**, **53**, **60**, **85**, **100**, **133**, **150**, and **175**.

WARNING

Setting the screen frequency and/or angle (described next) with the Riders file can produce unwanted side effects when used with Illustrator. If the Illustrator file has the Riders embedded with these options enabled and is printed from Illustrator, all the plates will get the same screen frequency and angle. The screen frequency and angle should be set from within Illustrator, in which case the selected PPD will set the appropriate screens for the individual plates. If any of the other Riders options are enabled, they will also be applied to each plate but will not cause problems if used correctly.

➤ **Screen Angle**. The screen angle determines the angle in which the rows of halftone dots will be printed. Setting **0** degrees, for example, will cause the rows of dots to be printed vertically, and **90** degrees will cause them to be printed horizontally. Typically, for black-and-white printing (like to a LaserWriter), the angle is set to an angle that is not straight up or down, such as **45** degrees, to make the dot rows less conspicuous to the eye.

The screen angle can be set to **None** (for black-and-white line art with no tints) or any value between 0 and 360.0000, but the drop-down menu suggests common settings: **0, 15, 30, 45, 90, 105, 120**.

➤ **Spot Function**. The spot function determines the halftone dot's shape when it is drawn. Using a **Round** spot function, for example, will result in round halftone dots. The shape of the halftone dot can affect how well gradients blend together, the quality of the midtones, and other variables of halftone screening. Different dot shapes can also be used for special effects.

Seven spot function options are included with the Riders filter. To use one of them, select the spot function from the pop-up menu. To get a visual idea of what each of the included spot functions does, try printing a gradient from black to white with a coarse line screen, using the different spot functions.

You may also import a spot function. To do so, select the **Import** option from the drop-down menu. An imported spot function must be correctly formed PostScript and be correctly formatted. The Spot Function Template file, in the Riders folder with the Riders filter, is a skeleton file you can use to create your own custom spot function definition.

When importing a spot function, the Riders filter first checks the beginning of the file for the signature (**%!RM1_Spot**). It then searches for the first Return, and reads in the entire text that follows. Since everything but the first line of the file is included in the Riders file that is written out, it is important that any commentary be commented out. To comment out lines of text, put a percent (%) character at the beginning of the line.

Here is an example of a simple round spot function within the required curly braces (for more information about writing a spot function, please refer to Adobe's PostScript documentation):

{ dup mul exch dup mul add 1 exch sub }

Importing a incorrectly formatted spot function could cause your Illustrator document not to print, or worse, corrupt the document.

WARNING

➤ **Flatness**. Flatness determines how accurate the PostScript interpreter is at drawing curves. Curves are described as small line segments within the interpreter. The smaller the line segments, the more accurate the curve will look. However, the smaller the line segments, the more of them it will take to define the curve, and thus the more complex the curve will be to print.

Curves can be too complex for a PostScript interpreter to rasterize and can result in a PostScript error (usually a "limitcheck" error). Setting the flatness higher may simplify the curve enough to make it printable. The higher the flatness is set, the less accurately it will be drawn, but it will print faster a PostScript error is less likely to occur.

The Riders Flatness setting is applied globally to all curves in an Illustrator document. Note that within Illustrator you can set the output resolution of individual objects, which is the equivalent of setting flatness, through the **Object > Attribute** command. If a curve is extremely complex and you do not wish to lose any of the curve's quality, Illustrator has a **Split long paths** option in the File > Document Setup dialog box, which affects all new curves drawn in Illustrator (but does not change existing objects).

The flatness can be set to **None** (for artwork with no curved paths, only straight lines) or to any integer between 1 and 5080, but the drop-down menu suggests common values: **1**, **3**, **10**, **100**, and **200**.

➤ **Annotation**. You may enter an annotation of up to 254 characters by choosing **Setup** from the Annotation drop-down menu (Figure 11.19). The Base-13 fonts are available in the Font pop-up menu, and a point size of 4 to 30 can be entered for the annotation text. The annotation will appear at the bottom-left corner of the page in the font and size selected— be sure to select **Include** from this drop-down menu before closing the dialog box.

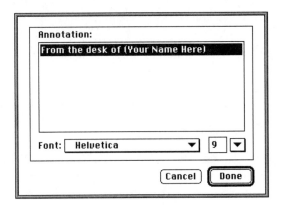

Figure 11.19 The Annotation Setup dialog box.

➤ **Error Handler**. This option lets you include a general-purpose error handler that will print error information on the page if a PostScript error occurs. If you are using the Apple LaserWriter driver, which has its own error handling capabilities, do not include the error handler.

NOTE Illustrator allows you to print using its custom screens, which enhance the output of gradients to low-resolution printers. You turn on these screens by unchecking the **Use printer's default screens** checkbox in the Document Setup dialog box. Since these custom screens have their own custom screen frequency, screen angle, and spot function, you will probably want to turn them off if you plan to use the Riders file to set the frequency, angle, and/or spot function. Be aware, however, that if you leave the custom screens on and install a Riders file, the Riders file settings will override the custom screens.

3. When you are done setting up the Riders filter options, click the **Make** button and save the Riders file into the Plug-Ins folder.

Using the EPSF Riders File

Once you create an EPSF Riders file, it is invoked automatically when you print. Simply use the **Print** command to print an Illustrator document if you want the effects of the Riders file to apply to this printing only or open a document and use the **Save As** command to save the document in EPS format with the Preview option set to **None** if you want the effects of the Riders file to apply to future printings when the Riders file is not in the application folder.

Illustrator looks for the presence of a Riders file named Adobe Illustrator EPSF Riders in the Plug-ins folder whenever a document is printed or saved as

EPSF or with a preview. If the Riders file is present, Illustrator appends the Riders file's PostScript text to the Illustrator document.

NOTE

It is possible to have several Riders files, each with a unique descriptive name and modified to create different effects. When a certain effect is desired, simply rename that Riders file "Adobe Illustrator EPSF Riders" and move it into the Plug-ins folder.

WARNING

If the EPSF Riders file is not being used, it should not remain in the Plug-ins folder since it can slow down the program's performance. Linescreen frequency and angle settings contained in an active Riders file will override similar settings in Illustrator.

WARNING

The *Adobe Illustrator User Guide* warns that "This file is intended only for users who are fluent in the PostScript language." We agree that this file is not for everyone, but if you think you can understand how to use the file from the instructions given here, you can experiment with it by printing and saving only test files when the Adobe Illustrator EPSF Riders file is in the Plug-ins folder—and moving it out of the Plug-ins folder (or back into the folder called Riders files) before opening, printing, or saving files that you do not want to affect.

Editing the Riders File

To edit the Adobe Illustrator EPSF Riders file, you can use the plug-in that comes with Illustrator 6.0, as described earlier in this section. If you are familiar with the PostScript language, you can instead make these and other changes the hard way. Open the file as a TeachText file by double-clicking its icon or use any word processor, and modify the code. The EPSF Riders file consists primarily of lines of code that have been made into comments only (that is, disabled) by the addition of a percent sign (%) at the beginning of the line. Lines that begin with a percent sign and a bullet (%•) are precoded lines that you can activate by deleting both characters from the front of the line. You can then modify the code as desired. Lines in the EPSF Riders file that begin with a percent sign *not* followed by a bullet are permanent comment lines that should not be activated (by deleting the percent sign).

Disabling the Riders File

As long as an Adobe Illustrator EPSF Riders file is in the Plug-ins folder or the same folder as the application, the changes specified in that file will be applied to every document printed from Illustrator. To disable the Riders file, delete it (by choosing **Filter > Other > Delete Riders**), move it to a different folder, or rename it.

To remove the Riders information from an Illustrator document that has been saved with a Riders file, the Riders file must be removed from the Plug-ins folder and then the document resaved. Illustrator may remain open while the Riders file is created or deleted.

Printing doesn't add the Riders to the file on disk, only to the file sent to the printer.

N O T E

Dot Density Calibration

If you are printing film for color separations or black-and-white halftones, you may need to calibrate Adobe Illustrator to compensate for dot gain or loss on your imagesetter. Imagesetter calibration insures that a given color value specified in Illustrator actually prints with the correct halftone screen value from your imagesetter.

This section is addressed primarily to service bureaus or production departments that have their own imagesetters for outputting film. You also need a densitometer for the readings to be able to use Table 11.1.

N O T E

Table 11.1 lists density conversions. Choose a maximum density (D-Max) column and then read down that column to find corresponding density values for percentage black:

Table 11.1 Density conversions.

% Black	3.0	3.6	4.0	4.4
0%	0.000	0.000	0.000	0.000
10%	0.046	0.046	0.046	0.046
20%	0.097	0.097	0.097	0.097
30%	0.155	0.155	0.155	0.155
40%	0.222	0.222	0.222	0.222

50%	0.301	0.301	0.301	0.301
60%	0.397	0.398	0.398	0.398
70%	0.522	0.523	0.523	0.523
80%	0.697	0.699	0.699	0.699
90%	0.996	0.999	1.000	1.000
100%	3.000	3.600	4.000	4.400

When reading negatives remember that % black values are flipped. A 20% screen in your artwork is read as an 80% screen by the densitometer.

It is very important to obtain your chosen Maximum Density before you begin to fine-tune the intermediate densities with the tint adjustment table. The tint adjustment table cannot increase the D-Max. The values across the chart are basically the same until you get to the higher values. Values change dramatically at the high end, in the last 10% of density. Maintaining a 98% screen different from a 100% screen is critical (the same as 0% and a 2% screen).

Transmission densitometers return values from 0 to 5.0. You need to translate the values from percentage to this other unit/value. Table 11.1 may help.

If you still have Illustrator 5.0 or 5.5 installed, there's a Densitometer Control Chart—an Illustrator document you can print—stored in the Utilities folder in the Illustrator 5.0 program folder.

NOTE

Solving Printing Problems

Occasionally when printing a complex document from Illustrator, one that contains long paths, objects converted by Adobe Streamline, blends, masks, compounds, lots of grouping, or with patterns, an error message may be generated.

These messages include "-8133," "VM error," "The document is okay but cannot be printed," "please use the Chooser to select a printer." The phrase "Limitcheck; offending Command: Curveto, Fill, or Clip" may also be encountered. Sometimes no specific error is given, but the document simply does not print.

Printing errors are almost always the result of the document being too complex to be printed with the current memory available on the printer. Installing additional memory into the printer (if possible) or using a different printer with more memory may help, but there are several other ways to get around this problem.

It should be noted that the file size in megabytes on disk does not reflect the complexity of a file. In the same sense, making an assumption about a file's complexity based on the way it looks is not always an accurate indicator of whether it will print.

Here are some suggestions that may solve the problem. When trying any of these suggestions, *always work with a back-up copy of your artwork files.*

Make Sure You're Connected

If the printer just isn't working or you get the message that the printer cannot be found, there is most likely a problem with the connection to the printer:

➤ The printer is not turned on.

➤ The printer is not connected correctly to your computer or network.

➤ The printer is not selected in the Chooser.

➤ The printer is broken.

Pay Attention to the Error Message

A "-8133" error by itself generally means your file is too complex overall. You must reduce the number of elements within it or the complexity of the file using one or more of the suggestions given under the next headings.

Limitcheck errors usually indicate a specific part of the file is too complex for the memory the printer allocated for particular tasks. An indication of the problem's source is provided by the "offending command" message, such as Curveto (curve to), Fill, or Clip. *Curveto* usually means one or more paths are causing the problem. *Fill* can mean you have a blend in a mask or pattern that is causing the problem. *Clip* usually refers to a problem with a mask.

If an error message is not displayed on the screen, choose **Print** from the File menu and click **Options**. In the Print Options dialog box, select **Print Detailed Report** for the PostScript Errors option, and try printing the document again. If a PostScript error occurs, the printer will print an error page.

Test Printing Parts of the Artwork

VM error usually means your printer ran out of memory. Try printing the file in pieces. Copy one or two of the more complicated parts/objects, such as masked elements or pattern fills, to a new file and print that. Do this for all objects in your file. If they all print separately but not together, you need to make one or more of the objects less complex. If one object does not print separately, you have found another problem. Either redo/remake that object or make it less complex.

Reinstall Printer Drivers

Sometimes printing problems are caused by a corrupted printer driver, such as LaserWriter or Print Monitor. If this is the case, delete the existing driver and Print Monitor and reinstall fresh copies from the original disks.

Select Split Long Paths on Printing and Set Output Resolution

In Illustrator, you set the **Split Long Paths** and **Output Resolution** options in the Document Setup dialog box (**Command+Shift+D**). Illustrator also offers the ability to set the output resolution for individual objects, through the Objects > Attributes dialog box (**Command+Control+A**).

When you choose **Split long paths**, longer paths within the artwork will be "broken up" into pieces that can be processed by the printer more easily. The splitting occurs the first time the artwork is saved or printed. You should see a series of horizontal lines across your illustration, indicating where the paths are divided (theses lines will not print). When you are finished printing or saving, go back and turn off **Split Long Paths** or all new artwork that you create will be affected in the same way.

The **Split Paths** option does not affect text, masks, compound paths, or stroked paths. In these cases, you can use the Scissors tool to cut the path manually.

NOTE

Simplify the Artwork or Divide it into Separate Documents

Try a different approach to creating your image in Illustrator or eliminate some of the artwork if possible. If some objects are covered by other objects, consider deleting the hidden objects. Here are some elements that may be complicating your work·

➤ *Blends.* Whenever possible, use Illustrator's gradient fills, rather than "shape blends." If you do use shape blends, try to minimize the number of steps used or reduce the number of blends overall. Also, when making linear blends (ones that go in a straight line), using lines instead of rectangles can reduce the complexity. (Lines have only two anchor points, whereas rectangles have four.) Be sure to specify a thick enough line weight so there will be no gaps when it is printed. (You can check this by zooming all the way in and then previewing the blend.) When you start to make a blend, Illustrator automatically gives you the maximum usable number of steps, so if you are blending colors, setting this number higher will not make the blend smoother. It is fine to make this number lower, especially if you will be printing to a laser printer, because most 300 dpi printers can produce a maximum of 32 levels of gray.

➤ *Masks and patterns.* Make them simpler. Avoid patterns containing blends; they are extremely complex. Check the *User Guide* for tips on making simpler patterns. Sometimes it is better to make a series of copies of your art and place them side by side, as opposed to making the art into an actual pattern.

➤ *Paths.* Use the Pen tool instead of the Freehand tool to draw paths whenever possible. Paths drawn with the Pen tool tend to have fewer anchor points. Try to make shorter paths where possible. Split long complex paths into multiple, abutting pieces. If your path has curves in it, see if you can use fewer anchor points and readjust the curves to compensate. Use the Scissors/point deletion tool to remove unnecessary anchor points and readjust the remaining points. Choose **Filter > Objects > Cleanup** to delete stray anchor points (points with no text or path attached).

➤ *Fonts.* Be sure there are no unused fonts in your file. If you suspect that you have unused fonts, select everything in your file and copy it to a new file or choose **Select All** and change the font to Helvetica, save, and then change the text you want back to the font(s) you want to use in the file.

➤ Another thing to check is in **File > Page Setup, Options**. Be sure that **Unlimited Downloadable Fonts** is not checked. When it is checked, fonts can get flushed from the printer's memory and have to be downloaded again, which increases printing time and may cause the file not to print.

Eliminate Unused Patterns and Colors

When working with patterns or custom colors, one can collect several colors and/or patterns that are no longer used in the image. Simply deleting the object filled with a pattern or color does not remove it from the file. To get rid of the unused patterns or colors, choose **Object > Custom Color or Patterns** and click on the **Select All Unused** button in the Custom Color or Pattern dialog box. Then click on the **Delete** button. This eliminates the extra information that ties up valuable printer memory. Save the document and print.

Print at a Lower Resolution

You will find that the lower the resolution (1200 dpi vs. 2400 dpi, for example), the more likely your document will print. It is not uncommon for a document to proof on a 300 dpi laser printer but not print to an imagesetter. Likewise, certain documents can be printed at medium resolution but not at high resolution. Remember that in Illustrator you can set the output resolution for individual objects, so if you have determined that one object is causing a problem, you may want to try lowering the output resolution for just that one object.

Chapter 12

Case Studies

This part of the book presents a collection of finished works that were created by professional artists using Adobe Illustrator. The descriptions of each of these works include procedures and tips that can be applied to a wide range of applications. They refer to techniques that have been described in earlier chapters. You can adapt many of the steps described here in creating your own artwork.

The examples in this section can be divided into five broad categories:

➤ Four illustrations with a hand-drawn look that demonstrate techniques using the Brush and Pen tools

➤ Four illustrations that use gradient shading and other tricks to add dimension or special "stained glass" effects

➤ Four illustrations that demonstrate the use of layers, although you'll notice that some of the illustrations in other categories might also use layers

➤ Eight examples of "totally real things"—a bridge, jewelry designs, maps, anatomical diagrams, and product illustrations

➤ Nine examples of working between Illustrator and other applications such as Adobe Photoshop, Adobe Streamline, Adobe Dimensions, MicroFrontier's Color It!, Adobe Acrobat, and plug-ins such as KPT Vector Effects (although some Illustrations from the other categories also used Photoshop to modify scanned images to be used as templates)

These rough categories are in no way exclusive. You'll find interesting shading in the "real things" category and gradient fills in several categories. We think you'll find something of interest and use in each example.

Hand-Drawn Looks and Tint Shading

Hand-drawn looks can be difficult to accomplish with computer-based drawing applications. Illustrator offers a few tools and commands that help, and several techniques were described in Chapter 9. Here we offer examples of four artists' approaches to this problem:

➤ Robin Bort uses a drawing tablet with the Brush tool set to pressure-sensitive to create her illustration of a musician.

➤ Stephen Czapiewski starts with a solid black shape outlining Michaelangelo's David and then creates shaded areas as closed paths with no stroke and fills of white or tints of black.

➤ Curt Mobley uses the Pen tool to create closed paths that look like uneven brush strokes to create his cartoon-style illustrations.

➤ Ian Shou's comic-style drawings are based on his free-flowing hand-drawn illustrations, which are then scanned and re-created in Illustrator.

Robin Bort's Musicians

Robin Bort was on the staff of the Live Oak Music Festival (outside of Santa Barbara, California) and did all the graphics for the festival for six years. The black-and-white image titled *Kristina*, shown in Figures 12.1 and 12.2, is of Kristina Olsen, a folk singer/songwriter. A color image titled *Peru*—shown in the colorplates—is the flute player from the group Sukay. Both illustrations are loosely based on images from a Photo CD that was made from slides. Here, we describe the steps in creating Kristina.

Figure 12.1 The hand-drawn look of Robin Bort's black-and-white *Kristina* was created using a drawing tablet and the pressure-sensitive Brush tool © 1995 Robin Bort.

Figure 12.2 Kristina in Artwork view.

Accustomed to doing very detailed hand-drawn images using programs like Fractal Design's Painter, here Robin wanted to try for the same feeling in Illustrator. Here are her basic steps in creating Kristina:

1. Robin had slides of the artist put onto a Photo CD.

2. She opened the photo on the CD and printed it out on paper.

3. Using a 12-inch × 12-inch CalComp tablet, she put the laser print under the plastic cover and, with the brush tool in Illustrator, very loosely sketched Kristina varying the pressure, especially in the hair. For this she had the brush tool set to 1 point (minimum) and 12 points (maximum).

4. From here on, she simply looked at the photo from time to time. It was very time consuming, but the image is made up of many tiny brush strokes with the brush tool set to 0.5 points (minimum) and 2 points (maximum) with a rounded tip. Robin either used white to make little nicks out of the original thick and thin sketch or added little stray strokes in black.

5. Where possible, to simplify the file, she used the Pathfinder filters to cut out the white nicks (with Minus front) and to incorporate the extra black strokes where they touched the main drawing (with the Unite filter).

6. The musical notes were clip art which she roughened in the same manner—making little nicks with the brush tool and then using the Pathfinder filters Minus front and Unite. "I'm not particularly fond of the **Roughen** command. It looks too much like a computer did it!"

7. Robin signs all her computer creations by importing a file that originated as her actual signature (on paper), which she scanned and ran through Streamline.

Robin Bort has been an illustrator and graphic artist for ten years. For the last three years, she has posed as the entire art department for a software publisher. Robin also does freelance illustration and graphic design. You can reach her at P.O. Box 659, Santa Margarita, CA 93453, 805-438-3325.

NOTE

Linda Oates' Mayan Storyteller

Linda Oates' storybook cover was illustrated entirely using the Brush tool in Adobe Illustrator. The original shading is in color, but you can get the feel for it in this black-and-white image.

Figure 12.3 Linda Oates' Mayan Storyteller—initial sketch with Brush tool, then shaded.

Linda started outlining the figure and his adornments roughly using her tablet pen, with the Brush tool set to Variable (pressure-sensitive), with the tip varying between 1 and 3 points. This yielded closed paths that looked like brush strokes.

She then used the Brush tool to add shading into the outlines—this time set to 6-12 points, and the Paint Style palette set to a gray fill and no stroke. She worked on a lower layer, with the top layer locked.

 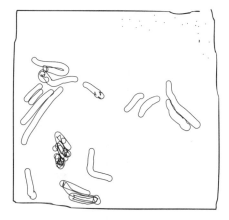

Figure 12.4 Mayan figure in Artwork view—initial sketch lines (left),
and the shading on a lower layer (right).

Linda Oates is a story writer who illustrates her own work. She can be contacted by e-mail to Anna Sahzi @aol.com.

Stephen Czapiewski's David

Stephen Czapiewski's representation of Michaelangelo's David was originally commissioned as part of a logo for an art festival. It began as a pen and ink drawing of the statue that he then scanned and redrew entirely in Illustrator. Stephen notes, "Even though I have a Wacom tablet, I didn't use it for this illustration. I found that the tablet was a little too random for this project. I wanted the illustration to be unmistakably *David*.

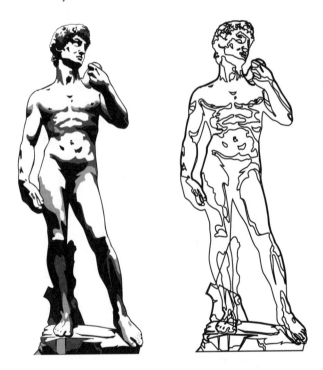

Figure 12.5 Michaelangelo's David recreated by Stephen Czapiewski
(© 1995 OOMM Studios), in Preview and Artwork views.

The final *David* is composed of several layers of shapes, each having a different tint of black as a fill (Figure 12.6):

➤ The lowest layer is a solid black-filled outline of the body (first image in Figure 12.6).

➤ The next layer is various shapes that have a white fill with no stroke. He varied the space between the black outline shape and the white shape on top of it to give the illusion of a painted brush stroke, since "the way that the 'stroke' varies would have been extremely difficult, if not impossible with a tablet."

➤ The next two layers include various shapes in two different tints (third and fourth images in Figure 12.6).

Figure 12.6 David shading is composed of various shapes assigned four tints of black (from 0 to 100 percent).

NOTE Stephen Czapiewski and his wife Maureen run OOMM Studios (P.O. Box 43, Holly MI 48442, 810-634-6533) where they provide graphic services to "all kinds of cool clients!" Stephen is a former Desktop Publishing Project Leader for Ross Roy Communications. He has designed several fonts (using Illustrator), logos, automotive illustrations, and renderings. He also publishes several comic book series.

Curt Mobley's Computer Boy

Curt Mobley created this illustration for the *Colorado Springs Computer Times* (Figure 12.7). He usually makes a pencil sketch first and scans it for use as a template in Illustrator. In this cartoon, the lines with varied thicknesses were created as closed paths with the Pen tool with a stroke of none and a fill of white or black or whatever tint was used. He created the rain pattern as white lines and used it to fill the window shape.

Figure 12.7 Curt Mobley's illustration in Preview and Artwork views. Rain effect is actually a pattern of white shapes. The basic tile is shown against a black background in the center here.

Curt Mobley is a cartoonist and animator in Colorado Springs, Colorado. He can be reached at 719-520-5040 or via e-mail at Curt943@aol.com.

NOTE

Ian Shou's Cartoons

Ian Shou's comic style and great sense of humor are shown in his illustrations, two of which are shown in Figure 12.8 and 12.9. (His more serious illustration of Golden Gate Bridge is an example later in this chapter.) The flag is a personal concept piece he calls *Shakedown*, re-created from an original hand-drawn illustration he did based on the "shakedown of government." (The original colors were done using color pencils on photocopied pencil drawings.) His penguin, *Lucian*, was an exercise to create an animated character. There are no tricks here, just a great talent for illustration.

The brick wall behind Lucian the penguin was built brick-by-brick (or sets of bricks were copied and pasted), rather than by using Illustrator's built-in Brick pattern fill.

Figure 12.8 Ian Shou's flag in Preview and Artwork views (see also color plate).

Figure 12.9 Ian Shou's penguin in Preview and artwork views (see also color plate).

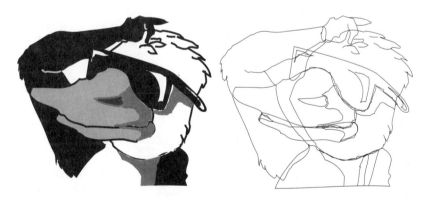

Figure 12.10 Penguin's head in Preview and artwork views shows artful detail (see also color plate).

NOTE

Ian Shou is a graphic artist and illustrator. He can be reached at Apartment 49 Design, 2250 Latham St., #49, Mt. View, CA 94040, 415-968-7846, e-mail: lshou@aol.com.

Gradient Shading and Other Tricks

Gradient fills, or gradient effects created using the Blend tool, are a great help in creating three-dimensional shading in Illustrator. The next four examples show both methods of creating gradient fills for dimension, plus two examples of creating a stained-glass effect. In addition, these other special techniques are highlighted:

➤ Alvin O'Sullivan creates shapes from a composite of simple ovals and rectangles and then uses the Unite filter to create the single shape he desires.

➤ Gary Allen Smith's *Cyberwoman* is an exercise in simplicity as well as dimension.

➤ Larry Rosenstein creates a stained-glass effect using gradient fills and KPT Vector Effects.

➤ Rob Marquardt's stained-glass effect is created with the Knife tool, which easily cuts through his many layers of artwork.

Alvin O'Sullivan's Pen

Alvin O'Sullivan's approach in Illustrator is a direct extension of his traditional drawing (pen and ink) techniques (Figure 12.11). Using the simplest shapes, he defines the spatial layout and then suggests depth using different fills.

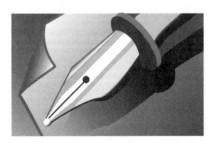 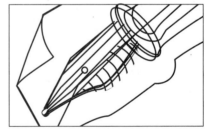

Figure 12.11 Alvin O'Sullivan's Pen in Preview and Artwork views.

Here's how he developed the pen:

1. He started with a pen-and-ink drawing to work out the linear design aspects.

2. When he had what he thought was a good beginning, he opened Illustrator. The piece was developed much as the pen and ink drawing was.

3. He used the Oval and Rectangle tools to block out some of the smaller shapes.

4. These forms were arranged and eventually consolidated using the **Filter > Pathfinder > Unite** command to make larger shapes.

5. Individual shapes were filled with different shades of gray or gradient fills to give it dimension.

6. The final artwork included three masks: the outer rectangle that frames the piece, the shape of the pen nib, and a shape around the wide dark lines over a gray background that composes the ink-gathering mechanism under the nib (Figure 12.12).

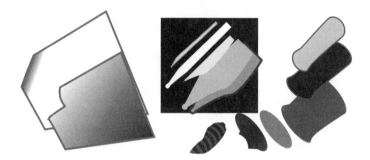

Figure 12.12 Some components of the pen.

 Alvin O'Sullivan's art can be viewed at his Web page http://users.aol.com/Taoberry/ or you can contact him at Taoberry@aol.com. He lives in New York.

NOTE

Gary Allen Smith's Cyberwoman

Gary Allen Smith has been doing portraits of one kind or another for a long time. His *Cyberwoman* was an attempt to integrate his earlier traditional work. He received a BA in visual arts at the University of California, San Diego, with an extended minor in computer science, and he notes "both disciplines seemed very similar to me—the study of the analysis and restructuring of information including how various presentations of that information are perceived by all types of individuals. It's just that art tends to be more visual and computers tend to be more algorithmic."

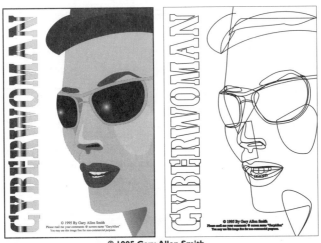

Figure 12.13 Gary Allen Smith's *Cyberwoman*, here in Preview and Artwork views, is a masterpiece in economy of lines (see also color plate) © 1995 Gary Allen Smith.

Gary's explanation of his work was so eloquent, we decided to let him speak for himself:

"In college, my drawing courses were designed to investigate the nature of three-dimensional perception in two-dimensional media. We did all sorts of exercises in trying to draw representational imagery without using the conventional techniques of perspective (things getting smaller and hazier as they get farther away.)

"One of the strongest observations I made during this period is that layering plays an important role in visualizing three dimensions. When the edge of an object goes behind another object, our visual system projects that line in a way that makes sense of what we are seeing. The behavior of the lines converging on the point of overlap is critical to what projection is made. This can be illustrated with two hearts.

"The only difference is that the small line segment protruding below the cleft of the first heart has been rotated slightly counter-clockwise so it lines up with the left slope of the cleft. It turns a heart with a small vertical cut into a more three-dimensional heart. You can take this phenomenon further into three dimensions as in the example of a cat's eye, by adding a single dot of white.

"When I got out of college I worked in traditional oils on canvas or acrylic on masonite. I mostly did animal portraits and found that I could make areas less and less shaded and still maintain a three-dimensional look to them. The ultimate example of this, I suppose, is paint-by-number art. There, the representationalism is entirely in the shapes of the lines. Similarly, I often experiment on the computer by taking scanned photographs and converting them into stained-glass designs.

"The cyberwoman drawing exhibits an economy of shape and line that is a natural evolution of my experiences. I did use a scanned template from a black and white cosmetic advertisement I found in an old newspaper. I find tracing is usually unacceptable so I drew all the lines with the mouse and used the template for positional information.

"The only shaded areas are the eyes, the teeth, and the cleft of the neck. However, there is a shaded effect by layering the different shapes making up the nose. I gave her eyes a more alien look by using a spherical blend that takes the white highlights out of the plane of the black glasses. This made them look like glowing sensors beneath the surface of the glasses.

"The text uses a custom blend created in the paint style window's gradient editor. The teeth and other shadings were accomplished similarly but with simpler gradients."

For the last four years Gary has been producing gallery-quality fractal artworks. His art has appeared in several shows in San Diego, including TechnoArt '94 and CyberFest. In 1995 he won the Director's Choice award at the Con Dor Science Fiction Festival. He can be reached at garyallen@aol.com.

NOTE

Larry Rosenstein's Stained Glass

Larry Rosenstein's simple stained-glass window (Figure 12.16) is done with the help of Vector Effects (ShatterBox and Neon). Here's how he created the illustration:

Figure 12.14 Larry Rosenstein's church window in Preview and Artwork views (see also colorplate).

1. Larry started with a stained-glass pattern designed by his wife, Karen, a glass-art designer (left in Figure 12.15).

2. He applied KPT ShatterBox to add panes to the window, using the options: radial, 8 segments, no offset or disruption. (If you look closely, you'll see that the impact wasn't quite centered horizontally, which was not intended.)

3. Next he made a copy of the window in a separate layer and set the fill to black. He applied KPT Neon to the copy to create the leaded lines using the following options: 50%, 8 point. This outlined each piece individually, which looked funny because they overlapped (see Figure 12.16).

4. To create continuous lines, he first used Outline Path to convert the lead to filled shapes.

5. Finally, he repeatedly selected one shape, then chose **Filter > Pathfinder > Same Paint Style, Unite, and Hide** until all individual shapes were merged.

6. Finally, he used the **Show All** command to make everything visible again (Figure 12.16).

Figure 12.15 Church window before and after KPT Shatterbox.

Figure 12.16 Before and after steps 4 and 5.

NOTE

Larry can be reached at 182 Muir Avenue, Santa Clara, CA 95051, e-mail: LarryR9@aol.com.

Rob Marquardt's Stained Glass

Rob Marquardt has been experimenting with Illustrator 6.0's knife tool and finds it makes creating the individual glass "breaks" a lot easier than using Pathfinder filters alone (Figure 12.11). Here's how he created the illustration:

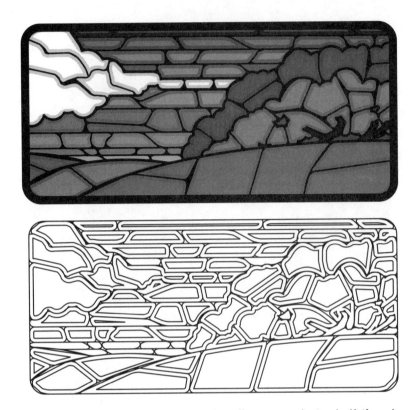

Figure 12.17 Rob Marquardt's stained-glass effect is created using the Knife tool.

1. Draw the border of the artwork, placing one at the bottom layer, filled with black. A copy goes on the top layer, with no fill and a black stroke. Create your artwork between these layers using primitive shapes.

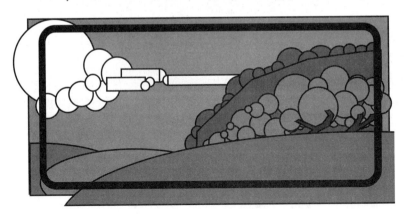

2. Select all the color artwork and apply the Pathfinder Merge filter. Then, using a copy of the top stroke path, apply the Crop filter. Ungroup the cropped artwork.

3. Make a copy of this art on a higher layer, with no fill, a fatter stroke and rounded caps. Lock and hide this layer for now.

4. Use the knife tool to cut lines in the glass. Since the knife affects any artwork it touches, move the artwork to a temporary cutting layer — locking the other layers — where you can work on each piece independently of the others. When finished with each segment, put it back on the layer it originally came from. Repeat until satisfied with the look. (Rob had to use Pathfinder filters to start in on the center trees — the knife didn't want to cut apart the compound path.)

5. Apply the Round Corners filter (here he used a value of 5). Go in and tweak any areas that have too big of a gap created, or greatly overlapping artwork.

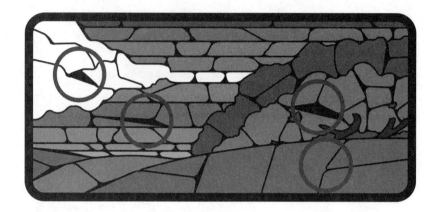

6. Inset the paths of the artwork—4 points in this example—and move them to their own layer.

NOTE

Rob used KPT Vector Effects—KPT Inset—in this step. You could instead use Pathfinder filters (Offset Path then Divide) and then delete excess paths, but with so many paths, as Rob explains, "it would be a real pain."

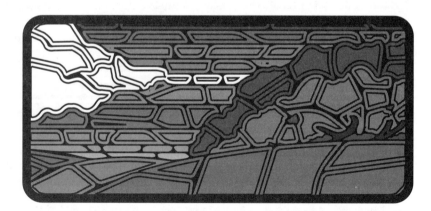

7. Remove any strokes remaining on the inset artwork and darken the underlying art using the Adjust Colors filter or any third-party color filter.

8. Make the layer that was hidden in step #2 visible again and the artwork is complete.

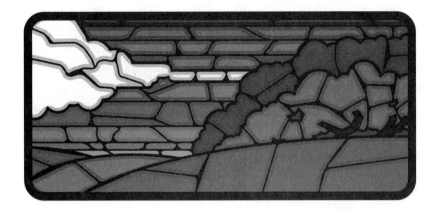

Rob's artwork is also an example of working in layers: he worked in ten layers all together, including a temporary cutting layer where he could position objects to be cut and then hide all other layers before cutting with the knife tool. This is a clever solution to what can be a problem with the knife tool: it cuts all artwork that falls in its path, not just selected objects. (The next section of this chapter focuses on layers.)

Rob Marquardt can be reached at Benyas AD Group, 126 North Third Street, Suite 300, Minneapolis, MN 55401, 612-340-9804, e-mail: rob@bpsi.net or guyspam@aol.com.

NOTE

Layer Meisters

The next section of our art gallery describes the work of three artists whose complex illustrations were simplified by working in layers.

- ➤ Scott Winkowski uses nine layers to develop his inviting Doorway into a bright future.
- ➤ Eve Elberg developed her self-portrait in 12 layers.
- ➤ Marina Thompson's winter scene used 8 layers.

Other examples in this chapter that also use layers include Rob Marquardt's stained glass—the preceding example—and Sue Sellar's anatomical illustrations, Gary Symington's furnace, Sandee Cohen's push pin, and Paul McBride Mahan's Greek columns.

Scott Winkowski's Doorway

Scott Winkowski created this doorway illustration for a graduation card. All of the areas that look like gradient fills in preview were actually created using the Blend tool (see Chapters 5 and 6).

In Figure 12.18, adjacent paths that resulted from blending the sun shades appear as a black area in Artwork view, but we omitted the sky and ground elements, which were composed of many adjacent rectangles created with the Blend tool (and appeared as a solid black areas in Artwork view).

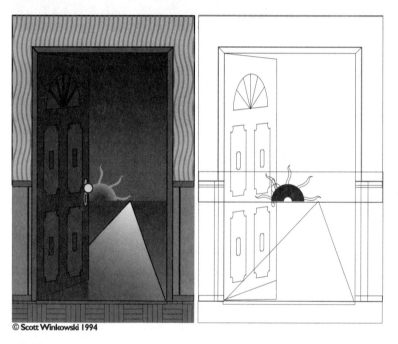

© Scott Winkowski 1994

Figure 12.18 Scott Winkowski's Doorway in Preview and Artwork views (see also colorplates).

He worked in 10 layers, enabling him to create some of the foreground elements before he completed the background. Figure 12.19 shows nine of those layers. A tenth layer was used for lettering (not shown here).

NOTE

Scott Winkowski is a cartographer and freelance artist. He can be reached at 11815 Cornwell Rd, Manassas, VA 22111, e-mail: Blackrose1@aol.com.

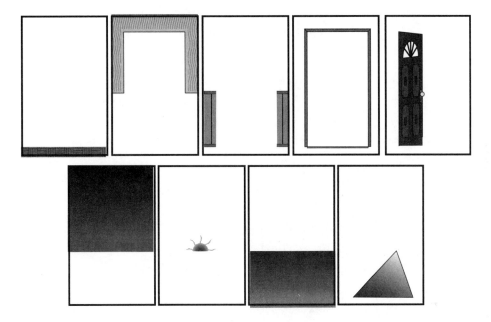

Figure 12.19 Nine of the layers used in creating the Doorway, shown here with the four lower layers positioned before five upper layers.

Eve Elberg's Self Portrait

Eve Elberg is an illustrator and multimedia designer whose self portrait with dripping hair and terry-cloth robe is, as she quips, "naturally, it's a bit self-flattering!" It's also a great example of using blends, gradients, patterns, custom colors, and layers (Figure 12.20).

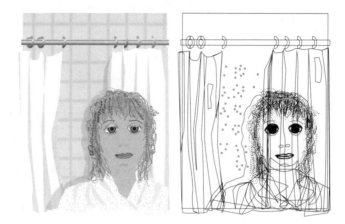

Figure 12.20 Eve Elberg's After the Shower in Preview and Artwork views (see also color plate).

Eve worked in 12 layers to produce this piece. This made it easy to lock or hide elements selectively as she worked.

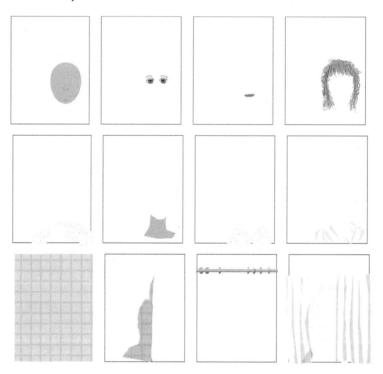

Figure 12.21 The 12 layers in After the Shower, starting with the lowest layer in the bottom-left corner.

Without using layers, not only would it have been progressively harder to select individual elements but the screen-redraw time would have become a significant factor. Many of the objects have pattern fills (the wall, the shower curtain, the towel, her robe), and most of the gradient effects were created using the Blend tool rather than gradient fills. Figure 12.22 shows a crude dissection of Eve's hair and eyes (ouch!).

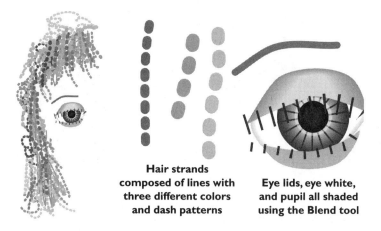

Hair strands composed of lines with three different colors and dash patterns

Eye lids, eye white, and pupil all shaded using the Blend tool

Figure 12.22 Eve's hair and eyes dissected.

Eve Elberg, Eve Design, Brooklyn, NY, Phone: 718-398-0950, Fax: 718-398-2995, e-mail: eve@interport.net.

NOTE

Marina Thompson's Outer Visions

Most of Marina Thompson's work is done in Illustrator, but some is then carried into Painter or Photoshop. It is usually colorful, often whimsical, and as spontaneous "as I can keep it." The Winter illustration described here was a cover for a New York-based magazine called *WorkForce Diversity*. The Summer piece (shown next) was for the *New Age Journal*.

Marina notes, "I think the most difficult part of the Winter illustration (Figure 12.23) was anticipating the volume of snowflakes it would take to create the image." As you'll learn in the following steps, she uses KPT Vector Effects (on the snowflakes).

© Marina Thompson 1995

Figure 12.23 Marina's Winter scene in Preview and Artwork views (see also colorplates).

Here's a summary of Marina's steps in creating the winter scene:

1. She started by scanning her pencil sketch and bringing it into a first layer as a template. Then she traced it and scaled the artwork to the right size and locked the layer.

2. The next layer is a basic background—sky and ground gradients—"mostly for color reference at this point." Once she had the background blocked out, she hid the layer so she could see her pencil sketch again.

She toggled this second layer on and off as needed until she didn't need the scan anymore, at which point she deleted the scan layer.

NOTE

3. In the next layer, she made the building structure by creating several custom pattern fills using varying color saturations for light, medium, and dark blue snow fills. "At first I wanted the building to be transparent," Marina notes, "but in the end I added a solid color fill behind the building shape."

4. Next layer was a scattering of small snow.

5. Then another layer for the large foreground snowflakes. These were generated in a separate file and then pasted onto this layer (being careful to leave room for the masthead of the magazine). She used mostly Dingbats as starting points for the snowflakes, creating outlines, adding and subtracting shapes with the Pathfinder filters Unite and Divide, and finally using KPT Vector Effects—Shadowland and Sketch filters—to give them a little more depth.

6. In the file she sent to the client, she included a layer called "Place Masthead here" because she wanted the large snowflakes and a few small ones in front of the masthead.

7. Another layer of small snow was added to really build up the density. She selected groups of dots and option-copied for rapid accumulation.

8. All the blue snow was "becoming monotonous," so she created a layer with just yellow snow. That way she could hide the layer to see if it worked better with or without it.

9. Lastly, she created the snowdrifts, "since the ground was looking too flat." She did this with the Brush tool set to a variable width (Minimum 1 point, Maximum 36 points), filling with the same gradient as the original ground.

Figure 12.24 Layers in Marina's Winter scene.

In Marina's beach scene, illustrating an article called "Summer Sizzlers," the trick was creating the shadows on the beach towel going across a gradient with stripes. She used the Divide filter (with some difficulty because of the many grouped objects) and then added 15% black to the stripe-colored shadows. The shadows in the gradient were mostly just "eye-balled" colors but including 15% black.

To keep the color palette clean, she tries whenever possible to overlap the use of custom gradients. For example, Marina used the same gradient for the sky, surf, chairs, book, boom box handle, and antenna. Duplicating gradients and making small changes to them is another way to stretch a color palette without getting too busy.

© Marina Thompson 1995

Figure 12.25 Marina's *Summer Sizzlers* illustration (see also colorplates).

NOTE

Marina Thompson can be reached at 31 Willow Road, Nahant, MA 01908, Phone: 617-581-1725, Fax: 617-581-5808, e-mail: MarinaTh@aol.com.

Totally Real Things

The next examples demonstrate the amazing ways in which Illustrator—and some wonderfully talented artists—can represent very real objects with total realism:

➤ Ian Shou reproduces the Golden Gate Bridge in architectural detail.

➤ Ben Gorman uses Illustrator to create designs and cutting templates for his Navajo silver jewelry.

➤ Doug Heinlein creates a bird's-eye view of Park Avenue.

➤ Steven Gordon illustrates a bird's-eye view of Huntsville, Alabama.

➤ Sue Sellars graphically represents the human anatomy.

➤ Scott Crouse illustrates a saw and a truck ready to drive off the page.

➤ Gary Symington takes us inside a glowing furnace.

Other illustrations in this chapter that might have fit in this section include Alvin O'Sullivan's pen tip, Sandee Cohen's push pin, Scott Gordon's map of Utah, and Scott Crouse's steel can.

Ian Shou's Golden Gate Bridge

Ian Shou's Golden Gate Bridge was created for a multimedia game company (Figure 12.26). (His more comic illustrations are used as examples later in this chapter.) It was created entirely in Illustrator without use of a template. He built it the way the real bridge would be built. He studied the blueprints and images of the construction of Golden Gate Bridge and designed the girder structure, then the foundation bars, etc., and finally connected all the parts together the way he thought the actual bridge would be constructed (Figure 12.27).

Figure 12.26 Golden Gate bridge in Preview and Artwork views.

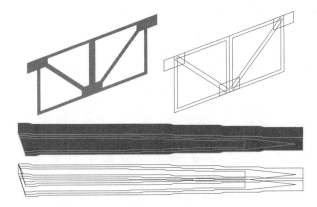

Figure 12.27 Two details from the bridge, in Preview and Artwork views (tall piece has been rotated 90°).

NOTE

Ian Shou is a graphic artist and illustrator. He can be reached at Apartment 49 Design, 2250 Latham St., #49, Mt. View, CA 94040, Phone/fax: 415-968-7846, e-mail: lshou@aol.com.

Ben Gorman's Jewelry

Ben Gorman is a Navajo Indian who designs contemporary Native American jewelry using Adobe Illustrator. Figure 12.28 shows a few of his designs. Of course, they do not do justice to the actual jewelry pieces.

Figure 12.28 Two of Ben Gorman's Navajo jewelry designs (see also colorplates).

Here is a brief description of how Ben works:

1. He begins by sketching a design using paper and pencil and then scanning the design into Adobe Photoshop where the image is prepared as a template for Adobe Illustrator.

2. The design process includes making a rendering of the jewelry piece by providing gradient shadings to give some three dimensionality. Also, the stones are colorized to match the stone color that will be used in the jewelry. This rendering is used primarily for show.

3. Another set of illustrations are created from the first illustration to be used as a template for sawing on a sheet of sterling silver.

NOTE

Most of Ben's silver work involves silver overlay. The silver overlay technique involves two sheets of silver soldered together. The top sheet will have designs cut out of it and the bottom sheet is used as a background. One illustration template is needed for the top layer and one for the bottom later.

4. To apply the final design from the computer to the silver requires a special type of paper called laser appliqué film. This is a very tough film that can be printed on by a laser printer. It is sticky on one side, so it can be applied to a smooth surface. He prints the final design on this paper and applies the paper to sheets of sterling silver as cutting templates.

Figure 12.29 Two of Ben Gorman's Navaho jewelry designs as simple line art used as a cutting template.

NOTE

More of Ben Gorman's jewelry can be seen on Sunshine Studio's web pages: http://www.trail.com/sunshine. He can be contacted at 520-674-5070, e-mail: BGorman100@aol.com.

Doug Heinlein's Bird's Eye Views

Doug Heinlein's cityscapes are based on his childhood recollections of the small town where he grew up. *Puzzle #2* is shown in Figure 12.30. They will be used as three levels of difficulty in a maze–chase like game from a CD-ROM, *The Virtual Erector Set: The E-Force Rescue* (©1995 Imagination Pilots Entertainment).

Figure 12.30 Doug Heinlein's Puzzle #2 from The Virtual Erector Set:
The E-Force Rescue (©1995 Imagination Pilots Entertainment)

Without attempting an actual step-by-step description of this complicated art-work, we will highlight a few interesting tricks Doug used:

➤ Doug started with an underlying quadrille grid, which he used as guides in building this and similar mazes—all the same size and with the same perspective. He added a one-point perspective grid: two diagonal lines that crossed at the center of the quadrille grid.

➤ The grid was eventually concealed behind a large black rectangle and, on top of that, a rectangle filled with a radial black-and-white gradient that represented the paved street surface. It also gave a feeling of light coming from the center of the maze.

➤ Each city block is created individually with unique buildings that follow the one-point perspective—as if you were hovering in a helicopter over the center of the image. The following figure shows one such block, enlarged, in Preview and Artwork views.

➤ Trees are shaded with a green linear gradient to give the effect of light coming from one direction. Note that this is a linear gradient rather than radial, since trees don't have the shiny surface of a sphere that often take a radial gradient reflect a point of light.

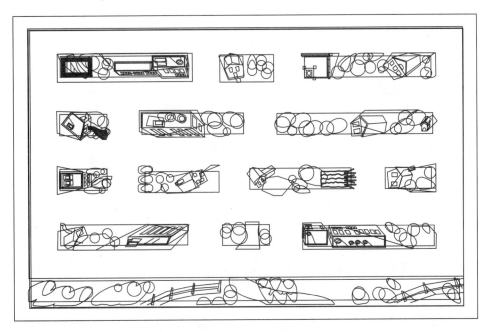

Figure 12.31 Artwork view of Puzzle #2.

Doug Heinlein is Creative Director at Imagination Pilots Entertainment, 640 N. LaSalle, Suite 560, Chicago, IL 60610, Phone: 312-944-9471, Fax: 312-642-0616, e-mail: dhein-lein@aol.com

NOTE

Steven Gorton's Maps

A popular but demanding element of city tourism maps is a representation of major buildings and landmarks, and Steven Gordon's map of downtown Huntsville, Alabama does it beautifully. Steven saw that his main challenge in this example was drawing enough detail to express the character of each building but not enough to look like a miniature architectural rendering.

Steven notes, "Perspective city views are harder to draw if you can't visit the buildings in person." For nearby Huntsville, he took a camcorder trip around downtown to supplement his reference materials. By contrast, a recently completed map for Columbus, Georgia (a 1996 Olympic venue), was done long-distance. His client provided aerial photographs, photocopies, postcards, a Polaroid, brochures, a blueprint and a hand-drawn sketch for reference.

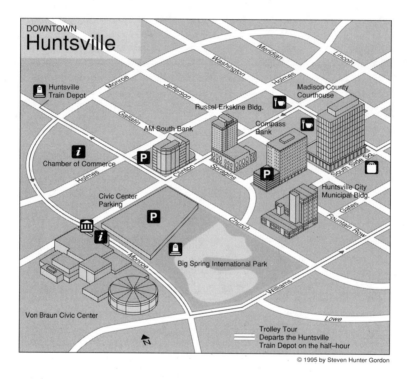

© 1995 by Steven Hunter Gordon

Figure 12.32 Steven Gordon's map of downtown Huntsville (see also colorplates).

Steven comments: "I switched over to Illustrator last spring when Adobe offered cross-grades to FreeHand owners. I've found Illustrator 5.5 superior for map-making because of its type placement and manipulation, selection tools, on-screen color fidelity, and reliable output."

NOTE

Without detailing the hundreds of steps involved in creating this map, we note a few important points here:

➤ Lines composing a building were set with butt caps and rounded joins for clean intersections.

➤ The title block employs lighter tints for the green background and gray road casings.

➤ The two paths cutting through the title block (the white street and the wider gray path behind it) had to line up with the paths defining the same street outside the title block. To accomplish this, the path for the entire street was cloned (copied and pasted in back), then cloned again and given a wider, light gray stoke.

➤ A rectangle was drawn for the title block background and assigned a lighter version of the map's green background. He masked the rectangle and the two cloned streets to create the discrete area of the title block.

NOTE

Desaturating color values is one technique that allows map features like roads and rivers to extend into and behind title and legend blocks in maps where page space is at a premium.

Figure 12.33 Downtown Huntsville title block.

➤ The roof and two sides of each building are drawn in plan view and then angled and scaled to create a perspective version. Figure 12.34 shows an enlarged detail in Preview and Artwork views. (See Chapter 9 for tips on drawing in perspective and creating three-dimensional effects.)

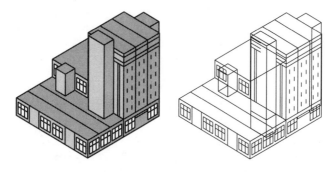

Figure 12.34 A Huntsville building in Preview and Artwork views.

Another example of Steven's work appears later in this chapter. It's a map of Utah that includes an imported image.

N O T E Steven Hunter Gordon has been designing and producing maps with desktop software since 1987. His techniques include shaded relief rendering, perspective views, and integrating maps, text and graphic images. He has produced city, tourism, transportation, accessibility and recreation maps, for books, brochures, magazines and computer screens. Currently, he operates GordonMaps by computer, modem and overnight delivery from Madison, Alabama. In addition to making maps, he has participated in cartographic software and knowledge-based development. He can be reached at P.O. Box 752, Madison, AL 35758; 205-772-0022, e-mail: GordonMaps@aol.com.

Sue Sellar's Anatomical Illustrations

Sue Sellar's anatomical and biological illustrations are masterpieces of stippling. We describe one here, an illustration of the stomach (Figure 12.35). This one plus three others are shown in the colorplates.

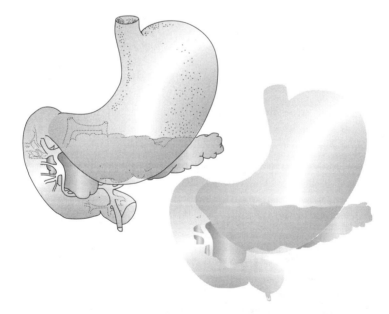

Figure 12.35 Sue Sellar's illustration of a stomach, with background shading elements pulled to the right.

Sue works in Illustrator using some of the same techniques she used "before the Macintosh" to illustrate textbooks. She still starts with a hand sketch in some cases and scans the sketch for use as a template in Illustrator. The shapes are meticulously drawn, but the real tricks lie in the shading techniques:

➤ The background color in most of her illustrations is created by drawing shapes and filling them with different gradient or linear fills. Figure 12.45 above shows the background elements separate from the full illustration. The trick here is to get the gradients in adjacent shapes to match up.

➤ The stippling for added dimension is created using the traditional technique: each individual stipple is created using the Brush tool set to 0.5-point with a drawing tablet. The tremendous advantages of using Illustrator over the old pen-and-ink method include the ability to work in magnified views (so her hand doesn't actually have to stipple at 0.1-point intervals) and the ability to view on-screen or print drafts to assess the effects (Figure 12.36).

Figure 12.36 The black lines from Sue Sellar's illustration, with an enlarged detail of the stippling effect.

Sue Sellars is a freelance artist and performance artist at MacWorld and other conventions, where she can be found demonstrating CalComp drawing tablets and various drawing programs. She can be reached at Two Blue Heron Studios, P.O. Box 136, Philo, CA 95466, 707-895-3067.

NOTE

Scott Crouse's Saw and Truck

Scott Crouse is a full-time product illustrator and a freelance graphic artist. He usually works from some kind of template in beginning a product illustration.

Sometimes he scans a photo into Photoshop and creates many of the paths in Photoshop and then copies them to Illustrator, or he'll place an EPS image on a separate layer and use it as a template, but he notes "this is not my favorite way of tracing an image because it tends to slow down and mess up screen redraws."

Two of his illustrations are described here (Figure 12.37 and 12.38), and a third is discussed later in this chapter (see also colorplates).

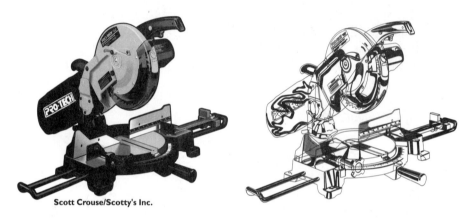

Scott Crouse/Scotty's Inc.

Figure 12.37 Mitre saw illustration by Scott Crouse in Preview and Artwork views (see also colorplate). Lines that appear thick in Artwork view are actually adjacent paths created in blending for shading.

Scott believes that what really makes the saw illustration is the transparent effect of the plastic blade guard. By copying parts of the underlying image of the blades and recoloring them in the color of the blade guard and softening them with blends they give a pretty convincing effect of transparency to the illustration. Notice the areas where the translucent, plastic blade guards pass over the yellow saw body (See colorplate).

Scott notes that the secret to doing an involved piece such as the truck on the next page is to decide on a base tone and blend from it to both the highlights and shadows. On the body, he used the dark red for the base tone and made blends from it for the highlights. To Scott, the wheels are the hardest part because it is easy to make them look something less than round if you don't do the shading right.

Scott can be reached at Scott Crouse Illustration, 59 Coleman Rd., Winter Haven, FL 33880, 941-294-8146, e-mail: ScotMan421@aol.com.

NOTE

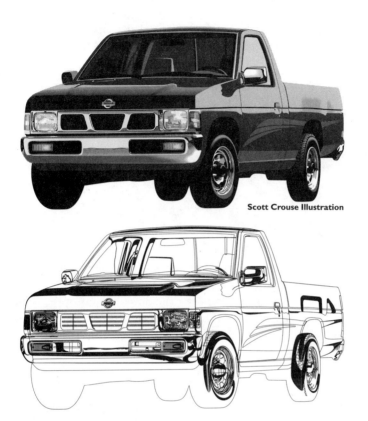

Scott Crouse Illustration

Figure 12.38 Nissan truck illustration by Scott Crouse (see also colorplate),
in Preview (above) and Artwork views. Lines that appear thick in Artwork view are
actually adjacent paths creating in blending for shading.

Gary Symington's Furnace

To start this furnace illustration, Gary was given a "very bad" black-and-white
photo to work from—so bad, in fact, he had to redraw it. He then scanned his
hand-tracing and used it as a template. The perspective was done with as much
copying and pasting as possible—"more than you might think"—of the little
round wire "conduits," which he then reworked a little. "Those bars were tricky,"
he notes, "I believe I just worked with them until I had them right. If I get stuck
on perspective I may work out a single point perspective sketch to help out."

Illustrator's gradients made this job feasible—and much needed to get the look
of heat and the "glow." The hot wire itself is four layered lines of diminishing size.

719

Each line was copied and pasted in front, then adjusted. By changing the colors, Gary got the glow effect, more evident in the color plate than in Figure 12.39.

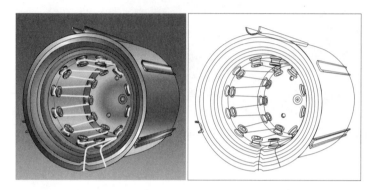

Figure 12.39 Gary Symington's furnace in Preview and Artwork views (see also colorplate).

He worked in a number of different layers during the development of the illustration and then consolidated some so he ended up with only three (Figure 12.40). "I can tell you that this would have been pretty much impossible before Illustrator had layers," he adds. "I turned off layers and hid various layers so I could see what I was doing"

Figure 12.40 Final set of layers in Gary's furnace, from bottom (left) to top. Top layer is shown against black here to make white lines visible.

Gary Symington, of Meadow Vista, CA, is a freelance illustrator and graphic designer. He can be reached at 916-878-6876 or e-mail: Drummer 911@ aol.com.

NOTE

Mixing Illustrator with Other Tools

These last illustrations were created using Illustrator and at least one other application. (A few of the earlier examples used Photoshop to clean up scans for use as templates in Illustrator, but we don't count that unless the Photoshop art was included as part of the Illustrator artwork, as in some of these examples.)

➤ Lester Yocum's Santa Star came through Streamline on the way to Illustrator.

➤ Sandee Cohen's push pin, Scott Crouse's steel can, and Paul McBride Mahan's Greek columns all enlisted the help of Adobe Dimensions for the three-dimensional effects.

➤ Arthur Saarinen's postcard design, Ray Villarosa's dramatic poster, and dr. Zox's *New tricks for an old dog* used Photoshop and Streamline as well as Illustrator.

➤ Steven Gordon's map of Utah is backed by a colorful mountain profile created in MicroFrontier's Color It! He then takes the whole thing out to a PDF file for viewing with Adobe Acrobat.

➤ Stephen Czapiewski's *Nephthys* started with elements in Illustrator that ended up in Photoshop.

Lester Yocum's Santa Star

Lester Yocum loves to play with light and lines in his greeting card designs. In this example, the artwork was drawn with thick black lines in ink, then scanned in at 300 dpi and autotraced through Streamline in outline mode, with cleanup and coloring in Illustrator. He used Illustrator to light up the border from the star to Santa's face, subtly reinforcing the image's glow (Figure 12.41). The background snowflakes started as perfect circles, Points were added using the Add Anchor Points filter then distorted using Scribble with various settings. The resulting objects were copied, scaled, and rotated to add variety.

Figure 12.41 Lester Yocum's Santa Star greeting card, shown here in Preview and Artwork views, is also a colorplate.

With over 15 years of traditional and digital illustration and design experience, Lester Yocum's credits range from posters, books, and signage to Web pages. He is currently a graphic artist and systems administrator in Glen Burnie, Maryland. He can be reached at LYOCUM@aol.com.

NOTE

Sandee Cohen's Push Pin

Shadows Push Pin originated as an exercise for Sandee Cohen's Illustrator classes. It basically shows many different ways to play with light and shadows (Figure 12.42). The push pin was created in Dimensions with the light highlighted off certain areas of the pin. Two shadows were created using KPT Vector Effects. Three gradients were used to curl the paper. Finally a tiny pinhole shadow was created using blends (Figure 12.42).

Sandee Cohen is a consultant and trainer based in New York City. She can be reached at 33 Fifth Avenue, New York, NY 10003, 212-677-7763, e-mail: SandeeC@aol.com.

NOTE

Figure 12.42 Sandee Cohen's Shadows Push Pin in Preview view (see also colorplate).

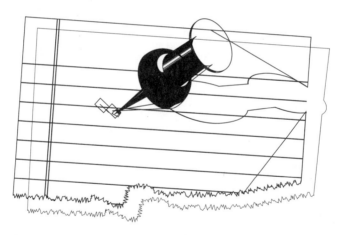

Figure 12.43 Push Pin in Artwork view.

Scott Crouse's Steel Can

Scott Crouse's steel can required several exchanges between Illustrator and Adobe Dimensions (Figure 12.44). (Two of his other illustrations were described earlier in this chapter.)

Scott Crouse/Scotty's Inc.

Figure 12.44 Scott Crouse's steel can illustration in Preview and Artwork views. Extra paths added in blending color transitions have been removed in the third image (see also colorplate).

1. Scott started this steel can by drawing a basic half profile of a can in Adobe Illustrator.

2. He copied it to Adobe Dimensions where he revolved it 360 degrees, adjusted the perspective, saved the image and exported a copy of it in Illustrator format.

3. He used this exported Illustrator image only as a template on a separate layer for the illustration so that he could reproduce its shape and perspective accurately. He used a photo of a can to guide him in the details and finished the illustration without a label.

4. Then he went back to the Dimensions document and exported a map of the side surface of the can in Illustrator format. This gave him a flat, two-dimensional set of guides that represented the side of the can which he used to make the label.

5. He set the type, converted it to outlines, and arranged the graphics on the guides.

6. He selected and copied all this back to Dimensions and mapped it to the side of the can. He then exported this version of the can with the label in Illustrator format.

7. He copied only the label from this Illustrator file and pasted it onto the completed can illustration and colored it appropriately.

NOTE

Scott notes, "Although using envelope-type plug-ins might be a little less time-consuming, I don't think they give the same kind of realistic results that you get with Dimensions. Remember to start the illustration in Dimensions and use that image as the guide for the rest of the work. It's a lot easier than making a really nice cylinder- or cone-shaped piece of art in Illustrator and then trying to reproduce its shape and perspective in Dimensions in order to map a label to it."

Scott can be reached at Scott Crouse Illustration, 59 Coleman Rd., Winter Haven, FL 33880, 941-294-8146, e-mail: ScotMan421@aol.com.

NOTE

Arthur Saarinen's Full Table

Arthur Saarinen's design for AVID was a printed postcard mailer with additional text placed on it in Quark Express (Figure 12.45). The table spoon, salt shaker, and measuring spoon where scanned, saved in Photoshop as EPS files, opened in Illustrator and traced, and sized and rotated to fit in the image. The wood table was a scanned photo that was brought into Adobe Streamline where a CMYK wood grain file was created (Figure 12.46).

© 1995 Arthur J. Saarinen, AVID

Figure 12.45 Arthur Saarinen's postcard design for AVID.

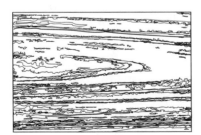
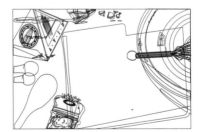

Figure 12.46 Artwork views of wood-grain lines (left) and other objects with blend lines removed (right).

Arthur J. Saarinen is a computer illustrator. He can be reached at Saarinen Associates, 7 Forest Court, Lexington, MA 02173, Fax: 617-674-0452, e-mail: ASaarinen@aol.com.

NOTE

Ray Villarosa's Crime-Comic Style

Ray Villarosa works for OHS, a Dental Health Organization in Miami. The illustration shown in Figure 12.47 was one of the presentation materials used in a seminar on domestic violence. Ray notes, "Because of the subject matter, I felt that a rough, nasty, gritty look was best suited for this." As you'll see in the following steps, he used a combination of Adobe Photoshop and Illustrator.

Figure 12.47 Ray Villarosa's domestic violence posters show both sides of the problem in graphic crime-comic style. The right half of this illustration is also shown as a colorplate.

Here's how Ray did it:

1. Ray sketched the figures on paper and then scanned them.
2. In Photoshop, he added more lines and played with the contrast to delete any light gray areas, and then saved it as a PICT file.
3. In Illustrator, he opened it as a template and added more lines and shapes after retracing it in a rough manner.

4. He took the image back into Photoshop where he ran a Gaussian Blur of 3. Here he notes: "I suppose I could have just Streamlined it, but the result was way too clean and the extra Photoshop step really did the trick, especially under the tight deadline I was under."

5. He used Adobe Streamline to trace it again.

6. Back in Illustrator he added final color and the type.

7. The shading effect on the man's hand in the foreground was done with the Blend Tool. He simply drew an amorphous shape that closely resembled the hand, filled it with a dark value, and used the default settings for blending.

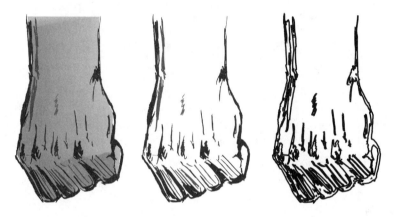

Figure 12.48 Hand in Preview mode (left), with shading removed (middle), and in Artwork view with shading removed.

Ray Villarosa, 16850 South Glades Drive #7D, North Miami Beach, FL 33162, 305-940-8556 after 8 p.m. EST, 1-800-223-6447 x303, e-mail: rvillarosa@aol.com, industrial@eworld.com, and 102510.3142@compuserve.com

N O T E

Steven Gordon's Map of Utah

Steven Gordon's map of Utah integrates a Southwest landscape painted in MicroFrontier's Color It! with tourism elements (roads, symbols) rendered in Illustrator. "Merging raster images with the precision of a vector drawing allows mapmakers to add interesting backgrounds to otherwise simple maps," he notes.

In this Utah map, Steven painted a flat landscape in MicroFrontier's Color It!, treated it with a noise filter, and brought it into Illustrator as an EPS file.

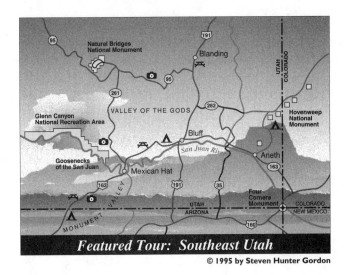

© 1995 by Steven Hunter Gordon

Figure 12.49 Steven Gordon's map of Utah (see also colorplate).

When combining raster images with a map, file sizes have to be watched. Maps with complex paths, lots of text objects, and a 300 ppi raster background can stress an imagesetter. Steven usually uses 144 ppi images for rendered back-grounds (which are not meant to be photorealistically sharp and clear anyway) to conserve file size (Figure 12.50).

Figure 12.50 Imported EPS (left) and Illustrator art (right) that compose map of Utah.

Raster images provide another challenge to the mapmaker. Visually judging and screen-proofing line color and weight may be difficult with a low-resolution EPS preview in the background. One solution is saving the Illustrator file (with its embedded EPS file) in PDF format, and viewing it in Adobe Acrobat. This can provide a smoother, higher-resolution view of the background EPS art overlaid with the accompanying Illustrator artwork.

Steven Gordon can be reached at P.O. Box 752, Madison, AL 35758, 205-772-0022, or e-mail at GordonMaps@aol.com.

N O T E

dr. Zox's 50,000 Year Old Dog

dr. Zox (his e.e. cummings-esque pseudonym, lowercase *dr.* intended) used Photoshop. Illustrator, and KPT Vector Effects to create this extrusion of a wolf (or tail-less hyena) cave painting (Figures 12.51 and 12.52). (We discussed the matter of starting with someone else's art, but couldn't give the "original artist" his due credit since it is cave art from 50,000 years ago!)

Figure 12.51 dr. Zox's New Tricks for an Old Dog (see also colorplates).

1. Dr. Zox took a GIF bitmap image and placed it as a layer in Photoshop. There he traced it using his Wacom tablet, working on a new layer. After tracing, he deleted the original scan.

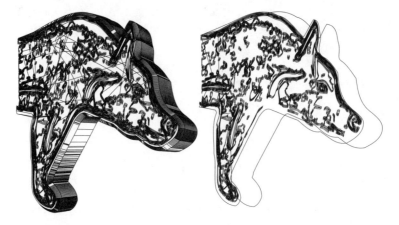

Figure 12.52 dr. Zox's New Tricks for an Old Dog in Artwork view.

2. He then rasterized the image in Streamline and used several KPT Vector Effects on it. He imported a photograph of a stone, which he captured with a Quicktake 100 digital camera. These layers were merged to create the background art (see colorplate).

3. In Illustrator, he imported the EPS TIFF file of the cave art and the streamlining of the background stone art into separate layers.

4. He cropped off half of the Streamline file to create the right half of the image.

5. The color values were adjusted by selecting the same paint style and using KPT Color Tweak.

6. To get a clean background outline of the front half, he used the pen tool to hand draw the vectors. KPT 3D Transform was used on this outline to create the three-dimensional extrusion. The KPT settings were saved to use again on the top layer.

7. He used KPT Vector 3D Transform, Emboss and Shatter on this top layer to create the "stucco-esque" look.

8. Since the vector 3D setting were reused the alignment of the art was precise, some paste in front/behind was used to adjust the layering of elements in this layer.

9. He also was dissatisfied with the eye so he "cheated" and dropped in a hand-vectored eye that was embossed to match the rest of the image.

NOTE

dr. Zox is easily contacted via e-mail to drzox@aol.com.

Stephen Czapiewski's Nephthys

Figure 12.53 Stephen Czapiewski's Nephthys is composed of six separate Illustrator files incorporated into a final Photoshop file © 1995 OOMM Studios, by Stephen Czapiewski (see colorplate).

Stephen Czapiewski's *Nephthys* was created primarily using Illustrator. All of the elements (a pink goose, Nephthys and Anubis) were done in Illustrator. These images were then imported into Photoshop where the clouds were painted. Stephen comments, "The piece was inspired by artist Michael Parkes. It contains a great number of oddball blends and strange techniques."

Some points worth noting:

➤ The only things that he traced for these images were the original drawings that he did by hand. He sketched the goose from a photo in a wildlife book.

➤ Each element was created individually in Illustrator and then combined on several layers in Photoshop. Stephen notes "I choose to combine the elements in Photoshop because the service bureau that I'd planned to have print it informed me that keeping everything in Illustrator may cause problems for their printer. I don't buy that either, but better safe than splattered. Since then, I've hooked up with another service bureau."

➤ For the blend that runs the length of the bird and the front of the fanned wing, Stephen created strokes blended to other strokes. There are seven such blends on the bird's body.

➤ The individual feathers are mostly auto-gradients. There are four slightly different gradients used for the feathers. The real trick was using the gradient vector tool to get the feathers to look as real as possible.

➤ Stroke to stroke blends were primarily what he used on the other elements also with a few exceptions.

➤ He used a tablet to sketch the clouds in the sky in Photoshop:

➤ He brought Anubis in first and painted the clouds around him. He then brought Anubis's left hand in and brushed in some clouds around his hand to give the illusion that he was parting the clouds.

➤ He placed the slab next and applied a bit of noise to it to make it look more natural.

➤ Nephthys was next. She was not edited at all in Photoshop.

➤ The goose was last. It wasn't edited in Photoshop either.

➤ The glyphs are a font that he picked up off America Online called Nahkt Hieroglyphics. On the slab face the glyphs are simply placed helter skelter, with some symbols combining to read basic terms like *worship*, *water*, and *heaven*. He applied the KPT Vector Effect KPT Emboss "to make them look like they were doing something other than just stuck to the rock like Egyptian fridge magnets." The glyphs are also used on Nephthys' headband. Here each glyph had to be manipulated to make it appear to be part of the headband. He used KPT Warp Frame for those effects.

N O T E Stephen created the Photoshop file specifically for printing to poster-sizes. The image is 18-inch x30-inch and is 100 dpi. The LZW compressed Tiff is 4.9 MB. He suggests, "Shop around for prices on poster printing. I've seen prices for large format color output ranging from $12 to $18 per square foot in the Detroit area! Look around, ask questions, check out samples. Great art is worth getting the best quality reproductions without becoming a starving artist!"

N O T E Stephen Czapiewski and his wife Maureen run OOMM Studios (P.O. Box 43, Holly MI 48442, 810-634-6533) where they provide graphic services to "all kinds of cool clients!" Stephen is a former Desktop Publishing Project Leader for Ross Roy Communications. He has designed several fonts (using Illustrator), logos, automotive illustrations, and renderings. He also publishes several comic book series.

Paul McBride Mahan's Columns

Paul McBride Mahan's Greek columns were created in pieces that originated in Illustrator and were then made three-dimensional in Adobe Dimensions (Figure 12.54).

Figure 12.54 Greek columns in Preview view.

1. A square was the original starting point for the base and capitol. The squares were created in Dimensions and then extruded with bevels in Illustrator.

2. The body of the capitol was created in Illustrator and then extruded in Dimensions. The columns were then aligned and a perspective view set. After rendering as a wire frame and as a shaded render, the completed column was opened in illustrator.

3. Shading was completed in Illustrator using various graduated fills made up in shades of gray.

4. He set the vanishing point by copying the line that defined the top of the cap and the line that defined the bottom of the base and then enlarging them one at a time from the "closest" endpoint. Where the two paths

crossed established the perspective point used to anchor the vanishing lines used to create the steps and the cornice and to copy and reduce the column to create the row of columns.

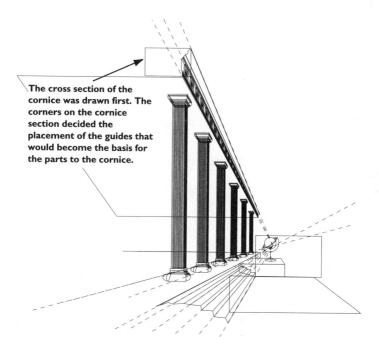

The cross section of the cornice was drawn first. The corners on the cornice section decided the placement of the guides that would become the basis for the parts to the cornice.

Figure 12.55 Artwork view of columns, including guides for perspective.

Paul McBride Mahan can be reached at PM Graphics, 404 S. Westland, Tampa FL 33606-2040. Phone: 813-251-5199. Email: PMnight@aol.com.

NOTE

Glossary

Actual Size—A command on the View menu (**Command+H**) that displays a view of a page on the screen, scaled to approximately the same size it will print (i.e., 100% scale), depending on the characteristics of your screen display.

additive primary colors—Red, green, and blue. The three colors used to create all other colors when direct or transmitted light is used (television, for instance). See also *primary colors* and *subtractive primary colors*.

Adobe Separator—Adobe's add-on color separation software package that can be used in conjunction with Illustrator but is not needed with Illustrator 6.0 and later versions. Adobe Separator prints your files color separated (i.e., each color is printed on a separate sheet of paper or film). See *color separation*.

Adobe Type Manager—See *ATM*.

alignment—The positioning of lines of text on a page or in a column: aligned left (flush left, ragged right); centered; aligned right (flush right, ragged left); or justified (flush on both left and right). The alignment of a block of type is indicated by the position of its alignment point.

alignment point—The point used to align a block of type. The alignment point is also used to select and move the type. Each block of type has one alignment point. The point appears as a solid square when the block of type is selected; otherwise, it appears as an x.

anchor point—The point on a segment that determines where the segment starts or ends. Anchor points are invisible unless any segment of the path they form is selected. Anchor points that end curved segments have direction lines and points associated with them. A single anchor point with no segments connected to it appears as an *x* when it is not selected.

area graph—A line graph with the area below the line filled in with colors, patterns, and so on. An area graph is more effective if you use several sets of data.

area type—Type that is bound by a path.

Area-type tool—A tool that enables you to enter text inside an open or closed path. The text flows to match the shape. See *type tool*.

Artboard—The work area on which one or more pages of an Adobe Illustrator document is displayed. An 18-inch square on which you work in Illustrator. The document size is indicated by a solid rectangle, and the print area is indicated on the artwork board by dotted borders.

artwork—The paths and type created with Illustrator that constitute an image. Stroke and fill attributes are not visible in an artwork image. Artwork is saved as a POSTSCRIPT program. Compare with *preview image* and *template*.

Artwork view—A display of an Adobe Illustrator document with lines that define the artwork without color effects. See also *Preview view*.

ascender—The part of a lowercase letter that rises above its main body. Technically, only three letters of the alphabet have ascenders: *b*, *d*, and *h*. Uppercase letters and the lowercase letters *f*, *k*, *l*, and *t* also reach the height of the ascenders. See also *descender*.

ASCII—A standard format for storing text files (i.e., American Standard Code for Information Interchange). A numbering scheme that assigns unique binary numbers to each text and control character. The form in which text is stored if saved as Text Only, an **Export** command option in Illustrator as well as a Save command option available for most databases, spreadsheets, and word processors. ASCII files include all the characters of the text itself (including tabs and carriage returns) but not the non-ASCII codes used to indicate character and paragraph formats. See also *text-only file*.

ATM—Adobe Type Manager, a font management utility developed by Adobe Systems. Illustrator uses fonts that are managed by ATM. ATM also downloads the fonts you use in your Illustrator documents to the printer you output to. See *printer font*, *screen font*, and *type manager*.

auto trace—To trace around the shapes or lines in a template automatically using the Auto Trace tool.

average—To find the average location of selected anchor points and move the selected points to that location. When you average points, the points remain distinct points. Compare with *join*.

axis—A reference line on a graph. See *x axis* and *y axis*.

bad break—Refers to line breaks and column breaks that result in widows or orphans, or to line breaks that hyphenate words incorrectly or separate two words that should stay together (for example, *Mr. Smith*). See also *nonbreaking space* and *orphans/widows*.

backup—Saving or making an extra copy of the current or an original file or disk.

banding—An undesirable striped effect that prevents a blend or gradient fill from appearing uniform.

bar graph—See grouped column graph.

base—The shiny, nonphotosensitive side of film. See *emulsion*.

baseline—A horizontal line that coincides with the bottom of each character in a font, excluding descenders (i.e., the bottom of letters such as *a* and *x*, excluding the tails on letters like p and q). In Adobe Illustrator, the baselines of a block of type are visible when the type is selected. You click on a baseline to select type and drag it to move type.

Benday—An old printing term for *screen tints*. Taken from the name of a company that used to produce screens for the printing industry.

bevel join—A squared off corner that is created when the notch that is formed when two lines meet is filled with a triangle. Compare *miter join* and *round join*.

Bezier curve—A curve, named after Pierre Bezier, that is defined mathematically by four control points. These control points are the four direction points at the ends of the two direction lines that are tangent to each curve. All curves in Adobe Illustrator are Bezier curves. See *curve*.

bit—Smallest measurement of computer information.

bit depth—The number of bits used to describe each pixel in a bitmap. The bit depth describes the amount of color or grayscale information conveyed by a pixel. A black-and-white bitmap has a bit depth of one. Each pixel can be either 0 or 1, which correspond to black and white, respectively. Grayscale images can have bit depths of either 4 or 8. A 4-bit grayscale image has 16 shades of gray; an 8-bit image has 256 shades of gray. Color images can have bit depths of 4, 8, 16, and 24. A 4-bit color image has 16 colors, an 8-bit image has 256 colors, a 16-bit image has thousands of colors, and a 24-bit image has millions of colors.

bitmap—A graphics image or text formed by a pattern of dots. Photoshop and Painter produce bit-mapped graphics, for example, as do scanners or digital cameras. Low-resolution images are sometimes called *paint-type* files, and these images usually have fewer dots per inch (dpi) than high-resolution TIFF images. Also, an electronically displayed graphic image made up on a matrix of dots. Templates and Preview images are bitmap images. Contrast with *object-oriented graphics*.

bleed—Used to describe a printed image extending to the trimmed edge of the sheet or page.

blend—To create a series of successive shapes or shadings between two selected paths.

blueline—A prepress proofing material, used to proof black-and-white art before printing. This test printing is done by using a photochemical process (instead of printer's inks) that produces a blue image on white paper. See also *prepress proofs* and *press proofs*.

blue pencil/blue line—Traditionally, a guideline drawn with a blue pencil or printed in light blue ink on the boards and used as a guide for manually pasting up a page layout. The blue ink is sometimes called *nonrepro blue* because the color is not picked up by the camera when a page is photographed to make plates for offset printing. In Illustrator, you can create nonprinting margins, column guides, and ruler guides on the screen to help you position text and graphics; these lines do not appear when the page is printed.

BMP—A bitmap graphics file format used by Microsoft Windows. A BMP image is an indexed color image that can be read by computer system environments or graphics software. Illustrator 6.0 can save files in BMP format on the Macintosh, but only the Windows version of Illustrator (and other applications) can open or import this format. See *bitmap* and *file formats*.

board—A sheet of heavyweight paper or card stock onto which typeset text and graphics were traditionally pasted manually. See also *blue pencil/blue line*.

body copy—The main part of the text of a publication, as distinguished from headings and captions. See also *body type*.

body type—The type (font) used for the body copy. Generally, fonts that are used for body copy, as distinguished from display type. See also *body copy*.

boilerplate—A document set up with text and graphic elements that will be included routinely in a series of documents based on the boilerplate without the need to recreate the repeated elements each time. See also *template*.

bounding box—An invisible, nonprinting rectangle that Illustrator defines as the boundaries of artwork and how it will be cropped when trim marks are applied through the Trim Marks filter. Also defines the size of the illustration when it is saved in EPS format and imported back into Illustrator using **File > Place** or placed in another application such as PageMaker or QuarkXPress.

butt cap—A square line cap that is perpendicular to the end of a line. It is called a butt cap because the cap butts up against the end of the line. Compare *round cap* and *projecting cap*.

bounding box—Rectangular space that contains all of the artwork. Also, the rectangle that defines the size of a pattern tile.

brochure—A folded pamphlet or small booklet.

calligraphic—Style of font that mimics fancy handwriting, such as that created with pen and ink or beveled pens. See *font*.

callouts—In publishing, text that points out and identifies parts of an illustration. Also, headings that appear in a narrow margin next to the body copy. See also *pull-out quote*.

camera-ready art—The complete pages of a publication assembled with text and graphics and ready for reproduction. Literally refers to pages ready to be photographed as the first step in the process of making plates for offset printing. See also *mechanicals* and *offset printing*.

cap height—Height of a typeface's capital letters.

caps—(in text) Editors' short-hand for capital (uppercase) letters. Illustrator offers the ability to set text in Uppercase through the **Type > Change Case** command, in which all characters of the selected text are automatically converted to capital letters regardless of how they were typed or to mixed case, in which the first letter of each word in the selection is capitalized.

caps—(on paths) Defines how the end of a graphic line looks: square, butt, rounded, or projected. See also *line cap*.

caption—Descriptive text that identifies a photograph or illustration. See also *callouts*.

carriage return—A line break you insert by pressing the **Return** or **Enter** key at the end of a line or paragraph. Sometimes called a *hard carriage return* to distinguish it from the soft carriage returns that result from word wrapping at the right margin of area text or right edge of a column. The term originated from the typewriter, which actually had a carriage that "carried" the paper back and forth in front of the keys and "returned" the paper to the left margin position when you pressed the **Return** key.

cell—The intersection of a row and a column in a graph work sheet.

CGM—Vector file format that is widely accepted among both DOS and Windows applications. The acronym stands for Computer Graphics Metafile. The Windows version of Illustrator can import CGM files. See also *file formats* and *vector images*.

check box—The small square to the left of certain options in dialog boxes. You click the check box to turn an option on or off (to select or deselect it). An *X* appears in the check box after it is selected, or turned on. The check box is empty if is it deselected, or turned off.

choke trap—The intentional overlap of a lighter background onto a darker object to compensate for misregistration on the press, accomplished by spreading the background color slightly thereby, "choking," or squeezing, the edges of the lighter object.

Cicero—A unit of measure equivalent to 4.55 millimeters, commonly used in Europe for measuring font sizes, but not supported by Illustrator. See also *measurement system*.

click—To press and then immediately release the mouse button.

clip art—Off-the-shelf art.

Clipboard—A feature of the operating system. Temporarily stores text or graphics cut or copied by the commands on the Edit menu. The **Paste** command brings the contents of the Clipboard to the page. The **Edit > Show Clipboard** command displays the contents of the Clipboard.

clipping path—A mask as defined by Illustrator's **Objects > Masks > Make** command. The effect of a mask is to "crop" background objects by making parts of them invisible and nonprinting.

closed path—A path with no endpoints. A loop. Compare with *open path*.

CMYK—Shorthand notation for *cyan, magenta, yellow*, and *black*. Sometimes written *CYMK*. See also *process color* and *subtractive primary colors*.

coated stock—Paper that has a light clay or plastic coating. A glossy or slick paper is coated. Often, the color you want depends on the type of stock on which you are printing.

coincident—Occupying the same position. In a straight line, an anchor point and its two direction points are coincident.

collinear—Occurring along the same straight line. The anchor point and two direction points of a smooth point are collinear.

color bar—A strip of colors printed on color separations that tells the press person how consistent the color is during the printing run.

color keys—A color overlay proofing system produced by the 3M Company. See *overlay proofs*.

color-matching systems—Methods, or recipes, for mixing ink used by commercial printers to create consistent colors. By choosing a desired color for your print job from a booklet of color swatches, a pressman follows specific recipes from the color swatches for mixing different inks to get the desired color.

color separations—In offset printing, separate plates used to lay different colors of ink on a page printed in multiple colors to reproduce the proportional amount of cyan, magenta, yellow, and black in the original. Illustrator prints color separations of documents.

color swatch—In Illustrator's Paint Style palette, the fill and stroke of the selected object displays as a color swatch. Illustrator also allows you to choose a fill or stroke color from color swatches that you can arrange in the Paint Style palette. Also, a color sample in a swatch book for a color matching system. See also *color matching systems*.

comp—Traditionally, a designer's comprehensive sketch of a page design, showing the client what the final page is to look like after being printed. Usually a full-sized likeness of the page, a comp is a few steps closer to the final than a pencil rough and can be composed by using ink pens, pencils, color markers, color acetate, pressure-sensitive letters, and other tools available at art supply shops. A comp created by using Illustrator resembles the finished product, featuring type-set text, ruled lines, and shaded boxes created in Illustrator. The comp can be used as a starting point in building the final document. A paper proof printed on a color printer before you print the final negatives is the equivalent of a comp.

compound path—A group of two or more paths, with at least one reversed path. The reversed path or paths can create the effect of transparency, or "holes," in the artwork.

compression—A method of making an image or file take up less storage space on a disk or in memory. Several techniques are commonly used to compress bitmap image data:

- ➤ Run Length Encoding (RLE) is a compression technique that maintains color quality (i.e., a "lossless" technique), supported by the TIFF file format and some common Windows file formats.

- ➤ Lemple-Zif-Welch (LZW) is also a lossless compression technique supported by TIFF, PDF, and PostScript language file formats.

- ➤ CCITT encoding is a family of lossless compression techniques for black-and-white images that is supported by the PDF and PostScript language file formats (CCITT is an acronym for the French spelling of International Telegraph and Telekeyed Consultive Committee).

➤ Joint Photographic Experts Group (JPEG) is a compression technique that sometimes results in color degradation. It is supported by the PDF and PostScript language file formats.

condensed type—A narrow typeface having proportionally less character width than a normal face of the same size. Although you can achieve this effect by graphically scaling characters from the normal font, usually condensed characters are individually designed as a separate font. Condensed typefaces are used where large amounts of copy must fit into a relatively small space (tabular composition being the most common area of usage). See also *kerning*.

constrain—To restrict drawing, moving, or transforming to an angle you specify, usually a multiple of 45 degrees. You constrain the movement by holding the Shift key as you drag the mouse. See also *x axis* and *y axis*.

continuous tone image—An illustration or photograph, black-and-white or color, composed of many shades between the lightest and the darkest tones and not broken up into dots. Continuous-tone images usually need to be converted into dots, either by scanning or by halftone, to be printed in ink or on a laser printer. When you scan an image, it is converted from a continuous tone image to a halftone. See also *halftone*.

Control Panel—An Apple menu item on the Macintosh used to adjust mouse and screen settings, and to change options for some extensions.

Control palette—A movable window in Illustrator that enables you to manipulate the selected object through numeric entries.

copy fitting—Determining the amount of copy (text set in a specific font) that can fit in a given area on a page or in a publication. Making copy fit on a page in Illustrator by adjusting the line spacing, word spacing, and letter spacing.

corner point—An anchor point in which the anchor point and its two direction points are not positioned on a straight line. Corner points are used to join two segments traveling in different directions. Compare with *smooth point*.

corner radius—The radius of the circle used to form rounded corners in a rectangle.

Cromalin—An integral proofing system produced by DuPont. See *integral proof*.

crop—To use Illustrator's masking feature to trim or hide the edges from a graphic to make the image fit into a given space or to remove unnecessary parts of the image.

crop marks—Lines printed on a page to indicate where the page is to be trimmed after the final document is printed and bound. Illustrator prints these marks if the **Crop Marks** option is selected in the Print command dialog box. You can also set up crop marks using the **Object > Crop Marks > Make** and **Filter > Create > Trim Marks** commands. See also *printer's marks*.

crossbar or **crosshair**—The shape of the pointer after one of Illustrator's tools for drawing lines and shapes has been selected. See also *pointer*.

current attributes—The fill, stroke, and type attributes that are in effect when you create a path or specify type. The current attributes appear in the Paint Style palette when no objects are selected.

cursor key distance—The distance that selected objects move each time that you press a cursor (arrow) key.

curve—A smooth trajectory defined by two anchor points and two direction points. The anchor points define where the curve starts and ends. The direction points determine the shape of the curve.

custom color—An ink color that you assign to objects in your drawing. With custom color, you can produce one negative for each color used in the artwork or opt to convert all custom colors to process colors when printing color separations. Compare with *process color*.

custom view—A named display of a document that retains the view settings, including the current zoom level, layer options, and Artwork or Preview view.

cutout—See *Knockout*.

cyan—The subtractive primary color that appears blue-green and absorbs red light. Used as one ink in four-color printing. See also *subtractive primary colors* and *process color*.

CYMK—See *CMYK*.

dash pattern—The pattern of lines and gaps between lines that make up a dashed line. You create a dash pattern by specifying the length, in points, of each dash and of each gap between the dashes.

data series—A column of data in a graph work sheet.

default—The initial setting of a value or option. Used to describe the value(s), or mode that Illustrator will use in processing information when no other value or mode is specified. A preset response to a question or prompt. Default settings can be changed.

density—The degree of opacity of an imagesetter negative or positive. The laser's effect on the imagesetter media, combined with the effect of the chemicals used to process the media, determine the density of black on the film.

descender—The part of a lowercase letter that hangs below the baseline. Five letters of the alphabet have descenders: *g, j, p, q,* and *y*. See also *ascender* and *baseline*.

deselect—In Illustrator, to select another command or option or to click a blank area of the pasteboard to cancel the current selection. Also to turn off (remove the X from) a check box. See also *select*.

Desktop—The screen display when the Macintosh Finder is active and application windows are closed or hidden.

desktop publishing—Use of personal computers and software applications such as Illustrator to produce copy that is ready for reproduction.

dialog box—A window that appears in response to a command that calls for setting options. See also *window*.

digitize—To convert an image to a system of dots that can be stored in the computer. See also *rasterize* and *scanned-image files*.

digitizer—See *scanner*.

Dingbats—Traditionally, ornamental characters (bullets, stars, flowers) used for decoration or as special characters within text. The laser-printer font Zapf Dingbats includes many traditional symbols and some new ones.

direction line—The straight line connecting an anchor point and its direction point. A curve touches the direction line at the anchor point.

direction point—A point that defines the direction from which a curve enters the curve's anchor points. The position of a curve's two direction points determines the curve's shape.

directory—A named area reserved on the hard disk where a group of related files can be stored together. Identified as a folder on the Macintosh desktop. Each directory can have subdirectories. See also *hierarchical filing system*.

discretionary hyphen—A hyphen inserted when **Command+** - (hyphen) is pressed. Identifies where Illustrator can divide a word to fit text in the specified line length if Hyphenation is on (as specified in the Paragraph palette). The hyphen appears on-screen and on the printed page only if it falls at the end of a line. See also *hyphenation*.

display type—Type used for headlines, titles, headings, advertisements, fliers, and so on. Display type is usually a large point size (several sizes larger than body copy) and can be a decorative font.

document—The file that you create by using a graphics, word processing, or desktop publishing software package.

dots—See *halftone dots* and *pixels*.

dots per inch—(dpi). See *resolution*.

dot-matrix printer—A printer that creates text and graphics by pressing a matrix of pins through the ribbon onto the paper. These impact printers usually offer lower resolution (dots per inch) than laser printers and are used only for draft printouts from Illustrator.

double-click—To quickly press and release the main mouse button twice in succession.

downloadable font—A font that is sent from your computer to your printer each time you use it. See *font*.

drag—To hold down the mouse button while you move the pointer.

drag and drop—Dragging a selected item from one open publication to another open publication.

Draw-type files—See *object-oriented files*.

drop cap—A large capital letter used to start a paragraph or chapter, dropping down a few lines with the text wrapping around the drop cap. Drop caps can also extend above the text.

drop-down menu—See *pull-down menu*.

dummy publication—Traditionally, a pencil mock-up of the pages of a publication, folded or stapled into a booklet, that the offset printer uses to verify the correct sequence of pages and positions of photographs. See also *template* and *thumbnail*.

Duotone—A process for printing a grayscale image using one color of ink that represents different degrees or percentages of the grayscale.

Dylux—A brand name for blueline proofing material.

ellipse—A regular-shaped oval created by using Illustrator's Oval tool, as distinguished from irregular ovals, which are egg-shaped.

ellipsis—Series of three dots in text (…) used to indicate that some of the text has been deleted (usually from a quotation). A single character created by pressing Option+; (semi-colon). An ellipsis appears after every Illustrator menu command that opens a dialog box (for example, **File > Open...**).

em—Unit of measure equaling the point size of the type; for example, a 12-point em is 12 points wide. The width of an em dash or an em space. See also *en*.

emulsion—The photosensitive layer on a piece of film or paper. Emulsion side up or down may be specified in the Print command dialog box.

en—One-half the width of an em. The width of an en dash or an en space. See also *em*.

Encapsulated PostScript (EPS) format—A file format that describes a document written in the PostScript language and contains all of the code necessary to print the file. See also *PostScript*.

endpoint—An anchor point at the beginning or end of an open path.

Enter key—Key you press to break a line if the Text tool is active or to confirm the selected options in a dialog box. Also called the **Return** key. Usually has the same effect as the **Return** key on a typewriter. Also used to apply options selected in a palette. See also *carriage return*.

EPS—See *Encapsulated PostScript format*.

export—To save Illustrator text to a word processing file. Illustrator lets you specify whether to export the text in text-only format (ASCII), WordPerfect formats,

MacWrite formats, Microsoft RTF formats, Microsoft Word formats, or Write Now format.

export filter—A process that tells Illustrator how to convert its files so that the files can be understood by the word processing program that imports them. See list under *export*.

file formats—Sometimes referred to file types, or simply formats:

> ➤ Illustrator 6.0 can open or import any Illustrator file formats (including those created by previous versions), any EPS format, PostScript language print file format, PICT, TIFF, Photoshop 3.0 (or later), Acrobat Portable Document Format (PDF), Photo CD format, PC Paintbrush format (PCX), ASCII text, MacWrite, Microsoft Word, and some other word processing formats.

> ➤ Illustrator 6.0 (and later) can save Illustrator artwork in a variety of other formats (besides native Illustrator format), including EPS, Acrobat (PDF 1.1), Amiga IFF Format, Windows bitmap (BMP) Format, earlier versions of Illustrator (back to 1.0), PCX Format, Pixar Format, Photoshop JPEG, and Targa Format.

> ➤ The Windows version of Illustrator comes with a Computer Graphics Meta import module (CGM), Micrografx Drawing import module (DRW), AutoCAD Drawing Interchange import module (DXF), Lotus 1-2-3 Picture import module (PIC), Macintosh PICT import module (PCT), AutoShade Rendering import module (RND), Microsoft Windows Metafile import module (WMF), and WordPerfect Graphic import module (WPG). The Windows version of Illustrator can import Encapsulated PostScript File (EPS), Bitmap File (BMP), Paintbrush File (PCX), and Tagged Image Format File (TIF). See also *BMP, CGM, DRW, EPS, GIF, PCT, PICT, PCX, RND, TIF, TGA, WMF,* and *WPG*.

fill—To paint an area enclosed by a path with a color or tint of black.

film—Photosensitive material, generally on a transparent base, that receives character images and may be chemically processed to expose those images. In phototypesetting, any photosensitive material, transparent or not, may be called film.

flatness—The maximum distance, in device pixels, of any point on a rendered curve from the corresponding point on the true curve.

flush—Aligned with, even with, coming to the same edge as. See also *alignment*.

flush right (or **right-justified**)—Text in which lines end at the same point on the right margin. Opposite of ragged right or left-justified. See also *alignment*.

folio—Page number on a printed page, often accompanied by the name of the document and date of publication. See also *running head* and *running foot*.

font—One complete set of characters in the same face, style, and size, including all of the letters of the alphabet, punctuation, and symbols. For example, 12-point Times Roman is a different font from 12-point Times Italic, 14-point Times Roman, and 12-point Helvetica. Screen fonts (bit-mapped fonts used to display text accurately on the screen) can differ slightly from the printer fonts (outline fonts used to describe fonts to the laser printer) because of the difference in resolution between screens and printers.

font outlines—Paths that represent text characters created by using the **Type > Create Outline** command. Creating outlines gives the character(s) anchor points so you can manipulate the shapes, add colors and patterns, and so on. Also, the designs or formulas that define fonts mathematically, such as PostScript fonts.

footer—See *Running foot*. See also *folio*.

format—Page size, margins, and grid used in a publication. Also, the character format (font) and paragraph format (alignment, spacing, and indentation).

formatting—Using the type and paragraph attributes to modify the page.

freehand tolerance—A value that controls how sensitive the Freehand tool is to variations in your hand movement, set in the **File > Preferences > General** dialog box.

gamma—The measurement of contrast in the midtones of an image. Images have black points and white points and between these two points is a range of brightness that contains valuable visual detail called the midtone range. Gamma adjustment is done by increasing or decreasing only this midtone range. Adobe Photoshop is generally the preferred software package for graphic manipulation of this degree.

gamut—The possible range of color values in an image. TrueColor, 24-bit images have a gamut of 16.7 million colors. Gamut is also thought of as the range of color that a color printer or a commercial press can accurately produce.

ghosting—The shift in ink density that occurs when large, solid areas interfere with one another. Also, a procedure in which two images are combined together electronically. The images are given specific weight in relation to each other to create the effect.

GIF—(Graphics Interchange Format) A bitmap graphics file format developed by CompuServe and commonly used on CompuServe forums and the World Wide Web. See *file formats.*

gradient fill—A graduated blend between colors, either linear or radiating from a specified point. A gradient fill may be a blend between a single starting and ending color, or it may consist of multiple intermediate blends between a number of colors. See also *blend.*

graph—An illustration that represents values entered in a spreadsheet or in the graph data dialog box—a visual representation of data. See *pie graph, area graph, line graph, grouped column graph, stacked column graph,* and *scatter graph.*

graphic—A line segment or path that you draw in Illustrator. An illustration brought into a Illustrator publication from another application.

graphics tablet—A drawing tablet that is electronically sensitive, transmitting information from the tablet to the computer. Artists use the tablet, writing or drawing with a stylus, or pen. Today, many varieties of graphics tablets are available to select from for use in graphics environments.

grayscale image—An 8-bit image that can hold up to 256 different colors. Grayscale images are not actually full color but different shades of black. No other color besides various intensities of black in a grayscale image can be used. Also, grayscale images are not file formats for images but a variation that can be used in different file formats.

Greek text—Traditionally, a block of text used to represent the positioning and point size of text in a designer's comp. Standard "greeked text" used by typesetters looks more like Latin: *Lorem ipsum dolor sit amet.* Also, the conversion of text to gray bars or boxes that show the position of the text on the screen but not the real characters. Body text usually is greeked in the Fit in Window view in Illustrator; small point sizes may be greeked in closer views on some screens.

grid—The underlying design plan for a page. In Illustrator, the grid can be composed of a series of nonprinting horizontal and vertical lines that intersect to form a "grid."

gripper—The top part of a page where the printing press grabs the paper. Nothing can be printed in this area.

group—To combine two or more objects so that they act as a single object. You can manipulate groups just as you do individual objects.

grouped column graph—Bar graph; represents data by the height of each column or bar. A column graph is valuable for comparing one item to another or comparing different items over a period of time.

guide—A nonprinting line (margin guide, ruler guide, column guide, or custom guide) created to help align objects on a page. In Illustrator, nonprinting guides look like dotted lines, dashed lines, or blue lines, depending on the screen's resolution and color settings.

guide objects—Lines or shapes used to help you position or align the objects you draw or text you create. See *grid.*

gutter—The inside margins between the facing pages of a document; sometimes describes the space between columns. In some word processors, the gutter measure is entered as the difference between the measures of the inside margin and the outside margin. See also *margin.*

hairline—The thinnest rule possible, generally 0.25 point.

halftone—An image composed of dots of different sizes. Using a scanner, you can convert continuous tone images, such as photographs, into halftones. Contrast with *continuous-tone image.* Also, the conversion of continuous-tone artwork (usually a photograph) into a pattern of dots or lines that looks like gray tones when printed by an offset printing press.

halftone dots—Dots as they appear on the printed page. The size of the halftone dots depends on the screen ruling used.

hanging indent—A paragraph in which the first line extends to the left of the other lines. You can use a hanging-indent format to create headings set to the left of the body copy. See also *indentation.*

hanging punctuation—Punctuation marks that fall outside the text margins.

hard carriage return—See *carriage return.*

hard disk—Disk storage that is built into the computer or into a piece of hardware connected to the computer. Distinguished from removable storage.

header—See *running head*. See also *running foot* and *folio*.

headline—The title of an article in a newsletter, newspaper, or magazine.

hidden objects—Objects that are concealed from view so they cannot be selected or modified in any way.

hide—To remove a path or block of type from the artwork temporarily. Objects that are hidden do not preview or print.

hierarchical filing system—A disk storage system in which files can be stored in separate directories (folders), which, in turn, can contain subdirectories. See also *directory*.

highlight—To distinguish visually. To select text by dragging the I-beam, which usually reverses the normal appearance of selected text (black text on a white background, for example, appears as white text on black background after it is highlighted).

hinting—Built-in font instructions that scaleable fonts use to make adjustments to the pixels making up a letter so that the letters look crisp and clear at lower resolutions. Hinting affects smaller point sizes. Point sizes above 14 or 18 points are not affected as much by hinting.

horizontal scale—The proportion between the height and width of type.

hyphenation—Hyphenation can be achieved in several ways: (1) Illustrator automatically hyphenates text (based on a built-in dictionary) as you place or type text on the page; (2) Illustrator recognizes hyphens inserted by the word processing program; (3) you can insert *discretionary hyphens* (displayed only if they fall at the end of a line) by pressing **Command+** - (hyphen) within a word. See also *discretionary hyphen*.

I-beam—The shape of the pointer after the Type tool is selected. See also *pointer*.

icon—Graphic on-screen representation of a tool, file, folder, or command.

image area—Area inside the margins of the page or the printable area of the page.

imageable area—The printable page area. The imegeable area is the page size less a border that the printer uses to feed the paper or film.

import—To bring text or graphics into Illustrator from other programs, such as text from a word processing program (**File > Import Text**) or graphics from other sources (**File > Place** or **File > Open**). See also *file formats*.

import filter—A process that tells Illustrator how to convert files from other programs for use by Illustrator.

increment—Distance between tick marks on a ruler. See also *measurement system*. Also, distance moved using the arrow keys, as specified in the general preferences dialog box.

indentation—Positioning the first line of a paragraph (or second and following lines) to the right of the left column guide (to create a left indent), or positioning the right margin of the paragraph to the left of the right column guide (to create a right indent), relative to the other text on the page. In Illustrator, you set indentation through the Paragraph command dialog box or by choosing the **Indents/Tabs** command. See also *hanging indent*.

indexed-color bitmaps—8-bit images that include a color table that defines a 24-bit color for each of 256 values that can be represented by an 8-bit value. An 8-bit image can thus use colors usually available only for 24-bit images. The indexed-color image is limited to 256 colors, however.

insertion point—A blinking vertical line that indicates where characters you type will appear.

inside margin—Margin along the edge of the page that is to be bound. In single-sided publications, this is always the left margin. In double-sided publications, the inside margin is the left margin of a right-hand page or the right margin of a left-hand page. See also *gutter* and *margin*.

integral proof—A color proofing system that bonds all four process colors to a single sheet.

interpreter—Software built into PostScript-compatible printers and typesetters that converts PostScript commands into a form the printer can use to draw an image.

isometric drawing—A drawing of an object that looks three dimensional. Usually, the horizontal edges of the object are portrayed at a 30-degree angle and all verticals are projected perpendicularly from the horizontal base.

italic—Letters that slope toward the right, as distinguished from upright, or Roman, characters.

invert—See *reverse*.

join—(noun) See *line join*.

join—(verb) To connect the endpoints of an open path. When you join the endpoints of one path, Illustrator closes the path with a straight line segment. When you join the endpoints of two open paths Illustrator combines them into one longer path. Compare *average*.

JPEG—Compression scheme developed by the Joint Photographer's Experts Group that retains most of an image's visual information, compressing the file by anywhere from 5 to 100 times the original file size. See also *compression*.

justified text—Text that is flush at both the left and right edges. See also *alignment*.

kern—To adjust the spaces between letters, usually to move letters closer together. See also *kerning*.

kerning—The amount of space between letters, especially certain combinations of letters that must be brought closer together to create visually consistent spacing around all letters. The uppercase letters *AW*, for example, may appear to have a wider gap between them than the letters *MN* unless a special kerning formula is set up for the *AW* combination. In Illustrator, you can adjust the space between letters manually by using the Text tool and pressing **Command+[** to decrease space or **Command+]** to increase space. See also *kern*.

knockout—A generic term for a positive or overlay that "knocks out" part of an image from another image. The most obvious example of this is white type on a black background. The white type is knocked out of the background.

landscape—A printing orientation in which the "up" direction is along the short side of the page. Compare *portrait*.

laser printing—Used to describe printing on a toner-based laser printer. These printers use laser technology—light amplification by stimulated emission of radiation—to project an intense light beam in a narrow band width (1/300 inch in 300 dpi printers). This light creates on the printer drum a charge that picks up the toner and transfers it to the paper. See also *phototypesetting*.

layer—To place objects in layers that are in front of one another. See also *painting order*. Also, a named layer in Illustrator's Layer palette.

layout—The process of arranging text and graphics on a page. A sketch or plan for the page. Also the final appearance of the page. (In platemaking, a sheet indicating the settings for the step-and-repeat machine.)

layout grid—See *grid*.

leaders—Dotted or dashed lines that can be defined for tab settings in some applications. Illustrator does not support tab leaders.

leading—Historically, the insertion of thin strips of metal (made of a metal alloy that included some lead) between lines of cast type to add space between the lines and to make columns align. In modern typography, the vertical space between the baselines of two lines of text. To give an example of the terminology, 12-point Times with 1 point of leading added is called *13-point leaded type*, or *12 on 13 Times*, and sometimes written as *12/13 Times*. In Illustrator, leading is entered in points in the Character palette.

legend—A label placed next to or above a graph to define a series of data.

letter spacing—Space between letters in a word. The practice of adding space between letters. In Illustrator, unjustified text has fixed letter spacing; justified text has variable letter spacing, which is adjusted within the limits entered in the Spacing Attributes dialog box. See also *kerning* and *word spacing*.

ligatures—Character combinations that are often combined into special characters in a font. Some downloadable fonts, for example, come with the combinations *fi* and *fl* as special characters. Illustrator can set ligatures automatically through the **Type > Smart Punctuation** command.

line—The straight line between two anchor points. In a line, each anchor point and its corresponding direction point occupy the same location.

line break—The end of a line of text, created by automatic word wrap and hyphenation. See also *carriage return*.

line cap—A cap is placed at the end of a solid line or segments of a dashed line. Illustrator provides three kinds of line caps: butt, round, and projecting.

line graph—Consists of a series of points (data) that are connected by a line. The movement of the line indicates the trend over a period of time.

line join—The style of connector used when Illustrator strokes a path. The choice of joins becomes important when stroking paths that contain corners. Illustrator provides three kinds of joins: miter, round, and bevel.

line length—Horizontal measure of a column or a line of text.

line spacing—See *leading*.

line weight—The weight or thickness of a line, expressed in points.

lines per inch—(lpi) See *screen ruling*.

link—Connecting two or more separate objects together so the text in one object flows to the other.

linked file—In Illustrator, an EPS graphic that has been imported using the Place command. See also *object linking and embedding*.

linked text areas—Text rectangles that are connected across the columns on a page from the beginning to the end of an article. As you edit linked (or *threaded*) text, Illustrator moves words from one text block into the next text block in the chain to adjust to the new text length. See also *area text*.

list box—Area in a dialog box that displays options.

lock—In Illustrator, using the Lock command to anchor selected objects and prevent them from being selected subsequently. Locked objects cannot be inadvertently selected or moved while laying out other text and graphics.

lowercase—Small letters that make up the alphabet. The term comes from typographers storing the small letters in the lower part of a printer's typecase.

LPI—Refers to lines per inch, denoting the measurement standard of halftone dots arranged in a line to simulate variations in tones found in Grayscale and other continuous-tone images. These lines of halftone dots compose a linescreen (the LPI) that when viewed from a distance, represents a grayscale image using patterns of black and white visual information. See *DPI* and *halftone*.

Macintosh—Personal computer developed by Steve Jobs and Apple Computer in the early 1980s. Macintosh computers dominated the graphic arts world in the early days of the influx of the personal computer. Macintoshes are known for their ease of use.

Macintosh PICT—See *file format.*

magenta—The subtractive primary color that appears blue-red and absorbs green light. Used as one ink in four-color printing. See also *subtractive primary colors* and *process color.*

margin—Traditionally, the distance from the edge of the page to the edge of the layout area of the page. The margins guides in Illustrator are normally used to define the limits of print area. See also *gutter* and *inside margin.*

markers—Column symbols that represent the data in your graphs.

marquee—A dashed rectangular region that appears when you drag the pointer tool to select objects.

masking object—An object that acts as a stencil in an artwork document. Portions of the artwork that extend beyond the boundaries of the masking object are "clipped" by the masking path and therefore do not preview or print. See also *clipping path.*

measurement system—Units chosen through the **File > Document Setup** and **File > Preferences > General** commands: inches, millimeters, or picas/points. The chosen units appear on the rulers and in all dialog boxes that display measurements. You can enter a value in any unit of measure in a dialog box, regardless of the current Preferences selection, by typing the abbreviation for the unit in your entry. For example, *3.5in* indicates *3.5* inches, *3pt* specifies 3 points, *3.5mm* indicates 3.5 millimeters. See also *pica.*

mechanical—Traditionally, the final pages or boards with pasted-up galleys of type and line art, sometimes with acetate or tissue overlays for color separations and notes to the offset printer. See also *camera-ready art* and *offset printing.*

mechanical separations—Also called *mechanicals,* the traditional name for color separations printed as black-and-white art. See also *color separations.*

memory—A hardware component (chip) in a computer system that stores information and instructions that are currently in use. The area inside the computer where information is stored temporarily while you are working (also called *RAM,* or *random access memory*). The amount of memory a computer has directly affects its speed and the size of the documents you can create.

menu—A list of choices presented in either a drop-down or pop-up window from which you can select an action.

menu bar—Area across the top of the publication window where menu titles are displayed.

mirror—To create a mirror image of an object. In Illustrator, you can do this to selected objects by using the Reflect. You can also print mirror images of the artwork by using the **Flip Horizontal** and **Flip Vertical** options in the Print Options dialog box.

miter join—A corner created by extending the edges of two converging lines until they meet. Compare *bevel join* and *round join.*

miter limit—The ratio that determines the angle at which Illustrator switches from a mitered (pointed) line join to a beveled (squared off) line join. The miter limit is equal to the maximum ratio of the diagonal line through a line to the width of the lines producing the join. The smaller the miter limit, the less sharp the angle at which Illustrator switches from a mitered to a beveled line join.

Moiré pattern—A grid pattern (usually undesirable) that can result when two or more screen tints are overlaid incorrectly or printed at incompatible angles. Can also occur if a bit-mapped graphic with gray fill patterns is reduced or enlarged See also *rosette.*

monospace type—Typeface in which all the characters are of the same width. Courier, is an example.

negative—A reverse image of a page, produced photographically on a clear sheet of film as an intermediate step in preparing plates from camera-ready mechanicals for offset printing.

object—An anchor point, segment, path or type block, or a group of anchor points, segments, paths and type blocks.

Object Linking and Embedding—(OLE). A feature of System 7 and Windows 3.1 (and later versions) whereby objects created in one application that supports OLE can be pasted into another application that supports OLE either as embedded objects (i.e., part of the document into which they are pasted) or as linked objects (i.e., linked to the external source and updated when the source changes). In either case, the objects can be edited by double-clicking on them, thereby activating the application that originally created them. See also *linked file.*

object-oriented graphics—Draw-type files consisting of a sequence of drawing commands (stored as mathematical formulas). These commands describe graphics (such as mechanical drawings, schematics, charts, and ad graphics) that you would produce manually with a pencil, straightedge, and compass. Usually contrasted with paint-type files or bit maps. Contrast with *bitmap*.

oblique—Slanted version of a Roman typeface that simulates italic. See *italic*.

offset—To move the image away from the right edge of the film or paper on which it is printing.

offset printing—A type of printing that uses an intermediate step to transfer a printed image from the plate to the paper. The type of printing done using a printing press to reproduce many copies of the original that is printed out on a laser printer. The press lays ink on a page based on the raised image on a plate that is created by photographing the camera-ready masters. See also *camera-ready art*, *laser printing*, and *mechanicals*.

old style—Type style characterized by small variations in the stroke weight of the letters, bracketed serifs, and diagonal stress.

OLE—See *Object Linking and Embedding*.

open path—A path with two endpoints, that is, a path that has a beginning and an end. Compare with *closed path*.

option button—A large rectangular area in a dialog box that contains a command such as **OK** or **Cancel**. You can activate option buttons surrounded by a thick black line by pressing the **Return** key.

orientation—The Artboard and page positions: portrait or landscape.

origin point—The point that stays fixed while you stretch or drag the rest of the object with a transformation tool. See *scaling tool, rotate tool, reflect tool*, and *shear tool*.

orphans/widows—The first line of a paragraph is called an orphan if separated from the rest of the paragraph by a page break. The last line of a paragraph is called a *widow* if it is forced to a new page by a page break and separated from the rest of the paragraph. Most publishers generally consider widows and orphans to be bad page breaks (or column breaks). The term *widow* also is used to describe bad line breaks that result in the last line of a paragraph having only one word, especially if it falls at the end of a column or page. See also *bad break*.

outline font—A printer font in which each letter of the alphabet is stored as a mathematical formula, as distinguished from bit-mapped fonts, which are stored as patterns of dots. PostScript fonts are outline fonts, for instance. See also *bitmap*, *font*, and *font outline*.

outside margin—The unbound edge of a publication. In single-sided publications, the outside margin is the right margin. In double-sided publications, the outside margin is the right margin of a right-hand page and the left margin of a left-hand page. See also *inside margin* and *margin*.

overhead transparency—An image printed on clear acetate and projected onto a screen for viewing by an audience.

overlay—A transparent acetate or tissue covering over a printed page, where color indications and other instructions to the offset printer are written. Also, an overhead transparency that is intended to be projected on top of another projection. See also *color separations*.

overlay proofs—A color proofing system that uses transparent overlays for each of the four process colors.

overprint—To specify that a colored object print on top of another colored object that overlaps it, without "knocking out" the underneath color. See also *knockout*.

oversized publication—A publication in which the page size is larger than paper size. See also *page size*, *paper size*, and *tile*.

page size—The dimensions of the Artboard as set in the **File > Document Setup** dialog box. Page size can differ from the paper size, specified through the **File > Page Setup** command. See also *margin* and *paper size*.

PageMaker—The leading desktop-publishing package, now owned by Adobe. The current version, 6.0, is available for both Macintosh and Windows systems and is fully compatible across platforms and can import Illustrator artwork.

paint—To fill a region defined by a path with a gray shade or color or to draw a line that is centered on its path.

painting order—The sequence in which the objects in a document are painted. Objects are painted from back to front, meaning that in a number of layered objects the frontmost object will obscure all or part of the objects that lie behind it.

pair kerning—The Illustrator option that changes the amount of space between two letters to create visually consistent spacing between all letters.

palette—A movable window on the screen that contains tool icons or options for formatting text or graphics

PANTONE Matching System—A popular system for choosing colors, based on ink mixes. See also *color matching systems.*

paper size—The size of the printer paper. Standard paper sizes are letter (8.5 by 11 inches), legal (8.5 by 14 inches), European A4 (210 by 297 millimeters), and European B5 (176 by 250 millimeters).

pasteboard—The on-screen work area surrounding the pages on which you are working. You move text and graphics to the pasteboard, where they remain after you turn to another page or close the publication.

paste-up—See *Mechanicals.*

path—One or more connected segments. You can fill a path or you can draw a line that is centered on the path.

path type—Type that is placed along a path.

pattern—One or more objects that has been bounded by a rectangle and defined as a pattern. Once defined, patterns can be used to paint paths.

PCT—Suffix used for DOS and Windows systems when transferring Macintosh PICT file formats. See *file formats.*

PCX—Bitmap graphics file format first made popular by PC Paintbrush. Now an industry standard, supported by all major graphics applications. Illustrator 6.0 for the Macintosh can save files in PCX format. See also *file format.*

perspective—The artist's term for distance or depth in a drawing. To make an object look as though it goes back into the distance by distorting the shape and changing size, color, and position.

phototypesetter—A device that sets type photographically using a photochemical process and special film as output.

phototypesetting—Producing a page image on photosensitive paper, as when documents are printed on an imagesetter.

pica—A unit of measure equal to approximately 1/6 inch, or 12 points. Use the Document Setup and **Preferences** commands from the File menu to select picas and points as the unit of measure for the ruler lines and dialog box displays. You also can enter a value in picas and points in any dialog box by typing a *p* between the number of picas and the number of points: for example, 3p2 specifies 3 picas and 2 points. See also *point size* and *measurement system*.

PICT format—A format used to store some Macintosh graphics documents. Usually converted to PIC or PCT format when transferred to an MS-DOS/Windows system. **pie graph**—A graph shaped like a pie, with each piece (or wedge) showing a data segment and its relationship to the whole; useful for sorting data by presenting parts of the whole.

place—To import a graphic document from another source into an Adobe Illustrator document.

plate—A metal or paper sheet affixed to a press to transfer the image to paper. Plates are photographic and created from film. Ink is applied to the image areas on the plate and transferred to paper running through a press. See *plate-making*.

plate-making—The process of making photographic plates from film negatives. See *plate*.

plug-in filter—A module supplied separately from the Adobe Illustrator program for creating special effects in artwork.

point—Unit of measure, used in Illustrator for specifying type and line attributes. There are 12 points in a pica, and approximately 72 points in an inch.

point of origin—A fixed spot that you specify in your artwork from which a transformation begins.

point type—Type that is neither bounded by a path nor along a path.

pointer—The on-screen icon that moves as you move the mouse.

portrait—A printing orientation in which the "up" direction is along the long side of the page.

PostScript—A computer language invented by Adobe Systems that is used to define the appearance of type and images on the printed page. When you save an Illustrator document, you are actually saving a PostScript program. See also *Encapsulated PostScript*.

PPD file—PostScript Printer Description file. The document used by the Illustrator and the Chooser to set the default information for the type of printer you are using.

Preferences—The Illustrator submenu on the File menu used to select the unit of measure displayed on ruler lines and in dialog boxes, as well as other display variables. Also used to set hyphenation, color matching, and plug-in folder preferences.

prepress proofs—Sometimes called bluelines, these proofs are made by using photographic techniques. See also *press proofs* and *blue lines*.

preset attributes—The paint, stroke, and type attributes that are in effect if you haven't specified any other attributes. See also default attributes.

press proofs—A test run of a color printing job through the printing press to check registration and color. See also *prepress proofs* and *bluelines*.

preview image—The view of your Illustrator artwork that is displayed on your screen as a bitmap and approximates the printed output. You can specify whether paint and pattern attributes appear in the preview image. A version of the preview image is saved along with the PostScript language code for the artwork document when you specify one of the preview options before saving your artwork. Compare *artwork*.

Preview Selection view—Shows the artwork as it appears painted, letting you study one or more specific objects. The Preview views show all text and painting attributes you apply to your drawing as you create it. Text attributes include typeface, size, and special effects. Painting attributes include line width, colors, fill patterns, and so on.

primary colors—The elemental colors of either pigments or light. Red, green, and blue are additive primaries. White light is produced when red, green, and blue lights are added together. Cyan, magenta, and yellow are subtractive primaries. The inks used to print three-color process or four-color process with black. See also *additive primary colors* and *subtractive primary colors*.

print area—The area on a piece of paper where the printer reproduces text and graphics. It is always smaller than the paper size. See also *margin*.

PrintMonitor—A Macintosh application for sending files to the printer. When Background Printing is selected through the Chooser, Illustrator's **Print** command sends the publication to the PrintMonitor, or spooler, not directly to the printer. The PrintMonitor holds files in the print queue and prints them in the order in which they were received. You can continue working on other files while a file is being printed. See also *print queue*.

print queue—Files in the spooler waiting to be sent to the printer. Files are sent in the order received. See also *PrintMonitor*.

printer font—A bit-mapped or outline font installed in the printer or downloaded to the printer as a publication is printed. Usually distinguished from the screen font, which displays the text on the computer screen. See also *bitmap*, *font*, and *outline font*.

printer's marks—Crop marks and, if you are printing color separations or a color composite, registration marks, a density control bar, and color-control strips. Created in Illustrator by the Use **Default Marks** option in the Separation Setup dialog box.

process color—One of the four colors cyan, magenta, yellow, and black blended to produce colors in the four-color process. With process color, you produce a maximum of four negatives, regardless of the number of colors used in your artwork. Compare with *custom color*. See also *spot color* and *subtractive primary colors*.

process separations—Four-color separations made from color artwork.

progressive colors—The four process colors plus white and the various combinations of cyan, magenta, and yellow.

progressive color bar—Progressive color bars are printed on each sheet of a process color printing job to ensure proper ink coverage and color. The bar is usually trimmed off before the job is shipped. Sometimes the progressive color bar will also include black and screen tints of the combinations.

projecting cap—A square line cap placed at the end of a solid or dashed line. The cap is perpendicular to the end of the line and extends one half of a line width beyond the line's endpoint. Compare *butt cap* and *line cap*.

proofread—To read a preliminary printout of a page and check for spelling errors, alignment on the page, and other features that are not related to the technical accuracy of the content.

proofs—See *prepress proofs, press proofs,* and *bluelines.*

proportional spacing—The characters in which wider letters, such as W, take up more horizontal space than narrower letters, such as i, as seen in proportional fonts such as Helvetica and Times.

proportionally—When you resize an object, keeping the horizontal and vertical scaling percentages equal keeps an object in proportion to its original size.

pull-down menu—A list of commands that appears after you select a menu. In Illustrator, the menu titles appear on the menu bar along the top of the screen, and the menu commands drop down in a list below the selected menu title.

pull-out quote—Quotation extracted from the text of an article and printed in larger type, often set off by ruled lines.

QuickDraw—A graphics language built into the read-only memory (ROM) of the Macintosh.

radio button—The round area to the left of certain mutually exclusive options in a dialog box. You click the option button to turn on, or select, its option. Selecting one option button deselects, or turns off, all other option buttons in the group.

ragged right—Text in which lines end at different points near the right margin. Opposite of flush right or justified text. See also *alignment* and *flush right* (or *right-justified*).

RAM—See *memory.*

raster—Images made up of colored pixels arranged in an imaginary grid (bitmap images), the opposite of vector images. EPS images are vector based and must be rasterized before printing or viewing. Raster is another name for *bitmap* or *paint graphics.* See *bitmap, digitize, rasterize,* and *vector images.*

rasterize—The conversion of the mathematical outlines of letters to create the filled-in character with bitmap screen and printer representations. Illustrator 6.0's Object > Rasterize command lets you rasterize any object in Illustrator. See *bitmap* and *digitize.* Contrast with *object-oriented graphics* and *vector images.*

rectangle type—Type that is bounded by a rectangle.

reflect—To create a mirror image of an object.

reflected light—See *subtractive primary colors.*

Rectangle tool—Illustrator tool used to create squares and rectangles.

registration—The accuracy with which images are combined or positioned, particularly in reference to multicolored printing where each color must be precisely aligned for the accurate reproduction of the original.

registration mark—One of a number of small reference patterns placed on separations printed by Illustrator to aid the printer in positioning color overlays.

release—To let go of a mouse button.

resolution—Number of dots per inch (dpi) used to create an alphanumeric character or a graphics image on a screen or printer. High-resolution images have more dots per inch and look smoother than low-resolution images. The Macintosh screen has a resolution of 72 dots per inch; the Apple LaserWriter has a resolution of 300 dots per inch; typesetters print 1,200 dots per inch or more. The resolution of PostScript language image-setting devices (Agfa, Linotronic, and so on) is measured in pixels per inch. (See *pixels.*)

reverse—Text or a graphic in which the white areas are changed to black and vice versa. Usually, text and graphics are black on a white background; if reversed, they are white on black.

RGB—Shorthand notation for red, green, and blue. The primary colors used in displaying colors on a monitor. See also *primary colors* and *additive primary colors.*

right-justified—See *flush right* and *alignment.*

RIP—Stands for *raster image processor.* A device that converts computer instructions into bit maps to be output by a printer. RIPs are most commonly found on high-resolution imagesetters and typesetters. See *raster* and *rasterize.*

Roman—Upright text styles, as distinguished from italic. Sometimes used to refer to Normal style, as opposed to Bold or Italic, on Illustrator's Font menu.

rosette—The circular dot pattern that occurs when screen tints are overlaid correctly.

rotate—To revolve an object about a given point.

roughs—Traditionally, the preliminary page layouts done by the designer using pencil sketches to represent miniature page design ideas. See also *thumbnail.*

round cap—A semi-circular line cap placed at the end of a solid or dashed line. The diameter of the cap is equal to the width of the line. Compare *butt cap* and *line cap.*

round join—A corner created when two lines are connected with a circular arc whose diameter is equal to the width of the line. Compare *bevel join* and *miter join.*

ruler guides—Nonprinting extensions of the tick marks on the rulers, which form horizontal and vertical dotted, dashed, or blue lines on the page. Used to align text and graphics on the page. Select the **Show Rulers** command to display the rulers, and then drag the Selection tool from a ruler onto the page to create a guide. See also *guide* and *nonprinting master items.*

rulers—Electronic rulers, one of which is displayed across the top of the publication window and one down the left side. Also, the text ruler displayed on the Tab Ruler palette. Rulers show measures in inches, picas, millimeters, or Ciceros. Use the Rulers command to display or hide the rulers. Use the Preferences command on the File menu to select the unit of measure displayed on the ruler lines and dialog box displays. Increments (tick marks) on the rulers depend on the size and resolution of your screen, as well as on the view (Actual Size, Fit in Window, 200%, and so forth). See also *measurement system.*

rules—Black lines added to a page—between columns, for example—to improve the design or increase readability of a publication. Can be created by using Illustrator's Pen tool.

run-around—See *text wrap.*

running foot—One or more lines of text appearing at the bottom of every page. Also referred to as the *footer.* See also *folio.*

running head—One or more lines of text appearing at the top of every page of a document. Also referred to as the *header.* See also *folio.*

sans serif—Typefaces without serifs, such as Helvetica and Avant Garde. See also *serif.*

saturation—The amount/percentage of color in a pixel. A fully saturated pixel displays no gray component. Saturation is one of the three components in the HSB color model. Lack of saturation in a color pixel produces a dull image area that resembles a grayscale image.

scale—To change the size of an object either vertically, horizontally, or both.

scanned image—The image that results when a photograph, illustration, or other flat art is converted into a bitmap. Scanned images can be saved in a variety of graphic formats, including PICT, TIFF, and EPS. See also *digitize* and *bitmap*.

scanner—An electronic device that converts a photo, illustration, or other flat art into a bitmap. A video camera is a scanner that converts three-dimensional objects into bitmaps.

scatter graph—A line or data point graph that shows trends or patterns and how the variables affect each other. Scatter graphs are useful for developing a conclusion as to the relationship of two or more variables.

Scissors tool—A tool that cuts a path where you click and thus creates a separate object.

screen—Gray tone usually identified as a percentage. A 100-percent screen is solid black; a 10-percent screen is light gray.

screen font—A bitmap font used to display type on your computer screen. A screen font also sends information to the CPU, designating the printer font to be downloaded during output. See *font* and *printer font*.

screen ruling—The number of lines per inch in a screen tint or halftone. See also *halftone*.

screen tint—A screened percentage of a solid color.

segment—A line curve that is defined by an anchor point and its direction point.

separation—An individual piece of film or paper used to reproduce a process or custom color.

script fonts—Type designed to look like handwriting or calligraphy, such as Zapf Chancery. See also *font*.

scroll bar—Gray bars on the right side and bottom of the document window. Scroll arrows at both ends of each bar enable you to scroll the document horizontally or vertically. Each scroll bar has a scroll box that you drag to change the view within publication window. Dialog boxes and palettes also can have scroll bars for viewing long lists of files or options.

select—To define an object to be acted upon by the next command or mouse operation. You must select an object before you can change or edit it in any way. Generally, you select an object by clicking on it with the selection pointer or by dragging the selection marquee around it. Also, to turn on (or place an X in) a check box (or other options) in a dialog box. See also *deselect*.

selection marquee—A dashed rectangular region that appears dragging the Selection tool to enclose and select more than one graphic or text block at a time. See also *drag*.

selection pointer—An arrow-shaped pointer used for selecting and moving objects.

separation—Before having an artwork printed at a commercial print shop, you can print out a copy of the artwork for each color to be used in the printing. For example, everything in the art that is yellow prints on one page, everything that is blue prints on another page, and so on. You separate the colors so the camera person at a print shop can make a separate plate for each color. See *color separation*.

serif—A line crossing the main stroke of a letter. Typefaces that have serifs include Times, Courier, New Century Schoolbook, Bookman, and Palatino. See also *sans serif*.

service bureau—A graphic arts business (agency) specializing in typesetting, design, layout, high-resolution image setter output, stripping, and/or plate burning. A prepress company linking the desktop publisher with the printer.

shear—To slant an object vertically, horizontally, or along an arbitrary line.

signature—In printing and binding, the name given after folding to a printed sheet of (often 16) pages. The term is sometimes applied to page spreads printed adjacent to each other in the sequence required for offset printing of smaller booklets.

single sided—A publication designed for pages that are reproduced on only one side of each sheet of paper. See also *double-sided publication*.

size—To make a graphic smaller or larger.

skew—To slant an object vertically. See *shear*.

smooth point—An Anchor point connecting two segments in which the anchor point and its two direction points are located on the same straight line.

snap-to—The effect of various types of nonprinting guidelines, such as margin guides, ruler guides, and custom guides. These guides exert a "magnetic pull" on the pointer, text, or a graphic that comes close to the guides. Useful for aligning text and graphics accurately. Also, the effect that edges of palettes can have with each other and with the edge of edges of the document on the Artboard.

soft carriage return—See *carriage return*.

spacing—The amount of space, in points, that is added or removed between lines or paragraphs or pairs of characters in a type block. Spacing affects the amount of white space in a type block.

spec sheet—A mock-up, or copy, of the drawing showing the various color values.

spooler—See *PrintMonitor*.

spot color—A process that adds solid areas of colored ink to a publication. Same as *custom color*.

spot-color overlay—A page printed as color separations, so that each color on the page is printed separately and then combined by a commercial printer to form the completed page.

spread—A negative image that has been fattened to create trap. Also, a facing-page layout in double-sided documents. (Illustrator's Artboard is an area that can be divided into pages by making the Artboard size larger than the Page size and setting Tiling options in the **File > Document Setup** dialog box..

spread trap—The intentional overlap of a lighter object into a darker background to compensate for misregistration problems on the press, accomplished by spreading the lighter color slightly, thereby "spreading," or expanding, it into the background.

stacked column graph—Similar to a group column graph, but the columns are stacked one on top of the other. Stacked column graphs are useful for comparing progress over a period of time or to show the relationship of parts to the total. See *grouped column graph*.

stacking order—Order in which overlapping text and graphics are arranged on the page and on-screen. Also called *painting order*.

status line—A screen element located along the bottom of the screen; displays information about the objects, view, position of the pointer, and so on.

stripper—The person who takes the negatives and "strips" them in the proper position so that they will run correctly on the press. The stripper also usually cuts the color-separation masks when mechanical separations are made.

stroke—To draw a line that is centered on its path.

style—One of the variations within a typeface, such as roman, bold, or italic. See also *font* and *typeface*.

subtractive primary colors—Cyan, yellow, and magenta. The three colors used to create all other colors if reflected light is used (for example, in printed material). See also *additive primary colors*, *primary colors*, and *CMYK*.

system folder—The folder that contains the system software. It is located on the startup disk.

Tagged Image File Format—See TIFF.

tangent—Touching a line or curve at only one point. The direction line is tangent to the curve at the anchor point.

tangent line—See *direction line*.

template—The scanned image or the image in PICT format that you use as the basis for Illustrator artwork. A bitmap. The template appears on the screen as a gray image behind the artwork, it is not part of the final printed document. Compare with *artwork* and *preview image*. Also, a boilerplate document that has already been set up with a grid or other elements to be "cloned" in creating new documents based on the template. See also *boilerplate*.

text box—Any area in a dialog box in which you type text.

text-only file—Text created in another application and saved without type specifications or other formatting. Illustrator can import text-only files from any source. See also *ASCII*.

text wrap—Automatic line breaks at the right edge of a column or at the right margin of a page. Also, the capability to wrap text around a graphic on a page layout. See also *carriage return*.

threaded text—See *linked text*.

thumbnail—Traditionally, a small pencil sketch indicating the artist's plan for a page. Also, a small window showing a low-resolution bitmap representation of a graphic or a page displayed in a dialog box when opening or searching for a document, as with Adobe Fetch.

tick marks—Marks on the rulers or on a graph axis showing increments of measure. See also *measurement system*.

TIF—Refers to Tagged Image File Format. The file format extension for a TIFF file is TIF. See *TIFF*.

TIFF—Refers to Tagged Image File Format, originally developed by Aldus Corporation for the Macintosh. TIF files are in bitmap graphics file format and are accepted by DOS, Macintosh, Unix, and Windows applications. See *file formats*.

tile—(page) To divide Adobe Illustrator's drawing area into pages for the page size currently specified in the Page Setup dialog box. Used in oversized publications. A part of a page printed on a single sheet of paper. For a complete page, the tiles are assembled and pasted together. See also *oversized publication*.

tile—(pattern) To repeat a pattern in columns and rows across the layer of the document in which that pattern paints a path.

time-out error—Printer stops because it has not received information for a while. Usually occurs while you print complex pages and the printer takes a long time to print a large bit-mapped image. Saving before printing helps reduce chances of data loss.

tint—A percentage of black or one of the process or custom colors.

toggle—An on/off switch, command, or option. Used to describe cases in which the same command or option is invoked to turn a feature on and off. A command that lets you switch between two settings. The Show/Hide Rulers command is an example of a toggle.

tones—The shades of a photograph or illustration that is printed as a series of dots. Tones are percentages of black; lower percentages produce lighter tones.

toolbox—The set of tools displayed in a palette when a document is open.

tracking—The spacing between characters in a text object. Positive tracking values move characters apart; negative tracking values move characters together. See also *kerning*.

transforming—As used in conjunction with Illustrator tools, means to bend, stretch, exaggerate, or distort objects without redrawing them. You can mirror, reflect, rotate, scale, and shear objects with just a click and a drag.

transmitted light—See *additive primary colors.*

transparency—See *overhead transparency* and *overlay.*

transverse—Rotation of the page on the film or paper on which it is printing. Currently, this term is applicable only to Linotronic typesetting machines.

trap—Overlap needed to ensure that a slight misalignment or movement of the separations will not affect the final appearance of the job.

triple-click—To quickly press and release the main mouse button three times in succession. In Illustrator, for example, triple-clicking on text with the text tool selects a whole paragraph. See also *click.*

TrueType fonts—Fonts used in most Macintosh (System 7 and later) and Windows (3.1 and later) applications, developed by Apple and Microsoft as an alternative to Adobe PostScript font technology. TrueType is a scaleable font technology, meaning that, unlike bitmap fonts, you need only one font to create any point-size type you want. These fonts work best on desktop printers and are not commonly used in high-resolution imagesetters.

Type 1 fonts—Adobe PostScript fonts that provide the highest output quality.

Type 3 fonts—A PostScript-type format used by other font vendors before Adobe released Type 1 specifications. Usually, these fonts are not hinted. See *hinting.*

type manager—A utility that organizes font definitions and renders font outlines on-screen and for a printer. Adobe Type Manager (ATM) is generally the most commonly used type manager. See also *ATM.*

typeface—A single type family of one design of type, in all sizes and styles. Times and Helvetica, for example, are two different typefaces. Each typeface has many fonts (sizes and styles). Sometimes the terms *typeface* and *font* are used interchangeably. See also *font* and *style.*

uncoated stock—Paper that is not coated. Uncoated paper is usually less smooth and absorbs ink more readily.

ungroup—To separate groups into individual objects or into subgroups.

unit of measure—The units marked on Illustrator's rulers, such as inches, picas and points, or millimeters.

uppercase—Capital letters that make up the alphabet. The term comes from typesetters storing the capital letters in the upper part of a printer's typecase. See *caps*.

vector graphics—The type of graphics produced using Illustrator's drawing tools. See *object-oriented files*.

vertical shift—The distance that type appears from its baseline. You can adjust the vertical shift to raise or lower type.

vertical justification—Adjusting the spaces between lines of text (leading) in fine increments to make columns on a page end at the same point.

view—The size of the pasteboard and page as displayed in the publication window. View is determined by selections on the View menu, or it can be changed using the Zoom tool.

weight—The width of a path (stroke). Also, the variation in a character's stroke width. See *type style*.

white space—Empty space on a page, not used for text or graphics.

widow—See *orphans/widows*.

window—On-screen area in which an application runs or a dialog box. Each application window has a title bar, a menu bar, and scroll bars. Some dialog boxes also include a title bar. See also *dialog box*.

WMF—A graphics file format unique to Microsoft Windows capable of storing both bitmap and vector graphics. The Windows version of Illustrator can import WMF formats. See *file formats*.

word spacing—The space between words in a line or a paragraph. In Illustrator, unjustified text has fixed word spacing; justified text has variable word spacing, which is adjusted within the limits entered in the Paragraph palette. See also *kerning* and *letter spacing*.

word wrap—The automatic adjustment of the number of words on a line of text to fit a text rectangle or text inside a path (area text). The carriage returns that result from automatic word wrap are called soft carriage returns to distinguish them from hard carriage returns, which are entered to force a new line after you press the Enter key. See also *text wrap* and *carriage return*.

WPG—File formats produced in WordPerfect and DrawPerfect applications. The Windows version of Illustrator can import WPG formats. See also *file formats*.

wrap—See *text wrap* and *word wrap*.

WYSIWYG—"What You See Is What You Get" (pronounced "wizzy-wig"). Describes systems such as Illustrator that display full pages with all text and graphics on-screen. Preview views are more WYSIWYG than Artwork views.

X axis—The horizontal reference line to which objects are constrained as you draw in Illustrator. Also, the horizontal axis in a graph. See also *constrain*.

x height—A distinguishing characteristic of a font. The height of lowercase letters without ascenders or descenders, such as *x*, *a*, and *c*. Also called the *body* of the type.

y axis—The vertical reference line to which objects are constrained as you draw in Illustrator. Also, the vertical axis in a graph. See also *constrain*.

yellow—The subtractive primary color that appears yellow and absorbs blue light. Used as one ink in four-color printing. See also *subtractive primary colors* and *process color*.

zero point—The intersection of the two Illustrator rulers at 0 (zero). The default zero point is at the intersection of the left and bottom edges of the document area, but it can be moved.

zoom—To magnify or reduce your view of the current document.

Index